THE OXLEY FARM DIARIES

THE OXLEY FARM DIARIES
1814-1823

EDITED BY MICK HENRY
INTRODUCTION BY BRIAN SHORT

SUSSEX RECORD SOCIETY
VOLUME 104

PUBLISHED IN ASSOCIATION WITH
SUSSEX FAMILY HISTORY GROUP

Published 2024 by
Sussex Record Society
Barbican House
High Street
Lewes
East Sussex BN7 1YE
ISBN 978 0 85445 086 2

In association with
Sussex Family History Group
10 Fairford Close
Haywards Heath
RH16 3EF

© Sussex Record Society, Sussex Family History Group, contributors

The text is set in Palatino Linotype 11/14 and 9.5/12 in the footnotes

It was prepared in Microsoft Word and converted for print by Adobe PDF Library 22.2.244, PDF version 1.7 (Acrobat 8.x)

Printed by Hobbs the Printers Ltd., Totton, Hampshire

VOLUMES ISSUED BY THE SUSSEX RECORD SOCIETY

Vol. 1   Marriage Licences at Lewes, 1586-1642
Vol. 2   Sussex Fines, 1190-1248
Vol. 3   Post Mortem Inquisitions, 1558-1583
Vol. 4   Ecclesiastical Returns for East Sussex, 1603; Sussex Poll Book, 1705; Sussex MSS in the Harleian MSS; Bishop Praty's Register, 1438-1445.
Vol. 5   West Sussex Protestation Returns, 1641-1642
Vol. 6   Marriage Licences at Lewes, 1670-1732
Vol. 7   Sussex Fines, 1249-1307
Vol. 8   Bishop Rede's Register, 1397-1415 (Pt. 1)
Vol. 9   Marriage Licences at Chichester 1575-1730
Vol. 10 Subsidy Rolls, 1296, 1327 and 1332
Vol. 11 Bishop Rede's Register, 1397-1415 (Pt. 2)
Vol. 12 Marriage Licences at Chichester (peculiars), 1579-1730
Vol. 13 Cuckfield Parish Register, 1598-1699
Vol. 14 Post Mortem Inquisitions, 1485-1649
Vol. 15 Bolney Parish Register, 1541-1812
Vol. 16 Star Chamber Proceedings, 1500-1558
Vol. 17 Ardingly Parish Register, 1558-1812
*Vol. 18 Angmering Parish Register, 1562-1687
Vol. 19 Sussex Manors and Advowsons, etc., 1509-1833, A-L
Vol. 20 Sussex Manors and Advowsons, etc., 1509-1833, M-Z
Vol. 21 Horsham Parish Register, 1541-1635
Vol. 22 Cowfold Parish Register, 1558-1812
Vol. 23 Sussex Fines, 1308-1509
Vol. 24 East Grinstead Parish Register, 1558-1661
Vol. 25 Marriage Licences at Lewes, 1771-1837, A-L
Vol. 26 Marriage Licences at Lewes, 1772-1837, M-Z
Vol. 27 Preston Manor Court Rolls, 1562-1702
Vol. 28 Sussex Apprentices and Masters, 1710-1752
Vol. 29 Abstracts of Documents relating to the Dobell family, 16th-18th cents.
Vol. 30 Glynde Parish Register, 1558-1812
Vol. 31 Custumals of the Sussex Manors of the Bishop of Chichester, c. 1256-1374
Vol. 32 Sussex Marriage Licences at Chichester, 1731-1774
Vol. 33 Sussex Inquisitions (from Bodleian Library), 1541-1616
Vol. 34 The Book of John Rowe, Steward to Lord Bergavenny, 1622
Vol. 35 Marriage Licences at Chichester, 1775-1800, with Index 1731-1800
Vol. 36 Sussex Chantry Records, 1535-1652

Vol. 37   Hastings Rape Records, 1387–1474
Vol. 38   Chartulary of Lewes Priory (Pt. I), 11th–14th cents.
* Vol. 39 The Buckhurst Terrier, 1597–1598
Vol. 40   Chartulary of Lewes Priory (Pt. II), 12th–14th cents.
Vol. 41   Transcripts of Sussex Wills up to 1560 Vol. 1 Albourne - Chichester
Vol. 42   Transcripts of Sussex Wills up to 1560 Vol. 2 Chiddingly - Horsham
Vol. 43   Transcripts of Sussex Wills up to 1560 Vol. 3 Horsted Keynes - Pyecombe
Vol. 44   Records of the Barony and Honour of the Rape of Lewes, 1265-1466
Vol. 45   Transcripts of Sussex Wills up to 1560 Vol. 4 Racton - Yapton
Vol. 46   Chichester Cathedral Chartulary, 13th–16th cents.
Vol. 47   Survey of Robertsbridge Manor, 1567–1570
Vol. 48   The Town Book of Lewes, 1542–1701
Vol. 49   Churchwardens' Presentments, (Pt. I), Archdeaconry of Chichester, 1621-28, 1664-70
Vol. 50   Churchwardens' Presentments, (Pt. II), Archdeaconry of Lewes, 1674-1677
Vol. 51   Record of Deputations of Gamekeepers, 1781-1928

Jubilee Volume Sussex Views from the Burrell Collection

Vol. 52   Chapter Acts, Chichester, 1472-1544 (The White Act Book)
Vol. 53   The Manor of Etchingham cum Salehurst, 1597-1865
Vol. 54   Quarter Sessions Order Book, 1642-1649
Vol. 55   Ministers' Accounts of the Manor of Petworth, 1347-1353
Vol. 56   Lay Subsidy Rolls, 1524-1525
Vol. 57   Custumals of Sussex Manors of the Archbishop of Canterbury, 1285-1330
Vol. 58   Chapter Acts, Chichester, 1545-1642
Vol. 59   Chartulary of Boxgrove Priory, 12th-14th cents.
Vol. 60   Custumals of the Manors of Laughton, Willingdon and Goring, 1292-1338
Vol. 61   A Catalogue of Sussex Estate and Tithe Award Maps (Pt. I), 1606-1884
Vol. 62   Minutes of the Common Council of the City of Chichester, 1783-1826
Vol. 63   The Book of Bartholomew Bolney, 15th cent.
Vol. 64   Rye Shipping Records, 1566-1590
Vol. 65   Cellarers' Rolls of Battle Abbey, 1275-1513
Vol. 66   A Catalogue of Sussex Maps, (Pt. II) 1597-1958
Vol. 67   Estate Surveys of the Fitzalan Earls of Arundel, 14th cent.
Vol. 68   The Journal of Giles Moore of Horsted Keynes, 1655-1679
Vol. 69   The Town Book of Lewes, 1702-1837
Vol. 70   The Town Book of Lewes, 1837-1901
* Vol. 71 Accounts of the Roberts Family of Boarzell, 1568-1582

Vol. 72		Printed Maps of Sussex, 1575-1900
Vol. 73	*	Correspondence of the Dukes of Richmond and Newcastle, 1724-1750
Vol. 74		Sussex Coroners' Inquests, 1485-1558
Vol. 75	*	The Religious Census of Sussex, 1851
Vol. 76		The Fuller Letters, 1728-1755
Vol. 77		East Sussex Land Tax, 1785
Vol. 78	*	Chichester Diocesan Surveys, 1686 and 1724
Vol. 79		Saint Richard of Chichester
Vol. 80		The Ashdown Forest Dispute, 1876-1882
Vol. 81		Sussex Schools in the 18th century
Vol. 82	*	West Sussex Land Tax, 1785
Vol. 83		Mid Sussex Poor Law Records, 1601-1835
Vol. 84		Sussex in the First World War
Vol. 85		Sussex Depicted: Views and Descriptions 1600-1800
Vol. 86	*	Sussex Shore to Flanders Fields: Edward Heron–Allen's Journal of the Great War
Vol. 87	*	East Sussex Parliamentary Deposited Plans, 1799-1970
Vol. 88		Sussex Cricket in the 18th century
Vol. 89	*	East Sussex Coroners' Records, 1688-1838
Vol. 90		The Durford Cartulary
Vol. 91	*	Sussex Clergy Inventories, 1600-1750
Vol. 92	*	Accounts and Records of the Manor of Mote in Iden, 1461-1551, 1673
Vol. 93	*	East Sussex Church Monuments, 1530-1830
Vol. 94	*	Winchelsea Poor Law Records, 1790-1841
Vol. 95	*	Littlehampton School Logbook, 1871-1911
Vol. 96	*	Letters of John Collier of Hastings, 1731-1746
Vol. 97	*	Chichester Archdeaconry Depositions, 1603-1608
Vol. 98	*	Church Surveys of Chichester Archdeaconry, 1602, 1610 & 1636
Vol. 99	*	Facing Invasion: Proceedings Under the Defence Acts 1801-05
Vol. 100	*	The Great War Memoir of Ralph Ellis, Sussex Artist and Soldier
Vol. 101	*	Sir Stephen Glynne's Sussex Church Notes
Vol. 102	*	Brighton Mendicity Society: Lives of the Urban Poor
Vol. 103	*	Sussex Clergy Wills 1635-1714

In print volumes marked with an asterisk can be obtained from the Sussex Record Society, Barbican House, Lewes, East Sussex, BN7 1YE or through the Society's website: www.sussexrecordsociety.org

CONTENTS

Acknowledgements xi
List of illustrations xiii
Introduction xv
Editorial policy li
Glossary lii

The Diaries
    1814 3
    1815 47
    1816 123
    1817 214
    1821–23 287

Appendix 1: Farm accounts 341
Appendix 2: The Prosecuting Society of Heathfield and Warbleton 365
Appendix 3: 1816: The Year Without a Summer 367
Appendix 4: Family trees 369
Appendix 5: Nicholas Oxley Will 409
Appendix 6: Name index 413

ACKNOWLEDGEMENTS

Paul Oxley, the current owner of the Oxley Farm Diaries, first brought them to the attention of the Sussex Family History Group (SFHG). Paul lent them to SFHG, and contributed to the cost of conserving and binding the first volume. He has graciously approved their publication.

Members of SFHG contributed to the project in a number of ways:

- Madeline Cole made a major input to the transcription here. The farms and places around Bodle Street were particularly interesting to her as her Grandparents lived there; as a child she spent time travelling between Heathfield, Rushlake Green etc and exploring that area.
- Jayne Adams retired in 2020 to East Sussex, the home of her maternal family for more than 400 years. She contributed her extensive genealogical expertise, and has been responsible for much of the detailed family history here; she has also contributed the family trees and biographical notes in Appendix 5.
- In 1943, Norman Allcorn's family moved to East Sussex, eventually settling at Priory Farm, Rushlake Green. Norman started work in 1950, managing a dairy herd at Dean and Pilly Farms. He has been a fount of knowledge on the history and practice of farming in Sussex.
- Teresa Whetstone gave us permission to include her note on The Prosecuting Society of Heathfield and Warbleton (Appendix 2)
- Contributors to the SFHG Facebook group helped significantly in resolving difficulties in the text.
- Brian Cutler served as Chairman of the Sussex Family History Group from 2002 to 2007 and has been a member of the SRS Council for many years. He was instrumental in introducing the SFHG project to SRS and hence in producing this publication.

Mick Henry, Chairman of SFHG, led the project and oversaw the transcription of the diaries; Brian Short, Emeritus Professor of Historical Geography at the University of Sussex and President of the Sussex Record Society, contributed the Introduction.

The East Sussex and Brighton and Hove Record Office (ESBHRO) at The Keep are the current custodians of the Oxley Farm Diaries. The Sussex Record Society commissioned the present publication, which has been published in association with SFHG.

LIST OF ILLUSTRATIONS

Illustrations are © SRS/SFHG or public domain unless noted

Collecting Faggots	Frontispiece
Great Bucksteep Farm, 1920	xxii
Great Bucksteep Farm, 2020 © Oast House Archive; Creative Commons Licence	xxiii
Pilly Farmhouse, 2024	xxv
Christian's River, 2013 © Robin Webster; Creative Commons Licence	xxvii
Paying hop pickers	xxxvi
Hay harvest	xlvi
The Emperor of Russia and his Daughter and King of Prussia	27
Heathfield Independent Chapel © Andrew Hill; Creative Commons Licence	38
Thrashing	41
Carting faggots for Christmas	42
Trimming hedges	62
Beehive	76
Warbleton Priory	79
Mowing clover	89
Dr Goldsmith's Roman History	102
Mrs Selms and John Trill Lade married	114
The Mill, Bodle Street Green	115
Windmill Hill Mill	129
Carting hop pockets	185
Drilling and harrowing	200
Ploughing	216
Bucksteep Mill	244
Warbleton Church	246
Sheep washing	261
Summertree Farm	285
Sandhill Farm	289
Reaping and binding	327
Prinkle Farmhouse today	339

cont...

Colour Plates

1. The Oxley Farm Diary, page 1
2. Bucksteep and the surrounding area
3. Bucksteep Farm crop map 1814
4. Bucksteep Farm crop map 1815
5. Bucksteep Farm crop map 1816
6. Bucksteep Farm crop map 1817
7. Pilly Farm crop map 1821
8. Sandhill Farm crop map
9. Sand Hole Farm crop map
10. Summertree Farm crop map
11. Gravestone of Nicholas Oxley
12. Gravestone of Elizabeth Oxley

INTRODUCTION

Nicholas Oxley has allowed us to enter into the life and work of a Wealden farmer in the years following the Napoleonic Wars. His diaries, transcribed in this volume, were kept remarkably faithfully for much of the period 1814-23. He was born into a farming family on 6th December 1794 in Heathfield, the son of Thomas Oxley (1760-1830) and his first wife Elizabeth née Cornwell (c.1760-c.1795). He was baptised at the Heathfield Independent Chapel in Punnett's Town on 6th January 1795.

Probably originating from Derbyshire, members of the Oxley family had been in the area by the late sixteenth century and had developed connections with the iron industry. From Stream Furnace in Chiddingly the father of John Oxley produced 210 tons of guns in 1692 and 235 tons in 1693, all for John Fuller. In 1719 David Oxley purchased Kingsley Hill, near Warbleton itself, although selling it in the following year.[1]

Thomas, the son of William Oxley and Mary neé Dearing, was a farmer from Heathfield and later Wartling. His wife, Elizabeth, was the daughter of Robert Cornwell and Elizabeth née Diplock from Gill Hope Farm in Mayfield. She died in the year following Nicholas's baptism. Thomas quickly married again, in 1796 to widow Ann Bland née Crundell, also in Heathfield. As a result, Nicholas gained a step-mother and three half-siblings: William (1797-1830), David (1799-1847) and Elizabeth (1802-1830), from his father's second marriage.

On 27th October 1818, Nicholas married Elizabeth Pattenden (1788-1843) at the parish church of St Mary the Virgin in Warbleton. Elizabeth was the daughter of John Pattenden (1752-1815) and Elizabeth née Gorringe (1755-1822) from Warbleton. Elizabeth's uncle, Robert Pattenden (b.1754), brother of her father John, lived at Batemans in Burwash from 1787 until his death in 1821. Nicholas and Elizabeth had two sons, Thomas (1819-1883), and Othniel (1821-1864), both baptised in Warbleton by the pastor John Press, who features prominently in the diary. Thomas Oxley, a music teacher, emigrated to Syracuse, New York with his family in 1856 and died there in 1883. Othniel Oxley remained in Sussex until his death in 1864. As well as tenanting Cowden Farm, Othniel had a variety of other occupations in later life, including an appointment as an Overseer of Roads. At his death in

---

[1] East Sussex Brighton and Hove Record Office (ESBHRO), David and Barbara Martin, Rape of Hastings Architectural Survey P45/22 and P45/49 and Report 523; SAS RF 15/26, f.337.

1864 his will records him as a Tea Dealer. He is buried at All Saints Church, Herstmonceux.

Nicholas died in 1833 aged 38 and was buried on 25th June in the cemetery of the Independent Chapel at Punnett's Town near Heathfield, where he had been a faithful member all his life.[2]

THE DIARIES

The first part of the diary, for the years 1814 and 1815, was torn out of a larger ledger and bound and conserved in its present format in the East Sussex Brighton and Hove Record Office at The Keep in the early 2020s as AMS 7476/1/1. The Sussex Family History Group agreed to split the cost of rebinding with Paul Oxley, the diaries' present owner. The second part covers the years 1816 to 1823 and is at ESBHRO: AMS 7476/1/2.

The diaries comprised 350 original pages, and covered from Saturday 15th January 1814 to Friday 10th October 1817 for Bucksteep Farm, with only a small break of 5 weeks in 1814 when Nicholas was busy with the hop harvest. There is then a gap until Wednesday 3rd January 1821 by which time Nicholas had married, had become a father to Thomas, and was primarily concerned with his newly-acquired tenancies at Summertree and Sand Hill Farms. The diary then continues for these farms until Friday 12th October 1821. The entries for 1822 are very fragmented, and only 18 days are covered from January until May. The final days are from Wednesday 1st October until the last entry on Wednesday 15th October 1823.[3] A tabulation of farm income and outgoings covers the Summertree and Sand Hill properties only, beginning in December 1817 (Appendix 1).

In all there are 1,594 days covered, with entries outlining the day's work, those involved, their whereabouts on the farm, and the weather. In total there are just under 500 individuals mentioned. We see the routine, but the language and the terminology are also of interest.

We also see that their faith was an important element in the family's life. There was a long history of nonconformity in the Warbleton area, a feature of many of the large parishes in the Sussex Weald where the parish church

---

[2] The Oxley family history has been researched by members of the Sussex Family History Group, particularly Jayne Adams, in conjunction with Paul Oxley. Madeline Cole and Mick Henry transcribed the text as presented in this volume. For fuller details of the genealogies and family trees see Appendix 4. A transcript of Nicholas's last will and testament is at Appendix 5.

[3] Other documents relating to the Oxley family 1828-1829 are at ESBHRO: AMS 7476/2.

could be difficult to reach along atrocious roads, particularly in winter, and where the clergy of the established church might fail to gain the confidence and respect of their congregations.[4] When the religious Census for Sussex was taken in 1851 the Hailsham area, together with Battle, stood out as having the highest non-Anglican attendances. It is significant therefore that the Oxleys attended the nonconformist Independent Chapel at Heathfield on Sundays, frequently staying all day.[5] Given the difficulty of travel this would have made sense. Family members generally walked to the chapel although on occasion a cart might be used, especially for Nicholas's mother and sister Elizabeth.[6] The service was held every Sunday, and Nicholas outlines who went, including their maid, and who did not, how long they stayed, what chapter and verse was read out by John Press who normally presided over the Chapel, and what pages they sang from their Hymn Book. Sometimes other preachers visited, coming from places such as Herstmonceux (Mr Winchester), Brighton, Lewes and Burwash. On one occasion there was a visiting preacher from Ireland.

John Press (1783-1868) was a successor to George Gilbert (1741-1827), who, it is said, was a soldier who was converted to 'Methodism' in 1766 and subsequently established the Independent Chapel at Cade Street.[7] On Sunday 2nd February 1817 Nicholas records:

'Mother rode Father I Wm David Elizabeth and the maid walked to Heathfield Chapel in the morning our worthy Pasture [Pastor] Mr Press being ill our aged pasture [Pastor] Mr Gilbert preached from Galatians the 6 chapter and the 15th verse in his room[8] much to the satisfaction of

---

[4] See Jeremy Goring, 'Church and Dissent in Warbleton c1500-1900', Warbleton and District History Group 1980; B. Coleman, 'Southern England in the Census of Religious Worship, 1851', *Southern History* 5, 1983, 154-88.

[5] The chapel was returned as the Heathfield Independent or Congregational Chapel in the 1851 Religious Census, having most recently been built in 1808 on the site of two earlier eighteenth-century chapels. See J.A. Vickers, *The Religious Census of Sussex 1851* (Lewes: Sussex Record Society 75, 1989), 43.

[6] Nicholas's actual mother Elizabeth neé Cornwell had died in about 1795 and he refers throughout his diary to his mother, being Ann (neé Crundell), his step-mother and Thomas's second wife. Similarly, Elizabeth is his half-sister.

[7] M.A. Lower, *The Worthies of Sussex. Biographical sketches of the most eminent natives or inhabitants of the county, from the earliest period to the present time* (Lewes: Geo P. Bacon 1865), 76-9; and see Neil Errey: *Roots Branches and Leaves* (Adelaide, Australia: Privately published 1982). The Erreys and Gilberts were interrelated.

[8] Nicholas uses the phrase 'in his room' here and elsewhere to mean 'instead of' or 'in his place'.

his late hearesses.'[9]

As fiercely noncomformist employers, the Oxleys never encouraged any work being undertaken on Sundays. On 3rd September 1815 Nicholas recorded that 'Mr Harris the Painter Merchant [came] on Bussiness! What an awful thing to do Business on the Sabath day when God hath Commanded it be kept Holy and he is a Jelous God and will in no wise require without full satisfaction for His injured justice'.

There were also evening prayer and reading gatherings at other houses, often on Tuesdays, including at Bucksteep Farm itself. John Press would sometimes also attend such meetings. Other chapels might be visited on occasion, for example, Herstmonceux, but there are relatively few references to the parish church St Mary, although Thomas was an occasional visitor there and funerals made visits necessary. Warbleton was one of a number of parishes in the area with a strong Puritan emphasis, and although we do not find the extreme naming of children here by this period, Nicholas gave his second son the Old Testament name Othniel, and J.T. Lade named his first son Caleb.

On 23rd June 1816 there is the first mention of Mrs Sober at the Stone House in Rushlake Green. On the following week she spoke 'to a numerous and respectful congregation'. Mrs Ann Sober (née Kemp) (1775-1855) was now the widow of the late Abraham Cumberbatch Sober (1771-1813) who had managed a Barbadian plantation and whose grandfather had grown rich from the slave trade.[10] Abraham was also on the Committee of the British and Foreign Auxiliary Bible Society for the County of Sussex, which was chaired by his brother-in-law Thomas Read Kemp, who was also President.[11] Ann Sober was the daughter of Thomas Kemp MP for Lewes (1745-1811) and sister of the well-known Thomas Read Kemp, founder of Kemptown to the east of Brighton. On 10th September 1816 Nicholas records that 'The Honerable Lady Mrs Sobers her sister Miss Kemp and

[9] Hearers?
[10] ESBHRO: DUN 12/6, 25th April 1810 10-year lease Capital messuage called Stonehouse, coach-house, stables, cottage, barn, buildings and 177a 1r 19p to Abraham Cumberbatch Sober of Warbleton, esq.
[11] The British and Foreign Bible Society was founded in 1804 and there soon developed many auxiliary and branch societies in Britain. It may be that Mr Press talked in chapel of the work of the auxiliary branch in Sussex, founded in 1811, on the morning of 29th October 1815 when Nicholas describes that he 'afterwards gave an account of the Auxiliary affairs and the which Mother wass very much hurt'. Presumably meaning upset or affected.

two Miss Burts Visitors this evening'. Ann Sober later left to live in Sussex Square, Kemptown.[12]

As well as recording the work of the farm and the faith of the family, we have a great variety of local, national and even international history. The First Peace of Paris, signed on 30th May 1814, ended the war between France and the Coalition of Britain, Russia, Austria, and Prussia. Napoleon had abdicated in April and there was a state visit by various victorious dignitaries in June in England before leaving for Vienna.[13] And on Sunday 26th June 1814, following a military review at Portsmouth and breakfast at Goodwood hosted by the Duke of Richmond, 'the Emperor of Russia & his daughter, & King of Prussia & General Blücher past through Garner [Gardener] Street on their route to Dover & embark for France.' They left England on the following day. The 7th July 1814, which Nicholas records as a clear day, was the Prince Regent Thanksgiving Day, with treats for the Poor on Rushlake Green, and with nearly 800 people attending. And two years later, on Thursday 18th July 1816 he records a further Prince Regent's Thanksgiving Day 'for the blessing of peace England is at peace with all the World after a most dreadful war etc'. Unusually for a Thursday, 'Father I & David whent to Heathfield Chapel Mr Press preached from Thessalonians 5 Cha 18 verse sung the hymns on 264-471 and 444 pages Father whent to Cade Street.'[14]

We also have the 'Year with no Summer' in 1816, following the eruption of the volcano Tambora on 10th April 1815 on one of the Lesser Sunda Islands of Indonesia (see Appendix 3: 1816: the Year without a Summer). In Britain the summer of 1816 has long been recognised as one of the most unseasonable on record, and the July was the coldest July within the Central England Temperature series (extending back to 1659). The 1810s are

---

[12] Ann's first marriage had been to Rev. George Bythesea of Ightham in Kent, in 1797, but he died in 1800 just after the birth of his son George Kemp Bythesea. She married Cumberbatch Sober on 14th August 1806. She died in Ledbury, Herefordshire in March 1855, always wealthy through bequests from her late father. And see Appendix 4.

[13] The Congress of Vienna began in September 1814 and continued until June 1815. The Peace was, of course, premature because the final defeat of Napoleon did not come until the following year at the Battle of Waterloo followed by the Treaty of Paris in November 1815. Great celebrations in London, such as the July 14th Service of General Thanksgiving for the Allied Victory held in St Paul's Cathedral, where the Prince Regent and Wellington entered together, were somewhat tempered by sober reflections on the losses and consequences of the war.

[14] Thessalonians 5 Cha 18 'In all things give thanks…'

also among the coldest decades recorded over Europe and the northern hemisphere, with weather anomalies thought to relate to reduced sun spot activity at that time. Crop failure had also faced many at the end of the eighteenth century, again linked to generally cold conditions in the 1790s and early 1800s. Nicholas and the farm struggled, as did much of European rural society and we can certainly appreciate why he observed and noted the weather conditions at Bucksteep so carefully.

Across the country the winter of 1813–14 was exceptionally cold and harvest failure and famine added to the woes of the war. Winter 1815–16 brought heavy snowfalls, flooding, strong winds and a cold spring. A cold, wet summer followed with crops being damaged. Now there was growing social unrest and clear distress in the countryside with many farms failing altogether. Attendance by the Oxleys at the Prosecuting Society of Heathfield and Warbleton in an effort to counteract local crime may well have been one local impact.[15] Given the inherent problems of farming in the Weald (see below), together with the severe hardship and food shortages as a result of the war years, with a stagnating economy as over 400,000 men from the armed services entered the labour market at the same time as European markets for British exports was still disrupted, to have such an appalling weather situation made life very challenging:

'For extreme events during 1816 we might single out the severe winter with periods of flooding (5–6 January) and heavy snow (6–8 February); heavy rain and flooding on 7 and 15 April; a very cold spring with snow on 12 May; and a very wet and cold summer interspersed with high-amplitude storm events. One may conjecture whether these conditions were a function of normal weather, or of volcanic aerosols which would have produced a marked drop in surface pressure across the mid latitudes across the North Atlantic.'[16]

---

[15] Towards the end of Nicholas's life there were disturbances in Warbleton on 12th November 1830 against a parish overseer, part of a more general rural protest movement centred in eastern Sussex around Battle and Brede, coming to be known as 'Captain Swing'. See E. Hobsbawn and G. Rudé, *Captain Swing* (Harmondsworth: Penguin 1969) 79, 81.

[16] Lucy Veale and Geogina Endfield, 'Situating 1816, the "year without summer"', in the UK', *The Geographical Journal* 182 (4) 2016), 318-30. The period covered in the diaries was towards the end of what has become known as the Little Ice Age. The last Frost Fair on the Thames was in January 1814.

WARBLETON AND ITS FARMING ENVIRONMENT

Nicholas and his family farmed at Great Bucksteep, to which most of the diaries refer. Nearby, however, was Bucksteep Manor and Little Bucksteep but by the time of the diaries these were independent of the Oxley farm and merited no specific mention. There were connections, however, of long familial links: in 1700 the 'Manor of Buxteep and capital messuage called Buxteep Place with barns, stables, stalls and land (187a)', was occupied by Thomas Oxley, in Warbleton and Dallington.[17]

Great Bucksteep Farm is located along the banks of Christian's River above its confluence with the Nunningham Stream, which then joins the Ash Bourne to flow via Boreham Bridge to Pevensey Levels and the sea at Normans' Bay. The farm was in the southern part of the large parish of Warbleton in the Hundred of Hawkesborough. An early reference is *Bocestepe* (12th century) or *Bustepe juxta Dalinton* (1279), 'steep place overgrown with beeches', giving a flavour of the immediate environment.[18]

The farming environment of Bucksteep was not promising. The High Weald had a complex mosaic of soil types but most were poorly drained and deficient in lime, but also phosphate and potash. The geology underpinning Warbleton, primarily the Ashdown Formation and Wadhurst Clay with patches of Tunbridge Wells Sand, was not altogether a promising basis. The Wadhurst Clay, often intractable and still heavily wooded, was described as a 'sportsman's paradise but a farmer's hell', The soils, according to Horsfield in 1835, varied from poor black sand on Warbleton Down; loam in the south and southwest, clay in the east and southeast and a gravel-loam mixture in the centre.[19]

---

17 ESBHRO: AMS 5729/106, Conveyance, 'Manor of Buxteep and capital messuage called Buxteep Place with barns, stables, stalls and land (187a) occupied by Thomas Oxley, in Warbleton and Dallington'.
18 ESBHRO: Historic Environment Record, MES 21385 Bucksteep: Great Bucksteep Farm; A. Mawer and F.M. Stenton, *The Place Names of Sussex*, vol. 2 (Cambridge University Press 1929), 469.
19 T.W. Horsfield, *The History, Antiquities, and Topography of Sussex* vol. 1 (Lewes: Sussex Press 1835), 556. Farming was precarious at times on the poor soils and higher altitudes of the north of Warbleton. Watkins Down Farm, part of the Ashburnham Estate, had no fewer than nine tenants in the 20 years after 1830 (B. Short, 'The turnover of tenants on the Ashburnham Estate, 1830-1850', *Sussex Archaeological Collections* vol. 113 (1975), 157-74.

Great Bucksteep Farm, 1920

The farm was set within a hilly landscape of scattered homesteads and plentiful woodland on the edge of the High Weald where the land drops away southwards towards the Pevensey Levels. The fields of the farm sloped uphill from the farmstead's location on the Christian's River. Rushlake Green and Punnett's Town to the north and Bodle Street Green to the south were the largest hamlets, scarcely villages. This was an ancient landscape, carved out of former marginal land, and historically granted to Battle Abbey from the twelfth century, and with the manor of Bucksteep, created out of the larger Warbleton manor in the following century locally important.[20] The area in the southern part of Warbleton was the most inviting for early settlement, and we find Bucksteep manor exacting work services and having slightly larger medieval holdings than on the lands elsewhere in the area.

[20] There is a single rental for Bucksteep in 1375 and for the Battle Abbey lands in Bucksteep in the fifteenth century; but by the 1460s 'Buckstepe' was only nominally within the jurisdiction of Battle (M. Gardiner, 'Medieval Settlement and Society in the Eastern Sussex Weald before 1420' (University of London, PhD 1995), 212-26; E. Searle, *Lordship and Community: Battle Abbey and its Banlieu 1066-1538* (Toronto: Pontifical Institute of Medieval Studies 1974), 407.

Great Bucksteep Farm, 2020

Great Bucksteep seems to have become the site of the manor house for Bucksteep manor by the sixteenth century, when it was part of the Pelham family interests, and field names on the tithe map incorporating 'chapel' and 'pound' point to its local significance (see colour maps).[21] In the early eighteenth century Bucksteep Mill, to the south, with c.264 acres, was sold off, leaving Bucksteep Place with c.210 acres. By 1788 it was in the possession of John Tourle of Landport near Lewes, by 1810 it was owned by William Stanford and by 1838 it was still in his possession and occupied by John Whiteman.

Great Bucksteep, or Bucksteep Place, was in its essentials a substantial Wealden hall house originally of mid-fifteenth century date. It was set on a north-south axis and later modified with chimneys and an additional parlour range allowing the construction of a grand staircase in the late seventeenth century. Maintenance costs would have been high and the building was later reduced in size commensurate with its status as a farmhouse, although the north, south and west walls were encased with bricks.[22]

21 'Buckstepe' was of sufficient significance for it to be included on John Norden's map of Sussex (1595).
22 ESBHRO: HER MES25138, Great Bucksteep, Warbleton; David and Barbara Martin,

The area was unaffected by the later enclosure movement, and the landscape was one very typical of the eastern High Weald of Sussex: small fields edged by substantial shaws, their shapes determined as much by natural features as by any later endeavours. Field sizes here and around Heathfield and Burwash were the smallest in the High Weald, generally under 10 acres.[23] With average farm size in Warbleton's former commons and wasteland being 50 acres by the time of the tithe redemption award of 1837, Bucksteep itself at over 230 acres, was exceptionally large, and the family concern including the other farms, as we shall see, was considerable.[24]

By contrast much of the northern part of the parish consisted of small farms reclaimed from common or waste as recently as the eighteenth century. On the commons and waste of northern Warbleton 13 of 31 recorded leases for tiny properties were first granted in 1790-91, with the last in 1796.[25] Labourers, tradesmen and absentee speculators were mainly involved. As late as 1808-1820 there was an ongoing dispute as to ownership of the waste in Warbleton between the Earl of Ashburnham, as Lord Paramount of the Rape of Hastings, and the 2nd Earl of Chichester concerning the former's claim to all waste in the surrounding Manors.[26] The population of the parish increased only slowly from its first recorded 908 in 1801 to reach 1,167 by 1821, and thereafter continued to a peak by 1851 of 1,509 and then slowly declined, a pattern common to many rural parishes in Sussex.

BUCKSTEEP FARM

In 1797 a lease was granted by John Tourle to Thomas Oxley of Heathfield, yeoman for seven years at £104 for a messuage and lands called Bucksteep Farm (213 acres) in Warbleton. This was Nicholas Oxley's father, who remained a significant presence during the years of the diary.[27] By the will

---

23 'Warbleton: Great Bucksteep' (ESBHRO: HBR 1/523).
24 Based on calculations from the later Ordnance Survey sheets c. 1875 where field sizes are given.
25 ESBHRO: TD/E 50.
26 Jayne Kirk, 'Colonists of the waste: the structure and evolution of nineteenth century economy and society in the central Forest Ridges of the Sussex Weald' (University of Sussex MA Dissertation 1986), 29-30.
27 ESBHRO: Ash 524
28 ESBHRO: ACC 6077/6/3.

Pilly Farmhouse

of John Tourle in 1801, when Thomas is named as occupier, the property was devised to Henry Jackson of Lewes and to John Tourle's brother-in-law William Cooper of Lewes, gent.[28] On 2nd December 1814 Nicholas records that 'Mr Stanford Mr Tourle Mr Tourle Came to Shooting'; again on 9th December 1816 'Mr Stanford and Mr Tourle came here the evening about six o'clock on purpose to have a little shooting to morrow if the Weather permits', and the next day 'yesterday David carried the Game Bag for Mr Tourle and Gamekeeper Phillips they Kild 2 Hares 2 Rabbits 3 Pheasants and a Wood cock Mr Stanford not well layed a bed nearly day'. On 1st October 1817 he records that 'David is a gentlemans footman to day waiting on Mr T Tourle Esquire and his wives Father who came here yesterday'.[29]

The Oxleys' occupation of Bucksteep presents us with another phenomenon which is rarely documented. Thomas Oxley had taken on Bucksteep by the seven-year lease in 1797, and his sons continued working on the farm but with Nicholas also going on to rent the adjoining nearby properties of Pilley, Sandhill and Summertree, sometimes also referring to Sandhole (later named Lower Sandhill). There are also many references to Combish in the diary, almost certainly Combe Ash, between Pilley and Sandhole. All these latter were rented in conjunction with J.T. Lade from Mr Noakes and all were effectively run as a family concern. The family also

[28] ESBHRO: SAS/WS 146 Copy of the will of John Tourle of Landport, gent; Land Tax Assessments for Warbleton 1780-1832 (XA/31/29).

[29] John Tourle of Landport, Lewes (1728-1802) had a daughter Mary (1780-1846) by his second wife, Mary Cooper (1728-1802), sister of William Cooper, a Lewes attorney. Mary Tourle married the wealthy William Stanford on 2nd March 1802. Stanford had purchased Preston Manor in 1794 and lived at Preston Place.

rented Cowden Farm and the small farm adjoining Bucksteep, Cold Hodges, just below Bucksteep Mill. Cowden in the parish of Wartling belonged to the neighbouring Ashburnham estate and at just under 272 acres was one of the largest and best on that estate.[30]

During the Napoleonic wars there were general complaints about the 'monopoly of small farms by the great farmers', and although the Oxleys could not really be described as 'great farmers', nevertheless the occupation of at least five or six farms by one family would have had significant impacts on the society and economy of this part of Warbleton parish between the Christian's River and the Trullilows Stream.[31] According to Nicholas' will, he also owned freehold land in the Herstmonceux area which he leased out. One unit, with a house, buildings and a small poultry farm, was called Iron Croft, situated in Lower Road, Herstmonceux, and was leased to Richard Hoad. Another was leased to Charity Collins, although the name of the property is not given. In September 1817 Nicholas expressed difficulties in keeping track of all the interactions: on 3rd we find 'Wm went to the other farms a harvesting etc I cannot keep a proper account of the goers and comers I so often forget and seldom know when they happen.' And then on 23rd October 'I shall now turn book into a book of account on my own business seeing if have not time to attain to the above particulars and instead of saying any thing about Bucksteep and Cold Hodges Farms I may perhaps make some remarks on Summertree and Sandhole Farms'. On that same day 'J T Lade and I entered on Summertree and Sandhole Farms'.[32]

Entering a Wealden farm at this time was not straightforward for a new tenant. By the 'custom of the country' or tenant-right, the incoming tenant would pay the outgoer for husbandry already undertaken which left crops in the ground, hay in the stack, for any drainage operations from which the newcomer could benefit, manures (or half manures if one crop was taken

[30] By 1830 Cowden Farm was recorded as being tenanted by Nicholas and David Oxley (1830-34), then by Nicholas's widow Elizabeth Oxley (1834-44) and then his son Othniel Oxley (1844-50) (ESBHRO: ASH 1993 and Short, 'turnover', 157-74. Cold Hodges, sometimes just Hodges, originally a medieval farmstead, was another of the Oxley adjoining properties; in the 1851 census it was returned as comprising 21 acres.
[31] Roger Wells, 'Social protest, class, conflict and consciousness, in the English countryside 1700-1880' in M. Reed and R. Wells (eds), *Class, conflict and protest in the English countryside, 1700-1880* (London: Frank Cass 1990), 121-214.
[32] Sandhole farm was adjacent to Sandhill and seems to have been incorporated into the latter farm. For the Lade family tree see Appendix 4.

Christian's River, 2013

from that ground), hop poles and implements and so on. Appraisers or valuers were called in to calculate the sums involved and the calculations could become complex and drawn out.[33] It was believed that Sussex had the heaviest ingoing valuations in England, saddling the new tenant with a debt which often had to be paid off in instalments. The whole process attracted opprobrium from later agricultural writers.[34]

At Summertree and Sandhole it seems that Thomas Oxley initially paid for the lease and valuation in 1817, which was later repaid. On February 13th 1821 we hear 'Paid the appraisement (for Summertree and Sandhole] to Mrs Waters … Mr John Waters my Land Lord died Tuesday February 7th and left the Sandhill etc Comwish to Mrs A Maria Waters and Family

[33] See Appendix 1, Table 11, 'The Apprisement of Sandhill Combish and Pilly Farms in the Parish of Warbleton in the County of Sussex from Mrs Maria Waters to Nicholas Oxley Jany 2nd 1821 consisting of all the stock and tackling of woodland ploughings & Woodlands & Hoath'.

[34] A well-respected critic was James Caird in his *English Agriculture in 1850-51* (London: Longman 1852), 506.

and the Pilly to Mr Ths Waters and Family'. On Tuesday 7th October 1822 Nicholas records 'Masters Thomas & Holman apprised me out of the Sandhills & Pilly farms Mr Wm Isted took the Sandhills & Mr Wm Waters Mr Thomas slept here last night ….' 'On the next day 'Fine weather… Oxen cleared the Pilly & Sandhill of all my old tackling and carried it to Frankwell to be sold at their sale.'

The period dealt with in the diaries was generally a hard one for farmers. The small farms here had thrived in the wartime period of high corn prices up to 1815; but between 1816 and 1842 a post-Napoleonic farming depression ensued, nearly half the small farms were lost in nearby Chiddingly, and many of the remainder changed from owner-occupancy to tenancy, with only a few additional ones appearing on newly-enclosed land.[35] The end of the wars saw a slump in the corn prices which had been high enough in the war years when the export of corn had been forbidden, to make profits. But now a succession of poor harvests was combined with high outgoings for taxation, poor rates and tithe payment. As a fiercely difficult area for arable farming, this Wealden location fared badly when corn prices tumbled. But cereals continued to be grown at Bucksteep, as elsewhere at this time. Only slowly did the need to put more land down to grasses take hold. Nicholas Oxley certainly attended meetings concerned with the level of tithes in Warbleton, part of a more general intensification of feeling among farmers, and an issue near to the heart of nonconformists such as the Oxleys who might resent payment to representatives of the established church. Criticism comes through diary entries. We hear that on Wednesday 9th October 1816 'Father whent to Rush lake to pay his Tithe but did not Our Parson Cole is got greatly in Debt so that we hardly know who to pay it too'.[36]

The economic and environmental difficulties in this area were prolonged and were mediated by a range of personal and holding characteristics that resulted in varying abilities to withstand economic pressure. Outgoings frequently exceeded income and many farm businesses went under. We therefore hear on Tuesday 15th June 1816 that 'Father and I went to sale at the Halfmoon Mr Ellis's property Father brought a hind harness and an ox

35 June Sheppard, 'Small Farms in a Sussex Weald Parish 1800-60', *Agricultural History Review*, 40 II (1992), 127-41.
36 A mural in St Mary Warbleton records that Benjamin Thomas Halcott Cole died in 1850 in Bangor aged 68 but had been rector of Warbleton for 57 years. ESBHRO: AMS 6146/231 gives his dates at Warbleton as 1813-50. And see ESBHRO: AMS 6146/237 for negotiations in 1828 to enable Cole to pay off £2,000 of debts.

chain. And on October 31st that year 'William David and I whent to Mr Newman's Sale at Herrings Dallington it is full of sales now, there wass one on Tuesday last at Boreham and tomorrow at Jollinghous and one this week at Heathfield two last week in this Parish and one just by at Redpale in Dallington.'

Warbleton was within that part of Sussex whose small farms relied heavily on hop growing to survive and the parish was part of a marked concentration in far eastern Sussex. It was also within an area which was later defined as important for the rearing, fattening (cramming) and marketing of poultry, although Nicholas Oxley gives no indication of it having any importance at Bucksteep or on his other farms.[37] Geese and 'Foulls' get little mention. Nor was there any mention of concerted drainage operations, but only ridging up to allow furrows to drain excess water away.[38] However, the Oxleys were certainly alive to the need for rotating the crops in their fields (see colour figures 3-6). The fields given over to hops, Upper and Lower Pound Field and Grimes Croft, for example, were so used in 1814-16 but then sown to tares and peas for 1818. To the east of the farm was the 9 acres, with the four year rotation being potato and roots/wheat/oats undersown with seeds/grass for a hay crop. Only three fields in the far south-east were permanently in grass: Great and Little Silver fields and Calves Lodge Meadow, the latter yielding a hay crop in two of the years. There is little mention of fallows, although fallowing must have been practised, and no mention of marl, elsewhere still commonly used in the High Weald, although far less so than in earlier centuries.[39] The area of crops and grass can be approximately calculated from entries in the diary, and related to the later tithe map to give the location of the different crops. Overall, the areas of crops and grass at Bucksteep were approximately:

[37] Brian Short, 'Agricultural regions, improvements and land use c.1840' in K. Leslie and B.Short (eds), *An Historical Atlas of Sussex* (Chichester: Phillimore 1999), 96-7.
[38] The Soilscape map for the Bucksteep area describes the soils as 'Slightly acid loamy and clayey soils with impeded drainage' (LandIS - Land Information System - Soilscapes soil type viewer).
[39] Topley believed that marling had been discontinued by the 1820s (W. Topley, *The Geology of the Weald* (London: HMSO 1875), 387-8. But in many areas it, together with liming, had been heavily used during the Napoleonic Wars when high wheat prices made the high extraction and carriage costs economic (J. Brown and H. Beeecham, 'Farming practices' in G. Mingay (ed), *The Agrarian History of England and Wales VI 1750-1850* (Cambridge: Cambridge University Press 1989), 280.

1814: 171 acres (hops 14, corn/tares 76, roots/potatoes 40, grass 41)
1815: 138 acres (hops 10, corn/tares 70, roots/potatoes 8, grass 50)
1816: 153 acres (hops 8, crops 84, roots/potatoes 4, grass 57)
1817: 173 acres (hops 11, crops 94, roots/potatoes 2, grass 66)

The actual size of the farm in the tithe survey was 234¾ acres of which 48¼ acres were woodland, and included tracks, buildings, yards and orchards, the latter recorded in the tithe survey as just over one acre. The survey also includes, for example, a Forestall or green open space near the centre, which was classed as three acres of pasture near the farmhouse.

There is some mention of other crops: onions, for example, in connection with 'gardening' on Tuesday 26th March 1816, and he records pruning fruit trees on 9th February 1815, and his brother William gathering apples on 25th September 1816. Other ancillary activities included bees – swarming is frequently reported, from an old hive, a lower hive, and 25th September 1815 he records that 'Wm Hoad Henry Fowl help me take 3 Hives of Bees one was dead which is four in all Wasps are verry numerous this year'. Four hives are mentioned elsewhere. Fallow is mentioned on 13 August 1816: 'I was mowing thistles in the 7 acres vallow'.

As the farm emerged from the high prices for corn during the war, there was still an emphasis on cereals (and hops) rather than pasture. Livestock did not feature as prominently in the diary as the crops and cropping. In 1815 and again in 1816 Nicholas does give the results of a census of livestock during later autumn when most animals had returned from the marsh. Summarising the stock on 8th November 1815 there were:

Four working (plough or draught) horses, a cast off stallion, five colts including one kept for Mr Diamond, and a riding horse. There were a number of bullocks, four milk cows, a bull, a two-yearling heifer for Butcher Watten 'when he means to Fetch it'; a pair of Oxen for sale otherwise to be fattened; a black runt cow also to be fattened; six working oxen, seven yearlings, six weaning calves, a cow kept for Thomas Hoad, and six two-yearlings in the Marsh. The sheep consisted of 15 ewes 3 Down, 24 'Lambs of our own and 30 (should be but one Dead) marsh lambs for Mr Thomas Winchester'.

The 1816 stock as at 13th December consisted of:
Four Cart Horses and two colts and 'Old Jack the Poney' six cows and two being fattened; four two-yearling steers; four oxen and a bull; six yearlings, ten calves and a two yearling heifer; three or four ewes with the tegs etc lambs 'which are to be kild when it suits and a ram, in all of ours 29 and 22 marsh lambs Once 30 but we have lost 8 of them in good

keep'; and three hogs in the pound 'a fattening', seven shuts 'and a Quantity of Geese and Foulls which I seldom tell'. The bull was hired out for servicing his neighbours' cows. During the winter months Nicholas had the time to visit to collect his 'bull money': in January 1815 'I went round by Ashburnham and Dallington gathering of Bull money' and similarly in 1816.

In 1813 Arthur Young Junior's survey of farming in Sussex criticised the fact that the Weald 'presents to the eye hardly any prospect but a mass of wood' and condemned 'the singular custom of shaws' then still prevalent. However, he also admitted that demand for wood was rising and therefore 'some people consider them the most profitable of any land whatever'.[40] Much attention, as we shall see, was certainly paid to the woodland on Bucksteep, including the environing shaws which essentially cut up the landscape into small and irregular fields. The tithe apportionment of 1837, in allocating 48¼ acres of woodland to the Bucksteep total area, carefully distinguished the larger areas of shaw: those around Kiln Field, Gutter Field and West Pound Field were all ¾ acre; while even more substantial were those around Nine acres (2 acres) and Red Pale (one acre), and even larger were Rough shaw (2½ acres) and Kiln shaw (2 acres). In excess of 10 acres was taken up in this way.

Grimes Wood, mentioned frequently as a source of wood, is given on the tithe survey as 25 acres. Broom Wood is mentioned as a source of faggots but its location and size is uncertain, and Furze Wood is also noted, presumably that area of woodland next to Furze Field. On 24th November 1815 Nicholas records drawing sixty ash, three alder, three willows and two oak poles from there. On 22nd April 1816 he also refers to having 'carried 100 house faggots from the wood at the bottom of the 12 acres to Mr Russels'. This may be a reference to what is named on the later Ordnance Survey maps as Marlpit Wood. The tithe apportionment also includes Squires wood (5½ acres) although this is not mentioned by name in the diaries but is presumably the woodland adjacent to Great and Little Squires Fields. Additionally, on 25th November 1816 there is mention, of Thomas Oxley buying Wartling Wood with Mr R. Purs[t]glove, a block of wood south of Boreham Street, surely an indication of the economic

---

[40] Rev. A. Young, *General View of the Agriculture of the County of Sussex* (London: The Board of Agriculture 1813), 9-10; 169. This had been written at the beginning of the war but only published in 1813.

importance of woodland at this time.[41]

The commercial exploitation of this woodland, which, importantly, was tithe free, being in the Weald, was ongoing even though now having lost its former market into the now defunct Wealden iron industry. Warbleton had been a thriving area for ironworking, but the last remaining ironworks, at neighbouring Ashburnham, had closed around 1813.[42] But faggots, bark, building timber, fence posts, hop poles, farm implements and sundry other uses for the woodland remained an important feature of the Bucksteep economy. In view of the large amount of woodland, it is also interesting that Warbleton parish could provide 22 felling axes according to the returns collected under the Defence Acts, more than most other parishes in Hastings Rape.[43]

THE SOCIAL AND ECONOMIC RELATIONS OF FAMILY AND WORKERS AT BUCKSTEEP

Nicholas, his father and his half-brothers were by no means 'gentlemen farmers', but worked alongside their employees, undertaking all the tasks necessary to maintain the farm's output. His father, however, was also frequently absent on visits to neighbouring farms, to markets and fairs, to their marshland etc, absences sometimes mystifying Nicholas, such as on 3rd December 1816 'Father gone somewhere Southward has been gone all day Mother is in trouble about him', and later this is compounded by other undertakings: on Wednesday 30th May 1817 'Father is often out some where being Overseer Assessor and surveyer I cannot always tell where he goes I shall not pretend to keep a regular account'.

The five men in the Oxley family worked hard, but if things were difficult for farmers in this area, things were certainly no better for farmworkers. Nicholas was clearly concerned that labour costs might increase: he notes on 9th October 1815 that 'There is great Talk about

---

[41] Wartling Wood is just over 89 acres according to the 25-inch OS map 1899; Grimes Wood is given as 32 acres, Marlpit Wood as 9 acres, and Furze Wood, being part of the larger Sprats Wood, 30 acres but probably not all belonging to the Oxleys. On the revised 1908 map Sprats wood is divided into Big and Little Sprats, with Little Sprats, the Bucksteep portion, being 7½ acres.

[42] H. Cleere and D. Crossley, *The Iron Industry of the Weald* (Cardiff: 2nd edtn 1995), 310-11. The forge closed in 1827.

[43] Roger Pearce, *Facing Invasion: Proceedings under the Defence Acts 1801-1805* (Lewes: Sussex Record Society vol. 99, 2019), 69.

alteration of Price of work to 2s per day'. But soon after the end of the war numbers of discharged soldiers swelled the labour force: on Wednesday 20th December 1815 his diary entry includes 'a Chap Loitered about the Barn after work nearly all Day but we have none for him.' And many workers also feared the introduction of the new threshing machines. Such a machine for the threshing of wheat is mentioned for Bellhurst, home to John Bland, Ann's son by her first marriage: on 23rd October 1816 we hear that 'William whent to Bellhurst to help them threshing Wheat with the mechien'. On 9th December 1816 we again hear that 'William whent to Bellhurst threshing Wheat with the Machine'.[44]

Warbleton was by no means without problems of poverty. In 1795 it was reported that subscriptions to relieve the poor had been raised in the parish, as in other parts of the county, and there were reports of thefts of foodstuffs.[45] There were two charities for apprenticing poor children of the parish from bequests by Thomas Stolyon and Ann Hawksworth.[46] A poor house near the church existed by Nicholas's time and was in use until the parish was incorporated into the Hailsham Union after 1834. From 1816, the year that the Bellhurst machine was operating, attacks on threshing machines, alongside arson and threats to employers and parish officers (as at nearby Burwash in 1822) developed in the South East as unemployment also increased. In April 1822 John Darby JP of Markly in Warbleton wrote to Peel 'at the request of chief inhabitants of this place' to report that the earlier sheep stealing in the parish had been halted by the conviction and execution of a gang leader, but that the 'Practice has again commenced' with two or three individuals killing and stealing from a butcher in Rushlake Green.[47]

Workers were paid by the day, with no pay if they were absent, the absenteeism sometimes frustrating to Nicholas and meticulously recorded in the diary. And on March 13th 1815 he recorded that he was laying off some workers because of wet weather. Conversely there had been payment

---

44 The threshing machine, becoming more widely adopted in the 1810s and 1820s, was to be a source of great concern for men and women whose winter employment in barns using flails was threatened.
45 *Sussex Weekly Advertiser* 26th January 1795; 1st December 1795.
46 ESBHRO: PAR 501/24/1.
47 C. Griffin, *The Rural War: Captain Swing and the Politics of Protest* (Manchester University Press 2012), 54–5; The National Archives: HO 641/1 ff 229-30 John Darby to Peel 9th April 1822. I am grateful to Professor Carl Griffin for drawing my attention to this source. Peel had become Home Secretary in January 1822.

for hop pole shaving 'by 6 Romanies' in April 1814. The farm workers are named together with the tasks undertaken. Appendix 1, Tables 2-8 for 1817 and 1818 detail payments.

For Bucksteep we have good information about the workforce, and among the first pages of the diary, for the week beginning January 17th 1814, for example, we hear of Tom Daw lime spreading, John Marten and Thomas Hoad thrashing, which they continue to do all week, Old Dann grubbing and William Farmer wood cutting in Grimes Wood. By Friday 4th February we have John Marten still thrashing; Tom Daw, Master Piper and William Dann grubbing; Joseph and Jesse Marten joining William Farmer in wood cutting; and Thomas and Henry Hoad (his son, then aged 14) hedging. By Thursday 10th February we hear of old Piper and Dann Grubbing; John Marten ditching; Joseph Marten and Jesse, William Farmer and James Message's boy wood cutting; Thomas and Henry Hoad still hedging, Martha Hoad, then aged 12, shaving hop poles; and rather ambiguously 'spreading little John'. The diaries continue in this vein throughout to offer a real insight not only into the routines of the farm, but also into the working week of the men and women employed.

The Hoad family were certainly closely involved with Bucksteep and were also nonconformists, attending the Heathfield chapel. Thomas Hoad (1772-1838) was in his 40s at this time. We hear of Dame Hoad, sometimes referred to as mother Hoad, chopping and later stripping hops, turning seeds, haying, and on occasion working alongside Dame Dann in haymaking and branching hops.[48] Dame Hoad may well have been Thomas's mother. His daughter Ruth (1804-55) was baptised at the chapel in July 1804 and, as a young teenager, was also at work in haymaking. On the 21st July 1814 we also find her sister Mary (1806-30) together with Master Hoad (possibly young Thomas, aged 17) and William Oxley also aged 17, mentioned as helping. On 15th April 1822 in an entry for Sandhill and Summertree 'Henry Hoad left me at Lady tide after having lived with me (excepting a fortnight that he went to Wighten) for 3 years by half yearly bargains altering his wages and settling with him every ½ year

[48] Dame Dann was also noted as undertaking dogwood scraping, as, for example, at 13th June 1815. This was *Frangula alnus*, Alder Buckthorn or dogwood and was prized in the Battle area for use in the making of gunpowder. We hear that 'When the underwood in the district was being cut, the dogwood was carefully reserved, peeled and tied into bundles.' (http://ramblingsofanaturalist.blogspot.com/2011/04/explosive-plant.html). It also had medicinal uses as a somewhat violent purgative.

giving him the liberty to go away every time before we bargained again'. Farmwork for women and children was primarily confined to seasonal piecework employment in hop preparation and picking and the hay harvest. Nicholas paid much attention to the work involved, and in the hop garden he was careful to enumerate the pairings and positionings, or standings, in the alleyways of the pickers. On Friday 1st September 1815 he listed the regular standings in the Croft hop garden:

1st standing Mrs Morfey and Family, 2 Ends Mrs Beal and Mrs Foster the other bin

2nd Standing Elizabeth and Mrs Selmes 1 Bin Mrs Hoad and Family the other Bin

3rd Standen Ann Isted and Harriot Bradford Bins and Mary Barton and Elizabeth Ratten the other

4th standing Dame Hoad and Maid 1 Bin and Dame Dann and Mrs Baker the other Charity Collins to come to stand when the Maid does

On Thursday 14th September he returned to the listings, now giving: 'The Nine Hopers are Dame Easton Dame Honeysett 1st Bin Dame Lambhurst and Dame Cornford 2nd Bin Dame Pook Tom Pook and Mrs Isted's Maid and Family 3rd Bin Francis Dann Mrs Effick 4th Bin.'

The pickers were mostly regulars from one year to the next. They were paid off at 1s. per bushel; although by 21st October 1816, when labour was becoming more plentiful, he was paying them off at 3d per bushel with a dinner given, and by 8th Oct 1817 they were receiving 2½d per bushel, quite a dramatic decrease over three years. But no other activity on the farm required so much human labour.

There is no obvious mention of Ann Oxley or her daughter working in the fields alongside the other family members. We hear of mother and daughter attending chapel regularly, and also prayer meetings on weekday evenings, often at the Stonehouse and normally on Tuesdays. Ann was a frequent visitor to Bellhurst to visit John Bland and her grandchildren. The visits became more frequent during the summer of 1816 when John was taken ill, dying in September. Nicholas records a period of 'deep mourning'.[49] Elizabeth (1802-1830) seems to have had a childhood free of farming cares. Nicholas records her visiting friends, sometimes staying overnight, or having friends to stay at Bucksteep: on 22nd July 1816, 'Sophia and Ann Smith come to see

---

[49] Ann (née Crundell) had married John Bland Sr in 1779 in Brenchley, Kent. He died in 1794, being buried at Heathfield, leaving her with two children, Ann and John, the latter being the John Bland who died at Bellhurst. (See Appendix 4 for family tree).

Paying hop pickers

Elizabeth and are weather bound and stay all night they are now very noisy in the room just by, Elizabeth Ann and the Maid with them'. On Saturday 16th August 1817 he complains as a big brother 'Elizabeth Hannah [Verrall] and Ann [Smith] went to Gardener street Etc they are frequently on the run I seldom know were'.[50]

Nicholas's wife Elizabeth Pattenden is hardly mentioned in the diaries. They married on 27th October 1818, one week after her sister Sarah who married Daniel Lade, but we unfortunately have no diary entries for that period, nor at the time of his first-born son Thomas in 1819. Elizabeth is, however, mentioned on Wednesday 11th June 1817: 'Elizabeth Lade Harriot Phillips Elizabeth And Sarah Pattenden where here to night I went

[50] It would be wonderful to know whether Elizabeth fitted the criticism of William Cobbett, made in 1815, that if one stepped into one of those large farm houses 'he would no longer see the farmer's daughters, Madge or Dolly, feeding the pigs, fetching in the cows, milking them, or churning and making cheese ... No, no: he will find the young ladies in a back parlour, playing upon the forte piano, drawing or embroidering, perhaps making themselves up new caps or dresses to appear in at the next county ball.' (W. Cobbett, *Political Register* (25th February 1815), 247-8.

home with the Pattendens I hope that the Lord has begun his good work of grace on their hearts'. The latter may refer to the fact that the Pattendens may not have been nonconformists: Elizabeth had been baptised in the parish church and when her sister Sarah married it was after banns had been read in the parish church, but Nicholas and Elizabeth were married by licence, a not infrequent procedure adopted by nonconformists or where the bride and groom were of different persuasions.[51] Elizabeth died in 1843 but in the 1841 census she was described as a farmer aged 50, at Cowden Farm, with Mary her unmarried sister aged 45 and Othniel, then aged 15.[52]

Nicholas documents the interactions between the Oxleys and those families closest to them, either as kin or as neighbours. The intersections, fostered by visits, are numerous and span more than one generation: Oxleys, Lades, Selmes, Pattendens and Blands form a farming community based around Warbleton and adjacent parishes. Simon Selmes (1776-1809), a widower from Northiam, and Ann Bland married in 1806; on his death Thomas Oxley was an executor, and Ann then went on to marry John Trill Lade in 1815. Simon and Ann had a daughter, Ann Maria, in 1809 shortly before his death. Ann Maria later married Vincent Lade, John Trill's brother. Another brother, Luke, together with Elizabeth Oxley, Nicholas's half-sister, was a witness. Vincent and Ann Maria moved to Southwark where, by 1838, he was a hop porter.

The relations with the Lade family were particularly close. John Trill (JT) Lade is mentioned very frequently. His father Thomas from Priory Farm, Warbleton, had married Elizabeth Trill in 1781 and John was the third son from that marriage, born in 1789. His brothers Thomas and James farmed at Priory with their father.[53] Nicholas recorded on 19th Oct 1815 that John

---

[51] 'Oxley, Nicholas, of Warbleton, farmer, bachelor, aged 23 and upds. & Elizabeth Pattenden of same, spinster, aged 30 and upds.: bondsmen, said N. O. and Thomas Oxley of Warbleton, farmer. 20 Oct. 1818. [Lewes.]' (Edwin H. W. Dunkin & E. W. D. Penfold, *Marriage Licences at Lewes 1772-1837, M TO Z* (Sussex Record Society vol. 25, 1919), 317.

[52] The census ages were rounded down to multiples of 5. In fact Elizabeth was then about 55, Mary 48 and Othniel 19.

[53] Priory Farm was on the site of the Augustinian New Priory, dedicated in 1417, originally founded to replace the Priory of the Holy Trinity, at Hastings at the time of the abandonment of that priory, when the monks were removed to Warbleton until its dissolution in the 1530s (V.C.H. Suss. vol 2. 77). The Lades' farmhouse was in part constructed in the sixteenth century from the stones of the Priory and its ruins would have been obvious around the house and oasthouse. Thomas Jr sold the farm to George Darby in 1828 (ESBHRO AMS 6146/242).

Tryll Lade comes weekly and sometimes twice a week to see Mrs Selmes in Courtship etc'. Ann Selmes appears by this time to be living at Bucksteep. John and Ann Selmes (1786-1871) married in November 1815. Nicholas recorded this in some detail:

'This day after nearly seven years widdowhood and nearly two years courtship and several disappointments Mrs Selmes has got a fresh husband John Trill Lade son of Ths [Thomas] Lade at the Priory they where married by the Rev Mr Young of Heathfield at Warbleton church father wass old father and Elizabeth Lade bridemaid they dined with mother Mrs Lade Mrs Trill (James Trill's wife) David and I Mrs Lade and Daniel C Lade came here in the evening had roast pig for dinner'[54]

Their first son, Caleb was born on 15th April 1816. At first the couple actually seemed to spend much of their time apart, John often staying at Bucksteep and Ann either there or at Priory. Caleb was born at Bucksteep, and Nicholas recorded John visiting his wife and son four days later. Then on 28th 'Mrs Lade came down stayers the first time since the 15th Inst her husband came to see her'. Throughout that summer the couple were back and forth from the Priory. On 17th May 1817 Nicholas notes 'Mrs Lade and her son are gone to the Priory I would hope for good till she and her husband have business for themselves'. Was he becoming unhappy about the couple's uncertain movements? Even more forcefully he noted on 20th July 'J T Lade sleeps here to night Mrs Lade and her Family stayed at home all Day this ought not to be her permanent home but the Priory'. And on 31st August 'J T Lade came with his son and wife here this evening he went home again that is her home till the 11th of October but she is oftener [here] than she is there by far'.

In 1817 Nicholas entered into partnership with John Trill Lade to become joint tenants at the nearby Sandhill and Summertree farms, both less than 50 acres in size. After Nicholas's death John and Ann went on to have a large family and by the 1840s had moved to Woodingdean Farm just outside Brighton where John had a farm of over 400 acres.

---

[54] Parish gives the term 'old-father' to mean the person who gives away the bride at her wedding (Rev W.D. Parish, *A Dictionary of the Sussex Dialect and Collection of Provincialisms in use in the County of Sussex* (Lewes: Farncombe & Co. 1875). Among working families in Sussex the bride was not accompanied to church by her father. The bridal procession normally simply consisted of just four people, the bride and bridegroom, the bridesmaid, and the old father, here Thomas Oxley and Elizabeth Lade, John Trill's younger sister. It appears that Ann would have been about 3 months pregnant at the time of her marriage.

The Oxley household always had a maid: on 18th March 1816 'a girl by the name of Eastland from Windmill Hill after a place' and on Monday 25th Lady Day, 'Philadelphia Eastland the new maid' presented herself. On 21st March 1817 'the Maid Phillidelphia Eastland whent away not for any misdemeanour or ill intent but [b]y mutual consent of Mother and herself'. On 25th March 'Ruth Hoad [noted above] came to live with us' to replace her. On 7th March 1822 'My Wife Bargained with one of Master John Awards Girls for a Maid for to come here at Ladetide but how and on what condition I know not'.

NICHOLAS OXLEY'S FARMING YEAR

An annual cycle of tasks characterised the social and economic life of Bucksteep and the diaries allow us to follow the routines. The diary begins in 1814 during the Napoleonic war when there had been much attention to cereals: wheat, oats and barley, and these remained important. The woodland was also an important resource and one yielding a decent income. And a third was the growing of hops, and one perhaps receiving an undue amount of attention. Hops were 'the gambling of farmers', about which Arthur Young Senior noted that 'we have general assertions of profit, and when we come to examine, we find particular accounts of loss.'[55] A good yield brought profit, but only if yields all around elsewhere were not so good – then there could be a glut and prices would be low.

For livestock, the traditional Wealden cattle-farming system, which involved the retention of all male calves, their use as plough oxen between the ages of three and six, followed by fattening for the butcher, was generally practised, and the abundant supplies of manure which the winter stall-fed cattle provided were very beneficial for the hop fields. The high price of corn during the war had seen many turn to potatoes, both as animal feed and for human consumption. Young devoted some space in his account of Sussex farming to 'this very valuable root' with the neighbourhood of Battle seen as having large quantities.[56] In 1801 when the census of farming was undertaken during the concern over possible French invasion, it is notable that Warbleton had more draft oxen than draft horses (142 to 116). The same ratio still held in 1803.[57]

We tend to hear more about sheep, sometimes referred to in the diaries

---

[55] A. Young, 'A Tour in Sussex', *Annals of Agriculture* 11, 1789, 255.
[56] Young, *General View*, 115.
[57] Pearce, *Facing Invasion*, 286.

as marsh sheep or what were elsewhere called keep sheep, maintained inland over the winter from about Michaelmas to Lady Day (29th September to 25th March or 5th April) and returned to the salt marshes in summer, where they stayed for perhaps six months.[58] The Bucksteep livestock, cattle as well as sheep and sometimes a colt, destined to spend the summer on the marsh, were driven there in small numbers during April and May. We find a reference in April 1814 to 'marsh lambs driven to Black Horse Inn' and 'father drove six 2-yearling heifers and a yearling colt to Winchelsea'. The marsh seems to have been rented from Mr Thorp of Fairlight, briefly mentioned on 14th December 1816, and the Oxleys probably overwintered some of Mr Thorp's own sheep at Bucksteep. Mr Thorp was either John Thorp of Fairlight or his son William Thorp of Winchelsea. Other than the Winchelsea location, mentioned several times, we have little detail about the marshland or its precise location and extent. On their return, normally in September, some cattle were penned up to be fattened using potatoes. Thus we have for 22nd September 1815 'Father went down in Marsh in morning Drove home 3 Bullocks'. By early November or December nearly all the stock had been driven to their winter quarters.

Here we use the UK meteorological calendar definitions of the seasons: spring being March, April, May; summer June, July, August; autumn September, October, November; and winter December, January, February. This makes the seasons appear to be in a linear progress, but of course farmwork was a cyclical progress from winter on to spring and so on.

THE FARMING YEAR: SPRING

Spring was the time for ploughing, 'shiming' (to break up weeds) and harrowing in preparation for the summer season. Horses were used for the ploughing in March through to May. Tares, barley, long tail white oats, clover and trefoil were sown and rolled. Potatoes were also planted, a job for the younger girls in May.

In the barns there might still remain oats and wheat to be threshed, and malt to be dried. Preparations for the summer crop and beyond were heralded by purchases of sacks of rye grass seed (April 1815), of tares (January 1816), of barley (April 1816), clover seed and long tail white oats.

[58] J. Farncombe, 'On the Farming of Sussex', *J. Royal Agricultural Society of England* 11, 1850, 75-88.

In April 1821 Nicholas summarised the cropping situation at Sand Hill and Summertree:

'I have this year sowed and what wass sowed before I took The Farms 13½ Acres of Wheat 6¼ Acres of Oats 1 Acre of Barley 1 Acre of Spring Tares 2 Acres of Peas 15¾ acres of Clover 2¾ of Trefoil 9½ Clover and Trefoil Mixed and 4½ Acre of Rye grass Also we have planted 1678 Hills of Hops and there is 5¼ Acres of Hops to Pole Also there is 8 Acres of seeds to Mow this summer and 4 Acres of Old seeds to feed off or mow as may seem more proper this the particulars of My Arible land this year'

The terminology employed here – '… sowed and what wass sowed before I took The Farms…' relates to the complex tenant-right procedures noted above.

Sacks of oats were sold at Cross in Hand, sold more locally, or taken to the mill. Something of an informal exchange economy supplementing more commercial operations can be glimpsed when on 15th march 1821 Nicholas records 'I went to the Halfmoon Market in the afternoon and exchanged 4 Sacks of Barley for 5 sack of Oats with Mr James Harmer and I afterwards Bought 15 Sacks of Oats of Mr Everest of Gardener street at 19s per Quarter.' A further indication of the local interactions is also seen at this time as he records 'the best Sow went to Hog to J Harmer's Boar', and similar arrangements, as we have seen, were made for the hiring of the Oxley bull.

The maintenance of soil fertility was ongoing, a very necessary task on the difficult Wealden soils. Dung was carried from various mixens, from the stables and ox yard, to replenish hop gardens. Ditches and watercourses needed to be maintained, and weeds, such as kilk (charlock) pulled. And extremely important for the arable fields was the spreading of lime: chalk was obtained from (East)Bourne during the Spring although this too was a more-or-less continuous operation during the year.

The hop gardens certainly received attention: the ground required repair, and horses drew ash poles from the woods, some 3,000 by May, to be sharpened, shaved, and individually erected in hills for the bines to twine around. There was also the dressing of the hops and there was nidgetting: using a triangular horse-hoe, an implement used in Kent and Sussex chiefly in cultivating hops or here also for peas. By May the hop tying could begin, the fastening of the hop plants to the poles.

The continuous round of wood cutting was also recorded. Timber fellers had cut 125 trees by mid-May 2014 and oxen hauled the timber out so that sawing could begin, with a saw pit dug for the sawyers. Hop, fencing poles and cord wood were sold, as were huge quantities of faggots for domestic heating, cooking and for firing kilns, together with bark for tanning – visiting tan flawers are mentioned in May 1815 – and wood for the maintenance of farming tools, such as the Sussex rist-plough, and rods for thatching.[59] In May 1817 the cutting of heath faggots also reminds us that parts of the farm were subject to the incursion of heath, but that this too was put to use.

And as March progressed lambing might begin. But other stock would now be on the move: in April 1815 Nicholas was driving three barren cows and 2 yearling heifers into the marsh and in May he 'went down in the marsh' with another two cows and two calves. In the unseasonable year 1816 there were thirty lambs in the marsh in March, but four had died. Thomas was a frequent visitor with stock, to inspect the grass or to conduct business. On 20th April 1816 'Father whent down into the Marsh to see if the grass grows but says it does not the frosty mornings and cold winds hinder it'. In late May that year the backwardness of the grass continued to raise anxieties for livestock: 'there is but little grass the weather being so unforeseeable the grass don't grow and we are so short of fodder we cannot keep them in any longer'.

SUMMER

Now came the busy summer months of haymaking and harvesting on top of the ongoing farming routines of ditching, weeding, mowing thistles, clearing bracken and carting dung.

Soil improvement was again a theme to which Nicholas responded at some length. There is much repetition throughout the summer of 'moul' and 'mouling' which must refer to the use of mould and scrapings (rather than marl) which were applied as a fertiliser across the fields. This would

[59] Cord wood was a pile of wood cut up for burning, 8ft by 4ft and 4ft thick. As such it had been a standard input to the Wealden iron industry. Nicholas refers to the rist plough, which Rev. Arthur Young calls the Kentish turn-wrest (Young, *General View*, 55). On 11th July 1815 Nicholas recorded that 'Foster with Horse plough in 12 acres which was so very dry and hard it broke some chains and the rist and where obliged use the round plough'. The heavy plough turned the furrow in one direction only, but the wooden mouldboard (probably the 'bat' to which he refers in the diaries) could be fitted on either side to throw the furrow to the left or right. It had no wheels and while good on heavy soils, required a skilled ploughman. The replacement round-plough was probably a wheeled plough, deemed less useful on these soils.

then be 'dredged', whereby bushes, perhaps thorn, were bound together and drawn across the field to pulverize the dung or mould.

In July 1816 we also have 'drift sand from river' being applied, together with ashes from the charcoal pit. Horses went to Wallsend (Pevensey Bay) after 3½ tons of beach, shingle for bottoming local roadways which could be nearly impassable on the clays during wet conditions, and this was repeated in July 1817. Large amounts of chalk now came again from Bourne but also from elsewhere on the Downs via Hailsham. There is also mention of chalk from Amberstone and Swains Hill, and 13 loads coming from the Trulilows stream, one of the many such small rivers originating in the ghylls of the High Weald and flowing under various names to the Pevensey Levels. On 7th July 1817 'Horses went to Mr Ades Limekiln near Wannock after Lime'. On 2nd July 1816 we hear that 'the Martins litt the Lime Kiln this morning' and 'Lime burners whom I forgot to mention filled the kiln on Saturday fired her today morning'. In June 1815 'horses went to Brightling after lime for Mr Adds', almost certainly to Glazier's Forge where the Ashburnham lime works supplied lime from an inlier of the Purbeck Beds to farms within a 16-mile radius by the late eighteenth century, gaining much praise from Arthur Young Senior.[60] Fuel was also now supplied in the form of coal, collected from Pevensey.

Work in the woods and the selling of faggots continued, for example, but with many faggots retained for firing the Bucksteep kiln and for making charcoal in a pit for the hop drying to come. Then the coal pit was fired (by Master Robbins in 1815).[61]

Harvesting now began in earnest. By July 1815 the oats and tares could be harvested, followed by trefoil, and horses carried loads of roots from the fields. Tares and trefoil were fed to the oxen, welcome because weather could be so variable, such as in August 1815 'Cows short of food because of drought'. A further task concerned the reaping and mowing of clover in August. At this time many hands, perhaps four or five, now turned their attention to haymaking, with oxen and horses carrying loads home. Haystacks were built and thatched – always it seems by Honeysett. But in July 1816 Nicholas remarked that 'it has been a most remarkable Wett time for Hay and most considerable quantity is no doubt spilt', and later that

---

[60] Young, 'A Tour in Sussex', 759; ESBHRO, ASH 1835 General accounts for lime works 1786-1812.

[61] The use of 'master' here and elsewhere in the diaries was to denote a married workman, young or old.

month 'It is a most extraordinary summer for Rain and will be the means of spoiling a great deal of Hay we had done all our Haying last year by this time and this year we have not carried any Meadow Hay there is a plenty of grass in the meadows'. Furthermore 'We had 47 Loads of Hay from about 45 acres this year'.[62]

Sheep washing is recorded in June 1817, together with shearing ('shaving'), including the new lambs, who were weaned and washed. On 7th July 1815 we hear of 'shearing sheep in Mill Barn where the shearer sleeps', presumably an itinerant workman who would come about midsummer. Fleeces, including lambs' wool might be sent to Hailsham.

And then the important task of preparing for hop picking would begin: hop tyers were at work. The best poles were seen as ash, chestnut and larch, with oak, beech and hazel deemed inferior.[63] In July 1816 we hear that 'hops have a plenty of bine but do not promise for much Bud'. On 3rd to the 6th August 1814 we hear of Dame Hoad, whose work revolved much around the hop gardens and haying, stripping hops for the pickers to begin work.

AUTUMN

By October the wheat harvest was finished, and now came the time to assess the results. In September 1816 Nicholas noted 'it is such weather a wass scarcely ever known in Harvest after such a Wett summer the Corn is greatly swollened and the much battered with the Winds'. In September at Sandhole 'It is verry Wett Harvest and by all appearance a Great deal of Corn must be spilt' and on the following day 'Showry weather Horses and Carters Bosseling[64] It hass been a verry gagery[65] Harvest and I doubt not but that a Great Deal of Corn is spilt but through Mercy I hope there is none of Mine that will catch much hurt'.[66]

Crops were still being gathered: potatoes were being dug; tares and

[62] With a produce of about one load per acre, or about a ton per acre, this 'year without a summer' was some way below the figure of 2 tons and upwards for meadows and 1½ ton for upland grass given by Young for the Sussex hay harvest (Young, *General View*,154). Weights and measures were, however, notoriously localised.
[63] J. Y. Stratton, *Hops and Hop Pickers* (London: Society for Promoting Christian Knowledge 1883), 18.
[64] Bosseling: see glossary.
[65] Poor.
[66] Parish gives 'gagy' as showery.

clover were mown, and a good yield of peas enabled ten sacks to be taken to Woods Corner in September 1817. Threshing of oats, barley and Cobham wheat could begin, and this was intensified during November, with sacks of wheat going to mills in the area.

But the main focus of activity during the autumn were the hop gardens. The years 1815–1818 saw a greater acreage of hops being grown across the High Weald than at any time during the war. Picking began on 3rd Sept 1821 at Sandhole, where Nicholas grew 'abot 39-3-14 acres hops this yr sold some at 46s per hundred in London and locally for 42s and 45s'.[67] Hopping finished on 29th September 1823 at Sandhill, or at Bucksteep in 1814 on the 5th October.

The oast would now be prepared to receive the hops for drying and bagging, and in 1816 details were given of the demolition of an old oast and the building of a new one, which began operations that September. Sea coals (probably Welsh coal) were brought from Pevensey, or later via Lewes and Laughton, and together with charcoal, were fed in to dry the hops, which were then bagged into pockets and trodden down. Operating the kiln, the 'hair' or drying mat, the pockets in which the hops would be pressed down tightly, all required experience. Oxen then carried the pockets to Heathfield, or, in September 1817 horses carried six and then another nine pockets to Cade Street. From there the hops were carted by waggon to be sold in Borough High Street market by the hop factor, Samuel Latham, who acted for Bucksteep. Prices were notoriously fickle: in October 1816, the year with exceptionally cool summer, 'Father received a letter from Latham our Hop Factor yesterday he has sold 6 Pockets of Hops at 145s per hundred weight'.[68] In 1815 they had fetched £14.15s cwt. On 2nd October 1816 Nicholas complains of 'such weather for Harvesting and Hoping as I think wass never known we have 12 acres of Oats 8 acres of Barley and 5 or 6 load of Wheat ... we can't meddle with it and grows in the Ear and many of our Neighbours are worse of than we are and some peopel at some places have not carried any Hops are very Slite and much damaged with the late winds and Rains'. Following the hopping the poles were stacked and the old bines cleared away.

---

[67] That is 39 acres 3 roods and 14 perches (4 roods = one acre, 40 perches = one rood).
[68] By 1816 the London price per cwt for Sussex hops in October was very high at 231s, reflecting the terribly cold summer. Wealden hops never reached the higher prices of those from Kent but even so Latham's sale was rather poor. The poor summer of 1816 and that following of 1817 yielded high prices, but by 1819 they were 65s. (G. Clinch, *English Hops* (London: McCorquodale & Co 1919), 48)

Hay harvest

And always attention was paid to the soil. Lime, mould and dung were spread together with coal siftings and ashes, and also river gravel in 1815, presumably from Christian's River. This was a time also for the clearance of bracken, especially from Furzes Field, to be carted with stubble (the harvest aftermath) into yards and the calves' lodge. And in the woods, there was the cleaving of logs and selecting of hop poles.

Now stock must be brought inland from the marsh. Thomas was active in this, driving bullocks home, and we hear that there were purchases of lambs to keep over the winter. On 27th September 1815 'Master Elfich the Looker and Boy drove the stock home from the Marsh by reason of a disorder in the head amongst them'. But by the 8th November Nicholas was able to say that 'We have driven nearly all the stock to their respective places where they are to Winter except the Beast in the Marsh'. In October 1816 a cart fetched '100 oil cake' from Cowden, considered efficient though expensive for fattening cattle, but further evidence for the economic integration with the Oxley's Cowden Farm. We hear of the same task repeated in December, this time being brought from Windmill Hill.[69] The wheat season for the following year would now be addressed and Nicholas is able to report that by Saturday 28th October 1815 'Finised sowing the 12 Acres with Brown Cobham Wheat from Windmill hill'. Rather unusually he expands on his farming thoughts, explaining that 'there is several different ways of Sowing which any one that lives to see the difference next Harvest May judge of the best plan the two End headlands with 4 Warpps this end and small Warp on the other end ploughed in and left 6 Warpps next to the 4 Warps where plough is and Harrowed a draft afterwards and there are 5 Furrows not struck out all the rest is ploughed and sowed the general way some with Oxen and some with Horses no lot Furrows'.

This is difficult to follow but he is clearly thinking through the optimum ways of creating furrows and ridges on the heavy soils.[70] The Brown Cobham wheat is also noted as covering 27½ acres at Summertrees and Sandhole.[71] Oxen were employed for ongoing ploughing, rolling and harrowing, but the wet conditions brought other problems: on Monday 9th September 1816 'the weather has been so unfavourable we have not had opportunity to work our Oxen enough to keep them to Rights so that we cannot keep them out of the Chapel Meadow which is very Wett as well as the other pastures'.

WINTER

Indoor and outdoor work continued as winter weather allowed. Oats and barley remained to be threshed in the barns, especially if there was snow,

[69] Oilseed cakes, from rape and linseed at this time, later joined by cotton seed in the 1850s, were produced by crushing to leave oil. For long these oils were primarily for industrial purposes, paint-making and cloth-dressing for woollen manufacture, but were becoming more widely used in farming by the later years of the Napoleonic wars, first as a manure but latterly as cattle-feed, with the crushing mills located more in Yorkshire and Lincolnshire.

[70] Parish offers 'warp' as 'a piece of land consisting of ten, twelve, or more ridges, on each side of which a furrow is left to carry off the water'. The term in Sussex is distinct from the term used in parts of northern and eastern England to signify flooding of lower lying fields to acquire silt, the water afterwards being allowed to drain off.

[71] Cobham wheat is mentioned as being grown in Gloucestershire in Henry Colman, *European Agriculture and Rural Economy*, Volume 2 (Boston: C.C. Little and J. Brown 1849), 210.

and oats and wheat were to be taken for milling. Some were sold and conversely barley seed was purchased.

Soils could still not be ignored, and dunging, spreading lime in January and ashes in February continued. Troublesome anthills were cut up in 1815. Any remaining stubble was carted to the ox yard. Wood cutting also continued, with faggots being sold, the chopping of hop poles and cutting of ox goads which were sent to Preston, north of Brighton. And the cutting and mending of hedges and trackways was also undertaken.

And now whenever possible winter ploughing for the next Spring season could begin. On 31st December 1816 'this is the last days account for this year This has been a Remarkable Wett Year and the Fruits of the Earth very backward'. On 7th January 1817 it was reportedly very wet but the first winter ploughing took place. As well as the fields, the old hop gardens would also be dug and ploughed. Hop pole shaving for the next season would be under way by February. Beans and peas were now planted (1815), and in February 1817 tares and peas were sown where hops had previously been, in an effort to rest the soils from the exhausting hop crop.

And then came Spring again and the cycle would recommence.

CONCLUSION

There has been a strange gap in the history of British agriculture. There has been much, of course, on the great estates, on farming techniques, farm inputs and outputs, but the farmers themselves have been curiously neglected. The landowner has been well studied and we now, thankfully, have uncovered more sources for the history of the farmworker. But in the middle comes the farmer, not so much as a category but as a person. To help reinstate the farmer within the heart of rural society we again need the sources, and although farmers clearly kept accounts and papers, their preservation might be problematic. Farm accounts and crop books are useful here but without doubt we can learn huge amounts from the study of farmers' day books and diaries. Here we may have a problem: farmers were busy people, preoccupied with their daily tasks and problems, and may not have necessarily had the time, the inclination or writing skills to keep a day-to-day diary.[72]

Of the relatively few such diaries contemporaneous with those of the

---

[72] An attempt to rescue the farmer as an individual is recognised in R.W. Hoyle, 'Introduction: Recovering the Farmer' in R.W. Hoyle (ed), *The Farmer in England, 1650-1980* (Farnham: Ashgate 2013), 1-42.

Oxleys, we might note that of Thomas Doubleday of Gosberton, Lincolnshire (1812-33) or the set of 41 farm diaries belonging to the Beale Family of River Hall Farm, Biddenden, Kent which document the daily lives of Richard Beale Snr and Jnr during the years 1804-13. These diaries, part of a longer time span, describe tasks such as harvesting, ploughing, animal husbandry, fencing and woodland management. There are insights into the personal lives of the family, their visits, meetings and correspondence.[73] And from a different environment from the Sussex Weald we also have the Wiltshire diaries of the yeoman farmer Thomas Pinniger between 1813-1847, providing detailed daily accounts of the sheep and corn husbandry practised around Avebury. Again, we hear of farming practices, corn and livestock prices and the weather. Pinniger also noted the births, marriages and deaths of relatives, friends and acquaintances, revealing the social milieu in which he lived.[74]

To join these we now have the diaries of Nicholas Oxley. They were faithfully kept between 1814 and 1823, albeit with some gaps, and they provide an account of the daily life of Nicholas Oxley, his family and his workers in the Sussex Weald at Warbleton. He also meticulously records the local weather conditions, because for most farmers this interest was not just curiosity but a demonstration of the great concern in that vital factor of farm life. His concerns for his farming in the dreadful year of 1816 are particularly striking.

What comes through most strongly in studying farm diaries such as those of Nicholas Oxley is the depth of engagement with the land and community. Seemingly concerned with mundane events and routines, the diaries are valuable historical documents, the record of a particular family, place, time and culture. Written after a full day's work and probably just before bedtime by the light of a candle, they are a running commentary on that day's work and on the all-important weather, perhaps sometimes careless in spelling and lacking punctuation, but withal a surprisingly faithful record. Thus, on 10th November 1815 'I write thiss and yesterday's account in the Great Window of the Kitchen about 7 o'clock in the Evening'; or on 29th November 1815 'Trill Lade sleeps here to night he is

---

[73] Museum of English Rural Life: Merl FR DX1000 (Doubleday); FR DX2147/17 (Beale). And see Jeremy Burchardt, 'Farm Diaries 1770-1990' in Paddy Bullard (ed), *A History of English Georgic Writing* (Cambridge: Cambridge University Press 2022), 79-98.
[74] Alan Wadsworth (ed), *The Farming Diaries of Thomas Pinniger 1813-1847* (Gloucester: Hobnob Press 2021)

now a reading in the 116 Psalms the clock is a striking 8 in the Evening I am against the Great window in the kitchen etc.'. And at the end of another day, 14th July 1817, we hear that 'Mr Steer is here the evening on Bussiness I suppose he and Father is now consulting Browns Bible just at my elbow in the great Window about ½ past 8 O'clock'.[75]

[75] Browns Bible: the Scottish minister John Brown's (1722-87) Self-interpreting Bible was originally published in 1778, and went through several editions through to Nicholas's time, containing illustrations of biblical scenes, notes and explanations in heavy leather-bound volumes.

EDITORIAL POLICY

The diaries have been transcribed *verbatim*, reflecting Nicholas Oxley's idiosyncratic and variable spelling, and his typical lack of punctuation. They are handwritten, and occasionally either the script or the condition of the pages makes reading difficult.

Interpolations are shown thus within the text: [letter], [word]

Uncertain readings are shown thus: [?]

Uncertain but suggested readings are shown thus in the footnotes: [suggested?]

Explanatory notes are included in the footnotes, but definitions and explanations of terms, in particular of farming terms, are included in the Glossary.

In the diary, the names of days are typically abbreviated, and Sundays are normally indicated by 'A' or 'B'. Days of the week are sometimes not shown. In the transcript below, these dates have been rationalised and expanded as an aid to comprehension: the first day of each month is headed, eg., *Thursday 1 February*, and subsequent days in the month *Friday 2* etc.

GLOSSARY

axle-tree		the fixed bar or beam of wood, etc, on the rounded ends of which the opposite wheels of a carriage revolve (OED)
bait		afternoon refreshment, with strong beer, in the hay and harvest field
bastard		harrow with iron teeth
bedsteddle		bedstead
beech		variant of beach; = gravel, shingle
bine		the climbing stem of the hop
bosseling		also boseling, bozling, etc. Used particularly in hop picking to describe people moving around a job in progress but doing nothing to help = bozling around. Used in East Sussex until fairly recently: about people in the oast who weren't there working 'what are they doing up in here bozling about'?
brishings		hedge cuttings
brushings		small crop of hay
bubbage		rubbish, weeds
bullace		wild plum
cast		a piece of ground to be worked (in a wood)
chaldron		= cauldron; a dry measure of 4 quarters or 32 (or 36) bushels, in recent times only used for coals (OED)
chep		the share-beam of a plough; esp. a horizontal beam forming the sole of a turnwrest plough, to the end of which the ploughshare is fixed (OED)
chucks		small pieces of wood
clog		sticky mud or clay for blocking up
cone		small stack of hay
cord (of wood)		a stack 8 feet x 4 feet x 4 feet
coulter		an iron blade fixed in front of the ploughshare
crib		the bin used in hop-picking (OED)

GLOSSARY

ditching	digging out ditches, which was regular work on this wet land
downwards	(of wind) from the south
drudging	chain harrowing grass to spread dung pats, remove dead grass and aerate the soil
dryth	dry spell
Dutch blue	variety of potato
fell, felloe	each of the curved pieces making up the outer rim of a wheel, to which the spokes are fixed (OED)
filbert	hazel-nut
frith	thin, scrubby wood, with little or no timber, and consisting mainly of inferior growths (OED)
gapping	mending holes in the hedges
grist	corn to be ground; grist to the mill
grubbing	hoeing, but for deep rooted weeds like docks which needed digging out for which there was a grubbing tool, a single tine with a fork on the end
hacking up	earthing up (potatoes)
haulm	the stems or stalks of various cultivated plants, as peas, beans, vetches, hops, potatoes (OED)
heal (v)	'to cover; Sussex. As, 'to heal the fire'; 'to heal a house'; 'to heal a person in bed' (OED)
heave-gate	a gate which is opened by being lifted out of the sockets or mortices (OED)
hoath	hoth, hawth, heath; scrub
hog jet	a small bucket fastened onto a long handle to feed the pigs
kibe	a chapped or ulcerated chilblain, esp. one on the heel
lease wheat	ears that have been gleaned after harvest
leet	manorial court
lew	shelter
maxon, mackson	variants of mixen, dungheap, midden

moul	mould; earth, soil; a small lump or clod of earth; loose or pulverized earth or soil (OED)
neb	end of the pole that connects the waggon or tug to the animal pulling it. Called so because it looks like a bird's beak
nidgeting	horse hoeing
nidget	horse hoe for weeding the ground between rows of hops
pocket	large sack for hops
pook out	to heap up; spec. to put up (hay, wheat, corn, etc) into cocks or pooks; to gather in (a crop, etc) for this purpose (OED)
pook	a heap, a haycock; a roughly assembled heap of hay, oats, barley, or other unsheafed produce (OED)
pug	clay or loam that has been pulverized, thoroughly mixed, and kneaded into a soft, plastic condition without air pockets for brickmaking, pottery, etc; any earth or other material having a similar consistency or use
quiler	variant of quoiler; a leather strap passing around the hindquarters of a carthorse, which allows the cart to be driven backwards or downhill; the breeching (OED)
redger	variant of ridger, a tool for ridging soil
rist	any of various parts of a plough; specifically (a) the share-beam (obsolete); (b) a mouldboard; (c) a piece of wood or iron fixed beneath a mouldboard (OED)
shay	variant of chaise; cart for people
shiming	to hoe crops with a shim, a kind of horse-hoe or shallow plough
shut	young pig
spindle	axle
spud	a type of spade

GLOSSARY

steddle	the lower part of a stack of corn, hay etc (OED)
sturr	harrow
tailing	small oats
ted (v)	to spread out, scatter, or strew abroad (new-mown grass) for drying (OED)
treddle	sheep or goat dung (OED)
trunk (v)	to turn a crop
tug	timber waggon
upwards	(of wind) from the north
vore	variant of furrow; narrow trench made in the earth with a plough, esp. for the reception of seed
waggon leat	an iron shoe to put under the wheel to act as a brake when going down a steep hill
wint	two ridges which are ploughed by going to one end of the field and back again; arable land which is harrowed twice over is said to be harrowed a wint

Abbreviations:
Qr: quarter of a ton
B: bushel
D: Dutch

THE DIARIES

1814

Saturday 15 January 1814
Daw Lime spreading[76]

[Sunday 16]
Frost up on the Gar[den]……

[Monday 17]
Tom Lime spreading John Thrashing Cleaned up 4 Sacks Oats[77]
Thos Hoad Thrashing Old Dann Grubbing Wm Farmer Wood Cutting Grimes Wood

[Tuesday 18]
John Marten Threshing Cleaned up 6 Sacks of Oats
Tom Daw Carried 10 Sacks of Oats to Mr Russell Warbleton
Ths Hoad Thrashing

[Wednesday 19]
Verry Wett
Tom Grubbing Old Dann Half Day
John Marten Thrashing Ths Hoad Thrashing

[Thursday 20]
Very windy & snow Tom Daw grubbing 9 acres John Marten thrashing
Ths Hoad thrashing

[Friday 21]
Very clear Tom & Old Dann grubbing John Marten thrashing
Ths Hoad thrashing

[Saturday 22]
Fine Morn Rough After Noon Tom Daw Thrashing
John Beal Grubbing up in 9 Acres John [Mar]ten & Nick Threshing
Ths Hoad Threshing

---

[76] Throughout the diary we have chalk being brought to the farm to make lime in their own kiln and occasionally brought in from other places. This was achieved by heating the chalk in a kiln. Also referred to in the diary is 'making places for lime' helping make 'lime lump places'.

[77] Winowers were around, but we suspect Nicholas did not have one and most likely threw up the corn into the breeze between the barn doors which separated out the chaff and then most likely through sieves to separate the weeds and tail (small corn) from the corn. Cornford is mentioned as a 'sieve bottomer' in the diary.

[Sunday 23]
Very Cold and Some Snow

[Monday 24]
Snow Morning John Marten Thrashing Tho Thrasg Tom Daw Went to Gardner street[78] after for 10 Sacks of Barley I have ….ed Nick Cleaned up 32 Sacks …ing John Threshing

Tuesday 1 February
and [Chapel C]loase [Hen]ry Hedging[79] [cut]ting Old Dann Grubbing 9 acres

Wednesday 2
Wm Carried 26 Timber sticks and 3 Ash racks[80] I Bashed fields down to House
2 Load Stubble from 12 acres to Ox Yard John thrashing Ths Hoad son Hedging Wm Farmer Joseph Marten and Jesse H Cutting Wm Dann Mr Piper Grubbing 9 Acres Thawed all Day

Thursday 3
Tom Grubbing Old Dann & Piper Josph Marten Jesse & Wm Farmer Wood Cutting Ths Hoad & H trudging
Frosty Morning Sun Shine Ried Verrall from Lewes

Friday 4
Frost and Sun all Day John Marten thrashing Tom Daw Master Piper Wm Dann Grubbing 9 Acres Josh Marten Jesse Marten Wm Farmer W[ood] Cutting Ths Hoad and Henry Hedging Father Sheep

Saturday 5
Tom Old Dann Mr Piper Grubbing 9 Acres Jack R Nail John Thrashing Tom Hoad and Henry Hedging Joseph Marten Jesse & John Farmer [cut]ting Fine Frosty morn some Snow After Noon

Sunday 6
Very Misty and some Rain in afternoon

Monday 7
Tom I Father Carried 50 H Faggots[81] 9 Acres to T Hoad Plough up 9 Acres

[78] This is the High Street through Herstmonceux.
[79] Hedges were cut with a swap or hedging hook.
[80] Timber that was carried.
[81] Types of faggot noted in the diary are Hoath, House, Hop, Top, Kiln, Lew, Luse,

Brought 9 Acres Faggots Broke Open & Old Dann Josph Marten & Jesse Wm Farmer Hedging Henry Dole

Tuesday 8
Horses plough up 9 acres Wm Farmer W[ood] Cu[tting] Thos Hoad & Henry thrashing half day hedging after noon Henry hop pole shaving[82] John Marten thrashing spindle mended[83] very wett misty day

Wednesday 9
Horses plough up 9 acres Father & Nichs clean up 31 sacks of potato Oats[84] John carried them to the mill 4 oxs cart Josph Martin Jess & Wm Farmer wood cutting man from G [Gardner] Street Thos Hoad hedging & Henry Old Dann grubbing 9 acres Fine day

Thursday 10
Very foggy Horses plough old Piper & Dann Grubbing up 9 acres John Marten ditching at garden Joseph Marten & son Joseph & Jesse Wm Farmer James Message boy wood cutting Thos Hoad & Henry Hedging Marther[85] shaving pols spreading little John

Friday 11
Horses plough Old Dann grubbing Piper Do stacked up 2 carts roots[86] John Marten & Nichs Dung spreading Poun[d] hop garden Thos Hoad hedging James Message Joseph Marten & Jesse wood cutting F[ine] Weather

Saturday 12
Josph Marten Jesse & Josph James Message & boy wood cutting Thos Hoad hedging John dung sho'ng[87] Horses plough Old Dann grubbing Nichs Do

Bush, Spray, Hawth, Peabow, Brush, Hazel & Bush.
82 Removing the bark from the pole.
83 Repaired the axle of the wagon.
84 The potato oat was first discovered in Cumberland in 1788 under rather peculiar circumstances. 'Mrs Mary Jackson of Threepland, who died in the year 1810, at the advanced age of 82 years, whilst working in one of her fields observed a single stem of oats growing on a potato ridge, the seed of which had been carried thither by the wind. Observing that the straw was uncommonly strong, when the grain was matured she preserved it and used it for seed the ensuing season, which succeeding in a very extraordinary degree, the method was soon after adopted by a number of farmers.' *Dublin Journal of Temperance, Science and Literature*, Volume 2, 1843.
85 Martha.
86 A valuable resource for feed or for making manure.
87 Shoveling?

Half day fine day sun shine
Elias put on some shoe on the horses

Sunday 13
Very foggy weather

Monday 14
Foggy Morn John Marten Edwn Whitman dig Hop digging[88] up Pound
Hop Garden Horses plough up 9 acres Old Dann Nichs Father grubbing up
9 acres Thos Hoad hedging up Grimes wood some wood cutting

Tuesday 15
Sunshine Horses plough Old Dann grubbing Father & Nichs finish
John dung spreading morning After John & Nichs cleaned up 12 sacks of
potato oats John Baker Josph Thompson hop diging Wm Foster Half day
Thos Hoad hedging Josp Martens son Joe & Jesse Marten wood cutting
Plough share that I laid[89]

Wednesday 16
Horses finish plough up 9 acres Old Dann Grubbing John Marten John
Baker Wm Foster Joseph Thomson hop digging Nichs half day Do Thos
Hoad Hedging Josp Marten Josph Do Jo boy & Jesse Barker Wood cutting
Frosty morn sun shine day

Thursday 17
Very .. frost morn C afternoon
Horses plough up 7 Acres began corner gain the river
Old Dann grubbing John Marten Nichs John Baker Rd Whiteman Wm
Foster & Joseph Thomson hop diging Josph Marten son Josp boy Jesse
Marten wood cutting Thos Hoad hedging Mather Hop pole shaving

Friday 18
Horses plough Old Dann grubbing John Marten Nichs thrashing oats
Joseph Thomson Edd Whiteman Wm Foster John Baker hop diging
Josph Marten son boy & Jesse Marten Wm Farmer Mr Gander Wood
cutting Thos Hoad hedging Mather Shaving frosty morn

Saturday 19
Misty morn cloudy afternoon horses plough John Marten & Nichs
thrashing Thos Hoad half day Josph Marten Jesse Josph Marten Thos Hoad

---

[88] Preparing for hops.
[89] Fitted a new share to the plough.

half day wood Cutting Edd Whiteman Josph Thomson John Baker Wm Foster

hop diging finish Began orchard Old Dann grubbing half day

Sunday 20
Frosty morn fine day

Monday 21
Frosty sun shine day Horses fetched 1 load o roots from Bushy Fields 1 Do from 9 acres Old Dann grubbing Josph Thomson cording roots[90] John Marten thrashing Thos Hoad Josph Marten Josph Do Jesse Marten John Baker

Wm Foster wood cutting Nichs & David drove Rush cow up to Mr Press Elias Standen shewd[91] 1 horse Naild Do slept Over & Wm Gilbert married at Warbleton church[92]

Tuesday 22
Frosty cloudy morning fine afternoon Horses fetched 1 load of roots from 9 acres plough up 12 acres John Marten Nichs & Josph Thomson cleaned up 7 sacks 2 B of oats Morning felled some bushes from Silverfields to mend hedge down Aust Brook Josph Marten Josph Do & Jesse Do boy John Baker Wm Farmer Thos Hoad gapped Old Dann wood cutting

Wednesday 23
Frosty sun day

Horses fetched 1 load very large roots from 9 acres plough up 12 acres south side of the warp[93] John Marten Josph Thomson gaping Redpale Thos Hoad Josp Marten Josp Do Jesse Do J boy Wm Farmer Josph Pankhurst Saml Stephen John Baker Wm Foster wood cutting garden Old Dann Do

Thursday 24
Frosty fine day Horses plough up 12 acres John Marten Joseph Thomson gapping Wm Foster John Baker Thos Hoad Josph Stephn Saml Pankhurst Josph Marten Josph's girl Do Jesse & Wm Gander Do Wm Farmer wood cutting Jerry Reid boy hop pole shaving plough share sharp Nichs spread 5

---

[90] The only mention of this phrase in the diary; probably just tying up the roots.
[91] Shoed.
[92] William Gilbert married Hannah Hall at Warbleton Church on Monday 21st February 1814. He was the youngest son of George Gilbert (founder of the Chapel) & Ruth Wright.
[93] Warp or warping: ploughing in small lands or cants to aid drainage.

bushels of ashes at Hodges Old Dann CW[94]

Friday 25
Frost too hard for plough Horses fetched 1 load of roots from 9 acres John Marten Josph Thomson Nichs got in half oat stack Thos Hoad wood cutting no body been to see who their has twin cow calved

Saturday 26
Freshly fine day Horses drawing poles from 1 end garden to young part Carried 27 sacks of wheat to Mill oxen John Marten Josph Thomson [crossed out] Nichs Finished getting in oat stack in all 9 loads Thos Hoad Josph Marten Josph boy & Jesse Wm Farmer Josph Stepn Saml Pankhurst John Baker Wm Foster Old Dann wood cutting 2 boy shaving

Sunday 27
Frosty morning sun shine day

Monday 28
Frosty morng cloudy day been very dry frost that has been known for 19 years Horses drawing poles from Croft garden to Pound field Oxen John Marten Nichs Josph Thomson cleared rubbish from oat stack morning afternoon drawing poles Do Josph sharping Thos Hoad Wm Farmer Old Dann Josph Josph boy Josph John Marten Saml Josph Stepn Pankhurst John Baker Wm Foster Gander wood cutt[ing] 5 boys girl shaving most snow this winter that has been known for 19 years

Tuesday 1 March
Very rainy day John Marten Josph Thomson threshing oats Thos Hoad Henry threshing oats Do Horses plough up 12 acres 1 hour plough share laid

Wednesday 2
Horses plough John Marten Josph Thomson sharping poles pound garden Thos Hoad boy Josph John Josph boy John Marten Wm Foster John Baker Old Dann Wm Farmer wood cutting 6 shave storm hail cloudy day

Thursday 3
Cloudy day Horses plough John Marten sharping poles Josph Thomson Do half Day Josp Josp boy Jesse John Marten Wm Farmer John Baker Wm Foster Old Dann Thos Hoad Josph Saml Pankhurst 6 shaving wood cutting

[94] Cutting wood.

Friday 4
Little frost Horses plough John Marten sharping poles Josph Josph boy Jesse John Marten John Baker Wm Foster Old Dann Message boy Thos Hoad
Wm Farmer wood cutting 6 hop pole shaving

Saturday 5
Windy cold day Horses plough John Marten Josph Thomson hop digging Josph Josph boy Jesse Marten Josph Saml Stepn Pankhurst Message boy Wm Farmer John Baker Wm Foster Old Dann Thos Hoad wood 5 shavers

Sunday 6
Windy cloudy day little snow

Monday 7
Snow morning cloudy day Horses plough John Marten threshing Josph Thomson hop digging hops Morning afternoon thrashing Thos Hoad Wm Foster wood Elias mended spindle

Tuesday 8
Windy little snow at times Horses plough John thrashing & Josph Thomson Do Thos Hoad Father Nichs cleaned up 15 Qr 2 B long tail D Blue Josph Jesse Marten Wm Foster John Marten Message Wood cutting Thos Baker Do

Wednesday 9
Tom Nichs plough John Marten Wm Father carried 1 load oat straw to Hodges John Josph Thomson thrashing Thos Hoad thrashing wheat two Pankhurst's Wm Farmer Josph Marten boy John Baker Old Dann Message John Marten wood cutting 7 hop pole shaving

Thursday 10
Frosty snow thawed Horses plough oxen John Mar[ten] carried poles from wood into pound garden Thos Hoad thrashing Josph Thomson thrash Old Dann John Baker three Pankhurst Josph Marten boy Message Wm Farmer Wm Foster John Marten wood cutting 6 shavers tug chase mended Share sharp spin[dle]

Friday 11
Snow night frost cloudy day Tom Chaff cutting John Marten Josp Thomson thrashing Thos Hoad Do John Baker Old Dann Wm Foster Josph Marten boy Wm Farmer wood cutting Thos Cow calfed bull

Saturday 12
Snow night little morning plough half day Mr John Marten Josph Thomson thrashing Thos Hoad thrashing Wm Foster John Baker Stephn Pankhurst Wm Farmer John Marten 2 pole shavers bought 1 ton of hay J Lade

Sunday 13
Freze. Cloudy thawed shut up 3 shuts to fast

Monday 14
Frost windy cloudy cold day Horses plough John Marten Nichs Father carried poles from wood to pound garden morning afternoon John sharping Do Josph Thomson thrashing Thos Hoad Do Wm Dann John Baker Wm Foster Wm Farmer John Marten wood cutting some shavers 2 Pankhurst's W cutting

Tuesday 15
Frost windy cloudy day Horses plough John Marten sharping poles Joseph Thomson diging Hop brook Thos Hoad thrashing cleaned 3 qr 3 bush wheat John Baker Wm Foster two Pankhurst Gander Wm Farmer John Marten Old Dann some shavers 3 old links put on plough chains I Do that John I Do 1 link

Wednesday 16
Little frost windy cloudy sun day Horses plough Hodges Millfield at Bottom John Marten carried up 5 sacks of wheat at 12£ per+ load to Mr Russells Josph Thomson diging between apple tree Thos Hoad thrashing John Baker Wm Foster Gander John Marten wood cutting Wm Foster finished some shav[ers]

Thursday 17
Little frost warm clear day Horses plough Hodges John Marten sharping poles Thos Hoad thrashing Colly Cow Calfed bull Wm Foster John Baker Old Dann John Baker two Pankhurst Message Gander Wm Farmer John Marten some shavers

Friday 18
Little frost foggy morning Horses finished Hodges Thos Hoad ditching Grimes Brook half day David Honnissett John Baker hop digging croft John Marten sharping poles croft & diging Old Dann Wm Foster two Pankhurst Message Gander Wm Farmer some shavers

Saturday 19
Foggy day Horses plough 7 acres Wm Foster John Marten John Baker

David Honnysett Nichs hop diging Thos Hoad ditching Grimes Brook the boy Wm Farmer Gander wood cutting some shavers boy finished fence poles shavd 32 score at 8d per score

Sunday 20
Foggy morning sun shine

Monday 21
Rain mist foggy day Horses plough John Marten threshing hop diging half day Do carried little dung into brook hop garden Nichs Titus Cornford Wm Foster John Baker David Honnesett hop diging Thos Hoad ditching Wm Farmer John Marten W Gander wood cutting some shavers

Tuesday 22
Foggy morning fine day Tom chaff cutting[95] Thos Hoad thrashing John Marten thrashing Wm Foster John Baker David Honnysett Wm Cornford Nichs hop diging finished Wm Farmer some savers

Wednesday 23
Foggy cloudy sun shine day Horses plough John Marten Nichs carried little dung from mixen Chaple meadow in to hop B garden David Honeysett John Baker Titus Cornford Wm Foster hop diging Aurcherd[96] Thos Hoad Wm Farmer John Marten wood cutting Gander Do some shavers plough irons sharped

Thursday 24
Foggy morning rain & mist afternoon Horses plough finished 7 acres oxen dung from stable carrying morning finished in all 30 load afternoon John Nichs fetching ash poles together Wm Foster John Baker Titus. Cornford hop diging Thos Hoad wood morning afternoon thrashing John Marten wood cutting some shavers

Friday 25
Foggy morning Horses drawed out 66 ash poles from the wood John Baker Wm Foster Titus Cornford hop diging Thos Hoad ditching & wood cutting John Marten wood Do some shavers John Marten gone to live at John Blands Sarah Eton Sanhill[97] Father agreed with John Baker to drive oxen at times for 16 shillings per week

[95] Cutting straw into short lengths with a machine for horse feed.
[96] Orchard.
[97] Sandhill?

Saturday 26
Foggy morning sun shine day Horses drawing fence poles out of the wood into Poun[d] field John Baker spreading dung Nichs Cornford Foster diging Thos Hoad John Marten wood Cutting some shaving poles

Sunday 27
Sun shine Deep Red cow calved cow

Monday 28
Foggy morning sun shine Horses sowing tares up 9 acres John Baker Wm Foster Nichs Titus Cornford dressing pound hops Thos Hoad brishing Old lane again Grimes wood John Marten Message wood cutting some shavers Father purchased of John Venus 6 sacks of spring tears[98] at 24s per sack Sheep began to lamb

Tuesday 29
Windy night cloudy day some rain Horses finished sowing 9 acres David Honneysett Foster John Baker Titus Cornford George Guy Nichs hop diging Thos Hoad thrashing half day John Marten wood

Wednesday 30
Foggy night sun shine day Horses sowing 7 acres with long tail white oats & Trefoil Thos Hoad thrashing John Baker Wm Foster David Honneysett George Guy Nichs Titus Cornford dressing hops[99] croft John Marten wood cutting finished some shaving

Thursday 31
White frost cloudy showers rain Horses finnished harrow 7 acres Thos Hoad thrashing David Honeysett cutting hop sets[100] Father Nichs uncle Wm Oxley cutting sets Do John Baker Wm Foster Titus Cornford George Guy dressing & grubbing hops upper end croft some hop pole shavers

Friday 1 April
Rain morning sun afternoon Thos Daw chaff cut Thos Hoad thrashing John Baker thrashing David Honneysett cutting hop sets Afternoon some shavers

Saturday 2
Fine day shower rain Horses carried 75 House faggots & bushes from 9

[98] Tares
[99] Applying manure.
[100] Perhaps taking cuttings from new hop shoots to propagate new plants.

acres to Thos Hoad morning afternoon Tom cutting chaff David Honeysett John Baker Wm Foster George Guy Titus Cornford dressing & cutting hop setts Brook & Croft Thos Hoad thrashing

Sunday 3
Fine day

Monday 4
Fine day Horses drawed some 12 feet poles into pound hop garden 14 Do poundfield John Baker laying out poles poun[d] garden George Guy hop diging Brook Wm Foster wood cutting some shavers

Tuesday 5
Clear sun shine day Horses sowing potatoe Oats & Clover in 12 acres John Baker sharping poles Pd garden George Guy hop diging Thos Hoad thrashing borrowed 1 horse of Wm Harmer for harrowing purchase 3 bush clover paid at £2 2s per B Wm Foster wood cutting some shavers

Wednesday 6
Foggy morning cloudy sun shine day Horses finished harrow 12 acres John Baker sharping laying out poles poun[d] garden George Guy hop diging Thos Hoad thrashing Wm Foster wood cutting some shavers borrowed Wm Harmers horse Father drove marsh lambs to B horse[101]

Thursday 7
Cloudy morning sun afternoon Horses harrow at Hodges Mill field with long tail wites & clover & trefoil finished oat season harrow tolerable well John Baker laying poles George Guy diging hops finished Thos Hoad thrashing Wm Foster wood cutting some shavers

Friday 8
Clear sun day Good Friday John Baker laying sharping poles George Guy sharping poles Auchard Blacksmith move 4 shoes[102] and made new waggon seat out of old iron some shavers Thos Hoad thrashing Wm Foster wood cutting

Saturday 9
Clear day Horses plough Whenhouse field Thos Hoad thrashing Josph

---

[101] This probably means Father drove the Marsh lambs to the Black Horse Inn near Battle. This seems to have been a stopping/exchange place for farmers and drovers, as it is mentioned on several occasions.
[102] See fn. Wednesday 13 March.

Marten Wm Foster wood cut[ting] John Baker Nichs cleaned 1b 1 sack Dutch Blues Share sharp

Sunday 10
Clear fine day

Monday 11
Clear day Horses plough oxen John Baker Nichs drawing poles pound & orchard garden Wm Foster sharping poles & George Guy poling orchard Thos Hoad thrashing some shavers

Tuesday 12
Clear day Horses plough oxen stirring Gutter field George Guy Wm Foster poling Thos Hoad thrashing Josph Marten wood cutting shavers Thos Hoad cows calf died share sharp

Wednesday 13
Clear day Horses plough oxen stirring Gutter field George Guy Wm Foster poling Thos Hoad thrashing Josph Marten wood cutting shavers Thos Hoad cows calf died share sharp

Thursday 14
Clear day Horses & oxen plough Wm Foster George Guy Old Dann poling Thos Hoad thrashing Josph Marten wood some shavers Heathfield fair very dull little sold

Friday 15
Cloudy morning thunder storm & rain afternoon Horses carried 40 of sacks of long tail Oats to X in Hand[104] to meet Mr Best at Bucksted Thos Hoad Wm Foster George Guy cleaned 2 loads of wheat Wm Dann poling Josph Marten wood cutting some shavers oxen plough Coller Linded with lether[105]

Saturday 16
Showery day Horses plough oxen carried 2 load of wheat to Joph Balcombe at 17£ 10s per load Ths Hoad Wm Foster George Guy cleaned 14 sacks 2 bush morning Hoad thrashing Foster Guy poling afternoon Old Dann

103 '2 Removes' is Farrier terminology for taking off a horse's shoe, in order to dress the hoof and replace the shoe in a proper manner on the same or another foot, hence an old shoe used over again. This is probably what he means on the 8th 'Blacksmith move 4 shoes'.
104 Cross in Hand.
105 Leather collar oiled with linseed oil.

poleing Josph Marten Message wood cutting Some shavers

Sunday 17
Rain morning clear afternoon

Monday 18
Rain morning cloudy day Horses plough finished oxen drawing poles into pound hop garden Old Dann Wm Foster George Guy poling Thos Hoad thrashing some pole shavers

Tuesday 19
Sun & cloudy day Horses harrow gutter field Barley Oxen carried 500 14 feet poles up to Carrots Green[106] I broke Neb Thos Hoad thrashing Wm Foster George Guy Old Dann poleing Josph Marten wood cutting some shavers Father drove 6 yearling & Dann cow & Hailsham Down in the marsh

Wednesday 20
Horses harrow oxen carried 500 – 14 feet poles to Carrots Green for Mr Weller both lots 10£ & 150 house faggots[107] 2 cord of wood to Mr Stone 3£ 4s 0d Thos Hoad thrashing Old Dann Wm Foster George Guy poleing Josph Marten wood cutting Some shavers [illeg]

Tuesday 21
Fine morning showery afternoon Horses harrow Oxen rolling sowed trefoil & clover Thos Hoad thrashing barn out cleaned up 32s 2 b wheat Wm Foster George Guy poleing pound garden Thos Hoad Do Old Dann poleing Josph Marten wood cutting some shavers

Friday 22
Cloudy and sunny day Horses drawed 2 load 12 feet poles into pound garden harrow whenhouse 2 went rold tares gutterfield[108] Do some oxen drudging Chapel W meadow rolling Do barley Thos Hoad Old Dann Wm Foster George Guy poling Josph Marten wood cutting some shavers

[106] Carrick Green in Dallington was occupied by a Richard Ticehurst in the 1861 census. His obituary in the Hastings and St Leonards Observer (14 December 1872) states he was 'for many years of Carrots Hill Farm Dallington'. In the 1841 census for Dallington, Carrots Green appears as a residence. Carrick Green, Carrots Green and Carrots Hill Farm are probably one and the same thing [Jayne Adams].
[107] For the bread oven.
[108] Harrowed Whenhouse field twice across and rolled tares in Gutterfield.

Saturday 23
Fine day Horses rolling kiln field oxen drudging chapel meadow Thos Hoad Wm Foster George Guy Old Dann poleing Josph Marten wood Cutting some shavers Winchester crew timber Felling Father cut[109] the lambs

Sunday 24
Cloudy some showers

Monday 25
Cloudy showers rain from north Horses drawing poles from wood to P garden oxen drudging Silverfield & Crofts lodge yoke up pair three yearling steer[110] Thos Hoad boy Wm Foster George Guy Old Dann poling Josph Marten wood cutting timber felling Do some pole shavers 6 Romaes[111]

Tuesday 26
Showery day Horses drawing poles into pound garden & Archard oxen carried 100 pea bough to Mr Russell & 100 house faggots to Mr Guy Thos Hoad Wm Foster George Guy Old Dann Henry Hoad poleing Josph Marten wood cutting pole shavers Do Timber fellers new pug ring & ling[112] hop tiers in the pound garden cut 2 calves

Wednesday 27
Cloudy day little rain afternoon Horses nidgeting peace pears kiln field & drawed firs[113] for potatoes Frost killed the pears afternoon rolling B field oxen fetched chucks from pound field Thos Hoad Henry Wm Foster poleing morning Old Dann Do Josph Marten wood cutting boy Do some shaving Poles hop tiers

Thursday 28
Cloudy day Thos Daw trunk up again pound rolling 2 upper fields at Hodges Thos Hoad Thos & Henry Wm Foster George Guy Old Dann finished poleing young garden morning poleing in croft Wm Foster Auchard John Baker Nichs bringing chucks from young garden home hop

[109] Castrated.
[110] Training them up to work. Once trained they will only work as a pair so if sold must be sold together.
[111] Romany people?
[112] Perhaps an iron ring on the pug with a link in it; Nicholas might have shortened the word linking to ling.
[113] Marked out first for potatoes.

tyers Josph Marten & boy wood cutting 2 shoes remove plough irons laid David finished scrapeing dog wood timber fellers

Friday 29
Cloudy day Horses plough in croft oxen carried C wood kiln house faggots from pound shaw & waggon load Of the feet poles into orchard Thos Thos Henry Hoad Old Dann George Guy poleing croft Wm Foster orchard Josph Marten & boy wood cutting timber Father smokey cow calved cow

Saturday 30
Cloudy morning clear afternoon Horses harrow and streking[114] firs croft morning afternoon harrow nidgeting firs Bush field oxen carrying root from bush field & brought 300 poles from the wood to orchard Josph Marten & boy finished wood cutting Thos Hoad Thos Henry George Guy Old Dann poling Wm Foster Do timber fellers

Sunday 1 May
Clear day

Monday 2
Clear day Horses nidgetting pound garden finished 1 went[?] Oxen plough in 13 acres again the hoth[115] Thos Hoad Thos Henry top cutting Grimes Wood[116] Wm Foster George Guy Old Dann poling hops timber fellers Father David drove 3 cow calves 2 two yearlings steer & 1 yearling colt in to the marsh

Tuesday 3
Cloudy morning clear afternoon Horses nidgetting P garden oxen plough George Guy Wm Foster Old Dann poling Thos Thos Henry Hoad top cutting timber fellers Oxen share sharp ……….I and orchard some

Wednesday 4
Horses nidgetting first part P garden 3 went in all second Do 2 went oxen plough Mast Thos Henry Hoad top cutting timber fellers Wm Foster Old Dann poling George Guy poling Archard oxen sharp at Standen Rushlake[117]

---

[114] Streking is some form of cultivation, possibly going crossways.
[115] Hawth, scrub.
[116] Perhaps taking out tall trees and leaving the coppice.
[117] Elias Standen, at Rushlake, sharps the plough

Thursday 5
F cloudy morning rain afternoon Horses clearing chuck in croft oxen plough Wm Foster Old Dann poling Brook George Guy orchard Thos Thos Henry Hoad top cutting timber fellers Jesse Jarvis fetched 7½ hundred of 14 feet poles at 18s pr hundred for the place

Friday 6
Clear day Horses & G Guy carried 3 load of wheat straw up side oxen yard oxen clearing hop garden Mast Thos Henry Hoad top cutting Wm Foster Old Dann poling in Brook timber fellers Jarvis fetched 7 ½ Hund. Of poles oxen Do carried 12 sacks of wheat to the Mill 18£ 4 Nidget tines laid

Saturday 7
Clear day Horses nidgetting C orchard garden oxen carried 1 chord of wood to Mr Russell and 30 rist bats to P Pankhurst & 3 ½ poles into Brook garden Mast Thos Henry Hoad top cutting timber fellers Wm Foster poling morning George Guy 2 girls & Wm Foster planting potatoes in kiln field Father Purchase Wm Harmer's bull calf hop tiers

Sunday 8
Cloudy day Yearling colt jumped over the Grimes Brook hedge & stake himself under the flank

Monday 9
Cloudy day Horses plough in 13 acres oxen Carried 100 H[ouse] Faggots to Mr Russell & 100 Do ½ chord of wood for John Baker Thos Thos Henry Hoad top cutting Wm Foster George Guy David Hoad's girls potato planting in the croft Timber fellers finished felled down 125 trees Mr Tomlins from Brighton & 2 gentlemen come to look at cold Hodges traveler J Jarvis 7½ poles hop tiers

Tuesday 10
Cloudy day windy Horses plough oxen carried ½ C wood 100 faggots & W Waters shoemaker ½ C wood 50 faggots drawed 250 poles top squires field for Jarvis Thos Henry Hoad top cutting Wm Foster David & girls potating hop tiers W Crouch tailing sheep[118]

Wednesday 11
Cloudy morning clear afternoon Horses plough morning afternoon Loaded 4½ loads of bark oxen carried 100 faggots to Mr Russell and getting bark

[118] Removing the tails for hygiene purposes.

together Thos Hoad chopping hops in the orchard Wm Foster George Guy David girls potatoing finished croft began B fields Thos Henry Hoad picking up chucks in the wood hop tiers killed hog

Thursday 12
Cloudy windy day Horses & oxen carried 2 loads bark to Mr Baker Heathfield Thos Hoad Henry & Thos chopping hops Wm Foster G Guy potatoing morning afternoon clearing hop gardens hop tiers Jarvis 7½ poles in all 3000

Friday 13
Cloudy day some rain Horses nidgetting croft & brook gardens oxen loaded up some bark & Wm Foster Do G Guy clearing hop gardens Mast Thos Henry Hoad chopping hops morning afternoon thrashing oats Old Thos ditching at Hodges in the plat John Baker G Guy Wm Foster casting up dung[119] in Chapple Yard hop tiers oxen turn[?] Hodges

Saturday 14
Cloudy misly showers Horses plough oxen carried 1 load bark to Heathfield Mast Henry Hoad hop chopping G Guy Wm Foster casting up dung share sharp

Sunday 15
Cloudy warm day

Monday 16
Cloudy warm sun shine day cold weather of late stop things from growing Horses plough oxen carried 1 chord of wood & ½ hund'd faggots & carried 33 prong bats & lot of old iron to the Blacksmith Mast Thos Hoad thrashing Henry Hoad chopping hops in the Brook Wm Foster G Guy David potatoing in the Brook hop tiers Whichesters men diging saw pit plough irons laid

Tuesday 17
Clear day Horses rolling parts 7 acres and the Mill field at Hodges oxen drawing trees for the sawyer morning afternoon plough in 8 acres long ways Mast Thos Hoad thrashing Henry Do chopping hops G Guy Wm Foster & David finished potatoing in the Brook Old mare foaled a horse colt Mr Pursglove Cowden fetched 100 house faggots Father drove 6 two yearling heifers and one yearling colt down to Whincelsea hop tiers

[119] Making a maxon or dungheap.

Wednesday 18
Cloudy morning clear afternoon Horses & oxen plough Mast Thos Hoad thrashing Henry Hoad hop chopping G Guy Wm Foster casting up dung in O Close & C Lodge timber sawyers hop tiers share sharp yoke up pair 3 yearling steers

Thursday 19
Clear day Horses plough oxen Do Mast Thos Hoad thrashing Henry hop chopping G Guy Wm Foster Casting up dung hop tiers timber fellers Mr Purglove Fetched 400 house faggots at £1 5s per hund'd in the place Thos Hoad cleaned up 23 sacks of long blue tail oats

Friday 20
Clear day Horses plough finished & plough 10 acres oxen carried 171 ash poles to Rushlake for Mr Tanner at Buxted Mast Thos Hoad thrashing Henry hop chopping Brook G Guy carried chucks into the Garret & picking potatoes in the oast David Do Mast. Daw gone away agreed with Wm Foster for 15s per week & 900 top faggots Break fast Sunday morning hop tiers [sawyers crossed out] Do saw[120] farrowed & pigs

Saturday 21
Clear windy day Horses plough oxen plough & drawing trees for sawyers Mast Thos Hoad thrashing G Guy David moving potatoes Henry Hoad hop chopping Share sharp Mr Pursglove to 1 chord half wood H^d Marten some faggots 1 link to chain

Sunday 22
Cold windy cloudy day

Monday 23
Cold windy cloudy morning warm afternoon Horses plough oxen fence & hop pole drawing Mast Thos Hoad bedding poles into the pound field G Guy helping & Do in the wood Henry Hoad hop chopping carpenter mended yard gate & hewing trees over 2 links shot & ring to hedging chain shot[121] Wm Marten afternoon faggots

Tuesday 24
Cold windy rain all day Horses plough 3 Hoads[?] oxen David G Guy

---

[120] Sow.
[121] It appears that two links of the measuring chain had been broken. See also 13 June.

drawing poles Thos Thos Hoad bedding poles morning afternoon thrashing squire cuirtes[122] 150 top & 100 spray Faggots

Wednesday 25

Showery morning cloudy afternoon Horses oxen drawing poles G Guy Father David Do Thos Thos Henry Hoad bedding poles hop tiers

Thursday 26

Fine frost warm day Horses carried 200 of house faggots to Mr Pocock WM Hill[123] Oxen 1½ chord of wood Mr Barnes Dallington 100 faggots to Mr Hoad Hodges Mr Hoad gapping between P fields Mast Thos Hoad thrashing Do clean up 19 sacks Dutch Blues G Guy casting dung morning P field afternoon helped cleaned oats Henry Hoad chopping hops Pound field Old Dann ditching Grimes wood sawyers Do hop tiers Wm Marten Finished carrying faggots thrashing wheat Squires[?] & mended the redger with old links

Friday 27

Clear day Oxen carried 200 kiln faggots to Goldsmith B Kilns morning afternoon loaded up horses 150 Do Morning afternoon Do Thos Thos Henry Hoad chopping hops P field G Guy casting dung P field sawyers Old Dann ditching Esqr Curttis Afternoon faggots Pursglove top faggots & cord wood

Saturday 28

Clear warm day Horses & oxen carried 350 Kiln faggots In all 1100 Thos Thos Henry hop chopping G Guy casting dung Old Dann ditching sawyers hop tiers Mr Curttis finished carrying faggots No: 450 New Hoops Hog jets

Sunday 29

Cloudy Morng little Rain Clear Aftn

Monday 30

Clear Morng Cloudy Aftn Old Dann Ditching all the Rest Hallow [day] Keeping Horses and oxen Carried 150 Faggots and ½ Chord Wood

Tuesday 31

Cloudy Day Drops Rain Night Oxen Carried 150 House Faggots to Mr Loydd Windmill hill Horses Got in the Wheat stack with 2 Waggons Borrd 1 other Bill Harmer No Loads 9½ ditto Fetch home some Oats from the

---

[122] Curtis?
[123] Windmill Hill.

Barn shop in the Garret Thos and Hoad Helping Get in the W Stacks Old Dann Ditching two weeders hop tiers

Wednesday 1 June
Cloudy Day Rain Aftr Horses plough 8 Acres Oxen Carried 200 Faggots Mr James Goldsmith Old Dann Ditching Sawyers Master Tho Hoad clearing out Ditches Poun[d] Garden Henry Hoads girls Wheding Hop tiers

Thursday 2
Cloudy Day Horses plough finished Oxen carried 100 Faggots to Mr Erry & Drawing Trees for the Sawyers 4 Loaded 1 Chord of Wood Master Thos Hoad Killd Hog and clearing Ditch and Gapping G Guy Henry Hoad Carrying in Potatoes from the Brook to Oast and Diging Orchard and Hop tiers Old Dann Ditching I have Laid

Friday 3
Cloudy and Rain Day Horses carried 100 Faggots to Mr Lullham Herstmonceux Oxen 1 Chord Wood to Mr Whisham & 100 Faggotts to Mr Lullham ditto at £1. 16. 0 Master Henry Hoad Thrashing Wheat Master Hoad turning Maxon[124] at Hodges plat G Guy Diging in Orchard Old Dann Ditching Sawyers ditto

Saturday 4
Cloudy sunny Showr Rain Horses Carried 200 Top & Spray Faggots for Wm Foster and Drawed 3 trees for the Sawyers Oxen carried 22 trees Chord to Mr Fox R L G[125] and Carried 100 Top Faggots to Mr J Water for the Boord Master Hoad & Henry thrashing Master Hoad G Guy shoveling dirt into 4 pole Hills P Garden Old Dann Ditching colly from the Marsh to Bull Hop tiers John Waters Fetched 100 Kiln Faggots from Wood

Sunday 5
Cloudy Morng showers Rain afternoon

Monday 6
Cloudy Day Horses & Oxen Carried 350 Kiln Faggots to Mr Smith B kilns Master Henry Hoad threshing Master Hoad Hop shoveling Orchard G Guy help Loading Faggots Old Dann Ditching Sawyers Hop tiers Workers chairs Mended Oxen Do Drawing trees Dung Rake Mended Blacksmith nailing horses[?]

---
[124] Mixen.
[125] Rush Lake Green.

Tuesday 7
Cold Cloudy Day Horses & Oxen Carried 700 Faggots to Goldsmiths Do Master Hoad Henry threshing Master Hoad turning Maxon Hodges Hop tiers weeders Sawyers Old Dann Ditching Blacksmith New Plates our Waggon

Wednesday 8
Cold Windy Rainy Day Horses & Oxen carried 350 Faggots to B Kilns Load up Do Mr Hoad help Horses Master Henry Hoad thrashing G Guy loading Faggots & Shovelling Hops croft Old Dann Ditching David and William Drove two 3 yearlg steers and Russells Cow on the Marsh fetched out 2 Cows & Calves Hop Ties Pursglove fetched 100 House Faggots Coller landed with Leather

Thursday 9
Clear Warm Day Oxen and Horses Carried 750 Faggots to B Kiln Mast Henry Hoad thrashing Mr Hoad turning Maxin G Guy shovelling Hops Old Dann Ditching Sawyers Do Hop Ties Weeders line hop new oxen turn out load[?]

Friday 10
Clear and Cloudy Day Horses & Oxen carried 750 Faggots to Mr Goldsmith & Horses Drawing Trees Mast Henry Hoad thrashing Mr Hoad finised Turning Mixon Casting up Dung in the Yard G Guy Hop shoveling & Thistle Mowing Old Dann Ditching Sawyers Do Hop tiers Weeders Mr Lade Priory fetched 300 Hop Poles at 19s per Hundred

Saturday 11
Clear Warm Day Horses & Oxen finised carryg Faggots to the B Kiln in all 4000, Horses Do Carried 90 fence poles to Dill Gate for Mr Squires at 6d per pole Carried Load Faggots Do to our Kiln Oxen 2 loads Do Thos Henry thrashing Mr Hoad casting up Dung G Guy Shovelling Hops Old Dann Ditching Sawyers Hop Ties Weeders Oxen Broke Yoke

Sunday 12
Clear Warm Day

Monday 13
Cloudy Day Drops of Rain Aftern Horses fetched 2 Loads Faggots from 9 Acres & 3 Trees from G Wood Oxeg Hop Ties Weeders Mr Stanford from Preston come to Look at the Sawyers 2 link to chain shot 3 Calves left to weaned in the Stall

Tuesday 14
Clear Warm Day Horses Nidgetting Hops Croft I went finised Oxen fetched Chord Wood & Faggots Home Mast Henry Hoad thrashing Mr Hoad Casting up Dung Hodges finised & chopping Hops Archard G Guy shoveling Hops Archard Brook & Croft Old Dann Ditching sawyers Father found a swarm Beese Crofts Garden

Wednesday 15
Cloudy Rain Thunder Morng Aftern Cloudy Suny Horses & Oxen Carried 27 loads of Dung from the yard & Maxon in the P field G Guy Help filld Do Tho Hoad Mowing Thistles P field finised Mast Henry Hoad Thrashing Corn Oxen in the B field

Thursday 16
Cloudy Day Oxen Drawing Trees Horses & Oxen 3 Carts Carried 5 L Loads of Dung Do Mast Thos Hoad Nick Cleaned 25 Sacks 2 Bushels of Wheat Old Dann ditching Sawyers Weeders put Broad Wheels on the Horse Waggon Tug N Link 1 has Line New Do piece of Iron for Head of a Gate[126] Wm Oxley Warbleton Sussex

Friday 17
Cloudy & Sun Day. Horses Drawed up Load of Rafters to Windmill hill Oxen helpd Ditto & David timber & Carried drawed 2 Load of Wheat up to Mr Pinyon Old Evenden Lot Clearing Sawyers Old Dann Ditching Thos Hoad G Guy Chopping Hop Croft. Mast Henry Hoad thrashing Yoke piece Old Dice put on tug link mended 12 New Hoe Weeders 2 Quilers Hoops Battle Market

Saturday 18
Cloudy Morng Misty Aftn Horses Carried Load Rafters to Laughton & Mast Lanhard Team Oxen Carried 2 Load of Wheat to Mr Newington Burwash mill sh 15£ per load G pay the Gate Mast Henry Hoad Thrashing G Guy Ths Hoad Chopping Hops Ditto Old Dann Ditching Sawyers Weeders Evenden Lot Cleaving

Sunday 19
Rain Hard Morng Showry Aftn Stop Home

Monday 20
Cloudy Morng Showrs Rain Aftn Oxen & Horses 3 Carts Carried 5 L Loads

---

[126] Entry by William Oxley; obscure.

of Dung into P field G Guy Helping Do Ths Hoad Digging Gravel Old Lane Mast Henry Hoad Thrashing Old Dann Ditching Evenden Lot Cleaving pick sharp at the little Forge

Tuesday 21
Cloudy Day Horses Drawed Load principle Rafter up to Windmill Hill Oxen Helpd Ditto Do Oxen Drawing Trees & fetched home load of Top Faggots Old Dann Ditching G Guy Helping Load Rafters Ditto Chopping Potatoes B fields Morng Oxen New Link & Ring Open Ditto 4 O'clock Barnes cut the pigs

Wednesday 22
Rain Morng Cloudy Aft, Horses Carried Load Principle Rafters to Laughton Ditto Oxen Drawing was finised Old Dann Ditching Old Evenden Lot Cleaving Thos Henry Hoad Thrashing Mr Hoad Throwing Faggots & Chord Wood over the River Grimes Wood Morng Aftn Chopping Potatoes P Field Weeders Ditto Washed the Sheep in Mr Couchman Pond

Thursday 23
Cloudy little showrs mist Horses fetched 4 Chord of Wood to Coal pits Oxen Dung Carrying 3 Carts 55 Loads G Guy Thos Hoad Helping Mast Henry Hoad Thrashing Old Dann Ditching Sawyers Old Evenden Lot Cleaving way Hop tier Horses fetched

Friday 24
Cloudy Day Horses Carried 50 faggots to W Wisdom Do 50 top to Anne Marfer[127] Ditto Carried load Rafters to Windmill Hill Oxen Carried 1 Wood to Wisdom & Help us to Windmill Hill
Thos Henry Hoad Thrashing Thos Hoad Chopping Potatoes Kiln field G Guy Ditto Bushey field Old Dann Ditching Sawyers Old Evenden & Wife Lott Cleaving Hop Tiers Mr Couchman Bought 160 fence poles at 8d per pole fetched them away with Oxen

Saturday 25
Cloudy Cold Day Horses Carried Rafters to Laughton Oxen fetched Load Chalk from Hailsham Mr Whoodhams laid it out at 1£ per Load Broke Axel Thos Henry Hoad Threshing Thos Hoad Potato chopping Kilnfield finished G Guy Chopping Potatoes Croft Old Dann Ditching Sawyers Hop Tiers

[127] Morfey?

Sunday 26
Cloudy Morng Aftn few Drops Rain Mr Dirkel from Lewes preach Chapel twice Evening Mr Day the Emperor of Russia & his Daughter & King of Prussia & General Blucher past through Garner Street on their Route to Dover & Embark for France

Monday 27
Cloudy Showr Rain Morng Aftn showers Do Horses Slurying in 13 Acres turned up Hill Oxen 9 Acres turned up Hill Do Thos Henry Hoad Threshing G Guy Thos Hoad Chopping Potatoes in Croft and Chopping Hops Orchard Old Dann Ditching Sawyers Thos Thos Hoad & Nichs Slaughtered the last Hog Hop Tiers Old Evenden Tho Pankhurst fetch new Exil[128] to Waggon Thos Pankhurst for mending wagon Exil

Tuesday 28
Cloudy & Suny Day Horses Carried 100 Faggots up in Dill Gate Lane & Chord Wood & Faggots to House & Rafters Slabs & Laths up to Windmill Hill Oxen Do Carried Faggots and Chord Wood to House Thos Henry Hoad Threshing Morng Aftn Thos Hoad Topping Tree P T Shaw Carpenters Hall[129] it Down to Day Old Dann Ditching Thos Hoad G Guy Chopping Hops Old Evenden Lott Cleaving Hop tiers New Link to Chain New Shaft pin key 1 horse 4 removes

Wednesday 29
Clear & Cloudy Day Horses Carried Load Timber to Laughton Oxen fetched Chord Wood & Faggots home Thos Hoad Cut Top of a Tree in the Wood & Hop Chopping Thos Hoad Chopping Hops Ditto Henry Hoad Weeding Gutter field Sawyers Old Evenden & wife Lott Cleaving

Thursday 30
Cloudy & Suny Day Horses Nidgetting Pound Garden Cross Ways Oxen Carried 50 Faggots ½ Chord Wood to Mr Judge Meckam Down[130] & fetched Load Chalk Back Sawyers Old Evenden Lott Cleaving Thos Thos Hoad G Guy Cleaned 24 Sacks 1 Bush Whe at Morng Aftn Do 3 Chopping Hops & Potatoes Henry Hoad Chopping Hops New Linch pin

---

[128] Axle.
[129] Haul.
[130] Magham Down.

The following is an excerpt from a letter written August 24th 1887 by Sarah NOAKES (born Sept. 25th, 1805 Herstmonceux; sailed for America April 5th, 1831; settled in New Providence), daughter of Thomas NOAKES (1780 son of John NOAKES and Mercy née NOAKES) and Frances née NOAKES:

" In 1814 a treaty of peace between the King of France and his Britannic Majesty, George the Third, caused great rejoicings in every town in England-- illuminations, etc. Why, I remember it so perfectly, and what pleasure is caused by what I saw at that time! Many distinguished foreigners visited England, amongst whom were the Emperor of Russia, King of Prussia, Duke and Duchess of Oldenburg, Blucher and Platof. They drove in open carriages close past my father's house. We had prepared boquets for the occasion, and as we stood on the balcony threw them into the carriages, which they acknowledged with a graceful bow and pleasant smile, looking as much pleased as we were. I was then a very little girl, though it is as vivid today in my memory as an occurrence of yesterday."

by Joanne Mays Becker, SFHG member; John and Mercy Noakes were her 3x great grandparents, and she is descended from Thomas's sister Frances.

28 THE OXLEY FARM DIARIES

Friday 1 July
Cloudy & Suny Day Horses I Nidgetting P Garden Thos Hoad David finised 2 Wenh[ouse] Carried timber Windmill Hill Oxen 3 Carts Carried 14 Load to the Maxin finised Load in all 204 began Nother Mixin Top field Carried 29 Loads Thos Hoad G Guy felling Henry Hoad tending sheep out on the Road[131] Carpenter Winchester Making heave Gates & Bars Old Evenden Lott Cleaving New hop Strap Link squl[?] slapl[e?]

Saturday 2
Cloudy Suny Day Horses Rafters to Laughton Oxen Carried 50 Load Dung Thos Hoad G Guy felling Thos Hoad Chopping Potatoes Old Evenden Lott Cleaving Henry Hoad Sheep Tending on the Road Plough Share laid

Sunday 3
Cloudy & Sunny Day

Monday 4
Cloudy & Sunny Day Horses Plough Oxen Do Henry Hoad Thos Thos Hoad Mowing Oats Aftn Nichs David G Guy Hacking up Potatoes Brooke Garden Kiln field Winchester sawing felled 2 trees Old Evenden Lott Cleaving

Tuesday 5
Cloudy & Sunny Day Horses Nidgetting Orchard 2 Nidgett 2 Wents Brook 2 Wenh[ouse] 1 Nidge Croft Do 1 Nidgett 1 Wenh[ouse] Thos Thos Hoad Mowing G Guy Harrow Potatoing Oxen Plough Henry Drove Morrow Mr Delves Wheel Plough Horses Carried Load Timber up to Windmill Hill Oxen Do help Sawyers Old Evenden & Wife Lott Cleaving Drawed Silver field Pond[132]

Wednesday 6
Cloudy Sunny Day Horses Carried Load Timber to Laughton Oxen plough G Guy Nichs Hoeing Potatoes Croft P Garden B fields Thos Thos Hoad Mowing finised & Began Round Banks at Hodges Trefoil Old Cornford Chopping Hops

Thursday 7
Clear Day Prince Regent Thanksgiving Day treats for the Poor on Rush Lake Green nearly 800 People to Dine Show Land

[131] Making the most of the road verges.
[132] Cleared out the weeds.

Friday 8
Cloudy Showry Day Horses & Oxen Plough G Guy Chopping Hops Mr Cornford Do Thos Hoad Mowing Father found Pincher Mare Dead in a Ditch in Grimes Brook

Saturday 9
Cloudy Showry Day Oxen & Horses plough Thos Hoad Thrashing G Guy Mr Cornford Hop Chopping Thos Hoad Half Day Do 7 Prongs Sharp[ened]

Sunday 10
Cloudy Showry Day 2 strayed sheep into Bushe fields Marked JT

Monday 11
Cloudy Morng Clear Aftn Horses & Oxen Plough Thos Hoad Mowing thawn[133] Croft Garden & Helping sheep Shearer Thos Hoad G Guy Chopping Hops Morng Wm Hoad shovelling Hops Brook Morng Aftn Do 3 & Nich turning Seeds 10 Acres Hoe laid Weaned Lambs & washed them B fields Old Cornford Chopd

Tuesday 12
Cloudy & Sunny Day Horses & Oxen plough till 10 O'Clock Do Carried 7 Loads of Hay Stack up at Home finised John Baker stack Thos Henry Hoad G Guy Nich David Old Cornford Dame Hoad Haying Mr Hoad Do Plough Key made out of Old Ox Bone Key slight Crop Seeds Old Evenden & Lot cleaving

Wednesday 13
Cloudy & Sunny Day Horses & Oxen Plough Thos Wm Hoad Mowing Grass at Hodges Thos Hoad G Guy Old Cornford chopping Orchard David Nich turning Seeds at Hodges Aftn Evenden & Dame Hoad Lott Cleaving

Thursday 14
Cloudy & Sunny Day Oxen plough finish plg Do 13 Acres Horses Do Thos Wm Hoad Mowing Tares began C Lodge Meadow Thos Hoad G Guy Old Cornford chopping hops 3 plough shares sharp[ened] Old Evenden Lott Cleaving

Friday 15
Clear & Cloudy Day Horses & Oxen Plough finised Thos Wm Hoad Mowing & Finised & Began Chaple Meadow Ths Hoad G Guy Old Cornford Chopping Hops finised Began Croft Dame Hoad Weeding Silver

---
[133] Thorn.

field Old Evenden Lott Cleaving Mr Crouch share[134] Lambs

Saturday 16
Rainy Day Horses & Oxen Carried 22 Sacks of Wheat at 15£ per Load to Mr Whoodhams Hailsham & fetched back 2 Load Chalk Thos Wm Hoad Mowing little while Thos Hoad Old Cornford shovelling Hops Brook 3 stake New Nails put in the Wheel

Sunday 17
Cloudy & Sunny Day

Monday 18
Cloudy & Sunny Day Horses & Oxen Carried 100 Faggots to Mr Judge & fetched 2 loads of Chalk back Thos Wm Hoad Mowing Thos Hoad Nich David Mother Hoad turning Seeds at Hodges Do Chopping Hops Croft New plate and rails to Waggon 2 Staples

Tuesday 19
Cloudy & Sunny Day Hoses fetched 1 Load Chalk & fetched 1 Load Seeds Hay home Borrowed Delves Horse Oxen Carried 4 Load from Round Banks & 3 Loads in the other two Meadows stacks up Hoad Maid Mother Hoad David Nich Thos Hoad Father haying Thos Wm Hoad Mowing Roling Squash[?] mendied 2 Staples

Wednesday 20
Cloudy & Sunny Day Horses Carried Old Evenden Chucks Do 50 Faggots to Mr Pankhurst & fetched load of Chalk from Chithurst[135] Oxen plough Headlands at the Banks Hodges Do Loaded 1 Load at Calves Lodge Thos Hoad Chopping Do Haying Mowing Thisles & Fields Dame Haying Thistles Do Martha Haying Thistles Do Thos Wm Hoad Mowing finisd began P Croft New plate for Ring Pin

Thursday 21
Cloudy & Summer Day Horses & Oxen plough Morng Aftn Carried 2 Load Hay Calves Lodge finised Do 2 C Meadow 1 Home 1 C Lodge Mast Hoad Dame Martha Nich David Mary Hoad Haying Thos Wm Hoad Mowing finished began C W Meadow 2 plough shares Sharp 1 Cother[136] laid Prong

134 Shear.
135 The text does appear to read Chithurst but this seems very unlikely, Chithurst being a parish in the Western Rother valley between Midhurst and the Hampshire border, and remote from the chalk outcrop of the South Downs.
136 Coulter.

steel put on Carpenter Winchester

Friday 22
Cloudy Sunny Day Horses & Oxen plough finised Morng Aftn Oxen Carried 3 loads Hay Home Horses Do fetched Load Roots from 9 Acres home and Carried 1 load Hay Thos Hoad Nich David unloaded hay Calves Lodge Do Haying all Women Do Thos Wm Hoad Mowing finised Boy Clearing Chalk turned Horses into 9 Acres Old Robbins made Coal pit

Saturday 23
Clear Hot Day Horses fetched 2 Loads roots Do Finisd & Carried 8 Load Hay to Oxen Stack Oxen Do ploughing in Peas 9 Acres Thos Hoad pooking out[137] W Hoad Mowing Round Hodges Do carried 1 Load home stack & 2 Do to Oxen Stack Thos Hoad Haying Woman Do finised Chapple Meadow Winchester set up Gate at the poun[d] Boir Old Robbins Do New set Gate Irons

Sunday 24
Clear Day Very Warm

Monday 25
Clear Day Horses fetch Chalk Do Carried 2 loads of Hay from C W Meadow Oxen Carried Ashes into C Meadow & Carried 3 loads Hay from Pond Croft & 1 from C W Meadow Thos Hoad Haying Do Women Thos Wm Hoad Threshing Wheat Old Robbins Fird pit borrowed 2 horses W Harmer lent Delves Ox Do

Tuesday 26
Clear Day Horses fetch Load Chalk Borr'd 1 Horse Mr Delves Oxen plough Elias David Pooked out Thos Hoad Nich Haying Round[?] Hodges Thos Wm Hoad Threshing Kiln Barn tilling Old Robbins Do New shoe for traveler Horse

Wednesday 27
Clear Day Horses Carried Load Hay from Hodges & tip C Lodge stack Oxen plough Thos [Hoad] Thrashing Thos Hoad Mowing Thistles Foot Laid[138] rivet Drove in Rods & Hodges Old Robbins Kiln Burnt

Thursday 28
Hot Clear Day Tempest Night Oxen plough Horses Do Headland Thos Wm

---

[137] Using a three pronged (pooking) fork to push hay into bundles.
[138] Mr Foot did some laying; or as they were haying, this may be the foot of a haystack.

Hoad Thrashing Thos Hoad Thistle Mowing Brook Kiln Burns put out Old Robbins Foot Laid

Friday 29
Clear & Cloudy Horses Oxen plough Thos Wm Hoad Thrashing Thos Hoad Gapping Making Lime places 13 Acres Thistle Mowing Old Robbins put on 2 Staples & Haps[139] for Gate

Saturday 30
Cloudy Morng Clear Aftn Oxen plough Horses emptied Lime Kiln Carried 5 Loads into 13 Acres Thos Wm Hoad Do Kiln Burns Do Thos Wm Hoad Thrashing Thos Do Casting Dung Stable to 4 New Shoes for Mare

Sunday 31
Clear Day

Monday 1 August
tempest Morng Hard Showr Cloudy afternoon Horses & Oxen plough Hoad pooking out share sharp Wm Hoad Mowing Trefoil Hodges Broke Wheel plough Do Chop of foot plough

Tuesday 2
Cloudy Day Horses & Oxen Plough Thos Hoad Pooked out Thos Wm Hoad Thrashing Finised Cleaned 17 Sacks 3 Bushel Wheelers mended two Plough Wheat Grown on Both Farms 23£ 2s 3d peas 2.5 B oats 14.5.4.

Wednesday 3
Foggy Morng Clear Day Oxen plough Horses Carried 65 Loads of Moul into 9 Acres with 2 Carts 3 Hoads Filling Foster shovlg Henry Hoad spreading Do 3 Hoads Do Spreading plough share sharp Dame Hoad Stripping Hops P Garden

Thursday 4
Clear Day Oxen plough Horses Carrd 71 Loads Moulings 2 Hoads Do Dame Stripping Hops New timber chain

Friday 5
Cloudy Day Showrs Misty Rain Horses carried 60 loads of Moul Do 3 Fillers 1 Spreader Oxen plough. Dame Hoad Stripping Hops

Saturday 6
Cloudy Showry Rain Oxen Carried 2 Loads Straw from Barn to Hay Stacks

[139] Hasps.

& ploughed 9 Acres Do Carried 1 Load Trefoil to Oxen yd stacked Horses Carried 51 Loads of Moul 4 Hoads Do Do Carried 1 Load Trefoil Hoads Do Honeysett Thatched Stack Hodges Dame Hoad Stripping Hops & Blacksmith to Remove Finised Carrying Mould No Loads 253

Sunday 7
Cloudy & Windy Day

Monday 8
Cloudy Windy Day Showr Rain Morng Horses & Oxen Curtis' Harmer's Delves Teams fetched 13 Loads Thos Hoad Bagd 3 Do Hoppers began

THERE IS A GAP IN THE DIARY FROM TUESDAY 9 AUG –FRIDAY 23 SEPT, DURING HOP PICKING

Saturday 24
Cloudy Day Horses plough Oxen Carried 15 Pockets Hops to Heathfield Do Load Bins Carrd P field Hoppers Finishd Brook Thos Hoad baged 3 Pockets Thrashed Flourin Oats sold 5 lambs Waters 39s per lamb

Sunday 25
Cloudy Day Showry Morng

Monday 26
Cloudy Day Horses fetched 35 Cwts of Sea Coals from Pevensey Oxen Rolling 9 Acres Thos Hoad Trod 7 Bags[140] Hoppers began P Field Weighed of 9 pockets 3 Lamb straid into B Farm

Tuesday 27
Cloudy Day Horses fetched 12 Hop bins from Wm Harmer Do Loaded timber Drawed to Windmill Hill Oxen plough 9 Acres Thos Hoad Thrashing Wheat 2 Removers for 2 Horse staple[141]

Wednesday 28
Rainy Day Horses to Laughton John Baker Thrashing Oats Thos Hoad Wheat Do Hoppers

Thursday 29
Rain Morng Horses Warping Round Banks Hodges John Baker spreading Mould Huglet Field Thos Hoad Thrashing Hoppers Do Bogt 2 Pockets Weighed 5 Pockets 2 Masons & Boy 2 Carpenters

[140] Of hops.
[141] Two new horse shoes.

Friday 30
Windy Day Horses Load timber drawd to Turner Green John Baker spreading Mould Thos Hoad trod 3 Pockets Thrashing Hoppers 2 Masons & Boy Father Bought Ram for 43£ at Pinyons [Bo]ldle Street 47£

Saturday 1 Oct
Cold Windy Day Horses to Laughton & to Lewes for 2 Chals[142] Coal for E Standon Oxen plough 9 Acres Hoppers Thos Hoad Thrashing Oats

Sunday 2
Clear & Windy Day

Monday 3
Clear & Windy Horses Warping Oxen Plough Hoppers Thos Hoad Bag 22 Pockets Thrashing Do David fetch Beast from Winchelsea Very Poor

Tuesday 4
Clear Day Horses plough Finised Oxen 1 Cart spreading Lime 2 spread Cart Coals Siftings Chapl Meadow Helping hoppers Thos Hoad Thrashing Cleaned 6 Sacks 3 Bushls Wheat

Wednesday 5
Clear Day Horses Harrowed R B field Foster Seeds Bro[w]n Cobham wheat John Baker Thos Hoad P poling[?] Finish Hoping Father Bought 10 Lambs for £9 of Mr Whoodham Hailsham

Thursday 6
Cloudy Day Horses Plowing in Cobham Wheat in 13 Acres John Baker Hn Hoad Spreading Lime 13 Acres Thos Hoad Thrashing Oats Hoad Do Wheat Old Striping Poles

Friday 7
Cloudy Day Horses Plough Oxen spreading Lime Old Hoad striping Poles Thos Hoad Thrashing Hoad Do Payd Hoppers 1/- Bush

Satturday 8
Clear Day Horses Plough Oxen finished Lime spread both fields Old Hoad striping Poles Croft Thos Hoad Thrashing Hoad Trod 6 Pockets

Sunday 9
Frosty Morng Clear Day Mr Winchester Preach Chaple

[142] Chaldrons.

Monday 10
Frosty Clear Day Horses & Oxen Plough Thos Hoad Thrashing Hoad Do Thrashing Old Hoad Stripping Poles Hny Hoad Do

Tuesday 11
Cloudy Day Horses & Oxen Plough Thos Hoad cleaned 12 Bush'l Wht Thos Henry Hoad thrashing Thos Hoad Thrashing Old Hoad Striping Poles

Wednesday 12
Cloudy Day Horses & Oxen Plough Thos Hoad Trod 7 Pockets Hops Finished Hnr Hoad Thrashing Thos Hoad Cleaned 2 Qtrs Barley 10 Bushel Oats Old Stripping Poles

Thursday 13
Cloudy Day Horses Oxen Plough Finished Thos Hnr Hoad Thrashing Nich fetched 2 Sacks Wht from Cowden

Friday 14
Cloudy Day Showr Rain Horses Draft 13 Acres Finish & Oxen 3 Carts Carried 24 Loads Dung from P field 10[?] Acres Thos Hoad Nichs Do Thos Hnr Hoad Thrashing Cleand 21 B Wht Old Hoad Stack Poles I Weighed of Hops 99 cwt 2 qtrs 15 lb in the whole growth

Saturday 15
Showry Day Horses Ploughing in Wh[ea]t old brown Straw in 8 Acres Oxen 3 Carts Carried 21 Loads Dung Do Nich Thos Hoad Thos Hnr Hoad Scouring out firs[143] in the 13 Acres Do Thrashing Old Stacking Poles Hnr Gilbert Painted 2 Gates

Sunday 16
Clear Day

Monday 17
Cloudy Day Showry Morg Horses & Oxen plough Thos Hoad Spreading Dung 8 Acres finish Thos Hnr Hoad Girls Nich David Diging up Potatoes Kiln field Old Hoad stacking Poles put 3 Hogs in the Pound

Tuesday 18
Showry Day Horses & Oxen plough Thos Henr Hoads Girls Nichs Potatoing Croft Garden Thos Hoad Carried 3 Loads Dung 8 Acres Carried 3 Do Wht to Garden fetched 5 Sacks Wht Back Old Hoad stacking poles

[143] Furze.

Wednesday 19
Showry Day Horses & Oxen plough Thos Hnr Hoad Thrashing Old Hoad Stacking Poles drove 4 Others to Mr Erry Heathfield Thos Hoad & Car

Thursday 20
Cloudy Day Horses plough [oxen fetched] John Baker Scowring out Water Carrng spdg[144] Dung 8 acres Thos Hnr Hoad Thrashing Thos Hoad Thrashing Oats Old Hoad Stakg Poles sold 1 pair of 3 yearlg steers at Rotherfield Fair for 2.2.15

Friday 21
Frosty Morng Clear Day Horses finished 8 Acres Oxen Carried 98 Pockets Hops to Mr Parker Thos Hnr Hoad Girls Potatoing Old Hoad stacking Poles G Guy stripping poles P Garden fetched New Waggon from Wheeler

Saturday 22
Misty Morng Cloudy Day Horses Warpg 9 Acres Thos Thos Hnr Hoad Girls Potatoing John Baker fetched Fo[s]ter home I pooking out plat 3 Hoad scouring firs & Tares

Sunday 23
Cloudy Day Tethered Oxen Hay Straw Several weeks before

Monday 24
Clear Day Horses plough Oxen Do Broke plough Dung Carry 9 Acres Thos Hoad Do G Guy Striping Poles

Tuesday 25
Rain in the Night Cloudy Day Horses fetch 2 Sacks Wht from Cowden ploughed Thos Wm Hoad Thrashing Wht G Guy Striping Poles

Wednesday 26
Cloudy Day Horses Harrowed 9 Acres Father herdsmans Oxen plough Thos Wm Hoad striping Poles Archard Thos Hoad Thrashing Oats 2 Carpenters

Tuesday 27
Cloudy Day Horses Harrow Oxen plough Thos Wm Hoad Stacking Poles 2 Carpenters Thos Hoad Thrashing

Friday 28
Cloudy Day Horses Harrow sow'd with old straw Wht Oxen plough

[144] Spreading.

finished Thos Wm Hoad Stripping Poles pound Garden G Guy & Thos Hoad spreading Mouls Hugt field Hodges

Saturday 29
Rain Aftn Thos Hnr Hoad Striping Poles Morng Aftn Thrashing Horses & Oxen plough Huglt field Hodges Thos Hoad cleand 4 Sacks Oats Thrashing Barley G Guy Striping Poles

Sunday 30
Cloudy Day Mr Beaufay preached at Chp

Monday 31
Cloudy Day Horses Harrow plough Hodges Finished sowing Old straw & Cobham Wht Oxen Do plough Thos Wm Hoad G Guy stripping Poles Thos Hoad Thrashing Cleaned 1 Sack of Wheat

Tuesday 1 November
Misly Day Horses 2 Carts Carried 23 Loads of Dung in Hodges spread Headland Baker Do Thos Henry Hoad Thrashing Thos Hoad Thrashing Morng Aftn Cleaving Logs fetched Hailsham Cow home from Marsh Shut up to fat with Potatoes & Barley Straw

Wednesday 2
Cloudy Day Horses Carried 34 Load Dung Ashes finishd Thos Hoad Baker Do Thos Hnr Hoad Thrashing Cleand Nichs I 3 Sacks 2 Bush Barley Carried to Windmill#7+

Thursday 3
Cloudy Day Horses Carried 2 Load Hop Bines from Croft Garden to P Field 1 Load Poles home & 1 Load Bines in Orchard to Hodges yard stack I Do Oxen 2 Carts Carried 30 Loads of Dung from Chl yard to CH Meadow Thos Hoad Do Thos Hnr Hoad Thrashing

Friday 4
Cloudy Day Drops Rain Horses 2 Carts Carried 32 Loads Dung from P Field to Croft Garden I shevld[145] Oxen Carried 28 Load Dung CWM & 12 Chpl Meadow Thos Hoad Do Thos Hnr Hoad Thrg

Saturday 5
Rainy Day Horses 1 Cart Carried 16 Loads Dung from yd to the Meadow Oxen Carried 28 loads Dung C Meadow & Thrashing Thos Hoad Do Thos

[145] Shovelled.

Heathfield Independent Chapel

Wm Hoad Cleand 15 Sacks 3 Bushl Wheat

Sunday 6
Cloudy Day Mr Chuttende from Brighton preached at Heathfield Chaple

Monday 7
Clear Day Horses 1 Cart Carried 19 Load of Dung into Chaple Meadow from yd Finishd John Baker Thrashing Oats Cleand 5 Sacks 2 Bushels Thos Hoad Stubb Mowing High Field Hodges Thos Hoad Fersy field[146] Do Hnr Hoad 8 Acres Mr Gilbert Painted 2 Gates

Tuesday 8
Cloudy day Horses Carried 16 Sacks 1 B of Wht to Mr Blackmans Mill Wheat 56½ lb per Bushl Head Do Tails 50½ per Bushl at 17£ per Load Do Loaded load Slabs[147] & Brought home John Baker Thrashing Barley Thos Hoad Hnr Thos Hoad Stubb[148] mowing

Wednesday 9
Frosty Morng Cloudy Day Horses Carried Hop Bines from Orchard Garden Ox's Yard Nichs Load Slabs from Grimes Wood John Baker

---

[146] Furzes field.
[147] Slab: to dress (timber) by removing the outside slabs; to clear of bark-wood (OED).
[148] Stubble.

1814

Thrashing stubb Mowers G Guy Stubb Mowing B Field

Thursday 10
Clear Day Horses Carried Hop Bines into P Field Hop poles Home John Baker Thrashing Stubb Mowers

Friday 11
Frosty Morng Cloudy Day Horses Clear P Garden from Poles David I stack Stubb Mowers Finished Thos Hoad Mowing Litter[149] Firsy Field[150]

Saturday 12
Rain Morng Clear Aftr Wm Foster sprdg Dung Chaple Meadow Thos Hoad Thrashg Thos Wm Hoad Thrashing

Sunday 13
Cloudy Day

Monday 14
Cloudy Day Horses Carried 1 Load Brakes[151] & 1 Do Stubble to Calves Lodge 2 Loads from 8 Acres to Chaple Yd I Raked Thos Hoad Thrashing & Foddering Baker ill Thos Hnr Hoad Thrashing

Tuesday 15
Showrs Misty Rain Horses Carried 3 Stubble Chapple Cloase I Do Home Thos Hoad Thrashing Thos Wm Hoad Thrashing

Wednesday 16
Rain Morng Clear Aftr Horses Carried 2 Loads Stubble Chp Yd 1 Load Fircy Field 8 Load 8 Acres Thos Hoad Thrashing Thos Hnr Hoad Thrashing

Thursday 17
Frosty Morng Cloudy Day Horses Carried 5 Loads Stubble into Hodges Yard I Rake Thos Hnr Hoad Cleand 12 Sacks 1 Bushl Wht Thrashing Oats Taing[152] Oats Nichs Do G Guy Cutting Grimes Brook Gill[153]

Friday 18
Cloudy Day Horses carried 10 Sacks 3 Bushl Wht to Mr Smith Mill at £17 pr Load Thos Hoad two Carpenters raking Lodge Pound Field Hnr Hoad

---

[149] Probably bracken for animal bedding.
[150] Furzes field.
[151] Bracken.
[152] Tailing.
[153] Ghyll.

Saturday 19
Rain Night Cloudy Day Wm Foster Thos Hoad Thrashing Henry Raking up straw Chaple Meadow Thos Hnr Hoad Thrashing G Guy Wood Cutting Drove Oxen into Yard Put Pair 2 Yearling Steers out to keep at John Bland spreading Dung Chp Meadow G Guy Wood Cutting Horses Carried 2 Loads Stubble Hodges 2 Loads Grinets 5 Loads High Field

Sunday 20
Showry Day

Monday 21
Cloudy Day Horses Jobbing Both 1 Carts John Baker Thrashing Thos Hoad Hawth Faggots Fircy Field[154] Thos Hnr Hoad Thrashing G Guy Wood Cutting 2 Carpenters Marking sheep Bridge Huglett river

Tuesday 22
Clear Frosty Day Horses Drawing Hop Poles of Garden to the other End Baker Thrashing Thos Hoad spredg Dung Chpl Meadow Thos Hnr Hoad Thrashing

Wednesday 23
Frosty Morng Cloudy Day Horses 2 Carts Carried 32 Load of Dung into first part Pound Garden John Baker Do Thos Hnr Hoad Nichs cleaning Oats G Guy Wood Cutting 1 Cart fetched 100 Oil Cake from Cowden

Thursday 24
Frosty Morng Cloudy Day Horses Carrd 30 Loads Dung Baker Do Thos Hnr Hoad Nichs Cleand 25 Sacks 2 Bushls Oats Do Brishing Old Lane Lew Faggots[155] Do in the Wainhouse field Thos Hoad Spreading Dung G Guy Wood Cutting

Friday 25
Misly Day All 5 Thrashing

Saturday 26
Rain Night cloudy Day Foster Baker Nichs Cleand 15 Sacks 3 Bushl Barley

---

[154] Gorse faggots from Furzes field.
[155] Lee (sheltered) faggots, which grew tall with long stems.

Thrashing

Thos Hoad spreading Dung CH Meadow Hnr Hoad Pound Croft Hop Garden spreading Dung CH Meadow Thos Hoad spreading Dung Diging Post holes at Hodges 2 Carpenters G Guy Wood Cutting

Sunday 27
Clear Morng Rain Aftern

Monday 28
Clear Day Horses fetched Hawth Lew faggots Hop Bines Load straw pit top pound field Lodge David Father Helpd pit out Grimes Wood Thos Hnr Hoad the Horses began Lents G Guy Wood Cutting

Tuesday 29
Rain Night Cloudy Day Horses Carried 3 sack 3 Bush Barley to Mill Clearing Roots Baker shoveling Dirt about house mended Cribs Poundfield Wood Cutters

Wednesday 30
Rain Night Morng Foster Hoad Baker Raked Bush field Stubble Wood Cutters Wm Marten Do

Thursday 1 Dec
Cloudy Day Horses Carried 13 Sacks of Barley to Mr Everest Gardner street

Carting faggots for Christmas

fetched straw from 12 Acres to Pound field Baker Thrashing W Cutting

Friday 2
Clear Day Horses Fetchd Load top End from Wood Dung spreading Croft & Pound Garden Wood Cutters Baker Thrashing Mr Stanford Mr Tourle Came to Shooting

Saturday 3
Frosty Morng C Cloudy Day Horses fetchd 2 Loads Stubble from Bush Field to Pound field Nichs Do Baker Thrashing Wood Cutters

Sunday 4
Rain Morng Flood Clear Aftr

Monday 5
Fine Morng little Wett afternoon Carters Dung spreading Baker threshing Barley Workmen Wood cutting

Tuesday 6
Clear sunshine day little shower afternoon Horses 50 Faggots to Brigden Hill morning Carter Spreading Dung afternoon Baker & Nichs Cleand 5 sacks 3 Bushls Barley & threshing Workmen wood cutting

Wednesday 7
Misty rain Horses Caried 12 bls Oats to Mrs Yorkes moved Dung Calves Lodge 3 bu Barley to Mill Baker & Henry threshing Oats Home Barn Workmen Wood cutting

Thursday 8
Fine Morning till 11 Misty showers till 4 & a Wett Evening Foster spreading Dung P F hop Garden Baker H Hoad Thrashing Workmen Wood Cutting

Father Bought Horse of £3 Reeves T Hoad 2 bush potatoes

Friday 9
Fine morning showry afternoon Wett evening Foster threshing Barley Baker & Henry Threshing of Oats Nichs fetched Horse home Workmen Woodcutting George 1 bushel Potato's

Saturday 10
Cloudy nearly all day with a well[156] afternoon Foster threshing Barley Baker & Henry oats Workmen Wood cutting

Sunday 11
Wett morning Cloudy Afternoon

Monday 12
Cloudy & Misty rains Foster threshing Barley Baker Do Henry spreading dung Thos Hoad Senr & Wm Hoad threshing Oats Thos Hoad Kild the wight Fat Hog rest workmen Wood cutting

Tuesday 13
Windy with some rain afternoon still Evening Weighd the Hog 52 stone 3 lbs Horses Carried it to Mr Isted Pignole Ashburnham Carried 10 sacks Barley to Gardner street Mr Everest's worked new Horse first time Baker & Nichs Cleaned 5 sacks of Barley Baker mending and triming track through Gutterfield shaw Workmen Woodcutting Mr Press Preached in evening from Hebrews 2 Chapter 3 Verse New skids[157] to new Waggon & Lock boards

Wednesday 14
Cloudy all day showry afternoon Windy Wett Evening Horses Plough Grinnetts Baker Finised the track in the Gutterfield shaw Thos Hoad

[156] Wett.
[157] Iron shoes placed under the wheels when going down steep hills.

threshing Oats rest workmen Wood cutting Father Mr Woods Lime feast Cow shut in yard for good[158]

Thursday 15
Windy Cloudy & Showry Horses Plough H Gdn Baker threshing stub mowing Kiln Field Workmen Wood cutting

Friday 16
Windy showrry & Cloudy day with a still Evening Nichs bought a watch of Thos Hoad Junr & sold it to Thos Hoad Senner[159] Foster & Baker threshing Oats Chapel Barn Thos Hoad Senner & Wm Hoad threshing Oast House Barn Henry Bozling[160] Woodcutters not known

Saturday 17
Windy & cloud all day with some rain in afternoon & Evening Foster & Baker stub mowing Kilnfield workmen Woodcutting Nichs & Henry fetched the Cold[161] home from the Marsh

Sunday 18
Windy & Cloudy no Wett much be few drops morning some sunshine

Monday 19
Windy Cloud a little Showr about 4 O'Clock Horses Plough Finnised the Grinnetts Baker stub mowing Kiln Field Workmen Woodcutting

Tuesday 20
Frosty morning Clear sunshine day & Frosty Evening Foster Henry & David stub Goading mowing and raking Baker to Battle Father to Burwash Mr G Adams Look'd at the 11 feet Poles work men wood cutting

Wednesday 21
Frosty morning snow'd & raind soon after 10 O'Clock and a most all sorts of weather afterward & Evening Foster with Traveller & the cart brought home Betsey from Schooll in the morning & stubble mowing with Baker afternoon workmen woodcutting Master Hoad Kild a sheep at night Father went to Egypt [farm] in Morning to rushlake green afternoon

Thursday 22
Frosty all day Cold SE wind sun shone out till 3 O'Clock afternoon Cloudy

---

[158] That is, to fatten.
[159] Senior.
[160] Bosseling: see glossary.
[161] Colt.

& Cold Horses carried 6 Quarters of Oats to Mr Blackman's Mill & Load of Stubble from Bush field to home yard Baker & Nicholas Cleand 3 sacks Head & 4 sacks tail. Baker after threshing Potato Oats the same sort that they Cleand Workmen Woodcutting G Guy Wm Hoad Thos Hoad Senner & Thos Hoad Junior received meat for Christmas Dinner

Friday 23
Snow in morning from the East lasted all day about an inch thick Cloud to all day Horses sell[162] the Waggon in the Lodge in the morning Foster & Baker threshing Oats C Barn Thos Hoad Junr & Wm Hoad threshing home Barn Thos Daw Wood cutting Grimes Wood Henry Choping hop poles. Candle went out

Saturday 24
Verry Cold day & Cloudy Foster & Baker threshing Oats C Barn Henry choping Hop poles Workmen woodcutting

Sunday 25
Freezing Snowing Day Christmas Day D N Oxley

Monday 26
Snow in the morning afterward rain thawd all day Cloudy & by night snow nearly all gone wind in NE Wm Hoad Woodcutting wether any more is not known Nichs & David wrote out some bill Father is gone to Ashburnham Place on Mr Pattenden's account & 1st Holy day

Tuesday 27
Cloudy & Showry all day wind SE Horses holy day keeping & Carter Thos Hoad Senr & Wm Hoad threshing Wood cutters unknown Wm & Saml Oxley came to see us

Wednesday 28
Rained from the preceding Evening till about 9 or 10 O'Clock a little rain afterward & some sunshine wind moved to the NE Cloudy Evening Foster & Baker threshing Henry bosling[163] Thos Hoad Senr & Wm Hoad threshing wood cutters not known Wm & Saml Oxley visitors I forgot the flood

Thursday 29
Cloudy with some rain in Evening Foster & Baker thrishing Workmen woodcutting Father gone to Mayfield John Oxley came to see us & went

---

[162] Set?
[163] Bosseling; see glossary.

home again with his Brother William

Friday 30
Horses Carried 1 Load of straw to Hodges in the morning Baker & Foster threshing Oats afternoon Henry Bosling in afternoon all to Hodges in the morning Father came home from Mayfield Workmen woodcutting Cloudy morning Wett afternoon

Saturday 31
The last Day in the year Fine weather all day not much Cloudy Foster & Baker threshing and Cleand sack of Oats in C Barn Henry threshing home Barn Workmen wood cutting Saml Oxley went home & Wm to stream Mill wind N

DIARY FOR THE YEAR OF OUR LORD 1815

Sunday 1 January
Clear clouds in the morning clear sunshine afternoon wind in the north Father, Mother David and Elizabeth & me went to Heathfield Chapel an excleent sermon preached by Mr Press from Matthew 20th chapter 32 verse

Monday 2
Foster & Henry with 2 Horses and cart fetched a parcel from windmill Foster Baker Henry cleaning of oats in Home barn James Eaton cutting up ant hill rest of the workmen wood cutting I went to Cade Street in the morning to hear the fate of my uncle but did not know until about 4 O'clock when we had the awful tidings of his departure about half past 8 o'clock this morning

Tuesday 3
Foster and Henry with the horses to plow in Furze field Baker and David cleaning oats Nicholas and Father went to Mayfield in Sussex Rest of workmen wood cutting G Guy come to wood cutting about 3 O'clock James Easton gutting upp[164] ant hill J Pain & Benjamin came to see us Nicholas Oxley got in the bed first David put the candle out and then to get in the bed by dark Amen David forgot to put in how that Nicholas on fell from horse on coming home from Mayfield a little below swife gate[165] dark all the way home got home about half past eight O clock in the evening

Wednesday 4
Horses with 2 carts dung carrying carried 42 loads Foster Baker & Henry with them from Poundfield to the young hop garden James Easton cutting up ant hills rest workmen wood cutting John & Benjamin visitors

Thursday 5
Foster Baker & Henry carried 43 loads of dung from Pound field to the young hop garden James Easton cutting up ant hill in Silverfield rest workmen wood cutting John and Benjamin left us for Cade Street in afternoon I brought new hat price 12/6d off Mrs Fox Rushlake Steer brought me new sute of mourning in evening

---

[164] Cutting up.
[165] Swiffe Gate is about 1 mile east of Broak Oak on the Burwash road, marked on map as Paygate Cottage.

Friday 6
Horses dung carrying Poundfield garden finished some in the Croft Baker & Easton thrashing oats workmen Mr Adams came to see the 14 feet poles Father and Nicholas gone to the funeral of Nicholas Cornwell

Saturday 7
Horses stubble carrying finished Easton thrashing workmen wood cutting Father came home from Mayfield

Sunday 8
Nicholas came home from Mayfield to Chapel in the morning Mr Press preached from Jerimiah 15 chapter 19 verse all to Chapel except Mother & Anne

Monday 9
Horses with 2 carts carried 19 sacks of potato oats to Bucksteep mill and dung carrying from dung mackson[166] in Poundfield to the young hop garden Baker Beal and Easton cleaning oats Chapple Barn rest workmen wood cutting Father to Rushlake Green I went round by Ashburnham and Dallington gathering of Bull money[167] the Waldron heifer calved before morning with a bull calf began the hay stack for the heifer in morning they cleaned 16s head 6s 1d tail longtail wight oats

Tuesday 10
Horses plough in the Furzefield and finished Baker thrashing barley B Bale[168] thrashing oats H.B. Easton cutting up ant hills rest workmen wood cutting I went Heathfield for Mr Press who preached this evening on the new birth from John's Gosble 3 chapter 3 verse

Wednesday 11
Horses plough Squire field Baker C.B. threshing Beal threshing H.B. Easton cutting up ant hills in the Silverfield rest workmen wood cutting Father went to Hailsham Market I went up to Attwood's at Bodle Street wrighting out of bills for James Harmer horses brought some oats from the Chaple Barn home into the garret by assistance the Carters Baker & Beal

---

[166] Mixen, dungheap.
[167] Money from other farmers for sharing a bull. By several contributing they were able to buy a better quality bull.
[168] Beal.

Thursday 12
Horses plough in the Squire field Baker threshing barley C.B. Beal squabed a little against the large Window afternoon threshing oats HB Easton cutting up ant hills rest workmen wood cutting Father went to Ashburnham I went to the Halfmoon market and tea'd at Mr John Wethers Junr.

Friday 13
Horses all shoe'd & all went to dung carrying 2 att the time & Foster feld and shelv'd[169] Henry had the horses up to blacksmith's 2 att the time carried the dung from before the lime Kiln to the orchard hop garden Baker cleaned 1 sack of barley after wards threshing of oats CB Beal threshing oats HB Easton cutting up ant hills Thos Hoad & son Hedging nine acres rest workmen wood cutting Mr Thos Wathers brought 8 fatting sheep of Fathers at 37s per head wich is 14£ 16s Mr John Gain visitor

Saturday 14
Horses plough in Squirefield Baker & Beal cleaning oats C.B. morning Baker threshing CB afterwards Beal Do oats H.B. Easton cutting ant hills rest workmen wood cutting Mr John Gain went home in afternoon

Sunday 15
All went to Heathfield Chapple except EA & Mo Mr Press preached a most excellent discourse from Genesis 24 chapter 31 verse he spoke of the feeling of Christian and then spoke in what reason they ought to come in to join the church of Christ here below

Monday 16
Killed the fat Barren Hog in the morning & Thos Hoad cutting out in the evening weighed according to Davids calculation 55 stone & 6 cwt Horses finished carrying the dung mackson away from up against the Kiln into the orchard hop garden Baker threshing C.B. & began the hay stack again after weighting from wheat sowing Beal threshing HB Thos Hoad headging 9 acres Easton cutting up ant hills rest workmen wood cutting David brought the Tom cat in almost dead and is now if not dead apparently in a dying situation

Tuesday 17
Tom cat was found dead this morning Horses kept holiday Foster seeking

[169] Shovelled.

after a bacon reek[170] Henry chopping hop poles Baker threshing CB Beal threshing HB in morning afterwards dung spreading up in the Croft Thos Hoad hedging 9 acres Easton cutting up ant hill rest workmen wood cutting Father went to Heathfield I went round to Dallington gathering in Bull money David drove in 7 wheel barrow loads of dung in the House garden

Wednesday 18
Horses plough in Squirefield Baker & Beal cleaned 8 sack head & 5s 2b tail potato oats Easton finished cutting up ant hills about 4 o'clock then went to spreading dung in orchard hop garden Thos Hoad & son hedging 9 acres rest workmen wood cutting Father went to the woods corner Club for the first time I have got a cold which is not very pleasant but bearable through mercy should the Lord be pleased to remove it to his own Glory in his own good will and time is my desire

Thursday 19
Horses dung & moul carrying from about house Beal & Eastone dung spreading Baker threshing Thos Hoad hedging workmen wood cutting I went to the Half Moon Market

Friday 20
Horses carried some wood to Hodges & afterwards Baker & Easton threshing oats CB Beal dung spreading Poundfield hop garden Thos Hoad hedging 9 acres rest workmen wood cutting Father went to Crawl

Saturday 21
Horses moul carrying Hodges in Grinnets Baker & Beal threshing oats CB Thos Hoad's threshing wheat HB rest workmen wood cutting I went to Grovely to find out a boar but he was cut[171]

Sunday 22
All went to Heathfield Chapple except Mother & Ann. Mr Press preached from Colossians 3 chapter 11 verse But Christ is all and in all.

Monday 23
Foster Baker & Horses holiday keeping Easton and Beal threshing CB Thos Hoad Senr & Junr & Wm Hoad threshing wheat HB Henry hop pole chopping other workmen not known Father went to Warbleton Church as

---

[170] Rack.
[171] Castrated. Grovley was a small farm next to the Priory.

Pall Bearer for Mrs Coal[172] Brother Wm visitor Mr Thos Hoad had the sow to hog to Mr Christmas bore[173] at the Hole[174] in the morning

Tuesday 24
Horses moule carrying in the Grinnets Foster Henry & Easton with them Baker & Beal threshing CB Wm Hoad threshing Thos senr Afternoon Thos Hoad junr all day Do … workmen besides if any wood cutting Mr Richardson & James Oxley cousins visitors Mr Press preached up tale from Roman's 8 chapter 33 verse brother Wm & I went up to Gardner Street afternoon we all went to Mr Smith's except David & Ann

Wednesday 25
Horses carried 99 faggots from Grimes Brook shaw & our faggot stack to Mr John Guy Senr afterwards carried 1 load of wheat straw to Hodges Baker & Beal threshing CB 3 Hoads threshing wheat HB Easton throwing faggots over the river into Grimes Brook and turning moule up in the Bushey field there has owing [to] the present snow Been no wood cutters since Wm Hoad has been to threshing Mr Richardson James Oxley & Wm my brother all went to their respective homes in the afternoon about 1 O'clock then went from here

Thursday 26
Horses moule carrying in the Croft garden Thos & Wm Hoad Senr threshing Easton felling of moule Baker & Thos Hoad went aft. barrels for Wm Akehurst Wm Hoad went in the afternoon Father & I went to Halfmoon Market & to the Parish meeting at Rushlake Green Beal felling[175] moul cart

Friday 27
Horses Foster Henry Easton & Beal mouling Croft garden Baker threshing oats C.B. Thos Wm & Thos Hoad threshing wheat H.B. I begin the seed hay stack for the cows at night Mr Russell visitor in the middle of the day Father went to Priory in the evening

Saturday 28
Horses carried moul in the Croft garden Foster Henry Beal & Easton helped Baker threshing oats C.B. Thos Hoad's threshing HB Wm Hoad wood

[172] Mrs Ann Cole.
[173] Boar.
[174] Darvel Hole.
[175] Fixing or repairing the fells or felloes.

cutting Grimes wood G Guy Do Grimes Brook I had p[lo]ugh[e]d Jack's moved all Bodle Street Green

Sunday 29
We all went to Heathfield Chapple in morning except Ann Elizabeth & Mary Beedle Mr Press preached from Exodus 14th C 132 I liked his discourse very much Father went to our church in afternoon and heard the Hailsham Parson preach from these words 'Blessed are the dead that die in the Lord yea saith the spirit for they rest from their labours and their works do follow them.' He said it was not much of a discourse

Monday 30
Horses ploughing Squire field Baker threshing CB Thos Hoad threshing HB Easton and Beal hop diging Poundfield garden rest workmen wood cutting David & I planted some Filbird[176] Plants and gaping betwixt the chaple mead... and Pond Croft John Soland visitor

Tuesday 31
Horses plough Baker threshing CB Thos Hoad's threshing HB Easton & Beal hop digging rest workmen wood cutting all as yesterday Father went to Rushlake Green David & I planted some beans & peas my uncle Robrt Cornwell visitor to a late [h]our

Wednesday 1 February
Horses Hoad's Beal Easton and wood cutters all as yesterday Baker threshing CB in morning cleaning up the wheat straw stack in afternoon

Thursday 2
Horses plough Easton Beal hop digging as yesterday Baker threshing CB rest workmen wood cutting I went to Halfmoon Market

Friday 3
Horses Beal Easton as yesterday Baker threshing & gaping six acres rest workmen wood cutting

Saturday 4
Horses plough in the Squire field Baker threshing CB Easton & Beal hop digging Croft Father and I took some of George Guy's work against and in Grimes Brook and gainst Vinesses field rest workmen wood cutting Carters were granted some hay for the old horse or Bowler before they sole[177] it

[176] Filbert.
[177] Sold.

Sunday 5
Mother & Ann stopt at home all the rest went to Heathfield Chapple Mr Press preached from Ephesians 1 Cha 13 & 14th verse

Monday 6
Horses finished plough in Squire field Baker gapping & threshing Beal & Easton hop digging Poundfield garden to Thos Hoad's & I cleaning wheat HB cleaned 25s 2 bu Head 2s tail they had cleaned 2 sacks before rest workmen wood cutting

Tuesday 7
Horses ploughing in Croft hop garden Easton and Beal hop digging as yesterday some workmen wood cutting Baker threshing CB I went to meet Mr Press who preached this evening from Proverbs 12 Cha 25 verse

Wednesday 8
Horses plough Orchard Garden Baker Beal & Easton with cutters as yesterday I went with Mr Press to Rushlake Green Father & Elizabeth went to Warbleton Church to Mr John Pattenden[178] who died last Friday morning about 3 o'clock aged 62 Years cousin Sam G Oxley visitor

Thursday 9
Horses plough 10 acres tried the Bushey field put it would not do Baker threshing CB Beal Easton and David Honeysett Senr hop digging Poundfield garden rest workmen wood cutting Mr John and Richard Pursglove and Phillips & C hunting around about here Mr Russell visitor and pruned the fruit trees

Friday 10
Horses went twice to Bucksteep WaterMill with 25 sacks of wheat and 2 sacks of Barley carried 1 load of wheat straw after ward up to Oxens Close for their fodder rest all as yesterday to w[h]at I knowd Mr Steer visitor in evening

Saturday 11
Horses plough Baker threshing oats HB 3 hop diggers rest workmen wood cutting Father I & David took an of Mrs Martin cast[179] in Grimes Wood

Sunday 12
Father Elizabeth and Ann stopt at home rest of us went to Heathfield

---

[178] John Pattenden's funeral.
[179] Take a cast: measure a piece of land.

Chapple Mr Press preached from the 2 Book of Peter last chapter and the last verse

Monday 13
Horses stood in the stable in the forenoon till about 3 O'clock afterwards carried 7 sacks of barley to mill Baker threshing in forenoon He and I cleaned 9 sacks of barley Thos Hoads threshing HB George Guy Wm Hoad and Thos Daw [with one eye] wood cutting rest if any not known

Tuesday 14
Horses plough 10 acres Baker threshing CB Thos Hoad junr threshing oats HB Easton and Honeysett hop digging Poundfield garden rest workmen wood cutting Mr Reed rat catching catched 7 I went to hear preaching at John Honeysett preached from Luke 19 Cha 10 verse

Wednesday 15
Horses plough Beal Honeysett & Easton hop digging Baker threshing CB Thos Hoad junr threshing all day Thos Hoad & son afternoon rest workmen wood cutting David & I took Thos Daw cast Mr John Reeves from Rushlake visitor from 1 O'clock till about or after 8 O'clock

Thursday 16
Horses plough in the forenoon Baker threshing in the forenoon He and I went to the Halfmoon Market and fetched the bull home Cost 18£ Thos Hoad's threshing HB some hop diggers and wood cutters but not known

Friday 17
Horses plough Thos Hoad and Baker cleaning oats HB I Cornford and Beal hopp digging in Pound field garden Honeysett and Easton stub raking Kiln field rest of the workmen wood cutting I went to Mayfield at the appraisements of my uncles goods and found 2 more securities Father went to the Club at the Star Inn Heathfield for posicuting thieves[180]

Saturday 18
Horses plough Thos Hoad threshing wheat HB 4 workmen hop digging Baker threshing barley CB rest workmen wood cutting I came home from Mayfield stopt the preceding night at Frog Hole

Sunday 19
Mother and Ann stopt at home rest went to Heathfield Chaple Mr Press preached from the 68 Psalm the 18 verse Beal has not been to work since

[180] See Appendix 2 for a note on the Prosecuting Society of Heathfield and Warbleton.

Saturday

Monday 20
Horses plough some hop diggers and wood cutters and threshers as Saturday

Tuesday 21
Horses plough some hop diggers woodcutters and threshers as yesterday David Father and I took G Guy's cast in Grimes Wood Mr Winchester spoke in prayer Mr Press gave out the hymns and preached from Romans 6 Cha 23 verse and baptised a child and an Irishman concluded in prayers at Mr Smiths

Wednesday 22
Horses plough in 10 acres hop diggers finished Poundfield garden Easton Honeysett & Cornford began the orchard G Guy Do in the afternoon David & I spreading dung in orchard hop garden Baker threshing CB Thomas Hoad's threshing HB Wm Hoad wood cutting some hop pole shavers Father went to Hailsham Market Mr Squires team came after fence poles

Thursday 23
Horses plough broke the red plough 4 hop diggers 3 threshers and 2 men and a boy wood cutters David and I fetched 1 lump of potatoes with a pair of oxen a cart from Kiln field into the oast I went the Halfmoon market

Friday 24
Horses plough Baker and I cleaned 18 sacks of barley Guy Cornford Honeysett and Easton hop digging in Orchard garden Thos Hoad threshing HB Thos Pankhurst put a handle to a plough Wm Eavenden[?][181] Has been three days log cleaving att two and sixpence per day Wm Hoad Wm Farmer wood cutting Mr Reeves Rushlake Mr James Dann Mr Jesse Jarvis and Mr Delves visitors

Saturday 25
Horses carried a load of straw to Hodges and finished plough in the 10 acres finished it Easton Cornford and Honeysett hop digging Baker threshing CB Thos Hoad's threshing HB Wm Hoad wood cutting I took Wm Farmers cast in Grimes Wood David went to Gardner Street Father to the Priory in the morning

[181] Lavender?

Sunday 26
Father Mother Elizabeth David and I went to Heathfield Chapple in the morning Father Elizabeth and Mary Do in afternoon an Irishman preached in the morning from John 17 Cha 2nd verse in the afternoon from Isaiah 27 chapter and the last verse

Monday 27
Horses plough one went in an alley in the crofts hop garden afterwards plough in the Bushey field Baker threshing in the afternoon Thos Hoad threshing HB Wm Hoad wood cutting Guy Easton Honeysett and Cornford hop digging finished the orchard and began the Croft Father went to Warbleton Workhouse sold the old sow Master Grant visitor David and I planted some potatoes I planted some beans in the upper garden our young doe went to buck

Tuesday 28
Horses plough Bushey field Baker Easton Guy Honeysett and David stub goading and raking some all day Thos Hoad threshing killed the old sow in the afternoon Baker helpt Father sold the Old Doumadary or Hailsham Cow to Mr Noakes for 25£ if in calf 28£ if not Master Cornford hop digging in the croft Wm Hoad wood cutting Mr Noakes visitor as he past by from Dallington a going to Blackford's Heard odd noise about ½ past 5 O'clock rumbling thunder but see no clouds around in the East

Wednesday 1 March
Horses plough Bushey field Baker and I with oxen and a cart went to our workhouse with the old sow she weighted 49 stone and 7 lb and carried 6 sacks of potato oats to Mr Russell 4 hop diggers in the Croft 2 threshers Wm Hoad wood cutting James Harmer and Mr J Smith visitor Father went to the Club at Woods Corner Two heifers calved and lost both the calves

Thursday 2
Horses plough 4 hop diggers in morning Mr Honeysett went home in the afternoon Baker moul spreading in the Croft 2 threshers 1 wood cutter some hop pole shavers Father Went to Bellhurst I went to the Half Moon Market Wm visitor Mr Newman Do

Friday 3
Horses plough 4 hop diggers finished Croft began the Brook 2 Hoad's and Baker cleaned wheat head 22 s 3 Bus Tail 2 sack total 24 s 3 bu Wm Hoad wood cutting some hop pole shavers I sowed my onions Wm went home in the afternoon Father went to Mr Walters at Beastons

Saturday 4

Horses plough Oxen getting in the Traifoil seed stack Baker & Thos Hoad seed Do Wm Hoad finished wood cutting Honeysett Easton Guy Thos Hoad Junr David & I hop dressing Oxen Thos Hoad Baker and Father gathered up one load of stubble James Harmer Thos Soper Junr and Terry[?] Visitors

Sunday 5

All went to Heathfield Chapple in the morning except Mary & Ann Mary went in the afternoon Mr Press preached in the morning from Psalm 11 3 verse

Monday March 6

Horses plough in Bushey field Honeysett Baker Easton Guy Wm Hoad and I hop dressing finished the Croft in the forenoon and began the Poundfield garden Father cutting hop setts a few in the Croft afterwards in the Pound field garden David dressing in the Croft afterwards cutting hop setts Thos Hoad's threshing trailfoil Home Mr Noakes sent two boys for the fat cow in the afternoon I planted some Dwarf Marfat[182] Peas

Tuesday 7

The carters say that they begun plough the High field at Hodges yesterday about 12 O'clock and were there to day Baker Honeysett Easton Wm Hoad G Guy and I dressing hops in the oldest part of the young garden in the morning afterwards in the new part Thos Hoad's threshing as yesterday Father and David cut out sett in the morning Mr Press preached in the evening from from Hebrews 4 chapter and the three last verses

Wednesday 8

Wet weather Horses carried 2 load 4 bushels of wheat to this mill for Mr Smith at 16£ load Baker and Wm Hoad threshing of barely CB Thos Hoad's finished threshing traifoil in the forenoon Helpt carters in the afternoon Mr Press went home from here at almost 4 O'clock Henry went with him to bring Old Jack[183] back

Thursday 9

Horses plough Highfield Baker Guy Wm Hoad Honeysett and Easton hop dressing in the young garden Thos Hoad and I cleaned 16 sacks of Traifoil

---

[182] Marrowfat.
[183] The pony.

in the pug in the morning Thos Hoad's threshing wheat in the afternoon I and Father went to Halfmoon Market

Friday 10
Foster and Henry hop pole chopping in the forenoon Baker and Wm Hoad threshing barley in the forenoon Thos Hoad Senr threshing HB Baker and Hoad cleaned … barely in afternoon Foster Henry Easton Guy David and Honeysett stubble rakeing Kilnfield in afternoon Wm Hoad Do a little and finished 1 horse fetched 5 sacks of barley from CB to HB fetched the bull from among the oxen and put him into the stall where the fat cow was John Bland visitor

Saturday 11
Horses went to Waldron with seed Wm Harmer and carters four teams Honeysett Baker Easton Guy and Wm Hoad spreading moul further end of the Croft Garden in the forenoon all these and Father David and I finished dressing the young hop garden and cutting out setts in the afternoon Thos Hoads threshing HB Thos Oxley visitor Tailor and Walters Shoemakers Do 16 verse

Sunday 12
Father went to Mr Noakes on account of his Adagio Volti[184] in the forenoon Mother Elizabeth David and I went to Heathfield Chaple in the morning Father and Elizabeth Do in the afternoon Mr Press preached in the morning from the 61 Psalm latter part 2nd verse in afternoon from Galations 4 Cha 16 verse

Monday 13
Horses plough finished Highfield and ploughed Mr Thos Hoads plat in rent in the morning before Snackfast to tell G Guy David Honeysett James Easton not to come to work for we had nothing for them to do owing to the whet weather Wm Hoad and Baker digging in the morning in the upper corner of the Orchard Garden afterward in the young Orchard or Wenhouse Brook Thos Hoad's threshing Father went some where Heathfield ward but I don't know where from morning till night Mr Harris and Mr Jas Phillips Game Keeper visitors a few minutes In the afternoon

Tuesday 14
Horses plough further end of the Croft Hop Garden Baker Baker spreading moule at the same place Wm Hoad digging young orchard Thos Hoad's threshing Mr P Pankhurst and a man from Winchelsea to see the lambs

[184] Singing style.

visitors

Wednesday 15
Horses finished further end of the Croft at plough in morning afterwards ploughed Bakers plat Baker digging Garden ground in Orchard Hop Garden in morning afterwards helpt horses plough his plat Thos Hoad's threshing Wm Hoad hedging 13 acres David Honeysett witeting[185] Lodge and Barn I went to Mayfield on my uncles business Coley Cow calved in the morning about 7 or 8 O'clock

Thursday 16
Horses helpt holy day[186] except Colier who went to mill for Hog Corn Foster chaff cutting rest of the day Henry digging Headland of the Poundfield Hop Garden Baker Do in afternoon Thos Hoad's threshing Father went to Mr Counts and Mr Parker and Half moon I came home from Mayfield Wm Hoad hedging

Friday 17
Horses carters and Baker brought 3 loads of oat straw from Wm Isted's to Chaple Barn Wm Hoad hedging Father went to Burwash in afternoon Thos Hoad's threshing

Saturday 18
Horses carried some ash from Grimes Wood to Penny trap Daws in the morning afterwards fetched some clog and some thatching rods from Grimes Wood and set it down a gainst the pound David Father and I helped David and Father took Wm Hoads cast of wood I went to carry a note for Mr Hall to Mr Parker's Cade Street Baker digging poundfield Wm Hoad hedging Thos Hoads threshing home barn

Sunday 19
Father Elizabeth David and I went to Heathfield Chaple in morning Mary Do all day Mr Press preached in morning from Kings 2 Book 4 chapter latter part 26 verse in afternoon from Hebrews 11 Chapter 2 first verses Mr Ellis told Father of his Adagio Volto et Staccato

Monday 20
Horses carried two hundred Kiln Faggots from Grimes Wood to Wm Harmers Baker Easton Guy & I hop dressing in Orchard Garden David

---

[185] Applying whitewash.
[186] Holiday.

cutting setts Father went to Cade Street I went to Priory in the evening Thos Hoad's threshing Wm Hoad hedging

Tuesday 21
Horses carried 2 loads stubble in home yard and 2 loads into Ox yard from kiln field finished David helpt Thos Hoad's threshing Wm Hoad hedging Baker Easton Guy and hop dressing Father cutting setts Father David and I went to Mr Smith's to Mr Press preached from 2 Thessalonians 1 Cha 8 verses Mr Chas Woodhams Mr Delves Mr Sam'l Verrell Visitors Mr John Fox Senr died at 11 O'clock Thursday

Wednesday 22
Foster bosling[187] Henry hop pole chopping morning hop dressing afternoon Baker David and I W[ork?] all day in Brook garden Three Hoads and Easton stacking kiln faggots in Grimes Wood
Father went to Hailsham Market Mr Verrell went home Mrs Selmes left her place

Thursday 23
Horses drawed 2012 13 feet from the wood to the Pound field garden not into it Baker helpt 2 Hoad's Easton & Guy stacking Kiln Faggots David and I cutting setts in Brook garden and dressed a few hills in the Orchard in the morning but twas too wet Father went to the Halfmoon market Wm Hoad hedging

Good Friday 24
Spreading at Chapple but more went to hear from here Horses drawed 2400/12 feet poles from the wood to Pound field Baker helpt them 2 Hoad's and Easton stacking of faggots John Marten came after 14100 hop setts in afternoon man came to see the stray sheep but did not own them

Saturday 25
Horses drawed 3000 12 feet poles in to the Pound field Thos Hoad Senr & Easton finished stacking Kiln Faggots Baker helpt carters Wm Hoad David & I finished Brook and orchard hop gardens and cut out the set in the forenoon Wm Hoad gaping afterwards at Hodges Father went to Heathfield

Sunday 26
All went to Heathfield Chaple except Ann in the morning Mr Press

---

[187] Bosseling: see glossary.

preached from Philipians 2 chapter 9th 10th and 11th verses I stopt down at the Crown instead of going to Chaple in the afternoon with Mr Steers and Mr Mepham Wm Foster left the horse

Monday 27
Wm Hoad took the horses wet weather all day all at holiday keeping Father went the Easter meeting at church Mary Beadle went away

Tuesday 28
Thos Hoad and John Baker made the Garden hedge Wm Hoad chaff cutting I went to Mayfield Father went to Heathfield

Wednesday 29
Wm Hoad 2 horses and Millers cart went to MayField Thos Hoad Baker and Easton making a bridge up in the wood I came home from Mayfield John Bland too Mr Phipps visitors Forgot to mention T Hoad Baker & Easton cleaned 2. cwt 2. Qt 3. lb Wheat in afternoon

Thursday 30
Horses had the cart home in the morning carried 15 sacks of Barley to Dallington and carried some stakes and chucks from the wood to Hodges Baker moul spreading in Grinnitts Thos Hoad killed a hog boar and I helpt Thos Hoad and Easton threshing wheat HB Father went to the Halfmoon Market Mr Batup visitor

Friday 31
Horses carters and Baker carried 600 12 feet poles and 1388 13 feet poles in to the Pound field from the wood Thos Hoad and Easton the last of the Brown Eyeshell[188] Wheat in the morning then and I clean 15 bushels the last of the same above mentioned Father went to Heathfield

Saturday 1 April
Hoad drawed 1900 13 feet poles into the Pound field from the wood Baker helpt Thos hedging orchard hop garden against the Brook I went to Priory in morning

Sunday 2
Father Mother Mrs Selmes Elizabeth and I went to Heathfield Chapel in morning Mr Press preached from Deuteronomy 33 Cha middle part 16 verse in afternoon from last Chapter 14 verse [deletion] Jinny [deletion] went David went to Hurstmonceux in morning Malachi 4 Cha 2nd verse

---

[188] Eggshell (wheat variety).

Trimming hedges

was the priest surmon text

Monday 3
Horses drawing hop poles in young garden from old part to the new carter sharpening hop poles Thos Hoad hedging Baker David and I helpt Horses Father went down in marsh Wm visitor

Tuesday 4
Horses carried poles from the Wood to the Pound field afterward fetched in the potatoes from the Brook and Kiln field Easton sharping hop poles Thos Hoad hedging Baker helpt horses Mr Press preached from 2 Corinthians 5 Chap 14 & 15 verses

Wednesday 5
Horses and Baker carried some wheat straw from Home Barn and stacked it up against the Ox yard Thos Hoad hedging Guy Foster and Old Dann hop poling in Croft I went to Cowbeach and Gardner St Wm Oxley went home Mr T Mepham and a boy visitors with 48 sheep

Thursday 6
Horses went to Saunders Mill after seed Baker hop digging in morning and he and I cleaned about a load of oats he afterwards went to hop digging in Brook Mother and Elizabeth went to Uncle Wm Oxley's Father went to Heath field David went sheep to Black horse Thos Hoad hedging Foster Guy and Dan hop poling Croft Mr Batup borrowed Duke & Diamond

Friday 7
Horses harrow in the 10 acres Baker and I sowed 10 acres of Black except 2 bushels of white oats and carried 9 sacks of wheat to mill with 4 oxen & a cart Thos Hoad hedging Guy Dann & Foster hop poling Croft Mr J Ellis visitor Father Mother and Elizabeth out visiting at J Waters Easton sharping poles

Saturday 8
Horses harrow 10 acres Baker & I with 4 oxen yesterday and to day carried 26 sacks of Head and 1 sack Tail wheat to mill Baker went with oxen to Priory with 4000 hop setts and to J Wood after 5 sacks of Rye Grass seed he and with oxen drawed 350 12 feet poles from wood to Croft garden rest workmen as yesterday J Bland Uncle Wm Oxley Mr Buss visitors Father went to four mile[189] to Mr J Blackman

---

[189] Foul or Fowl Mile, between Cowbeech and Rushlake Green.

Sunday 9
Father Mother David Elizabeth and I went to Heathfield Chapple in morning Father Elizabeth and Jinny in afternoon Mr Press preached from James 2 Cha 19th verse in morning Deuteronomy 33 Cha 25th verse afternoon Mrs Selmes Went to Hurstmonceaux Chapple Morning

Monday 10
Horses harrow 10 acres and Bushy field oxen fetched 350 12 feet poles from wood to Croft Garden Baker David and I helpt and measured up 18 sacks of oats morning Baker threshing David harrow and I & Wm Hoad sowed Bushey field with 5 sacks of White Oats after wards 3 hop polers in Croft Easton sharping poles Thos poling young Garden Father went to Heathfield

Tuesday 11
Horses & Wm Hoad harrow in the Bushey field Baker threshing and dug watering in Kilnfield David and I sowed the Bushey field with seeds and drove our three barren cows 2 yearling heifers from Thos Isted's[?] down into marsh Old Smoke calved Guy Foster and Old Dan poling Croft Thos Hoad and I carters poling young garden I went to prayer meeting J Honeysett's in evening

Wednesday 12
Horses drawed hop poles from the Pound field into the young garden Baker helpt rest of the workmen as yesterday Father Elizabeth David and I went to the Heathfield Association in morning Father and I staid the evening Mr Winchester and Mr Drury[?] in morning and Mr Thomsett an Irishman in evening

Thursday 13
Horses harrow in Squires field Baker and I sowed 19 sacks of Oats in Squire field and found some Winttles[190] around the wheat stack David I and Father turn[?] the Friesians the 5 calves and 4 colts into the Kiln field Easton and Thos Hoad poling young garden Foster Guy and Dan finished Croft yesterday and began the orchard garden and were there to day Crowerst farrier visitors and drawed a dead lamb that had not the sheep and they killed her

Friday 14
Horses harrowed in the Squirefield and Baker sowing seeds three hop

---

[190] Possibly loose straw blown out of the stack.

polers in orchard Garden and 2 in young garden and Dame Dann hop tying Father David and I went to Heathfield Fair and sold Beast & Lively to Mr Gorringe beyond Brighton for 41£ 15s 0d

Saturday 15
Horses finished harrow in Squirefield and fetched the poles from Thirteen acres to the young garden Baker scouring out vero[191] in Bushy fields in morning he and I cleaned the last of the oats 4 sacks of Head and Tail and 7 sack and a bushel of barley Father David I Wm Hoad and Baker loaded 1000 14 feet poles on two waggons rest workmen as yesterday Mrs Selmes came home from Silverash after having been there some time Baker had Duke and Diamond home

Sunday 16
Father Elizabeth & I Chapple all day Mother David and maid in morning Mrs Selmes in afternoon Mr Press preached from Luke 15 Cha and 2 verse in the morning and from the 7 verse in the afternoon

Monday 17
Horses and oxen drawed 1000 14 feet poles to down gate and loaded 500 14 feet and 1000 12 feet on 2 waggons a woman and a boy came after the strayed sheep after having been with us ever since the 1st of December last Dame Dann hop tiers and some other with her Thos Hoad & farm carters in young garden and Wm Foster in Brook and Old Dann & G Guy in orchard hop polers Richd Winchester visitor and marked some in Grimes wood we worked new waggon first time with oxen

Tuesday 18
Horses and oxen drawed hop poles as yesterday rest as yesterday except G Guy who left at noon all went to meeting at Mr Smith's except Mrs Selmes & Ann Mr Press preached from Gallations 1 chapter   verse Mrs Bland visitor and Eliza her daughter visitor in afternoon Mr Nathan Tailer in evening

Wednesday 19
Horses harrowed and shimed the Furze field I sowed it with barley and helpt them shim Baker & oxen roling Eight Acres Mr Button team came after 2000 Old 12 feet poles Thos Hoad & Easton young garden Foster Guy in Brook & Old Dann in orchard hop poling Master Buss came after sack of barley and 1 sack of oats

[191] Probably furrow.

Thursday 20
David & I sowed the Highfield with oats and seeds[192] and horses harrowed them in Baker with 6 oxen roling Eight Acres rest workmen as yesterday Father and I went to Halfmoon But[t]ons team came after 1000 more 12 feet poles 2 heifers calved

Friday 21
Father I Baker & David helpt carters load 100 peabow faggots[193] Horses drawed them to Mr Russells rest workmen came but did not do much because of the wet weather

Saturday 22
Wm Hoad chaff cutting and had 2 Horses shewed[194] Baker finished threshing barley and Henry and I helpt clean it Thos Hoad and Easton casting up dung in Calves Lodge & Poundfield Old Dann hop poling orchard Foster hop digging in the Brook a little wile showery weather all day

Sunday 23
All went to Chapple except Mother & Ann in morning I stop afternoon Mr Press preached in morning from John 10th Cha 3rd and 4th verse Proverbs But the righteous are not so for they shall shine forth more and more unto the perfect day. Was his text in afternoon

Monday 24
Horses Wm & Henry Hoad's & Baker David drawing 13 feet poles and chord wood from Grimes Brook Foster Guy poling hops in Brook Wm Dann in archer[195] Easton & T Hoad poling Pound garden Dame Dann tighing hops in the P garden Thos Parker visitor I went to Frog Hole and the start for London

Tuesday 25
Horses Wm & H Hoad's and Baker and David a clearing chucks from the Croft Brook and archer gardens and also the top of Poundfield Foster poling hops in brook & orchard Guy Eastone and Thos Hoad poling hops in Pound garden Thos Hoad killed at patherish[196] sheep I went to London

---

[192] Undersowed the oats with a mixture of clover and grasses.
[193] For peas to grow up, or faggots of small twigs.
[194] Shod.
[195] Archer field or garden.
[196] Of a sheep: showing symptoms of giddiness or ataxia. (OED).

Wednesday 26
Horses Wm Hoad Baker fetched some bushes from the wood to Chapel mead[ow] and silver field afterward fetched 1 load of hay from Calves Lodge to the hay loft and then cleared croft and Brook garden of old poles Wm Dann sharped poles in top Poundfield T Hoad Eastone & Guy poling pound garden Wm Foster finished pot[ato]ing Archer H Hoad and David went into the market with 5 yearling calves and 2 2 yearling colts Jn Bland and T Delves visitors

Thursday 27
Horses Wm & H Hoad's and Baker carried 49 loads of dung up into the Kiln field Thos Hoad Eastone Foster Guy and Dann sharping poles from the great stack in Poundfield Father David Selmes went to Sobers sale

Friday 28
Horses Wm & H Hoad's harrow for John Waters Hodgeskins oxen Thos Hoad and David drawing pole into Pound afterwards Thos Hoad poling and Eastone Foster and Dann David carry of poles from that garden Dame Dann potatoing I forgot for this 2 day past She was a dog wood scraping Mrs Flurence Mrs Waters and Mr Waters visitors

Saturday 29
Horses Wm & H Hoad's and Baker carried 45 loads of dung in to the kiln field oxen Thos Hoad and David chuck carrying Foster Eastone Dann poling hops finished in morning Eastone & Foster casting up dung afterwards some hop tieing croft Father went in to the marsh 1 Heifer calved

Sunday 30
All went to Heathfield Chapel in morning except the maid maid we[nt?] in afternoon Mother & Ann stopt Mr Press preached in morning from Isiah 41 Cha 17 verse in afternoon from Job 17 Cha 9 verse I came home from London

Monday 1 May
Wm Hoad & Henry shiming Poundfield garden David & I shiming young orchard T Hoad & I drawed vere[197] in morning David & I shiming with carters rest day Thos Hoad and Easton potato planting Wm Foster went to Frog hole to Mr Cornwell after a pig 2 week old cows turned out day Miss Gells visitor some hop tiers Baker oxen ordering 3 meadows

[197] Furrows.

Tuesday 2

Horses Wm & H Hoad and I shiming young garden David helpt in morning went down in the marsh with two cows and 2 calves in afternoon Wm Foster setting up hop poles to burn[?] and hop chopping in morning helpt shim in afternoon Thos Hoad gapping at several places Easton planting potatoes some hop tiers Mr Press preached in evening from 1 Samuel 2 Cha 8 verse David sore him I Baker oxen roling 9 acres

Wednesday 3

Horses shiming young garden till about 3 O'clock and then began the Croft oxen Baker druged Calves Lodge meadow and Hodges in forenoon Baker helpt maid carry up chucks in afternoon T Hoad & Easton hop chopping orchard garden Foster & I help carters Father went Hailsham Market Mr J Elis & Mr Counts maid visitors Mrs Selmes went to Mr Newington's at Bines in her road to Mayfield

Thursday 4

Wm & H Hoad's Foster & I shiming in Croft garden with 4 horses 2 shimers Baker gaping silverfield Thos Hoad & Easton hop chopping orchard garden Wm Oxley visitor Father went to Half moon Market

Friday 5

Horses & oxen Wm Hoad Henry Hoad Thos Hoad Baker Foster James Phillips & dogs Father & I got the wheat stack on in 10 loads in the morning finished about ½ past 1 O'clock carters Foster Baker & I with two teams in 2 load fetched the chord[198] wood and faggots from the 13 acres Easton all day Thos Hoad afternoon hop chopping orchard garden Father & Mother went to Mr Smith's is Visitor some hop tiers yesterday and to day Mr T Bennett visitors. Wm Oxley went home in morning

Satturday 6

Horses carried 1 chord of wood to Mr Goldsmith at Rushlake and 100 faggots to Wm Hoad's Bodle Street oxen 100 faggots to Mr Goldsmith's Rushlake and loaded 100 faggots and sett out at sannells T Hoad Foster & Easton hop chopping Mr James Dann sons visitors with with a two yearling heifer Russell school Master & J Viger visitors yoked steers first time[199]

---

[198] Cord.

[199] Training by getting them used to a yoke. They will only work in their own pairs after training.

1815

Sunday 7
Maid and Ann stayed at home in morning rest Heathfield Chapple Father & I stayed all day maid came in the afternoon Mr Press preached in morning from Isiah 32 Cha first part 2nd verse and afternoon from Jeramiah 32nd Cha 37th and following verses

Monday 8
Horses harrow & plough Grinetts oxen went twice to Mr Goldsmith's with 100 faggots & 1 chord of wood T Hoad & David shiming part orchard & part Crofts Garden Foster Easton hop chopping Croft Thos Easton visitor to J Easton yoked steers 2nd time Baker & I alone

Tuesday 9
Horses plough Grinnetts finished it oxen carried last 100 of House Faggotts to Mr Goldsmith sett 100 out at Sannell the 2 workmen hop chopping Baker mowed trap[?] in upper garden Mr Ellis visitor in morning Mr Charles Verrel and his wife visitors late in evening I have forgot the hop tiers and the tan flawers began last Saturday Winchesters and party Thos Hoad top loping

Wednesday 10
Horses carried 100 house faggots to Mr Russell's oxen 100 Do Mr Crouch Flitter Brook [Lane Punnetts Town] Foster & Easton hop chopping Thos Hoad top loping timber fellers hop tiers etc Mr Mrs Verrell went from here at 10 O' clock David & I fishing at night

Thursday 11
Horses harrow and drawed rows for potatoes in Grinnetts oxen 100 faggots to Crouchers and fetched all the 82 faggot fro' oast brook to our house tan flawers T Hoad top cutting and hop tiers Foster & Easton hop chopping man & boy from Alfriston & J Bland visitors Father went to Lewes this morning

Friday 12
Horses & oxen carried 100 faggots & 1 chord of wood to Mr R J Russells oxen sett 100 faggots out at Sannells carters took harnis to pieces ready for oiling Foster helpt Baker T Hoad top cutting Easton top chopping tan flawers hop tiers etc David & I drove 2 Heifers to Burwash Fair did not sell them Father came home from Lewes Mr Delves short visit

Saturday 13
Foster & David shiming Brook garden carters Saml Fox & Boy oiling

harness T Hoad work for self timber fellers hop tiers etc oxen carried last 100 faggots to Mr Russells that he is a going to have sett 100 faggots ½ chord of wood out at Sannells turned horses out in Bushey field night carter hop choping in Poundfield in morning Father & he afternoon Do in Brook

Sunday 14
All went to Heathfield Chaple in morning except Ann & maid she went in afternoon Mr Press preached from Corrinthians 1 cha 23 & 24 verses in morning & afternoon Wit Sunday Mrs Dann visitor

Monday 15
Horses Foster & Henry roling oats and something else David says as he is all most or quite a sleep about ½ past 10 O'clock at night. Oxen load of wood consisting of 100 faggots and ½ chord of wood carried to Mr J Waters Rushlake T Hoad top cutting timber fellers finished in afternoon some hop tiers Wm Hoad went yesterday to Horsham Great[200] number of visitors the chief of which are Mr James Lade & wife Sarah & Ruth Reeves George Ellis Thos Goldsmith Chiddingly & etc several on account of some bulocks to be drove to Winchelsea to morrow by G Ellis T Goldsmith and John Waters Forgot to mention oxen carried one 100 of faggots to John Baker and brought waggon home had a pair wheels to wheelers to be mended a treaty deal more[201] perhaps I cannot recollect not all

Tuesday 16
Horses roling ten acres & Bushey field Henry alone oxen carried 100 faggots & 10 bundeles thatch rods to Mr Wenhams Boreham T Hoad top cutting Foster hop chopping in Brook Father I David Elizabeth & Mrs Dann went to meeting at Mr Smith's Mr Press preached from Numbers 14th Cha 24th verse G Elis & T Goldsmith started early in the morning

Wednesday 17
Horses & oxen carried 200 Hund Faggotts to Boreham shop and 15 bundles of thatch rods to M J Scrace T Hoad top cutting Easton & Foster hop chopping Pound field hop tiers Wm Hoad with horses Mr J Elis Uncle Wm Oxley and wife aunt Bet cousin Ruth Oxley's visitors took faggots in Broom wood

[200] Great Fair.
[201] Good deal more.

Thursday 18
Horses & Oxen carried 200 faggots to Mr Pocock and fetched 200 faggots from Broom wood to Dill Gate T Hoad top cutting Easton & Foster hop chopping Pound field hop tiers Messr Jer & Thos Ellis Mr Diamond & Wm stopped for enquire visitors S Winchester carpenter mending wattles etc[202]

Friday 19
Horses & Oxen went Boreham shop with 200 faggots and loaded up 200 from our wood T Hoad top cutting Foster & Easton hop chopping orchard garden Dame Dann who has lodged here some time except Sundays has her Pound field hops & scrapt the Dog wood was to day a weeding with the maid in the two upper Wheat fields some hop tiers David went with oxen Mr Hilder & Masr were visitors brought timber Mr Stanford went home in afternoon Mr Reed visitors I forgot to mention 15 bundles thatch rods to Mr Scrace which makes 30 in all

Saturday 20
Horses carried 100 faggots to Mr Verrell Meachams Wartling and fetched 700 bricks from Tilly Kiln oxen carried 100 faggots to Mr Loyd's Windmill Hill and 100 to Mr Wm Grant T Hoad top cutting Easton Foster hop chopping orchard weeders hop tiers etc Messr J & T Ellis Wm Oxley and J Phillips game keeper visitors Father bought Mr Ellis's house & 6 quarters of S Goldsmith oxen turned out at night in silver field

Sunday 21
All went to Heathfield Chapple in morning Father I & Elizabeth in afternoon Mr Press preached from Hebrews 11 Cha 6 verse in morning and Isaiah 45 Cha 17 verse afternoon

Monday 22
T Hoad Baker & I killed hog in morning Horses carried 50 faggots to Loyd's Windmill hill and 50 to Park Gate near Wartling ground sett[?] rows Grinnetts oxen 100 to Park Gate X Do and fetched home 6 sacks tares from carters T Hoad top cutting Easton all day & Foster half day hop chopping hop tiers Dame Dann weeding half day Father went down in marsh 2 boys visitors Forgot to mention horses carried ½ quarter Kiln Faggots to Bodle Street for the Parrish to go down to Huglets river & oxen carried 6 bundles

[202] These would have not been the woven hazel type, but more likely to have been split oak or sweet chestnut hurdles, like a small gate. Old shepherds called all fencing used to fold sheep by the common term of 'wattles'.

thatch rods to Bellhurst to go to Mr Elfick Looker

Tuesday 23
Horses & oxen carried 400 Kiln Faggots to Mr Goldsmith's B Kiln and 100 House faggots and 14½ feet wood to Thos Hoad's Easton Foster & Dame Dann potato setting Grinnetts David cut setts hop tiers Hilder Harriss Reed Bennett and some other visitors about the timber Father bought top wood took trees to draw to the Tet[?] and to agreed to carry the timber to Pevensey sold Heifer and calf to Mr Baker near Amberstone for 13£

Wednesday 24
Horses carried 200 faggots to B Kilns & 100 House Do to Wm Hoad's oxen carried 200 Do to Do throwed new waggon over first with 200 Kiln Faggotts[203] in Mr Squires field in Morning carried 100 House Do to T Hoads Foster Easton potato planting Grinnetts Dame Dann Do half day hop tiers Father Went to Dallington Fair T Hoad top cutting some timber hewers David help potato planters Mr Hall visitor Father sold Tegs for 58£ Ram died in Kilnfield Baker & I flawed him

Thursday 25
Horses & oxen carried 400 Kiln Faggotts to the B Kiln & horses Do 50 House Do & 10 chord of wood to Wm Hoad oxen fetched 150 from the to[204] wood to our Kiln T Hoad top cutting Easton & Foster finished planting the Grinnetts David helpt but was unwell yesterday afternoon and today Dame Dann & maid pulling Kilk[205] in Round banks some hop tiers Mr & Mrs Delves visitors

[Friday 26]
Dame Dann & maid pulling kilk Round banks Mr Newman & Mr Thos Walters visitors

Saturday 27
Horses & oxen carried 800 faggots to B Kiln and brought home 600 bricks T Hoad top cutting half day Easton & Foster casting up dung some hop tiers & kilk pullers Thos Waters J Reed[?] visitors David went to Gardener Street

Sunday 28
All went to Heathfield Chapple except Maid & Ann in morning and except mother Ann and I in afternoon Mr Press preached from Timothy 2 Cha 4

---

[203] The waggon was overloaded with 200 kiln faggots, and overturned.
[204] Top?
[205] Charlock (wild mustard).

verse in morning & the 2 following verses afternoon

Monday 29
Both teams carried 400 faggots to Brick Kiln and sett 400 out at Sannells T Hoad river cutting between our Brook and Mill Brook Easton & Foster casting up dung at Hodges Hop tiers David puld kilk half day in Round Banks Mres Wimble Newman at Alfriston & Mr & Mrs Press visitors Old Hive bees swarmed

Tuesday 30
Teams carried 800 faggots to B Kiln T Hoad river cutting Foster & Easton carried rist bats to gather in the wood & carried them up to the top of G brook shavers hop chopping hop tiers sawyers David puld kilk a little to wett for it E Standen & his housekeeper & Mr Hilder visitor Mr Press preached in evening from Hebrews 4 Cha 9 verse

Wednesday 31
Teames carried 400 faggots to B Kiln and completed the 4000 T Hoad dicking[206] in Brook & part day yesterday Foster & Easton Hop chopping & pulling Sawyers teams for Bark hop tiers team for load top faggots David finished pulling kilk Father Hailsham Market Mr & Mrs Press went to Hurstmonceux Forgot horses got up and carried T Hoad top cutting wood home oxen carried 100 top faggots to Joseph Morfey's

Thursday 1 June
Horses carried 50 rist bats to the wheelers & chord of top wood 5 fence poles to Mr Russell's oxen carried 1½ chord of wood to Mr Barnes Dallington & 100 top faggots to Mr Morfie T Hoad dicking Foster & Easton shovling hops hop tiers Father went To Mr Buckland Heathfield Mr Squires visitor

Friday 2
Carters Foster & David shiming hops in Croft Easton shovelling & T Hoad dicking oxen carried 100 faggots & 1 chord of wood to Mr J Baker's & 500 hop poles into the red pale field from the wood

Saturday 3
Horses Foster & David shiming hops Easton I helpt ox boys load 1500 14 feet poles and back to wood & faggots out of the bottom drawed poles into red pale field Thos Hoad dicking some hop tiers weeders sawyers etc Mr

[206] Ditching.

Squire came here henceforth I shall not keep a particular account of the visitors but write chiefly of our own business

Sunday 4
Father mother Elizabeth & I went to Heathfield Chapple in morning Father I Elizabeth & maid in afternoon Mr Press preached from John 21 Cha 17 verse in morning & Luke 22 Cha 31 & 32 verses in afternoon David went Herstmonceux in morning

Monday 5
Horses & oxen carried 3000 of 14 feet poles into the red pale field Easton helpt them T Hoad & Foster stacked them Mr & Mrs Gilbert visitors at pleasure Steer & Fox & Hewers of timber hop tiers weeders etc

Tuesday 6
Horses carried 200 faggots from Broom Wood to Gardner Street [& sett 100 out Dill Gate] oxen carried 600 poles to redpale field and bought kiln faggots from nine acres to the pole stack drawed tree to sawpit and fetched 150 kiln faggots to our kiln T Hoad & Foster finished stacking poles in red pale field and some or all the 12 feets in Pound field Father & David fetched Colly & Smoke cows & calves home from marsh sold Heifer to Step'n Brook 10£ 10s there is in the red pale field 5600 of 14 feet poles timber hewers

Wednesday 7
Horses carried 100 faggots from Broom Wood to Mr Morres's Boreham oxen 100 from our wood to Benj'm Guy near wind mill hill Foster and T Hoad finished pole stacking & went shovelling hops in orchard Dame Dann weeding Mr & Mrs Smith Mrs Harmer Mr Robt Russell visitors with Mr & Mrs Gilbert.

Thursday 8
Both teams carried 100 faggots from Broome Wood to Haisham and fetched 2 load of chalk Thos Hoad finished dicking in the Brook and stripping hops Wm Foster shovelling hops half day finished Croft began Pound[?] field timber sawyers weeders etc carters & 3 ox teams fetched 2 hundred faggots 2 chord of wood from Grimes Wood Mrs Pettitt visitor Father went To Waldron

Friday 9
Horses carried 100 top faggots to Mr Scrace Akhurst and fetched load Kiln

home to Kiln Oxen heald[207] 14 feet hop pole stacks and with Kiln faggots from wood and drawed trees to sawpit Thos Hoad Foster threshing wheat H Barn Dame Dann weeding 10 acres J Bland came here in afternoon and mother[?] & supt etc and went away Mr Barnett called at the house

Saturday 10
Horses oxen carried 200 faggots to Hailsham from Broom Wood and fetched Home 2 load chalk except the Lee tailings[?] T Hoad Foster threshing Dame Dann weeding 10 acres

Sunday 11
All went to Heathfield Chaple in morning except Ann and the maid and all except mother I and Ann in the afternoon Mr Press preached twice from Romans 8 Cha 14th, 15th, 16 & 17 verses Lower hive of bees swarmed

Monday 12
Horses & oxen carried 2 hundred faggots from Broom wood to Hailsham and fetched home some chalk T Hoad & Foster threshing Easton hop chopping orchard garden Dame Hoad weeding same people came here on business

Tuesday 13
Horses carried 100 house faggots from Broom wood to Mrs Brocks[?] & Mrs Pain.... against Herstmonceux Park Gate near Wartling hill oxen drawed tree the pitt and fetched home load of Kiln faggots in morn ... and carried 100 house faggots from wood to Mr John Christmas Faveham in afternoon T Hoad and Foster threshing Easton hop chopping Dame Dann Dog Wood sraping Mr Barnett cutt 2 colts Violet Marefold and my bees swarmed the old stock the second time all went to Mr Smith's in evening except David Mr Press preached from 34 Psalm 4 verse

Wednesday 14
Horses Carters & Baker carried 50 loads of dung out of the yard to below the barn threshers sawyers & Dame Dann weeding ½ day Easton shovelling some neighbours business

Tuesday 15
Father sowed the tares & horses harrowed them in in the upper part of the Croft afterwards fetched the new plough home from summer tree and used her in the Kiln field oxen plough in Do Foster David & George Guy cleaned

[207] Covered.

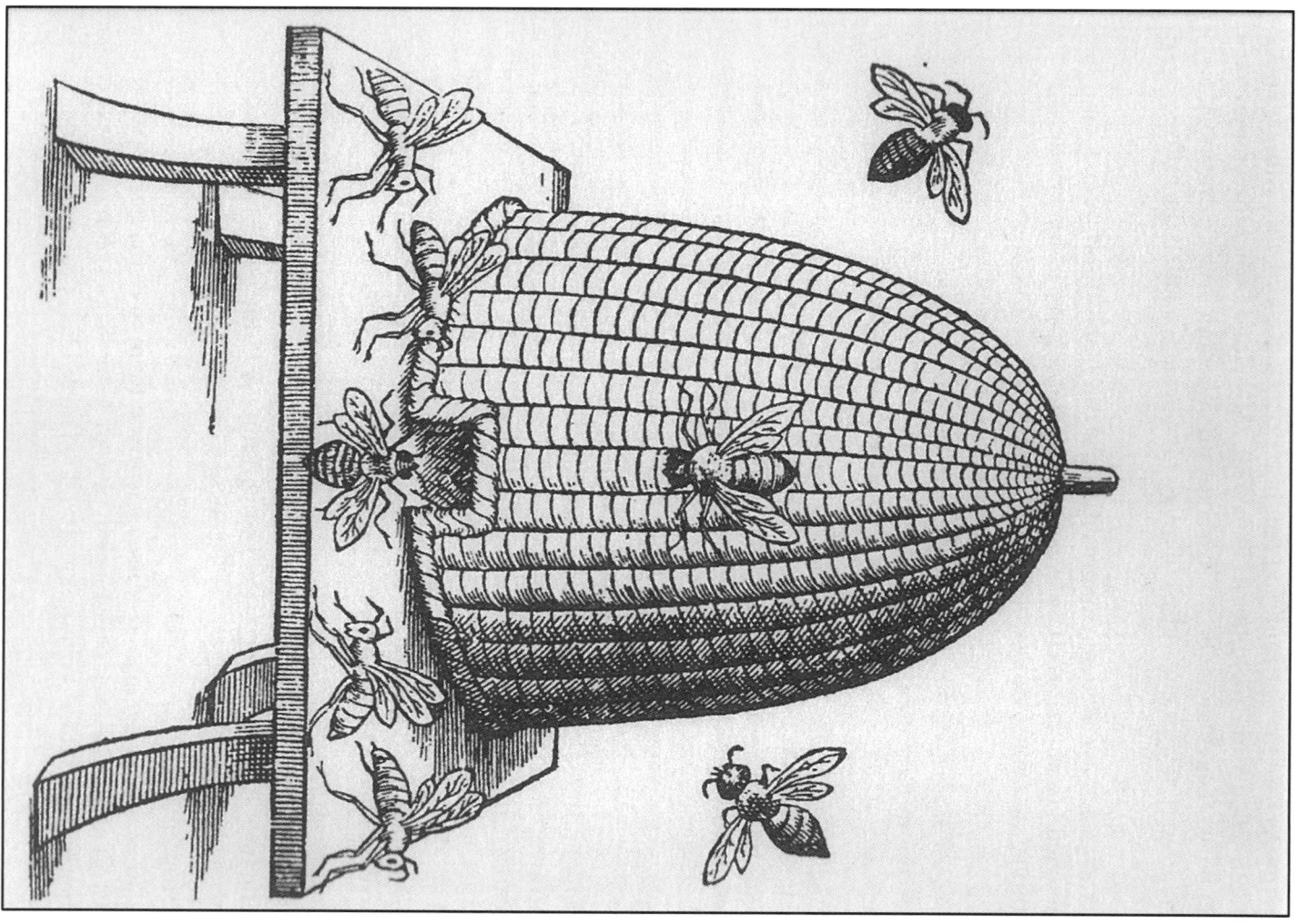
Beehive

11 sacks & 3 bush Head and 1 bushel Tail in morning David plough in my room[208] in afternoon Guy & Foster threshing wheat in afternoon Thos Hoad & Easton began mow in the 12 acres seeds Father and I went to sale at the Halfmoon Mr Ellis's property Father brought a hind harness and an ox chain

Friday 16
Horses & oxen plough in Kiln field mowers threshers weeders etc David plough in my room Father went to Dallington etc shut up Colly's & Smoke's calves to weaned

Saturday 17
Horses carried 100 faggots and oxen 1 chord of wood from Broom wood to Hailsham and fetched home 2 load of chalk threshers mowers weeders etc David went with oxen Sepr Brook[?] had his cows calf home I went to Rushlake Green

Sunday 18
All went to Heathfield Chaple except Ann and the maid in the morning and except Father David & Ann in afternoon Mr Press preached from Isaiah 40 Cha 6 & 7 verses in morning & From 2 Timothy 1 Cha later part 10 Verse

Monday 19
Tames[209] went to Hailsham with 100 faggots and chord of wood from Broom wood & fetched home some chalk Foster threshing mower began the Wenhouse field. Dame Hoad and maid and David haying 12 acres Father went round Cowbeach Fowl Mile Rushlake etc

Tuesday 20
Horses plough in Kiln field oxen ploughed the pett in the pettfield at attwood[?] farm Wm Harmer help with a pair of steers mowers etc Dame Hoad & Dame Dann haying 12 acres David went to Frog hole and borrowed an old mare named Violet

Wednesday 21
Teames plough in Kiln field mowers Foster threshing etc Father went to Chaple on ad[?] meeting of the members Mr Press preached in evening from 1 Peter 2 chapter first part 7th verse I forgot to mention that Mr

[208] In my place.
[209] Teames.

Richardson came here on Monday evening and stop all night and repaired Elizabeth dial. etc next day Mr Reeves Buckle on business etc

Thursday 22
Horses plough in Kiln field & got up a load of hay from 12 acres oxen drawing trees till about 10 O'clock afterwards plough and got up a load of hay Mowers and hayers Mr Benjn Field Senr from Mayfield came here on business

Friday 23
Horses plough in Kiln field & got up a load of hay from 12 acres oxen plough and got up 1 load of hay there was 4 loads of hay at 12 acres mowers finished gutter field and began mill field Foster threshing hayers etc Father went somewhere westward I don't know where but dined at Mr Reeves at Rushlake

Saturday 24
Horses and oxen plough mowers finished mowing seeds Foster threshing Dame Dann and Dan old[210] haying Father went to Lewes on Mr J Waters horse

Sunday 25
All went to Heathfield in morning and all except mother and I in afternoon Mr Press preached in morning from Ephatians 1 Cha 7 verse in afternoon from 43 Psalm 5 verse swarm of bees

Monday 26
Horses and oxen finished Kiln field plough following Foster T Hoad & Easton cleaned 130 s 1 Bu wheat T Hoad clipt hedge Easton mowed thistles etc helpt Baker & I unload 2 load of hay David went to Stream Mill Father to Rushlake etc

Tuesday 27
Horses went to Brighting after lime for Mr Adds oxen fetched last 5 chord of wood out of the to the house and coal hearth T Hoad & Easton hop chopping Foster threshing Dame Dann and David haying unloaded Wm Harmers May horse Horses had it home Mr Press preached in evening from Job 29 Cha 13 verses Mrs Press also came

Wednesday 28
Teames went to Hailsham with 100 faggots & 1 chord of wood and fetched

[210] Old William Dann.

Warbleton Priory

home some chalk and a mangle got up 2 large loads of hay from wenhousefield Easton and T Hoad helpt us and chopt hops etc Foster threshing hayers etc Father went to Hailsham Market

Thursday 29
Teames got up 16 load of hay from Wenhousefield unloaded last load hay from 12 acres Foster threshing all the rest haying

Friday 30
Carter Easton & David shiming croft and Pound field oxen hay carrying 2 load from Wenhousefield and 4 load from Millfield hodges there is 20 load of hay from Wenhousefield except a piece of ground about ½ an acre which makes in all 21 fair load of hay and the other 8 loads makes 29 load of seed in all this year Wm Foster threshing rest haying Father went to Dallington and Rushlake Wm Oxley visitor

Saturday 1 July
Horses oxen Mill with 1½ load of wheat at 14£ 10 loaded up some timber sett out dillgate Baker T Hoad David & I unloaded a load of hay that came out of the bottom of the Wenhousefield oxen 2 carts[?] Easton Hoad dung got 50 load out carry up hops close to below the barn Foster threshing Wm went home

Sunday 2

All except the maid & Ann went to Heathfield Chaple in morning Father I and the maid in the afternoon also Elizabeth who went home with James Lade and his wife to Stream Mill Mr Press preached twice from Romans 8 chapter 6 verse

Monday 3

Horses went to Pevensey with timber and brought back 2 chaldrons of coals oxen fetched home six hundred of Kiln faggots to Kiln Foster threshing T Hoad & Easton began mow meadow grass at Hodges Lime burners whom I forgot to mention filled the kiln on Saturday fired her today morning Father went to down in Marsh I went to Cowbeach etc

Tuesday 4

Horses carried load of coal to Mr Press'es and loaded another load of timber from wood to Dillgate Oxeners Foster etc dung carrying mowers began Chapple meadow finished hodges etc attended to wash the sheep washing sheep Bushey field David Father helpt made lime lump place etc below Old Hoad's house but did not answer Elias Standen brought a new share for the Ox plough Saml Winchester and boy made a new gate chept[211] Dame Hoad haying Oxen left beach up ag[ain]s[t] huglet hill carried gate to Wartling toll

Wednesday 5

Horses and Oxen carried some timber to Walsend brought back 30 Hand post welsh coul and 2 ton beach mowers Foster drying sand priory help empty lime kiln 3 cart upon kilnfield mowers lime burners filling the Kiln again rest get up 3 load meadow hayers at Hodges

Thursday 6

Horses carried a cart load of lime and some sand from Priory at choice[212] to Cade Street and brought some sand home oxen Foster Baker David and I

Friday 7

Horses plough 12 acres oxen drawing trees in forenoon got up a small load of hay from the Chaple Meadow Foster threshing Mr Crouch sheared sheep in Mill Barn and sleeps here etc

---

[211] Chepped. Chep is the share-beam of a plough; esp. a horizontal beam forming the sole of a turnwrest plough, to the end of which the ploughshare is fixed. (OED).

[212] There was a sand pit at The Priory.

Saturday 8

Horses plough 12 acres oxen fetched home a load of chalk from Trolilo river in morning and in the afternoon got up about 3 load hay in 4 times with Duke and Diamond alone up to oxens hay rick Foster threshing in morning haying afternoon mowers mowed Hoad's croft hayers etc

Sunday 9

All went Heathfield Chaple except mother and Ann & the maid in morn[ing] Father & I stopt & maid went in afternoon Mr Press preached from Exodus 33 Chapter 14 & 15 & 16 verses in morning from Romans 8 Cha 28 verse Elizabeth came home from Stream Mill

Monday 10

Horses carried 100 faggots 28 fleeces and some lamb wool to Hailsham picked up the last of 13 load of chalk oxen carried 2 poles & 6 rails to Mr Isted's and fetched home a load of chalk from Trolilo river and carried 5 load of hay from Chaple Meadow we finished it making about 9 loads mowers in Chaple wood meadow Foster threshing in Mea ... afternoon haying hayers etc Mr T Barker[?] Senr Heathfield & Mr Newman Senr visitors Weeler chept raded plough etc

Tuesday 11

Foster with Horse plough in 12 acres which was so very dry and hard it broke some chains and the rist and where obliged use[213] the round plough Wm Hoad cattle market Baker David and I finished the 2 home stacks got up the three load of hay from Ponds Croft mowers in Chaple wood meadow Mr Press preached at Toll from Ephesians 5 Cha latter part 25th & 26th verses

Wednesday 12

Horses plough Foster Baker David and I unloaded a load of hay in morning and carried a load of straw to Calves Lodge cleared Chaple wood meadow 3 small load 2 to the Ox yard and 1 to C Lodge mowers who began Calves Lodge medow yesterday finished it to day mowed round hop garden hayers etc Father went to Hailsham Market sold Deep Red Cow for 20£ 10s and twin for 20£ Mr R Russell Mr & Mrs Press visitors

Thursday 13

Horses plough oxen drawed 1 load of straw to the upper hay rick and 1 to the Ox yard Baker carried some ashes from Kiln and ash lump David & I

[213] Were obliged to use.

went after Mr Christmas's plough with Stout and Valiant etc in morning all except horse haying Calves lodge and finished it (there was 3 small loads) in afternoon Easton mowing in the wood Dame Dann & Dame Hoad branching hops[214] in the forenoon Honeysett thatched the last of the stacks of seed hay in the home hay rick etc

Friday 14
Teams fetched the chalk that was dropt at amber stone[215] and carters carried home oxen put up in Poundfield and six acres Honeysetts thatched the other seed hay stack Foster threshing mowers began the seven acres with Trefoil for seed Dame Dann branching hops etc Pound field was a going to pull and trim the stack I built at the Ox Close but did by reason of some rain there has not been no rain for some time before the grass is almost dried up and the ground is parched for thirst etc David went mate with oxen to day Father went to Heathfield Chaple on bussiness etc

Saturday 15
Teames plough 12 acres broke Christmas's plough chopp[216] which did not want much doing as it was nearly asunder before threshers mowers hop branchers & I trimed my stack mowed thistles etc

Sunday 16
All went to Heathfield Chaple in morning and Father Elizabeth and I stopt in afternoon Mr Press preached both times from 2 John 9 verse

Monday 17
Horses plough Father David and Baker Rond in some Trefoil before Brackfast Oxen got home the last of chalk from Trolilo River for this year David help get loaded 150 Kiln faggots from wood and Father helpt get up the hay (or what you may please to turn it) from the wood David I and Baker Do round the Poundfield & Croft garden Baker has a bad hand is trouble to work Mowers finished the Trefoil about noon and lumped the hay in the wood etc in afternoon Dame Hoad hop branching afternoon Lime Burners tild[?] the Kiln Master Reed catched 15 rats Peter Pankerst chopt Christmas's plough if I have to write so much every night I must some enlarge my book

[214] Training the hops up the poles.
[215] Sometimes the Oxleys went to the South Downs for chalk, but at other times it was dropped half way.
[216] Chep.

Tuesday 18
Teams plough and got up to loads of Trefoil Easton & Baker with oxen Father David and I help get up Trefoil Easton David and I unloaded the last of our hay which was about 18 load of meadow hay and 2 from the bottom of the wenhouse field wood etc 29 load of seeds and forgot 3 load meadow att Hodges which makes of all sorts 50 loads etc Foster threshing yesterday and today Thos Hoad brushing the road up the Chaple wood maid and Dame Dann branching hops etc Elizabeth and Ann went to Warbleton Church

Wednesday 19
Horses and oxen plough in morning came home at noon by reason of the rain Easton T Hoad David and I laid on the rest of the Trefoil in seven acres before Brackfast David and I howed some potatoes in morning in Young Orchard afterward nocking out Trefoil Thos Hoad Do all day and Easton in afternoon who was with oxen in morning Foster threshing Lime burners lit the Kiln in evening Mr J Christmas

Thursday 20
Horses plough oxen got home the last of the Kiln faggots 800 and 3 tree stems[?] Easton Baker and I & T Hoad Foster and David cleaned 18 sacks of wheat T Hoad chopt a few hops afterwards Dame Hoad branching hops Lime burners etc Father went to Halfmoon Market Elizabeth & Ann went to Bellhurst & brother Willm visitor

Friday 21
Horses plough and got up 2 load Trefoil oxen finished plough in the 12 acres Volowing[217] David & I helpt carters 1 load 2nd Father Do Easton with oxen Foster threshing T Hoad mowing thistles in silver field Dame Dann hop branching Pound field Mr John Fox visitor bought my flute Walking[218] but I bought in London for 19s he gives me 21s for it Wm went home Mrs Selmes came home from Mayfield Wm Harmer borrowed the role Lime burners put Kiln out

Saturday 22
Horses ploughing up and shiming amongst the potatoes in the Grinnetts oxen plough at 5 different places on the Roads for the parish got up the last of the Trefoil in 2 load which makes 6 load carried into the Chaple Barn

[217] Following?
[218] A walking flute is dual purpose, a walking stick and a flute combined.

Easton helpt get up Trefoil and Thos Hoad and he nocking of it out in former part of the day Baker and David helpt them unload a load in morning I went down in Marsh in morning Mrs Selmes and Ann went to Mr Phillip's Mr H or Richd Purstglove visitors Mr Steer brought me a new Barogan Jacket his brother and niece came with him forgot to mention Wm Harmer borrowed the role yesterday and had it home to day & Foster threshing H Barn

Sunday 23
All went to Heathfield Chaple in morning except Ann and maid Father David Elizabeth and maid in afternoon Mr Press Preached in the morning from Romans 3 Cha 7 and 8 verses in the afternoon from Phillipians 3 Cha former part of the 9 verse ' and be found in him.' Smiler Mare had fole this Morning in the silver field

Monday 24
Horses plough Kiln field oxen emted[219] the Lime Kiln carried 1 waggon load to the Grinnetts Hodges and some for wheat and Masons rest went kiln field Baker with Foster put up his chucks in the wood with oxen T Hoad and Easton made lime lump places and nocking out trefoil Foster threshing Morfee Beal and Boy laying a pinick over the small river against the chaple meadow gate J Bland and uncle R Cornwell visitors

Tuesday 25
Horses plough Baker with Stout & Valiant carted some dirt about to new pinnick Beal and Boy finished the pinnick and did some paring in the Brewhouse T Hoad & Easton finished nocking out the trefoil Foster threshing Messers Creel the Parson and Walters the Church Warden visitors Mr Vion[?] Blackford Do Mr Press preach in evening from John 6 Cha 45 verse

Wednesday 26
Horses plough Baker and I with oxen carried home the rest of his chucks and fetched the last lot of bushes out of the wood to 4 different places in Chaple & Chaple wood meadows 7 acres etc Unloaded the last load of the Kiln Faggotts for the house in morning Baker gaping David & I had the wheel plough home from the Blacksmiths which came from Mr Stanford's Preston by his and Mr Stephen Goldsmiths teams etc T Hoad mowing thistles Easton hop chopping in Orchard Foster threshing Father went to

[219] Emptied

Hailsham Market to sell a hip fallen cow but did not Mr Press went home Mr R Russell came after some chickens etc

Thursday 27
Horses plough with the wheel plough and broke the share Bak[er] and I fetched home the chord of wood from Poundfield to Coal pitt Baker with 4 oxen carried 6 sacks of wheat to Mr R Russell David and I carried from Kiln and Ash Lump 3 load of ashes Father Baker I David etc loaded up 2 waggons with timber and set out at Dillgate Foster threshing Easton and T Hoad hop chopping Da Hoad branching

Friday 28
Carters Baker and his wife Mrs Selmes Ann Selmes Elizabeth and I with teams went to Wallsend with timber and fetched 1½ tons coal and about 2½ beach back Easton T Hoad hop chopping in morning afterward David helpt them Clean trefoil Foster threshing Blacksmith made a new shear for wheel plough Father went to Silverash in evening

Saturday 29
Horses roling in Kiln field and plough with the wheel plough Baker Easton and I mowling with oxen along by the Bigest River against to new bridge ploughed 2 ploughing got out 60 loads into the Chaple meadow on the Barn side Thos Hoad hop chopping in morning Father David helpt him Clean Trefoil Foster was no[t] threshing Father had colts home from the hole and 2 calves from Mr Veness's Mr Christmas from hole with 4 boys came after Smilers colt I think had home Mare and all but don't know because David is a sleep Mr Mannington from Horeham call up on us Drank tea etc

Sunday 30
All except maid and Ann went to Heathfield Chaple in morning Father Elizabeth and I in afternoon Mr Press preached in morning from Luke 19 Cha 10 verse in afternoon from Esaiah 62 Cha 12 verse

Monday 31
Horses plough with 5 horses mainly Bowler Collier Traveller Violet and Smiler Oxen finished mowling against the river and and carried the dung away from Chaple Barn door in morning carried 2 Trefoil home to Calves Lodge in afternoon Easton helpt all day Thos Hoad a little while in morning and all the afternoon Father and I finished cleaning Trefoil in forenoon I fetched Smiler home from the hole in morning David had uncles Mare to Cade Street and the other calf from Sandholl Mr George Verrell

visitor Foster threshing Master Robins preparing coal pitt

Tuesday 1 August
Horses plough broke the red colt Foster Baker and I with oxen fetched the last 2 load Trefoil and 1 load of straw from CB to the Hay Loft and Old Hay rick T Hoad and Easton finished chopping orchard and began Poundfield Gardens Collier fired the pitt G Verrell went home David went to Garden[er] Street Father and mother gone visitors to the Hole I eat the few raw plumb

Wednesday 2
Horses plough and roling Easton Baker Foster David and I with oxen 3 cart fetched 37 loads of moul from Bushey field pitt to Kiln field T Hoad hop chopping Collier & Father went down in marsh Mrs Selmes gone to Sliverash Beal the Meason paring Bark Court Mich ham[220]

Thursday 3
Horses and oxen as yesterday but carried 43 loads of moul T Hoad hop chopping Mr T Delves dined here Father and he went to Halfmoon Market Collier etc

Friday 4
Horses plough oxen Baker Easton Foster David & I got out 44 loads mowl T Hoad hop chopping Collier heald his pitt Honeysetts thatched Oxen's Stack Forgot to mention broke the Black Colt yesterday had it shoed to day

Saturday 5
Horses plough oxen mouling got out 50 loads Workmen as yesterday Colier drawed his pitt Mrs Selmes came home from Mr Phillips Turned oxen in silver field etc Foster spreaded 20 loads of moul last night Honeysetts thatched Calves Lodge stack the stack at Hodges has been thatched for some time but I did not know when Shoed red colt

Sunday 6
Mrs Selmes & Ann stopt at home rest went to Heathfield Chaple in morning Father David & Elizabeth all day Mr Press preached in morning from John 3 Cha 3 verse in afternoon from Matthew 11 Cha 6 verse J Bland went to Heathfield chaple in morning and came here in afternoon

Monday 7
Horses finished ploughing Kiln field and roling part thereof oxen carried

[220] Michelham?

the rest of the moul in 37 loads from the Mack son that was dug out of the pitt by some mudmen in November 1813 ploughed some moul up against the Mill 16 acres Easton Foster Do T Hoad hoeing potatoes in Grinnetts Wm Oxley visitor

Tuesday 8
Horses plough oxen carried 70 loads moul from Bushey field to Kiln field T Hoad hop chopping Brook garden Baker Easton Foster David and I mouling 3 carts Father went to Battel Market Mr Press preached at Toll from years God's Building 1 Corinthians 3 Cha 9 verse David I and maid with Mother Elizabeth etc went

Wednesday 9
This morning I missed my key I had it last night to put my hymn book in the Beaurough[221] Horses plough 12 acres Easton T Hoad Baker Foster and David with 3 carts 6 oxen carried 72 loads moul I went to Hailsham Market sold a hip fallen cow (late T Hoad's to milk) to Mr Noakes Gardner Street at 16£ 5s

Thursday 10
Horses plough oxen 3 carts Baker Easton Thos Hoad David I carried 32 load of moul or Maol from just in Dillgate to Kiln field T Hoad and family began reep this morning at Hodges in Round Banks Dame Dann Do in 8 acres T Hoad spread some moul part after noon Foster finished threshing wheat in morning Baker and I helpt clean it in afternoon 6 sacks 2 bushels Head 2 Bushels Tail Broke the axel to the new cart Glide and Ann Reeves came yesterday and went home to day J Bland was here a little while in Morning

Friday 11
Henry has left the horses Wm Hoad and David plough Baker and I with 4 oxen carried 30 load dung from yard to the faggot stack placed against the Kiln all rest on reeping T Hoad and family Round Banks Easton and Foster 13 acres Dame Dann 8 acres Baker and I fixed the water cart up Father went to Rushlake in morning Buckle Reeves and Master S Latham on business Mother went to Bellhurst

Saturday 12
Horses plough Baker and I carried 33 load of dung to as yesterday Father help fill 13 loads in afternoon reeping as yesterday Mr Russell supt here in

[221] Bureau.

evening

Sunday 13
All except maid and Ann went to Heathfield Chaple in morning Father Elizabeth and I stopt the Afternoon Mr Press preached twice from the Two[?] Covenants Galations 4 Cha 34 verse

Monday 14
Horses plough oxen Baker Father and I brought the Trefoil seed home from CB to the Oat Garret Baker and 1 pair oxen got some straw out of the Home Barn and stacked against the blunt Trees in the yard T Hoad and Easton mowing clover Wenhouse field rest reeping our Blacksmith has the Baily[222] in his house a second time this year Forgot to mention I found my key yesterday morning in my breeches

Tuesday 15
Horses Plough Oxen Roling 12 Acres mowers Finised there Field rest Reeping Father went down to Marsh J Bland Eat supper here David went to Rushlake Blacksmith in morning with Plough Share Forgot to mention T Hoads Family Finised Round Banks and began Huglets

Wednesday 16
Horses Plough Oxen Baker and I Cleaned the Barn out Carried 1 Load straw from Barn and the the Brush Faggots from Chapelwood Meadow to the Lodg on Poundfield Bottom throwed up 1 Load straw and Trefoil down in the yard etc Reepers Father went Woods Corner Market

Thursday 17
Wm Hoad Baker Mowing 10 Acres onto T Hoad and Henry Began 9 Acres Wheat rest Reepers as yesterday David and I Tying up Hopoles a Man from Winchelsea Messrs Rouds and Russell of Bussiness Etc

Friday 18
Father David and I with Horses went to Mr Holders Mill Burwash with 8 Quarters Wheat at 12£ per Load and 7 Gur for 1 Guianea Father sold 10,000 of 14 feet Hopoles to Mr G Adams (near Perrymans) at 1 pound per Hundred Workmen as yesterday Elizabeth Lade (who hass been very ill inclining to Consumption is now by the Divine Providence nearly well) I visited Messrs Reed Beecham Ada Bodeham Delves Redpale Visit Hoad's finised Reeping Huglets

[222] Bailiff.

Mowing clover

Saturday 19
Horses and Oxen Caried 3 Loads of Wheat from round Banks 2 from Huglets which is all from Hodges and 1 from 13 Acres Wm Hoad and Baker helpt and finised Mowing 10 Acres Reepers etc Sam'l Winchester mending Oast etc

Sunday 20
Mrs Selmes and Ann stopt at home the Rest went to Heathfield Chapel in morning Father David Elizabeth and Maid stopt Mother and I came home in the afternoon Mr Press Preached in morning from Ephesians 2 chapter middle part 12th Verse', and stranger to the covenants of Promise' in afternoon from Psalm 73 and 26 Verse a Funeral Sermon for Mr John Parris

Monday 21
Wm Hoad and Baker Mowing Oast[223] Bushey field in Morning Horses they David Sam'l Winchester Father Dame Hoad Haying in Winhouse field Caried 4 Loads to Old Hayrick Sam'l Winchester mended this my Barrow in Morning Etc Dame Hoad Haying half day Father David I and Maid Do All day Reepers as yesterday Benny Selmes Visitor Mrs Selmes gone to Mayfield Drove 2 Two yearling Heifers to Hodges put Cows in Rowings but they are verry short By Reason of the Drought

Tuesday 22
Wm Hoad went to Battel got Benjamin Isted in his room finised Mowing Bushey Field Caried 3 Load Wheat from 13 Acres and the last of the Clover in Winhouse 3 Loads which makes 7 Loads Mrs Selmes came home from May field Reepers

Wednesday 23
Wm Hoad Baker Mowing Squirefield 8 Acres rest Reeping Mrs Selmes went to Silverash Cloudy day and some showers prevented Corn Carring Messrs Blackpole and John Oxley the Blacksmith Visit

Thursday 24
Horses Wm Hoad David I Father Got up 2 Load Wheat from 13 Acres 2 from 8 Acres and 2 from 9 Acres unloaded 4 etc Baker Mowing Foster Reeping in 8 Acres the rest as they where John Oxley Visitor again Benny Selmes Harriet Phillips Do Elizabeth went to Bellhurst etc I got a cold

[223] Oats

Friday 25
Father I David Wm Hoad Baker and George Guy 4 Load Oats from Bushey field and 5 Load Wheat from 9 Acres Finised 7 Load Old Mr Hoad his Wife and Mrs Baker laying on Oats Bushey field and 10 Acres Hoad finised Reeping 9 Acres all Reepers In 8 Acres Easton Finised 13 Acres Master Dann helpt his Wife

Saturday 26
Horses and Oxen Finised Wheat Carring 1 Load from 13 Acres 3 from 8 Acres which is 7 Load from 13 Acres and 5 from the 8 Acres which is 24 Load in all Carrid 10 Acres oats 7 Load Reeper finised Reeping about 5 O'Clock and helpt Us etc

Sunday 27
Maid and Ann staid at home Rest went to Heathfield Chaple in Morning Father Elizabeth and I stopt in afternoon Mr Press Preached in Morning from Isaiah 29 Cha 24 verse in the afternoon from John 20 Cha 31 verse

Monday 28
Wm Hoad and Henry with Horses Plough 12 Acres Baker finised Mowing Squirefield T Hoad and Easton Mowed the high field Oats and the Furze field Barley G Guy spreading Moul Chaple Meadow Weaned the lambs Foster and I measured 13 Acres and part of the 8 Acres Foster helpt Guy in afternoon Wett weather nearly all day and in Evening I bought David's sheep and Lambs 1 Lilbro 7 Solidties[224] Father went to Sannels in Evening Master Dann a Preparing Oast for Hopping Mr Russell Visitor The sow farrowed on Morning

Tuesday 29
Horses Plough Baker Easton and T Hoad threshed a Load of Oats in CB Baker threshing Oats Easton T Hoad Tying up hopoles and Moul spreading Guy and Foster Do in Chaple Meadow and Kilnfield I went to Stream Mill Elizabeth went to Priory Messrs Waters and Veness fetchd Beast home from Winchelsea Brother Wm came home with me this evening

Wednesday 30
Horses Plough Baker pair Oxen Carrid some Moul away from about the Oast and Brought some Gravel etc in morning buy river Casting between the Two foot Bridges from here to Ashburnham one way and to Dallington the other rest Moul spreading in Morning Carrid 3 Load Oats in afternoon

[224] £1 7s.

etc from Squire field. Wm Drove Messrs Goldsmith Balcombe Mephams etc Bullocks home David helpt him part way Mrs Selmes went to Bellhurst Waters and Veness fetchd their Beast away Morfey Beal and Boy Masons work repairing the Oast

Thursday 31
Horses Plough Baker laid some Gravel round by the House Workmen Moul spreading S Winchester mended Hop bins Morfey Beal and Boy Nailed Oast hair Down[225] I went down in Marsh

Friday 1 September
Horses Plough Oxen Carrid the Bins to the upper of the Croft Gardens Hoppers 8 Bins Easton and Foster Pole pullers. I measured Picked 161 Bushels Father Baker T Hoad David and G Guy Finised Carring Squirefield Oats 4 Loads and all the Barley in Furze field 1 Load and Last of Hoppers in their Regular standings in the Croft Croft 1 standing Mrs Morfey and Family 2 Ends Mrs Beal and Mrs Foster the other bin 2nd Standing Elizabeth and Mrs Selmes 1 Bin Mrs Hoad and Family the other Bin 3 Standen Ann Isted and Harriot Bradford Bins and Mary Barton and Elizabeth Ratten the other 4 standing Dame Hoad and Maid 1 Bin and Dame Dann and Mrs Baker the other Charity Collins to come to stand when the Maid does but did not Forgot took the first 3 Bushels out of Dame Hoads End with the new Bushel Old Wm Dann dries

Saturday 2
Horses plough in morning helpt the Harvesters Finis Harvest in afternoon with 5 Loads of Oats from Hillfield Hodges which is 23 Loads of Oats in all. Hoppers picked 254 Bushels Big as with two nice warm days Messrs George Adams and Friston Visitors.

Sunday 3
All Except Mrs Silmes and Ann went to Heathfield Chapel in morning Father I and Elizabeth in afternoon Mr Press preached in morning from Galatians 2 Chap 19 verse in afternoon from Acts 4 Chap 14 verse Two new Sermons. Mr Harris the Painter Merchant on Bussiness! What an awful thing to do Business on the Sabath day when God hath Commanded it be kept Holy and he is a jelous God and will in no wise require without full satisfaction for His injured justice Samuel Wood the gardener hong his self this Morning Gardner street

[225] The covering on top of battens in an oast house.

Monday 4
Horses plough in the 12 Acres and Finis drawn some Tares in Brook hop garden and began Warp 10 Acres oat gratin Baker with a pair of Oxen Graveling about the House T Hoad and G Guy shoveling hops Brook garden and Cutting the moul in the H Barn Charity Collins and Girls hoping hopping with Dame Hoad Maid stood with Mrs Selmes in morning Mrs Selmes went to Silverash in afternoon Hoppers Pick'd 273 Bushels Foster Trod one Pocket in Evening David went to Gardner street Henry went to Woods Corner with Plough Share which is Carried sometimes there and some times to Rushlake

Tuesday 5
Horses Plough Baker spread One Cart Load Lime but did not do afterwards Carried 20 Loads of Dung from Ox yard to Ponds Croft Meadow & Hoad mowd Tares the uper part Crofts hop garden G Guy striping and struck Poles Croft Hopers Picked 282 Bushels Foster Trod one and T Hoad 2 Pockets this morning Saml Winchester and Boy made hop Cart and a hop stool for T Hoads Wife Bowler has[226] here to for fetched in the hops but is not strong Enough he has done no work with the Team for this 3 weeks last Sunday he is almost Wrise out[227] at 18 years old Father went down in the Marsh

Wednesday 6
Horses Plough Baker with a pair of Oxen Carried 30 Load of Dung as yesterday Carried Hop Bins to the Lower Corner young garden against 12 acres and fetched Last Load of Hop fetched in first Load with Duke and Diamond and helpt Carry the Bins etc Finised Croft Pickd 240 Bushels which is in all from that garden 1210 Bushels Guy striping hop poles etc T Hoad threshing wheat H Barn Doctor Atree shooting yesterday and today Wm Foster Trod 2 Pockets in morning

Thursday 7
Horses Plough Baker Carried 25 Loads Dung Hoppers Picked 264 Bushels hops in Poundfield Old Part they are very rough Wanted 300 Bushels but did not get them T Hoad Trod 3 ½ Pockets in morning David puts in Father went Black Horse after the Marsh Lambs 30 Our share Fill[228] Lade and Venuss whent had Sack of Malt from Everist's of the street[?] I have not

[226] Was.
[227] Worn out.
[228] Trill.

kept particular account before which perhaps has been several Times

Friday 8
Horses Plough Oxen Baker Carried 29 Loads Dung heah[229] Ponds Croft over Hopers Picked 290 Bushel T Hoad threshing G Guy hopole striping Mr Wm Winchester of Herstmonceux hop Assistant Wheighed 12 Pocket from Croft 20 Cwt 2 Qtrs 2 lbs Father wint to Mr John Ballcomb Heathfield & C with sheep T Goldsmith and neighbours Fetchd their respective Lots away Foster Trod 2½ Pockets

Saturday 9
Horses Plough Oxen Carried Mangle to Rushlake and 4 Sacks of Char Couls to Priory in morning Carried some sea Couls and Char Coul[230] to T Isted's Oast and Brought back 4 Bins Father hired more Hoppers and T Blands oast Father went somewhere in search of a loust[231] Heifer did not find her picked 281 Bushels T Hoad Trod 4½ Pockets Weighed 8 Pockets 13C 1 Qrts 12 lbs T Hoad threshing G Guy hop pole striping

Sunday 10
Father Mother Elizabeth David and I went went to Heathfield Chapel in morning David Elizabeth stopt afternoon Mr Vicker from Lewes Hailsham Minister Preached in morning from Ephesians 5 chapter 25th, 26 and 27 verses and afternoon from Revelations 2 chapter 10 verse an Improvement on the Death of a Mrs Clark

Monday 11
Horses Plough Oxen Carried 12 pockets of hops to Cade Street in morning Baker gaping in afternoon Hopers Picked 296 Bushels T Hoad threshing Guy hop pole striping Foster Trod 2½ pockets in morning is now Treading about 9 O'Clock in Evening 1 Pocket

Tuesday 12
Horses Plough T Hoad threshing and Foster Trod 3 Pockets 4 fresh Bins Hopers Picked 420 Bushels J Bland Messrs T Watters and Steers Visitors Guy striping Poles Baker puld Poles

Wednesday 13
Horses Plough furnished the Bins Complete with pickers picked 427 Bushels T Hoad Trod pockets in the morning afternoon threshing Guy hop

---

[229] Here.
[230] Coal and charcoal.
[231] Lost.

pole Striping Brother Wm Messrs Furrance and Russel Visitors

Thursday 14
Horses Finisd Plough in the 10 Acres Warpt for Tares The Nine Hopers are Dame Easton Dame Honeysett 1st Bin Dame Lambhurst and Dame Cornford 2nd Bin Dame Pook Tom Pook and Mrs Isted's Maid and Family 3rd Bin Francis Dann Mrs Effick 4th Bin hops go off very fast Picked 436 Bushels Master Robins Dries and Boys Isteds Oast. Foster Trod 4 Pockets at home William wint to Half moon Market and Back again Mr Couchman Came and told us he has our lost Heifer Guy shaving poles Poundfield began there yesterday etc

Friday 15
Horses went to Wallsend for Couls but did not gett none Fetched Home 3 Tons Beach 2 More Bins Mary Honeysett Daughter of Mrs Honeysett Picker there is now 14 Bins and Picked 427 Bushels All the Oldest part T Hoad Helps newcomer etc Guy striping and stacking poles Wm went to Gardener street

Saturday 16
Horses wint out to Mr Couchmans after Coul and Lime spreading in Kiln field in morning Carried 17 Pockets of Hops to Heathfield in afternoon Emma Hoad Wm Hoads Daughter Fresh Picker All Pickt 421 Bushels Wheighed 12 Pockets 19Cwt 2Qrt 26lbs —Wm Foster trod Pockets in morning is gone to tread Wm Harmers we borrowed his Bushel Basket Tis now Wett weather this Evening it hass been very hot before all most ever since we began Hop Forgot that Wm went home this morning

Sunday 17
All except Maid and Ann wint to Heathfield Chapel in morning Father and maid in afternoon Mr Press Preached twice from 3 Cha Romans 31 verse Smiler Drawed the Cart the first time this Morning etc

Monday 18
Warping in Kilnfield Hopers Picked 454 Bushels T Hoad Trod 4 Pockets in morning Weighed 7 Pockets 10Cw 3Qtr 23lbs Ruth Reeves Visitor There is Now Picked in All 71C 1Q 1lb Uncle Cornwell and Mr Warner the Supervisor Came etc

Tuesday 19
Horses spreading Lime and Roleing Kilnfield Hopers Picked 454 Bushels

sent 7 Pockets to go to London by Mr Smiths Waggons Mr Debries[232] and Mr Smith Visitors on Bussiness etc

Wednesday 20
Horses Plough in Kilnfield Hopers finised Poundfield garden picked 476 Bushels Brought the Bins away to the Brook gardens G Guy Worked Constantly hopole striping

Thursday 21
Horses Plough Hopers picked Brook 383 Bushels began Orchard picked 173 Bush Wheighed 8 Pockets 12C 1Q 1lb T Hoad Trod 3 in morning Father had Bussiness about among neighbours about the Way Tax etc

Friday 22
Horses Plough Hopers picked 577 Bushels Foster Trod in morning 1 Pocket Father went down in Marsh in morning Drove home 3 Bullocks went to Parrish meeting this Evening Buckle Reeves wass here this morning

Saturday 23
Horses Nothing Wett weather in the morning Carters hoping hopers picked 396 Bushel Crowerst the Farier came and drunk[233] and bled three Bullocks for being swimy headed[234] Winchester weighed 4 Pockets 6C 2Q 20lbs Robert Reeves came after the Heifer his Father had with us Ever since last May I went to Winchelsea he did not have it hance[235] now Mr T Watters Butcher wass here to night

Sunday 24
Father Mother and Elizabeth ride in Cart I rode Jack and David walked to Heathfield Chapel in morning Mr Press Preached from Malachi 1 chapter 6 verse Wett weather all most all Day

Monday 25
Horses Plough in morning Carried the Bins home Finised Hoping Baker picked the last Pole about ½ past One took the last bushel out of Mrs Morfeys Bin about three got hops and Bins off Complete by Four O'Clock Picked 356 Bushels Picked in all 7754 Bushels Father went to Burwash to Mr Hild[er?] the Miller for money Wm Hoad Henry Fowl help me take 3 Hives of Bees one was dead which is four in all Wasps are verry numerous

---

[232] Delves?
[233] Drenched; medicated.
[234] Dizzy.
[235] Hence.

this year T Hoad Trod 4 Pockets in morning Etc Mother and Elizabeth went to Mr Russell's

Tuesday 26
Easton Sowed part 10 Acres with 6 Sacks of Tares Horses Harrowed them in Baker mending Horse pond Foster Trod 2 Pockets Hops in morning after ward striping Poles in Orchard Guy Do Pfield Master Dann finised Drying about ½ past 4 O'Clock Paid off the Latter Pickers namely Dame Honeysett Dame Easton Dame Lannkhurst Dame Cornford and Husband Dame Pook Mrs Elfick Francis Dann Wm Isted's Daughter Wm Hoads 3 Daughters Tom Pook Mary Honeysett and Old Man Morfey at 1 ½d per Bushel 12£ 7s 10 ½d and paid Master Dann I think 1£ 18s 0d J Bland Visitor

Wednesday 27
Horses Harrowed the rest and Roled part 10 Acres Easton sowed the rest with 1 sack of Tares from S Goldsmiths T Hoad and Baker Lime spreading in morning Carried 25 Load Dung from Mackson in Kilnfield and Laid down a little way from the Gate in the flat on the Right hand of the Road Foster Trod Pockets of Hops Easton Choping Turfes to pieces in Kiln field after the morning Master Elfich the Looker and Boy drove the stock home from the Marsh by reason of a disorder in the head amongst them I drove Mr Reeves Heifer home in afternoon J Winchester and Boy Carpenters Put up two look over the Back Court to cost up some work etc

Thursday 28
Horses Harrowing etc in 10 Acres T Hoad spreading Lime with Bowler and Baker with a pair of Oxen in the Kiln field G Guy striping and stacking poles Easton Cutting of turffs to pieces as yesterday Foster not here today Mr John Gain brought some aples Father went with him part way home to Cade Street perhaps to Market to see T Ellis about some hops Warm Day but no rain there has been since fine showers to soften the Clods for the season there wass this year but little frute but little Grass and not a Great burden of Corn about 15 Hundred of an Acre of hops which are at a Good price we have about 9 Acres several of our Neighbours have sent their Teams to London and been there selves Father has Talked of going it hass been in general a dry Summer Potatoes are not very good stock is cheap Corn is cheap potato are cheap thing in General are low

Friday 29
Horses struck out the furrows in 10 Acres in morning Rain prevented doing any more wass a going to Cade Street with hops with Oxen Sept but did

Saturday 30

Horses and Oxen Carried 48 Pockets of Hops to Cade Street Hoad threshing Foster hopole striping Guy Do little while Easton spreading Dung in afternoon do Croft

Sunday 1 October

Father Mother Elizabeth David and I went to Heathfield Chapel in morning I stopt the afternoon Mr Press Preached in Morning from John 15 Cha 14 Verse and in afternoon from 2 Corinthians 8 Cha 9 Verse Mr Stanford and Mr Tourl visitors in Evening etc

Monday 2

Horses Plough in Kilnfield Easton and Baker with 4 Oxen 2 Carts got out 31 Load of Dung from Ox yard to the Barn side Chapel Meadow T Hoad Cutt Mows and threshed Oats in C Barn Foster Striping Poles Messrs Stanford and Tourl shot 5 Pheasants Phillips the Game Keeper is Ill and could not go out with them in afternoon etc

Tuesday 3

Horses Plough Easton and Baker Carried some River Gravel from River to Oxen watering in Ox yard and Carried the mud from the Pond at Ox yard into the Ox yard Foster as yesterday T Hoad threshing Oats Cleaned 3 sack of wheat Wm Harmer Fetchd it away Shooters Kild 8 Pheasants 10 Partridge and 1 Hare etc

Wednesday 4

Horses Plough Oxen Carried rest of mud from the pond into yard at the Oxens Close perhaps it may be thought od of Carring Mud into the Close but it hass been dry for some time Carried 20 Loads of Dung from the Mackson in Kilnfield hie up to the Left hand of the same field in afternoon I have not seen Foster today T Hoad threshing Wheat in H Barn Easton and Baker work with the Oxen I have heard that John Oxley the new Blacksmith at Bodle Street came there yesterday morning at 7 O'Clock in the morning Mr Tourl and Mr Stanford went home morning Father went to

not T Hoad trod 3 pockets 6 Ends and 2 tubs in morning Winchester finised weighing here and at T Isted's we growed 137C o Qtrs 15 lbs[236] of hops this year which almost 7 Tons Foster striping Easton Gone to or talked of going to Horsebridge Fair Carters T Hoad and Baker unloaded the barley which hass been up on the Waggon ever since harvest

[236] 137 cwt zero qt 15 lbs. Nearly 7 tons.

Hailsham Market Bought Load of wheat of Mr E J Currtes Esq at 15£ 10s for Wm Harmer and himself David and I Drove the strayed Heifer home from Mr Couchmans, Forgot that Mr Barns the Sow Spayer Cut and spayed the Pigs and Cutt[237] the Bore yesterday

Thursday 5
Horses Plough Oxen Carried the mud from the Horses pond and Mould about the House into Kinfield Guy finised striping and stacking Poles in Brook T Hoad threshing Easton and Baker work with Oxen Wm Foster stacking poles Orchard garden this night is the Treat paid off the other Hopers £ s d Whose names are at another place in this book Master and Mrs Dann and Wm Hoad sleep here to night Etc forget name John Hoad Senr Joseph Morfey (Mrs Morfeys husband) Master John Beal and Our own Family

Friday 6
This morning before I wass up Wm Hoad with the light Cart and Smiler had Elizabeth and Mrs Silmes to Windmill hill to take the Cart for Lewes Elizabeth is gone to school to Mrs and Miss Browne's Cliffe Lewes Mrs Silmes is gone to visiting. Rained nearly all the Morning Carters shovelled out Water Turning up the Poundfield and helpt Father David and I lay some poles up a top of the stack that was laid up One End of the stack in afternoon T Hoad threshing Master and Mistress Dann went home John Waters Visitor otherwise on Business, Forgot David and I fetched the Calves home that had strayed to Sanhills and Carters strowed the straw stack about the Cows Close

Saturday 7
Horses Plough Oxen Baker and I fetched 140 Bushels of Lime from Sanhill Kiln to the Grinnetts Hodges and David helpt us Carry 2 Waggon Load of Dung from Poundfield Bottom and spreaded in along the Bottom of the 12 Acres T Hoad threshing Easton Dung Spreading in Kinfield Bowler and he fetched 3 casks of water for the Women in afternoon Foster striping hop poles in Orchard John Oxley the new Blacksmith cald but I don't know what about it has been a fine warm day it is in general Mild for the season

Sunday 8
Father I David and Maid went to Heathfield Chapell in morning Maid [c]ame home at noon rest stopt Mr Chittenden Preached in morning from 2

---

[237] Castrated.

Corinthians 8 Cha 9 Verse in afternoon from 9 Cha Hebrews 27 and 28 Verses

Monday 9
Horses plough Baker David and I with Oxen Carried 4 Waggon Load of Dung and spread about in 12 Acres T Hoad threshing Foster Finised striping Poles in Orchard in morning Easton spreading Dung in Kilnfield Father Drove 4 Two yearling steers and 2 Two yearling Heifers into Marsh had Jack shoed the first thing at the new Blacksmiths for Us There is great Talk about alteration of Price of work to 2s per day

Tuesday 10
Horses Plough in Kilnfield Oxen Carried 2 Waggon load strained the axel and 2 Cart loads of Dung into 12 Acres as yesterday David and I helped in morning and went to Rushlake fair in afternoon Easton spreading dung Poundfield Ths Hoad threshing Foster Diging up of potatoes in Brook Orchard etc

Wednesday 11
Horses Harrow in Kilnfield Father and Henry with them Wm Hoad Sowed the Wheat Foster and David Old Bowler Horse struck out the Furrows Wm Hoad sowed the Old Brown Straw Wheat Baker and I with Oxen Carried 10 Cart Loads of Dung and I shelved[238] in 12 Acres T Hoad Cleaned part of 21 sack some wass cleaned before for Grists in Morning Foster and David helped him Easton striping Poles in youngest part Poundfield Mrs Selmes come home from Lewes last night and went to Bed before I come home It hass Rained very fast since about 3 O'Clock and still Rains Wind in the North East etc

Thursday 12
Horses Plough in Kilnfield Oxen Carried 12 Haisel Faggots from Pound Field and 38 Hop pole Do From Brook and Croft Gardens and 50 House Do which have stored for some time up against the Whin house which put together is a load of wood for the new Blacksmith and fitch'd[239] home the Poles and of the Faggots of the the Bridge over the River in the Wood Father and Thos Hoad puld it up T Hoad yesterday afternoon and today Morning Made 50 House Faggots afour mentioned. Easton Hop pole striping Foster Diging up potatos etc

[238] Shovelled.
[239] Fetched.

Friday 13
Horses Carters Wm Foster and David and Harrowed most of bigust part of the Kilnfield Oxen plough in 12 Acres Easton striping Poles T Hoad thresh'd his own and Brothers Lease Wheat[240] and cut and Faggotted some Hawth up against Red Pale Uncle Wm Oxley Visited the Excise man to swears instead of Mr Warner at Heathfield this Hop Season Cald here this Evening verry Drunk Vomited in the Porch etc We put him in the Great Stall for a Nights Lodging. Shut up 3 Hogs to Fatt Wheaned the 5 Pigs that where Farrowed about the 28 of August Last

Saturday 14
Horses Finised little part of the Kilnfield Sowing and Ploughing Froter[241] did out Furrows etc Horses went to Plough in 12 Acres at about 2 O'Clock Oxen there All Day Easton Striping hop poles Thos Hoad mowing the stubble Hodges David went to Mr Curtis's with 9 Sack to fill with but it wass not ready Mrs Selmes went to Sliverash the Excisman went home we give the Oxen Hay they have had Fodder for some Time we don't work the Old Oxen steady etc

Sunday 15
Maid and Ann stay at home Rest went to Heathfield Chappel in morning Father and I stopt in afternoon Mr Press who hass been to London and wass there taken Ill with a stoppage wass this day by Providence permitted to Preach to his Beloved Congregation from Matthew 5 Cha 13 Verse in morning and from the same Book 16 Cha latter part 18 Verse in after noon 'and upon the Rock' etc Jack the Pony is put in the stable as Father Entends to go to London tomorrow

Monday 16
Father set out this Morning about 1/4 before 3 O' Clock to Nutley or Maresfield to Take the Coach for London. Horses and Oxen Plough in 12 Acres T Hoad Stubble mowing Easton hop pole stacking Foster threshing Oats C Barn 2 Plough Horses shoed new Blacksmiths first time etc Mr Delves Windmill hill Visitor etc etc

[240] Crop from leased field.
[241] Foster.

DR. GOLDSMITH'S ROMAN HISTORY,

ABRIDGED BY HIMSELF,

FOR THE

USE of SCHOOLS.

A NEW EDITION, CORRECTED,

AND WITH NEW COPPER-PLATES.

LONDON:

Printed by Rider and Weed, Little Britain,

FOR G. LEIGH AND S. SOTHEBY; W. J. AND J. RICHARDSON; J. SOTHEBY; F. AND C. RIVINGTON; SCATCHERD AND LETTERMAN; WILKIE AND ROBINSON; C. LAW; LONGMAN, HURST, REES, AND ORME; CADELL AND DAVIES; AND T. KAY.

1807.

Tuesday 17
Horses and Oxen Plough Foster and David with Duke and Diamond and Old Bowler with narrow Wheeled Waggon fetch'd 9 sacks of Wheat from Mr Curtis's afterward Foster spread the Dung that wass Carried into the 12 Acres with Carts T Hoad stubble mowing etc Easton not at work Mr Press Preached this Evening from Hebrews 3 Cha 1 verse for the first time this Winter

Wednesday 18
Horses Harrowed and Oxen Plough David and Henry Horses Foster Breaking Clods Wm Hoad Seedsman Brown Cobham Wheat David and Foster with Bowler struck out Furrows in 12 Acres T Hoad mowing stubble Easton stacking hop poles Mr Press went home Father returned from London the Evening about 6 O'Clock did not sell his hops thier sale is dull etc

Thursday 19
Horses Plough Oxen Baker and Foster Carried 16 Loads Dung at Calves lodge from the yard into the meadow and 10 Loads Do at Hodges into Horse Meadow Easton Finised stacking poles in Poundfield garden and began mow stubble in 13 Acres T Hoad mowing stubble at Hodges Mr Squires Eat his Dinner here Some Body at the back Door now whilst I am writing about 20 minutes after 2 O'Clock the person proves to be J Blands Boy with a Cart and Horse with 2 Sack of Peas Saml Winchester and Michael Collins Carpenters mended Cribs in Ox yard and sett up 2 posts One in Grimes Wood against Christians river fields and the other at to uper Kilnfield Gate there is a rumour about that Latham our Factor spoke but it is false but caused Mr Potter and Mr Richd Purstglove to Call to know. John Tryll Lade comes weekly and sometimes twice a week to see Mrs Selmes in Courtship etc

Friday 20
Horses Plough and Harrow Baker and Foster with Oxen Carried 17 Loads of Dung into the House Meadow and 16 Loads Do into the Mill field Hodges had the Cart home Easton mowing stubble in 13 Acres Thos Hoad Dug up his own Potatos I went to Rushlake Green and Bodle street Green S Winchester and Michael Collins Carpenters had several fruitless jobs

Saturday 21
Horses Plough and Harrow Baker and I with Oxen Picking up Chucks after the Carpenters who where not here today and fitched 52 Hawth Faggots

from up against red pale and laid on the Kiln Foster wass here a little while in morning helpt Baker Ring the Pigs[242] Baker and with Jack fitched some up from the Brook Orchard for the hogs I went to Mill with a Goristel[?] to Baker scoured the Ditch out down by the Court Lodge etc Foster went home to Kill his Hog Easton Foddered the young Beast in Pound Field with Trefoil home in morning afterwards mowing stubble Mowing T Hoad Do in 9 Acres Foddered the Oxen and Cows with Straw to night It hass been to Wett for Oxen at Plough

Sunday 22

Father Mother David I and think the Maid Father and I stay'd the afternoon at Heathfield Chapel Mr Press Preach'd Twice from 55 Psalm 22 verse

Monday 23

There hass not been till this afternoon any Rain since Saturday of any account So that we Sett the Oxen to Plough before the Horses in the Twelve Acres and keep it sowed up close to the Plough T Hoad Kild Baker's Hog in morning and mowing stubble in 9 acres Foster foddered in morning for Baker afterwards threshing Oats C Barn Wether Easton wass at work or not I don't know Mrs Selmes is gone to Sliverash Mr John Waters Junr Visitor in Evening he says he began Sow Wheat to day Mr Smith too nearly done some have not begun

Tuesday 24

Horses Plough and Harrow I sowed it Father and David with Bowler Struck out Furrow Baker finised Ditching down by the Cart Lodge and did some gaping in Busheyfield Turned the yearling's (5 in number) and 2 yearling Colt up There and put six Oxen and the Bull in to the Pound field Foster threshing Wheat in Home Barn Ths Hoad mowing stubble and Martha Raking after in 9 Acres Easton Do 13 Acres Mr Delves from Windmill hill Visitor it is now Wett Weather about 9 O'Clock in the Evening days begin to draw in a pace Tis inclinable to be showery

Wednesday 25

Carters spreading and scoured a littel ditch[ing] in the Chapel meadow one just in the gate the Other up above the Barn Baker threshing Oats CB Foster threshing Wheat HB rest stubble mowing Father went to Heathfield Chapel about Auxilary buildings Mr Press preached there in Evening from 1 Peter 2 Cha former part 7 verse. Elias Standen an Old Blacksmith Cald and had

[242] Put rings in their noses to stop them rooting up the grass.

some Bread and Cheese and Beer Mr Jarvis Called but did not come in. It keeps being Showry and pr..ment[?] the season. Maid went out Visiting

Thursday 26
Wm Hoad sowed and Horses ploughed in the Wheat in 12 Acres Baker Brishing along the Top of the 12 Acres for a foot path and helpt Foster and I Clean 4 Sacks of Wheat Foster Threshing before rest stubble mowing Mr Ths Waters and his son Stephen come here and supt[243] Bought 7 Ewe sheep at 1£ 4s per Head David went to Cade street. Maid Came home

Friday 27
Carters sowed Wheat and Plough in Baker and I with 4 Oxen and Cart Carried a load of Head Wheat at 14£ and 4 Bush Tail for Grist to Bucksteep Mill in morning Baker Shoveling the Borders of the Dung Mackson up on the Macksons David helpt him get a sack of Potatos with Old Jack from the Brook Orchard I helpt them drive the six Calves from the Whinhouse field to the Calves Lodge Meadow etc David and I sett up a post at the Barrowway between the shaw against the Squirefield and the Red pale field. Foster threshing rest stubble mowing J Honeysett Brought his Thatching bill[244] in morning J Phillips Game Keeper brought a Note and bought Waist coat of me for 3£ etc Fodder the Cows twice a day with Trefoil once

Saturday 28
This day we have Finised sowing the 12 Acres with Brown Cobham Wheat from Windmill hill there is several different ways of Sowing which any one that lives to see the difference next Harvest May judge of the best plan the two End headlands with 4 Warpps this end and small Warp on the other end ploughed in and left 6 Warps next to the 4 Warps where plough is and Harrowed a draft afterwards and there are 5 Furrows not struck out all the rest is ploughed and sowed the general way some with Oxen and some with Horses no lot Furrows Baker and I made some tracks across the lower headland in afternoon Baker wass gaping in Calves Lodge Meadow and threshing Oats in Chapel Barn in forenoon. Foster threshing H Barn rest Stubble Mowing Mrs Selmes who hass been to Silverash all this week nearly come here to night Mr R Russell Visitor etc

[243] Supped.
[244] A light form of hand bill for trimming thatching rods.

Sunday 29

Father and I went to Heathfield all day Mother and David in morning Maid Do Mrs Selmes and Ann stayed at home all day Mr Press Preached in morning from 5 Cha 25 verse of Ephesians and afterwards gave an account of the Auziliary affairs and the which Mother wass very much hurt Preached in afternoon from the 35 Psalm 3 and 4 verses. The Lord wass pleased to give me much comfort under this discourse as I have of Late become much distressed in mind on account of Sin but blessed be the Lord he hass I trust in some measure delivered me from that state of bondage wherein I had fallen through the prevalence of corruption

Monday 30

Carters Baker and Foster with 4 Horses and a pair of Oxen Carried 52 Load of Dung from Home yards to Mackson in the Poundfield with three Carts Thos Hoad and I with 4 Oxen had the newest Waggon to the Grinnetts he and his two Girls Dug up 28 Bushels of Potatos which partly Loaded the Waggon T Hoad with a pair of Oxen and a Cart fetched 15 Bushels of potatos from his Fathers to our Oast meaning to take them out from ours at Hodges etc Easton subble Mowing 13 Acres J Bland and Gamekeeper Phillips come in afternoon Mr Jesse Jarvis and Trill Lade Visitors to a late hour in Evening We heard from Latham our Factor yesterday he hass sold 68 Pockets at the Reduced price of 6£ 15s per hundred etc Hops having sold for from 9£ to 12£ per hundred Sussex Kent a little more the Duty hass been sett at as Low as 82,000£ but it is now sett at above a 100,000£ Which makes considerable difference in the price There is a general complaint of shortness of money in all most all Trade. Taxes and Tythes are Heigh and also the Rents in general and commodities Low which makes a great scarcity of money

Tuesday 31

Horses Carter Oxen Baker and Foster Carried Loads of Dung as yesterday T Hoad Potatoing Easton Mowing Stubble Wm Oxley my Brother Visitor he Father I David Mr Selmes and Maid went to Mr Smiths in Evening Mr Press Preached from Job 35 Cha 14 verse

Wednesday Nov 1

Horses Carried 3 small Load of Hop Bines from Orchard garden and 1 load of old poles from Do and 1 load hop Bines and 2 Cart loads of Potato from Brook garden Oxen fetched 64½ Bushels of potatos from Grinnets and 2 Loads hop Bines from pound garden to the Ox yard Carters laid there in home yard Foster Finised Diging Potato in Brook or new Orchard 52 Bushel T Hoad dug up 36½ Bushels of Potatos yesterday and 42 today Easton Mowing stubble Wm Oxley whent home Father whent to Hailsham Market I whent to Rushlake Green [in Evening] Wass measured for a new pair of Breaches etc

Thursday 2
Horses Carried some Potatos home from the Grinnets to Hodges Close and Plough in Grinnetts had home a Cart Load of potatos But[?] 1 Cart pair of Oxen spreading Lime in grinnets David and I with 4 Oxen and a Cart Carried T Hoad 15 Bushels of potatos home and Fetch'd 4 sacks of Peas from J Blands and 2 Bush Pollard from Windmill Foster threshing Wheat in Home Barn Easton mowing stubble etc

Friday 3
Horses plough and harrow Baker with a pair of Oxen Finised spreading Lime David and I Carried rest of the potato home to the the Calf's[?] and loaded up the rest of the potatos afterwards Baker and I with 4 Oxen helpt plough Wm Hoad sowed the side land and one headland and Baker the other Headlands with a sort of wheat We know of no Broper[245] name to it formerly came from Essex to Gillridge on or under the Hill Mr Waters of Beastons Calls it Essex Red Baker and I fetched it (5 Bushels) from Sannels in morning Father helpt some times and sowed into Lot Furrows thus we Finised the grinnits of Sowing and had the rest of the potatos home with the Orchard Garden to Be Laid up 2 Cart Load nearly which makes in all 125 Bushels from Grinnetts and 52 from Brook which is in all about 177 Bushels T Hoad Brishing the Hedges from Litter at Hodges and in pound field etc Foster not at work Easton as yesterday Clover stack, tumbled down to night

Saturday 4
Baker I and Carters put the Hay that fell down in to the Hayloft It hass Broke 2 Postes and 5 Rails I shot a rook the first that ever I shot in the Whinhouse above 9 rod where I wass. afterward Carters Carried 2 Loads of Hop Bines to Ox Close and a Load of Old Poles to home stack from Croft Oxen Carried small load of Litter from High field 2 Load of stubble from the Huglets and 1 Load from the Round banks in to the Close at Hodges Ruth Hoad Raked after the Waggon Foster threshing he hass bought the

[245] Proper.

Dalling[246] Pig for 12 shillings T Hoad and Easton mowing stubble David went to Stream Mill Chiddingly Father hurled[247] the Potatos with dirt in the Orchard Garden Honeysetts mended the thatch of Haystacks and buildings

Sunday 5

Father and I stayed all day at Chapel Mother and David in morning the Maid went to hear Preacher at Gardener Street in afternoon Mr Press Preached in the morning from 107 Psalm 43 Verse and in the afternoon from John 8 Cha Latter part 31 and all the 32 verses. Last week it wass verry Wett and dirty this week it has dried up and got good walking there having been no rain since Last Sunday as I remember

Monday 6

Forgot on Saturday to sett down Master Morfey mended the Windows etc Horses Carried 1 load of Bines to the Calves Lodge 2 Loads to Oxen Close and 1 Load to the Pound field pottom Oxen Finised stubble Carring at Hodges 2 more Loads from Round banks there wass 3 there and 2 in the Huglets Carried 1 Load from 9 Acres to the Calves Foster threshing rest stubble mowing Marry Hoad helpt us stubble mowing Father went to the sheep shaveing at Warbleton Church the Shepard is not at home What is to be the sheep Shear'd I don't know or Whether he hass more Composion[248] them nearly a month sooner perhaps he knows but I mean the Tithe Trill Lade Visitor in the Evening

Tuesday 7

Carters spread the Dung in Calves Lodge Meadow and set the load of Old poles up from the Croft in afternoon Henry and I cleaned the Great Stall out in readiness for a Barren Cow Foster threshing HB Baker threshing C B rest mowing stubble Father is gone Rushlake this Evening I went to Pray Meeting at Thos Martins Bodle street Mr Wooten Spoke in pray 1st Time sung a Hym Mr Carter read the 14 Cha John sung a Hym Spoke from the 13 Verse etc Wass Wett Weather in morning etc

Wednesday 8

We have driven nearly all the stock to their respective places where they are to Winter except the Beast in the Marsh Our Stock consists of 4 Working

---

[246] Dallington.
[247] Covered up.
[248] Compassion.

1815

Horses a Cast off stallion a Weanier Colt a Yearling Colt and a ride horse in home yard two yearling colts in Silver field and a yearling Colt a keeping for Mr Diamond in pound field the Bullocks and 4 Milk Cows a Bull a Two yearling Heifer for Butcher Watten when he means to Fetch it a pair of Oxen for Sale otherwise to be Fatted and a Black Runt Cow to be Fatted in the Stall at Home yard 6 Working Oxen in the Close 7 Yearlings in Pound field 6 Weanin Calves in the Calves Lodge meadow cow at Hodges for Thos Hoad and 6 Two Yearling in the Marsh. The Sheep Consist of 15 Ewes 3 Down 24 Lambs of our own and 30 (should be but one Dead) Marsh Lambs for Mr Thos Winchester

Horses Carried 1 Load of poles from Croft and 2 Load from Poundfield David and I sett the 1st Load up and put the Black Cow in the Stall and Drove the yearlings from the Bushy field into the Round field and Mr Diamonds Colt Do Baker and David put the Oxen into their Close Baker threshing in the forenoon I helpt him Clean 7 sacks and Bushels some White and some Black Oats it is this Year impossible to tell how many Oats We Grew for the Carters have gone and got Oats with or without measuring or any how ever since Harriet Foster threshing HB Easton is at work on mowing stubble I do not know what T Hoad wass at neither yester day nor to day John Fox Visitor

Thursday 9
After a Wett night Horses kept Holiday Carters Bozling[249] Baker threshing Barley Foster Wheat Do Father I and Carters put the Ram among the Ewes at Hodges Easton mowing stubble Thos Hoad Began Make the Hedges of the Furze Wood against the 8 Acres yesterday and wass at it to day Stephen Watters Visitor etc

Friday 10
Horses have done nothing Carters diching at the Corner of the Silver field against the Calves lodge meadow and Mr Smiths Pill field in the Corner rest of the workmen as yesterday Father went to Mr Russell's Robt Reeves came after Ram Master Rud and his Boy etc Catchd 20 Rats I write thiss and yesterday's account in the Great Window of the Kitchen about 7 O'Clock in the Evening

Saturday 11
Horses David and I the Carters Carried 2 Load of stubble from the 13 Acres to the Home yard and Loaded up a Load to Carry up to Ox Close and

---

[249] Bosseling: see glossary.

would have unloaded it only the Carriers Haffendens Team came after to Ash Trees of Mr Phillips from Bucksteep Wood that were through into our thirteen Acres for Mr Bray our Wheeler Carters helpt them in afternoon Easton hass Finised mowing the 13 Acres and began the 8 Acres T Hoad Hedging Foster thrashing Wheat and Baker Do Barley I went down into the Marsh and to Mr Everest's Gardener Street saw my Cousin T Parker at John Honeysetts after Charity Collins their ness his wife hass sent out etc Mr Russell at Church Visitor and John and Henry Purstglove staid the Evening and Bought the old Oxen Duke and Diamond at 42£

Sunday 12
Father Mother David and I went to Heathfield Chapel in morning and Father and Maid Do in afternoon Mr Press Preachd in the morning from 1 Isaiah 42 Cha 16 Verse and in the afternoon from the last Cha and the latter part of the 14 verse of the same Book

Monday 13
Carters drove Duke and Diamond to Prinkle and their Chains mended at Blacksmiths by the road in forenoon and helpt Baker Clean 3 Sacks of Barley in afternoon Baker threshing in the forenoon Thos Hoad and Wm Foster threshing in H Barn Easton I know nothing about I was a going to Mayfield Fair but it being such verry Windy and Wett Weather in the Morning I did not go There was a Flood Stephen Watters come after the Hip fall Heifer and I went with him home with her Trill Lade Visitor in the Evening

Tuesday 14
Horses Ploughed 8 ½ Went in the farther Silver field between the Calves Lodge meadow and the pit against Mr Smiths Pillfield Hedge and 4 ½ Went against the Meadow Hedge in the same Corner afterwards Brought 3 Cart Loads of Gravel to the gateway between the Silver fields Forgot that they unloaded the last Load of stubble they fetched from the 13 Acres last Saturday in the Oxen Close and fetched the Cleaned Corn home and Carried some Hog corn to the Mill in the Morning Foster threshing HB Baker Do in the C Barn of Oats T Hoad Hedging Easton mowing stubble Mr Phillips had a dinner Since John Bland and his a wife with his youngest Child came and had it Baptised in the Evening named William Mr Steer Brought David and I each a pair of Breeches and a waistcoat Mr Press Preached in the Evening from the 1 Book of John 3 Cha latter part of the 8th Verse

Wednesday 15

Carter casting up Moul they ploughed up yesterday all the rest of the workmen as yesterday Mr Press whent home Mrs Selmes whent Gardener Street I staid over at Gardner street at Mr Daws etc

Thursday 16

A Little Frost in the Morning Horses Carried the last Load of Hop Bines from the Pound field Garden and David and I help them Get up One Load of Old Poles and should have Carried More but it snowed and put us by it Left off Snowing by the time We left off Carters Cast up some Moul the rest of the day in the Silver field T Hoad threshing along with Foster rest workmen as yesterday Father went to the Tithe feast at Wartling to Boreham Bullhead Inn Collier the Horse that Father Bought of Mr Reeves on 8th December last wass Kicked yesterday in the afternoon by Traveller above the knee of the near fore leg wass perceived to be worse I told the threshers to get him in I went after Wm Harmer and David whent after Mr Crowhurst the Farier at Rushlake they both said his leg wass Broke and advised to Kil him I went to meet Father but he wass come home I then had Mr Phillips the Game Keeper to come down and shoot the Horse who came and shot him in the yard at 20 minutes before 8 O'Clock in the Evening in his 10th year of age in good working order worth about 18 Guineas

Friday 17

Game keeper Phillips and the Carters Flawed the Horse cut it to picies Wm Hoad with a Cart and 2 Horses Carried the Carcass to Bodle Street for Phillip's Dogs and Henry with Jack the Pony carried the skin to the Collar makers at Rushlake Green in the morning Carters casting up Moul in the afternoon rest of the Workmen as yesterday Mrs Selmes whent to Silverash Father went to Cade Street Joseph Morphey White washed the Hall etc there was this morning a sharp Frost considerable than yesterday

Saturday 18

The Frost continues Horses Finised Carring Old Poles 3 Loads from the pound field garden. Baker threshing Oats Foster Do wheat T Hoad Hedging and Easton made a sort of Finising mowing stubble in 8 Acres David and I setting up hop Poles and David had Jack to be Shod Mrs Selmes came home from Silverash Father Bought a pig of Mr Harmer for a

Sunday 19

Father Mother David and I whent to Heathfield Chapel in morning Father stayed the afternoon Mrs Selmes whent to Herstmonceux Chapel in morning The Maid and Ann stayed at home Mr Press Preached in the morning from the 72 Psalm the latter part of the 19th verse and in the afternoon from Romans 8 Cha 1 verse

Monday 20

Horses Wm Hoad David and I Carrid 2 Load of stubble from the 8 Acres to the pound field bottom and 1 Load to the Oxen Close Baker threshing CB Foster Do HB T Hoad Hedging Easton and Henry had 2 two yearling Colts to Croft in hand First and Father whent and exchanged them for a Mare coming 4 Year Old and gave 7£ the runt

Tuesday 21

Horses Carters and David Carrid 2 Loads of stubble from the 13 Acres to the Oxen Close and worked the new Horse the first time and had her shoed at night at the Blacksmiths rest workmen as yesterday Father whent to Battisford in the Evening etc

Wednesday 22

Horses Plough began the 8 Acres Baker with a pair of Oxen Mouling for himself T Hoad Hedging Foster whent or said he should go Mayfield and Easton to Battel Fair at there own pleasure. David and I whent to Battel etc

Thursday 23

Horses Plough and Fetched 250 hop Poles from the 8 Acres against the Lower Hedge to the Corner of the young garden in the Pound field T Hoad Hedging or Wood cutting in the Furze Wood Foster Baker and I Cleaned 18 Sack of wheat and got more out of the Chaff I don't know anything about Easton David shot a Hawk with my Gun the first Bird ever he shot a flying Father whent to the Half Moon Heathfield to prove the Debt on Parker and stopt the Market and whent to Mr Grants[?] in the Evening and Whent all day without a Dinner Trill Lade Visitor in the Evening Father says that Mr Reeves the Horse Dealer says that the new mare is but a Colt coming Two years old he ought to know he saw her at Cross in Hand Fair and wanted to Buy for himself J Bland sent 4 sacks of Peas

Friday 24
Horses Plough and Fetchd from the Furze Wood against the Plough field to the pound field against the Pound 60 Ash 3 Willows and 2 Oak Poles Baker and I with 2 pair of Oxen and a Cart Carrid 26 Sacks of Wheat to Bucksteep Mill at Four times at 14£ 5s per Load Foster Baker and I Cleand the rest of the wheat there wass in all what wass Cleand now 22 sacks 2 ½ Bushels of wheat there has been some cleaned before I don't know rightly how much but enough to make it up 17 Quarters – – – – – – – – – – – [six words crossed out] and 1 ½ Bushels at 4s per Quarter is 3£ 8s 9d for threshing Thos Hoad wood cutting Easton preparing for Grubing at Hodges Forgot Foster threshed a few Oats at night and a few Chogs and his own Leas wheat in the afternoon Father whent to Dallington at night and came home before late in the Evening

Saturday 25
Horses Plough and Fetchd a part of a load of Stubble that wass left in the 8 acres to the Poundfield bottom I raked after the Waggon Baker threshing CB Foster Do HB T Hoad wood cutting and his Girls a hop pole shaving Easton Grubing J Bland Visitor Trill Lade Do but did not come in Father whent to Dallington Trill Lade visitor again in Evening We have began all the hay stacks

Sunday 26
Father Mother David I and the Maid went to Heathfield Chapel in the morning Father stayed the afternoon Mr Press Preached in the morning from Colossians 2 Cha the first line of the 10th Verse and 25th Psalm 4 verse in afternoon

Monday 27
Horses Plough and fetchd home to against the pound 1 Load of hop poles, fence poles, Ash poles and Chord Wood Baker and I Cleaned 3 Sacks of Black Oats he wass threshing rest of the day. Foster threshing Ths Hoad wood cutting Easton Grubing, Mr Couchman Called on business Mr R Russel brought a new broom[?]
This day day after nearly seven years widdowhood and nearly two years courtship and several disappointments Mrs Selms hass got a fresh husband John Trill Lade son of Ths Lade[251] at the priory they where

---

[251] This text is emphasized in larger and heavier script.

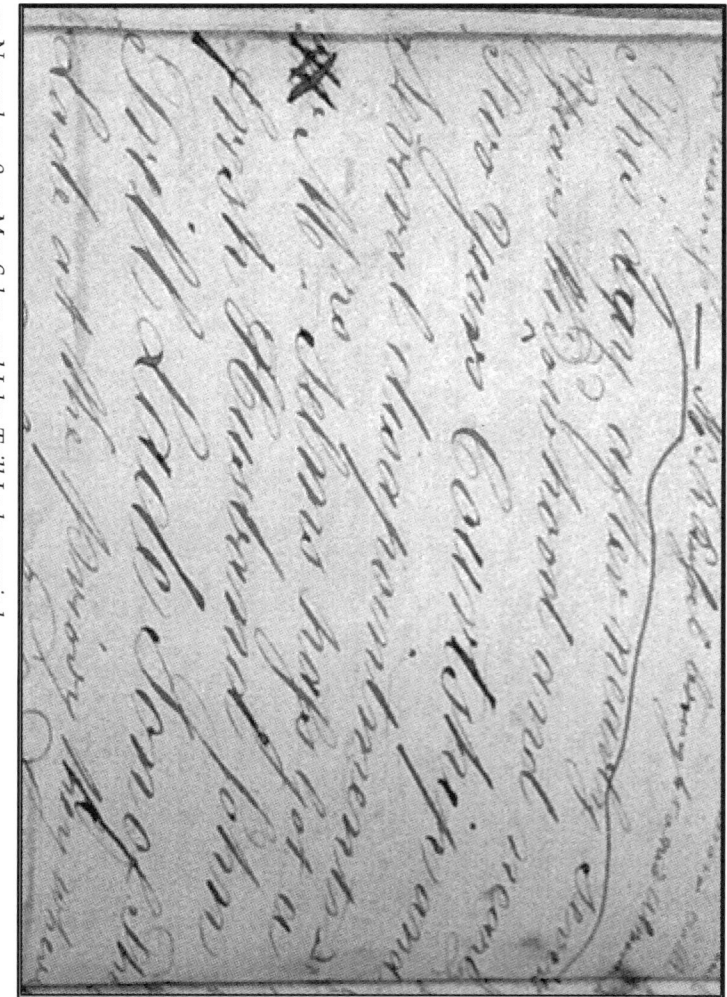

27 November 1815: Mrs Selms and John Trill Lade married.

married by the rev mr young of heathfield at warbleton church father wass old father and elizabeth lade bridemaid they dined with mother mrs lade mrs trill (james trill's wife) david and i mrs lade and daniel c lade came here in the evening had roast pig for dinner

Tuesday 28
Horses Plough Baker threshing in the forenoon Carrid 4 Sack of Hay corn to Bodle Street Mill with a pair of Oxen and a Cart in the afternoon rest of the workmen as yesterday Mr Steer of Cowbeech Visitor Father David and I went to Mr Smiths in the Evening Mr Press Preachd from the 146 Psalm the 8th Verse

Wednesday 29
Horses Carried the remaining part of a Load Stubble from the 13 Acres to the home yard and 2 Loads from the 9 Acres to the Oxen's Close and stacked, Baker threshing W Hoad and I helpt him Clean 7 Bushels of Oats at night Foster not at work T Hoad Wood cutting Easton Grubbing David whent to Bellhurst Father to the Priory and to Heath field Chapel in Evening Maid whent to Gardener street tril Lade sleeps here to night he is

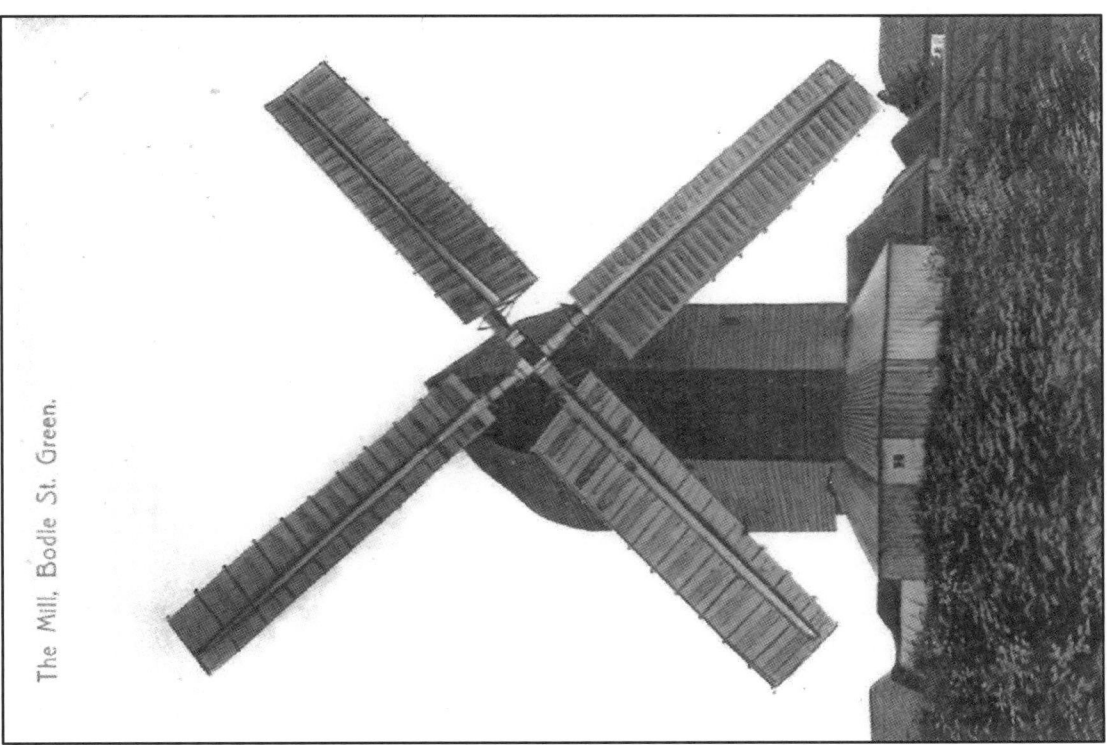

The Mill, Bodle Street Green

now a reading in the 116 Psalms the clock is a striking 8 in the Evening I am against the Great window in the kitchen etc

Thursday 30
Horses Carrid 11 Loads of Dung from the Mackson up against the Kiln to the Orchard hop garden Baker helpt them they would have done more but it Rained and thawed nearly all day Baker threshing Foster threshing T Hoad Wood cutting Easton Grubing the Honeysetts have undertaken to

Friday 1 December

Horses Plough Baker threshing Foster and Easton Casting up of Moul in Carves Lodge Meadow T Hoad wood cuting G Guy a new workman Hidging[252] between the 12 Acres and the 8 Acres I whent to Lewes etc make a small piece of the Hedge just below the uper gate of Kiln field and from the Corner of the Old Lane to the shaw below the Orchard hop garden Forgot Wm Hoad had Violet Shoed and brought some hay corn from the Windmill John Trill Lade sleeps here to night etc

Saturday 2

Horses plough Foster Baker and David Cleaned about 36 sacks of Oats in the Cha Barn rest workmen as yesterday I come home from Lewes Mrs Lade whent to the Priory David says the Hunters have Trod the and poutched the Kiln field when about to day

Sunday 3

Father I David and the Maid whent to Heathfield Chapel in the morning and Father stayed all day Mr Press Preachd in the morning from Acts 2 Cha and the latter part of the last Verse and from the 42 verse the same Chapter in the afternoon

Monday 4

Horses Carrid 10 Sacks of Oats and 5 sacks of Oats to Bucksteep Mill in the afternoon it Rained in the forenoon a Team from Wartling came after some Timber for Mr Reed at Boreham and got a stand in Grimes Wood Wm Hoad with 3 Horses helpt them out they came also last Saturday Thos Hoad wood cutting G Guy Hedging Honeysetts began their hedge in the Kiln field as here afore written Baker threshing CB Foster Do HB Easton I believe wass not at work Father whent to Cade Street and David to Windmill hill with some game to go to Lewes Mr Lades Boy came with a Pheasant and a Hare

Tuesday 5

Horses fetched the Hay Corn from the Windmill and a Load of straw from Thos Isted's to Hodges and David and I helpt them unload David and I helpt Foster clean 11 sacks and 2 Bushels of Oats Carters fild the saw pits up in Grimes Wood in the afternoon Easton Grubing rest of the workmen as yesterday Wm Harmer put a Ring into Old Boiler and took a Chaff from the Bulls Eye in morning David and I according to our Custom whent out

[252] Hedging.

to look at the Fatter Cow in the Evening and perceived she wass Blow'd I whent after Wm Harmer who came and gave her a Drink and opened her stomach lowered her considerably Father whent to Stream Mill in the morning and did not come home till between 12 and 1 O'Clock at night Wm Came home with him they have brought a spaniel and 2 Running Dogs[253] home with them

Wednesday 6
Horses Carried 31 Sacks of Oats to the Carriers at Cade Street Oxen helpt them part of the way had the mangle home from the Millrights Rushlake Foster threshing T Hoad wood cutting Honeysetts and Guy Hedging and Easton Grubing Father whent down into the Marsh and coming home lit of a Sale and bought goods to the amount of 11£ 5s 2d he stand a late hand This is my brithday I am now 21 and we have had a few friends on the occasion Viz Cousin Parker, Robert Reeves and David Lade who whent home and Thos Goldsmith of Chiddingly Elizabeth Lade Ruth Reeves Glyde Reeves and Ann Reeves who stayed night Trill Lade Sleeps here to night Brother Wm Oxley whent to Gardener street and back again a Tolerable little Company Forgot that Baker wass threshing after he came home with the Oxen and the Honeysetts began make a Hedg at Hodges between the High field and Roundbanks and the Millfield

Thursday 7
Horses whent to Windmill Hill and brought the Goods home that wass bought at the Sale of Mrs Fullers Carrier rest of workmen as yesterday Father whent to Windmill Hill with the Horses all the rest of My Company whent home after dinner etc

Friday 8
Horses Carrid the rest of the dung Mackson away from against the Kiln to the Orchard hop garden 47 Loads Wm Hoad Sholved Foster Filld the Carts Henry Choping hop poles they did tell their Loads of Dung all the rest of the workmen as yesterday

Saturday 9
Horses and Oxen Carrid 32 Loads Dung from below the Barn to the Oldest part of the Pound field garden Baker Filld the Carts Henry Drove between Wm Hoad sholved Foster David and I Cleand 13 sacks of Oats in the Home Barn rest of Work men as yesterday. I whent to Rushlake in the Evening I

[253] Lurchers.

understand that the Honeysetts have began another Hedge a small part of the Hedge on the North side of the Grinets

Sunday 10
Father I and David whent to Heath Chapel in morning Maid Do in field afternoon Mr Press Preached in the morning from the 74 Psalm 19 and 20 verses and from Romans 4 Cha the Maid hass forgot what Verse but she thinks the 20th and 21st verses. Mrs Lade and her Husband Whent to Church Last Sunday wass verry Dirty this Sunday is nice and Frosty

Monday 11
Horses Oxen Carters and Baker Carrid 35 Loads of Dung as on Saturday Father threshing Wheat in Home Barn Honeysetts T Hoad and Guy Hedging and Wood cut[ing] Easton Grubing Father whent to Rushlake Foster and I tied the Black Cow up Mrs Lade whent to the Priory Mr Standford and Mr Tour] Visitors Joseph Morfey and Mr R Winchester pland out the building of a new Oast

Tuesday 12
Horses Carters Carrid 18 Loads of Dung from the Mackson and Finised it in 85 Loads in all Baker threshing Foster not at work Honeysetts Finised their work Easton Grubing Guy Hedging Ths Hoad wood cutting I whent to Rushlake the shooters Kild a Partrige and a pheasant Mr Press Preached at John Honeysetts from Ruth 1 Cha 20th and 21st Verses Mr R Winchester came here and whent with David and I up there in Evening

Wednesday 13
Horses Carters and I Carried 33 Loads of Dung from the Mackson in the pound field in to the Crofft Hop garden Baker threshing in the Morning helpt the Timber Team out of the Wood with the Oxen in the afternoon Honeysetts left working have the others as yesterday the shooters Kild 5 pheasant and a Morehen and whent home in the afternoon Phillips and his Dogs was with them a shooting Joseph Morfey mended the Hall Chamber window Mrs Lade came home and had her husband home with her he wass here some nights last week that I have not sett down

Thursday 14
Horses Carters and I carried 38 Loads of Dung into the Crofft and 2 Load in to the Pound field Gardens rest of the Workmen as yesterday nothing Else in particular today only it wass a verry clear fine day

Friday 15
It rained in the morning and the frost is nearly gone away Wm Hoad Cutting Chaff Henry Cleand the stall out and made 2 Birch Brooms for the House I Drove the sheep from Hodges to the Bushy field in the Morning David and I a Gaping there in the afternoon Baker threshing Oats CB Ths Hoad and Foster Do Wheat HB Guy and Easton where at each at their work in the afternoon etc

Saturday 16
Wm Hoad Cutting Chaff Henry Choping hop poles etc T Hoad threshing in the morning and a wood cutting in the afternoon Wm Foster threshing all day Baker Do in CB Easton Grubing Guy Hedging. It wass Windy and Wett in the Morning Still afternoon snow in Evening tis verry Dirty Two Waters just cald from Cade street

Sunday 17
Father David and I Whent to Heath field Chapel in the morning Mother whent part of the way but returned on account of Weather the Maid whent in afternoon Mr Press Preachd in the Morning from the 73 Psalm the 1st Verse and in the afternoon from Nahum the 1st Chapter and the 7th Verse

Monday 18
Horses Fetch the Wood away from the Hodges that G Guy made to several Different places 51 House Faggots and Chord Wood Enough to make it up 70 — 155 Faggots as Kiln Faggots or Bush Faggots Carried to several place to mend gaps with 225 Hop poles and 9 Ash poles G Guy Finised the Hedge Between the 8 Acres and the 12 Acres and began a Cast in Furze Wood T Hoad wood cutting Easton Grubing in the Round banks at Hodges Baker Casting up Moul in the Silverfields and Foster threshing David and I had the Six Two Yearlings home from the Marsh and drove the 4 Steers to Hodges and the 2 Heifers into the pound field. We had a letter from Mr Latham yesterday he hass sold 12 more Pockets at 6£ 8s he wass bid in or just after Hopping 9£ 15s for the same Hops

Tuesday 19
I helpt the Horses and Carters gett up a Load of Stubble in the nine acres and they unloaded it at the Calves Lodge Henry borrowed a prong of Master Delves's thresher and I struck at a mouse and broke it and whent to the Blacksmith and had it mended they got up another Load and Carried to the Hodges Close afterwards brought a Load of Kiln Faggots Home from where Easton wass a grubing rest of the workmen as yesterday John

Bland and Wm Harmer come here perhaps on business David and I whent to Windmill hill and Gardener Street after Elizabeth from Lewes by Fullers Cart but she did not come John Trill Lade sleeps here to Knight Frosty morning snow an Inch and half Deep Till late at night and then Rain

Wednesday 20

Carters Shoveling up Dirt and Chaff cutting T Hoad wood cutting in the morning threshing along with Wm Foster in the afternoon Baker threshing rest of workmen not know wither at work or not. The si[e]ve bottomer Cornford brought 3 new Clothes Baskets and the Butcher come about the Christmass Beef in the forenoon Phillips the Game Keeper and Mr Russell was here this afternoon a Chap Loitered about the Barn after work nearly all Day but we have none for him. The Weather is extremly c[h]angeable yesterday it freesed on Monday it wass verry Dirty on Sunday and a few days it freesed. Today there hass been Two Floods one in Morning that had not quite sunk but what it come on again there wass a Flood again in the afternoon its verry Dirty indeed

Thursday 21

Wm Hoad with the Horses Carried 4 sacks of Hog Corn for us and a sack of Oats for Baker in morning Cleand the Hog pounds out and Whent to Gaping at Hodges Rest of the Day. Baker and David Cleand 6 Sacks and 3 Bushels of Oats and sifted the Chaff and put it into Bed Ticks[254] for the Women Bung the Pigs Baker Mouling in the afternoon Foster threshing T Hoad and Guy Wood cutting Easton Grubing or Faggoting up the stuff Father is gone to Rushlake about the Dole's Mr Nathan Tailor Visitor John Trill Lade sleeps here tonight

Friday 22

Horses Plough in 8 Acres Foster not at Work all the rest workmen as yester day in the afternoon David and I helpt Mr Wood the Gardener plant 20 Apple Trees against the Brook Hop Garden and 1 Cherry against the Hall Window in morning He Trimmed the Tree in the afternoon David and I with a pair of Oxen and a Cart fetchd the Hay Corn home from the Mill in the afternoon Messrs Russell and Delves Visitors Wm Hoad had Elizabeth my Sister Home from Gardener Street who came from Lewes by Fullers Cart Father whent to Sannels and I whent to Stephen Goldsmiths in the Evening Father Trill Lade and his Father looked Clippenham Farm over to Day

[254] Mattress covers.

Saturday 23
Horses Plough in the 8 Acres in the Winhouse field and 7 Acres T Hoad any Guy Wood cutting T Hoads Girls shave the Hop poles Baker threshing Easton Leveling or working about the Silde in the Calves Lodge meadow Settled for his Grubing 7 Chord of Roots 44 House Faggots and about a 100 of Kiln Do it Come to about 4£ Foster not at work Trill Lade Sleeps here to night the Rushlake Wheelers Exeld a Cart[255] that wass Broke the 10th August and put a new Exel to the fore Wheels of the Bigest Waggon strained the 10th of October Last

Sunday 24
Father Mother David and I whent to Heathfield Chapel in the morning Mr Press Preachd from 2nd Thessalonians 1 Cha the latter part of the 7 and the 8 verses 'When the Lord etc' J T Lade sleeps here to night

Monday 25
Christmas Day Father David Elizabeth Mrs Lade and I whent to Heathfield Chapel Mr Press Preachd from Galatians 4 Cha and the 4 verse Mrs Lade whent to the Priory and stays all night David and I whent there to Dinner and supper

Tuesday 26
I think there wass only Wm Foster threshing or at anything else to day it being a Holiday Several people came a Boxing[256] and paying for wood etc Mr Press Preached in the Evening from Luke the 2nd Cha and the 14 verse Tis a very windy Wett Dirty and Dark Evening consequently but few attended

Wednesday 27
Wm Hoad Cutting Chaff Henry whent to the Blacksmiths with the plough Iron Mr Press whent home he had a small boy with him and had it away with him again It wass Wett weather all the forenoon and nearly all the after noon Cold and Dirty the wind being Upwards most likely to Freese again to night the weather is uncommonly changeable David Honeysett came after his money for his and his Brothers Hedging Baker threshing

Thursday 28
Horses Plough in either the High field or the Round Banks Hodges and fetch a load of Roots and Faggots away Baker I and David casting up of

[255] Put in a new axle.
[256] Boxing Day: bringing presents.

Moul in the Wenthouse field against the Gutterfield shaw T Hoad and Foster threshing the rest I know nothing about John Trill Lade sleeps here to night Frosty morning Maid is gone to Holiday keeping

Friday 29
Horses Plough and Fetch'd home a Load of Roots Baker David and I casting up Moul T Hoad and Guy Wood cutting Foster threshing Easton casting up Moul in the Calves Lodg meadow J Bland and his Son Horatio Visitors. Tis very Dirty the wind is downwards

Saturday 30
Horses as yesterday Foster David and I Cleand 15 Sa 2 Bu Head and 7 nearly threshing measures Wheat Baker threshing Oats CB Wood cutting and Easton as yesterday a fine Drying Day the wind upwards John Trill Lade sleeps here to night and the Maid came home from Holiday keeping to night

Sunday 31
Father Elizabeth David Mrs Lade and I whent to Heathfield Chapel in the morning Mr Press Preached from the 84 Psalm the 11 Verse the Maid whent in the afternoon she did know rightfully where the Text wass but thought it wass the 103 Psalm the 1st Verse It is Fathers Birthday he is 56 years old John Trill Lade Sleeps here to night Is the Last days account to be written in this Book. All to one which is September 9th 1816 which is tury[?] not day
Wm Oxley
Bucksteep Warbleton
Sussex

THE DIARY OF NICHOLAS OXLEY 1816
THE FRUITS OF THE EARTH VERY BACKWARD

Monday 1 January

Carters Foster and I with the Horses and wagon fetched 7 sack and 2 Bushels of Wheat in from the Barn in the morning Baker/Henry and I Cleaned about six sack of Oats Wm Hoad helpt Kill his Hog in the rest of the forenoon Horses carried 4 sacks of Hog Corn to the mill and Baker threshing in the afternoon. T Hoad and G Guy Wood cutting in the Furze Wood Foster Casting up moul in the 7 acres and Easton Do in the Calves Lodge meadow Old Master Fowle from our work house John Oxley from Waldron and Dame Dann visitors Father went to Rushlake Green Mrs Lade Elizabeth and I went to the Priory in the evening Fine weather overhead but verry Dirty walking.

Tuesday 2

Horses Wm & H Hoad plow in High field Foster casting up moul in 9 Acres Easton casting up mould Calves Lodge Meadow Baker threshing CB T Hoad and G Guy wood cutting I went to Mayfield Father went to Priory Mr Delve visitor killed Hog in morning

Wednesday 3

Horses Wm and H Hoad plow brought home 1 load of Roots Foster Easton casting up mould in 7 Acres Baker threshing CB G Guy T Hoad wood cutting T Oxley J Steer S Fox Visitors I whent to the Club at Fishers Mayfield[257]

Thursday 4

Horse plough and brought home a load of roots Baker Mouling in the Wenhouse field Foster mouling in the 7 acres against the Squirefield Easton Do against the Chapel wood meadow Hedge T Hoad and G Guy wood cutting and came home from Mayfield in the evening

Friday 5

David helpt Baker all the rest of the workmen as yesterday but the horses did not fetch home any roots there is somebody just called I do not know

---

[257] The club may have been an annual Bible Society Meeting held at The Star Inn in Mayfield, where the innkeeper was Thomas Fisher. There were also Bible Society Meetings held at various other places, and they seemed to be common for many decades.

who it is. Mr Waters the shoemaker and Wm Oxley are the people.

Saturday 6
Horses plough and fetched home a load of wood Baker threshing – C Barn T Hoad G Guy wood cutting Cooter and Foster mouling – I whent after some Bull money North East ward got £3.12s.6d it has been very changeable weather all this week but no rain till today morning it was foggy and misty and dirty.

Sunday 7
Father Elizabeth David Wm and I whent to Heathfield Chapel in the morning Mr Press preached from Exodus 28 Cha. the latter part of the 24 verse In all places etc sung the hymn on the 270, 374 and 478 pages L.H.C.[258] Mrs Lade came home and had her husband with her Wm whent home.

Monday 8
Being Wett weather the horses did not do any thing Wm Hoad cutting chaff T Hoad and Foster threshing Oats in H.B. and Baker in the C.B. Guy wood cutting Foster mouling Easton not at work. Mr Henry Purstglove visitor G Verrell whent to Burwash etc Father I David and G Verrell whent Mrs Smiths in the evening Mr Press preached from the 106 psalm the 1st verse and sung the Hymns on the 324 & 256 and the 328th pages of L.H.C. a small moon.

Tuesday 9
Horse carried load of straw from Mr Thos Isted's to Hodges and finished ploughing the Bound banks and Highfields Baker threshing T Hoad and G Guy wood cutting Foster mouling Easton not at work. Mr Henry Purstglove visitor G Verrell whent to Lewes visitor I wrote out Wm Harmer Farming Bill paid and John Oxley £3 12s for his watch.

Wednesday 10
Horses plough at the further end of the Croft David & I casting up moul in the Wenhouse field Foster Do in the 7 acres Baker threshing Hoad and G Guy wood cutting Easton not at work Father whent home and Mr Press visitor. Tis now mild weather.

Thursday 11
The Carters and David mouling in the Wenhouse field Foster Do on the 7

[258] Lady Huntingdon's Collection of hymns, used in all the chapels of her 'Connexion' and in other non-conformist chapels.

acres Baker threshing T Hoad and G Guy wood cutting T Hoads girls shave the hop poles Dame Hoad hass undertaken to shave some Easton not at work Father whent to Rushlake and I whent to the Halfmoon Market

Friday 12
Horses carried 2 Ash Trees to Rushlake Wheeler Baker threashing David Easton and Foster mouling at 3 places T Hoad and G Guy wood cutting I whent to Dallington in the morning and to Mr Reeves at Rushlake in the evening Elizabeth to Mrs Reeves Do Father whent to Ashburnham Place in the forenoon and with Mrs Lade (at Priory) (who dined) to Windmill Hill and Gardener Street etc. In the afternoon Dry morning wett evening hop pole shavers

Saturday 13
Carter David and I mouling in the Wenhouse field Easton and foster Do in the 7 acres T Hoad and G Guy wood cutting Hop poles shaving etc. John Trill Lade sleeps here to night nothing else perticular as I know off to day.

Sunday 14
Father mother Elizabeth David & I and the maid whent to the Heathfield Chapel in the morning I staid all day Mr Press preached from Hebrews 11 Ch 20th verse sung the hymns on the 484, 403 and 150 pages and from the 24 Cha Matthew 44 verse and the hymns on the 401-398 and the 128 pages home John Trill Lade sleeps here to night etc

Monday 15
Carter fetched a sack of peas from Stephen Goldsmith I helpt him clear 8 sacks and 2 bush oats mixt 3 sacks with the peas and horses drawed them to mill in the morning Wm Hoad with 2 horses and a cart whent to Mr Delves Windmill hill with Elizabeth who is a going to Lewes to morrow in Fullers cart Baker killed his hog in the morning and spreading dung in the Pound Field Hop garden till the rain drove him into the barn in the afternoon David and I finished mouling and Henry bound the brishings up in the Wenhouse field Easton and Foster mouling 7 acres Thos Hoad and G Guy wood cutting Furze wood hop pole shaving etc a young man out of the workhouse came with a note to Father from Mr H Blackman etc

Tuesday 16
Horses etc Carters began ploughing the 9 acres and fetched home the last load of stubble David helpt them gett it up rest of the workmen frost in the morning and rained in the afternoon nearly as yesterday Mother whent to Mrs R Russell's Josse Smith … etc visitors I drove Venus's sheep out of the

Kilnfield wheat David and I slopt the Hogs out of the orchard hop garden etc.

Wednesday 17
Horses carried 6 sacks of wheat to mill for the parish in the morning afterwards plough 9 acres Foster threshing Oats H.B. Baker Do In CB Easton mouling T Hoad and perhaps G Guy wood cutting Mr T Delves visitor J. T. Lade sleeps here to night last night was windy and wett weather nearly all night and a flood in the morning

Thursday 18
Prince Regents Thanksgiving day for the blessing of peace England is at peace with all the World after a most dreadful war etc Father I & David whent to Heathfield Chapel Mr Press preached from Thessalonians 5 Cha 18 verse sung the hymns on 264-471 and 444 pages Father whent to Cade Street

Friday 19
Horses not at work Wm Hoad sharping hop poles in the Grand field Henry chopping hop poles for the women and cleaned the hog penns out Baker threshing CB T Hoad and Foster Do HB Easton mouling G Guy wood cutting David and I drove the Ewes from Hodges to the 11 acre silverfield in the morning I had Old Jack shod in afternoon Butcher Walters visit for brought the old Black Fatten Cow by weight 4s 8d per stone etc there was a flood nearly all last night and showery to day.

Saturday 20
Carter gaping at different places and Had Gider and Smiler shod Baker threshing CB Foster Do HB T Hoad and G Guy wood cutting hop pole shavers – Easton mouling J Bland visitor J. T. Lade sleeps here to night – clear mild weather nearly all day rather freezes this evening etc.

Sunday 21
Father David & I whent to the Heathfield Chapel in morning Mr Press preached from John 17 Cha first part of the 24 verse sung the Hymns on the 11, 374 and 124 pages L.H.C. there has been so many showers of rain of late that it hass made rather better walking than it has been.

Monday 22
Horses plough in the 9 acres Baker threshing in … C.B. Foster Do in the afternoon in the HB T Hoad and G Guy wood cutting (hop pole shavers) Easton mouling I gapping in the hedge loading from the corner in the Old

1816

Lane to the gate against the mill flood gate hop garden David whent to Hunting Phillips the Game Keeper Dogs I have wrote very badly to night

Tuesday 23
Horses plough Baker spreading dung in the Pound field Hop garden Foster finished threshing oats in the Home Barn in the morning and mouling 7 acres in the afternoon I believe the other workmen where as yesterday. Mr Press preached a funeral sermon for Mrs Reinsford Ashburnham from Job 1 Cha and the latter part of the 21st verse The Lord gave etc. sung the hymns on the 403-398 and the 401 pages there was A good assembly altho it is dark & dirty chiefly women Mrs's Press and Bartlett and Mrs Dann stay all night John Trill Lade sleeps here tonight.

Wednesday 24
Horses plough Bakers whent to Burwash to pay his and Master John Hoad's Tithe to Mr Philcox's office for Our Parson who is now in Frame for debt. Foster not at work Easton mouling T Hoad & G Guy cutting (hop poles shavers) Mr Walters the butcher came to settle his account with father his son Stephen and Pledwell their journey man and drove the Black Fatten Cow to their shop Rushlake Green P brought a new hat of[f] Mrs J Fox for 3/9 Mrs Press and Bartlett whent away from here in the afternoon.

Thursday 25
Horses plough Baker finished spreading dung in the pound field hop garden Foster David and I cleared 19 sacks of head and 1 sack & 2 bushels Tail Oats all have is in this barn with 25 sacks and 3 bushels we cleared before Foster in morning threshing wheat in the afternoon T Hoad and G Guy wood cutting Easton not at work I whent to Sumertree to Dallington and Padgham after money but did not get a farthing in the after noon Mrs Lade whent to the Priory and had her husband home with her who sleeps here to night etc.

Friday 26
Horses plough Baker spreading Dung in orchard hop garden Easton mouling (in Fosters part) Foster threshing HB T Hoad & G Guy wood cutting Martha Hoad hop pole shaving David and I digging a piece of ground in the Brook Hop garden for to plant some Ash Key's Father whent to Mr Phillip's sliverash and to Rushlake green – Old Butcher Pledwell has been here to day they killed the cow yesterday he says she was at calf and weighed upwards of 16 stone a quarter or 64 stones whole.

Saturday 27
Horses plough Baker I and David cleaned some Oats over once and measured up some tail 14 bushells – Wm Harmer looked at a heifers foot and he and I whent to Dallington in the morning David and I got 6 wheel barrow loads of dung up into the up[p]er Garden at night Foster threshing Easton mouling T Hoad and G Guy wood cutting Girls hop pole shaving Father whent to windmill hill – J T Lade sleeps here to night it has been mild weather thiss 3 or 4 days.

Sunday 28
Father mother David and the maid whent to Heathfield chapel in the morning Mr Press preached from James 2nd Cha 24th verse sung the hymns on the 332-36 & 457 pages Mr Thos. Richardson came home with me to clean and repair our clock to morrow. J. T. Lade sleeps here to night he hass had his father ride home with him for Father to ride to Lewes on to Preston to morrow.

Monday 29
Horses mouling and picking up moul about house and carried into the orchard hop garden Baker hop digging in Do in morning Easton mouling T Hoad and G Guy wood cutting Old Dame Hoad hop pole shaving Foster threshing Baker and David stacked a 100 of hop poles out of furze wood into the 8 and 12 acres in the afternoon & Mr Richardson cleaned the clock and David and I helpt him move it from against the Brewhouse Door against the great window near the pantry door he also cleaned T Hoads and Mr Walters clock and sleeps here to night Father is Gone to Preston J T Lade sleeps here to night frosty yesterday and to day – I whent to Bodle Street in the afternoon.

Tuesday 30
Horses fetched a 1000 hop poles 25 fence poles and 5 ash from the 8 and 12 acres to the Poundfield Hop garden and the Polefield Baker and I spreading dung in the Croft and Finnished Hop garden we were freezed out from hop digging in the orchard T Hoad & G Guy wood cutting Easton finished mouling in the 7 acres Foster threshing Dame Hoad and Martha Hoad hop pole shaving Mr Richardson whent from here this morning J T Lade sleeps here to night wether Father will come home to night or not I don't know J Bland visitor.

1816

Windmill Hill Mill

Wednesday 31

Horses & David carried the rest of the dung that was mackound[259] up in the Pound Field last year and some of it taken away some time in December 5 lambs in the Brook orchard 3 into the Croft Hop garden in the morning I helpt them bring a load of ash from the Furze wood in the afternoon Foster threshing Home Barn Baker threshing in CB Easton sharping hop poles in the pound field in the hop garden Mrs Lade is gone to silverash Mr T Delves visitor Father slept last night at Mr Fowlers at Lamport came home to night at 20 minutes before 8 o'clock in the evening.

Thursday 1 February

Horses Baker David and the Carters carried 2450 12 & 13 feet poles into the Poundfield hop garden Easton sharpening Do Foster threshing T Hoad and G Guy wood cutting Father took T Hoads hop poles 4100 12 & 13 feet and 1000 14 feet I had Mr Lade's horse home and whent to Half Moon Market it is remarkable the wind being in the south there should be such a severe frost as there is.

Friday 2

Horses Baker David and I draw 1000 of 14 feet poles in to the Red Palefield and 1050 of 12 & 13 feet in to the poundfield hop garden Easton sharping Do T Hoad wood cutting Dame Hoad and Martha Hoad shaving hop poles Foster & G G not at work. Mrs Lade came home from silverash the frost seems to be going away.

Saturday 3

Carters unloaded the ash loaded last Wednesday and fetched a load of straw from Mr Thos Peter's to Hodge's I helpt them unload it – Baker dicking gaping loging up of ash etc. Easton sharping hop poles Foster threshing T Hoad and G Guy wood cutting hop poles shavers Reed the rat catcher and boy catched 20 rats Father and I have each got nose runny colds The frost seems to be gone away tis very dirty.

Sunday 4

Father mother David and I whent to Heathfield Chapel in the morning I stayed the after noon Mr Press preached from Isiah the 56 Cha the 10 verse Who is among you th[at] feareth the Lord, that obeys the voice of his servant that walketh in the darkness and hath no light? – Let him trust in the name of the Lord and stay upon his God – sung the hymns as on the

[259] Maxoned, mixened.

324 355 and the 309 pages in the morning and from Solomons songs 2nd Cha the first part of the 16 verse My beloved is mine and I am his sung the hymns on the 473-140 and the 238 pages in the afternoon J. T. Lade sleeps here to night.

Monday 5
Horses plow W & H Hoad T Hoad W Foster J Baker killed 2 hogs in morning Easton sharping poles in P garden after and of the stack in Poundfield afternoon T Hoad Wood & G Guy Foster threshing Baker gapping Will[?] Wood I Went to Mayfield on the road for London Father went Sliverash Mr Russell visitor

Tuesday 6
W & H Hoad & Horses plowed oxen Baker Carried old sow to Ashburnham Foster threshing T Hoad G Guy wood cutting morning afternoon. Threshing David went to Mr Russells for 4 gall[ons] of salt R Cornford brought off two our horse from being minded

Wednesday 7
T Hoad threshing Home Barn Baker threshing C Barn Wm Hoad chaff cutting John Honeysett visitor I mowed all day over in Grimes Wood

Thursday 8
W & H Hoads & Baker cleaned 35 sacks of oats CB T Hoad wood cutting Hodgshaw H Hoad shod 2 horses to be shoed & Fost[er] threshing in morning Eastone sharping poles in the P Field.

Friday 9
Horses W and H Hoad and Baker drawed 500 poles into P Garden from furze wood afterwards I fetched oats home carried into garret afterwards loaded 500 hundred poles in P field T Hoad cutting furze in 13 acres Eastone sharping poles in P field garden Foster threshing Mr Bennett brought 4 bushel of malt broke down borrows A dung cart to go to Brightling borrowed A ox off him to take the wheat with Mr Mannington visitor

Saturday 10
Horses carried 500 of the 14 feet hop poles to Brightling down Father and Baker made a round into Mr Couchman's hop garden from out of the 13 acres Baker carrying chucks up into the garret afterwards and threshing in the afternoon Easton sharping hop poles T Hoad wood cutting at Hodges G Guy Do in the Furze wood Foster not at work Forgotten Carter loaded up

Sunday 11

Father I David Mrs Lade and the maid whent to Heathfield Chapel in the morning Mr Press preached from 1 Corinthians 6 Cha and the two last verses sung the hymns on the 300 352 and the 177 pages J T Lade sleeps here to night

Monday 12

Wm Hoad and I with the horses carried 500 of the 14 feet poles to Brightling down and loaded up 500 more Henry not at work he has a bad hand David gaping etc C Baker threshing C B Foster Do HB T Hoad and G Guy wood cutting at 2 places (See Saturday) Easton not at work Father whent to Ashburnham Place Messrs John Trill James Trill Thos Pinyon Thos Lade Junr and John Trill Lade spent the evening with us in company I have ceased saying anything about the weather

Tuesday 13

Horses Wm Hoad and I as yesterday Henry not at work Baker threshing C B Foster Do in HB T Hoad wood cutting Hodges G Guy Do in the Furze wood Easton not at work Father whent to Battle Market David whent to Rushlake green in the evening.

Wednesday 14

Horses Wm Hoad and I as yesterday Wm Harmer had his waggon to the stack and Father and David helped us load it with 400 of 14 feet to go with us to morrow if the frost holds Baker threshing C B Foster Do in HB T Hoad wood cutting G Guy Easton and Henry not at work Robert Reeves had the ram home they have borrowed this season Father is gone out some where I don't know where

Thursday 15

Horses Wm Hoad and I carried 500 and Wm Harmer and his team 400 of 14 feet poles to down gate – David and Baker loaded our waggon with the rest of the poles in that stack. In Poundfield 437 in this load being 3337 in all Baker and David cleaning some oats over once in the forenoon Foster at work with G Guy wood cutting Easton sharping hop poles in the Poundfield T Hoad wood cutting Hodges Henry not at work Father and I whent to Halfmoon Market received the account of the Black cow she weighed 65 stone 6lb at 4/8d per stone £15 6s10d Mr G Adams the man we sold our poles to visitor J T Lade sleeps here to night The Waldron 4 year

---

again Deame home from London John Walters spent the evening with us J T Lade sleeps here to night Forgot Mrs Lade whent to Bellhurst old cow calved this forenoon I think I have wrote very badly to night

Friday 16

Horses Wm Hoad and Henry Hoad with 4 oxen and Baker to help them cleared the 437 hop poles to Redpalefield and loaded up 63 more to make it up a load of 500 and drawed them to down gate the frost is gone away Wm Hoad David and I loaded the waggon again with 500 new Poles in the Redpale field that came from the furze wood David and I cleared 14 sacks 1 bushel of Black Oats the last time over Baker helpt latter part Baker threshing in afternoon in CB Foster Do all day in HB Easton sharping hop poles G Guy wood cutting in the furze wood T Hoad Do at Hodges Mr Kemp successor to Tayton Heathfield[260] brought me a new pair of halfboots at 16s

Saturday 17

Horses and oxen carried the 500 of poles that was loaded up yesterday to Brightling Down Wm Hoad David & I loaded the waggon again Baker threshing whilst – David & I cleared 11 bushels of wheat and father helpt us carry 63 poles from furze wood to the Redpalefield I whent to mill with 2 bushels of wheat for a grist David flawed[261] one of the Marsh lambs Easton finished sharping 12 feet hop poles on the Poundfield G Guy & T Hoad wood cutting Martha shaving hop poles Foster not at work father whent to Windmillhill David whent to Rushlake J T Lade sleeps here to night

Sunday 18

Father Mother Mrs Lade David and I whent to the Heathfield Chapel in the morning Mr Press preached from Exodus 14th Cha the latter part of the 15th verse spoke unto the children of Israel that he go forward sung the hymns on the 286 295 and 138 pages J T Lade sleeps here to night

Monday 19

Horses oxen with the Carters and Baker whent to Brightling Down with 500 of 14 feet poles and brought home from the Chapel Barn 140 sacks 1

---

[260] Thomas Read Kemp (1782-1844) was MP for Lewes 1811-16, and for Arundel and Lewes again 1823-37. Between 1816 and 1823, he founded an evangelical sect and preached regularly. He initiated the development of Kemptown, named after him. Trayton Heathfield was more properly known as John Trayton Fuller (1743-1811). He married the daughter of George Augustus Elliot, Baron Heathfield, and lived at Heathfield Park; he signed his letters 'Heathfield'.

[261] Flayed, skinned.

bushel of Black Oats to the parlour Foster threshing Easton digging hop pound field garden G Guy wood cutting furze wood T Hoad Do at Hodges John Bland's team brought 6 sacks and 3 bushels of peas to Hodges – Mr R Russell visitor a lot of hunters called in the evening after beer J T Lade sleeps here to night

Tuesday 20
Horses plough in the 9 acres Easton digging hop & poundfield Baker threshing in morning helpt Foster and David clearing wheat in my room in afternoon I helpt them in the morning 8 sacks head and 3 bushels of tail wheat T Hoad hedging between the Squire and Furze fields G Guy I understand was with Pettitt Jesse Smith London away all day yesterday he was not at work to day I whent to the Heathfield Chapel in afternoon with the pony for Mr Press it being very dirty he preached a funeral sermon for Mr Wm Errey who took with a fit near the Half Moon Market whilst a going home and died at 4 O'Clock on Friday afternoon a sudden removal Mr Press preached from Revelations 14 Cha 13 verse Write blessed are the dead that die in the Lord from henceforth; yea saieth the spirit they may rest from their labours and their works do follow them sung the hymns on the 108 page George Gilbert's selection and the 398 and 279 pages L.H.C. – preached here this evening from Romans 8 Cha 9 verse sung the hymns on the 36 – 295 and the 4 pages L.H.C. Mr Bartlet and Mr Press stayed all night Mrs Lade whent to Priory she was at Heathfield Chapel

Wednesday 21
Horses finished ploughing the nine and the 8 acres Baker threshing Easton & Foster digging hops Master Pook and his boy 2 fresh commences with them in the Poundfield Garden G Guy and T Hoad wood cutting David & I digging off[f] ground in orchard for beans and peas Misses Press & Bartlett whent away from here in the afternoon Heathfield woods.

Thursday 22
Horses plough in the 13 acre & Baker and David digging hops in orchard I Do in the morning whent to the Half Moon Market in the afternoon Easton Foster Pook & his son digging hops Poundfield Garden T Hoad wood cutting and helpt his daughter shave some fence poles G Guy wood cutting J T Lade first called in morning on bussness can't recall any one else visitors

Friday 23
Wm Hoad sowed the Round Bank Highfield with peas Father and Henry with the horses harrowed them in I digging hops all day and believe all the

rest of the workmen as yesterday Mr T Delves eats his dinner here in a hurry M J Purstgove just called – and John Bland came to see Foster in the afternoon etc a fine sunshine day mild and warm

Saturday 24
Horses plough in the 13 acres I think I am certain David and I with all the workmen were at the same as yesterday – Father has been gone all day he said he should go to the Priory David whent to Rushlake and found Father at Mr Reeves but he did not come home with him Frost in the morning warm sunshine day

Sunday 25
Father I David and the maid whent to the Heathfield Chapel in morning Mr Bartlet preached from Isiah 6 cha first part of the 9th shall I bring to birth and not give strength to bring fourth sung the hymns on the 256-11 and the 281 pages I saw Mrs Lade there who is at the Priory

Monday 26
Horses plough in the 13 acres Baker I and David digging hops in orchard Easton Foster Old Pook and the boy Do in Pd Hop Garden Foster in Do afternoon T Hoad and G Guy wood cutting yesterday was a misty and windy day to day was a still sunshine day

Tuesday 27
Horses plough a little while in the morning but the rain drove them off Baker David catching mice in Chapel Barn in morning Baker David and I Wm Hoad and Henry Hoad digging hops in orchard Baker spread some dung Do in afternoon Easton digging hops in the Pound field garden I know but little about the other workmen Mr R Russel visitor etc

Wednesday 28
Horses plough in 13 acres Baker David and I digging hops in orchard in morning the two yearling colt at Calves Lodge broke out and came down here Father and David had him back again David dug a few more hops Father moved some gooseberry trees in the house garden Baker and I planted some peas beans and Early Blouoye Potatoes[262] in the upper garden all in the afternoon Easton Foster Pook & his boy digging hops on the Pound field T Hoad and G Guy wood cutting Mrs Lade came home from the Priory in the forenoon John Saunders the grinder[263] at Bucksteep Mill

[262] Blue-eyed potatoes.
[263] Miller.

came to look at some Wheat tonight etc

Thursday 29
Baker Carter and horses fetched some chucks from the Poundfield hop garden to the forcourt in the morning afterwards plowing hops Croft Baker and David digging Do Easton Foster Pook and boy digging of hops in Poundfield T Hoad wood cutting Hodge I know nothing about G Guy I whent to the Halfmoon Market called at Mr Reeves coming home John Trill Lade sleeps here to night frosty morning wind upward all day Bull pooked Jack the pony Mr Daimond Visitor to see colt

Friday 1 March
Horses plough in croft Baker David and I digging hops in Do after the plough I know but little about the other 4 hop diggers they were nearly freezed out in the morning T Hoad wood cutting Hodges and his girls shaving hop poles I know nothing about G Guy I broke my spud and had it mended Father whent to Bellhurst Mrs Lade is gone to Silverash

Saturday 2
Horses carried some kiln faggots from Poundfield to James Eastons Bodle Street afterwards plowing hops in the Croft and the orchard garden Baker David & I carried the chucks from the Court into the Garrett afterward digging hops in the Croft Easton Foster Pook & boy do in Pound field garden T Hoad and G Guy if at work wood cutting Mrs Lade came home last night before I came home

Sunday 3
Father I David with the maid whent to Heathfield Chapel in morning I Stayed the afternoon Mr Press preached in the morning and afternoon from John 11 chapter the latter part of the 36 verse sung the hymns on the 332-343 and 31 pages in the morning & from 351-295 and 161 pages in the afternoon Mr Wilmshurst at Jollinghous[264] was in here when I came home The words of the poet where Behold how he loved him

Monday 4
Horses plough in the 13 acres Baker David and I digging hops in croft

---

[264] The identity of this place was initially elusive. However, it appears to be Jollithous. From a marriage settlement of 1770 between Martha Baker and Henry Harcourt both of Warbleton, clause 10: 'A messuage, barn, buildings and [blank] acres called Jollithous in Warbleton, occupied by Thomas Waters'. (TNA ref: DUN 15/45, 46). Elsewhere Nicholas uses the correct form Jollithous.

Easton Foster Pook & son Do in Poundfield T Hoad and G Guy wood cutting Father whent to Jollinghous in the morning and is not come home tis near ½ past 8 O'Clock Messrs Dann & Buckland from Heathfield and Mr Reeves Rushlake visitors J.T.Lade sleeps here to night David flawed another marsh lamb in the morning

Tuesday 5

Horses plough Baker David & I finished digging hops in Croft at noon digging the ends of the alley after the plough etc in afternoon Baker and David throughed[265] a stubble stack into the ox close and carried 2 bundles of hay from there to the Calves Lodge a bad sine[266] that that stack is nearly gone Easton Foster Pook & boy digging hops in the Poundfield garden T Hoad and G Guy wood cutting – Father and I whent to Mr Smith's in the evening Mr Press preached from Genesis 3 chapter 9 verse sung the hymns on the 216=200 and 230 pages a slite[267] congregation

Wednesday 6

Horses plough David and I Baker killed 3 geese and hop digging in the Brook Easton Foster Pook & boy finished the Poundfield garden at noon not at work in afternoon T Hoad and G Guy wood cutting – Mr Wilmshurst Jollinghous visitors Father whent to the Hailsham Market and sold a hog at 4s per stone showery dirty weather

Thursday 7

Horses plough Baker digging hops in the Brook in forenoon David and he cleared some oats in afternoon Thos Hoad killed a hog in the morning afterwards wood cutting I think G Guy was wood cutting Father paid Old Pook and his son off Easton and Foster not at work John Bland visitor I whent to Silverash with a goose and dined there Father whent to the Priory in the evening Henry Fowle at Mr S Goldsmith came in evening and wanted a place

Friday 8

Wett weather all the forenoon we weighed the hog 30 stone 6 lbs Wm Hoad with 2 horses and a cart carried it to Pevensey to meet a man from Bourne at 4s per stone was £6-3s-od brought home 2 sacks of tares From Bellhurst Baker cutting chaff in the forenoon carried some hay to the Calves Lodge in

---

[265] Throwed.
[266] Sign.
[267] Slight.

the afternoon G Guy and T Hoad wood cutting Foster Easton not at work Henry Boseling[268] sometimes doing nothing Mr Wilmshurst at Jollinghous visitor Wm and James Harmer Do

Saturday 9
Horses brought some oats from the Chapel Barn home and carried 6 sacks to Mr Russell Warbleton Charles Baker etc David gaping at several places in forenoon Baker made a dridge in the Silverfield in the afternoon T Hoad wood cutting Hodges and made a small part of a hedge between the springfield and the millfield near the river G Guy wood cutting I suppose no other work man to day tis dirty walking frequent showers of rain hail and snow the wind is upwards and rather cold

Sunday 10
Father mother I David whent to Heathfield Chapel in morning Father and I stayed the afternoon Mr Press preached both times from Revelations 3 chapter 10 verse Mr Luck Our clerk not being there Mr Press gave out and we sung the hymns on the 11=13=446=274 324 and 328 pages – a fine drying day wind upwards J T Lade sleeps here to night

Monday 11
Horses finnished Ploughing in orchard and plough in 13 acres afterwards Baker Easton David and I finished our hop digging in the brook and planted some ash keys[269] etc Foster threshing wheat T Hoad wood cutting G Guy Do if at work Father talked of going to wind mill hill in morning whent to Warbleton church in the evening a misty wett day a windy and wett evening Father did not come home till late in the evening

Tuesday 12
Horses finished ploughing 13 acres about noon Baker through[270] the dung out of the cow lodge and put in some straw carried a bundle to the ox close and carried some hay to the Calves Lodge etc etc Foster threshing Easton and G Guy not at work etc perhaps not T Hoad wett weather nearly all day windy and wett in the evening I whent to Rushlake and Mr Russell Warbleton church Mr T Delves visitor and carried off a goose he had brought of Father alive there is a young gander left beside what are for breeders

[268] Bosseling: see glossary.
[269] Long seed of the ash tree.
[270] Threw.

Wednesday 13

Horses plough in the 7 acres Baker David and I way mending in the chapel and Chapelwood Meadow Foster threshing I suppose G Guy and Thos Hoad wood cutting Easton not at work Mrs Goldsmith Rushlake visitor in the morning Father whent to Mr John Cooks Herstmonceaux in evening came home at 8 o clock Mr Wm Wilmshurst on the common visitors a few minutes at night A clear sun shine drying day I made a mistake in saying that Father came home at 8 o clock it was shoemaker Waters called with a pair of halfboots for David Father did not come home till late.

Thursday 14

Horses plough Baker Easton Father I and David dressing hops in croft Foster threshing I understand that T Hoad finished wood cutting at Hodges yesterday and was a faggotting in the Furze wood to day and I suppose G Guy Do Mr T Delves and John Bland visitors John Trill Lade sleeps here to night Forgot the Dann's lite Red Heifer calved up in the six acres pell shaw Baker David and I had them home into the stall a bull calf

Friday 15

Horses drawed some hay from the Home stack to the Calves Lodge afterwards plough Father David I Easton and Baker Finished dressing croft about 10 o clock and begun The orchard hop garden Father cut some setts in the orchard Thos Hoad and G Guy wood cutting Mr Watters visitor in evening a windy day at work Henry Bosling some time doing nothing Mr Wilmshurst at Jollinghous visitor Wm and James Harmer do wrong leaf look back [comment to himself]

Saturday 16

Horses plough Father cutting setts David I Baker and Easton dressing. orchard in them at noon and dress the Brook hop garden T Hoad wood cutting I under stand it is uncertain Guy is at work or not – Mr J Reeves Rushlake visitors a sunshine day wett evening

Sunday 17

Father Mother David and I whent Heathfield Chapel in the morning Father and I stayed and the maid whent in the after noon Mr Press preached both times from Ephatians 6 chapter 13th verse sung the Hymns on the 406=256=404 pages in the morning was not soon enough to hear the first hymn on the afternoon the others where the 410 and the 462 pages J T Lade visitor sleeps here to night I had a New watch of Mr Richardson etc a pleasent day wett all evening

Monday 18
Horses plough a little while in the morning holiday keeping the rest of the day Baker Easton and I digging potato ground In the brook orchard about 2 hours in the morning Baker and Easton at it again in the after noon I at nothing David something in the sheep way in the morning at nothing else of consequence Foster not at work for us T Hoad wood cutting I know nothing about G Guy it rained nearly all the forenoon a fine afternoon – a girl by the name of Eastland from Windmill Hill after a place John Oxley and boy come to shoeing traveller etc Women brewing

Tuesday 19
Horse plough Baker Easton David and I dressing hops in the Poundfield Father cutting setts Foster threshing T Hoad wood cutting perhaps G Guy Mr Press preached in the evening from Luke 15 chap 20=21=22 23 and 24 verses sung the hymns and the 287 295 and 36 pages Forgot Easton had the seed to T Isted's Barn in the morning

Wednesday 20
Horses plough Father cutting setts Baker Easton David and I dressing Poundfield garden T Hoad wood cutting Foster threshing – I know nothing about G Guy Mr Press whent home forgot horses carried 14 sacks for Mr Smith Wheat to Bucksteep Mill

Thursday 21
Horses finished ploughing seven acres fetched the waggons from the Calves Lodge and loaded the trefoil pug Father cutting setts Easton Baker David and I dressing hops poundfield T Hoad wood cutting G Guy Do who hass been to Mayfield a hop digging Mr John Walters Junr and Preston visitors John Trill Lade sleeps here tonight Samuel Winchster has been here to day and mended our stairs made some rivits and mended the cribes and a pour of little jobs

Friday 22
Horses whent to Mr Saunders mill Waldron with the trefoil seed in the pug and left the waggon till it is done out Father cutting setts Mr Hall at Grovehill sent a cart a pair of oxen and a man after 14600[?] setts Baker Easton David and I dressing hops poundfield Foster threshing T Hoad and G Guy wood cutting some boys and girls after wood Mr Purstglove Visitor

Saturday 23
Horses plough in the Huglets at Hodges Father cutting setts Baker Easton I And David dressing hops in poundfield Foster threshing in the forenoon

not in after Noon Thos Hoad and G Guy wood cutting Messrs S Over John Fox and Mr Barns on Business

Sunday 24
Father mother I David and I whent to the Heathfield Chapel in the morning maid whent in the afternoon I stayed the afternoon Mr Press preached from Ephesians 6 chap 14 and 15 verses in the morning and from Philippians 1 chapter the fore last words of the 21st verse 'to die is gain' sung the hymns on the 266=406=91=403=394= and 107 pages Mr Richardson from Mayfield with two children visitors John Trill Lade sleeps here to night

Monday 25
Lady Day Horses plough Wm Hoad and Henry Hoad are the carters Easton Baker David and I finished dressing the hops and cut out the setts the whole number of setts is that 26100 this is Bakers last day Jane Gower is a going away T Hoad wood cutting G Guy is gone to Bourne I hear Father is gone to the meeting called Easter meeting at church Vincent David and Luke Lade's come after a stray sheep that strayed into our fields on the 19th of Febuary last forgot Foster threshing and master son Reed and boy catched the rats

Tuesday 26
Horses finished ploughing the Huglets and carried 3 loads of dung into T Hoad's orchard garden Easton David and I cleared 17 sacks and a bushel of oats and had them home with Oxen and a cart and carried a cart load of hay to the Calves Lodge in the forenoon Easton digging in the young orchard David and I gardening sowed the onions etc in the afternoon Foster threshing T Hoad wood cutting Dame Hoad who has been laid up some time with her sore leg hop pole shaving Mr J Erry horse and cart brought some Rye up for John Bland and Mr Peers Tyler James Oxley same after Mrs Richardson and her two daughters Wm Hoad and I whent to Gardiner Street after Elizabeth from Lewes Jane Gower whent away Philadelphia Eastland the new maid some sheep began to lamb

Wednesday 27
Horses harrow in the 7 acres Easton sowed two sacks tares and afterwards gardening David and I with oxen dredging in Silverfield T Hoad wood cutting (perhaps Dame Hoad shaving hop poles) Foster threshing Mr H Hall after the next of his hop setts J Bland sent after his 2000 Mr Richard Purstglove came with a heifer to bull J T Lade sleeps here to night

Thursday 28

Horses and carters sowing Black Oats and harrowed in the 13 acres oxen David and I dredging Silverfield Easton gardening heald the ash up dug the pound dicking in the Poundfield bottom and dug a piece of ground in the chapel wood meadow and T Hoad wood cutting Father not at work J Oxley the blacksmith put a ring on to the role[271] Mr John Lade Wm Isted and son come after some trefoil seed in the pug etc

Friday 29

Horses harrow in the 13 acres and carters sowed some oats oxen dredged the Pondscroft and carried the ashes out into the Chapel Meadow David and I the oxen Easton gardening etc Foster threshing T Hoad wood cutting a heifer has calved in the Poundfield this morning Colly was called at night between 9 & 10 o'clock Father whent to Rushlake Mr Wilmshurst at Jollinghous hass resigned his effects over to father and Mr Benn Walters Mr John Purstglove at Herstmonceaux is broke

Saturday 30

Horses finished harrowing 13 acres oxen fetched a load of straw from Mr Isted Easton helped us in the forenoon David and I planted a piece of ground with potatoes in the Chapel Wood meadow and Easton threshing oats in CB in afternoon Foster threshing wheat in the HB T Hoad wood cutting Father whent to Mayfield Mrs Lade is gone to the Priory

Sunday 31

Father I David Elizabeth and the maid whent to Heathfield Chapel in the morning Father stayed the afternoon Mr Press preached from the 6 chapter of Ephatians[272] the 14th, 15th, 16 and 17 verses in the morning and after noon with the 18 verse sung the hymns and the 21=13 and 158 pages in the morning Father has forgot two of the hymns in the afternoon one was on the 460 page hymn

Monday 1 April

Horses carried a 100 of Peabow faggots from furze wood to Mr Russell's I helpt them load them David and I heald 18 ash poles up in the wood planted the pound with potatoes etc and carried with a pair of oxen and a cart some hay from the home stack to the Calves Lodge Easton threshing CB Foster Do in the HB T Hoad and G Guy wood cutting forgot the carters

[271] Roller: a Cambridge or ring roller.
[272] Ephesians.

whent to the Priory after some barley and rye grass seed – Father whent to Rushlake guess I did not mention that on last Saturday David and I flawed a 4th dead Marsh Lamb out of 30 a few weeks back thing where drownded with wet now they are dry deep with cold winds and frosts

Tuesday 2
Horses went to Waldron after trefoil seed oxen fetched 250 kiln faggots 200 house faggots from the eight acres Easton finished threshing oats in the Chapel Barn and helped us carry faggots Father backed them out of the gill G Guy finished wood cutting David and Father took it T Hoad wood cutting Dame Hoad hop pole shaving Vincent Lade visitor Old Bowler died about 20 minutes before 6 O'Clock in the morning aged nineten old Smoke Calved in the afternoon David and I Elizabeth and the maid went up to Mr Smith's in the evening Mr Press preached 1 book of Thessalonians 5 chapter and 9 verse sung the hymns 229=230= 400 pages Forgot that Game Keeper Phillips flawed The old horse and carried him off with horse and cart

Wednesday 3
I sowed 3 sacks of barley and the horses shimed it in with Wm Harmer's great shim in the 8 acres T Hoad finished wood cutting in the Furze Wood G Guy and Easton began pole the Poundfield hop garden Foster threshing foderd for me at night I not being well Father went to Hailsham Market Mr Jesse Jarvis visitor in the evening and stopt till about 110'clock Wm Harmer and boy came after some rye grass seed

Thursday 4
David and I finished sowing the 8 acres with barley and sowed. sowed one sack of trefoil Horses shimed it in Easton and G Guy hop poling Foster threshing T Hoad hedging in the Huglets Hodges against the road David and I cleared the last lot of oats in the CB 6 sacks Head 3 bushels Tail Maid Wheat to windmill Hill

Friday 5
Horses shiming 8 acres Father sowed some trefoil seed I helpt a little while David I and Foster cleared 21 sacks and 3 bushels wheat G Guy and Easton hop poling T Hoad hedging Hodges Drove his cow to bull I supper Dame Hoad hop pole shaving Mr James Jarvis came after a sack of trefoil Mr Mepham and his boy drove his Marsh Lambs here to go home with Otto Morrys Mr Wilmshurst Jollinghous visitor Jesse Smith came and brought the wheat at 15£ 1

Saturday 6
Horses harrowed in the 8 acres and carried 14 sacks of wheat to Bucksteep Mill oxen carried 7 sacks to Do and whent to Mr Russell's with a 180 of faggots Father and I helpt Foster clear 3 or 4 bushels Tail Wheat afterwards Foster helpt me with the oxen G Guy and Easton hop poling T Hoad hedging David whent to Blackhorse near Battle with the sheep did not get home till rather late

Sunday 7
Father Mother I David and Elizabeth whent to Heathfield Chapel in the morning I stopt the afternoon Mr Press preached from Romans 5 Cha 28 and 21 verses both times sung the hymns on the 324-23-217-249-307 and 36 pages

Monday 8
Horses Carters sowing Long Tail White Oats in 9 acres and harrowed I whent to Windmill Hill after 2 bushels of clover seed of[f] Mr Curtis David and I with a pair of oxen and a cart carried some hay from the home stack to the Calves Lodge T Hoad hedging G Guy and Easton Hop poling Gamekeeper Phillips brought the money for of Bowlers hide 9s Foster is gone to Mayfield Mrs Lade came home from the Priory.

Tuesday 9
Father David and William Hoad finished sowing the 9 acres with oats and seed horses harrowed with a pair of oxen and a cart whent to Bectons with trefoil seed 4 sacks Foster threshing T Hoad hedging G Guy and Easton hop poling Messrs Benjn and John Waters visitors In the evening yearling heifer calved in the forenoon a cow calf

Wednesday 10
Horses and oxen carried a 1000 of 14 feet poles to Down Gate Foster threshing G Guy and Eason hop poling T Hoad brushing up some stuff in the orchard hop garden Father whent to Ashburnham a two speaned two

Thursday 11
It being wett weather there was not any body at work for Father he David and I took T Hoad's wood cutting J Bland and William visitors

Friday 12
Called Good Friday Horses carters sowed the Huglets and harrowed the long tail wight oats and the seeds in T Hoad and Easton Hop poling in the Pound field garden Foster and G Guy not at work Mr Mannington visitor

William whent home Hogs began eat a lamb alive and for a punishment are put in prison but I should suppose they will find bail before they are brought before the jury on cause of murder

Saturday 13
Horses and oxen carried 1000 hop poles to Down Gate at twice T Hoad and Easton hop poling Foster threshing G Guy not at work Father whent to Rushlake Mr Bennett and his brother brought a sack of malt forgot J T Lade slept here last night

Sunday 14
Father mother I David Elizabeth and maid whent to Heathfield Chapel in the morning Father and I stayed the afternoon Mr Press preached from the 24 cha Luke the 46 and 47 verses both times sung the hymns on the 332=415 199=404=407 and 189 pages There has been some snow to day an inch or more thick on the ground J T Lade sleeps here tonight

Monday 15
Horses and oxen carried 1050 = 14 [feet] hop poles to Down Gate T Hoad and Easton hop poling perhaps G Guy Do Foster not at work Mrs Lade was this day delivered of a son and are like to do well T Hoad whent after the doctor Mrs Diamond Dame Hoad in the nurse Wm Harmer and Henry Fowle came here this evening

Tuesday 16
Horses and oxen carried 1050=14 feet poles to Down Gate Foster threshing T Hoad Easton and perhaps G Guy hop poling David and Henry loaded the waggons and croling[273] a usual David and I whent to Mr Smiths in evening Mr Press preached from 1 Corinthians 1 cha part 21st verse It pleased God etc sung the hymns on the 332 151 and 420 pages Father was gone some where all day I never knew where

Wednesday 17
Nearly all as yesterday amongst us Harriot Phillips visitor – we carried only 1000 poles

Thursday 18
I with oxen carried the last 500 of poles to Down Gate horses helpt part of the way and finished harrowing the 9 acres we have completed the 10,000 poles for Mr Adams T Hoad hedging in the Redpale field against the pitt

[273] Crawling?

Friday 19
Foster threshing Easton and G Guy hop poling Elizabeth Lade visitor Father whent to Egypt in the evening

Saturday 20
Horses carried some stakes from Hodges to T Hoad's hedging and shining a piece of ground the uper and of the Croft for potatoes – I with 4 oxen dredged the chapel and chapelwood meadows T Hoad hedging Easton and G Guy hop poling Foster threshing Mr Reed and boy with dogs etc catched 36 rats J T Lade came to see his wife

Sunday 21
Father I Elizabeth and David whent to Heathfield Chapel in the morning Father stayed the afternoon Mr Press preached from Isiah 29 cha the 18 & 19 verses in the morning and from the 145 psalm 18 & 19 verses in the afternoon sung the hymns on the 247=318 & 267 pages in the morning and the 77=&121 in the afternoon I don't know the others David and I came home about the Tegs that where out of their pasture and have been very troublesome all the last week they where up against Couchmans John Trill Lade came to see his wife.

Monday 22
Horses drawed the potatoes harrowed Further part of the Croft and carried 100 house faggots from the wood at the bottom of the 12 acres to Mr Russels I with 4 oxen dredged the calves lodge meadow and the two meadows at Hodges in the forenoon roling in the Kilnfield in the afternoon T Hoad hedging Easton and G Guy hop poling Foster not at work Mrs Diamond came to see Mrs Lade Mr Wilmshurst Jollinghous came about some thing Mrs Bland visitor

Tuesday 23
Horses carried a chord of wood to Mr Russels Horseford a two yearling colt The first time I Father and David cut Some potato setts and planted Do further end of the Croft rest workmen as yesterday Master Callis and

Stephen Over on business J T Lade came to see his wife

Wednesday 24
Horses whent to Mr Russels with a chord of wood and loaded up another chord I with oxen roling 10 acres Foster and David helpt father cutting lambs cleared 6 sacks 3 bushels wheat helpt Dr Diamond men and Crowhurst there's lunge Dr Diamond colt[274] (they had him away) and cutting potatoes rest workmen as on Monday Messrs Willis from Wadhurst West carpenter and Ashley miller Kenwards grinder on business and perhaps more

Thursday 25
Horses whent to Mr Russels with chord wood and brought a load of Kiln Faggots from the 12 acres to The Kiln I finished roling 10 acres and began the 12 acres David and Foster potatoing T Hoad hedging forgot the Easton began pole the croft yesterday G Guy and he where here to day Mr Wilmhurst team Heathfield came after 5 sacks of wheat for S Over Messrs Delves Edmonds and Ven visitors Father whent to Heath field J T Lade came a short visit to see his wife in evening

Friday 26
Horses drawed all the hop poles and 150 house faggots (for T Hoad) from the Huglet shaw the hog plot Hodges I finished roling the 12 acres and Kilnfield David bosling Foster helpt carters rest workmen as yesterday Wm Stanford Esq and his man came setting out timber to fell Father whent to Gardener Street with them J T Lade came to see his wife Harriot Phillips visitor (pen wants mending)

Saturday 27
Horses harrowed and roled the peas at Hodges with S Goldsmith role who whent to harrowing his peas this is with us a new plow a farming to harrow peas after they are up[275] David and I with oxen drawed 550 hop poles from the wood to the Poundfield garden and 1500 out of the Poundfield into the Croft T Hoad hop poling Pd field Easton in the Croft Foster bosling G Guy not at work Crowhurst cut 4 calves David whent to Gardener Street this evening is not yet come home at ½ past nine O'clock Father has is and has been this for days rather unwell with a cold

[274] Train on a lunge rein.
[275] A new ploy for farming to harrow peas after they are up.

Sunday 28
Father mother Elizabeth David Ann and I whent to the Heathfield Chapel in the morning Father Elizabeth and I stayed and the maid whent in the afternoon Mr Kirby from Lewes preached from Isaiah 66 cha 13 and part of the 14 verse in the morning and from John 3 Cha 36 verse in the afternoon sung the hymns on the 352-177-215 268-121 I have forgot the other Mrs Lade came down stayers the first time since the 15th Inst her husband came to see her

Monday 29
Horses faggot carrying from Hodges to T Hoad's and Barton etc Foster and I drawed 139 hop pole from the wood to Poundfield garden and brought 13½ bushels of ashes from Mrs Yorkes to the Chapel meadow with oxen afterwards potatoing in the Brook Orchard T Hoad hop poling Guy and Easton not at work Wm Oxley from Heathfield and B Waters on business Father and David drove 2 of three yearling 3 two yearling and 6 yearling with 3 calves into the marsh

Tuesday 30
Foster helpt the oxmen and carters to carry 125 Kiln Faggots to Barton with 29 House Do 100 Kiln to Jo Clement[?] 200 Kiln Do brought home 2nd carried 200 home to Wm Hoad's rest workmen Hop poling Mrs Phillips visitor Brother Wm Oxley has left his place Father whent out somewhere I don't know where forgot Wm Harmer came 4 times after Kiln Faggots

Wednesday 1 May
Horses and oxen drawed 600 Kiln Faggots and stacked up in the Furzefield and drawed 600 home Wm Foster helpt us Do Easton G Guy and T Hoad hop poling in the Croft and Brook gardens Father whent to Hailsham Market and to Heathfield mother whent to Heathfield also to my uncle Wm Oxleys wives funeral at Chapel who died on last Saturday morning at a quarter past 4 o'clock Mr Press preached from ………………… Wm whent To Hailsham Market in the afternoon Elizabeth Lade visitor

Thursday 2
Horses and oxen stacked 600 kiln faggots as yesterday drawed 500 of 12 feet hop poles to the Brook garden 413 kiln faggots home Foster helpt in the 3 work men hop poling Mr Baker shaving hop poles Wm Harmer came twice more and hass gott all his 600 kiln faggots Wm had Mr Lade horse home that Father borrowed on Sunday last The Winchester's came to felling and flawing timber

Friday 3
Horses and 2 oxen Wm Hoad and I carried 150 house faggots to Loydes Wind Mill Hill David Willm and Henry cleared the Poundfield garden of old poles and chucks with 2 oxen and planted some potatoes in the Brook 2 hop polers in orchard G Guy not at work forgot the we brought 500 of 12 feet poles from Hodges to the orchard etc Cherry cow calved a bull calf she is the last of the seven 5 bull calves and 2 cow calves all a live – J Bland J T Lade and Mr Russel the School Master visitors and on business forgot Master Dann Tanflower[276]

Saturday 4
Horses carried 100 faggots to Mr Morris and 30 bundles of thick rods to Mr J Scrace Boreham I helpt them with 4 oxen out at Wind Mill Hill Wm fetched his boxes from Priory with a pair of oxen and a cart Foster bosling 3 workmen hop poling orchard Tanflower Messrs Reeves Jo Dann Barnes the shoemaker and others on business S Over has sent a rig horse[277] on trial at 18£ 10s Master Dann hop poling croft

Sunday 5
Father I and William whent to Heath field Chapel in the morning William stayed the afternoon A young man I don't know preached from Galatians 2nd Cha 20th verse and sung the hymns on the 11=354 and the 231 pages in the morning William forgot where the text was in the afternoon but says the (Luke 12 32) words where 'fear not little flock it is your Fathers good pleasure to give you the Kingdom' David whent to Gardener Street to hear Mr Pitcher

Monday 6
Horses drawed 150 poles into the Croft and a load into the orchard and Carried 100 faggots to the Blacksmith T Hoad Easton and G Guy hop poling orchard Old Dann Do in the croft Dame Dann hop tieing in the brook (she sleeps here) Foster threshing Winchester Tanflower William David and I bosling Wm Dray J Phillips and Master Buss on business Harriot Phillips Visitor

Tuesday 7
Carters David and I with the horses shiming Pdfield hop garden Dame

[276] Tan-Flawing: taking the bark off trees, the bark itself being called tan. The bark of the oak tree was used for tanning skins to make leather .
[277] One with only one testicle, or imperfectly castrated.

Dann Dame Baker hop ties 4 hop poles Tanflowers purchased a runt of Miller[?] Reeves for £5 10s Robt Reeves hawker have 2 other went to Beastons William lumping chuck in the Archard Foster threshing

Wednesday 8
Horses carried 725 hop poles from the wood to the orchard hop garden 3 hop polers there and one in the croft 2 hop tying another Foster threshing Mr Jo Dann drove a barren cow here Wm and I drove 2 barren and Old Smoke Cow and her calf Into the Marsh S Over had his horse pocked[278] Mr Russel visitor etc the bull poked The yearling colt in the thigh

Thursday 9
Horses carried 16 sacks of oats to Mr S Over Heathfield at 29s per Qr and carried 112 Kiln Faggots to Bodle Street for Wm Foster from the wood William Dann and I with oxen drawed 200 of 13 feet poles to the orchard garden in from the wood and a load of old poles from the croft the house etc we where boseling cinder[?] Foster threshing 3 hop polers in the orchard and I in the croft Dame Dann tieing in the orchard nothing particular besides but the Tanflower

Friday 10
Carters David and I shining with the horse in the Poundfield in the morning till the rain drove us home Dame Dann tieing hops in the morning 4 hop polers Do Foster threshing Wm drawed with a pair of oxen a part of from the Furze wood to the upper Redpalefield gate Messrs Winchester and Morfey came to see about the Oast forgot the Tanflower and I under stand a young man by the name of Apps has put a period to his Earthly existance by hanging himself In Mr Bennetts barn this forenoon[279] and Mrs Beal (Morfeys eldest daughter) sent out to night – shut the Waldron cows calf up to weaned

Saturday 11
Horses shimed T Hoads plot in The forenoon nothing in the afternoon T Hoad top cutting old Dann hop poling Paid G Guy off Foster not at work – Father whent to Warbleton Church William David and I whent to Mr Bennetts the Coroners verdict was sumary Forgot Easton casting up dung In the calves lodge ½ day Mr Purstglove and Mr Jn Waters Junr visitors

[278] Poked.
[279] Richard Apps hanged himself in Mr Bennett's barn; he was certified as a lunatic.

Sunday 12
Father mother William David Maid Elizabeth and I whent to Heathfield Chapel in the morning Father William and I stayed the afternoon Mr Press preached twice from Hebrews 2nd chapter 10th verse sung the hymns on the 185=316=49=194=329 and the 357 pages J T Lade came to see his wife

Monday 13
Horses carters and David clearing hop garden of chuck and old poles Wm and I getting chucks out of the orchard hop garden with a wheel barrow in the forenoon I all day William helpt Richard Winchester about setting up a post in the upper gate in the Redpale field Foster borrowed 4 oxen and a cart to fetch some bricks from the Tilly Kilns Easton and old Dann hop poling in the croft T Hoad top cutting Winchester flowing etc Mr Richard Purstglove had two heifers here and drove away two steers etc etc Messrs G Gillick[280] and Wm Wilmshurst on business

Tuesday 14
Horses not at work Wm Hoad and Easton gaping in the silverfield etc T Hoad top cutting Foster threshing Old Dann finished hop poling Winchesters Tanflowing this day we are in preparation of driving the beast to Winchelsea to morrow Mr Mepham and boy came with his 8 to Balcombe sent a man and his boy with his 5 and 2 colts Mr T Lade sent. sent 2 colts Mr James Lade and Mr Goldsmith had 10 of them[?] Wm Lade sleeps here to night and thinks of Going with me to morrow Mr Press baptised J T Lade's child its name is Caleb and Preached here to night from (I have Forgot where but the words where) 'and to know the love of Christ which surpasses Knowledge'[281]

Wednesday 15
Wm Hoad chaff cutting T Hoad top cutting girls hop pole shaving David and Henry cutting up thistles in Grimes Brook Wm Lade I John Waters and Trill Lade drove 3 bullocks and 6 colts to Winchelsea and bullock part of the way afterwards got as far as Ore Father whent to Wartling Hill and to Hailsham Market

Thursday 16
Horses Carters Easton David and Wm carried 54 loads of dung from the yard to below the barn in a Maxon T Hoad top cutting girls hop pole

[280] Gillard?
[281] Ephesians 3:19.

shaving Foster threshing forgot he was not at work yesterday Old Dann Hoath faggoting in the 13 acres Mesrs Cooper and Ellis Vinn on business. Tanflowers

Friday 17
Horses carters David and I shimed the Croft and part of the orchard garden Easton gaping Foster not at work T Hoad girls and Old Dann as yesterday Wm drove a cow and a calf into the marsh Mr Newman and a boy from Alfriston came to look at the bark Tanflower etc forgot the Joseph Morfey white washed the parlour and part of the kitchen yesterday Foster came after some alder poles to Build his house with

Saturday 18
Horses carters David and I shiming in the croft brook and Pound field gardens Foster Easton and Willm cleared 10 sacks and 2 bushels head and 3 bushels tail wheat T Hoad the Tanflowers and Old Dann as on Thursday Father whent Rush lake Green Mr Steer brought Wm a new sett of clothes

Sunday 19
Father Elizabeth Mr Lade I David and William whent to Heathfield Chapel in the morning Father William and I stayed the afternoon Mr Press preached from Corinthians 2nd chapter the 12th verse both times sung the hymns on the 404=295=411=474 and I think the 469 also the 150 pages maid whent to Herstmonceaux Wm whent to Mrs Sobers in the evening J T Lade slept Here last night and sleeps here again tonight

Monday 20
Horses carters David and William shiming in the Poundfield hop garden and fetched 600 of 12 feet poles from the Furze wood to the Poundfield Easton hop chopping in the orchard I roled the 13 acre oats T Hoad top cutting Old Dann Hoath faggoting some hop ties hop pole shavers and tanflowers Mr J Dann and Father whent down in the marsh and Father did business by way exchanging a heifer and the interest of 25£ for one year for a barren and two calves Mr John Waters Junr came here with a cow to bull Mr T Delves just called Charlotte Haffenden one of our old maids visitor Foster not at work

Tuesday 21
Horses carried 100 house faggots to Master Brooks Wartling Hill I roled the 8 acres with oxen Easton hop chopping T Hoad top cutting Tanflowers finished in the Furze wood hop pole shavers hop tiers etc Foster not at work Old Dann Hoath faggoting Mr Russel visitor I forget any more

Wednesday 22
Horses are gone to Bourne Pett after chalk and one to Ladye[282] at Wartling Hill to night I rolled the tares in the 7 acres some of the oats In the 9 acres and all the Huglets oats at Hodges David helpt me have William Harmers Great shim home Easton shim home chopping Old Dann Hoath faggoting T Hoad top cutting I think if they have not done his girls are a hop pole shaving – hop tiers – the tanflowers are at Hodges Foster not at work Wm whent to Purstgloves sale Hurstmonceaux J Bland and Aunt Elizabeth Oxley visitors

Thursday 23
Horses whent from Wartling Hill to Bourne pett and home oxen David & I carried 2 loads of hop poles from the wood to the Poundfield and 1 load from Hodges to the Poundfield and turned out in the further silverfield there is but little grass the weather being so unforeseeable the grass don't grow and we are so short of fodder we cannot keep them in any longer Easton hop chopping Old Dann Houth faggoting Foster not at work for us T Hoad top cutting Tanflowers hoptiers etc Farther whent to Heathfield Wm had a day home with him from the sale last night and he got out and whent home again Wm whent after him again to night and exchanged it with T Isted for his old snep[?] – Trill Wm Oxley and Mr Mannington visitors I whent as far as Heathfield Chapel with aunt uncle going home Elizabeth Do part of the way up Harrises Hill.

Friday 24
Horses carried 100 hop faggots to Mr Brooks Wartling Hill oxen David and I carried 100 top faggots from the wood to Wm Fosters new house and 462 hop poles from Hodges to the Poundfield Easton hop chopping Old Dann Houth faggoting Foster not at work I believe the Winchesters have done felling timber on our farms T Hoad hop cutting Mr Newman and a young lad with came about the bark – Harriot Phillips visitor I think Wm is gone home with her I whent to Dallington Fair to see Mr Wallis from Wadhurst but did not J T Lade sleeps here to night I think mine is very bad writing to night pen wants mending

Saturday 25
Horses carried 100 house faggots to Mr Waters the shoemaker Rushlake from the wood oxen carried 100 top faggots from the Calves Lodge

---

[282] Lade?

meadow to Wm Fosters new house and fetched the last of the hop poles at Hodges to the Poundfield two teams came after bark T Hoad top cutting Easton hop chopping Old Dann Hoath faggoting Dame Dann whent home yesterday maid weeding yesterday in the Kilnfield I know nothing about the other women folks Wm is gone to Stream Mill at Chiddingly I whent to Gardener Street in evening and was measured for a new pair of Buckskin Breeches

Sunday 26

Father Mother Elizabeth David and I whent to Heathfield Chapel in the morning maid whent in afternoon Father David and Elizabeth stayed all day Wm was there both times and came home with Mr Press preached from Isiah 22 cha 24 verse in the morning and sung the hymns on the 108=197 I have forgot the other page And preached from Matthew the 24 cha 44 verse in the afternoon the forgot the Hymns J T Lade sleeps here to night Mrs Lade Ann and mother whent to Redpale Mr Delves is very ill

Monday 27

Horse whent to Bourne after chalk to stay at Wartling Hill it was a very wett morning Foster threshing T Hoad top cutting Easton not at work Mrs Baker and Dame Dann came hop tieing in the afternoon David and I planted some cucumber seed at the Calves Lodge Wm whent to Mr Russels at Church in afternoon brought some small cabbage plants and some Redruff Beans etc we were gardening in the evening there has been frequent running too and fro to the Redpale from there here

Tuesday 28

Horses whent to Bourne and home with chalk oxen I David & Wm carried 44 loads of dung to the mackson below the barn Foster helpt us T Hoad top cutting Old Dann Houth faggoting Easton hop chopping in the afternoon hop tiers etc Father mother I Willm David Elizabeth and the maid whent to Mr Smiths in the evening Mr Press preached from Matthew 15 Cha the later part of the 13 and the 14 verse 'every plant etc' sung the hymns on the 307=78 and 318 pages

Wednesday 29

Horses carried 50 top Faggots ½ cart chopped up wood to Wm Hoad's and some chord wood and faggot home from the Calves lodge. Oxen drawed 2 oaks and 2 ash trees into the hay plot Hodges farm from the Huglet shaw and the 2 meadows and 27 oaks and 3 ash trees from the Calves lodge meadow into the silver field T Hoad top cutting Easton hop sharping

Foster threshing, Old Dann Hoath faggoting hop tiers Wm and I whent to Gardner Street in evening Father went to Hailsham Market J.T. Lade sleeps here tonight as team came after dark.

Thursday 30
Horses carried 50 top and 50 house faggots to old Master Honds and brought some rist leats and fence poles home from the wood David and William gardening etc. Easton hop choping in the Croft T Hoad top cutting Old Dann Heath faggoting. Foster threshing. Hoptins[?] and I whent to Mayfield Fair Father David and Elizabeth whent to Mrs Dobs[283] stonehouse to hear the Reverend T.P. Hugh preach from Hebrews 2 Cha first part of the 3rd verse.

Friday 31
Horses are gone after chalk Oxen ploughing the 7 acres rest of the work men as yesterday 2 teams fetched away the rest of the bark I think there was nothing else in particular.

Saturday 1 June
Horse came home with some Chalk …… Oxen plough rest of the workmen as on Thursday Father whent to Rushlake Green at the sale of Wilmshurst house I went to Gardner Street after my breeches J T Lade sleeps here to night

Sunday 2
Father, Mother and I William Elizabeth and the maid went to Heathfield Chapel in the morning. Father and I stay in the after noon. William went some where I don't know where in the after noon but perhaps to Horeham[284]. Mr Press preached twice from 118 Psalm the first part of the 3rd verse I here forget some of the hymns some where in the 161 = 256 = = and the 134 pages J.T. Lade sleeps here tonight Carter turned the horses out into the Millfield at Hodges.

Monday 3
Horses and oxen plough in the 7 acres and yoked a pair of 3 yearling steers the first time in the morning but did not work them. T Hoad top cutting Easton hop chopping Old Dann Hoath faggoting Foster threshing in the morning finished threshing wheat he killed 25 or 26 rats hop tiers etc Father whent to wind mill hill Elizabeth is gone with Elizabeth Lade to Mrs

283 Sobers.
284 Horam.

Bornor's[285] near the Black Horse Battle Vinette Lade had her horse home.

Tuesday 4

Horse plough Oxen went to Wartling Hill after chalk worked the steer the first time Father whent with us T Hoad hop cutting. Old Dann Hoath Faggotting Easton hop chopping Foster not at work hop tiers weeders etc I whent to Mayfield in the evening

Wednesday 5

Horses and oxen drawed 52 trees together in the furze wood Thos Hoad finished top cutting rest of the workmen as on yesterday Mr Preston Visitor forgot that we broke 3 chains. David had them mended

Thursday 6

Horses finished ploughing 7 acres and carried 100 top faggots Old master Hoad Oxen finished drawing 6 trees together and brought a 100 load of top faggots home and T Hoad and Easton hop chopping Old Dann Hoath faggoting hop ties etc Old Evenden and his Loth cleaving timber for wattle Elizabeth whent to Heathfield and to the Stonehouse in the Evening Father I William and David whent to Stonehouse Mr Kemp preached from these words 'for no other foundations can any man lay than that is laid which is Jesus Christ'

Friday 7

Horses whent to Bourn after chalk Oxen went to Wartling Hill after chalk Broke a pair of oxsteers and had a pair of Oxen of Wm Harmer rest of workman as yester day Wm Stanford Esq and his man on business JT Lade sleeps here tonight

Saturday 8

Horses came home with chalk Oxen fetched 2½ chord wood and 100 tops and 50 House Faggots T Hoad and Easton Hop chopping Foster not at work Old Dann Heath faggoting Hop ties Etc

Sunday 9

Father Mother I William David Elizabeth and the Maid whent to Heathfield chapel in the morning William also in the afternoon Mr Press preached from Isiah 33 chapter 22nd verse and sung the Hymns on the 254=438=467 pages Father Wm David and Elizabeth whent to Mrs Sobers in the evening

[285] This is likely to be Elizabeth Bourner née Lade (1766-1847), who married James Bourner (1752-1830); or possibly her mother-in-law Mary Bourner née Smith (1724-1816), who married Joseph Bourner (1725-96). The Bourners lived at Battle.

J T Lade came and had his wife and son away with him I had the swarm of bees today

Monday 10
Horses plough in the Furzefield Oxen whent to Wartling Hill after chalk had Wm Harmers 4 oxen with us Foster Wm and T Hoad cleaned the last of the wheat 6 sacks and a bushel Easton Hop choping Old Dann Heath faggoting Hop ties etc Father whent into the Marsh and had 3 cows and 3 calves home. Forgot he worked our steers the second time on last Saturday

Tuesday 11
Horses carried a load of Faggots Mrs Daws at the Cosway[286] and 75 faggots and a ¼ of a chord of wood Down against Hurstmonceux Chapel Foster Easton and I carried 58 loads of Dung with oxen from the Close to below the Barn T Hoad sharping Hop poles in the Poundfield several people after work etc Hop tiers Old Dann Hoath faggoting Mr Press preached this evening from John the 15 Chap 5 verse Sung the Hymns in the 352 = 264 = 16 pages Mr & Mrs Press and two children sleep here tonight I had a swarm of Bees 2nd first swarm

Wednesday 12
Horses gone to Bourn oxen I Wm David Foster and Easton mouling 7 acres carried 49 loads Old Dann Hoath faggoting T Hoad sharping Hop poles Hopties etc Mr Robt Cornwell came on business Mr Press whent home

Thursday 13
Horses at Bourn Easton Foster David & I mouling 7 acres carried 55 loads T Hoad Sharping Hop poles Old Dann Hoath faggoting Mrs Baker Hoptieing etc Mrs Press and her two children whent Hoam. Father went up to Belhurst Wm went Half Moon Market

Friday 14
Horses at Bourn I David Easton Foster mouling 7 acres Carried 62 loads T Hoad sharping Hop poles Old Dann Hoath faggoting Old Evenden & his Wife Lot cleaves timber for Wattles etc Father went to Heathfield Forgot that Wm whent to Heathfield on last Tuesday morning and Mr Purley too sent after his Heifers.

Saturday 15
Horses load 3 loads of chalk at Wartling Hill and brought one home Oxen

[286] Crossways?

mouling carried about 60 loads and Easton Foster David and I Do T Hoad finish sharping and stacking Hop poles in the Poundfield Mr Barnett Cut a 2 yearling Colt etc etc

Sunday 16
Maid went to Hurstmonceux all the rest of us whent to Heathfield Chapel in the morning Father Wm and I stayed the afternoon. Mr Press preached from Romans 8 Cha 2 verse in the morning and from Hebrews 11 Chap 24-25 and the 26 verses and sung the Hymns on the 294=274=224 177=184 and the 167 pages

Monday 17
Horses shiming Hops Poundfield garden Easton Foster T Hoad and I with the oxen got out 67 loads of Moul in the 7 acres Wm and David hoeing potato Maid weeding in the 12 acres Mrs Lade came home from Priory with her son. I had a swarm of bees come Father hived them

Tuesday 18
Horses shiming Poundfield and the Croft gardens Oxen carried 60 loads as on yesterday Wm and David with a Horse and cart brought some chucks home from the Poundfield and chopt some potatoes etc Maid weeding Mr T Woodhouse from Hailsham visitor JT Lade sleeps here to night I understand that David has left of keeping an account of the weather I think I shall do it for the future it has been a remarkably cold summer last Friday and Saturday were very cold Sunday mild Monday warm to day mild the wind chiefly upwards.

Wednesday 19
Sunday warm sunshine day the wind in the West Horses shiming Hops Oxen mouling as on Monday carried 80 Loads in field rather better began another range Wm and David Bosling etc

Thursday 20
Horses are gone to Bourne after chalk the lay at Wartling Hill Wm and David had the 2 yearling colt down in the Marsh Oxen and workmen as on Monday carried 70 loads Faggot[287] about the weather which should stand first a warm day rather cloudy in the afternoon the wind in the SWW and NW Mrs Lade and son are gone to the Priory again Father I Wm David and Elizabeth whent to Stonehouse in the Evening the Reverend T. R. Kemp preached from the 10th verse of the 2nd chapter of Luke

[287] Forgot.

Friday 21

A warm day a few clouds and the wind changeable from the North to the South West Horses are not at home Oxen workmen etc carried 76 load of Moul as on Monday Father whent to Horam Waldron Miss Philly Cornford and her brother Richd Cornford the Snr customer visitors.

Saturday 22

A cold foggy morning warm in the middle of the day and some clouds the wind in the East in the morning afterwards in the the South Horses laid out 2 loads of chalk at Wartling Hill yesterday and Thursday and brought a part of 1 load home today from Bourne Oxen and the workmen as on Monday Carried 64 loads we where a Fishing afterwards in the River catchd 57 Eels and 41 Trout the Honerable Lady Mrs Sober Mrs Cramp and her Daughter visitors Mr Robt Russell Do Father whent to Heathfield

Sunday 23

A Cold Cloudy day and but little sun wind in the West Father Mother I Wm David Elizabeth Ann and the Maid whent to Heathfield Chapel and left the House empty in the morning Father Wm David and Elizabeth stayed at home the afternoon Mr Day preached from Romans 3 Chap 21st and 22nd verses in the morning and sung Hymns on the 444=445=240 pages I have not enquired about the afternoon. Wm I David and Elizabeth whent to Mrs Sobers in the Evening Mr Press preached from Matthew 1 Cha 21st verse

Monday 24

This day is nearly as yesterday the wind more northward and rather colder Horses David and the Carter carried 1000 Heath faggots from the 13 acres to the Kiln oxen I T Hoad Easton and Foster [4 of us] carried 77 loads of moul in the 7 acres Father and Wm cleared the upper part of the oast out ready to be pulled down tomorrow Mr Gower a new comer hoeing wheat in the Kiln field Wm and I whent to Gardner Street Chapel in the Evening Mr Martel preached from Kings 2 Book the 5 Cha and the 14 verse

Tuesday 25

A very warm day clear in the morning rather cloudy in the afternoon the wind sometimes N and sometimes W etc Horses finished fetching home the Heath faggot from the 13 acres Oxen 3 workmen and I carried the coals from the Old Oast to the one near the Pound and finished mouling 7 acres carried 16 loads afterwards T Hoad and I got home some of T Hoad wood Chuck etc from the wood to his House with oxen Foster and Easton not at work in the morn while Master Gawen[288] Hoeing wheat and sowing turnips in the kiln field etc The Winchester's and Morssey[289] and his Men pulled the Timber work of the Old oast down Dame Dann and her grandaughter finished Hop thinning Ann is at school at Mrs York's all except David whent to Mr Smith and Mr Day preached from Mark the 16 Cha the 15 verse have forgotten some of the Hymns etc.

Wednesday 26
Mild warm day wind in the south cloudy morning rain all the afternoon and a wet Evening Horses ploughed the head lands where the Moul was in the 7 acres and drawed some of the old Timber from the Old Oast up into the Poundfield for the new oast Oxen carried 26 loads of dirt from the Hedgerow in the Poundfield against the Croft gate up into the Poundfield David Honeysett a new cowman Wm Foster Wm David and I do Filled and Shelved T Hoad and Easton began Mow in the Squirefield the rain drove us all off at noon Old Gower hoeing Wheat ditto David Honeysett and Foster cleaned one Head of the Home Barn out in the afternoon Mr Press and Mr Day Visitors Mr Day was not well he stays all night Wm whent part of the way home with Mr Press to have the horse back etc

Thursday 27
Wether it has rained all night or not I can't tell I slept to fast to know but it rained this morning till nearly noon and some showers in the afternoon the wind veered from the South to nearly north not very cold but a warm pleasant showery as there has not been no rain for some time that probably may do a great deal of good Carters T Hoad Wm David and I cleaned out the other Head of the Barn Moved the straw etc etc catch I think 12 Rats in the morning Horses drawed some old Timber from the oast to the Poundfield oxen Easton and Foster David Honeysett snr David and I carried 24 loads of the hedge away for the new oast and T Hoad clipping hedges in the afternoon turned the 4 oxen into the Bushey field Wm whent with Mr Day to Rushlake to take the horse back Father Wm David and I whent to the Stonehouse this evening the Reverend Mr Kemp preached from Johns Gospel 1 Cha the latter part of the 29 verse 'Behold the Lamb of God that taketh away the sin of the World'

Friday 28
A few clouds about but no rain rather inclining as be cold wind in the

---

[288] Gower.
[289] Morfey?

North Horses fetched 5 loads of sand from over Mrs York's to against the Pound to build the new oast with etc Oxen Foster David Honeysett Wm David I and G Gray (a new comer) carried 39 load of Moul Dirt away from the Hedgerow T Hoad and Easton mowing the Martins where filling the lime kiln they began on Wednesday not here yesterday etc John Bland his wife and Children Visitors Mr H Christmas Do called Master Delves mother has been very ill brought our close stool or sitting chair home Father whent to Horeham Waldron

Saturday 29
A warm sunshine day with some clouds the wind in the south and very still Horses carried 75 Faggots and 1/4 of a chord of wood to Master Lusteds against Herstmonceux Chapel and some Boards from the Old Oast to where the new one is to be Oxen 3 workmen (as yesterday) plowed up and removed 66 loads of Moul not in the Hedgerow by just by in the field T Hoad and Easton Mowing old Gower Hoeing wheat in the Kilnfield William whent to our proposed going to Rushlake to see Robt Reeves in the afternoon Elizabeth and I whent to Gardner Street.

Sunday 30
A Mild day some clouds about the wind from the SW to NW Father Mother I William David and Elizabeth whent to Heathfield Chapel Mother Wm and I stayed the afternoon Mr Day preached from Acts 11 Cha 23 verse in the morning and from Hebrews 9 Cha 28 or last verse and sung from the Hymns on the 490=492 pages Mother Willm David and Elizabeth the maid and Ann whent to the Stone House in the evening Mrs Sobers spoke from these words (I forget to where they were) 'Jesus says unto him I am the way' to a numerous and respectful congregation.

Monday 1 July
A showery morning very mild and still some sunshine in the afternoon and some clouds the wind moved from the south to the North west Horses carried a chord of wood to Mr Barns Dallington and brought a chord of wood home and laid it down against the Winhouse David & Foster & Honeysett G Gray and I with 6 oxen and 3 carts carried 66 loads or there about from home yards to the Poundfield upon[?] that Moul or Dirt carried from the Hedgerows T Hoad and Easton mowing the Bushey field I don't know much about old Gower and old Evenden and his wife etc. Father whent down into the Marsh Wm had the prongs sharpened at the Blacksmiths ready for Haying etc

Tuesday 2

A mild pleasant sunshine day some rain in the Evening the Wind in the South West Horses whent to Wallsend after 3 ½ tons of Beach to between Redpale and Dolves Oxen carried 40 loads of Dung from the home yards 13 loads of Moul and rot litter from the new hayrick and 2 loads of Dung from the Hog pound to the Poundfield and fetched one load of small chalk from the kiln to the Horse Pond Foster G Gray Honeysett David and I with them Wm and Mr Barrow Haying in the Squirefield T Hoad and Easton mowing in the Wenhouse field the Martins litt the Lime Kiln this morning Mr G Verrel Visitor all night R Russell Visitor Elizabeth is gone to Mr Smiths all night etc etc J Honeysett and D Honeysett clearing bracken.

Wednesday 3

To day was nearly as yesterday but rather more cloudy with some showers about one small one here at noon and one in the after noon at about 6 o'clock Horses carried Some Top wood to Hailsham and fetched home some chalk Oxen 3 workmen David and I carried loads of drift sand from the River to the Poundfield in morning and and carried 3 loads of Hay in the afternoon to the home hay rick from the Esquirefield etc Mowers Father Wm Mrs Baker maid and Ruth Hoad helpt us etc Martins put the kiln out G Verrell whent home Trill Lade had his wife and son home again the carters borrowed a horse yesterday of J Bland and had him today Old John Honeysett and his nephew David Honeysett clearing bracken yesterday and today for Mr G Morfey Elizabeth whent with Mr Smiths Family to Wallsend to see the Sea and home after we where abed

Thursday 4

A sunshine morning some rain in the forenoon and some in the after noon cloudy Evening wind in the SW Horses as yesterday oxen David and I are plough in the Esquirefield and loaded up the last load of Hay from that field Wm who tended the sheep and made the lime and lump places and the three work men Honeysett Mr G Gray and Foster who where spreading Moul in the 7 acres and Father helped us gett it up Mowers finished the sides Old Gower hoeing wheat in the Kilnfield Two Honeysetts cleaning bricks for Joseph Murfey

Friday 5

Showery weather wind in the SW Horses as yesterday oxen emptied the kiln carried one small load of Lime to the new oast that is to be and five loads up into the Esquire field borrowed a wagon of Wm Harmer Foster

Father and Wm help the Lime burners at the Kiln Do Honeysett helpt David and I unload and helpt G Guy spread the rest of the Moul in the 7 acres T Hoad and Easton planted some cabages in the upper garden and Hoeing up potatoes all day Foster and G Guy Do in the afternoon Do Honeysett shovelling Orchard Hops ditto Old Gower hoeing wheat Mr J Morfey had several men at work to day I don't know all their names cleaning bricks making mortar and began dig the Foundation of the Oast

Saturday 6
Some clouds and some sun no rain till the Evening and then not much the wind in the S and the SW Horses whent there last time to Hailsham as on Wednesday Oxen Foster David William and I carried 25 cart loads of bricks and stones from the old Oast up against the pound from the new oast we turned the Bushey field hay after wards I had Wm Harmer's Waggon home T Hoad Easton GG hop choping in the Pound field garden Honeysett shovelling orchard Old Gower in the Kilnfield hoeing wheat and sowing turnips Mr J Morfey and 2 men cleaning bricks one Carpenter the Master Man I forgot Father whent to Heath field yesterday S Wilmshurst visitor to day J T Lade sleeps here to night

Sunday 7
Father Mother I Wm David and Elizabeth went to Heathfield Chapel in the morning. Mr Press preached from Romans in the morning and afternoon 11 Chap 22 verse I forgot the Hymns Father I Wm David and Elizabeth went to Mrs Sobers in the Evening spoke from the first Chapter of Romans 1 clause of the 16 verse forgot the weather showery in the morning cloudy nearly all day the wind in the SW

Monday 8
Clear morning cloudy afternoon Rain in the evening wind in the S and SE Horses and oxen plough the Esquirefield and had home two trees for the new oast in the forenoon carried 4 loads of Hay from the Busheyfield (G Guy turned off[290] on Saturday night) T Hoad and Easton turning dung and moul in the Poundfield David Honeysett shovelling hops in the orchard and Foster piling chord and fetched timber of the old Oast some of it to Barn All on full force carrying hay in the afternoon Old J Honeysett cleaning bricks young D Honeysett diging a sawpitt in the Poundfield Elizabeth Lade called and Elizabeth whent with her to Windmill Hill and Bellhurst had word that one of of our Colts are unwell etc

[290] Dismissed.

Tuesday 9

A pleasant cooling wind from the South all day some clouds and a heavy shower of rain about 7 o'clock in the Evening Horses plough oxen brought home the rest of the Filchin chalk the carter throughed[291] out at Trolilos River and a waggon load of sand from near Mrs York's and carried of load of bricks from the old Oast to against the new one Foster finished shovelling hops in the Orchard and helpt us with the sand and the Bricks afterwards He David William and Ruth Hoad turned the Wenhouse field seeds T Hoad and Easton turning dung and Moul in the Poundfield paid Master Honeysett off 1 man cleaning bricks and I don't recollect of any thing else. Mr Press preached in the evening from the 146 Psalm the 8 verse I must give up thinking about the Hymns JT Lade sleeps here tonight John Bland visitor this afternoon.

Wednesday 10

Some showers in the forenoon a Fine afternoon wind in the South and in the West Horses and the oxen plough Foster a casting up Dung in the calves lodge and at plough at my stead[292] in the afternoon. T Hoad and Easton Finished the Marks on in the pound field and began carting the Dung up in the oxen cart 1 man cleaning bricks etc etc Father and I went to Mayfield.

Thursday 11

Some shower in the morning and one in the afternoon wind in the West Horses and oxen at plough in the forenoon carried 4 loads of hay in the afternoon T Hoad and Easton casting up dung and Foster setting up hop poles in the Garden in the morning All of us on haying in the Wenhouse field Wm Hoad Mr Lade's horse home that I rode yesterday Master Honeysett finished cleaning bricks for Mr Morfey a man and a boy hewing timber the sow farrowed about ½ past 4 o'clock 10 pigs Father Mother I Wm David and Elizabeth whent to the Stonehouse in the Evening the Rev Mr Kemp preached from Acts the 10 Cha the 36 verse J T Lade sleeps here tonight

Friday 12

Showery weather the wind in the West and North West Horses and oxen at plough the three workman casting up Dung in the Oxen Close The Martins lit the Kiln again two sawyers and one Carpenter Mrs Lade and Elizabeth

[291] Throwed.
[292] In my stead.

whent to Silverash William whent to Wind Mill Hill the Old Sow had but 8 pigs tonight

Saturday 13
Showery weather some sunshine and some cloudy weather the wind sometime in the West and sometimes in the North West Horses and oxen finished ploughing the Esquire field and drawed 2 trees and one log from the wood and 3 trees and one log from the Orchard field to the Sawpitt in the Poundfield the horses have drawed home a tree from the wood everytime they where at plough in the Esquire field Foster not at work T Hoad and Easton made some Lime lump places in the Furze and in the Esquire field's Washed the sheep in the River just above the Road leading up to the Poundfield and casting up Dung in the Poundfield bottom Sawyers and one man confer to Limeburner will put kiln out to night Mr Moonington[293] visitor Mr S Wilmshurst Do J T Lade sleeps here tonight

Sunday 14
Cloudy weather rained from about 11 o'clock to 7 o'clock in the evening rather Foggy no sun wind in the South Father Mother I William David and Elizabeth and Mr Lade whent to Heathfield Chapel in the morning William David and I stayed the afternoon Mother and Elizabeth ditto Mr Press preached from Ezekiel the 47 Cha the latter clause of the 9 verse 'And every creature' etc in the morning and from Romans 5 Cha 18 verse William and I whent to Stonehouse in the evening Mrs Sobers spoke from Romans 1 Cha 17 verse J T Lade sleeps here tonight

Monday 15
A Shower all the morning fine after noon wind in the south and south west etc the rain yesterday and today made it quite Dirty but it has dried up the afternoon surely Borrowed and a Waggon of William Harmer the Horses and Oxen Em[p]tied the Lime Kiln T Hoad Wm Foster and the Martins helpt us William Do. Easton casting up Dung Poundfield bottom in the afternoon Masons Carpenters and Sawyers laid Foundations of the under side and the upper Head of the new oast Elizabeth slept at Mr Wm Wilmshurst on the Common last night and came home today Mr H Purstglove visitor. Forgot that we unloaded one load of Lime in the Furzefield and 4 loads in the Esquirefield.

[293] Mannington.

Tuesday 16
Rained nearly all day wind in the South. Horses Carter Wm Foster David and I carried some bricks from the Old Oast to the new one Carpenters worked in the Barn Sawyers and Masons sometimes at work Wm T Hoad and Easton whent to Ponderling Wm Harmer was in here the Evening

Wednesday 17
Wett morning and a wett Evening wind in the South South West and South East Horses William David and I finished carrying of bricks from the place where the old Oast was to the new one and carried some old timber Horses drawed 4 Trees from the Wood to the saw Pitt sawyers carpenters and masons

Thursday 18
A cold windy morning showery day and cloudy Evening some what cold wind in the South West Horses carried 100 of House Faggots to Mr Reetus[294] in Gardner Street I helpt them part of the way with 4 oxen The three workmen mowing thistles etc at Hodges and in the Silverfield ox pasture Sawyer and Carpenters and Mason. Mr G Verrell Visitor whent with Father I and David to Mrs Sobers in the Evening William was there after having been to Half Moon Market Mr G R Kemp preached from Jeremiah the 33 chapter the latter part of the 13 th verse 'Shall the flocks pass again under the hands of him that teleth them saith the Lord'. JT Lade sleeps here tonight

Friday 19
It nearly like winter about Dirt and Rain and no doubt a great deal of Hay will be spoilt we have about 4 ½ acres of seeds but in the Wenhouse field Mr Smith our neighbour has upwards of 16 acres out Mr Lade at the Priory I believe has not carried any it rained all this forenoon and part of the afternoon. Windy in the afternoon rather cold wind in the Southwest by the south T Hoad and Foster mowing thistles in the after noon of yesterday Sawyers and Masons in the afternoon Mr John Waters Junr visited in the Evening I whent to Silverash in the Evening G Verrell stays here tonight

Saturday 20
No rain some few clouds about rather more in the Evening wind in the South and South East Verry warm Carter whent to Mr Petus's with 100 Faggots and to Master John Hoad's 100 Faggots ½ top and ½ house Oxen

[294] Reeves?

drawing Trees from the wood to the Pitt and Easton helpt me gett a cart load of sand with them Easton and Foster Boseling T Hoad helpt Master Cross shave the sheep and Lambs in the Mill Barn weaned the lambs drove them to the Bushy field and the old sheep to the Silverfield Father whent to Mr Harmers David whent to Gardner Street. G Verrell whent home Master Barns called and took Fathers Boots to Mend Sawyers Carpenters and Masons J T Lade sleeps here tonight. Father and I turned some hay in the Evening

Sunday 21
Some clouds and some sunshine a Thunder storm in the morning and a shower in the afternoon wind in the South West Father Mother William David I Elizabeth whent to Heathfield Chapel in the morning Father Mother and William stayed the afternoon Mr Press preached both times from Jude 1=2=3 and 4 verses Father Mother I William David and Elizabeth where at Stonehouse in the evening Mrs Sobers spoke from Timothy the 1 chapter 15 verse except the last clause Maid whent to Herstmonceux etc. J T Lade sleeps here tonight

Monday 22
Rather windy and Cloudy and a Wett Evening Wind in the South West Horses ploughing in the Tares in the 7 acres Oxen drawing trees and got up one load of Hay. T Hoad and Easton mowing round the Hop gardens in the forenoon and setting up Hop poles in the gardens in the afternoon Foster not at work Old Dann William Mr Baker and Father Haying T Hoad Easton Father William and Old Dann grubbed the Cherry Tree in the four court just before dinner Oxen ox pasture so that we fodder the oxen with the tares from the 10 acres just by. Sawyers Carpenters and Masons. One woman where a Bucketing to day and broke the pump J Morfy and Mr R Winchester got the buckets out in the evening.[295] Sophia and Ann Smith come to see Elizabeth and are weather bound and stay all night they are now very noisy in the room just by, Elizabeth Ann and the Maid with them

Tuesday 23
Weather it Rained all night or not I don't know but it rained this morning and some clouds and showers about all day Wind rather high from the South West in the morning and still (or nearly so) from the West in the evening Foster is laid up with a Sore leg Horses oxen 2 workmen 2 brothers

[295] Losing a bucket down the well was serious, as it had to be recovered by a rope with grappling irons.

I and Easton carried about 29 loads of Dung from the yard and 24 loads of Moul from where the Old Oast stood and mackoned[296] up in the Gutterfield Sawyers Carpenters and Masons Mrs Baker pulling thistles down in the Brook in the afternoon I understand Master T Hoad shut the Cherry Cows calf up to weaned he has been taken from his Mother and put to the Dann Heifer who has took it of her own since hers was weaned. Father Mother William David and I whent to Mr Smiths in the evening Mr Press preached from 2 Kings 5 Cha the 15 verse

Wednesday 24
Some showers about a still warm day cole[d] evening wind in the South West we all as yesterday afternoon Carried 53 loads Sawyers Carpenters and Masons Old Dann setting up Hop poles in the gardens Ruth Hoad pulling thistles Maid Do In the afternoon Elizabeth whent to the Priory Father whent to Heathfield Chapel in the evening J T Lade sleeps here tonight Mr R Winchester the Master Carpenter mended the pump it pumps five times as well as it did before.

Thursday 25
Some sunshine in the afternoon and showery nearly all day wind in the NE-N-NW-W and SW Horses and oxen finished carrying Moul away from the place where the Old Oast stood Turned some hay and mounded a Load but the showers coming hindered carrying any 2 workmen helpt and Dug a Ditch out on the Right Hand side as you go from the River to the Poundfield and helpt the Carters carried some Dung away and brought some stuf to the little Barn Doors etc etc. Masons where not at work the Sawyers and Carpenters where thus Thistle pullers

Friday 26
Some Clouds about a shower in the afternoon Horses and oxen whent to Wartling Hill after chalk T Hoad and Easton mowing the Calves Lodge meadow no Masons Sawyers and Carpenters and thistle pullers etc Father whent Down in the Marsh Mrs Fluorance visitor Forgot that we drawed the 5 calves from the Silverfield and 1 from Hodges into the Grimes Brook yesterday morning J T Lade sleeps here tonight

Saturday 27
Some clouds and a few drops of rain wind in the West Horses and oxen whent to Wartling Hill after chalk and carried 3 load of Hay it has been a

[296] Maxoned, mixened.

most remarkable Wett time for Hay and most considerable quantity is no doubt spilt Our stack laid open till the Toad stools growed upon it Mowers Hayers Sawyers and Carpenters etc J T Lade sleeps here tonight. Oratio Isted came home with us with some green peas and took the Basket home with him

Sunday 28
Some clouds and some sun and some Rain in the afternoon wind in the West Father Mother I William David and Elizabeth whent to Heathfield Chapel in the morning William and Elizabeth stayed the afternoon Mr Press preached both times from Ezekial the 20 Cha and the 37 verse Father Mother I William David Elizabeth and the Maid whent to Mrs Sobers in the Evening She spoke from these words 'For the law was given by Moses but Grace and Truth come by Jesus Christ'. Mr G Verrel and his friend Mr Knight visitor and whent with us to Chapel in the morning and to Mrs Sobers in the evening Mrs Lade is gone to sleep at the Priory tonight Etc etc

Monday 29
A clear sunshine morning and I under stand a very heavy shower about 11 O'clock lasted 2 hours there was but very little at Wartling Hill not enough to hinder there Haying Horses and oxen whent to Wartling Hill after chalk T Hoad and Easton mowing in the Chapel wood meadow. Old Dann boseling G Guy pulling thistles etc etc Carpenters and Masons have just the Floor up Mr Stanford and a son and Daughter visitors G Verrell and Mr Knight whent home Forgot the wind was in the North West and South

Tuesday 30
Some Thunder showers and some have a Frost in the morning wind was very still very changeable in almost all quarters Horses plough in the 7 acres oxen fetched a Cart load of sand from against Mrs Yorke's and 1200 Bricks from Tilley Kiln to the Oast Master Delves Fetched 1300 for Us it being such weather he did not know what to do Foster and G Guy Hop choping in the Orchard Garden Old Dann pulling thistles Mowers where in the Chapel Meadow Carpenters and Masons etc etc. Father whent to the Tilly Kilns T J Lade sleeps here tonight

Wednesday 31
Cold Frosty morning a shower in the afternoon that came so fast as to rais[e] a Flood in about 2 hours down in our Brook Cloudy Evening the Wind has been I think all ways not long at a place Horses plough oxen fetched some chalk from Wartling Hill and some from the Five Bells

Thursday 1 August

Cloudy a few drops of Rain wind in the North west and west rather cold Horses and oxen drawing Trees from the wood to the saw pit in the forenoon Horses fetched the Faggots from the Calves Lodge and Red Pale Fields in the afternoon we where all trimming the Hay Stack up in the afternoon Carters too I whent after one of our ladders Mr Veness borrowed he sent a man home with me with it showers etc Foster is laid up again with scurvy legs Turned G Guy off Old Dann at work on the road Masons have got the new oast up ready to rear[?]²⁹⁷ Sawyers and Carpenters Ruth Hoad pulling Thisties Mrs Lade and Elizabeth whent out a how do you doing to Mrs Russell's Warbleton Church Forgot William David and Ruth Hoad turned the Hay in the Calves Lodge meadow

Friday 2

Cold morning a few drops of Rain some clouds wind was in the North East in the morning before 7 o'clock afterwards in the South West all day Horses carrying Kiln Faggots from the Furzfield to the Kiln oxen fetched a Cart load of sand from against Mrs Yorkes for the Masons carried some faggots from the orchard hop gardens and the granary to the House and carried 3 cart load of Tiles from where the Old Oast was to the new one and got up one load of Hay at the Calves Lodge Father helpt us William and Mrs Baker and Ruth Hoad Haying Maid ditto Mowers Sawyers and carpenters Masons two men levelling the inside of the oast and laying tiles etc

Saturday 3

There was a long Flood in the night which made things verry Wett this morning sun shone nearly all day a very few drops of rain in the forenoon. Wind rather brisk from the South West Horses whent to Wallsend after 2

Mowers in the Chapel meadow old Dann mowing thistles in the 7 acres and Hoeing weeds in the Orchard Hop gardens Sawyers Carpenters and Masons Foster and G Guy choping Hops in the Orchard J Bland visitor and brought some Peas It is a most extraordinary summer for Rain and will be the means of spoiling a great deal of Hay we had done all our Haying last year by this time and this year we have not carried any Meadow Hay there is a plenty of grass in the meadows in general it seems a promising potato year Oats are Middling they say the worm or maggot in the ear is a great deal in the Wheat hops have a plenty of bine but do not promise for much Bud.

²⁹⁷ As in rear up, erect? Otherwise obscure.

Chaldrons of Coals for the Revd Mr Press and left them at Dillgate Oxen at nothing William David I Mrs Baker and Ruth Hoad Haymaking in the afternoon Sawyers Carpenters and Masons raised the new oast T Hoad and Easton mowing in the Chapel Meadow Mr A Russel the assessor on business etc. T J Lade sleeps here tonight

Sunday 4
Warm still sunshine day some clouds as the morning it had and appearance of fine weather wind in the South West Father Mother I William David and Elizabeth whent to Heathfield Chapel in the morning the Maid whent some where I don't know where Father Mother William David and Elizabeth staid the afternoon Mr Press preached from Hebrews 7 Cha 24|25 verses in the morning and from Isiah 47 Cha 17 verse in the afternoon Father Mother Wm I David and Elizabeth Whent to Mrs Sobers in the Evening and she spoke from 1 Corinthians 1 Cha and 18 verse Wonderful fine morning to be sure only little cloudy Bless her JT Lade sleeps here tonight

Monday 5
a Sunshine morning cloudy and some Rain in the afternoon wind rather still in the South and North East Horses carried the 2 Chaldrons of Coals to Mr Press Heathfield Oxen carried 4 cart loads of Tiles from the Brook to the Oast Easton and T Hoad mowing in the Ponds Croft GG Hop choping today 2 Carpenters J T Lade sleeps here tonight Hayers in the forenoon Martins began about the Kiln again

Tuesday 6
A sunshine morning cloudy afternoon wind In the South West Horses fetched the last load of Kiln Faggots from the Furzefield to the kiln drawed some timber from the furze field to the Redpale field and loaded 2 loads of Hay 1 in the calves lodge and 1 in the Chapel wood Meadow oxen finished carrying tiles in the forenoon 1 man laying tiles 3 Carpenters etc. David I William Father and the Maid Haying in the afternoon Mowers are at Hodges J T Lade sleeps her[e] tonight. Mother whent to Mrs Smiths a visiting forgot Father whent to Mr Russell's at Church yesterday afternoon

Wednesday 7
Wett weather all day till 4 o'clock then some sunshine but no Flood Wind in the South west and west It has been quite a idle day 3 Carpenters at work in the Barn Father whent to Lewes and rode Mr Lades Horse J T Lade had it down last night J T Lade sleeps here tonight

Thursday 8

Cloudy and some sun and a little Rain in the evening wind in the South West Carters I William and David unloaded 3 loads of Hay at the Calves lodge and loaded up a load of Cleft Timber. Mowers finished mowing in Grimes wood. All on a Haying and got up 2 load in Evening from the Chapel wood meadow etc etc Carpenters and Masons and Old Evenden cleavering[298] Laths J T Lade had their Horse home in the morning

Friday 9

A sunshine day some clouds and a little rain some heavy showers whent up Northward wind in the Southwest and West Horses and oxen drawed the load of Timber up to Wind Mill Hill and got up 4 load of Hay from the Chapel Meadow and 1 load from the Chapel wood meadow in the afternoon T Hoad mowed the garden and the Fore Court afterwards helpt William David and I unload 2 loads of hay at the Calves lodge Easton mending the Road in the Chapel meadow all afterwards on a Haying G Guy is sometimes a choping Hops and some times not as it Happens with Him Carpenter and Masons etc etc

Saturday 10

Some clouds but no Rain as I know on wind in the North West and west Horses whent to Laughton oxen carried 4 loads of Hay from Chapel Meadow Father William David I T Hoad Easton Mrs Baker Ruth Hoad and Sarah Morfy all Haying Carpenters and Masons J T Lade sleeps here to night

Sunday 11

Rather windy day some clouds and rather the appearance of rain in the Evening wind in the West Father I William David Elizabeth Mrs Lade and her Husband whent to Heathfield Chapel in the morning William & I stayed the after noon Mr Green from Burwash preached in the morning from 1 Peter 2 chapter first part of the 7 verse and in the afternoon from the words 'They that be whole need not a phisition[299] but they that are sick' evening She spoke from Job 33 chapter latter part of the 24 verse 'Deliver him' etc J T Lade sleeps here to night Forgot that the Bull got out and run away and William whent after him yesterday morning and found him between Rushlake Green and the Brick Kilns yesterday

[298] Cleaving.
[299] Physician.

Monday 12
Cloudy all day some Misty rain Wind in the south west Horses whent to Tilly Kiln after 800 of bricks and Harrowed the Esquirefield oxen did nothing T Hoad helpt Easton mend a gap against the Pound and helpt David and I carry some old tiles to the new oast and fetch the Chucks from the Barn to the Back Court and put some stuff up on the seed Hay Stack in the morning Easton helpt T Hoad gaping and mended the Road leading to Redpale in the morning T Hoad and Easton Hop choping in the Orchard In the afternoon David and I trimmed the Calves lodge stack up in the afternoon etc masons Father whent to Silverash in the Evening Mrs Delves at Redpale just cold in the Evening

Tuesday 13
Cloudy morning and some Rain a bright sunshine afternoon Wind in the South West and North West in the evening Horses Finished Harrowing the Esquire field and at Plough in the 7 acres got up one load of Hay from the Chapel meadow and carried to the oxens stack oxen carried 4 load to the Home Hay Rick and began another stack I was mowing thistles in the 7 acres vallow[300] and in the Furze field and the Bracken in the Silverfield in the forenoon Haying in the afternoon David Hoeing thistles in the 7 acres and Haying T Hoad and Easton Hop choping and Haying Father William Sarah Morfey and Ruth Hoad Haying Mason finished tiling in the oast J Bland Visitor T J Lade sleeps here to night this was the last time J Bland was at Bucksteep for once

Wednesday 14
Some sun in the morning Cloudy all day some Rain in the afternoon wind in the North and East and South Horses plough and T Hoad Easton David and I unloaded a load of Hay at Home and 2 loads at the oxen close and carried 2 load of Hay with the oxen to the Home stack which finishes the Chapel Meadow Father William Sarah Morfey Ruth Hoad and Mrs Baker Haying 2 Carpenters no Masons today Mrs Lade whent to Windmill Hill William whent to Warbleton Church in the Evening

Thursday 15
Some sunshine generally cloudy and a shower in the Evening ½ a Flood. Wind in the South West Horses plough oxen William David and I carried some straw from the home Barn to the oxen Hay stack and some Faggots

[300] Fallow.

from the Poundfield to the Kiln and put some kiln Faggots around the Cucumber bed carried the stuf around the Poundfield Hop gardens to the seed Hay sack and drawed an Apps[301] from the gutterfield shaw to the saw pit Hoad and Easton Hop choping G Guy ditto Sawyers Carpenters and Masons J T Lade sleeps here to night Mr G Verrell from Lewes came here this evening

Friday 16

A heavy shower in the morning and 4 or 5 heavy Thunder showers in the afternoon which caused a large Flood and the wind changed from the South West to the North in the afternoon Horses whent to the Tilly Kiln after five hundred of Bricks and carried a part of a load of Cleft Timber as far the Five Bells River and could not get no further oxen carried the other part on Mr S Goldsmiths Waggon as far as there Easton and William Hoad load it all on the Carters Waggon unyoked the oxen down here tonight and left both Waggons at Five Bells T Hoad and Easton choping Hops and helpt us Mr G Verrell whent from here soon after nine o'clock Masons and Sawyers

Saturday 17

Cloudy some little Sunshine showery and some Thunder Wind in the West it is very Dirty indeed I think it has rained every day or night for this 2 months since the turn of days such a Summer as is severely known in the memory of Man Horses whent Laughton Easton and David with 4 oxen Helpt them up to the Turnpikes from five bell River and had our Waggon to the Tilly Kilns I went with the other 4 oxen and come home with 800 of Bricks afterwards we had the Waggon home and got a Cart Load of sand against Mrs Yorkes and about 8 or 10 Bushels of Lime from the Redpale kiln for the Masons T Hoad Boseling Masons Carpenters and Sawyers G Guy hop choping in the forenoon he is so idle we have no more work for him at present Father whent to Wind Mill Hill Mr T Delves is not to live but a very little while of a Consumption. J T Lade sleeps here tonight.

Sunday 18

A Cold morning pleasant day not much sun Cloudy and a few drops of rain Wind in the North West Father Mother I William David and Elizabeth whent to Heathfield Chapel in the morning Father William David and Elizabeth stayed the afternoon Mr Press preached from Thessalonians 2 chapter the 13 verse in the morning if I mistake not and from the same

[301] Ash tree.

again in the afternoon according to Williams account William David I & Elizabeth whent to the Stone house in the Evening Mrs Sobers spoke from the words' and to know him and the power of his Resurrection' Maid whent to Herstmonceux Chapel in the morning she say Mr T Delves died last night at 10 O'clock J T Lade sleeps here tonight

Monday 19
Cold morning pleasant day some sunshine and a few drops of Rain Wind in the North west and West and south west Horses plough in the Furze field oxen drawing Logs from the Wood to the Redpale field and drawed a Top of a Tree home T Hoad and Easton and Foster choping hops etc and Haying William Haying Sawyers Carpenters and Masons Father whent down the Marsh Father I William David and Elizabeth whent to Stonehouse in the Evening the Revd Mr Kemp preached from the first Epistle of John the 4 verse

Tuesday 20
A misty Rain in the morning Cloudy and some sun in the afternoon wind in the North and North East Horses finished the Furzefield and where at plough in the 7 acres Oxen fetched the Deal Boards for the Oast Chamber from Mr Winchester Cowbeach in the morning nothing afterwards and T Hoad Boseling Foster and Easton Hop choping Croft sawyers Carpenters and Masons J T Lade came with a Horse and Borrowed our Shay Cart and Harness and had his wife and son off with him Mr Press preached here this Evening to a good Congregation from John 5 chapter and the 2nd-3rd and 4th verses

Wednesday 21
A Warm sunshine day the best we have had since Midsummer some Clouds wind in the North East very still Horses finished ploughing 7 acres and carried 1 load of Hay to the Oxen stack and 1 load home from the Ponds Croft Oxen carried 1 load home and turned that 4 out with the cows T Hoad I William David Maid Mrs Baker Sarah Morfey and Ruth Hoad Haying all day Foster and Easton Hop choping in the forenoon Haying in the after noon Sawyers Carpenters and Masons Father whent to Hailsham Market and sold a two yearling heifer for 10£ the market was very dull Mr Press whent home

Thursday 22
Cloudy morning with a few drops of rain sunshine afternoon some clouds Wind in the Northeast Northwest West and South west and back again to

Friday 23

the North east very still Horses ploughing Hops in the Croft and Carried the 2 last Load of Hay from the Ponds Croft Oxen carried 4 loads of Hay from the two meadows at Hodges T Hoad William David and I unloaded a load of Hay in the morning T Hoad for Faggoting of Hoath on the Pound loading to red pale in the forenoon Haying in the afternoon Foster and Easton Hop choping and haying Women Hayers Father ditto Sawyers Carpenters and Masons Crowerst cutt 4 bore pigs and spayed 3 sow pigs

Saturday 24

Rather Cloudy some sun Wind in the North west and Northeast Horses plough in the Croft Hop garden Oxen whent to Tilly Kiln after 1200 of Bricks and Carried our last load of Hay for this year from Grimes wood to the oxen and Calves lodge stacks we shall have no good Hay in all the lot. T Hoad Faggoting Hoath in the Road up the Kilnfield etc and helpt us in the field Oats and we turned them into the Chapelwood Meadow Carpenter and Masons Father and William ditto Foster and Easton Hop choping Carpenter and Masons The Supervisor and Hop assistant come the first time to survey the Oast

Sunday 25

Cloudy morning some rain warm sunshine day with some clouds wind in the N.E and S.W Horses whent to Bourn sea House after a load of chalk b[or]rowed two horses of Mr T Isted the 3 workmen with 6 oxen spreading Lime in the Esquire field Oxen gott out this evening into Mrs Smiths full field Oats and we turned them into the Chapelwood Meadow Carpenters and Masons have nearly finished the Oast

Monday 26

A clear sunshine morning some clouds in the course of the day and a clear starlight evening wind in the Northwest a small moon Father Mother I William David and Elizabeth whent to Heathfield Chapel in the morning Father I William and Elizabeth stayed the afternoon the Revd A Start from East Grinstead preached from 1 Corinthians 15 chapter the first part of the 10 verse 'But by the grace of God I am what I am' and in the morning from 2 Corinthians 8 chapter the 9 verse in the afternoon Father I William David and Eliza Beth whent to Mrs Sobers in the Evening she spoke from Acts 2 chapter the 12 Verse Maid whent to Herstmonceux

A sunshine morning Cloudy day the wind in the N. and NE. Horses fetched load of sand from against Mrs Yorkes for the new Oast and drawed 2 Oak and 1 Ash Trees from the Silverfield to the sawpitt Oxen 3 Workmen finished spreading Lime and Carried the rest of T Hoads wood home William David and I Trimming sacks and loaded a load of Wheat straw in the Home Barn T Hoad kild a Ram in the evening William whent to Gardner street after some Malt Mr Everest brought 6 Bushells in his Cart Mother whent to Bellshurst. J T Lade had his wife and son home this evening

Tuesday 27
Cloudy day and a few drops of rain etc but little sun wind in the NE Horses whent to Bourne pitts after a load of Chalk Oxen David and I at plough in the Esquirefield and drawed tree logs to the saw Pitt T Hoad Easton and Foster Hop choping Honeysett thatched the seed haystack Sawyers Carpenters and Masons Elizabeth whent to Heathfield and to Heathfield Chapel William whent to Chapel Do in the Evening , the Revd Mr Lucks from Islington who is out on the London Missionary preached from 2nd Corinthians 5 chapter the former part of the 14th Verse

Wednesday 28
A warm sunshine day and but few clouds wind in the NE & E not a cloud to be seen in the Evening Horses whent to Tilly Kiln after 900 of Bricks Carter loaded a load of Straw in the Home Barn the 3 workmen mowing Peas in the Bound banks[302] and Highfield at Hodges Honeysett thatched the Meadow Hay stack in the home Hay Rick and mended the Cow Lodge and the Chapel Barn Oxen plough Sawyers Carpenters and Masons Mother whent to Bellshurst

Thursday 29
A warm sunshine day some clouds Wind in the S and SW. Horses whent to Bourne pett after Chalk Oxen plough Father and William with one pair drawed and unloaded a load of straw at the Calves lodge and Hodges Stacks Honeysett thatched the oxon stack the 3 workmen finished Mowing peas about bait time and began the 10 acres Tares Sawyers finished there work so Carpenters Masons quit Strong forget William Hop choping in the pound field

Friday 30
Cloudy nearly all day wind in the W and NW Horses Plough in the Croft Hop garden and fetched the straw from the Calves lodge what was not wanted etc Oxen plough I had the share laid 3 Tare mowers 2 Masons

[302] Round banks.

William Hop choping Mr James Lade from Chiddingly Visitor J T Lade (his brother) sleeps here to night. Honeysett thatched the stack at the Calves lodge and the stack at Hodges We had 47 Loads of Hay from about 45 acres this year Wood the gardener pruned the Vines and Plum Trees

Saturday 31
Cold cloudy Wett day and Dirty walking Wind in the West South West South Southeast East Northeast North. Horses whent to Bourn Chalk pett[303] after chalk T Hoad and Easton fild the saw Pitt up in the forenoon T Hoad Kild a pig in the Evening Crowerst broke the Rear of its Belly a spaying and lett it's gutts down in a Large bunch there is another in a little so Foster not at work it has been an Idle day with us 3 Carpenters and 4 or 5 Masons

Sunday 1 September
After a cold Wett night it was a cold showery day and a cold North wind blowed the Hopoles down and so blowed the corn about. Father I William and David whent to Heathfield Chapel in the morning William and David stayed the afternoon Mr Press preached both times from Romans the 15 chapter and the 13 Verse William and David whent to Stonehouse in the Evening Mrs Sobers spoke from Solomons songs the 1 chapter and the 7 verse Maid whent to Herstmonceux Chapel in the afternoon J T Lade sleeps here tonight

Monday 2
A Cold cloudy morning some sun in the daytime clear moonlight evening wind in the North and Northwest Horses carried 4 Bundles of Rack staves 3 bundles of ladder staves to Gardner Street to go to Preston and fetched 300 of Bricks from the Tilley Kiln T Hoad finished filling the sawpitt up and he William David and I Tieing up Hop poles afterwards all day Foster and Easton not at work Masons in the morning nobody about the Oast in the afternoon Father whent down into the Marsh Father I William and David whent to Stonehouse in the evening the Revd Mr Kemp preached from Hebrews 10 chapter and the 10 verse

Tuesday 3
A Frosty morning Cloudy and sun shine day some rain in the afternoon wind in the North Northwest West Southwest and S and Southwest again. Horses whent to Bourn pett (the last time for this year) after chalk the 3 workmen mowing Tares in the 10 acres William David and I Tieing Hop

[303] Pit.

poles and gaping 2 Carpenters and one Mason Elizabeth whent to Mr Russels Mr Saml Latham our Hop Factor and Mr Dorsett from Frankwell Visitors T J Lade sleeps here to night

Wednesday 4
After a Wett night a showery morning and a Flood some Rain Hail and snow in the day some sunshine wind in the Southwest Rather warmer it is such weather a wass scarcely ever known in Harvest after such a Wett summer the Corn is greatly swollened and the much battered with the Winds Horses at nothing Carters stacking or pileing Chalk 3 workmen finished mowing Tares 3 Masons no Carpenters Father whent to Hailsham Market to sell a Cow from the Marsh but did not it wass a Dull Market

Thursday 5
Some clouds in the morning and some Sun in the day time Rather warmer than it has been wind in the Southwest a Drying day Horses Wm Hoad and a Cart gravelling the Barrow way between the Road and yard at Hodges and carried some stuff from the bank below the oast and laid before the Oast door Oxen David and I fetched all the Chalk the Carters had laid down at Wartling Hill these last 5 times a large load and came very heavy William and Hoad drove Old Smoke Cow down into the Marsh and had a Heifer and calf home with us T Hoad Easton and Foster began Mow the Black Oats in the 13 acres Morfey came about the Glass window to the Oast No Masons nor Carpenters Master Henry Beeny the shoe maker on business Mr J Steer visitor J T Lade sleeps here tonight forgot his wife whent to priory today

Friday 6
Cold morning sunshine forenoon cloudy afternoon and rain in the evening wind in the North and Southwest William Hoad with Horses raising the ground before the Oast and bringing home Chucks Henry helping in the morning afterwards turning Peas Oxen fetched a large load of chalk from the Five Bell River which is all for this year William David and I (with Henry) turned the Peas in the Roundbank and Highfield at Hodges the 3 mowers finished mowing the Black Oats and sett on Reeping the Kilnfield Wheat Old Dann Reeping in the Kilnfield 4 Carpenters no Masons Father whent to Mayfield Mr Johnson and his wife from Gardener Street cald to Buy some Peas and Cutt[304] Mrs Lade Elizabeth and M[arly hear they called again and drank Tea in the Evening and J T Lade sleeps here tonight Shut

[304] Cucumber?

the sow up to Wean her Pigs

Saturday 7

A few drops of Rain in the morning Rather windy day cloudy and some sun Wind in the Northwest Horses plough in the Esquire field T Hoad Easton Foster and Old Dann Reeping in the Kilnfield & Old Evenden and his Wife in the 12 acres David and I Tieing up Hop poles 4 Carpenters Peter Forkhouse put a new Hind Exel Tree[305] to the narrow wheeled Waggon Father and William whent to Blackhorse near Battle after the Marsh Lambs 30 Ewe Shears some Neighbours come home with Father and just cald in the evening in Mr John Purstglove and his Brother Henry where all this evening

Sunday 8

Cloudy day some sun Wind in the North west Father Mother I William David and Elizabeth whent to Heathfield Chapel in the morning William and I stayed the afternoon Mr Press preached both times from Ephesians the 6 chapter the 18 19 and 20th Verses – Father I William David and Elizabeth whent to Mrs Sobers in the evening she spoke from John 14 chapter the 16 verse J T Lade sleeps here tonight he and his wife have been to Bellshurst today

Monday 9

Wett weather nearly all day Cloudy all day and windy wind in the Southeast Horses plough part of the forenoon Oxen carried 1 Waggon load of Dung from the Poundfield bottom and carried home some more if the weather would let us some Reepers in the Kilnfield part of the day 1 Carpenter making a new gate the weather has been so unfavourable we have not had opportunity to work our Oxen enough to keep them to Rights so that we cannot keep them out of the Chapel Meadow which is very Wett as well as the other pastures

Tuesday 10

Windy drying day Wind in the Southwest some clouds Horses plough Oxen Carried 3 or 4 Waggon load of Dung as on yesterday T Hoad Easton Evenden and his Wife Reeping in the 12 acres Foster Old Dann and his Wife Reeping in the Kilnfield I whent to Mr Purstgloves at Princkel and measured between 11 and 12 Acres of ground for them The Honerable Lady Mrs Sobers her sister Miss Kemp and two Miss Burts Visitors this

[305] Axle-tree.

evening Forgot 1 Man and boy Masons 2 Carpenters

Wednesday 11
Some Clouds and a Little Rain in the afternoon Wind in the Southeast – Horses whent to Cowbeach after some Deal Board in the morning nothing else. Oxen carried 2 load dung as on yesterday this forenoon nothing in the afternoon Reepers as on yesterday William turning Tares in the afternoon David and Henry Hoad Sarah Morfey and Ruth Hoad ditto in the afternoon 1 Carpenter William Hoad William and I whent to helpt carry Old Mrs Lade from Mr W Lades to Church in the afternoon there was a Funeral sermon or cold[306] so to be by our Parson Lewes[307] from 1 Corinthians 15 chapter and the 53 verse JT Lade sleeps here tonight

Thursday 12
Weather nearly as yesterday wind more Westward Horses finished ploughing the Esquirefield and William Hoad the Carter had the Heifers calf to Mr Scraces Boreham in the evening oxen not at work William David and I Tieing Hop poles all day Reepers and Two Carpenters the Carpenters have done there work and made two new Hop bins to day several things besides New Chapel Meadow gate against the River

Friday 13
A sunshine morning cloudy all the rest of the day with a few drops of rain Wind in the southwest Horses and oxen carried 7 load of Peas from the Highfield and Roundbank Field Hodges to the Home Barn I must correct a mistake I made last night instead of T Hoad Easton and Foster being Reeping they where a mowing Oats in the Nine acres and finished them today in the forenoon afterwards William Foster helped us carrying Peas T Hoad Reeping in the Grinnetts at Hodges and Easton Reeping in the 12 acres Old Evenden and his wife ditto Dame Dann and her Husband Reeping in the Kilnfield J T Lade sleeps here tonight Dame Dann sleeps here a nights in general

Saturday 14
A Bright sunshine day not many clouds wind in the south and southwest Horses warping in the Furzefield and carried 1 load of Peas Oxen William T Hoad and I carried 1 load of Dung with the Waggon from the Poundfield

---

[306] Called.
[307] Probably Rev. Lewis David Lewis (1763-1826), apparently an outspoken clergyman who had no time for dissenters or non-conformists, and who ruffled a great many feathers. His stay at Warbleton was brief.

bottom to the 7 acres and some bracken from the hither Silverfield to the Chapel Barn and 2 loads of Peas from Hodges to the Chapel Barn Horses carried these there 10 loads in all Foster is a Days Man[308] he was on mowing oats in the Huglets Hodges T Hoad Reeping in the grinnets Easton Old Brendan[309] and his Wife reeping in the 12 acres and Dame Dann and her Mates (if she has any) in the Kilnfield Father whent to Bellhurst Mr John Bland is unwell and has been for some time

Sunday 15
A Clear Bright summers day not a cloud to be seen in the afternoon Wind in the Southeast and Southwest Father Mother I William David whent to Heathfield Chapel in the morning Father William and David stayed the afternoon Elizabeth and Maid whent in the afternoon Mrs Lade and her Daughter Miss Selmes whent to Heathfield Chapel and Mrs Lade whent to the Priory Mr Press preached from Colossians 1 chapter the 9th 10th 11th 12th and 13th Verses both times Father I William David and Elizabeth whent to Mrs Sobers in the Evening she spoke from Acts the 16 chapter and the 30 and 31st verses J T Lade sleeps here tonight

Monday 16
A warm clear day as on yesterday. Wind in the Southeast Southwest and Northwest Horses plough finished the Furzefield and carried one load of Oats from the 13 acres to the Chapel Barn Oxen David I and Father carried 3 Waggon load of Dung as before and carried 1 load of Oats Foster helpt us carry oats he finished mowing Oats in the Huglets and mowed a road through the 8 acre Barley etc T Hoad Old Evenden and his Wife Reeping in the 12 acres Easton not at work Dame Dann and her Mates Reeping in the Kilnfield Wm Mrs Baker Mary Honeysett Mary and Sarah Morfeys Haying on Oats all day Elizabeth whent to Bellhurst she said that J Bland was worse Mother whent there in the evening Mr R Russel Visitor

Tuesday 17
Not a cloud to be seen till about sun down a small cloud appeared in the Northwest Wind was very still in the Southwest very warm Horses plough began Warp[ling] the 7 acres and carried 1 load Oats from the 13 acres Oxen carried 5 loads in all day David and I with William Foster Mary and Sarah Morfeys ditto Easton not at work T Hoad Old Evenden and his Wife Reeping in the 12 acres Dame Dann and her Mates in the Kilnfield T Hoad

[308] Casual labourer.
[309] Evenden?

Family in the Grinnets. Father AJ since know where some where about Warbleton Church other things I know but little about

Wednesday 18
Warm and some sun in the Forenoon Cloudy and more Cold in the afternoon with a sort of sleet rain in the evening Wind in the Southeast East and North Horses Oxen with Father, I, William David & Foster and Mary and Sarah Morfey carried all the Tares 10 loads from the 10 acres Easton not at work rest of the workmen as on yesterday day Mr R Russel brought some Hop pocketing Oast Hair and Brimstone[310] – Phillips the Game Keeper shot two Partridges for us

Thursday 19
A cloudy day and but a little sun Rather cold wind in the North Horses plough Oxen William David and I carried 1 load of Wheat from the Kilnfield and 3 loads from the 12 acres to the Home Barn Forgot that we carried 1 load of Wheat last night from the Kilnfield Father helpt us today with two loads Easton not at work rest of the work men as on yesterday Father whent to Bellhurst this morning and said J Bland was no better J Blands Boy came this evening about 7 o'clock and said his Master was took unconsciouable and the Doctor thought he would not live but a very little while Mother whent home with him Foster threshing Peas in the C Barn

Friday 20
Cloudy morning clear afternoon and Evening rather cold Wind in the North East and North again Horses plough William David and I carried 4 loads of wheat with the oxen from the 12 acres to the Home Barn Father pitched off 3 loads and William Hoad one Father kild a sheep in the morning Easton came to Reeping again to day Foster threshing Peas Rest Reeping as usual Mother came home from Bellhurst in the morning she said J Bland was better J Waters came to borrow a Horse to morrow to send to Lewes Father whent to Brownings and Bellhurst in the Evening

Saturday 21
Cloudy morning a shower in the Middle of the day foggy Evening Wind in the North and East Horses and oxen carried 6 load of Wheat from Kilnfield to the Bushey field to a stack William Hoad built it Father and William assisted David I and Henry Hoad loaded with Horses and Carters carried some straw to thatch it we where quite Wett a carry of wheat to day and

---

[310] Sulphur was added to the kiln to kill any insects in the hops.

changed our cloths I and remember getting Wett through all my cloths carrying wheat in the year 1811 and a very Wett day from the 12 acres Foster threshing peas T Hoad Reeping in the morning threshing lease wheat for himself in the afternoon Rest of the Reepers as on Thursday Mrs Lade whent to Bellhurst she says J Bland is no better but has lost his spirit J T Lade sleeps here tonight

Sunday 22

Cloudy day some sun Wind in the East. Father I William David and Elizabeth whent to Heathfield Chapel in the morning Father William and I stayed the afternoon Mr Press preached in the morning from 2 Corinthians 8 chapter and the 9 verse and in the after noon from Isaiah 43 chapter the 1 and 2nd verses William and David whent to the Stonehouse in the Evening Mrs Sobers spoke from Jeremiah 8 chapter and the last 22 verse Mother whent to Bellhurst Maid whent to Herstmonceux Chapel and to Bellhurst J Bland is no better J T Lade sleeps here tonight

Monday 23

Cloudy and but a little sun and showers in the middle of the day Wind in the East and South west rained in the evening sometime a sort of an idle day with the Team Horses William Hoad carried 2 loads of Chucks home from the Oast Henry helpt them carry a Waggon load of Peas home from the Chapel Barn to the home yard I with a pair of oxen and a cart carried a Tub and helpt the Honeysetts gett some water out of the Bushey field gett to use Thaching the Wheat stack. William and I helpt Foster finis threshing peas Henry Hoad and David helpt us and cleared 5 sacks and 2 Bushels and partly cleared and put the rest up in sacks in the forenoon Foster and I threshing wheat in the Home Barn in the afternoon. William David making Hop pockets Reepers etc Mother came home from Bellhurst she say J Bland come to his speech again last night but is not consciousable Father whent to Rushlake in the evening

Tuesday 24

Cloudy some sun and some rain Wind in the Southwest Rather warmer Horses whent to Pevensey after 3 tons of Welsh coals and 2 sacks of House coals David and I with 2 oxen had the Cart and Tubs home again we where a gaping between the Chapel and ponds croft meadow the oxen are very troublesome. Oxen Father and William David and I with a Waggon carried the Bins into the Croft Hop garden ready for Hoping and afterwards William David and I cleaned the Oast Hair and drove the oxen into the

Carting hop pockets

silverfield Foster threshing wheat H B T Hoad and Easton mowing Barley in the Eight acres Old Evenden and his Wife Reeping in the 12 acres. Dame Dann and her companions in the Kilnfield Father whent and looked over J Blands business he is no better Mr R Russel wass here this morning Mr Hayward from Heathfield Visitor. J T Lade sleeps here tonight. Candle is nearly out this evening

Wednesday 25
Cloudy warm day wind in the South west Horses Warping 7 acres oxen William Foster David and I carrying Dung from the Ox Close just in the 10 acres we did not till the Loads David William I Foster and Wm Hoad turned the 9 acres afterward William gathered the Apples and helpt Old Dann who was getting the oast ready for Hoping J Morfey put the windows in T Hoad Easton and Old Evenden and his Wife Reeping in the 12 acres Dame Dann in the Kilnfield she is gone home tonight Mrs Lade whent to Bellhurst J Bland is no better. Father whent to William Harmer in the Evening

Thursday 26
Foggy morning warm day and rather cloudy and so still I scarce know where the wind is Horses plough and fetched in some Hops in the Evening we began Hop today T Hoad Foster Easton and my two brothers pulled poles I measured to 15 Bine tis almost needless to mention these now tonight for they not all have the picked 152 Bushels in the Croft Old Dann dries them Morfey and a Boy nailed the Oast Hair on and Beal his Man helpt put up a Grate in the Parlour I understand a person called last night in the evening after I was asleep and said J Bland Died between 7 & 8 O'clock he was born July 24th 1780 at Half past 7 O'clock in the evening and lived past 36 years 2 months and 5 days he has not been sensible since Sunday and his man came this evening about the Business and had his super here Mother whent to Bellhurst Etc

Friday 27
A warm day some sun not much wind Wind in the North and Southwest Horses Carter and William carried 4 loads of Wheat from the 12 acres and 1 load from the Grinnets Hodges to the Home Barn All the rest of us Hoping finished the Croft and Picked all the Brook and picked 137 Bushels I whent to Mayfield in the afternoon Forgot Old Master Dann is the Hop dryer

Saturday 28
Cloudy showery day Wind in the Southwest Horses carried 1 load of Wheat from the Grinnets to the Home Barn no more where there T Hoad kild a sheep Reeping in the Kilnfield and Trod 2 pockets of Hops Rest of us generally Hoping in the Orchard picked 160 Bushels T Lade sleeps here to night

Sunday 29
A still cloudy morning rained all the forenoon and part of the afternoon Cloudy all day Windy afternoon and Evening wind in the Southwest Father rode [to] the Heathfield Chapel in the morning William David and I whent in the afternoon Mr Press preached twice from Isiah 30th chapter the 20 and 21st verses we three whent to Mrs Sobers in the Evening she spoke from Romans 6th Chapter the 23rd verse J T Lade sleeps here to night

Monday 30
A Cold but not cloudy morning some sun in the day Cloudy and some Rain in the afternoon Wind in the South west Horses plough in the 7 acres T Hoad Reeping in the Kilnfield and Old Evenden in the 12 acres William and David boseling Hops picked 207 Bushels we are troubled to gett above

one Oasting in a day they are so small in general William whento to Bellhurst in the morning Mother and Father whent to J Bland's funeral he buried at Wartling Church according to his own wish He was a Lame Man from his left Hip being out of place by a certain disorder that came upon him when he was about 15 or 16 years old which did at times keep running till his Death his left leg and Thigh left of growing but the time before his other had got its growth which made him always Lame He was a Thin faced man dark hair about 6 feet High and a grave deportment ready Witt a good Scholar in the common branch of Farming and Parish business and generally known and respected the last time I saw him wass on the 13 of August last at this house and the last time that ever I shall this side of the grave and may the Lord prepare me and my other Brothers and Sister for that awful change that when Death may meet me or them we may be Ready

Tuesday 1 October
Windy and Wett great part of the day before I wass up till about 3 O'clock in the afternoon Some clouds and more still in the Evening Horses not at work all day the Hop assistant weighed 5 Pockets of Hops weight 7 cwt 3 Qrts 16 lbs Carters and great part of the Hopers picked 86 Bushels of Hops in the after noon all we did Mr Steer measured William David and I for each of us a new Waistcoat and is going to make T J Lade one J T Lade sleeps here tonight

Wednesday 2
Wett morning cloudy and rain nearly all day windy in the Middle of the day Wind in the Southwest such weather for Harvesting and Hoping as I think wass never known we have 12 acres of Oats 8 acres of Barley and 5 or 6 load of Wheat out we can't meddle with it and grows in the Ear and many of our Neighbours are worse of the we are and some peopel at some places have not carried any Hops are very Slite and much damaged with the late winds and Rains Horses William Hoad carried 5 Pockets to Cade Street to go to London in the morning T Hoad Reeping part of the day in the Kilnfield Old Evenden cleft a log just in the shaw above the pinnel against the Chapel meadow gate William and David Boseling Hopers picked 164 Bushels T Hoad trod 2 pockets in the morning Father whent to Hailsham Market and sold a Barren Cow at £12 10s Messers James and William Lade and Veness fetch the Beast home from Winchelsea Marsh I

suppose they have not growed much etc Crowerst drest a Cibe[311] in Hock near fore foot

Thursday 3
Cloudy day not much sun wind in the North and Southwest with an appearance of rain there wass a few drops Horses nothing Carters David and William Picking up Hops in the Poundfield Garden and helpt us gett in the Bins and Turned the 9 acres Oats again Hopers picked 46 Bushells in the Orchard and 100 in the Roundfield Gardens etc J T Lade sleeps here tonight Father whent to Bellhurst in the afternoon Forgot T Hoad and Master Evenden Reeping T Hoad Treds all the Hops I shall here give an account of the Hoppers names in the Regular standing down by the 12 acre Hedges just in the Poundfield Gardens and mention the southern Bin of every standing and the Western and of every Bin first Dame Hoad Elizabeth and Maid and T Hoad and Family 1st Standing William Burgess and Dame Dann one Bin and Ann Isted and Dame Reed and Children the other Bin 2nd Standing Elizabeth Wratton and Mary Honeysett one Bin Charity Collins and her girl and Mrs Honeysett the other 3rd standing Hannah Hoad and Sarah Morfey one Bin Francis Gander and Mary Morfey the other Bin 4th and Maiden standing Mrs Drew and Mrs Morfey and her Family ingaging the other Bin as yett a week standing this the 5th and last standing in their regular order I remember Foster and Easton pull poles

Friday 4
Misty rain nearly all day not much sun it is very Dirty Wind in the Southwest Horses plough in the Esquirefield Warping T Hoad trod some Hop pocket in the morning and afternoon and some time Hoping Hopers picked 160 Bushels the Hop assistant weighed off 8 Pockets of Hops weight 11 cwt 8 quarters 15 lbs etc

Saturday 5
A Warm day rather cloudy more sun than common Wind in the Southwest South and East Horses Carried 7 pockets of Hops to Cade Street in the morning Henry with one horse carried the Wool to Hailsham they where afterwards turning Oats T Hoad Finised Reeping and whent to striping Hop poles in the Brook Hop garden Old Evenden finished Reeping the 12 acres William and David turned the Barley that was mowed in the 8 acres Hoppers picked 174 Bushels made two Oastings for I thought they would have gathered more Old Nan Morfey came today a new comer to the 5th

[311] Kibe, chilblain.

standing and Father is gone somewhere to see about the Tithe

Sunday 6

Rather Cloudy Warm some sun a shower in the forenoon and one in the Evening several distant strokes of Thunder in the course of the day Wind very still I scarce know where she was JT Lade came here and whent with Father Mother I William David and Elizabeth to Heathfield Chapel in the morning William I and Mother stayed the afternoon Mr Press preached in the morning from Solomon's songs 2 chapter the 4 verse and from Philippians 1st Chapter beginning at the 6th verse in the afternoon he scarce mentioned his text all through his sermon or preached well too Father Mother I William and David whent to the Stonehouse in the Evening Mrs Sobers spoke from these words 'Consider the work of God' the 7 chapter Ecclesiastes and the 13 Verse according to J Blands desire only his Wife and Mother and Father whent into Deep Mourning but Mr Steer made Me My two Brothers and J T Lade each a New Waistcoat with Black Buttons and dark cloth Mr Steer brought them last night

Monday 7

Foggy morning and some Rain cloudy day and no sun Wind in the West in the afternoon but generally still Horses Plough in the Esquire field T Hoad striping Hop poles Hopers picked 152 Bushels etc

Tuesday 8

Foggy morning Warm sunshine day some clouds Foggy evening a Bright moonlight night coming by at this time about 9 O'clock Wind in the South and Southwest etc Horses Plough T Hoad striping Hop poles William and David turning Oats Hoppers picked 170 Bushels Father whent to Brownings etc

Wednesday 9

A sort of Black Fog in the morning not many clouds Rather cold day Wind in the Northeast Horses plough and carried 1 Load of Wheat sheeves from the 12 acres William David and T Hoad turning Oats and carried 2 Loads of Wheat sheeves from the Kilnfield and I from the 12 acres with the oxen which finis[h]es the Wheat Harvest Hoppers picked 182 Bushels Father whent to Rush lake to pay his Tithe but did not Our Parson Cole is got greatly in Debt so that we hardly know who to pay it too

Thursday 10

Cloudy and Foggy morning some clouds in the and not much sun in the daytime Wind in the Northeast East southeast and south etc Horses plough and carried one load of Oats from the Huglets Hodges Oxen T Hoad William and David carried two loads of Oats from Hodges etc Father with them hoppers picked 201 Bushels pole pullers had a suppore[312] here tonight J T Lade sleeps here tonight forgot that on Monday or Tuesday last Mr Couchman sent a man with a pair of Oxen and a cart after Six Hundred weight of Welsh Coal

Friday 11
Foggy morning some clouds rhymes[313] in the day and clear evening Wind in the southwest in the first of the morning afterwards in the Northwest and North rather cold Horses Plough and carried one load of Oats from Hodges oxen carried 2 Loads from 9 acres all the oats are carried into Chapel Barn T Hoad William David Father and Gamekeeper Phillips harvesting Hoppers picked 215 Bushels

Saturday 12
Cloudy Day a few Drops of rain in the evening Wind in the North rather cold Horses and Oxen carried the rest of the Oats from the 9 acres to the Chapel Barn some in the Barn 4 loads nearby in a stack against the Barn and lift two loads out of the barn Father William and David with Carters Wm Hoad John Oxley the Blacksmith Phillips the Gamekeeper and Joseph Morfey the Mason (who has been here this two or three morning about the Oast and the Parlour grate) Harvesting we have now carried all our Oats Hoppers Finished hopping in the Poundfield garden this afternoon and picked 153 Bushels the whole Number of Bushels of Hops we growed this year is ... the pole pullers and I helpt Harvesters after we had done. J T Lade sleeps here to night Mr Squires just called

Sunday 13
Cloudy day Rather cold wind in the North Father Mother I William and David whent to Heathfield Chapel in the morning Father William and David stayed the afternoon Elizabeth and the Maid whent in the afternoon Mr Press preached in the morning from the 14 chapter John 26th verse and from John the 12th Chapter and the 32 verse in the afternoon. William David and I whent to Mrs Sobers in the evening she spoke from Hebrews the 9th Chapter and the 27 verse Father received a Hop Letter

---

312 Supper.
313 Rimes, frost.

Monday 14
Rather cloudy day not clear Wind in the North and Southwest Horse plough in the Esquirefield Foster William David and I unloaded 3 load of Oats in the Chapel Barn and turned some Barley and gott and carried one load with the oxen to the Home Barn T Hoad and Easton mowing Barley in the 8 acres Old Dann getting Charcoals into the Oast etc William Hoad and his Mate helpt William David and I take 4 Hives of Bees fore me tonight Father whent the other farms and Down into the Marsh etc. Father received a letter from Latham our Hop Factor yesterday he has sold 6 Pockets of Hops at £145s per hundred weight

Tuesday 15
Some clouds very still Wind in the South etc Horses plough T Hoad and Easton finished mowing Barley in the 8 acres in the morning T Hoad stripping Hop poles in the Croft afterwards Easton put a Fence against the South end of the Oast to save the window and helpt gett up a load of Barley David and I unloaded a Load of Barley in the morning William went to Mr Russell's in the morning William and I carried two Cart load of Chucks from the New Oast home and William David and I with Easton carried a large load of Barley with the oxen in to the Home Barn Foster helpt us unload it he was threshing Oats all day in the CB Old Dann as on yesterday J Morfey and boy at work in the Back Court about the sewer and the well etc Father whent to Bellhurst etc

Wednesday 16
A cold morning clear day I have not seen a cloud all day wind in the South and Southeast Rather cold Horses Finished Warping the 8 acres and the 7 acres T Hoad I William and David with all the Oxen and 3 Carts carried 4 Pockets of Hops to Dillgate for Wm Harmer to carry to Cade Street and a load of clay from against J Morfey to the Back Court for J Morfey and his Boy J Reed and 47 loads of Dung from the Oxen Close into the 10 acres etc. Foster and Easton threshing Wheat in the Home Barn Old Dann striping Hop poles in the Orchard T Hoad two pockets of Hops in the Evening Mrs Lade whent to Silverash she says that Hops have sold at 28£ per Hundred at Wey Hill Fair I think it is a Ficktion Father whent to Hailsham Market J T Lade Sleeps here to night

Thursday 17
Cloudy showery day not much sun and North till I did know when the wind wass in the afternoon she wass in the Northwest in the afternoon still

evening with a kind of Foggy Mist Horses Wm Hoad whent to Wenhouse Hill after some Lime in a cart to Lime the Wheat with and sowing in the 7 acres Oxen I William David and T Hoad carried 1 load of Moul from against the back court to the 10 acres and 49 Loads of Dung as yesterday Foster and Easton cleaned some Wheat and threshing Old Dann striping Hop poles J Morfey and Boy as yesterday Mr Ticehurst the Wheeler at Ashburnham came and bought our ash poles and a small log Old Evenden came and settled for his work

Friday 18
A Wett dirty morning a Drying afternoon Wind in the Northwest and North. Horses and oxen carried 210 Ash boles a quantity of spokes and Waggon staves and a log of nearly 6 Foot of Timber to Mr Ticehurst Ashburnham with two Waggons David and I with the oxen Foster and Easton threshing in the Home Barn Old Dann striping Hop poles etc. T Hoad finised putting the Hops up 12 Pockets and an end a Tub and some small parcels one as yet to weigh on Monday next Mr J Purstglove and Mr R Chandler came and bought 31 sheep for 41£ this evening

Saturday 19
Cloudy some rain and some sun in the day Dark cloudy Evening some rain Wind in the Northwest and southwest Horses Harrow William Hoad sowed 7 acres Oxen Nothing T Hoad striping Hop poles in the Croft and Old Dann in the Orchard Foster and Easton threshing and cleaned 9 Bushels Wheat David helpt he and I drove the Calves from the Wain house field into the Croft Father and William Drove the 31 sheep to Cowden in the morning I measured 2 acres and a Half of J Thompsetts Reeping for Jesse Smith and William and David whent to Nutting[314] in the afternoon J T Lade sleeps here tonight

Sunday 20
Showery morning Cold windy day some clouds Wind in the Southwest and West Father Mother I William David Elizabeth and the Maid whent to Heathfield Chapel in the morning Father I William and Elizabeth staid the afternoon Mr Press preached from Galatians 4 chapter the 6 verse in the morning and from Luke 2 chapter 31 verse in the afternoon Father I William and David whent to Mrs Sobers in the evening she spoke from Isiah 44 chapter the 22nd verse

---

314 For cobnuts.

1816

Monday 21

A Cold Windy day some Clouds in the afternoon Wind in the North Northwest Horses Harrowing 7 acres I with 4 oxen fetched 5 sacks of Wheat and about a Bushell of Turnips from Bellhurst and moved the Waggon in the Furze wood for Master Evendens Chucks, William and David turned the Barley in the 8 acres T Hoad striping Hop poles in the Croft etc Old Dann in the Orchard Foster and Easton threshing Wheat in the Home Barn I suppose it yields very badly according to the custom of the year seed wheat at about 26 or 27£ per load Mr Warner weighed off the rest of our Hops 12 Pockets on hand and some small Barels and a Tub 20 cwt 2 quarters 13 lbs all our Growths – 46 cwt 1 quarter 3 lbs

This night we pay off our Hoppers the following manner at 3d per Bushel

	Talley	£. s d
	(Bushels)	
T Hoad Wife and Family	15. 11	2. 7. 9
Dame Hoad	9. 1	1. 7. 3
Ann Isted	8. 1	1. 4. 3
Mrs Reed	16. 7	2. 9. 9
William Burgess	9. 3	1. 7. 9
Dame Dann	10. 9	1. 12. 3
Hannah Hoad	11. 9	1. 15. 3
Francis Gander	11. 2	1. 13. 6
Sarah Morfey	11. 2	1. 13. 6
Mary Morfey	8. 6	1. 5. 6
Mrs Morfey and Family	8. 10	1. 6. 6
Old Nann Morfey	8. 4	1. 5. 0
Mrs Drew	4. 7	13. 9
Charity Collins	7. 0	1. 1. 0
Mrs Honeysett	18. 8	2. 16. 0
Mary Honeysett	10. 8	1. 12. 0
Elizabeth Wratten	11. 8	1. 15. 0
Sister and Maid	11. 0	1. 13. 0
	11. 9	1. 15. 3
Master Dann	15 Days drying	1. 17. 6

There was besides the Hoppers and our workmen Master Evenden and his Wife Phillips the Game keeper John Oxley the blacksmith J Morfey the mason and master John and David Honeysett the thatcher to supper have to night and Mrs Winchester's Girl ditto Charity Collins wass not here she is a Nursing. The wass several children I shall not mention

Tuesday 22

Wett weather all the forenoon some clouds in the afternoon and the wind so still I scarce know where she wass Horses Harrowing in the Esquirefield William Hoad sowed the Wheat I fetched yesterday William Hoad helpt them some times David and I with the Oxen Drawed one load of master Evenden chuck home to Rushlake green for him David and I fetched 8 of the Hop bins from the Poundfield Garden into the Oast Chamber and Changed and whent to Mrs Delves Sale at Redpale William there to Father ditto in the afternoon Foster and Easton not at work for us neither Old Dann T Hoad striping Hop poles in the Croft J T Lade sleeps here to night

Wednesday 23

A Bright sunny day rather cloudy morning and a few small clouds in the day forgot it wass a very cold frosty morning the wind so still I don't know where she wass a clear starry light evening Horses Harrow William Hoad sowing as yesterday David and T Hoad with the Oxen carried 1 load of Moul from the Back Court 1 load of Dung from the Hay pound 20 loads of Dung from the Oxen Close 1 load of Moul ditto 7 loads of Dung from the Great Barn doors of the Chapel Barn and 4 loads of Dung from the Poundfield bottom all into the 10 acres T Hoad threshed some Oats for the Carter in the CB at night Foster and Easton threshing all day and I helpt them clean 12 Bushels of Wheat at night in the Barn James Easton gathered the Bullice[315] afterwards Old Dann striping Hop poles in the Orchard William whent to Bellhurst to help them threshing Wheat with the mechien[316] the Honerable Lady Miss Kemp and Mrs Sobers visited and Drank Tea here this evening etc

Thursday 24

Windy day and cloudy afternoon rather cloudy morning and a Wett evening after 7 O'clock there wass no dew in the morning Wind in the Southwest or nearly south Horses struck the lot pease out in the Esquirefield etc William Hoad Sowed/Harrowed the Furzefield Oxen

[315] Bullace.
[316] Machine.

carried the rest of the Barley from the 8 acres just into the Corner of the 12 Acres in a little s[t]ack of 5 loads which finishes our Harvest for this year T Hoad Easton and Foster with David and I ditto William Hoad helpt us at night it was in good order I know nothing about Old Dann I suppose he wass at work as William whent to Bellhurst on yesterday Father whent to the other Farms etc

Friday 25

Cloudy showery day rather Windy from the south Horses plough warping in the 10 acres T Hoad Easton and Foster spreading dung in the 10 acres part of the day Foster and Easton threshing in the HB in the afternoon T Hoad threshing in the CB his Girls where striping hop poles in the Poundfield Garden yesterday and today Father had thought of not working the Oxen but Mr Jesse Goldsmith at the Tilly Brick Kilns had Liten[317] his Kiln and was drove out for Faggots and we carried him 200 Kiln Faggots from our Kiln piles he helpt us load Old Dann striping hop poles in the Orchard William whent to Bellhurst to threshing as yesterday

Saturday 26

Some clouds all day and some sun wind in the East Horses plough I set a Waggon in the Lodge with a pair of Oxen who drawed it from the 12 acres T Hoad spreading Dung in the 10 acres before the Horses Foster and Easton threshing Old Dann not at work William and David and I measured T Hoad and Easton Reeping in the 12 acres Father T Hoad David and I measured Dame Danns work in the Kiln field she looked on whilst and afterwards took her money Forgot that the Honeysetts thatched the Barley stack yesterday and part of the Tares stack against the Home Barn and today J Morfey and A Boy where here yesterday and today a paving the Back court and mending the Tileing of the House Father whent to Brownings in the morning William whent to gardener street in the afternoon Mr Waters brought a Letter from Latham who has sold 7 more Pockets of Hops at 14 per Hundred forgot his Brother William wass here from Beestons last night Messers Randel and Dunk where home the Evening Father sold to Mr Rangel[318] a pair of Oxen 7 years old last spring named Stout and Valient and a goose for 35£ Clock strikes nine J T Lade sleeps here tonight

[317] Lit.
[318] Randell?

Sunday 27

Sunny day Rather Warm some clouds Wind in the southeast Father Mother William I David Elizabeth and the Maid whent to Heathfield Chapel in the morning Mother Elizabeth William and David stayed the afternoon Mr Press preached in the morning from 1 Corinthians the 16 Cha and the 22nd verse and from 2 Chronicles 33 Cha the last clause of the 13 verse Father Mother I William David and Elizabeth whent to Mrs Sobers in the evening she spoke from Ezekial 37 chapter part of the 4 verse 'O ye dry bones etc'. J T Lade sleeps here tonight

Monday 28

Cloudy morning some rain in the forenoon some sun in the afternoon moonlight evening wind in the southeast and East Horses plough David and I with the Oxen drawed Master Evendens other load of Chucks home and some straw from the Bushy fields to the Home Close T Hoad Scouring out last Vores[319] in the sowed fields Foster and Easton threshing Old Dann striping Hop poles in the Archer and Orchard garden T Hoads Girl's ditto in the Poundfield Father whent to Rushlake green and Jollithous to Wilmshursts apprisements William and I whent to Boreham and looked Brownings and Masums Farms over and whent to Bellhurst etc Mrs Sober's Maids two of them Visitors Mrs Lade whent to Bellhurst Honeysett Finised thatching the straw stack and mended the Cow Lodge

Tuesday 29

A clear warm sunshine day Some clouds wind in the East and Northeast William Hoad and David with the Horses Plough in the 10 acres Henry not at work Oxen not at work William and I Finised spreading Dung in the 10 acres and threshed some Oats for the Horses in the CB Foster threshing in the HB T Hoad stacking poles in the Croft his girls striping in the Poundfield Old Dann ditto Orchard Easton not at work It has been a runing day with us Father whent to Brownings and Mr Randel bought a pair of Oxen from there at 35£ and came and bought a pair of 3 yearling steers named Peost and Lively at 30£ Mr and Mrs Dunk wass with him Elizabeth Lade visitor Mr Henry Purstglove and William Harmer whent home this evening

Wednesday 30

After a wett showry night a cloudy and showry morning some sun in the

[319] Furrows.

day a showry afternoon Cloudy and showry Evening wind in the southeast Horses plough T Hoad Finised the Croft and began stack the poles in the Poundfield garden his girls striping ditto Old Dann in the Orchard Easton not at work Foster not at work in the morning threshing in the afternoon William and David fetched a pair of Oxen from Brownings and spilt[320] my Team by driving the Two Older and the two youngest to Dallington with them to Mr Randels I Whent to Rushlake Father whent to Hailsham Market J T Lade sleeps here tonight

Thursday 31
Cloudy showry day some sun Wind in the Southeast and southwest Horses Plough Foster threshing Old Dann stacking poles in the Archer T Hoad and the Girls as yesterday Easton not at work Father and I fetched the two new Bins from the Poundfield into the Oast William and I did some gaping William David and I whent to Mr Newman's Sale at Herrings Dallington it is full of sales now, there wass one on Tuesday last at Boreham and tomorrow at Jollinghous and one this week at Heathfield two last week in this Parish and one just by at Redpale in Dallington It is dirty and very Wett weather generally and I Fodder my Oxen steady once a day with straw and have for this week past Forgot T Hoad kild a sheep Mr J Veness our neighbour wass here today Father is at Mr Waters sennells[321] this evening Messrs Everest and Preston Cald as they whent home from sale Forgot that my two Brothers and I with the Oxen carried some wheat and straw to the CB and the Honeysetts thatched the Oat stack

Friday 1 Nov
Friday showery weather and some sun and so still I don't know where the wind was a small breeze from the west or there abouts in the afternoon horses plough Carters began the sec[on]d hay stack yester day J Morfey borrowed 4 oxen and a cart to fetch some potatoes from Masum[322] near Boreham with 20 bushels and carried for us 347 Cooper staves to Mr Wratten Gardener also Mr Woodhams hops 20 Clee[?] to go to Hailsham by the carriers to morrow and carried 100 sheep skins to Mr Swetmans to Glovers at Gardener Street Foster and Easton threshing the forenoon Fosters wife was up tumbling to pieces in the afternoon T Hoad and family and Old Dann as yesterday Father whent to S Wilmhursts sale at Jollithous

[320] Split.
[321] Senior?
[322] Marsham.

in this parrish J T Lade sleeps here to night

Saturday 2
Showery dirty weather wind in the south west horses plough Foster threshing ½ day Easton all day T Hoad Old Dann etc as yesterday Mr J Waters senr visitor in morning he appraised Bellhurst Browning and Marsham Farms Father and Sophia Bland are going partners[?] in the above farm Father and I whent with him Mr John Purstglove at Cowden was with us Mother whent to Bellhurst we all dined at Bellhurst – Father brought a pair of oxen at sale yesterday for 7£ 10s and a Cheese Press and cube and I don't know their prices J T Lade sleeps here to night we have lost a marsh lamb the two days and think it was stolen one of them died to day

Sunday 3
Weather as yesterday generally – Father mother I William David Elizabeth and the maid whent to Heathfield Chapel in the morning William and I stayed the afternoon – Mr Press preached in the morning from the 3 Psalm the 9 and 10 verses and from Ezekiel 34 Cha 12 verse in the afternoon my two brothers and I where at the Stonehouse in the evening Mr Sobers spoke from the 89th psalm the 15 & 16 verses

Monday 4
A flood in the morning cloudy day some sun wind in the north southeast and south. I believe – but still Horses whent to Jollithous and drawed home in the narrow wheeled waggon – a cheese press weights etc a cube and barrell carters drove the oxen home their names are Luick and Nimble – Nimble the aft side they are 5 years off old – Old Dann has done striping and stacking the poles in the orchard garden – the other workemen as on Friday last except Foster who worked all day to day – Wm David and I boseling – Father whent to Warbleton Church Rushlake and Priory Elizabeth whent to Mr Russels and brought some earthen ware etc – etc

Tuesday 5
Showery dirty weather wind in the south west Carter threshing in the morning afterwards plough in the 10 acres with the horses rest work men as yesterday Wm and David fetched 6 yearling Beast from our marsh to Cowden Father whent after the other forman I have been nearly all day making new Taleys – J T Lade came home with Father and slept here last night

Wednesday 6
Showery weather S.S.W. Horses healed the Kiln up healed the Chalk Stack up with Kiln faggots Eastone & Foster threshing in home barn T Hoad threshing in Chapel Barn Master Dann stub morning in the afternoon David flawed two marsh lambs d[r]ove the marsh lambs into the Bushy Field & Luick and Nimble into the Silver Field Wm I whent from here about 3 O' clock and arrived at eight at Lewes this morning Lewes Tabernacle was opened for Devine Service today the Rev. Matthew Wilkes preached in the morning the Rev. R Stodhart in the afternoon etc The Rev. John Hayatt (or Kayatt) in the evening J T Lade sleeps here tonight

Thursday 7
Fine day Horses carried 12 pockets & one end of hops to Cade Street carried a load of kiln faggots from the Kiln to the House T Hoad hop pole stripping Eastone and Foster threshing and cleaning Old Dann mowing the stub in the Kiln Field Wm and I came home from Lewes to carpenters at work

Friday 8
A Frosty morning Horses harrowed Wm Hoad and I sowed 3 sacks of wheat Wm and Foster and David cleaned 1 ... wheat Foster threshing tears in the hoam barn[323] Eastone and Old Dann mowing the stubble in the Kiln Field T Hoad finished stripping hop poles to carpenters Mrs Lade went to the Priory Mr B Warters was here this evening Father went to the other farms

Saturday 9
Showery weather Horses striking out vers[324] Wm Foster threshing & stubble mowers T Hoad not at work Wm I David threshing oats in the Chapple Barn Father went to Mr Randel in the afternoon I drove the mars[h] lambs into the Pound field

Sunday 10
Cold morning with some snow a more pleasant afternoon with a cold evening wind in the north Father I William and David whent to Heathfield Chapel in the morning William stayed the afternoon Mr Press preached both times from the two last verses of the 59th Chapter of Isiah William whent to Mrs Sobers in the evening she spoke from Epations 2 cha the 13

[323] Tares in the home barn.
[324] Vores, furrows.

Drilling and harrowing

and part of the 14th verse the maid whent to Herstmonceaux Chapel in the morning

Monday 11
Cold frosty morning cold day cloudy windy and wett evening a large flood about midnight wind up in the north in the morning and moved gradually to the south west in the evening Horses plough in the 10 acres David and I with the oxen waiting in the carpenters and two loads of hop bines from the Poundfield Garden to the Ox Close and one load from the orchard to the home close lent Wm Harmer Easton T Hoad not here in the morning threshing oats in the CB in the afternoon I suppose Old Dann was at his work mowing stubble Foster not at work 3 carpenters mending lodges gates Barrow ways etc Wm flawed another marsh lamb in the morning it is strange what is the matter with them sheep they have lived well and have been after changed – Wm whent to Silverash and Bellhurst etc Father whent to Rushlake Green Mr John Purstglove has been here all the evening rather weather bound till midnight

Tuesday 12
Showery weather wind in the south west and North west – Horses finished

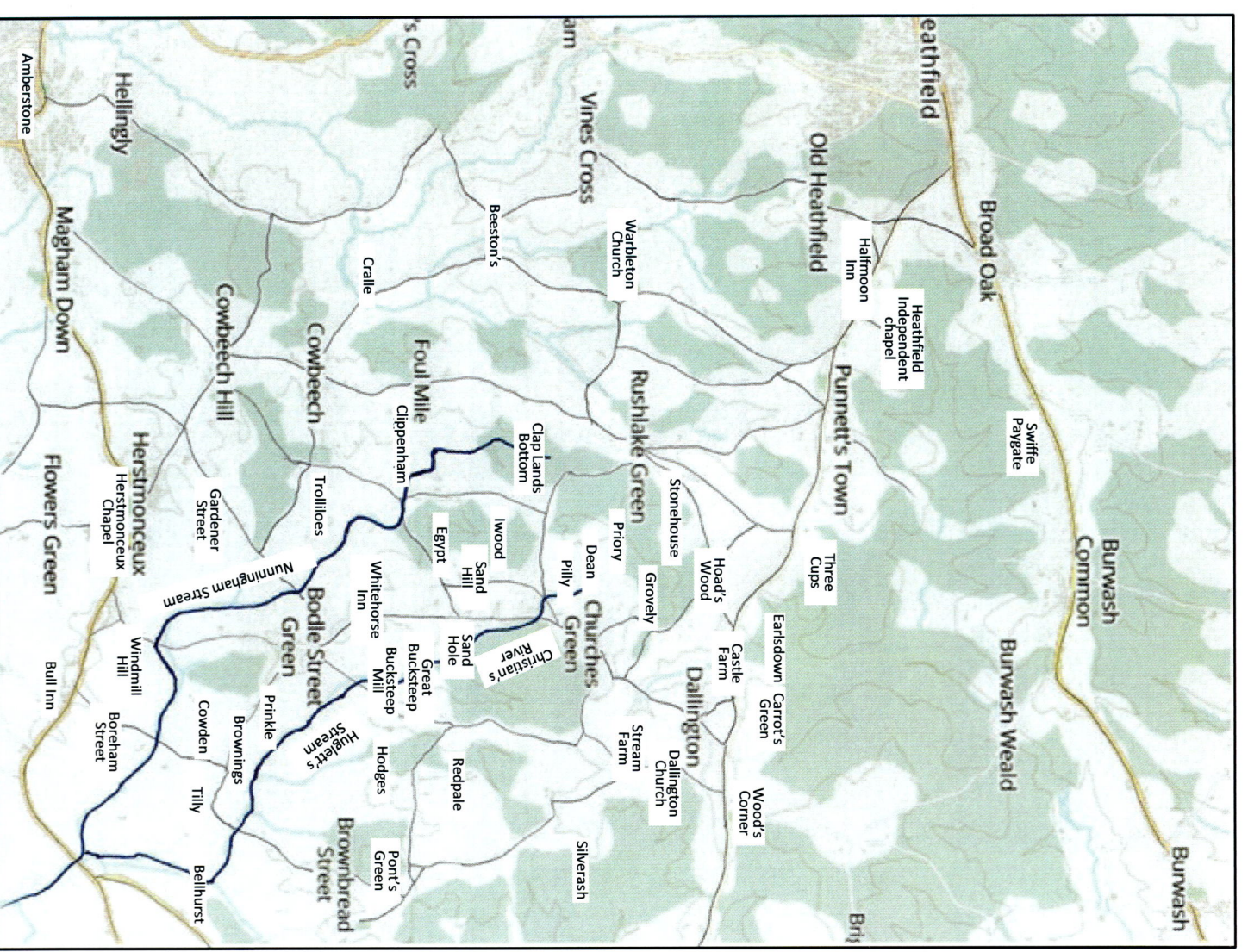

2: Bucksteep and the surrounding area

Scale 1 mile (1.6 km)

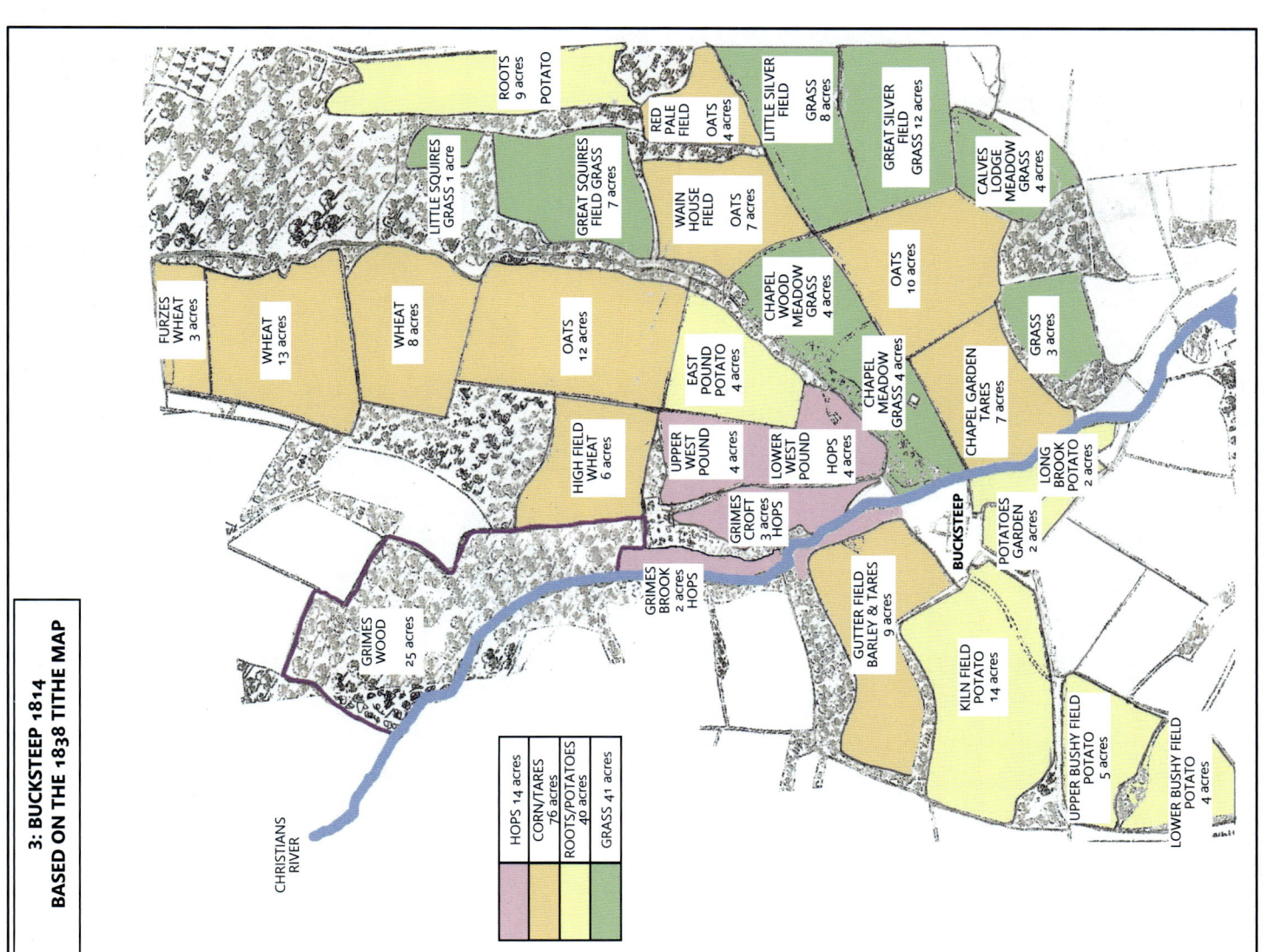

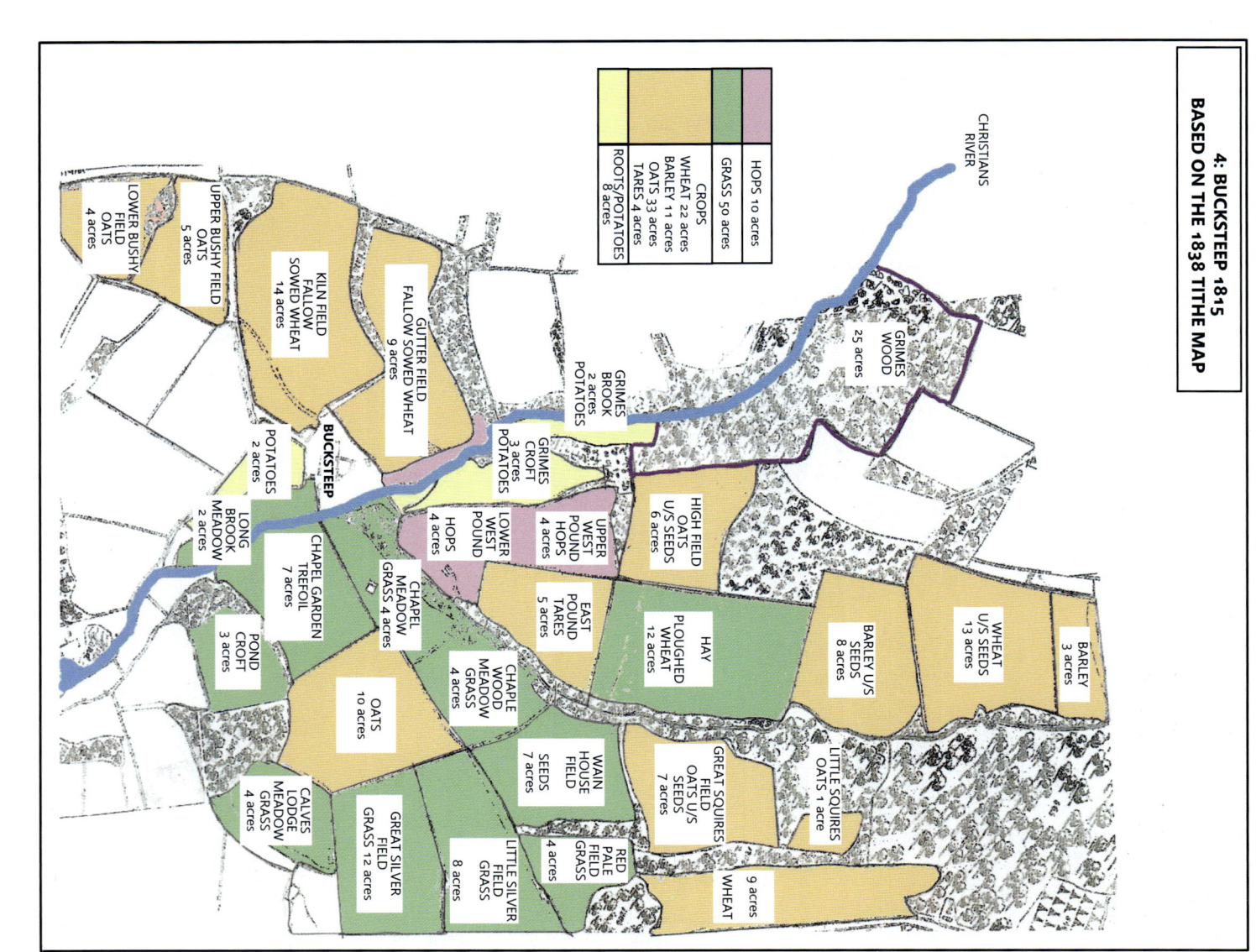

5: BUCKSTEEP 1816
BASED ON THE 1838 TITHE MAP

Fields shown on the map:

- OATS U/S SEEDS 9 acres
- RED PALE FIELD GRASS 4 acres
- LITTLE SILVER FIELD GRASS 8 acres
- GREAT SILVER FIELD GRASS 12 acres
- CALVES LODGE MEADOW HAY 4 acres
- LITTLE SQUIRES HAY 1 acre
- GREAT SQUIRES FIELD HAY THEN TURNIPS 7 acres
- WAIN HOUSE FIELD HAY 7 acres
- TARES PLOUGH WHEAT 10 acres
- FALLOW 3 acres
- OATS 13 acres
- BARLEY U/S TREFOIL 8 acres
- WHEAT 12 acres
- CHAPEL WOOD MEADOW GRASS 4 acres
- POND CROFT 3 acres
- HIGH FIELD HAY 6 acres
- EAST POUND ROOTS 5 acres
- UPPER WEST POUND HOPS 4 acres
- LOWER WEST POUND HOPS 4 acres
- CHAPEL MEADOW GRASS 4 acres
- CHAPEL GARDEN TARES PLOUGHED IN 7 acres
- LONG BROOK HAY 2 acres
- GRIMES CROFT 3 acres HAY
- GRIMES BROOK 2 acres HAY
- PEAS 2 acres
- GUTTER FIELD WHEAT 9 acres
- GRIMES WOOD 25 acres
- KILN FIELD WHEAT 14 acres
- UPPER BUSHY FIELD HAY 5 acres
- LOWER BUSHY FIELD HAY 4 acres

BUCKSTEEP

CHRISTIANS RIVER

Legend:
- HOPS 8 acres
- CROPS 84 acres
- GRASS 57 acres
- ROOTS/POTATOES 4 acres

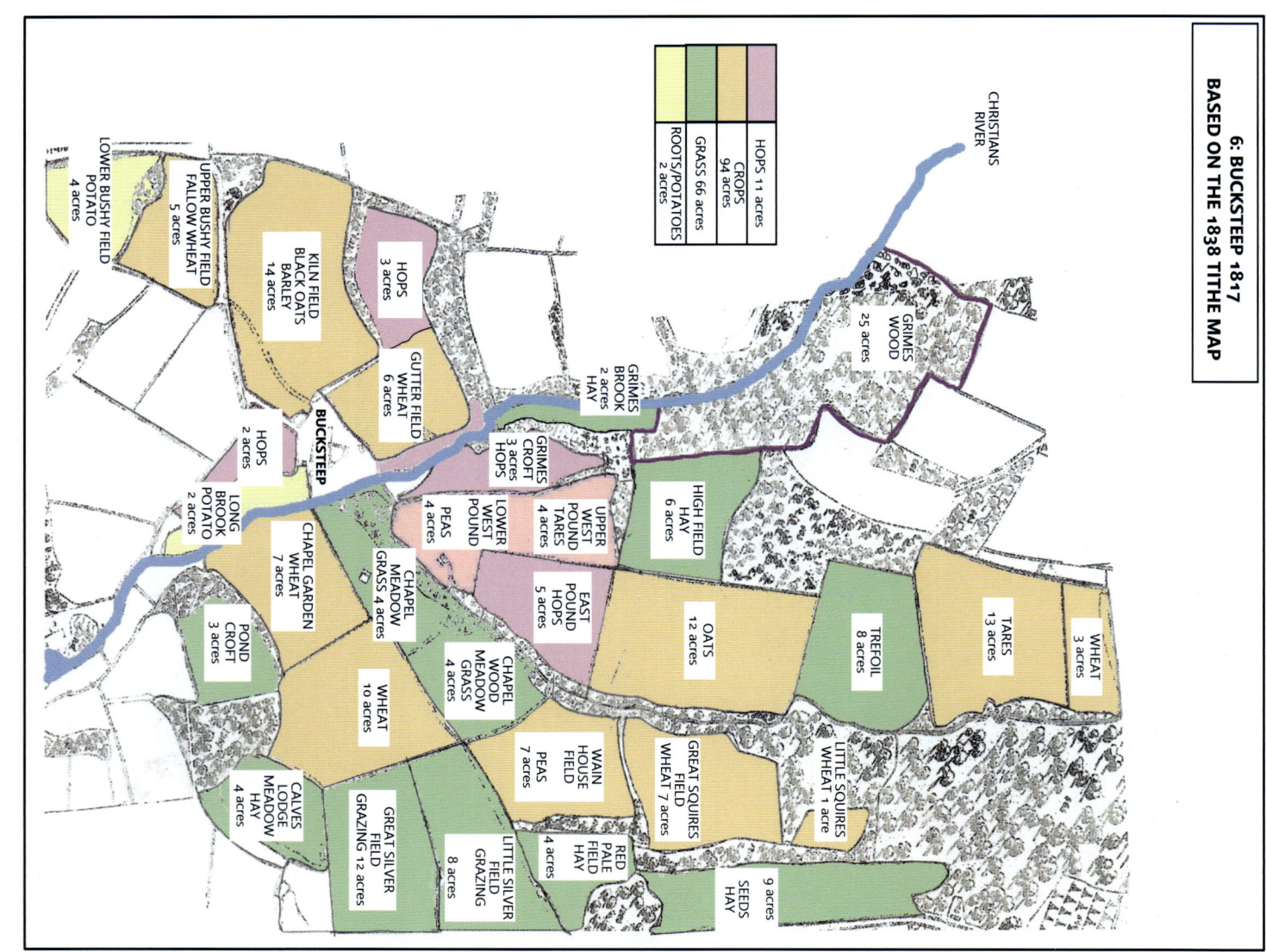

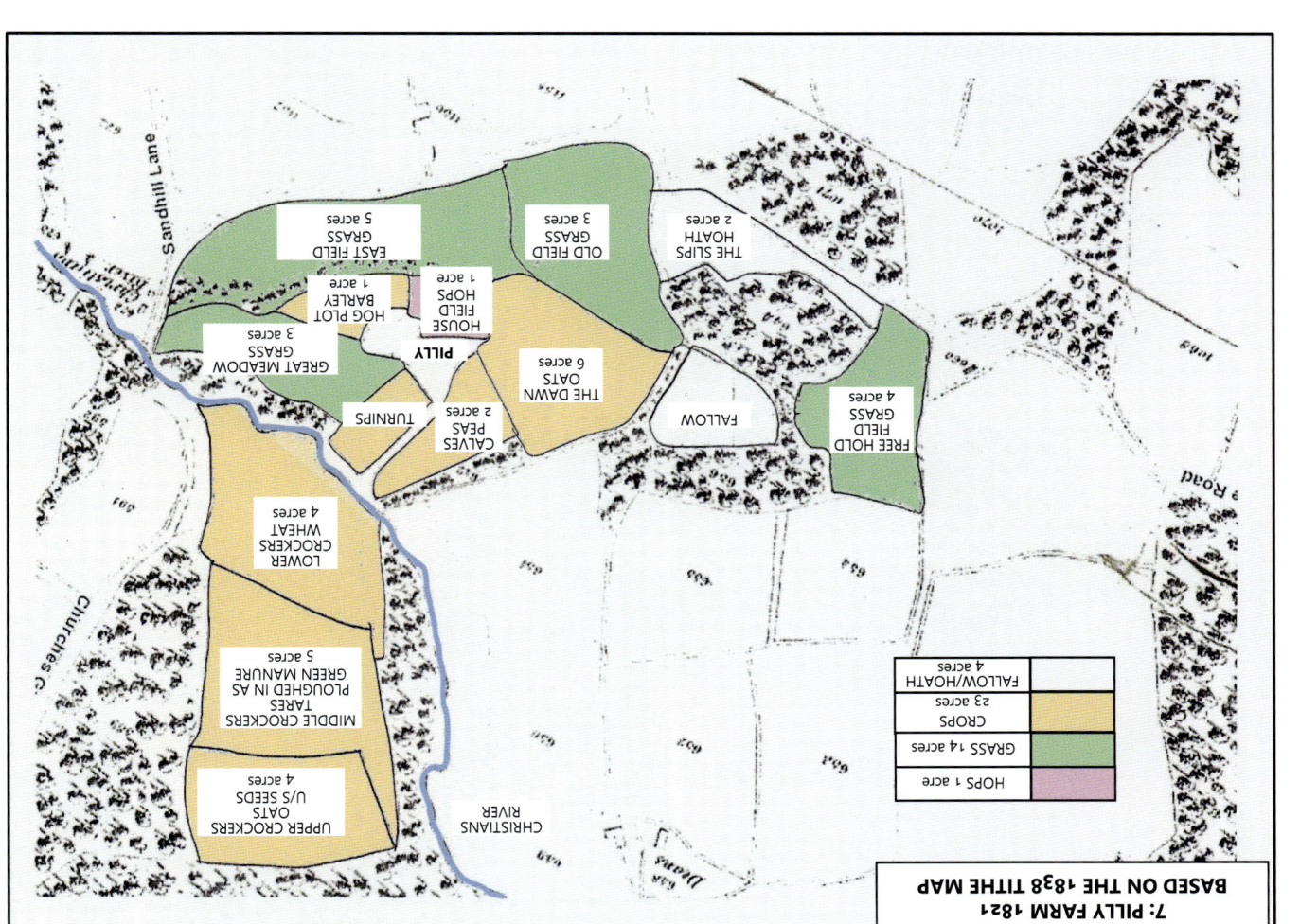

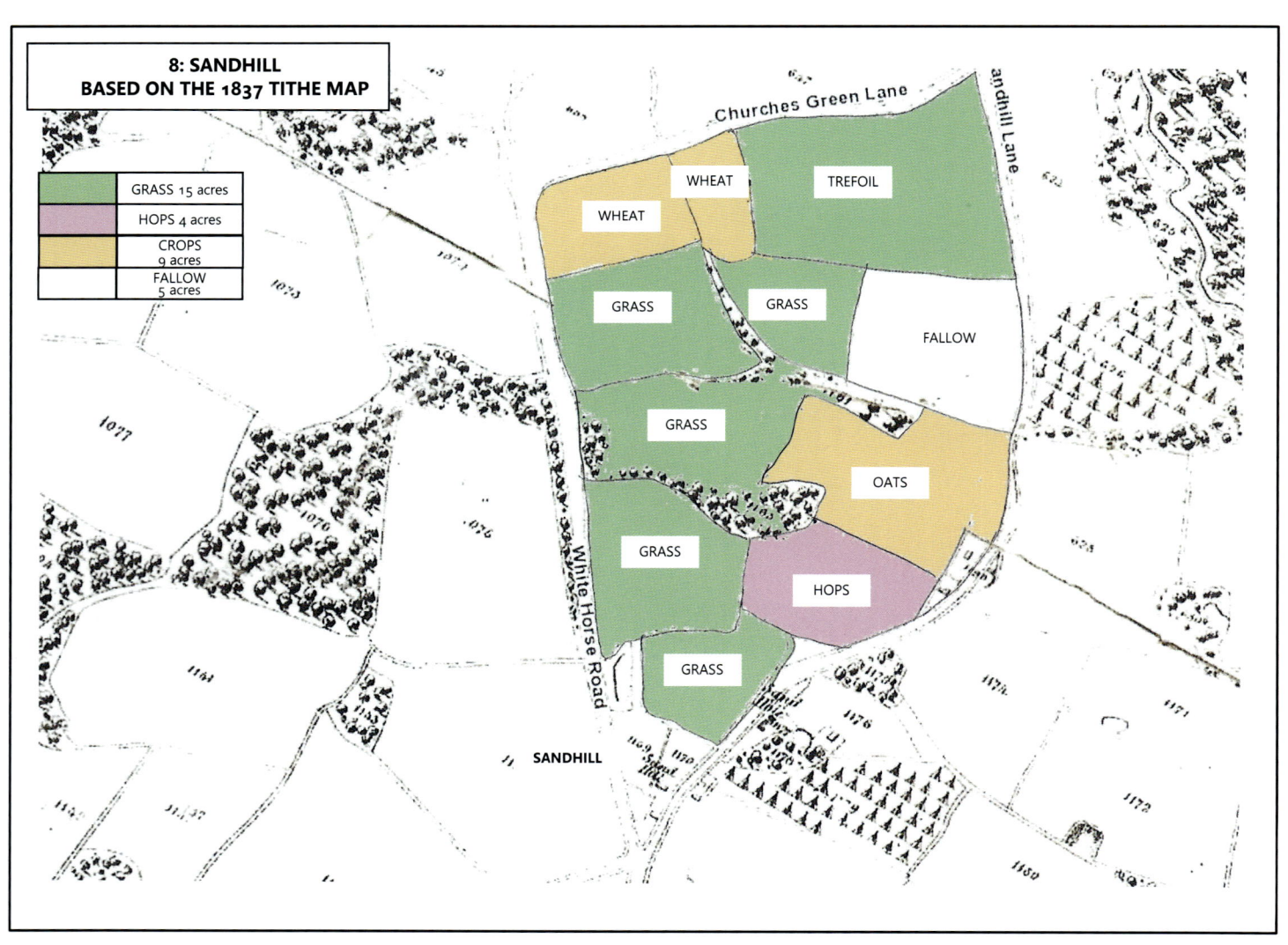

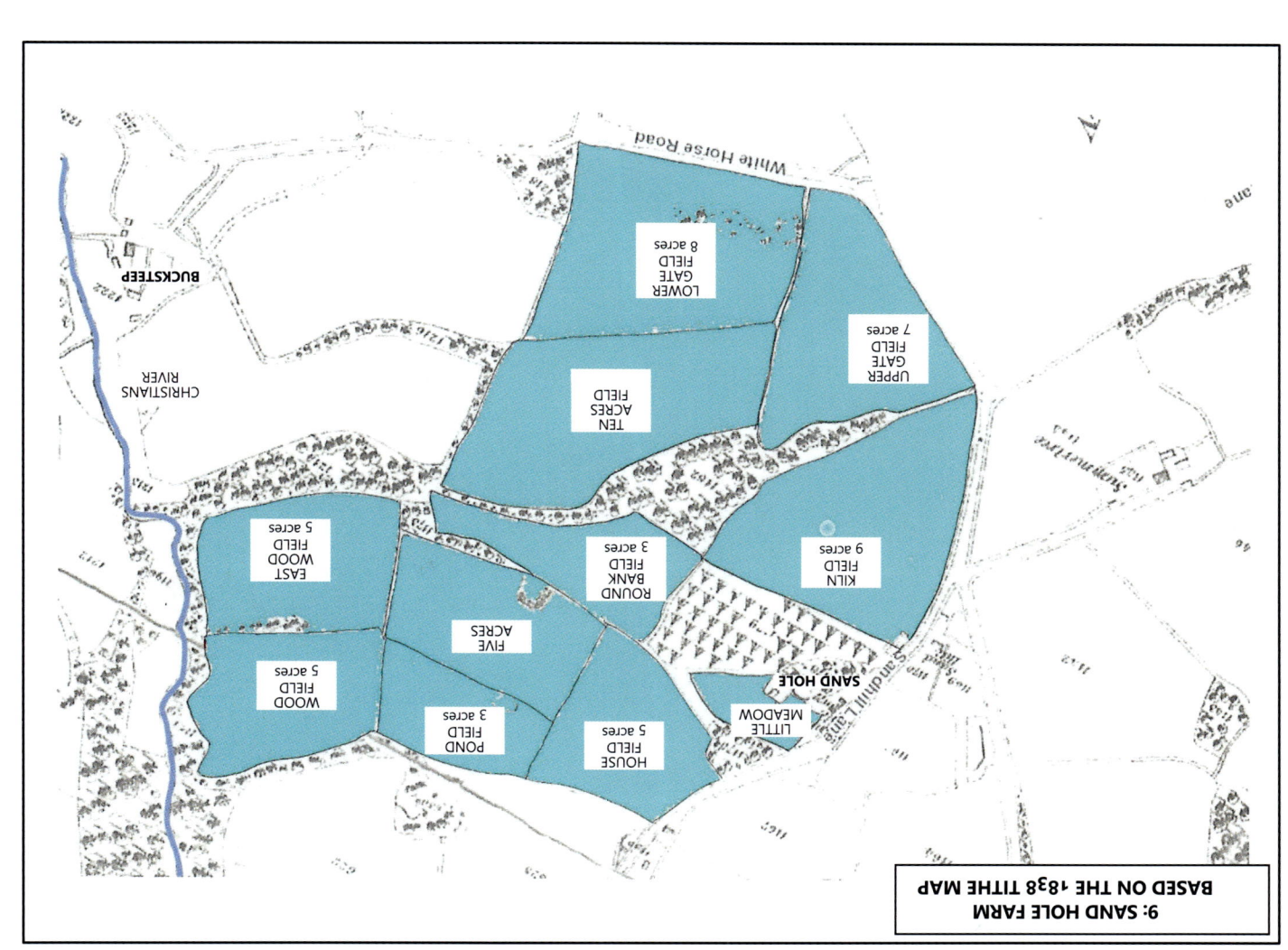

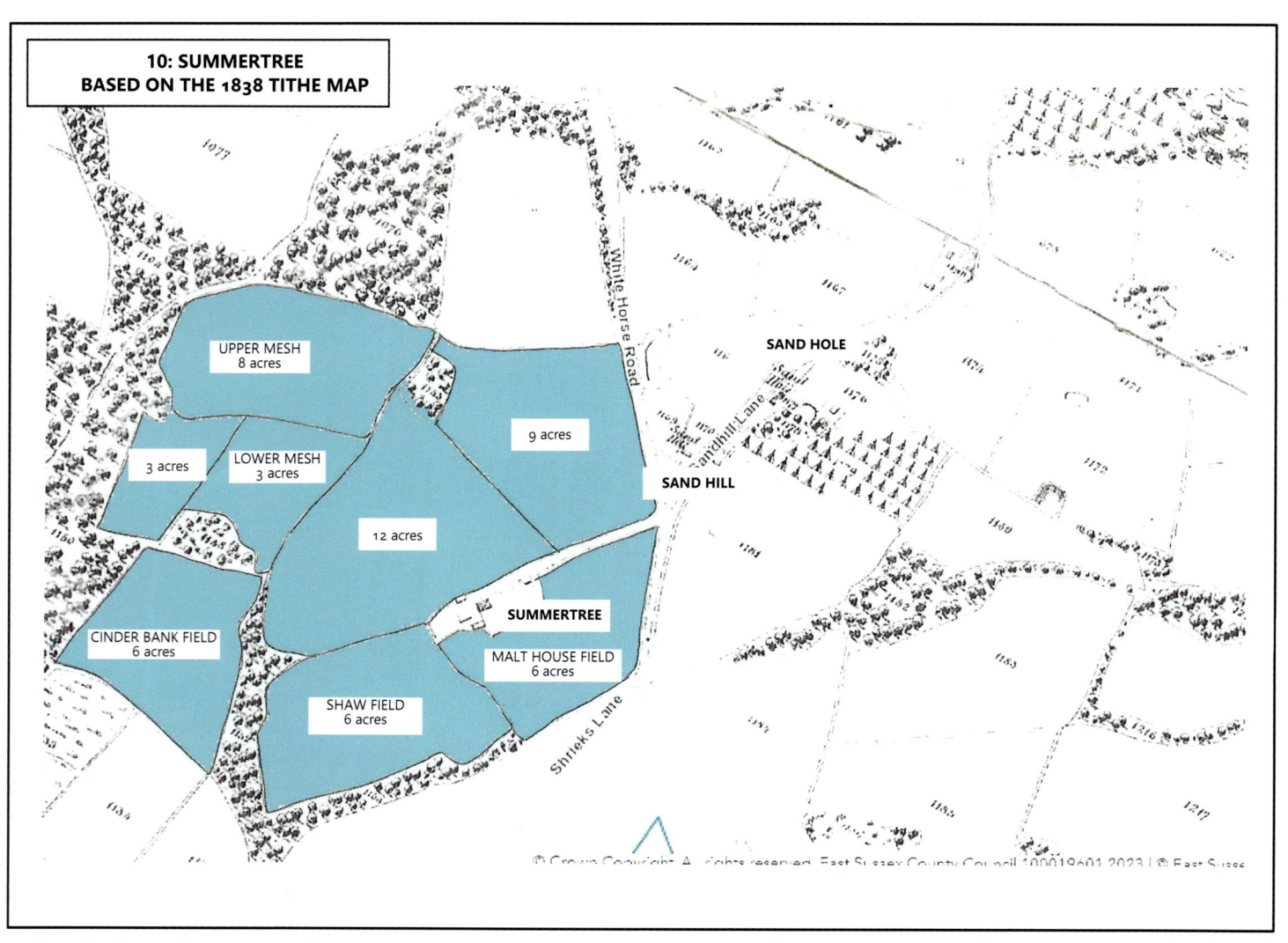

11: Gravestone of Nicholas Oxley

In memory of NICHOLAS OXLEY Late of COWDEN FARM, WARTLING, son of THOMAS WILLIAM? and ELIZABETH OXLEY, who departed this life the 21st? day of June 1833. Aged 38 . 'Many are the afflictions of the Righteous, but the Lord delivereth him out of them all'

12: Gravestone of Elizabeth Oxley

In memory of ELIZABETH OXLEY Who departed this life at COWDEN FARM, WARTLING, the 30th October 1843. Aged 55 years and whose dying words were:

Prepare me, Lord, for Thy right hand Then come that joyful day
Come Death, and come celestial band To bear my soul away
How vain appear the things of time and sense
How transitory all those earthly toys
When the Great Master calls the spirits home
To dwell forever in sublimer joys

ploughing the 10 acres – T Hoad threshing – Old Dann was at work a little while in the morning and Easton a little while in the afternoon Father whent to Battle Market Wm Harmer gave a calf a drink in the morning Mr Press preached here this evening from 2 Thessalonians 1 chapter the first part of the 7th verse

Wednesday 13

Cloudy but not much rain wind in the west some sun and sky very still horses Wm David and Henry harrow and Wm Hoad finished sowing the 10 acres Father and Wm b[or]rowed a horse off Wm Harman and struck out the verse[325] – I stoped the hogs out of the Archer and made a place ready for the potatoes and fetched a load and a part of another from the further end of the croft with the oxen T Hoad and family dug them Foster threshing in the HB – Old Dann and Easton mowing stubble in the Kilnfield – Mr Press whent home

Thursday 14

Horses plough in the Highfield and round bank Hodges – I with the oxen fetched home 40 bushels of potatoes to day I fetched home 33 bushels yesterday – T Hoad and family digging them William David and I dug up the potatoes in the garden – Foster and G Guy (a new comer) threshing tares in the home barn – Old Dann mowing stubble Carter not at work – Father whent to the other farms Wm whent to Rushlake Green – Mr T Waters J Wood and Mr R Russel called here today but did not get off their Horses

Friday 15

Frosty morning clear cold day some snow in the evening after 8 o'clock wind in the north – Horses ploughed and harrowed what they ploughed Wm Hoad sowed the wheat Wm helpt the carters – I with the oxen fetched home 20 bushels of potatoes and put them into the Toolroom David helpt me unload T Hoad and family dug them Foster threshing G Guy Do in the afternoon Old Dann and Easton mowing stubble Mr Wilmshurst on business Wm David and I heald the 73 bush[els] of potatoes up in the Archer and flawed another Marsh Lamb and put another into the CB which I think will soon die – drove the rest into the Chapelwood Meadow

Saturday 16

Frosty morning cold cloudy day wind in the north – Horses plough sowed

---

[325] Vores: furrows.

and harrowed what they ploughed oxen David and I carried 1 load of hop bines from the Archer to the Home Close and 1 load from the Poundfield and a small load of stubble from the Kilnfield to the oxen close – T Hoad threshing oats in the CB the lamb I wrote about yesterday was dead this morning Wm flawed it David says there are five more in danger Foster and G G threshing and cleared 11 bushels of tares – Eastone and Old Dann Mowing stubble Father whent into the Marsh William whent to Browning and met him at Bellhurst Mr J Purstglove sent mowers[?] and horse after a sack of peas

Sunday 17
Clear cold day wind in the north east Chaple at excepting maid Ann Father Wm Eliz ... afternoon preach morning 40 Psalm 6 7 8 verses afternoon from 2[?] Book Peter[?] three brothers Stonehouse in the evening preach from 6 chap 37 verse of St John

Monday 18
Showery day wind in the south west Horses plough 7 sown tares Foster G Guy threshing wheat Thos Hoad threshing oats Eaton mowing Dann and Father went to Ashburnham Mac[?] Boy jobbing moved our sheep into the Bushey field David Norringess[?] Settle His bill

Tuesday 19
A frost in the morning an eclipse in the sun between 9 and 10 o'clock in the forenoon cloudy afternoon some rain in the evening wind in the north west and south west – Horses as yester day – Wm David and I with the oxen carried a load of hop bines from the Poundfield and a load of stubble from the Kilnfield to the Oxen Close and put 23 bushels of potatoes into the Oast[?] unyoked the oxen in their Close the first time this winter they have been foddered twice in a day for some time in the Home Close with the cows two men threshing – T Hoad and family potatoing – Old Dann mowing stubble – Easton not at work he had a boy raking stubble Father whent to Windmill Hill and Gardener Street etc

Wednesday 20
A small frost and a small fog in the Bottom cloudy day some rain wind in the south west Horses as yesterday - oxen fetched home 43 bushels of potatoes into the oast – T Hoad and family potatoing – two threshers in the afternoon none in the forenoon – two stubble mowers etc a raker – Wm and David flawed another marsh lamb drove the rest into the Redpale field Father is gone I suppose to Cowden this evening he whent – talked of

going to Brownings this after noon

Thursday 21
Rather a cold cloudy day least I don't recollect any rain wind in the south east Horses as yesterday oxen fetched in 43 bushels of potatoes the threshers and I cleared 12 ½ bushels of wheat they threshing wheat again All the rest of the workmen as on yesterday – Wm and David boseling Wm whent to Brownings In the afternoon

Friday 22
Cold cloudy morning clear cold day wind in the east and north east Horses as yesterday T Hoad and Easton mowed the clover in the Bushy field for seed Wm David and I with the oxen loaded it all up on the carters broad wheel waggon and sett it against the Kiln – Foster and G Guy threshing and cleared 2½ bushels of wheat afterward threshing tares in the HB – Old Dann and Easton boy as yesterday – Father whent to Battle Fair etc Master J Gain came here with some apels etc in a cart

Saturday 23
Sharp frost in the morning clear cold day freezed all day except where the sun shone at some places wind rather more north than yester day Horses finished sowing at Hodges our is all Cobham Wheat this year – two threshers Old Dann mowing stubble he brought Wm and I each a new pair of halfboots from shoemaker Waters Rushlake this morning Easton mowing stubble – T Hoad mowing stubble in the Grinnets David and I whent to Browning and Marshams and into the Marsh and fetched in Old Barren cow by the name of smoke a runt a two yearling two speaned heifer and 4 calves into the Busheyfield left only two colts Forgot That Master Wood the gardener and his brother Brought 15 young appel trees and planted them In the Brook Orchard and pruned the vines And other trees etc

Sunday 24
Clear cold day as on yesterday wind In the north but generally still – Father Mother I Wm David Elizabeth and the maid whent to Heathfield Chapel in the morning Ann whent Dame Hoad and locked the House up – Wm stayed the afternoon Mr Press preached in the morning from 2nd Thessalonians 2nd chapter the last clause of the 16 verse – And good hope through grace and in the afternoon from Wm thinks from 1 chapter of Colossians the 19 verse Wm David and I whent to Mrs Sobers in the evening she spoke from these words – Who loved me and gave himself for

me – Galatians 2nd chapter the 28th verse

Monday 25

a few clouds in the forenoon cloudy after noon and evening a sharp frost in the morning afterwards it was in the give as tho there would be change of weather Wind in the south west Horses Wm Hoad the carter and Wm and I with two carts carried 28 loads of dung or slule out of the Pound field bottom in to the Poundfield Hop Garden oxen drawed a load of tare haum up to the Oxen Close at night Wm David and I unloaded it Henry Hoad is tired of horse and has left them – Foster and G Guy threshing tares in the HB – Old Dann and Easton mowing stubble in the Kinfield – T Hoad Do in the Grinnets Henry raking Do Father and David whent to the other farms – Mr R Purstglove and they looked Wartling Wood over he and and Father have brought the wood off the sule³²⁶ Elizabeth is gone out a how do you doing !!! Dallington way – forgot that Father and David drove the six yearlings coming two yearlings from Cowden to the Poundfield there to winter

Tuesday 26

Close cloudy morning rain nearly all day after 10 o'clock wind in the south west and north – Horses are gone to Brownings Wm Hoad with them to help get in the wheat season[?] I had the waggon down again with a pair of oxen in the morning afterwards threshing oats in the CB T Hoad with me in the afternoon – two threshers in the HB Old Dann mowing stubble a boy raking for Easton I suppose Easton not at work it being Bottle setting day Wm and David drive Quick and Nimble into the Ox Close from the Silverfield David has dried some wheat on the oast – Father whent to Brownings etc Father I William and David whent to Mr Smiths in the evening Mr Press preached from Hebrews 2nd chapter and the 3rd verse

Wednesday 27

Cloudy with some sun wind in the south west Horses are at Brownings T Hoad and family with his son Henry dug up the potatoes in the Brook Orchard Easton mowing stubble in the 12 acres his boy was in the Kinfield Old Dann mowing Do in the Kilnfield Master Reed came with his son [t]his day and ferrets and catched 2 rats in the wheat stack and 5 in the Home Barn Father whent to the other farms and to Hailsham Market I suppose Elizabeth is at the Priory – William Lade just called on business etc forgot moved the bull from the Home Close to the Ox Close and the 4 two

---

326 Sale?

yearlings from the Silverfield to the Poundfield and a cow from the Silverfield to the Home Close

Thursday 28
Foggy weather wind in the west Horses are Brownings – Foster and G Guy threshing tares – Old Dann and Easton mowing stubble in the 12 acres T Hoad and the rest I believe as on yesterday Wm David and I fetched about 6 bushels of potato in out of the Brook Orchard and heald the rest up there – Father whent to Tyth[327] feast at the Bullhead Inn Boreham for Wartling I whent to the Halfmoon Market etc Elizabeth came home from the Priory she has been to Mrs Pardons sale at Dallington which has been every day this week as yet

Friday 29
Cloudy at times some sun foggy morning clear moon light evening wind in the north rather still – I believe the workmen all as on yesterday David and I threshing oats in the CB in the morning Wm helpt us with the oxen carry a load of tare Haul[l]m some to the Ox Close and the rest to Hodges for fodder in the afternoon the bull in with the cows again he jumps a gate at any rate 5 feet high out of the Ox Close higher than him self !!! Father is gone around the parish after way fox[328] Wm whent to Brownings in the morning

Saturday 30
Frosty morning clear sunny day wind in the north I sowed the head land of the High & Round bank field Wm Harmer with his 3 horses harrowed I write last Saturday that our horses finished them that was [w]rong they only finished ploughing them and ploughed the Brook Hop Garden Wm Harmer and Father have exchanged a horse for a pair of oxen named Quick and Nimble we have not worked them since we have had them the horse is sent to the Bell hurst team the bargain is a secret no I shall not have invent it I believe all workmen where as on Thurs day except Foster who was not a threshing in the after noon T Hoad has mowed a field of stubble on Wm Isted Farm I did not know it before that Father had Brought the stubble of[f] him for 3£ Wm Harmer Had his oxen home Father whent to Brownings In the afternoon

[327] Tithe.
[328] Way tax.

Sunday 1 Dec

A little frost in the morning no moor at many places wind in the north – Father Mother I William David and Elizabeth and perhaps the maid whent to Heathfield chapel in the morning – Father and Wm stayed the afternoon Mr Press preached from Isiah 61st chapter the 3 first verses from a part in the morning latter part in the afternoon – Father William and David whent to Mrs Sobers in the evening she spoke from Isiah 53 chapter the 1st verse – Who hath believed our report etc

Monday 2

A sharp frost in the morning cloudy wind in the north west and west some sun T Hoad wood cutting in the shaw at the lower End of the Archer Hop Garden Henry with him Foster not at work G Guy threshing tares C Barn Easton at work a few hours Old Dann mowing stubble in the 12 acres William whent to Brownings helping them Harrow etc Father David and I moveing of Tackel etc from the stall to the Oast Forgot Elizabeth whent to Battle with Dame Hoad on Foot

Tuesday 3

A little Frost in the morning still cloudy day Finised sowing at Brownings Horses come home at night William as yesterday Foster and G Guy finised threshing Tare T Hoad and Henry Wood cutting Old Dann (and I Suppose) Easton Mowing Stubble in the 12 acres Boy Robing ditto in the Kiln field David and I threshing Oats in the CB and Tied two Cows up to fat in the stall Etc etc I whent to Mr Veness Summertree and borrowed a Potato Cutter[329] Father gone somewhere Southward has been gone all day Mother is in trouble about him Forgot that D Honeysett who has undertaken to make a small piece of hedge at the top of the Redpale field wass there today

Wednesday 4

Cloudy as yesterday David helpt carry the rest of the tare haum into the home ricks stedel afterwards Horses carried 3 Load of Stubble from the Kiln field to the Home Close Foster G Guy and I cleaned 7 sacks of Tears[330] in the hoam barn Old Dann drying William Harmers Oats Easton stubble mowing T Hoad wood cutting his Girl shaving hop poles I suppose Honeysett Hedging Mr Lade and Mr Reeves are this Evening Elizabeth whent to Priory

[329] To cut up potatoes for animal feed.
[330] Tares.

Thursday 5
Cloudy and rather windy day Wind in the south rain in the Evening after 7 O'clock Horses carried 3 loads of stubble to the Ox Close and one to the Home Close from the Kiln field David helpt the Carter I waiting on the Fatting Cows and threshing etc Foster and G Guy threshing wheat in the Home Barn T Hoad wood cutting Girls shaving Hop poles D Honeysett Hedging Old Dann and Easton and Boy as on Tuesday Except the boy who wass in the 12 acres William Harmer came after his Oats Father whent to Bellhurst etc

Friday 6
A Sunshine day some clouds Wind in the West and Northwest Rain in the evening Horse Carters carried 26 loads of Dung at the Calves lodge into the meadow all there is David threshing with me in the afternoon all the rest chiefly as yesterday Father is gone after Way Tar[331] Mrs Lade come home from the Priory

Saturday 7
Clear sunshine day cloudy evening wind in the north west Horses 1 load of Hop poles from the Croft and a load of stubble from the Kiln field to the Calves lodge I helpt the threshers clean 4 sacks and 3 Bushels of Wheat in the afternoon rest as yesterday Honeysett has finised his job etc William whent to Bellhurst

Sunday 8
After a very Blusterous night of rain hail frost and snow a sunshine forenoon Cloudy afternoon wind in the West Father Mother I William David and the Maid whent to Heathfield Chapel in the morning none stayed the afternoon Mr Press preached from 2 Thessalonians 2 chapter and the two last verses I suppose he finished this afternoon he did not in the morning William whent to Mrs Sobers in the evening she spoke from Isaiah the 54 chapter the Verse J T Lade came after his Wife and had her home to the Priory again Robert Reeves just call on his road from Bodle street to the Priory etc

Monday 9
Showry day Wind in the Southwest and South Rather cold Horses getting the Dung out of the Close at Hodges William Hoad and Henry with them two Carts David and I threshing Oast in the CB and drying of wheat in the

[331] Way tax.

Oast etc. Foster and G Guy threshing Peas in the HB T Hoad wood cutting Old Dann and Easton mowing stubble Boy raking etc William whent to Bellhurst threshing Wheat with the Machine Father has been somewhere that way Mr Stanford and Mr Tourle came here the evening about six o'clock on purpose to have a little shooting to morrow if the Weather permits

Tuesday 10
Cloudy showry morning fine sunny afternoon wind in the Southwest North west and southwest again Horses carried the stubble from the Grinnetts to the Close at Hodges I suppose about 2 loads Foster and G Guy threshing peas I helpt them clean them 4 sacks and 1 Bushel T Hoad Wood cutting Easton not at work Old Dann drying William Harmers Wheat William as yesterday David carried the Game Bag for Mr Tourle and Gamekeeper Phillips they Kild 2 Hares 2 Rabbits 3 Pheasants and a Wood cock Mr Stanford not well layed a bed nearly day William David and I whent to Mr Smiths in the evening Mr Press preached from John 10 chapter the latter part of the 3rd verse

Wednesday 11
Showry weather wind in the West Carters nesseling[332] jobs Foster and G Guy threshing Barley in the HB T Hoad wood cutting Old Dann and Easton I suppose mowing stubble in the 12 acres I did not see them when I wass there William as yesterday David and I boseling or rather walking about with the Gentlemen who have Kild nothing today they whent from here about 2 O'Clock the Carters where with 2 Horses and drawed them out to the Turnpike near Windmill Hill David and I fetched a stray sheep off ours from Mr Veness flock

Thursday 12
Cold Frosty Wett and still morning Cloudy and rain nearly all day Flood at night Wett evening Wind in the south Carters threshing Oats in the C B Foster threshing in the after noon not at work before T Hoad in the morning wood cutting I suppose none of the rest where at work G Guy I know was not at work for us Mr Holland's Mrs Sober's servant wass here to day with a letter [drawing of a man crossed out]

Friday 13
After a Tempestous Night Showery day Wind in the West Horses all Bad

[332] Nestling.

could not Work William Harmer gave a Drink to Guider and Violate. Henry went down in the Marsh after 2 Colts and have taken the Eldest in the Stable (to Fat it up a little). William Hoad was a Gaping in the morning Drove 4 calves and 2 yearling Hafer[333] up from the Bushey Field to the Calves Lodge 6 yearlings off from the Pound field to Hodges I helped him Foster a threshing T Hoad Hedgin against the Old Lane Old Dann mowing Stubble Easton not at work (still if I wass Father I would not employ him) Father William and David went to Bellhurst G Guy not at work We have now driven all our stock to the places where they are to Winter Namely 4 Cart Horses and a Colt in the stable Old Jack the Poney and a yearling off[spring] Colt in the home yards as yet 6 Cows and the two yearling off steers in the Home Close 2 Cows fatting in the stall 4 Oxen a pair of 2 yearling off steer and a Bull in the Ox Close 6 One yearling off at Hodges 4 Calves and a two yearling Heifer at the Calves Lodge 6 Calves in the Chapel and Chapelwood Meadow Sheep are move able or driven from place to place We have three or four Ewes with the Tegs etc Lambs which are to be kild when it suits and a Ram in all of Ours 29 and 22 Marsh Lambs Once 30 but we have lost 8 of them in good keep[334] and looked after 3 Hogs in the pound a fattening 7 shuts and a Quantity of Geese and Foulls which I seldom tell Forgot to write the Marsh homeland belongs to Mr Thorp of Fairlight in this County

Saturday 14

Rain Hail Frost and snow in the morning cloudy in the south all day not much sun clear in the North some small showrs Wind in the West William Hoad Cutting chaff etc Henry boseling I boseling jobs William and David threshing Oats in the C B in the forenoon Wm whent to Mr Russell's in the afternoon David and I cleaning in the afternoon T Hoad and Foster threshing in the H B ƒ G Guy and Easton not at work and I think Old Dann was not at work

Sunday 15

There was a large Flood in the night and a very high wind windy all day to day some clouds wind in the West Father I William David Elizabeth and the Maid whent to Heathfield Chapel in the morning Father stayed the afternoon Mr Press preached both times from Acts the 26th chapter the 22nd and 23rd Verses Father I William and David whent to Stonehouse the

---

[333] Heifer.
[334] Probably as a result of liver fluke.

Honerable Lady Mrs Sobers not being well her companion Miss Capper[335] a respected younger Lady spoke from Hebrews the 7 chapter and the middle part of the 22nd verse 'Jesus made a surety' she spoke sweetly of Jesus in a pleasing effecting manner I think it was all Noble discorrcs[336] I wass much delighted

Monday 16

Frosty morning still day some cloud Wind in the Northwest Carter boseling William Harmer drenched the two black mares as on Friday last T Hoad Hedging against the Archer Hop garden against the lane leading from Dillgate to the Mill Foster and G Guy finised threshing the two loads of Barley that was in the Barn Old Dann mowing stubble Easton not at work William and David threshing Oats I mending Cribs in the Home Close Father whent to Bellhurst etc

Tuesday 17

Misely Rain nearly all day some sun just at night Rain in the evening Wind in the West southwest south and Northwest Carters making a lew at the North Head of the C B and carried some Luse[337] Faggots from William Harmers to the wheat stack and building about home on there backs Honeysetts mending Roofs of Haystacks etc T Hoad Hedging William and David threshing in the CB none of the Rest at work

Wednesday 18

Frost in the morning a little while some clouds all day no rain to my knowledge Wind in the West Northwest and nearly North Carters making a lew at the North Head of the C B and carried some Luse[337] Faggots from the Archer shaw to theres and drawed the Load of Clover from the Kiln field that wass loaded on Battle fair day into the Home Barn I helpt Foster and G Guy clean 16 sacks and about 5 Gallons of Barley in the H B William and David threshing in the H B Old Dann mowing stubble T Hoad at the Wood work There is Talk that Easton is married to day to his woman by whom he has got 3 children. Father whent to Bellhurst and Hailsham market which is a week sooner than it should be on account of next Wednesday being Christmas Day after wards it is to Fall into the regular Channell

---

[335] Probably Selina Sarah Capper, Lady Sober's companion. Selina Sarah was born on 31 Dec 1781 in Wilmington, Sussex and died on 1 Dec 1860 at age 78. She never married and had no known children.
[336] Discourse.
[337] Loose.

Thursday 19
Cold windy day some snow in the afternoon it did not lay Wind in the North Carters at work as yesterday and made a Crib carried some more Luse Faggots to the Ox Close etc Wm and David threshing Foster and G Guy threshing the Clover they unloaded yesterday T Hoad Old Dann etc as yesterday I suppose Easton hass left us and no bad Rid[338] I whent to the Other Farms had the Ridering[?] move home from Bellhurst etc

Friday 20
There some snow in the night Frosty morning cold day some clouds Freezed at some places Carters setting up lew Faggots at the Ox close etc Foster G Guy and I cleaned the closure pug[339] they threshed 4½ Bushels of wheat I helpt them clean it T Hoad wood work and Kild a sheep I suppose Old Dann mowing stubble Father whent to Wartling Wood Uncle William Oxley Visitor Forgot William and David flawed a Black Calf that wass struck in the Calves Lodge window

Saturday 21
Clear Cold Frosty Weather Wind as yesterday in the Northeast William and David helpt William Hoad with the Horses carry 2 loads of stubble from William Isted's Freehold field to Hodges I helpt them the first load Dried about 5 sacks of Oats Blacksmith shoeing Horses G Guy threshing wheat Foster not at work T Hoad Wood work Easton mowing stubble and took his scythe away Old Dann I suppose as yesterday. William and I took a perished Lamb out of the Bogs against the River in the Winehouse field dead Father is gone to the Doleing at Rushlake Forgot I whent to Mr Howses last night Mr J Erry came after 4½ Bushels of wheat to sow Mr Purstglove sent after the Bull Father and he have exchanged the Bull for a steer to match an olde steer at Marsham

Sunday 22
Cold Frosty weather wind in the Northeast Father I William David Elizabeth Ann and the Maid whent to Heathfield Chapel in the morning Father and Elizabeth stayed the afternoon Mr Press preached from 1 Thesselonians 1 chapter 3rd Verse both times he was very lively in the morning my two Brothers and I whent to Mrs Sobers in the evening She spoke from 2 Corinthians 5 chapter and the 3rd verse

---

[338] Riddance.
[339] Clover pug.

Monday 23

Cold Frosty morning cloudy and some Rain in the day snow whent away and the Frost on going away Wind in the southwest Horses fetched the three other loads of stubble from William Isted's field carried 2 loads to the Ox Close left one on the Waggon I threshing Oats Foster and G Guy threshing wheat T Hoad Wood cutting I know nothing about the Rest William whent to Warbleton Church not in the Church but to Mr Russell's

Tuesday 24

Cloudy nearly as yesterday Wind in the Northwest and West Horses unloaded the stubble in the Ox Close and at the North Head of the C Barn and carried the last Load of Hop bines (we have this year) from the Pound field Garden to near the Calves Close at the North Head of the CB and fetched 200 of Oil cake from Windmill Hill Rest of the workmen as yesterday David and I threshinging Father round the Last Gone to Bellhurst to meet Mr J Pursglove there

Wednesday 25

Christmas Day a Clear sunny day Wind in the Northwest and Southwest Father I William and David whent to Heathfield Chapel in the morning Mr Press preached from 1 Timothy 3 chapter the first part of the 16th verse Father whent to Mr Ellises Cade Street for dinner he William and David whent to Stonehouse in the evening Mrs Sobers spoke from Luke 2nd chapter 9 and 11 verse I began my Haystack

Thursday 26

Very wet day Foster threshing half a day others hollow day[340] reeping it is very dirty wind in the southwest

Friday 27

Showery dirty weather wind in the south T Hoad Hedging around the Mill shaw at Hodges all the Rest not at work for us William and David threshing Oats Father whent to Cade Street Boys Boxing men after money etc etc

Saturday 28

Frosty morning showry day Windy evening Wind in the West etc Horses carried 6 Quarters of Barley to Bucksteep Mill at 38s per Quarter Carters Boseling T Hoad Wood cutting none of the rest at work Old Dann is at work on the Roads William and David threshing I whent to the Blacksmith

[340] Holiday.

with 2 Hay cutters and a Prong Gorge and William Oxley Visitors etc Crowhurst hass finised farriring[341] Guydor Mare she seem nearly well J T Lade sleeps here to night his wife came home on Thursday or Christmas Day

Sunday 29

After a Windy Blusterous night cloudy day some sun wind in the Southwest Father Mother I William David and Elizabeth whent to Heathfield Chapel in the morning Father and Mother staid the afternoon and Mr Press preached in the morning from 103 Psalm 1 and 2 Verses and in the pm from … chapter   Verse Father Mother William and David whent to Mrs Sobers in the Evening she spoke from Amos (4th) Chapter (12th) verse 'Prepare to meet thy God O Israel' J T Lade sleeps here tonight

Monday 30

Rain all day a Large flood at this time about 8 o'clock It keeps raining very fast wind in the Southeast Carters threshing Oats in the C B Foster and G Guy threshing wheat in the H B Such Weather no man could work out Doors without getting Wett William and David Drove 4 steers from Hodges to Marshams Father is gone to Rushlake

Tuesday 31

Cloudy Rainy weather very dirty Wind in the Southwest Carters ditching In the squirefield – Foster and G Guy threshing in the HB – Foster Carter and I Rung the Hogs[342] – William & David threshing in the CB this is the last days account for this year This has been a Remarkable Wett Year and the Fruits of the Earth very backward. Forgot T Hoad Wood cutting

---

[341] Pin firing, burning the leg to cure lameness; thermocautery.
[342] Put rings in their noses to stop them rooting.

A DIARY FOR THE YEAR 1817 BY NICHOLAS OXLEY

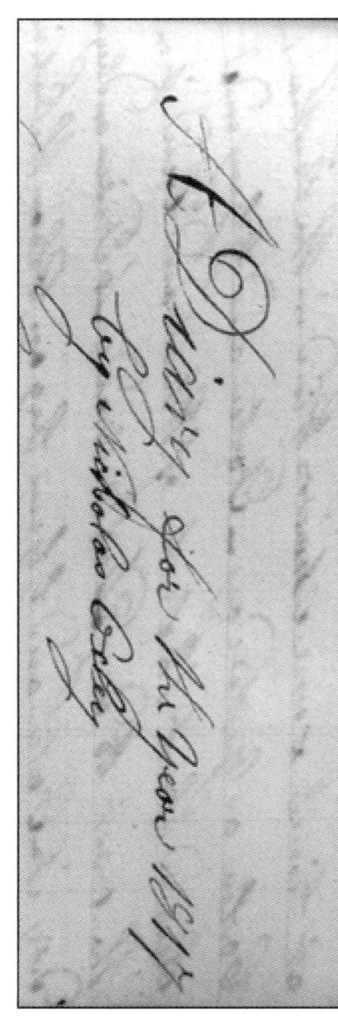

P.S. I shall not as I did last year give any account of the people the come here of business or visiting etc except they stay all night or once on things of great importance but plainly give an account of what the workmen are imployed about on Bucksteep and Hodges Farms and of the teanor also – I intend also to give a more particular account of the dung, lime, moul, hay, corn and straw: which I intend to put by its self – on a Sunday as usual in last year and of the weather as usual but I shall leave a line between every day account to distinguish one from the other the better that it might be the easier finding any thing – This is the plan I intend to persue if the Lord premitt otherwise without his permission I cannot do any thing

Wednesday 1 January
After a wett showery night Some sun on the morning showery after Noon very dirty wind in the south west rather Windy in the evening – Wm Hoad and Henry Hoad the carters ditching the upper part Of the Squirefield – T Hoad wood cutting Mill now Hodges Foster and G Guy threshing wheat in the Home Barn David and I threshing oats in the CB finished the South end Wm whent to Bellhurst etc Wm and David whent to the Priory in the evening Oratio Bland is here to night J T Lade sleeps here to night

Thursday 2
After a showery night a sunny day at times some showers wind in the south west Carters as yesterday – Foster and G Guy and I cleaned about 12 sacks of wheat and laid it on the cart to dry David made 4 fires and begun dry it – Foster and G Guy began clear the oats in the CB afterwards T Hoad as yesterday Wm whent to the Halfmoon Market

Friday 3
Showery weather wind in the south west a small frost at some places in the morning Carters ditching in the forenoon helping us in the afternoon finish drying wheat and clearing oats and laid them on the oast about 30 sacks and carried the wheat into the Home Barn again to be cleaned again Carters William David I and Foster had the horses moving the corn – G Guy not at work T Hoad hedging in the Archer Hop garden against the lane that leads from Dillgate to the Water Mill – Father whent to the other farms etc

Saturday 4
Wett weather flood all day wind in the south west rather brisk It is such a time for wett as I never knew before Carters threshing oats in the CB Foster threshing peas in the Home Barn G Guy is not at work and you may guess T Hoad is not. I have been working out the bills etc

Sunday 5
Bright sunny morning cloudy showery afternoon a dark blusterous evening before a moon light night wind in the south west Wm & Elizabeth Lade … and Father I David and the maid walked to Heathfield Chapel in the morning Mr Press preached From 1 Corinthians 2 chapter 2 verse J T Lade sleeps here to night

Monday 6
Cloudy showery morning clear afternoon sometimes and some cloud wind in the south west and north west Horses carters carried some oat straw from the CB to Hodges and ditching etc Wm and David drove T Hoads cow to Hodges and dried the oats – Foster and G Guy threshing peas I helpt them clean the wheat again we cleaned one Thursday last it has lost nearly 3 sacks there is now 9 sacks and cleared 2 sacks afterwards T Hoad on the wood work Father whent to Bell hurst etc forgot Horatio Bland whent home yesterday

Tuesday 7
Clear day rather cold and a sort of a London smuch[343] wind in the north a small frost in the morning if I mistake not Horses began plough the 13 acres this is the first winter ploughing for this year with us – Foster and G Guy threshing peas in the HB – T Hoad at wood work – Mr Press preached here this evening from 1 Cronicles 4 chapter the first part of the 10th verse And Jabez called on the God of Israel saying, Oh that thou wouldest bless me

---

[343] Smutch: soot, smut, grime, dirt (OED).

Ploughing

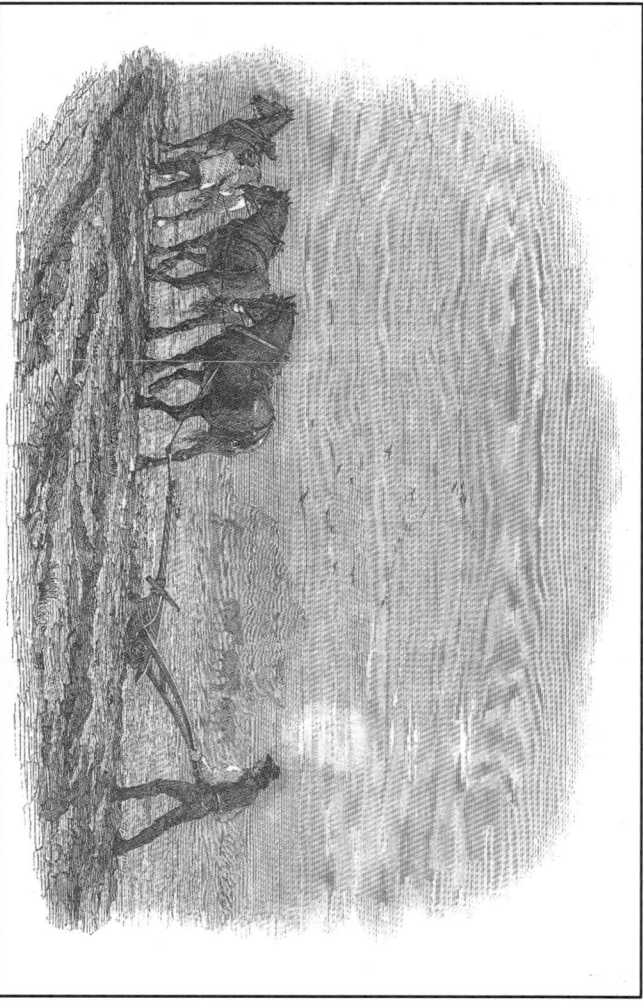

indeed J T Lade sleeps here tonight

Wednesday 8

Frost in the morning mild warm clement forenoon so that some of the birds sung like spring some part of the time some cloud afterward – very still Wm and David with the carter and Horses carried 1 load of stubble to the Ox Close and orchard and Calves Home 2 to the Home Close From the 12 acres – I threshing and whent to Mr Couchman's sale Wm whent there Foster and G Guy threshing and did my foddering for me to night Father whent to Hailsham Market – Old Dann and Easton finished the stubble work today I supposed they had done before they had not but now they have

Thursday 9

Frost in the morning some cloud and a London smuch wind in the north Horses plough – Foster Guy finished threshing peas in the eastern head of the HB I helpt them clear 8 sacks and 1 bushel and I fetched some oats from the oast and cleaned again 2 sacks and 3 bushels head pilkin[344] and tail about 3 bushels T Hoad at wood work – I thought Eastone had done his

[344] Inferior or discarded grain (OED).

work but I see him there to night and has still more to do – Wm whent to the Halfmoon Market Father whent to Dallington I whent to Mr Couchman's sale – J T Lade sleeps here to night

Friday 10
Frosty cloudy reemy[345] cold weather very still Horses and Oxen Wm Hoad Henry Hoad David G Guy Foster and I removed the barley stack from the 12 acres to the HB in 4 loads and a load of stubble from the 12 acres to the Home Close etc T Hoad at wood work Easton raking stubble in the 12 acres Wm whent to Dallington & afterwards to Catsfield etc

Saturday 11
Frosty and some clouds calm weather – Horses carrying old poles from the Poundfield garden to against the Faggot Stack – Foster threshing barley G Guy not at work – T Hoad wood work his cow calved to day a bull calf I shall drop mentioning much more about Easton as he is not now a steady workman – Wm Harman brought some oats to be dryed – Mr R Winchester and Mr J Morfey came and received their money for building the new oast Wm whent to Gardner Street and Bellhurst – Father whent to Bellhurst etc J T Lade sleeps here to night

Sunday 12
Frosty morning still mild warm day some cloud – Mother rode Father I Wm David and Elizabeth walked to Heathfield Chapel in the morning Father and Elizabeth where at Chapel the afternoon Wm whent to Heathfield church this afternoon Mr Press preached morning and afternoon from 1 John 2 chapter the 25th verse – Father and William whent to Stonehouse in the evening Mr Press preached from Acts 26 chapter the 24 and 25th verses the Honerable Lady Mrs Sobers is not well

Monday 13
Mild cloudy day some sun and rain in the evening wind in the west – Horses (carried poles from the hop garden) plough in the 13 acres – Foster and G Guy threshing barley T Hoad at wood work – Father whent to Rushlake – Wm is gone to Biddenham after a place and I suppose to Chiddingly sleeps this evening Mr Body and Mr T Pinion (Pinyon) came here on business etc J T Lade sleeps here to night

Tuesday 14
A small frost in the morning drying day some times cloudy wind in the

---

[345] Rimy, frosty.

Wednesday 15

A small frost some snow and rain nearly all day wind from the south west in the morning to the north in the evening cold winterly day T Hoad killed a hog in the morning afterward threshing oats in the chapel close Carter helpt kill the hog and cutting chaff etc Foster and G Guy threshing barley in the Home Barn – some tradesmen with bill etc

Thursday 16

A sharp frost in the morning soon after cloudy some few Drops of snow and rain nearly all day and in the evening wind in the north and south horses plough – Foster threshing ½ day G Guy all day – T Hoad at wood work I whent to Woods corner Wm whent to Gardener Street and David whent to Rushlake and to Warbleton church J T Lade sleeps here to night

Friday 17

Cloudy day some sun wind in the southwest Horses plough – David and I threshing – Foster and G Guy Do in the Home Barn – T Hoad at wood work Mr Jn Purstglove was here this evening and stayed rather late on what business I don't know perhaps to smoke a pipe or no

Saturday 18

A pleasant drying day some times cloudy wind in the south and southwest – Horses plough Foster and G Guy finished threshing barley David threshing T Hoad at wood work – Wm whent to Bellhurst – Mr J Waters is here this evening – J T Lade sleeps here to night

Sunday 19

Cloudy day some sun rather windy from the southeast rain part of the afternoon and all the evening – Mother rode and Father I William David and Elizabeth walked to Heathfield Chapel in the morning – Elizabeth stayed the after noon maid whent there in the afternoon Mr Press preached in the morning from Hezekia the 18th chapter and the 8 verse

Monday 20

A sunny drying day not many clouds wind in the south and southeast – Horses at plough David threshing – G Guy spread the dung in the Calves Lodge Meadow which was carried out in last year and helpt – Foster in the afternoon who was a ditching or clearing a ditch out by the Poundfield Hop garden hedge in the Poundfield – T Hoad at wood work – Wm whent north west Horses plough – Foster and G Guy threshing – T Hoad wood work David and I threshing oats – Wm came home this evening to Mr G Adams at Burwash etc Father whent to the other farms I don't recollect any thing else of any consequence only I whent to Fowle Mill and to Iwood in the evening

Tuesday 21
We have had all sorts of weather excepting[?] dusty weather to day a little frost in the morning and cloudy snow hail and rain in the forenoon windy and pleasant sunny weather with some bollowy clouds in the afternoon wind in the south southwest and west – Horses plough – David threshing – Foster and G Guy finished there ditching and began make the hedge at this lower end of the Poundfield shaw leading from the river that comes out of the shaw along by the road from the chapel meadow gate to the corner of the shaw northwards T Hoad wood work Father whent to Burwash sitting William whent to Westham Wm David and I whent to Mr Reeves Rushlake in the evening

Wednesday 22
Cloudy windy day with misty rains and verry dirty wind in the southwest Horses at plough – T Hoad threshing oats in the CB Foster and G Guy not at work for us – Father whent to Priory and to Hailsham Market J T Lade sleeps here to night

Thursday 23
Weather nearly as yesterday – Horses plough – T Hoad wood work – Foster and G Guy Do as mentioned on Tuesday with about 2 rods of hedge on the south side of the river to the corner of the shaw against the Chapel Meadow Gate – Father I William and David whent to Stonehouse in the evening where the Revd Mr Kemp preached from 1st Timothy the 1st chapter and the 15th verse except the last clause 'of whom I am chief'

Friday 24
Mild weather still foggy cloudy morning some sun and some clouds in the day and some sleet rain in the evening wind in the southwest Horses finished ploughing the arable part of the 13 acres rest of the workmen as yesterday – I dryed the clover pug Etc David sett up some hop poles etc Wm whent to Bellhurst and Wartliing Wood etc – Father whent to somewhere about Beech Mill in Ashburnham – Messrs J Waters junr and J Waters at Iwood where this evening J T Lade sleeps here to night

Saturday 25
Cloudy misty weather wind in the southeast Horses plough in the further end of the Croft – T Hoad Wood work – Foster and G Guy shovelled the

mud off From the road from the river to the Cart Lodge And ditching at several places not 40 rods from the House – J T Lade sleeps here tonight

Sunday 26
Foggy sometimes misty weather wind in the southwest Elizabeth Lade and Father I Wm and David walked to Heathfield Chapel in the morning Mr Press preached from Job 35 chapt and the 14th verse David and I whent to Stonehouse in the evening Mrs Sobers spoke from Luke 14 chapter and part of the 17 verse – Come for all things are now ready – I was this day admitted as a member to the Church of Christ at Heathfield Chapel

Monday 27
Foggy day some misty rain very still and warm some little wind in the afternoon from the east – Horses finished the further end of the Croft and began the Wainhouse field at plough I helpt Foster and G Guy clean the barley did not finish on account of sacks – T Hoad wood work forgot that on Saturday last Wm David and I with Old Jack the pony carried a part of a two brothers cut some Ox goads to send to Preston near Brighton – T Hoad was at work for Wm Harmer yesterday and to day making a new hedge near Hodgekins etc his girls and boy shaving hop poles for us

Tuesday 28
A mild still cloudy and some times foggy day Wind in the east and south – horses at plough in the Wainhousefield – William David and I help Foster and G Guy finish cleaning the barley in all 28 sacks with 16 sacks and 1 bushel before (not yesterday) is just 44 sacks and 1 bushel of from eight acres of ground. Foster not at work afterwards G Guy threshing wheat my lump of potatoes from the Archer to the little stall etc Father whent to Rushlake – Wm whent to Bellhurst etc – J T Lade sleeps here to night

Wednesday 29
Mild and some sun and sometimes Cloudy weather wind in the southwest and northwest Horses plough – G Guy threshing wheat in the Home Barn – Foster and throwed the mud out of the ox watering and let some water down out of the Silverfield pett David helped a part of the time afterward Foster cleaned hay pound out and shovelled some dirt up near the hay pound I cant [say] wether T Hoad was at work for us or Wm Harmer to day – Rat catcher Reed was here to day and catched 3 rats – Wm and Father whent to Wartling Wood – I whent to the prayer meeting Tom Martin's in the evening – J T Lade sleeps here to night

Thursday 30
Cloudy and some little showers in the afternoon after a pleasant sunny morning wind in the northwest – Horses plough – G Guy threshing Foster began dig the hops in the poundfield garden T Hoad at wood work in the millshaw at Hodges Wm and David planted some beans and an early sort of potato in the lower garden I was a gardening etc in the forenoon and whent to the Halfmoon Market in the afternoon – Mr H Purstglove was here this evening

Friday 31
Mild weather rather cloudy wind in the northwest – Horses plough and harrowed Wm Hoad sowed the peas in the hither part of the Wain housefield – G Guy threshing – Foster hop digging I cant tell about T Hoad – Mr G Adams was here this evening – Wm and David are gone to Ninfield sale this evening Mr Waters has the long red ladder home he borrowed some time ago – forgot th[at] Mr Bland from Bellhurst was here to day with some vinegar

Saturday 1 February
Horses finished harrowing in peas in the Wainhousefield – forgot the weather – A little frost in the morning a bright sunny drying day some clouds wind in the north – G Guy threshing – Foster drying hops Wm and David Do in the Croft – T Hoad wood work I whent to Silverash etc in the forenoon gardening In the afternoon – Father whent to the other farms J T Lade sleeps here to night

Sunday 2
Cloudy day not much sun wind in the northwest or there abouts – Mother rode Father I Wm David Elizabeth and the maid walked to Heathfield Chapel in the morning our worthy Pasture[346] Mr Press being ill our aged pasture Mr Gilbert preached from Galatians the 6 chapter and the 15th verse in his room much to the satisfaction of his late heareses[347] – Father did not come home till the evening he Wm David and I where at Stonehouse in the evening Mrs Sobers spoke from Proverbs 17 chapter and the 8 verse

Monday 3
Cloudy day wind in the northwest west and southwest – Wm Hoad sowing tares and the Horses harrow in the 13 acres – David and I cleaned the oats

---

[346] Pastor.
[347] Hearers?

in the CB and Wm helpt us clean 6 bushels of wheat in the Home Barn Foster digging hops in the afternoon Easton Whom I did not think of writing anything about in this book again is set to digging hops in the Poundfield hop garden – T Hoad wood work G Guy not at work

Tuesday 4
Some sun chiefly cloudy wind in the southwest – Horses harrow in the 13 acres Wm Hoad sowing tares and some peas where the hops where formally – William David and I with oxen carried the oats from the CB To the oast they measured 97 bushels of Head Oats and 15 bushels of tail oats – Foster and Eastone digging hops – T Hoad wood work – G Guy threshing William whent to Gardner Street – I whent to Dallington in the afternoon – Mr Jarvis and Mr Ths Waters at Iwood and Mr Thos Waters the butcher on business etc Mr G Verrell from Lewes is here to night – Mr Winchester the Hertmonceaux Chapel Minister preached here this evening from the 1st Epistel the 3rd chapter and the 1st and 2nd verses

Wednesday 5
Rather cold not many clouds in the morning more already in the afternoon and some rain in the evening wind in the northeast ... Horses finished harrowing in 13 acres – G Guy threshing and David and I helpt him clean in the afternoon – Foster and Eastone digging hops T Hoad at wood work etc etc Wm whent to Hailsham Market G Verrell whent to Cade Street and to Briteling[348] etc and have again – Mr Winchester whent home Mrs Lade is gone to Silverash

Thursday 6
A warmer and more cloudy day than yesterday wind in the northwest – Horses fetched a load of spill wood from behind the oast to the back court and a load of old hop poles from the Croft garden and a load of stubble from the 12 acres – one to the close and the other to the old hop pole stack Wm and David helpt G Guy finished the wheat 6 sacks and 2 bushels of wheat in the morning G Guy not at work after wards – Easton not at work – Foster drying hops T Hoad wood work – I threshing and stacked the Old poles in the CB Wm and David threshing in the CB – Black Oats – G Verrell whent home J T Lade was here this evening with the News paper but did not stop I know of nothing else to write to night to finish this side of the leaf with

[348] Brightling.

Friday 7

Weather nearly as yesterday rather more sun wind in the westerly quarters – Horses plough in the 12 acres Wm with them in Henry room[349] in the fore noon – Henry not at work in the forenoon plough in the afternoon – David and I threshing – Eastone digging hops – T Hoad wood work – the others where not at work – the millers carried 3 bushels of wheat and a pack of tares to Mr Goldsmiths Rush lake green for us – Wm Noakes from Dallington was here this night visitor

Saturday 8

Windy day sometimes cloudy wind in The northwest – A red light Father says it was like the northern lights some years ago passed over us to night between 8 and 9 o'clock the moon is in her last quarter and doth not rise till midnight or after but it was light as if it was moon light for at least a half an hour or more and all of us whent out to look at it – it came from the north and whent southward making the sky look like blood Horses harrowed the 13 acres again – T Hoad at wood work Eastone digging hops Foster do part of the day – I settled with G Guy and he packed up all his tools and is gone – Father whent to Boreham etc he had a new glass and a new key to my watch for me John Crouch was here to day and Wm whent as far as Prinkle to meet Father – Mrs Lade came home from silverash Mr Thos. Phillips my old school mate at Beckley in 1810 was married on Thursday last at Westham in this county to a Miss Smith at Dittens farm in Westham late of Kitchenham in Ashburnham I had a piece of his wedding cake – J T Lade sleeps here to night – the old sow that has been a fatting for some time farrowed to day 7 live pigs and some dead ones – J T Lade sleeps here to night.

Sunday 9

Cloudy some mist and rain in the morning some clouds afterwards and I understand it was lightest last night about 11 o'clock – Wind to day was in the northwest north and southeast very still evening it is remarkable to me it should be so mild when the wind is in the northerly quarter and sometimes pretty brisk Mother and Mrs Lade rode and Father I William

[349] Place.

> The appearance in the heavens on Saturday night of the *Aurora Borealis*, or Northern Lights, was more brilliant than had been known before for many years.— We find that it excited great interest on the Continent as well as in this country; such phenomena are no longer looked at with dread, but are now regarded with pleasure and hope, as the precursors of happier times.— The singular appearance on Saturday last took place about eight o'clock, and continued without intermission for a full half-hour, during the whole of which time the sky was illuminated from the horizon to the zenith, extending east and west for a considerable distance.— Broad streaks of light of various sizes rose from the horizon in a pyramidal undulating form, and shot with great velocity up to the zenith: they changed their forms very frequently and rapidly, and broke out in places where none were seen before, shooting along the heavens, and then disappearing in an instant. The sky, in various places, was tinged for a considerable space with deep purple, and the stars shone very brightly during the whole time through the clouds which formed the Aurora Borealis. A short time after this phenomenon had ceased, the rain began to descend, and continued to do so most of the night, though not violently.

The Aurora Borealis of 8 February 1817, as reported in many newspapers.

David and Elizabeth walked to Heathfield Chapel in the morning – Father and Wm stayed the afternoon Mr Winchester preached from Romans the 7 chapter and the 2 last verses in the morning and from the 5 chapter and the 1st verse in the after noon – Mr Press baptised his own child in the morning named Joseph Phillip – he is some what better but not well he has been very ill indeed J T Lade sleeps here tonight

Monday 10
Cloudy not much sun wind in the north west and southwest – Horses plough in the 12 acres I whent to Bellhurst with a move after 50 oil cakes Wm and David threshing Blackoats in the CB T Hoad wood cutting at the of the Wainhousefield against the river – Foster and Eastone hop digging Father whent to Bellhurst etc Mr Mannington was here to dinner The sow

that they said has 7 live pigs I suppose has only 6 now –

Tuesday 11
Foggy morning and sleet and rain rather cold some sun wind in the west north northeast and east – Horses plough – Foster digging hops Father and I took T Hoads wood work he has cut the shaw against the old lane below the orchard hop garden and made the hedge all up the lane to the upper corner of the hop garden on Buck steep and he has cut the mill shaw made the hedge that belongs to us and made the hedge at the bottom of the Grinnetts and made the hedge that is against the road in the House Meadow and cut the wood against the road in the spring meadow and Millfield this winter at Hodges Wm David and I helpt T Hoad kill a hog in the morning T Hoad helpt Father and I afterwards and was at his wood work again in the afternoon as yesterday – I understand the Honeysetts are making the hedge between silverfields to day and have been there two or three days before that hedge has not been made before since we have been here all the rest have – Eastone not at work Wm David and I threshing in the CB in the afternoon Mr J Erry came after some money Wm whent after some salt to Rushlake and Warbleton Church in the forenoon etc etc

Wednesday 12
Wet morning showery day wind in S west and north Horses plow T Hoad wood cutting Foster Eastone hop digging David & I threshing oats CB dryed 4 bushels of barley Wm whent to Cowden to shooting Father went to Hoods[350] Corner Club in evening

Thursday 13
Cloudy and some rain rather cold wind northwards chiefly – Horses plough – T Hoad wood cutting – Foster and Eastone hop digging – Wm David and I threshing & I whent to the Halfmoon Market

Friday 14
Sometimes cloudy and showery wind northwards – Horses plough – T Hoad wood cutting – Eastone digging hops Foster Do in the afternoon – Father whent to Bellhurst – Wm David and I bosseling – Mr R Russel was here this afternoon

[350] Woods.

Saturday 15
Cloudy windy and wet morning some sun afterwards a pleasant afternoon wind in the south and southwest – Horses plough T Hoad wood work – Eastone and Foster digging Hops in the Archer garden in the afternoon David and I threshing – I was at W Harmers this evening – Mr Ashe from Burwash was here on business J T Lade sleeps here to night

Sunday 16
A pleasant day some clouds a drying wind from the northwest rather cold – Mother & Elizabeth rode Father I Wm and David whent to Heathfield Chapel in the morning – maid whent and Father Wm and Elizabeth stayed the afternoon – Mr Press our reputed minister is in a great measure recovered of his late illness and preached to day from John 3 chapter the 14th and 15th verses, 'as Moses etc' in the morning and a funeral sermon from Romans the 6th chapter and the 7 verse for Mr Joseph Erry who died on Wednesday morning last aged 72 years and was buried this afternoon a Chapel he remembers and a Decon to the church – Wm and I whent to Stonehouse in the evening Mrs Sobers spoke from Malachi the 4th Chapter the later part of the first verse and the day cometh Etc J T Lade sleeps here to night

Monday 17
Cloudy foggy day wind in the west some sun – Horses plough and fetched home a load of stubble from the 12 acres to the Home Close – T Hoad wood work – I threshing In the forenoon and whent to Dallington In the afternoon – Wm and David digging hops In the Croft – Foster and Eastone Do in the Archer etc etc

Tuesday 18
Misty cloudy foggy windy weather wind in the southwest Horses and the work men as on yesterday – Wm David and I did nothing in particular more than common in the day but whent to Mr Smith's in the evening Mr Winchester preached from Isiah the 48 chapter to 17 verse – Father whent to Boreham etc

Wednesday 19
Clear warm still sunny day wind in the southwest northwest northeast south and north Horses plough – Wm David and I with the oxen carried 5 loads of rot dung from the mackson[351] below the barn to the upper garden

[351] Maxon, mixen.

and drawed 4 oaken poles to Mast. Beal's new house at Bodle Street etc the three workmen as on Monday last J T Lade sleeps here to night – Forgot Wm whent to Hailsham Market this afternoon

Thursday 20
Cloudy day some rain a very wett and stormy evening wind in the southwest – Horses plough and I helpt them get up last load of stubble from the 12 acres and unloaded it in the Ox Close this is the last load of stubble for this year T Hoad at wood work – Eastone and Foster digging hops – Wm David and I shut the two speaned[352] heifer calf up to weand at the calves lodge that was calved on the 18th of April last and has been with the cow ever since till now – drove the cow or heifer home to the other cows etc etc

Friday 21
Bright sunny morning some showers in the afternoon and evening wind in the west and northwest rather cold – Horses plough T Hoad wood work his girls and boy shave the Poles – Eastone and Foster digging hops – I whent to Gardener Street in the forenoon threshing in the afternoon – Wm whent to Bellhurst etc

Saturday 22
Cold windy day sometimes cloudy and stormy wind in the northwest – Horses plough in the croft hop garden – Eastone and Foster diging hops in the croft – T Hoad at wood work he toss out the alders and the other wood in the bogs and the shaw that is not fenced in from the croft against oast but has not finished faggotting it up – David and I threshing – Wm whent to Boreham etc some people on the by and on business here today – J T Lade sleeps here to night

Sunday 23
A misty foggy cloudy day wind in the northwest and west – Mother rode and Father I Wm and David Mrs Lade and Elizabeth walked to Heathfield Chapel in the morning Father Mother Wm and I stayed the afternoon Mr Press preached in the morning from Acts 3 chapter 19th chapter the 11 & 12 verses and in the afternoon from Job 19th chapter the 25 & 26 and 27 verses to a large congregation A funeral sermon for Mr T Dalloway who died on Wednesday morning the 12th Inst aged 69 years he died in this parish Father Mother David and Elizabeth whent to Stone house in the evening

[352] With two teats.

Mrs Sobers spoke from John the 3rd chapter and the 3rd verse – I have forgotten to write Elizabeth stayed the afternoon at Chapel.

Monday 24
Sometimes cloudy and not much sun wind in the west – Horses finished plough in the Croft and afterwards at plough in the 12 acres – T Hoad at work wood cutting – Eastone and Foster digging hop Wm and David gardening – I went to Bellhurst after oil cake which puts me in mind of butcher Waters being here this morning and is a going to take the runt when it suits him Father whent to Warbleton Church and Rushlake – Elizabeth Lade was here to day I suppose on a visit but I did not see her – Colly cow calved a bull calf this afternoon etc etc Forgot that we shut 3 shuts up to fat to day

Tuesday 25
Cloudy but not foggy in the morning some sun in the forenoon cloudy and sort of foggy mist or rain in the afternoon – wind between west and northwest – Horses finished ploughing the 12 acres – T Hoad wood cutting in the Bonds croft against the chapel meadow – Eastone diging hops Foster not at work – I went to Priory Wm went to Hailsham and Father whent to Wartling David helpt Mr Waters drive the fatted runt to his Fathers slawter house at Rushlake Green – there was a man from Mayfield came to see me to day after money.

Wednesday 26
A wett morning afterwards a drying day rather cold some clouds wind nearly southwest in the first of the morning afterwards in the northwest – Horses at plough in the Gutterfield – T Hoad wood work – Eastone and Foster digging hops – Wm whent to Bell hurst and David and I threshing in the forenoon David and I removed the best of the potatoes in the Archer hop garden into the Henhouse Father and Wm helpt us a little afterwards Wm David and I dressing hops in the Croft – Father whent to Wm Harmer's this evening – J T Lade sleeps here to night

Thursday 27
Cloudy morning cold windy day some showers about wind in the northwest – west – and north – Horses and oxen carried 93 loads of dung and moul from the mackson In the Poundfield into the hop garden Eastone Foster and I filled the carts Wm Hoad and Henry Hoad shelved 3 carts David spreading and sometimes threshing Wm dressing hops in and whent

to Halfmoon Market – T Hoad wood work – etc etc

Friday 28
Nearly as yesterday but not so windy a drying day wind in the northwest – Horses and oxen as yesterday Wm Hoad was not well and did not come till the afternoon David shelved in his room We removed about 93 loads Wm dressing hops in the Croft – T Hoad at wood work Father whent to Wartling etc

Saturday 1 March
Cloudy cold windy misty day wind in the southwest and west – Horses and oxen carried 86 loads as yesterday and heald the youngest part of that garden in all 272 loads and left about 5 loads more that was not wanted David whent afterwards the dressing hops with William in the Croft We afterwards carried 15 loads of dung from the Mackson below the barn into the Old Archer hop garden – T Hoad at Wood work his children shave the Poles J T Lade sleeps here to night

Sunday 2
Cloudy not much sun showery evening Wind in the southeast a Windy day Rather cold Mother and Father I William David & Elizabeth walked to Heathfield Chapel in the morning Father and Elizabeth stayed the afternoon Mr Press preached from John 11th Chapter and the later part of the 56th Verse 'What think Ye' etc in the morning – and from the same … Chapter and the same … verse in the afternoon William David and I whent to Stone house in the evening Mrs Sobers spoke from Hebrews the 10th Chapter part of the 7th Verse 'Lo I come' etc etc J T Lade sleeps here to night I believe

Monday 3
A Fine morning Cloudy and Windy Wett afternoon a Tempest in the evening. Wind in the southwest Horses finised ploughing a piece of Ground in the Gutterfield for Hops and sowed and Harrowed a piece of ground at the father end of the Croft garden T Hoad woodwork and threshing. David and I spreading dung and Moul in the Poundfield Hop gardens in the forenoon David threshing in the afternoon. William Dressing hops in the Croft Master John Honeysett threshing wheat in the Home Barn – Master David Honeysett Senr Eastone and Foster digging hops finished the Croft and where afterwards in the youngest part of the Poundfield Hop garden in the Oldest part is dug by Eastone and Foster. Peter Pankhurst checking a plough mending two Harrows etc Saml

Winchester and Michael Collins two Carpenters moving the Poundfield gate against the lower Corner of the southeast Head of the Oast to the upper Corner of the same Head of the Oast Pull the Old pound Down built a new one against the Oast for Coals etc

Tuesday 4
Rather windy stormy showry Weather Wind in the West chiefly Horses plough in the Kilnfield T Hoad wood work William David and I spreading Dung and Moul and threshing Eastone Foster and David Honeysett senr. and a Master Winchester from Rushlake Green Hop diging J Honeysett threshing wheat Mr Collins Carpentering etc Mr Winchester preached here this evening from Revelations the 22 chapter and the 2 verse J T Lade sleeps here to night

Wednesday 5
Frosty morning some showrs in the afternoon Wind generally between West and Northwest Horses Plough David and I spreading Dung and Moul Workmen and the Carpenter all as yesterday William whent to Dallington etc Mrs Lade and her son is gone to the Priory. The Waldron Cow had calved a Bull calf this morning Mr Winchester is gone from here

Thursday 6
A smart show'r and a small Flood in the morning Windy Blusterous day some showers Wind in the West and North quarters 2 Visitors Horses drawed 3 Harrows in a Cart to the Blacksmiths to have the Tines sharped afterward at plough in the Kilnfield J Honeysett threshing D Honey[sett] Hop diging Eastone and Foster ditto in the afternoon T Hoad Kild a lame shutt in the morning after ward I suppose at Wood work. William David and I threshing Black Oats in the Chapel Barn all day Father gone to Parrish Meetting at Rushlake Green

Friday 7
Frosty in the Morning showry stormy day Wind in the Westerly Quarter Horses plough. I whent to Bellhurst after the Rest of the Oil Cake and helpt William and David spread the rest of the Dung and moul in the Poundfield Hop garden J Winchester D Honeysett Eastone and Foster Diging in the ditto T Hoad Wood work M Collins Carpentering against the Oast Father whent to Mr Jarvis's crawl in the evening J Honeysett threshing

Saturday 8
Windy stormy showers of Rain Hail and Snow Wind in the Northerly Quarter still evening. Horses at Plough. David and I threshing in the C B J

Honeysett threshing in the H B T Hoad Wood work 4 Hop diggers as yesterday Father whent to Wartling and Herstmonceux

Sunday 9
Cold Windy day some flakes of snow but not to lie a drying day Wind in the Northwest Mother rode Father I William David and Elizabeth walked to Heathfield Chapel in the morning I stayed the afternoon Mr Press preached from Galatians 5th Chapter part of the 4th Verse 'Ye are fallen from Grace' in the morning and from Deuteronomy the 7 chapter 7 and 8 verses in the afternoon William and David whent to the Stonehouse in the evening Mrs Sobers spoke from 92 Psalm the 4 verse etc

Monday 10
A Frost in the morning still mild day scarce any Wind sometimes. Horses at plough William and David and I threshing and spread the Dung in the Archer Hop Garden etc T Hoad at Wood work his children shaving Hop poles John Honeysett threshing Eastone D Honeysett and James Winchester Hop diging Foster not here to day M Collins moving Croft Gate from just against the small window of the Oast to the Corner of the Oast etc Father whent to Bell hurst etc

Tuesday 11
A mild Foggy morning afterwards some clouds and a small wind from the South west Horses plough William David and I finished Dressing the Croft Hop garden – and finished Diging Hops the Brook Garden Foster and J Winchester diging Hops in the Poundfield garden T Hoad and his children as usual the Honeysetts are not at work for us to day Easton is gone to Battle and is put in Battle gaol for not aiding in keeping his Wife and his three base born Children Father whent to Battle Market

Wednesday 12
A Still Warm day Horses plough David and I Dressing Hops and Diging in the Brook garden William whent to Wartling and after wards helping us T Hoad wood work Foster J Winchester and D Honeysett Hop diging J Honeysett threshing Messrs Reeves and Daughter where here this afternoon. J T Lade brought the news paper here to night

Thursday 13
A Warm cloudy day it is now good Walking Wind in the Northwest and south west Horses Carters I and David Carried 36 loads of Ruff[353] Horse

---

[353] Rough.

Dung in to the Archer Hop garden William David spread it and Carters carried 6 loads of Ashes etc from against the Hog pound the Lime kiln and Oast into the Meadows I gardening and whent to the Halfmoon Market T Hoad at wood work J Honeysett threshing Foster D Honeysett and J Winchester Hop diging in the Archer garden J Winchester whent home unwell after Dinner M Collins Carpentering etc

Friday 14
A pleasant Warm sunny day scarce any clouds sometimes a cooling breeze from the Northeast and south Horses at plough T Hoad wood work David and I oppening of Hops etc William whent to Burwash and Father whent to Wartling Elizabeth whent to Heathfield J Honeysett threshing Foster and D Honeysett Hop dig I shall be very glad when the Fatting Cow is gone for she hass eat all her Oats

Saturday 15
White hoar frost in the morning some clouds rest of the day nearly as yesterday – Horses plough – Wm David and I opening hops – Foster and D Honeysett hop digging – J Honeysett threshing T Hoad wood work etc etc

Sunday 16
A clear pleasant day wind in the easterly quarters rather still it is now dusty up on Heathfield Turnpike – Mother rode Father I Wm David and the maid and Ann walked to Heathfield Chapel in the morning Father and I the maid and Ann stayed the afternoon Mr Press preached both times from Acts the 15th Chapter and the 11th verse Father Wm and David whent to Stonehouse in the evening Mrs Sobers spoke from the 16th Chapter of the Acts a series of verses nearly all the Chapter Elizabeth whent to Herstmonceaux

Monday 17
A white frost in the morning a clear bright summer day wind in the northeast the ground is dryer now than it has been the 9 months past for last summer was a most remarkable wet summer and this winter has been extremely wet it has now the appearance of a very forward spring and may the Lord grant that it may be so and likewise a fruitfull and an abundant year to remove the many ills which seem to threaten us – Horses plough J Honeysett threshing T Hoad wood work – D Honeysett and Foster hop digging – David whent to Bellhurst to help them dress[354] their hops – Wm

[354] Manure.

and I wetting barley dressing hops gaping etc Father helpt us gaping in the lower corner of the Redpalefield against the esquire field barrow – one is gone to the Parish Meeting to night etc M Collins carpentering

Tuesday 18
Frosty morning weather nearly as yester day – Horses plough – T Hoad wood work – Foster and D Honeysett hop digging – Master Wm Gur Senr and I dressing hops in the orchard and Hop garden William opening ditto David at Bellhurst as yesterday. J Honeysett threshing as yesterday. M Collins Carpentering. Father I William and Elizabeth whent to Mr Smiths in the evening Mr Press preached from the 1st John the 3 chapter and the 2 verse 'Beloved now are we the son of God etc etc'

Wednesday 19
Cold and chiefly cloudy weather. Wind in the Northwest chiefly Horses plough J Honeysett and T Hoad as on yesterday Foster and D Honeysett finised diging Hops and helpt David and William Gur finis dress the Orchard Hop garden Father was in the Malt way Mr Warner the Exciseman comes to survey it William and I Drove Old Smoke the other Fatted Cow to Hailsham Market and sold her to Mr Collins and Waters Alfriston at 3s/6d per stone The chief news on foot is Thms Honeysett shooting Sam'l Pettit senior in clapland bottoms for 'it' is exposed 'his informing against several Gin shops' the Gun blowed and he only slitely Wounded him and Pettit took Honeysett and had him to Burwash sitting where he was committed to Horsham gaol to take Trial at the next Sessions all this was done yesterday

Thursday 20
Cold windy and at some places Frosty weather Wind in the Northwest Horses finised ploughing the Kilnfield and drawed the Trees out off and began the Grinnetts T Hoad at wood work and Hedging J Honeysett David and I cleaned 13 sacks 3 Bushels of Wheat with 2 Bushels cleaned before makes it in all 14 sacks and 1 Bushel J Honeysett wass afterwards thereof threshing Clover pug and David and I helping D Honeysett Foster Gur and William Dressing Hops in the Poundfield garden etc etc Two Coopers mended the Mish Tub[355] Mr Warner surveyed the Malt Father whent to Warbleton. Church etc

---

[355] Mash tub.

Friday 21

Cold windy day warmer towards night Wind in the North Horses carried 1 load of wheat for 28£ to J Smiths Water Mill Bucksteep and 1 sack to Grind for us and carried 50 Faggots to J Morfeys and 25 to Mrs Eastons and fetched the Harrows from the Blacksmiths etc David and I helpt J Honeysett clean the Clover about 3 Gallons not at all good seed J Honeysett wass afterwards threshing wheat it wass too frosty to Dress Hops in the morning so we were all on a cutting setts and dressed some Hops at night Father whent to Wartling the Maid Phillidelphia Eastland whent away not for any misdemeanour or ill intent but [b]y mutual consent of Mother and herself Mr Russel was here this afternoon etc

Saturday 22

Frosty morning a still day warmer than yesterday Wind almost all ways chiefly East and southwest Horses carried 26 loads of Dung from the Mackson below the Barns to the further part of the Gutterfield to plant the Hops in etc David and I with a pair of Oxen and 1 cart carried together 11 load of Moul that wass dug out of ditches in farrows in the Chapel Meadow and fetched home 1 cart load of sare wood[356] from the Ox Close William helpt us. William David and I where afterwards cutting Hop setts and dressing Hops D Honeysett Foster and Gur cleaning Oats in the morning afterwards dressing Hops and cutting setts J Honeysett threshing T Hoad wood work I understand that James Winchester from Rushlake that came here to diging Hops and whent home ill on the 13th of this month Died this morning of an inflammation May the Lord of his infinite mercy prepare me for that solemn and awful change and keep me from sin while I tarry here Father whent to the Priory and William whent with him to Wartling Wood some what about the Hop poles

Sunday 23

Frosty morning a pleasant sunny day some Wind from the Southwest and south Father I William David Elizabeth and Ann whent to Heathfield Chapel in the morning William and Elizabeth and Ann stayed the afternoon Mr Press preached from the 2 Book 5 chapter the 20 and 21st Verses of Corinthians in the morning and from the 18th and 19th Verses of the same Chapter in the afternoon William and David whent to the Stonehouse in the evening Mrs Sobers spoke from Matthew 11 Chapter the 28th and 29th Verses etc

---

356 Share wood, shared or distributed between different people.

Monday 24
Showry Day Nick went to Mayfield to see Mrs Cornwell as she was taken worse but she was sensible but to weak to speak. William Harmer Borrowed the Roller Horses plough at Hodges in the Grinnets field Hop Dressing T Hoad Honeysett threshing Father went to Bell hurst setting out Hops I went to Mayfield

Tuesday 25
Showery Day Horses Harrow in the Gutterfield went to wheelers for a two new bastard harrow brought 1 Quarter spring Wheat that come from London Hop dress set out 1260 hills in Gutterfield Honeysett threshing Ruth Hoad came to live with us Henry Hoad gone to live at John Waters Sandhills Foster hass left us it was Father I William David T Hoad J Honeysett and Gurr set the Hops out

Wednesday 26
A cloudy day Misty Rain Wind in the Southwest rather brisk William Hoad and William with the Horses finised ploughing the Grinnets and ploughed T Hoads plot T Hoad I David D Honeysett and Gurr and his son Henry finised Dressing Hops Cleaned 15 sacks of Black Oats in the C B and Cutt a Quantity of Hop setts Old J Guy cutting setts all day J Honeysett threshing in the afternoon Father and Elizabeth whent to Heathfield Chapel to J Winchester's Funeral Mr Press preached a sermon from Judges chapter part of the Verse Mrs Lade come here from the Priory last night the Dann Heifer Calved a Cow Calf

Thursday 27
Rather cold morning a bright sunny Day Wind in the Northwest and North Horses Harrowing in the 12 Acres Henry Gurr drove them William Hoad sowed some Black Oats T Hoad D Honeysett and William Gurr senior Holeing and David and I put some Dung and Moul in the Holes for Hops in the Gutterfield William whent to the Other Farms in the forenoon helping David and I part of the afternoon Father whent to the Halfmoon Market My Aunt Lucy Cornwell at Mayfield is not like to live she hass been out of her mind for several years

Friday 28
Cloudy Rainy Foggy Misty Weather Wind in the Southwest Horses as yesterday I whent to Mr Blackman Mill with 5 sacks of Wheat with the 4 Oxen and a Cart My two Brothers and I cleaned 3 sacks and 3 Bushels of Black Oats and helpt J Honeysett clean 3 sacks and 2 Bushels of Head and 3

Bushels of Tail wheat in the morning T Hoad William Gurr D Honeysett and a chap by the name of Usher from Wartling preparing the ground for and planting young Hops in the Gutterfield William and David ditto Father whent to a sale at Little Bucksteep I whent but it wass all over before I got there Father whent or is gone somewhere else etc J T Lade sleeps here tonight

Saturday 29
Cloudy Foggy Showry Rainy Misty Raining day Wind in the South west and Northwest Horses at Harrow with the Bartard Harrows in the 12 Acres *William David and I with Usher T Hoad and Gurr finised planting Hops and afterward William David and I a Gardening Diging in the
* Left Handed writing
Brook and sharping down 2 Hop pole stacks while T Hoad wass a threshing and Gurr and Foster cutting Hop setts for Sale Father whent to Bellhurst

Sunday 30
A pleasant Day Wind in the N West All whent to Chapel in the morning except Miss Lade maid & Ann William Father Mother and I stop in the afternoon Mr Press preached in the morning from the 20th verse of the 4th Chapter of the 1st of Corinthians from Genesis the 18th Chapter and the 19th Verse in the afternoon William David Mother and Elizabeth whent to Stonehouse in the evening Mr Press preached from 11th Psalm the 3rd Verse J T Lade sleeps here tonight

Monday 31
A pleasant Day as on yesterday Horses Harrow in the 12 acres William and David at work in the Brook Hop garden on young Orchard and David Dried some Malt I a gardening J Honeysett threshing D Honeysett poleing Hop in the Croft T Hoad at Wood work Father hass agreed with Henry Gurr to live in the House and sleep at his Fathers to go with the Horse under mote[357] from this day I know nothing of the agreement only that they have agreed Father whent to Rushlake Our Wartling Ox Team brought some Barley and Beans etc etc Mr Barnett spayed 3 sow pigs and 1 Bore pig

Tuesday 1 April
A warm pleasant Day Horses at Harrow William and Henry with them

---

[357] According to an agreement.

William Hoad and I sowed the 12 acres with Trefoil seed J Honeysett D Honeysett and T Hoad as on yesterday David Dried the Barley and Beans that wass brought there yesterday Mr Press preached from Revelations the 14 chapter and 13 Verse a Funeral Sermon for a Mrs King at Ashburnham J T Lade sleeps here tonight

Wednesday 2
A Warm pleasant Day Wind in the East Horses finised Harrowing the 12 Acres and afterwards strike furrows down the alleys of the Poundfield Hop garden where it was not Dug David Maltstering and I helpt him pole some Hops in the Brook Hop garden I whent to Stonehouse with Mr Press William whent to Bellhurst a threshing with the Machine J Honeysett threshing D Honeysett Hop poling. T Hoad at Wood work Father whent to the Other Farms etc

Thursday 3
Pleasant day Horses Finishd hop then went to carting poles into that Garden and Oxen into the Croft from the Poundfield Honeysett threshing Honeysett and Barton Poleing in the Croft T Hoad wood Cutting William went to Bellhurst to Threshing finishd them[?] David calves into the Bush fields one sheep lamb Father went to Parish Meeting Old Wilem sale to day weaned the Pigs. J T Lade sleeps here tonight

Friday 4
Some clouds in the morning a pleasant sunny Day Wind in the Northeast Horses and Carters at Nothing J Honeysett threshing D Honeysett and Barton Hoppoling T Hoad at Wood work As it is what is called Good Friday David I Elizabeth and Ann whent to Heathfield Chapel in the morning Mr Press preached from Isaiah the 53rd Chapter the latter part of the 8 verse 'For the transgressions of my people wass he stricken' William went to Cowden and to Mr Adam's Burwash I went to the Priory William whent to Stonehouse in the evening I have not heard William say where Mr Presses Text was the Honerable and Virtuous Lady Mrs Sober is gone to Brighton and will be very greatly missed amongst the many Poor Families Mr John Purstglove was here the Evening

Saturday 5
Weather much as yesterday horses carried some Ash poles to Master Daws at Bodle street to make some Ox Bows with and where afterwards carr[y]ing Hop poles from the shaw below the Old Orchard Hop garden into the Poundfield Hop garden Old Master Gurr David and I placing

Hops in the Brook or young orchard J Honeysett Hops threshing T Hoad wood work David Honeysett and Barton poleing Hops in the Croft William went to the Blackhorse with Mr Thorps Marsh Lambs J T Lade sleeps here tonight

Sunday 6
A small Frost in the morning Rather cold and Cloudy Day Wind in the Northeast Mother rode Father I William David and Elizabeth walked to Heathfield Chapel in the morning William and David went to the Stonehouse in the evening Mr Press preached from 1 Corinthian's the 15th Chapter and the 21st Verse in the morning from the 22 verse in the afternoon and from Luke the 24th Chapter the 46 and 47 verses in the evening My Aunt Elizabeth Oxley (Fathers sister) and My Uncle William Oxley Visitors and sleep this night

Monday 7
Some Clouds in the morning and Rather cold a clear sunny afternoon Wind in the Northeast Horses at Plough in the Gutterfield David I and Master Gurr poleing the Brook in the forenoon Master Gurr poleing in the Old Archer Garden and David and I backing poles into it from the Shaw against it in the afternoon T Hoad a Wood work J Honeysett threshing D Honeysett and Barton poleing the Croft David Dryed some malt William and Uncle went to Boreham and here again Uncle and Aunt went home Father hass been ill since Thursday evening Elizabeth went for the Doctor Mr Dinmond Rushlake he was here this evening with a Lady etc I understand that Doctor Blackman of Boreham is Dead May the Lord prepare me for that solemn event

Tuesday 8
Warm Sun shine weather Wind in SW Horses plow Went to Brownings after some Wheat William Gurr with Oxen Carried 14 Loads of Dung into Gutterfield Field Workman as usual 6 of us Went Herstmonceux Chapel Morning 3 in the Evening Habakkuk 2 C 14 verse in the evening Psalm 9 Ch 9 verse Mr Kirby from Lewes in the morning and Mr A Start from East Grinstead preached it wass an Association of the Sussex Missionary J T Lade sleeps here tonight

Wednesday 9
Generally Cloudy and more cold than yesterday Horses and Oxen carried Loads of Dung from below the barn into the Gutterfield in the forenoon

Old Gurr and I filled William Hoad shelved and Harry drove between William David T Hoad and Mr Gurr spread it William Hoad sowed the spring Wheat on the ground where it is and the Horses Harrowed it in the afterwards. T Hoad at wood work William David and I at anything and Old Gurr was poleing Hops in the Old Orchard William and David moved the 5 Calves I have foddered in the Chapel Meadow this Winter into the Grimes Brook in the morning etc Father whent to the other farms etc Mr J Purstglove whent after all the Hop setts J Honeysett threshing D Honeysett and Barton poleing Hops in the Croft etc etc the Oldish Dann Cow the last of our Cows to calve this year Calved a Cow Calf this morning we have 5 all alive

Thursday 10
A cold day sometimes cloudy and some snow Wind in the North (Forgot that it Rained yesterday morning snowed about noon) Horses finised Harrowing the Wheat and after wards where Rolling the Kilnfield William David and I threshing in the C B I went to the Halfmoon Market in the afternoon J Honeysett threshing in the H B T Hoad sharping Hop poles in the shaw against the Oast in the Croft D Honeysett and Barton poleing Hops in the Croft Master Gurr poleing Hops in the Old Archer garden. J T Lade sleeps here tonight

Friday 11
Not quite as cold as yesterday Wind in the North and Northwest. Horses Rolling David and I poleing hops with Master Gurr in the Archer in the forenoon. William whent after some sacks and he and David and I cleaned 7 sacks of Head and 4 sacks Tail Black Oats in the afternoon T Hoad sharping poles J Barton and D Honeysett finised poleing the Croft began the Poundfield Gardens J Honeysett as usual etc etc

Saturday 12
Sometimes sunny and some times cloudy Weather some Rain in the morning Wind in the Northwest and North Horses at Harrow in the Kilnfield I whent with the Oxen with 7 sacks of Black Oats to the Fords Brownings and William and David help carry 2 wheel loads of poles into the Poundfield garden from the Poundfield we three where poleing in the Archer in the afternoon. T Hoad and Master Gurr Stumping Out the Road over Bodle street Green for the Herstmonceux and Warbleton Gentlemen Father wass there the other 3 workmen as on yesterday J T Lade sleeps here tonight

Sunday 13

Nice Morning surely I wrote this if Nick Wishes to know William Oxley Bucksteep Manor Warbleton Sussex in the hundred of Foxearle 1817 A pleasant morning Cloudy Hazze and sometimes misty Day Wind Northwards Mother Rode Father I William David Mrs Lade and Ann Selmes walked to Heathfield Chapel in the morning I stayd the afternoon William whent to Hurstmonceux Chapel in the afternoon Mr Winchester from Hurstmonceux preached at Heathfield from Revelations the 4 chapter and the 3rd Verse: And there was a Rainbow etc in the Morning and from Galasions the 3rd Chapter and the 3rd and 4th Verses the afternoon Mr Bates from Alfriston preached at Herstmonceux and I understand Mr Press preached at Alfriston

Monday 14

Cold morning Rather warm in the afternoon Wind in the North and Southeast Sometimes cloudy Horses at Harrow and Rolling the Kilnfield Drawed some pole from the Shaw below the Archer Garden in to the Archer Garden and some Chucks from about the Oast to against the Hog pound with the Oxen I with them My Brothers helpt me we afterwards helpt Old Gurr and his Boy Bob poleing the Archer Garden T Hoad sharping poles in the Ponds Croft shaw J Honeysett threshing D Honeysett and Barton poleing Hops in the Poundfield Gardens Father went to Heathfield Fair etc

Tuesday 15

A still Cloudy morning some sun in the day not very Cold Wind Northwards William Hoad sowed 3 sacks and 2 Bushels of Barley in the Kilnfield Horses working of it in Master Gurr And I with our 4 and William Harmans 2 Oxen and William Foster with 6 of Mr Smiths Oxen and Mr T Isted's help us Drive and John Lade to help us hole lane at places on Bodle street Green for Warbleton and Herstmonceux Parishes David Drying Malt all the Rest as on yesterday Father William and I whent to Mr Smiths in the evening Mr Winchester preached from Romans the 8th Chapter the latter part of the (31st) Verse 'if God be for us who can be against us' I wass wrong about Mr Press preaching at Alfriston on Sunday I have forgot the names of the places he preached at

Wednesday 16

A Cold Windy and chiefly cloudy Day Wind in the Northly quarters Horses as yesterday Oxen as yesterday excepting we had Mr Isted's 2 Oxen in the room of William Harmers William and David fetched a 2 yearling Heifer and a 2 yearling Steer from Hodges as the Hay is all gone from there into the Home close and helpt J Honeysett clean 16 Sacks of Wheat T Hoad Heath Cutting in the 13 acres D Honeysett and J Barton Poleing Hops Young Robert Gurr at any thing Father whent to Bellhurst etc etc

Thursday 17
Weather nearly as on yesterday but Rather Colder William Hoad sowed some Trefoil Clover and Ryegrass where he sowed the Barley in the upper part of the Kiln field all above the upper that leads to Dill gate and the Borrows that lett you into the Gutterfield out of Kinfield etc etc Gurr and I with the Oxen Carried the Hop pole Chucks to the House from the Pond Croft Grimes Croft and Wainhouse field shaws that have been cutt this Winter and fetched some Barley and Beans from the Oast to the H Barn for Brothers William David with J Honeysett to clean they made 5 sacks of Barley and 6 sacks and 3 Bushels of Beans they have also cleaned 9 sacks and 3 Bushels of Rye grass that wass [k]nocked off from the Hay by the Carters in the Hay Loft etc Bob was sometimes with me and sometimes with the Carters T Hoad Hoath faggoting Barton not at work for us D Honeysett poleing Hops J T Lade sleeps here to night

Friday 18
Cold cloudy and sometimes sunny Day Rather warmer than yesterday and the Wind not so brisk in the same Quarter Horses Harrow etc in the Kinfield William Hoad sowed some Black Oats My Brothers and I with the Oxen carried two wheel loads of Poles into the orchard Garden from the ponds Croft Old Gurr helpt us clean some Black Oats in the C B in the morning and we helpt him poleing Hops in the afternoon Bob wass with him T Hoad Hoath faggoting I took his wood work to night he hass cut all the shaws and Pitts and made all the Hedges around the ponds croft except that against the Tale wood (which wass made by Master James Honeyset who has cutt the Wood for Mr J Smith) and T Hoad has cutt the Alders on the shaw at this end of the Croft and made a Hedge from the River to the Oast and made a small piece of Hedg from the corner of the Croft Hop garden some few Rods above the Oast 12½ Rods long towards Grimes wood he has also cut the Alders and made the Hedge against the Brook Hop garden adjoining the shaw above described and hass also made 7 Rods of Hedge at the upper end of the Brook Hop garden from the Gutterfield shaw southwards all in the Wainhouse field last mentioned J Honeysett threshing wheat J Barton and D Honeysett poleing Hops in the

Poundfield garden Mr Warner wass here to day perhaps the last time on this Malting Bussiness

Saturday 19
Frosty morning a mild sunny Day not many clouds Wind Northeast wards Horses as yesterday David Mr Gurr and Bob poleing Hops in the Archer D Honeysett Ditto the Poundfield J Honeysett threshing I went to Crawl and to Boreham Father went to Boreham with me William went to Lewes on his own Bussiness I have not had a holiday like this for sometime before on a work day J T Lade sleeps here to night

Sunday 20
Some clouds Wind in the Northerly quarter Father I David Mrs Lade and Ann Selmes went to Heathfield Chapel in the morning Father and I stayed the afternoon Mr Press preached from Zechariah the 9th Chapter the 11th Verse in the morning and from Isaiah the 63rd Chapter the last clause of the 1st Verse 'Mighty to save' in the afternoon J T Lade sleeps here to night

Monday 21
A bright sunny Day Wind in the north and Southeast Horses Harrowing etc in the Kilnfield Henry and Robert Gurr with them William Hoad mussing[358] the Guider mare that is under the Farrier's Hands Crowhurst who thinks she has the staggers and attended Daily since Friday T Hoad Hoath Faggotting D Honeysett Hop poling J Honeysett threshing Peas David I Master Gurr and sometimes William poleing Hops etc Father went to the Other Farms J Waters is here this evening

Tuesday 22
A Rather pleasant Day and Rather Warm and still Wind chiefly Northwards Horses as yesterday William and I with the Oxen Drawed 450 poles into the Poundfield Hop garden from the Croft shaw against the Oast and I drawed the Oxens water out etc otherwise all as yester day Drawed 2 Dead Lambs from a sheep yesterday and the sheep Died to Day etc I went to Dallington in the evening William and David Flawed the sheep Drove 4 steers from Marsh on to the Marsh that where put there on 30th Dec last

Wednesday 23
Frost in the morning cold cloudy Day nearly all day Wind Northwards it has been a Long dryth and every apearance of a back ward spring so the Oats seasons a very Dry and hard beyond penetration some are without

[358] Missing.

Rain Horses as yesterday William went after Mr Ruben Knight to who came to see Guider he says it is presher[359] on the Brain Crowhurst met him here also we put the mare in the stall to night Horses as yesterday I was hop poleing with David and Master Gurr all the rest the Workmen see Monday both alike J T Lade sleeps here to night

Thursday 24
Weather as usual Horses in the Kilnfield as on Monday William Hoad nursing the Mare Oxen Old Gurr and I with T Isted's man and a pair of Oxen and two Horses ploughed the Warbleton part of Bodle street again after the other ploughing wass held up Etc Etc Old Gurr poleing Hops afterwards David helpt him and Dryed the Last lot of the Malt We have Malted 13 sacks of Barley but it did not yeold to but 10 Bushels of Malt out of 12 Bushels of Barley by reason of the Barley being Damaged in Harvest by Wett Warner has surveyed it D Honeysett and Barton poleing Hops in the Poundfield J Honeysett threshing T Hoad cutting Hoath in the 13 Acres etc etc

Friday 25
A Cold cloudy Day Wind in the Northerly Quarter Horses as yesterday William Hoad finised sowing the Kilnfield part with Barley and part with Black Oats all with seeds namely Ryegrass Clover and Trefoil Old Gurr David William and I with the Oxen carried 1 Wheel Load of poles from the Wain house field and Gurr and I 2 loads from the poundfield into the Poundfield Hop garden and Gurr and I with the Oxen and a Cart carried 15 sacks of Head Wheat for Mr Smith and 1 sack of [tre]Foil for us to Bucksteep Mill and also William and David helpt us carry a Waggon load of poles from the ponds Croft and load up another T Hoad cutting Hoath D Honeysett and Barton poleing Hops in the Poundfield Garden J Honeysett threshing in the Home Barn etc

Saturday 26
Cold cloudy morning a little but not much sun in the afternoon Wind rather stiller than this few days past in the evening the wind in the North and Northeast the Horses have at length after 14 Days hard Labour have succeeded in getting a season in the Kilnfield which is 13 ½ Acres finised it to day and Roled the peas in the Wainhouse field My Brothers and I with a pair of Oxen and Wheels carried the other load of poles from the Wain

[359] Pressure.

Bucksteep Mill

house field and 2 loads from the Croft gardens shaw into the Archer Hop garden and Drawed 4 loads of Old poles out to Burn David helpt J Honeysett clean 5 sacks and 3 Bushels of Peas J Honeysett finised threshing them and wass afterwards threshing Oats in the Chapel Barn William David and I helpt Old Gurr and his Boy poleing the Orchard Garden in the afternoon T Hoad cutting Hoath in the 13 Acres J Barton and D Honeysett poleing Hops Father went to Bellhurst J T Lade sleeps here tonight

Sunday 27
Cold cloudy morning a small shower of Rain some sun in the Day Wind in the Northly Quarters Mother Rode and Father I Elizabeth and Ruth (the Maid) walked to Heathfield Chapel in the morning William went to and from the 61st Psalm the latter part of the 2 verse 'When my Heart etc' The Mother Elizabeth and I stayed the afternoon Mr Press preached both times Colly Cow wass a Bulling in the morning and William and David drove her to Bull to Cowden Bull they also drove a 2 yearling Heifer of hers with her and left there to go to the Bull and had the Cow back again. They both went

to Herstmonceux Chapel in the morning etc

Monday 28
A still cloudy morning some sun in the Day Much Warmer than yesterday or for some preceding Days a Brisk Westerley wind toward night and a still evening Horses Rolling and Harrowing the Grinnets William Hoad sowed with Black Oats David and I with the Oxen carried the Hop poles that were loaded on the Waggon Last Friday into the Poundfield Hop garden and fetched 2 loads of old poles to the House William went to Bellhurst in the morning and after wards hept us hept J Honeysett clean 4 sacks of Oats at night. I set up the poles we drawed out on yesterday in the morning David hept me one load. J Honeysett threshing in the C B Gurr and his Boy Both poleing the Archer Barton and D Honeysett ditto in the Poundfield gardens T Hoad and I think somebody else but I forget his name cutting Hoath in the 13 acres etc Mrs Lade is gone to Bellhurst

Tuesday 29
A mild cloudy Day Wind in the south west Horses as yesterday David I Bob and his Father Gurr Finised poleing the Archer all to[ld] about 20 Hills no more poles Joseph Leeves from Woods Corner pay gate Cutting Hoath with T Hoad today the first day in the 13 acres the other three men as on yesterday William perposed going to Roberts Bridge with Mr Bland Mr Press preached here this evening from 4th Chapter of Hebrews and the 9th verse

Wednesday 30
A cold Winterley day two or three cold showers at night Wind in the North Horses finished harrowing and rolling the Grinnets Wm Hoad sowed it with trefoil rye grass & clover Seeds – Gurr Bob David and I with the oxen carried [C]arried 3 loads of old poles to the house one from the pound field one from the croft and one from the Archer gardens and yoked 4 three yearlings steers the first time and unyoked them in my yard with the 4 oxen 2 of them were before with the cart in the Home Close – My team is now renewed to 8 again I hope they will turn out well – T Hoad killed a shutt in the morning rest of the workmen as on yesterday – Wm went to Heathfield and to Hailsham Market – Mr Press went home etc Father is often out some where being Overseer Assessor and surveyer I cannot always tell where he goes I shall not pretend to keep a regular account

Thursday 1 May
A very cold cloudy day some sun towards night wind in the north Horses

Warbleton Church, Sussex. 439.

Warbleton Church

carried 100 of house faggots from The Ponds Croft to the Blacksmiths on Bodle Street John Oxley and 100 Do Do to T Hoad's from and at Hodges also fetched a load of cord wood home from Hodges Old Gurr and I with the 8 oxen 6 at a time Dredging the meadows – Bob and David sorting and setting up hop poles – T Hoad and Leeves cutting Hoath – D Honeysitt and Barton poling hops – J Honeysett threshing – Bray the wheeler and Mr Wm Martin were here to day on business Wm went to the Halfmoon Market Father went to see Buckle Reeves – Mrs Lade came here again to night Trill brought the news paper but did not stop Guider mare gets better in a slow degree but revives our hopes of serviving of her

Friday 2

A very cold cloudy and windy morning rather warmer in the afternoon wind in the north and northeast still evening – Horses carried 100 of House Faggots from the ponds croft to the Blacksmiths and made T Hoads up 200 as yesterday and 125 Kiln Faggots to the kiln – Master Gurr and I with oxen dredging in the forenoon we have dredged the Chapel wood the Chapel field and part of the Esquirefield drove the steers before – T Hoad and Leeves Hoath cutting J Honeysitt threshing Black Oats in the CBD and the ponds croft meadows yesterday and to day and rolled the Furze Honeysett and J Barton poling the Pound field Garden – William went to

Bellhurst David and Bob carving to the out side of the hop garden Father Mother and Elizabeth went to Warbleton church

Saturday 3
Frost in the morning warmer and more pleasant in the day than it has been for a considerable time past wind in the south west – Horses carried 100 of House Faggots to Mr S Waters the shoemaker at Rushlake and 100 Do to Wm Hoads etc etc Oxen finished rolling the Squirefield and began the 7 acres rest workmen Bob and all as yesterday – Father went to Bellhurst Wm and David drove one cow and heifer one steer etc 2 calves into the marsh Father went to Bellhurst & Mearsham very beautiful evening I hope we shall have some rain as we have not had any for some months past the ground is got very dry so that a great many cannot sow the oats for it so rough as I was looking out of the window I saw Nick agoing too foddering here this evening which is a very good plan when the oxen go too work hard D & I carried 2 B[lack]-Oats & peas to mill & fetched back the like quantity on our backs which was just enough for us therefore I conclude hallelujah Amen 1817

Sunday 4
Shower in the morning some clouds in the day mild but dry weather and some few clouds afterwards wind in the southwest and west – Father I Wm and David went to Heathfield Chapel in the morning – Wm and David stayed Mother rode and Elizabeth and the Maid walked to Chapel in the afternoon David went to Stonehouse in the evening Mr Press preached from the 1st Epistle of John the 3rd chapter and the 14th verse in the morning and from St John the 5th chapter and the 24th verse in the afternoon and at Stonehouse in the evening from Proverbs the 13 chapter and the 4th verse J T Lade sleeps here to night etc

Monday 5
Frost in the morning a bright sunny day I know not of any clouds all day wind SW Horses carried 75 faggots 74 chord wood to Loydd at Windmill hill and fetched some kiln faggots & C wood from Ox R[ick] & silv[e]r field Hodges home oxen Gurr 3 boys fetching chucks from Poundfield and croft hop garden Honeysett chopping hops in Brook I mean Old John shot Honeysett Barton poling in P Garden Mr Hoad Leeve Hoath cutting Father gone too looking at the roads[?] ..i[?] whether to night surely[?]

Tuesday 6
Foggy morning a warm pleasant day some cloud wind at various places

chiefly S West and sometimes N east – Horses carried Wm Hoads 100 House Faggots and 100 Kiln Faggots and carried Mr Gurr 100 Kiln Faggots my brother Master Gurr and Bob and I with a pair of oxen cleared the Brook and Archer Hop garden of chucks and old poles – T Hoad and Leeves Hoath cutting D Honeysett and Barton poling hops J Honeysett chopping hops in the Brook in the forenoon pretended to clean some black oats but it did not do he did not afterwards work for us – etc etc went to Burwash in the forenoon David and he are gone to Mr Russels Warbleton church this evening

Wednesday 7

A pleasant day but very few clouds chiefly none at all wind in the east rather windy Horses carrying Kiln Faggots to the kiln – oxen carried some for the House and loaded up a large load to get to the kiln David I and Gurr with them and built a chuck house against the Hog pound and rung the pigs and one hog etc Wm and Bob drove 3 cows and two calves and a colt into the marsh left only Colly cow and her calf at home besides the oxen and the yearling and she runs out in the Brook so that there are only my oxen to fodder till there is grass in the Silverfield which have not been laid in till since David calves have been at grass rest of workmen as yesterday – J T Lade sleeps here to night

Thursday 8

A still warm day some clouds at times wind in the southeast etc Horses went to Mr Errys Ma[r]shfoot Wartling Hill with 100 of House Faggots – Bellhurst team came after some House Faggots yesterday and to day fetched some potatos to day 225 Faggots and 74 cord of wood – our oxen Heath Faggots carrying we as usual – T Hoad and Leeves cutting Heath in the 13 acres – J Honeysett chopping hops ... Archer garden forgot to write there was yester day also D Honeysett and Barton poling hops – Bob at many things. That it happened – Father went to the Half moon Market as I thought when I wrote the above but it was wrong he went to Crawl and some other places of business

Friday 9

A very cold cloudy day wind in the northeast – quite a difference trait to yesterday and to day yesterday it was so warm I sweat stripped to the shirt – to day I had all my clothes and was very cold then except when at work and then could not sweat – Horses where removed part of Mr Reeves household from above & wife pay gate Heathfield to Mr Venis senr

Dallington Father was with them – oxen David I and Gurr carried 800 houth faggots as yesterday we carried 625 yesterday – T Hoad and Leeves cutting heath in the 13 acres D Honeysett and Barton poling hops in the Poundfield and Croft Garden Barton is not coming again – J Honeysett and Wm cleaned the Black Oats 15 sacks and 2 bushels of head and 3 sacks 2 bushels of tail in the CB

Saturday 10
Mild and cloudy day a pleasant rain in the evening there has not been such a shower for some weeks past not a hasty[360] shower but a very gentle mild rain – Horses drawed some poles from one part of the Poundfield to another and shimed the Brook hop garden etc etc Wm David and I with Gurr and his boy with the oxen removed some straw from the CB to the Ox Ric[k] stedle and stacked it – also removed the oats stack from the head of the barn in 5 small loads and collected 14 or 15 rats. – D Honeysett finished poling the Poundfield and Croft garden J Honeysett chopping hops in the Archer – T Hoad and Leeves cutting heath as usual – Father went to the other farms etc J T Lade sleeps here to night

Sunday 11
Some sun and some times cloudy a hail shower at Heathfield about one o'clock I have not been told wether there was any rain or not – wind in the northwest and southwest Mother and Elizabeth went in the cart and Father I William and David on foot to Heathfield Chapel in the morning Father I & William staid the afternoon Maid went to there in the afternoon Mr Press preached both times from Isiah the 44 chapter and the 3-4 and 5 verses – J T Lade sleeps here to night

Monday 12
There was a auellent[361] shower in the night and some small showers in the day but were all dryed up by night windy at night wind in the southwest & west – Horses carters Gurr and Bob shiming the young hops in the Gutterfield D & J Honeysett's my brothers and I potatoing in the Wainhouse Brook – T Hoad and Leeves cutting heath T Hoad has done his part Father went to Bellhurst etc etc

Tuesday 13
A windy day sometimes cloudy and more still in the evening wind in the

[360] Heavy.
[361] Excellent.

west – Horses carried some posts to Bodle Street Green and went to Mersham after 50 bushels of potatos etc Oxen 2 carts Old Gurr and I gravelling or removing gravel from from [sic] the cross ways beyond sannells Rushlake ward to[362] Bodle Street together with several more cart and men and boys load 48 loads 8 carts – T Hoad my brothers and the Honeysetts potatoing in the young hops etc Master Leeves has finished cutting the heath in the 13 acres he has 1337 Heath Faggots at 25s for thousand or 2/6d per hundred £1 12s 9¾ Father surveyed the roads etc etc

Wednesday 14
A smart shower in the morning and more in the afternoon windy weather wind in the west – southwest and south – Our horses and oxen with 4 carts graveling as on yesterday with 4 more carts not all the same as yesterday – Wm was with us to day loaded and carried 48 loads – T Hoad D Honeysett and David potatoing as yesterday J Honeysett Do and way mending against his house in the afternoon some hop tiers etc

Thursday 15
There was a very heavy shower about 3 o'clock in the morning a pleasant day not very windy nor many clouds wind in the southwesterly quarters – Horses and oxen graveling as on yesterday – carried 48 loads with the other teams T Hoad David and John Honeysett and brother David potatoing some women tieing hops – I saw Dame Dann a coming I suppose she will quarter here a night as she did last year and the year before etc – Mr H J C Waters from Hailsham is here at this present time about ¼ past 8 o'clock – J T Lade sleeps here tonight Master Crouch tail the sheep[363] and David assisted

Friday 16
Very nice morning quite pleasant I'm just agoing to work to carrying paving gravel to Bodle Street Green with several other cart horses are gone before us – fine weather all day very warm wind in the southwest – Horses and oxen as on yesterday T Hoad and D and J Honeysett finished planting potatoes in the Wainhouse Brook – David and Bob help the 3 men when after wards chopping hops in the Archer garden Bob and David back off from the Croft and the Poundfield Gardens etc etc Father went in to the marsh – I went to Gardner Street in the evening

[362] Toward.
[363] Remove the tails for hygiene purposes.

Saturday 17
Wm wrote that he was a very nice Morning yesterday but I will contradict him for there was a very sharp frost about 5 o'clock whilst foddering the oxen - I[t] was a still and more pleasant morning to day rather cloudy in the forenoon wind in the south and southeast Horses and oxen as on Thursday day – David and Bob at many things David had the guyde move[364] that is newly out of the farrier hand into the marsh – the three men finished poling hops and chopping hops in the Archer Garden – Mr Steer brought David and Father each a new jacket – Mr Russel the school master and Mr Barns the shoemaker on bussiness etc Wm went to Gardener Street this evening – Mrs Lade and her son are gone to the Priory I would hope for good till she and her husband have business for themselves

Sunday 18
A sort of cloudy morning a still warm day some showers in the afternoon – Father Mother Elizabeth and Ann rode in the cart and Wm David I and Ruth (all the family) walked to [crossed out] went to Heathfield Chapel in the morning I stayed the afternoon Mr Press preached from the 20th verse of the 6th chapter of Joshua And from [crossed out] in the morning and from Job I believe the 33rd chapter of the 28th verse 'He will deliver his soul from going into the pitt and his life shall see the light' or words to that effect

Monday 19
Cold cloudy day wett after noon and evening wind in the north easterly quarter – Horses carter old Gurr and Bob shiming hops in the croft William David and I with the oxen finished clearing the croft and pound field garden of chucks and old poles T Hoad gaping at various places we have t[w]o other workmen now – several women hop tieing – Mr Russel stays all night weather bound

Tuesday 20
Cloudy some sun and some rain warm growing day wind in the west south west in the day and east and northeasterly quarters in the evening Horses at plough in the Bushey fields Old Gurr David and I with carried 60 loads of dung from the Home Close and macksoned on the bank just below the orchard hop garden gate above where the oast used to be – Wm went to Bellhurst in the forenoon and helped us a little Mother in the afternoon he

[364] Guilder mare.

and I were at friends[?] this evening T Hoad and Bob gaping – Father and Elizabeth went to Heathfield Chapel in the afternoon the was a funeral sermon for a Mrs Dunk from Ticehurst

Wednesday 21
Wett weather till one o'clock the afternoon afterwards some clouds rather cold – wind southwest wards – Horses were at plough a while afterwards at nothing oxen drawed the threshed oats from the CB to the oast and sett the waggon in the Lodge T Hoad and Master Gurr threshing oats in the C Barn – I was at Samuel's this evening on business

Thursday 22
Cloudy some rain and some sun rather dirty at times wind in the south west – Horses and oxen gravelling Carters Master Gurr David and I Do see Friday or Thursday last or the day before or the day after T Hoad and Bob Hoad threshing several hop ties I scarcely know who all in all the gardens gaping at various places Father went to Battle – Wm went to Burwash the bines grow amazingly in general and other things too but rather backward Bless the Lords most holy name that he has sent such fruitful showers as he has done altogether beyond our discovering nought else to write as I remember but the Honeysetts mending the roofs of the barns and lodges with thatch

Friday 23
Showery dirty but very growing weather rather cold in the morning. Mild warm evening wind southwest and west etc oxen and horses as yesterday but William was with me instead of David who was boseling with Bob T Hoad threshing several hop ties I scarcely know who all in all the gardens

Saturday 24
There was a frost on the morning about 5 o'clock afterwards a warm pleasant day and but few clouds wind in the south Horses and oxen as yesterday but Wm was not with me but ½ day Bob was with me in his room he went to Cowden with a team after potatoes rest generally as on yesterday fetched home 39 Ox Bows from Master Daws in the ox cart

Sunday 25
Wett weather till the afternoon then some clouds and some sun wind in the south rather southeast – I only went to Heathfield Chapel in the morning and stayed the afternoon Father rode there in the afternoon Mr Press preached from the 1st verse of the 13th chapter of Hebrews in the morning and from the 9th chapter and I believe the 12th verse of the same book in the after noon Wm and David went to Herstmonceaux Chapel in the

afternoon

Monday 26
Cloudy morning a pleasant day some clouds chiefly sunny wind in the south T Hoad gaping at Hodges in the morning afterwards threshing oats in the CB all the rest keeping holiday – Father went and looked over the Wartling Farms Wm David and I went to Battle Fair Mary Gower one of our old maids stays Here on a visit to night

Tuesday 27
Mild pleasant weather – wind in the southeast south and southwesterley quarters – Old Gurr Bob and the carters with the horses shiming hops in the Poundfield garden David and I with the oxen dredged the Calves Lodge meadow and drawed some spare poles from the Croft into the Poundfield and Wm helpt us stack them in the after noon – T Hoad turning the mackson in the silverfield against the Calves Lodge Meadow and Mr Smiths pillfield – several hop ties Mr Mepham from Heathfield dined here to day with Mr Press and us Mr Press preached here to night from Mark the 16 chapter the 20th verse which in the last verse of that book Wm went to Burwash

Wednesday 28
A bright morning some clouds in the afternoon and a shower between 3 and 4 o'clock the wind has been in all the quarters very changeable – Horses as yesterday and shiming in the Archer garden – Oxen picking cord wood and faggots etc from reaaous[365] to the house and fetched 200 hoath faggots from the 13 acres to the kiln etc etc the Martins fired the kiln again to day morning T Hoad and the hop tiers as yesterday Mr Press went home – Father went to Hailsham Market

Thursday 29
Cloudy dirty rainy day wind in the northwest and northesterly quarters Horses at plough in the Bushey fields David helped Master Gurr and I load a ½ cart of cord wood and a ½ hundred of H faggots from the shaw against the orchard hop garden and the oxen drawed them to Mr Ste Water's Rushlake – the Martin's have put there fire out this evening to empty on Saturdy T Hoad and Hopsters as on yesterday Wm is gone Robert Bridge with Mr Bland Elizabeth is gone some where with him

[365] Areas? Various?

Friday 30

A very cold day for the time of the year cloudy and wind in the northerly quarters – Horses at plough T Hoad David and Master Gurr dunging carried 67 loads from the Ox Close and macksoned in the Chapel Meadow about 10 or 12 rods from the close gate against the road and made some lime lump places in the Bushey field – Hoptiers etc I went to Mayfield Fair

Saturday 31

Rather cold but more sun than yesterday I think the wind the same as yesterday – Horses and oxen carter limeburners Wm David I and Mr Gurr emptied the limekiln and carried the lime into the Busheyfields afterwards Father and not the limeburners helped us get the wheat stack in from the Busheyfields into the Home Barn 4 2/3. Loads – Forgot that the oxen eat the last of their hay at their close yesterday morning and where turned into the Home Close at night there not being enough grass to turn out into – T Hoad turning mould as on Tuesday hoptiers as usual – the Priory women Naney Lade and her sons came here again to day – J T Lade sleeps here to night

Sunday 1 June

More warm than yesterday rather cloudy wind westwards chiefly Father Mother and Elizabeth rode to and Wm David and I walked to Heathfield Chapel in the morning Mother and I rode home Father stayed and the maid went in afternoon Wm and David went to Herstmonceaux Chapel in the after noon and went with them to Stonehouse in the evening Mr Press preached from 2 Corinthians 3rd chapter and 13 and 14 verses both times at Heathfield and the 18 verse the same chapter at Stonehouse

Monday 2

A bright morning cloudy evening wind west and southwest – Horses at plough in the Bushey field – Old Gurr Bob David and I with our 8 and Wm Harmers 2 oxen graveling with 3 carts from the gravel pitt beyond the sannels to Bodle Street T Hoad turning mould in the silverfield – the limeburners began fill the kiln again it stood filled all the winter before Saturday – Wm went to Robertsbridge Father went to Rushlake – we turned the oxen out into the Wainhousefield seeds and tended them off the peas to night till they had filled their bellys Forgot that they shut Colly Calf up to weand today

Tuesday 3

Windy and rather cold day sometimes cloudy a few drops of rain in the evening Horses fetched 800 of hoath faggots to the kiln and the oxen Gurr Bob David and I rolled the spring wheat in the Gutterfield rolled the tares in the 13 acres and fetched 600 of Hoath Faggots to the Lime Kiln from the 13 acres – Martins finished filling the kiln and lit her again – T Hoad as yesterday Wm went to Bellhurst – Father has been somewhere I don't know where on horse back to day – Forgot that we turned the oxen into the silverfield the 1st time tonight

Wednesday 4
A little rain in the morning very windy all day so that the Wind Mills went without any sail out wind between west and southwest – Horses finished ploughing the Bushey field and began part of the Wainhouse field – Gurr Bob and I graveling 2 carts with the 8 oxen only see Monday – T Hoad moul turning – J Honeysett threshing wheat in the home barn he was there yesterday and Monday but I forgot to write his name down – several hoptiers also I know not particularly who lime burners etc Father went to Burnt Oak[366] Mr Reeves Warbleton

Thursday 5
A cold cloudy day windy but not so brisk as yesterday wind in the south west – Horses at plough in the Wainhouse field – Master Gurr and Bob with 6 oxen and one cart graveling I with 1 pair of oxen rolling the 12 acres Wm and David setting up poles in the Hop Garden – T Hoad killed a young hog in the morning afterward chopping hops in the croft – J Honeysett threshing several hop tiers etc

Friday 6
Cloudy some sun wind in the southwest – Horses at plough – oxen ploughed up some mould against the oast in the Poundfield Mr Gurr David and I with them afterwards I finished rolling the 12 acres with one pair and Mr Gurr went to Rushlake with 6 sack and 1 bushel of beans for the carriers with 2 pair and a cart the other pair have not worked all day Thos Hoad nailing fence up at Redpole And killed pig that was pooked[367] by a bullock Hop tiers as usual Elizabeth gone Mr Reeves Rushlake Green David and Wm afternoon cutting potatoes Do putting poles for them into the Brook farm on Hops as the wett has killed the potatoes in the Brook I thinks veryly our 3 brothers snarl brall[368] especially if we pay the tithe &

---

[366] Broad Oak?
[367] Poked.
[368] Shall brawl.

poor Taxes doth taking very ill old Newman visited us yesterday poor old man is very bad off he cusses about the oatbins at Hartridges gets a little of Ben & his wife cribbiges at Old Mrs Merricks and gits a mouthful of victuals I am very glad for this as they have a little to eat. This Wm rubbage not mine

Saturday 7

Cloudy morning a very warm summer like day wind in the southwest Mr Fox and his apprentice mending and the carts oiling the harnesses – Lime burners Gurr William David and I with 4 oxen and 2 carts emptied the lime kiln and carried the lime to put in a mackson against the oast T Hoad making trenches to put it in etc etc J Honeysett threshing – hop tiers as usual – My bees swarmed a large swarm it seems it has been very unaforable[369] as many people died in the winter and now a late cold summer but such is the will of the almighty who doth all things well then let us not repine … but bless him for mercies and then ask for more – Mr Jarvis called this evening on business J T Lade sleeps here to night

Sunday 8

Some misty rain in the forenoon colder and more clouds than yesterday wind in the SW – Father Mother Elizabeth and Ann rode to and William David I and Ruth walked to Heathfield Chapel in the morning Wm David I Elizabeth and Ann stayed the afternoon Mr Garnett preached from the 3 chapter of St John the 14 and 15th verses in the morning and from Acts the 16 chapter part of the 30 and part of the 31st verses in the afternoon si … [?] etc etc

Monday 9

Cloudy morning misty rain and a wett afternoon rather windy wind in the southwest Horses and the carters are gone with 100 House Faggots to Mr Gobbs and are going to take Mr Russels house hold and carry it to Brighton he is going to Chichester to live – David helped them load the faggots from Hodges afterward helped Gurr Bob and I get 50 loads of dung out the Ox Close to the place where the mould has been carried Away against to[370] road about the water dring[371] J Honeysett threshing T Hoad I believe hop choping – several hoptiers – Forgot that Master Morfey and his

[369] Unfavorable?
[370] The.
[371] Watering [place].

son tarred the oast last Friday and Saturday etc Wm went to Burwash and Father is gone to Warbleton Church – Mrs Lade Eliza and Caleb are gone to the silverash

Tuesday 10
Misty rainy morning a bright sunny afternoon after about 2 o'clock – wind in the southwest till in the afternoon then suddenly northwards afterwards west and then southwest ward again in the evening – Horses are gone to Brighton – Master Gurr David Bob and I with the oxen finished dunging at the Ox Close 45 loads to day in all there was 158 loads of Ruff Dung in the Ox Close – T Hoad hop chopping – J Honeysett threshing wheat in the Home Barn – hoptiers etc Father went to Battle Market and to Mr Smiths with Wm David Elizabeth Mr Press preached there from 2 Peter the 1st chapter the 10th and 11 verse – he came home with us and sleeps here to night

Wednesday 11
A warm pleasant day some clouds wind in the southwest – Horses came home to night they fetched 2 chaldrons of coals from Lewes to Master Standen's Blacksmith at Rushlake Green – Gurr Bob and I with the oxen finished ploughing the Wainhouse field – J Honeysett threshing in the H Barn T Hoad chopping hops and hived a swarm of my bees that flew over into Birtet Wood near Lottendens in Ashburnham Parish Hoptiers etc – David boseling – Father and Wm went to Hailsham Market Elizabeth Lade Harriot Phillips Elizabeth And Sarah Pattenden where here to night I went home with the Pattendens I hope that the Lord has begun his good work of grace on their hearts

Thursday 12
Generally cloudy and some rain some sun wind in the southwest – T Hoad Bob and the carters with the horses shiming hops in the Archer and Croft – Gurr David and I with the oxen the last of the hoath faggots from the 13 acres to the Kiln 1075 to day 3025 before makes it 4100 in all – J Honeysett threshing – hop tiers weeders etc Father and Wm went to Bellhurst and into the marsh and fetched home the Waldron and Cherry cows with their calves also fetched a Heifffer and calf from Bellhurst – Father was at Hurstmonceux Chapel this evening the Reverend T R Kemp preached here to night – Mr and Mrs Russel are come here one visit before they go to Chichester

Friday 13

Cloudy morning a wett afternoon wind in the southeast there was some sun – Horses as yesterday I don't know which Gardens – Oxen Gurr Wm David and I fetched 2 loads of Kiln Faggots from Hodges rain prevented our going again T Hoad and Gurr threshing oats in the CB in the afternoon – J Honeysett threshing wheat in the home barn – hop tiers etc etc I am sorry to think that Father has sett Easton to work again shoveting[372] hops in the oast Mr H Purstglove was here this evening on business – shut 3 calves up to weaned

Saturday 14

Clear windy drying day cloudy and wett evening – wind in the southwest horses finished shiming the hops etc my brothers Gurr and I carried 58 loads of dung from the Home Barn macksoned below the barn with the oxen 2 carts rest of the workmen and women I believe as yesterday – Mr and Mrs Russel are gone to day J T Lade sleeps here to night

Sunday 15

Rather cold for the time of the year some clouds wind in the southwardly quarter Father Mother and Elizabeth rode and Wm David and I walked to Heathfield Chapel in the morning Father and I stayed the afternoon Elizabeth Do the Revd Mr Press preached both times from the 15th chapter of John the 9th and 10th verses Wm went to Church in the afternoon and to the Stonehouse in the evening I have not heard him say where the texts were

Monday 16

A bright summer like day not many clouds wind in the southeast and east – the Horses are gone to Wonnick laying out of chalk Gurr David and I and Mastr Foots a fresh comer with the oxen carried 58 loads of dung as on last Saturday – Eastone shoveling hops in the Croft T Hoad chopping hops in the Pound field Garden Hoptiers and weeders as usual – put the weaning calves up into the silverfield – I had a swarm of bees to day

Tuesday 17

A warm summers day search any clouds wind in the east and northeast Horses are not come home yet – Gurr David and I with the oxen and 3 carts graveling Bodle Street T Hoad chopping hops – Eastone tieing hops with a stool – Foots healing the lime over with mould against the oast – Women

---

[372] Shoveling?

hoptiers and weeders etc

(Wm went up to the Windmill but there was no wind so I put the tail in and came home to bed but thy Boys was gone too bed that made know difference about my going for got to bed pretty Judith and up again in the morning but that makes no different for a great many people perhaps it might to some Wm Oxley)

– Forgot that Joseph Winchester was Here a carpentering to day – also I had Another swarm of bees to day

Wednesday 18

A clear warm day wind in the east Horses come home with a load of chalk they have 9 loads besides that that they had home oxen as on yesterday – T Hoad and Eastone tieing hops – Women weeding etc etc Foots as on yesterday – Father went to Woods Corner in the evening J Honeysett threshing

Thursday 19

A very warm day not much wind which was southwards – Horses carried 100 of House Faggots to Gobbs at church and 100 to Mr Wisdom at Bodle Street oxen fetched 2 loads of Kiln Faggots from Hodges and one load from the Archer shaw Gurr Wm David and I with them Father helped us the last load Trill Lade came here with the news paper and Wm went to Priory after it in the evening – rest generally as on yesterday I mean the workmen and work women and boys Etc etc

Friday 20

A very warm day wind generally N.E. and NW Horses harrowed the Bushey field with the bastard harrows – oxen Gurr Wm and David fetched the last load of Kiln Faggots from Hodges also carried T Hoads bundles to Hodges where he lives and turned out Wm and David went with the sheep to wash at Cowden and Gurr gardening afterward – I have had a holiday to day and went to Dallington and Bellhurst T Hoad and Eastone tieing hops Foots choping Do in the Archer – J Honeysett threshing – weeders etc etc Father went to Bellhurst

Saturday 21

Weather continues very warm wind very changeable in the forenoon chiefly south or southwest in the afternoon what little there was – Horses harrowed the ploughed part of the Wainhousefield – oxen not at work Jas[?] Honeysett Gurr and I cleaned 13 sacks and 2 bushels of head and 1 sack of tail wheat in the Home Barn there was 6 bushels cleaned before

Sunday 22

It continues being warm growingly summer weather with some thunder to day yesterday and on Friday towards evening each time on rain[?] have wind many ways We where all at Heathfield Chapel this morning and Father David and I stayed the afternoon – the Revd Mr Day from London preached from Micha the 6 chapter and the 8th verse in the morning and in the afternoon from John the 10th chapter and the 9 verse – Wm says he went to Herstmonceux Chapel this afternoon

Monday 23

Warm weather as usual rather more wind from the northeast still evening Horses the carters Gurr and his son Bob shiming hops in the Poundfield and Croft garden – oxen at nothing T Hoad and Foots as on Saturday hops chopping Eastone shoveling hops – J Honeysett and Jespier[?] Dann a mate he has gott threshing wheat in the Home Barn – D Honeysett (who has been here since poling hops) and David and I chopping hops in the Brook – hop tiers weeders etc – Father went to Mountfield this morning I believe as he sayed he should he is come back – Wm is frequently with Mr Smith millers milling shut the le[ft]³⁷³ Calf up to weaned

Tuesday 24

A few clouds in the morning a warm day not much wind – Wm Hoad and Bob shiming hops and Henry with 1 cart graveling with the horses – Gurr and I with 2 carts graveling with the oxen – David Honeysett and David chopping hops in the Brook and other places – T Hoad and Foots Do Eastone shoveling hops – Threshers weeders etc etc the Revd Mr Day preached here this evening from the 7th Chapter of Hebrews the 19th and following verses Mr C Hilder from perrymans Burwash and his son w[ere] here this afternoon

making it just 16 sacks in all this cleaning – Wm and David drove 5 yearling steers into the marsh and fetched home the youngest or 4 yearling Dann Cow and her calf Foots as on yesterday T Hoad & Eastone chopping hops in the Poundfield garden – etc I went to the Priory in the evening

---

373 Last.

Sheep washing

Wednesday 25

Foggy morning a warm day wind in the northwest – Horses at plough steering in the Bushey field – Gurr Foot David and I with the oxen 2 carts mouling in the Wain housefield laid out 50 loads the mackson was carried there from where the Old Oast was see about last July – T Hoad and Eastone mowing seeds in the nine acres this is the first day mowing for this year D Honeysett chopping hops – Threshers weeders etc Father went to Hailsham Market Wm at anything

Thursday 26

Cloudy morning a warm day and cloudy evening wind northwest and southwest – Horses and oxen and workmen as yesterday except that that the oxen had the narrow wheeled waggon to the Blacksmiths at night Wm went to the Halfmoon Market Heath field etc Winchester carpentering

Friday 27

There was a shower in the night and another this afternoon generally cloudy some sun wind in the southwest oxen and horses – nearly as yesterday oxen finished one mackson 115 loads and began another carried 25 loads of it to day against the gutterfield shaw in the Wain house field –

Saturday 28
Rather cold cloudy day not much sun wind in the southwest – Horses finished plowing the Bushey field the second time – Oxen Gurr David and I with 3 carts finished graveling Bodle Street (there was several more carts besides ours) and loaded up two small loads of hay from the nine acres J Honeysett and Dann have finished threshing our wheat to day and Foot helpt them clean 9 sacks of head 1 sack and 0 bushels of tail nearly the last for this year T Hoad and Eastone finished mowing the Huglets Dann Foot T Hoad Eastone Gurr Wm David I Mrs Dann Beth Dann and Susannah Morfey where all on haying in the after noon – Father went to Dallington to Mr Noakes

Sunday 29
Chiefly cloudy wind in the southwest Forgot that it was very windy yesterday – Father Mother Wm David I Elizabeth maid and Ann where all at Heathfield Chapel in the morning left none at home – Wm Elizabeth and I stayed the afternoon – the Revd Mr Day preached from Romans the 8th chapter and the 1st verse in the morning and from Phillippians the 3rd chapter and the 8th & 9th verses in the afternoon Wm David and Elizabeth where at Stone House this evening Mr Day preached there from 2 Corinthians 5th Chapter and the 19th–20th and 21st Verses

Monday 30
Cloudy morning Rather Cold more sun in the afternoon and scarce any clouds in the evening Wind chiefly Southwest Horses are gone to Wannock again afterward laying out of chalk Oxen Gurr T Hoad David and I unloaded the 2 loads of Hay we got up on Saturday in the new Rick Stedle or home Rick Stedle and Load up two more and stacked on it and ploughed the Mackson in the Wainhouse field against the shaw Foot spreading mould and Haying Easton choping Hops in the Poundfield and Haying Dame Dann and Ruth Dann Haying and Weeding Susannah Morphey Haying William is often Millering at Mr Smiths Wind Mill learning his trade as a Miller Father went to the Parish meeting this forenoon I have an unpleasant Cold

the mowers finished mowing the nine acres beyond the Huglett field Hodges – D Honeysett chopping hops J Honeysett and Dann threshing – rest of us with the teams Wm exempt – Master Winchester mending cart Mr Morfey his men and a boy tarring the oast etc etc etc Father went to Bellhurst – Sophia and Ann Smith visitors with Elizabeth

Tuesday 1 July
Cloudy morning Wett after noon Wind in the South and Southeast rather Cold Horses are not at home Gurr Easton Foot and I with the Oxen laid out 39 loads of mould in the Wainhouse field in the forenoon T Hoad mowing in Grimes Wood in the forenoon Gurr and T Hoad threshing Oats in the C B in the after noon William David and Robert choping potatoes in the Brook etc Father is gone to Bellhurst perhaps Weatherbound somewhere Forgot that Bob and Henry Drove the Cherry Cow to Bull to Cowden on the Sunday and William and Bob Drove the Waldron and the Dann Cows to Bull yesterday

Wednesday 2
Cloudy Day some Rain some Sun and Windy from the West the Wind turned last night after I had wrote yesterdays account to the West and wass very Brisk all night Horses are come home with some chalk they have laid out and fetched from the pett 8 loads this week and 10 loads before makes it 18 loads this year Oxen Eastone Foot Gurr and I Mouling removed 70 Loads T Hoad finised mowing in Grimes Wood and mowed around the Hop gardens William Millering David Boseling Father went to Heathfield Chapel etc etc

Thursday 3
Cloudy morning showry after noon a Mild evening Wind SW and SE Horses Carter carried 31 Loads of Dung from the home close and mackoned up in the Poundfield Oxen Mouling carried 2 Loads of Mould from near the House into the Wainhouse field and moved 50 loads in the Wainhousefield we ploughed the Mackson again and went into the nine acres to Haying but the Rain prevented us left the Waggons up there and went to Mouling again Men where with the Oxen as yesterday T Hoad choping Hops Dame Dann Weeding and Haying etc William and Bob fetched home a Cow and a Calf from the Marsh etc etc.

Why do not you say that Trill Lade your Partner in Summertree and Sand hil Farms his wife came here too knight but he's gone home again and that makes know difference too me Mr Woodyear[?] and a Girl went to Mr Marten Battle Road to examined too know what Parish she will Belong wether ours or Burwash but she aught too belong to Burwash this Ends but I want to finish etc etc Wm Oxley

Sir she came after I have written the above I am N Oxley

Friday 4

Cloudy morning and Drying afternoon Wind in the West Horses went after Chalk Oxen Easton Foot Gurr and I carried 2 Loads of Moul from aggainst the House into and removed 45 loads in the Wainhousefield in the forenoon T Hoad Choping the young hops in the Gutterfield in the morning after wards we where all on Haying fetched the last 2 loads from the nine acres there wass 6 in all and afterwards carried the 3 Loads of Hay from the Hugletts to the Rick steddle at Hodges this finises our seed Haying for this year Forgot that the carpenters where here at work yesterday and the sawyers ditto but the sawyers do not work for me I believe X

Saturday 5

Showry all Day Wind in the Southwest West and Northwest some Thunder Horses Carried 13 sacks of Wheat to Mr Edman's Mill at Boreham for 28£ per load I forgot the wass here yesterday and Bought it also they horses fetched 2 Chaldrons of Coals from Pevensey for Mr Press left at Dillgate Oxen drawed some straw into the Ricks Stedle and a load of straw to Hodges and turned out Old Gurr Easton Foot and I wass with them afterwards Old Gurr was threshing Oats in the C B and Foot and Easton were spreading Moul in the Wainhousefield T Hoad choping Hops Bob a Brown 5 yearling pony from Mr Holland's Windmill Hill it cost 15 Guineas it's a well made pony wite Down his Face his two Hind feet White and his fore feet Black

Sunday 6

Mist Driving Rain nearly all Day wind in the Southwest Wind in the Southwest Father and I went to Heath field Chapel in the morning William went in the afternoon Mr Press preached from the 27th Psalm the Last Verse the morning and from the Halter and the Verse in the afternoon David went to Herstmonceux Chapel this afternoon etc

Monday 7

Some times Cloudy and sun Wind in the southwest Horses went to Mr Ades Limekiln near Wannock after Lime for Mr William Isted Bellhurst Team Broke the Waggon Wheel Oxen Gurr and I went to Mr Presses with two Chaldrons of Coals afterwards Gurr wass tedding the Hay or Litter in the Grimes Wood. T Hoad choping Hops Eastone and Foot spreading Moul I went to Dallington in the evening William and David went to Gardner Street William and David where Hoeing Potatoes in the Brooke etc

Tuesday 8

Cloudy morning Drying after noon Windy Generally southwest or West Horses Carried some Timber to Cowbeech for Mr Richard Winchester and went to Amberstone after some Chalk Oxen Gurr Foot Easton and I removed 70 Loads of Moul in the Wainhouse field T Hoad choping among the young Hops David and Bob Boseling Father went to Battle Market Wm went to Bellhurst William David I and Mother went to Mr Smiths Mr Press preached there this evening from 1 Timothy the 2 chapter and the 4th Verse

Wednesday 9

Generally Cloudy some sun still evening Wind was West wards Horses went to near Wannock after Chalk Oxen Eastone Foot and I finished the Mouling in the Wainhousefield Removed 29 loads and ploughed the place up again afterward David helpt us 3 Carts Carry 18 loads of Dung into the Poundfield T Hoad choping among the young Hops David and Bob boseling Father and William went to Hailsham Market Mr G Verrall from Lewes is here to night William at Bellhurst and Marsham a carrying of Hay left Old Jack up their too Ordr Home but he Run home before him so he was Obliged to walk home. Elizabeth came home from Heathfield she went with us on Monday Sarah Press is come with her

Thursday 10

A warm sunny Day not many Clouds nor much Wind Wind in the East and South Horses at Plough Oxen carried 60 Loads of Dung as on yesterday afternoon Eastone and Foots filled and Gurr and I drove the Carts Father William David T Hoad and Bob are gone to Wartling Farms to Haying etc. Ends X

Friday 11

Mild Weather some Cloud and Wind southwest and West Horses at Plough the oxen and men as yesterday chiefly G. Verrel went to the other farms with them in the after noon Eastone Gurr Foots and I with the Oxen carried 46 Loads of Dung as on yesterday T Hoad chopping hops and helpt us Gett a Load of Hay from Grimes Wood in the afternoon Father William and David went to Haying as on yesterday in the afternoon G Verrall went with them his sister Hannah come here on a Visit Crouch shaved[374] the sheep

Saturday 12

Mild weather some smart showers from the North and Northwest Horses

[374] Sheared.

went to swains hill after Chalk Gurr Eastone Foot and I with the Oxen removed 15 Loads of Dung from the yard 2 from the Rick Steddle 2 from the Hog pound 3 from against the little Doors of the Barn and 7 from the Poundfield Bottom to the Mackson in the Poundfield and unloaded the Hay T Hoad went to Brownings to help Crouch shave the sheep there and finised Choping the young hops William and David went to Wartling I suppose Father also on Horse Back G Verrall went from here with an intention to go home just after Dinner Sarah Press is gone home etc J T Lade sleeps here to night

Sunday 13

Foggy morning Cloudy with some sun and some rain in the evening Father Mother Elizabeth Hannah Verrall William David and I went to Heathfield Chapel in the morning Elizabeth Hannah Verrall William and I stayed and the Girl went in the afternoon Mr Press preached from Luke the 13th Chapter the 24th Verse in the morning and from the 2 Kings the 2 chapter and the 11th and great part of the 12th Verse except the last part 'and Elisha took hold ' of his etc' William and David went to Stone House in the Evening Mr Press preached from Genesis

Monday 14

Showry Weather Wind in the West and South west Horses went after Chalk William and David Gurr and Foot with the Oxen Carried 3 loads of Straw from the Home Barn to the Ox Close and stacked up there and we all together Killed 77 Ratts in the Home Barn T Hoad and Eastone began Mow the Chapel Meadow J T Lade sleeps here to night Beal Morfeys gerniman[375] Mason was minding the Copper and stable etc Mr Steer is here the evening on Bussiness I suppose he and Father is now consulting Browns Bible just at my elbow in the great Window about ½ past 8 O'clock

Tuesday 15

A Wett morning showry Day Wind in the West and Southwest and Northwest Horses Harrowed the Busheyfield and fetched some Oats from the C Barn to the Oast Oxen not at work T Hoad and Gurr threshing in the CB in the morning afterward Gurr David and I Cleaned the Oats in the CB that are threshed for the Horse I have forgot the Quantity they are of no great value having been much damaged with Wett T Hoad and Easton where mowing Brushings in the Poundfield I have not seen Foots today Father went to Bellhurst Mr T Noakes was here this evening on Bussiness J

[375] Journeyman.

T Lade sleeps here tonight

Wednesday 16
A Drying Day some showers about a Cold Northerly Wind in the morning more West afterwards and rather warmer Horses and Oxen Carters Gurr and I went to Rush lake with Timber from Hodges Mr J Lade and Father helpt us load it etc Foots hoeing up Potatoes Mowers where in the Poundfield and Chapel Meadow again William and David went to Bellhurst to Haying etc Father went Ditto in the afternoon Master Gurr and I drove T Hoads Cow at night to Cowden

Thursday 17
Cloudy Cold morning some sun and some showers about Wind in the Northwest or there abouts Horses at Plough in the Wainhouse field Oxen Drawed 7 pieces of Timber from Hodges to Mr Brays the Rushlake Wheeler Father and Foot helped Gurr and I load it afterwards Foot cast up the Dung at the Calves Lodge T Hoad and Eastone Mowing in the Chapel Meadow William and David made some Lime lumps places in one of the Marsham field near Boreham they (I mean the Bellhurst Team) emptied a Lime Kiln to Day Bob is continually a Bosseller for which reason I do not always mention his name here

Friday 18
Some Rain in the morning a Drying Day scarce any clouds in the evening Wind Northwest and North Horses Went after Chalk Foot Gurr and I with the Oxen Carried 4 loads of Dung or shovellings from the Home yard to the Pound field Mackson and fetched 26 Loads of stuff from the Bank against the Oast into the Yard to fill up the Hollows and 1 load of River Gravel and laid against the Pond in the home yard William and David helped us in the morning and Haying in the Fords at Brownings in the afternoon Father and Mother went to Bellhurst. Mowers. Bob and I drove the Cherry Cow to Bull this evening

Saturday 19
Cloudy morning some sun in the after noon Wind in Northwest and West Horses finised sturring part of the Wainhouse field and unloaded or fetched some Chalk home from somewhere Oxen Gurr William David and I Haying Carried the Brushings from the Poundfield to the Home stack and Loaded up a load in the Chapel Meadow Foots threshing and helped us the last load Dame Hoad Susannah Morfey and Ruth the maid Haying Mowers finised Mowing the Chapel Meadow Father went to the Marsh etc J T Lade

Sunday 20

Cloudy some sun or Generally sun Wind in the West Father Mother Elizabeth Hannah Verrall William David and I went to Heathfield Chapel in the morning Father William David Elizabeth and Hannah stayed the afternoon and the maid went in the after noon Mr Press preached both times from Hebrews the 9 chapter and the Verse. J T Lade sleeps here to night Mrs Lade and her Family stayed at home all Day this ought not to be her permanent home but the Priory

Monday 21

Cloudy morning a sunny and Windy afternoon Wind in the Southwest Horses went to swains hill after Chalk Oxen carried 7 Loads of Hay from the Chapel Meadow to the home Hayrick in the afternoon Mr Phillips the Game Keeper stacked and Gurr Foots William David and I with Dame Dann her Grandaughter and Susannah Morfey and Bob all on a Haying also unloaded the load we loaded on Saturday Foots finised threshing the Oats about noon T Hoad and Eastone mowing trefoil in the 8 Acres and Brushings in the 6 Acres Master Richard Winchester moved the upper part of the Hayrick fence higher up to inlarge to Hayrick Old Master Dann wass Diging post Holes for him Mr & Mrs Smith and Mrs Ford from Battle Visitors Father went to Bellhurst

Tuesday 22

A Lowry morning some showers till noon a Dry afternoon not without Clouds Wind in the Southwest Horses carried some Timber to Mr Winchester at Cowbeatch and fetched a Load of Chalk from Amberstone Gurr and I with the Oxen at Harrow in the Wain house field with the Large Hook tined Harrow T Hoad and Eastone mowing Trefoil Foots went to Bellhurst at work Old Dann Toothing Rake Choping Hops and Haying David and Bob ditto William is gone to Bellhurst Father hass been to Bellhurst Mr Harmer wass in here when I came in to Dinner and Forgot that Father went with One of Mr Lade's sons with two of his Colts into our Marsh I have just mended this pen and as it did not write I have mended it again for some one else who may want it

Wednesday 23

A Lowry morning frequent Thunder showers in the afternoon made it Dirty Walking Wind in the Westerly Quarter Horses went to Swains hill after Chalk Gurr and I wass at Harrow till the Rain came and drove us away about noon we turned the Oxen out and Gurr went to Diging up mould where the old Pound used to be and he and I helped T Hoad kill an Old sow that hass been a considerable time a Fatting and is not very Fatt now She hass had a farrow of pigs in the meanwhile the mowers finised mowing the Trefoil in the 8 acres Foot turning the Lime and Mould together against the Oast Old Dann Chopping Hops in the morning and turning Lime and Mould in the afternoon Father went into the Marsh that is used by Mr Stace of Cow beach beyond a place called the New Bridge after a pair of yearling steers and Drove to Brownings I think William went with him William went to Bellhurst on some of them Farm Haying till the Rain prevented David went and helped them unload and Load of Hay this afternoon the Honeysetts thatched the seed Hay stack

Thursday 24
A Warm Day sometimes Cloud Wind the Southwest Horses went to Amberstone after Chalk Gurr William David and I and Bob cleaned 6 sacks of Oats (nearly) the last there is in the CB and cleared the Barn of straw 4 parcels some we stacked on the other and some we put in the close One pair of Oxen did to Day Old Gurr wass at same as on yesterday afternoon afterwards We Killed between 40 and 50 Ratts in the CB Mowers finised the Brushings in the 6 Acres and began Mow the Chapel wood meadow Dame Dann Old Dann Ruth Dann Dame Hoad and Mary Morfey turned the Hay in the Chapel meadow this afternoon William went to the other Farms Haying Father went there or some where else in the morning and to Rushlake Green in the evening Mr Squires wass here to day I suppose on Bussiness Foot not at work for us to day Father having so much bussiness he is but very seldom at home so that I cannot always tell where he goes

Friday 25
Cloudy Lowry morning till the after noon then sunshine Wind in the South west Horses went to Swains Hill after Chalk Oxen Carried 2 loads of Hay to the stack and left two loads in the Meadow Gurr David I Dame Dann Ruth Dann Dame Hoad Mary Morfey and Bob Haying in the forenoon and left off in being misty weather and the Hay not ready I went to Gardening Gurr Bob and David went to Diging up mould Foots and Dann casting Lime and mould together till about 4 O'Clock when the sun shone out and Father I David Gurr Dann Foots and Bob and Mary Morfey and the Carters helped sett to and Loaded up 4 loads of Hay in the Chapel Meadow by 8 o'clock when we all retired to Bait Mowers finised the Chapel wood meadow and began the Ponds Croft meadow Father went to the Other

Farms the morning William David to Haying all day

Saturday 26
Cloudy morning showry afternoon Wind in the Southwest Horses went twice to Trolilo River after Chalk Gurr William David and I and Bob unloaded the Hay we left loaded yester day 3 loads and the home stack Oxen Drawed 2 of them to the stack it being a Wett afternoon we did not do much besides Gurr and David went casting mould in the afternoon Bob and I drove the Isted Heifer to Mr Christmas to Bull in the Evening Foots and Dann Casting Lime and Mould William went to Bellhurst J T Lade sleeps here to night

Sunday 27
Showry weather Wind in the south west Father Mother Hannah Verrall William David and I went to Heathfield Chapel in the morning William and I stayed and Elizabeth went in the afternoon Mr Press preached both times from the 102 Psalm the 16 17 and 18 verses Father William David and I where at Stonehouse this evening Mr Press preached from Colosions the 3 chapter part of the 14 verse if mistake not the Text was 'Christ is all in all'

Monday 28
Windy weather some times cloudy Wind Westwards Carters Gurr Bob and I with the Horses and Oxen Ploughed and Carried 45 Loads of Drift sand from against the River between the Oast and Pinnick against the Chapel Meadow Gate up into the Pound field some distance is a Mackson in the forenoon Father went to Bellhurst William Ditto to Brownings Haying David Dame Hoad and Mary Morfey Haying here all day Gurr William Hoad Henry Gurr Bob Gurr and I Haying this afternoon Father helped us a little Carried the last 3 loads Hay from the Chapel Meadow to the Oxens stack and fetched the little Brushings from the 6 Acres to the Home stack etc Foots turning Lime and Mould Old Dann doth not work here any longer Mowers finised the Ponds Croft this morning and began the Calves lodge Meadow

Tuesday 29
Some Rain in the morning. Cloudy all day Wind in the Southwest Horses went to swains hill after Chalk Gurr and I with the Oxen carried 26 loads of Mould and drift sand as on yesterday morning Foot turning up Mould against the Oast where the Old pound used to be I suppose the Mowers have finised the Calves lodge and began the Meadows at Hodges David Mary Morfey Dame Hoad and Bob Haying William is gone to Brownings

Father hass been there I believe and perhaps some other places also Thatchers thatched the Other Home stack

Wednesday 30
Cloudy morning more sun in the afternoon some showers about Wind in the Southwest Horses and Oxen fetched 7 Tons of Beetch from Pevensey and laid on the Road above Master Busses house twixt Redpale and Woods Corner Foots Diging Mould near the Oast Eastone and Thomas Hoad finised mowing at Hodges Meadows David and some Women Haying as I was not at home I can not who-neither can I tell wether Father and William went any were but Elizabeth and Hannah Verrall went to Heathfield on a Visit I am rong in what I have written about my Father I suppose he went to Dallington to Mr Randles and wass gone nearly all day and wass not at home in the evening till after I wass in Bed

Thursday 31
Showry weather Wind in the South west the showers have made it Dirty Horses and Oxen with 4 Carts and William David I Master Gurr Henry Gurr Master Foot and William Hoad removed 68 Loads of mould from Eastone T Hoad David and I with Mary Morfey and Dame Dann laid on the Trefoil in the 8 acres and afterward went to Haying with Father William against the River in to the Poundfield see Monday T Hoad and Eastone Mowing Thistles in the Silverfield I cannot recollect any thing else worth setting down J T Lade sleeps here tonight

Friday 1 August
Some Rain about Noon Wind West wards Horses went for Chalk Oxen Carried 2 loads of Hay at night from the Chapelwood Meadow Gurr Eastone T Hoad David and I with Mary Morfey and Dame Dann laid on the Trefoil in the 8 acres and afterward went to Haying with Father William Ruth Dann and Ruth Hoad Haying in the Chapelwood meadow James Lade and Master T Luck Dined here to day

Saturday 2
Some clouds and showers but none here Wind in the West Horses went after Chalk Oxen Carried 4 Load of Trefoil from the 8 acres to the Chapel Barn and 3 loads of Hay from the Chapelwood meadow and 4 loads from the Ponds Croft meadow to the Oxen Stack We unloaded also the Loads on the Waggons and where all on with full force getting up the Seeds and Haying but Foots did not come till night J T Lade sleeps here tonight

Sunday 3
Some Rain this forenoon after ward fine weather some Clouds Wind as usual Father Mother I William David Mrs Lade and Ann went to

Monday 4

Very Windy Heazey Cloudy Day some misty rain before noon Horses went for Chalk Gurr Foot Eastone and T Hoad threshing Trefoil T Hoad and Gurr helpt David and I with the Oxen put 2 loads of Trefoil Haum into the Stack and fetched 3 Load of from the Calves Lodge meadow to the stack unloaded two and left one on the Waggon because it wass so Windy Foot and Eastone did not help us William Dame Hoad Dame Dann Ruth Dann and Mary Morfey Haying Mr Phillips the Game Keeper helped us

Tuesday 5

A Warm Day generally Cloudy still Weather wind chiefly Southeast Horses went for Chalk Oxen Carried the 4 small loads of Hay at Hodges is the last of our Haying on these Farms Gurr William and I tieing up Hop Poles in the Pound field Hop garden in the morning T Hoad and David helpt unload a load of Hay before Brackfast David Theethed[376] some Rakes Afterwards we where all Haying at Hodges Dame Dann Ruth Dann and Mary Morfey Branching Hops and Haying Foot and Eastone threshing Trefoil

Wednesday 6

A Bright Sunny Day not much Wind from the southeast William Hoad T Hoad Henry Gurr Old Gurr Eastone and David with 6 Carts Horses and Oxen Carried 72 loads of Dung from the Mackson in the Pound field into the Lower part of the 8 acres Each one his Cart Borrowed a Horse and a Cart of William Isted and an Ox Cart of Master Wisdom at Red pale the rest was all our own Foot choping Hops in the Archer William and I went to Hailsham Market with some Lambs and a Cow sold ten of the Lambs at 22s each Father wass there also I wass at Mr Smiths on Bussiness this evening

Thursday 7

Some Clouds and some sun Wind in the South and Southwesterly Quarters or there abouts Teams as yesterday excepting that I went with one Ox Cart in David's room finised the Mackson 72 Loads yesterday and 72 to Day is 144 Loads of Good Dung Large Carts and large Loads Foot as on yesterday Father I William David Elizabeth and Hannah Verrall went to the Stone

[376] Teethed.

House this evening the Revd Mr Kemp preached from 1 John the 3rd Chapter and the 9th verse 'whosoever is born etc' He is no great preacher May the Lord teach him what he knoweth not of the Word of Divine truth J T Lade sleeps here to Night

Friday 8
Cloudy and some rain in the forenoon some sun in the afternoon Wind Rather brisk in the from the West Horses and Oxen at plough in the 8 acres Gurr and I wass with the Oxen David and Foot spreading Dung in the 8 acres T Hoad and Eastone Cleaning and threshing Trefoil in the C B

Saturday 9
Some Rain and some Sun Wind in the West rather Brisy Horses & Oxen at Plough David and Foots spreading dung in the 8 acres Foots after wards turning lime and Mould S field T Hoad and Easton begin Mow Peas in the Wainhouse Field Father and William went to Bellhurst Gurr Trimming Hay Stack in the Chapel Cloase Somebody came too take Joseph Morfey Household for Debts on the 9th of August Messrs Randle Dunk and Dowland from Dallington are here this evening J T Lade sleeps here to night (E Oxley)

Sunday 10
Showry Weather Wind in the West Father Mother Elizabeth Hannah Verrall went to Heath field Chapel in the morning Father and I stayed the afternoon Mr Press preached from 1 Corinthians the 15th Chapter the 49 verse and from Luke the 1st chapter the 74 and 75 verses William David and I where at the Stonehouse this evening Mr Press preached from 1 Isaiah the 45 chapter and the 17th Verse

Monday 11
Showry Weather Wind in the Southwest South and Southwest again Horses and Oxen at Plough and William cleaning seed in Chapel Barn T Hoad and Easton mowing peas finised the Wainhouse field Foot is not here to Day Mr Robert Cornwell from Mayfield wass here to night on Bussiness Mrs Lade is gone to the Priory

Tuesday 12
Windy Showry weather Wind in the south west Horses at Plough Gurr and I with the Oxen had the narrow wheeled Waggon with an Ash Tree to the Wheelers at Rushlake Green and waited at the Wheelers whilst they took the Hind Wheels off and put new Ones on in the Room left the Old wheels to be took down for Court wheels Etc afterwards William David and Bob

helped us bring some Trefoil seed from the CB and put in to the Garrett and Rung the Hogs Ths Hoad and Easton mowing Peas in the 13 acres Foot not at work Father being so frequently gone to some places or Other that I cannot always Remember to sett it down he was at Rushlake with us today

Wednesday 13
Showry morning a Drying after noon very Windy from the Southwest Horses Harrow in the 8 Acres Oxen finised plowing of it about noon Old Gurr wass a Ditching between the two Lodges against the Wainhousefield Hedge afterwards and David helped him William and I would have trimmed the stack at Hodges but it wass too Windy T Hoad and Easton finised Mowing peas and began mow the Grimes Brook Father went to Bellhurst etc William and I went to Heathfield Chapel this Evening the Revd Mr Watson from Wivelsfield preached from Malaki the 3rd Chapter the 16 and 17 verses

Thursday 14
Misty Rain before noon Windy Day some Clouds in the afternoon Wind in the Southwest Horses went after Chalk Oxen Drawed the Rest of the Trefoil seed home from the Barn and one Load of the haum to the Oxen Hay stack Gurr and I finised the stack at Hodges except thatching and William and David helped us Clean the Trefoil seed and finis the Oxen Stack for the thatchers T Hoad and Eastone finised Mowing the Grimes Brook and mowed some Bracken in the pound field

Friday 15
A Windy Day still evening not much Rain Wind as usual Horses went after Chalk Oxen Carried 12 Sacks of Oats from Bellhurst and 20 Sacks from Mr Harmans to Mr J Balcombe Miller Heathfield T Hoad and Eastone mowing Litter[377]

Saturday 16
Still morning some Wind in the after noon and evening from the Southwest Horses went after Chalk Oxen T Hoad Gurr and Eastone with 3 Carts spread the Lime in the Bushey field David and I tieing up hop poles and tedding Hay in the Grimes Brook William and Father went to Bellhurst Elizabeth Hannah and Ann went to Gardener street Etc they are frequently on the run I seldom know were Honeysets thatched the Haystack at Hodges and began that at the Ox Close

[377] For cattle bedding.

Sunday 17
Cloudy some Rain Windy Wind as usual All of us went to Heathfield Chapel in the morning William David and I Elizabeth and Hannah stayed the afternoon Mr Press preached from St John the 1st Chapter and the 16 verse in the morning and from Amos the 4 chapter and the middle part of the 12 verse 'prepare to meet thy God' a Funeral sermon for Ruth Knight aged 16 this afternoon there wass a great many people on the Occation

Monday 18
Not so windy as it hass been but Windy from the same Quarters. Cloudy the Chief part of the Day and a Wett evening there hass not been much sun of late but very much Wind Horses went to swains hill after the last load of Chalk for this year from there Gurr Bob and David with the Oxen picked the litter up the T Hoad and Eastone have mowed in the pasture field I rolled places to lay some Lime and mould in the 8 acres and helped them T Hoad and Eastone tieing up poles and finised turning Lime and mould were afterwards Chopping hops in the Archer William went to Haying at Marsham Mr Richard and Mr Henry Purstglove where this evening and Mr R Russel from Chichester (late Warbleton) sleeps here to night

Tuesday 19
Wett weather all day Gurr T Hoad Eastone Bob and the Carters with the Horses were mending the Road on the hill below the Oast part of the Day Mr Russel is weather bound Mr Russel is gone from here this afternoon I suppose to Crawl mill on his journey home Our men killed 11 Rats in the Home Barn tonight and 10 in the C B yesterday there would have been preaching here this evening but it being unfavourable weather Mr Press did not come

Wednesday 20
Cloudy weather Rain in the afternoon Unpleasant harvesting weather Wind south and southwest Horses Carters shovelling Dung in the Home Close and carried to the Mackson below the Barn Gurr T Hoad and Eastone mending the Ox watering at the Ox Close and turned the Peas William David and I helped them some times we Drove the Weanier Calves from the Silverfield to the Ponds Croft forgot that the Messrs Purstglove sent us the 34 weather Lambs Father Bought of them at 15s per head 25£ 10s and put them into the Bushey field yesterday My Uncle William Oxley was here to Day he is a Heavenly Man

Thursday 21

A Warm morning Cloudy Day some Rain Wind in the North Rather brisk Horses went to amberstone after the rest of the Chalk at that place Gurr and I with the Oxen Dug 9 Loads of Gravel and removed 8 of them to Hodges Close etc and one into the Silverfield against the gate between the two fields Eastone began reep the 7 acres Evenden began the Esquirefield T Hoad was choping Hops in the Croft in the morning and Reeping in the 7 acres in the afternoon the Wheat is not ripe but the Weather seems very unfavourable We want the sun to shine out more if it is the Lord['s] Will William and David drove the Calves from the Ponds Croft Meadow (on account of their brutting the young Copes[378]) into the Calves Lodge Meadow Father William and David with Elizabeth and Hannah Verrall went to Stonehouse this evening Mr Kemp preached from Zachariah the 13 Chapter and the 1st verse. forgot that Mr Warner the Hop supervisor and Mr Russel the Hop assistant surveyed their rounds to day this first time this year

Friday 22

Sunny morning Cloudy Day Still evening Wind Northwards Horses fetched the last of all our Chalk home for this year from Chillhurst at three times Gurr and I Dug 12 Loads of Gravel in the Old Lane and removed up against the Kiln field gate further up with the Oxen – T Hoad and Eastone reeping in the 7 acres Dame Evenden all day and her Husband half day in the Esquire field to day is their first Day William and David Boseling Bob Ditto turned 4 Old Oxen into the Bushey field

Saturday 23

A Bright sun great part of the Day some few Clouds Wind Eastward chiefly not very Brisk Horses Plough the 3 time part of the Wainhouse field Gurr and I with the Oxen Carried 6 Loads Gravel as on yesterday afterwards Gurr and I with William David and Bob we're a Haying in the Grimes Brook they turned the Peas in the Wainhouse field in the morning all the Reepers were in their places as yesterday

Sunday 24

The Sea Roared very loud this morning Showry Day Wind in the Southeast Father Mother Elizabeth Hannah William David and I went to Heathfield Chapel in the morning Elizabeth and I stayed the afternoon Mr Press preached from Romans the 8 chapter and the verse in the morning and

---

[378] Brutting is a dialect word for breaking off young shoots (OED). Hence, brutting the young copse.

from Hebrews the 11 Chapter and the 25th Verse in the afternoon William David Ann and the Maid went to Stonehouse in the evening Mr Press preached from Isaiah the 40 chapter and the two first verses

Monday 25
Very Wet Day Teams at Nothing W Hoad Hoe Old Gurr chopping Hops in Croft in afternoon William went to Brownings in the morning shooting Small Birds for they Eat the Corn very much Ditto David shooting Nich Prowling about the Summertree and Sandhill Farms in the afternoon Weather cleared off this Evening Wind in the Southeast and Southwest J T Lade was here to night but did not stay long

Tuesday 26
Windy and heavy showrs Wind in the Southwest Horses went to Pevensey after 50 cwt of Welsh Coals and Bushels of House Coals Gurr William David and Bob Choping Bubbage between the hills in the Croft T Hoad and Eastone Reeping in the 7 acres Evenden was not in the Esquirefield I was gaping the Bushey field tieing up Hoppoles etc Father went to Boreham and Heathfield etc

Wednesday 27
Showry Weather Wind in the West The Teams were at nothing T Hoad and Eastone Reeping part of the Day T Hoad went to turning Dung at Hodges in the morning I have not seen Evenden to day Gurr and the Carters etc were Hop choping in the Croft and Orchard gardens Work is quite or all most at a stand it is to Wett for Reeping and the Peas are spoiling and the Hay Cannot be medled with and it to Wett for plowing or Mouling or any particular thing besides may the Lord God of Mercy's graciously grant us unworthy Creatures some sun and withhold the Battles of till we have gathered in the Fruits of the Earth and send us a Blessing there with and give us thankful Hearts for the Mercy for we are poor dependent Creatures and pentioners on his bounty Mr Stanford's sons and servant where here to Day with some Day for Phillips their gamekeeper William went to Bellhurst etc in the afternoon

Thursday 28
Some Rain but not much mild Weather Wind Southwest chiefly Horses went to the Blacksmith after fresh round plough to us and went to warping the Bushey field Gurr and Bob Boseling turning Peas etc Eastone Reeping in the Furzefield Old Dann and Evenden and his Wife in the Esquirefield T Hoad in the 7 acres his Family in the 6 acres at Hodges and J Beal in the 10

Friday 29

More Cloudy and more rain than yester day Also it wass a bright morning Wind in the Southwest Horses as on yesterday Gurr Bob David and I unloaded the Litter that was on the narrow wheeled Waggon in the Close and Home Barn afterwards gapping and setting up post and rail etc in the 6 acres and turned the four old oxen out there they would not be quiet in the Bushey field but would intrude on Mr Smiths premises I believe the Reepers are as yesterday William to Bellhurst and helped Gurr David and I turn some of the peas in the Wainhouse field and move some of Hay in the Grimes Brook Fine Weather this morning Rather Cloudy but I am afraid it will Rain but hope not

Saturday 30

Cloudy generally some rain and some sunn Horses as Thursday Gurr William David and I with the Oxen fetched a Load and a Half of Trefoil Haums and from the C B and about 2 Loads of Hay at 3 times from Grimes Brook to the Home Ricksteddle this is the last of our Hay this year Reepers as usual but Eastone wass in the 7 acres he hass finised the Furzefield Master Guy shovelled the Ricksteddle up for a shilling and went away again Father went to Bellhurst

Sunday 31

Mild some Clouds but no Rain Wind as usual in the Southwest Father Mother Elizabeth Hannah William David and I went to Heathfield Chapel in the morning Father William and David stayed the afternoon Mr Press preached from John 3rd Chapter the latter part of the 3rd verse 'Except a man be born again' a Funeral sermon for Mr Parris (who was buried last Thursday) as in the morning and from the 84th Psalm the 11th verse in the afternoon Mr Lower from Chiddingly come home with me and his Daughter Martha came home with Mother and Elizabeth etc she stay here tonight on a Friendly visit J T Lade came with his son and wife here this evening he went home again that is there by far I heard at Chapel that my Aunt Lucy Cornwell widow of my late uncle Nicholas Cornwell Died this

---

Acres all Reepers Messrs Jas Pinyon and Wm and Daniel Lade come here to Day and * we went with them to and about our Wartling Farms etc and home to Dinner and Mr J Smith junr wass with us at Tea * the 'we' was William and David and I Mr Noakes from Gardener Street sent his men after the fat Calf

morning about 5 O'Clock She has been not of her Mind for 8 to 9 years and has received little or no nourishment beside liquid since the 20th of March last past

Monday 1 Sept
A warm sunny Day Wind nearly still I forget in what quarter she was in Horses at Plough Gurr with the oxen Carried 15 Loads of Dung Moul etc from about the House into the Gutterfield William David and Bob turning Peas etc Horses Carters as on Thursday and Saturday last Mr Lower went home I went to Mayfield

Tuesday 2
A good harvesting day some clouds towards night – Horses at plough finished the Busheyfield warping – and afterwards were at plough in the Wainhousefield not warping and carried 3 loads of peas from Wainhousefield oxen carried 2 loads of peas from the 13 acres in the CB and 5 loads from the Wainhousefield into the HB – Horses fetched all the wheat from the Furzefield in one load into the home load Wm went to the other farms harvesting all the rest of ofunus where at home harvesting T Hoad at Hodges with his family Eastone finished the 7 acres all the rest as on Thursday last

Wednesday 3
Warm sunny day charming harvest weather and it seems as tho' the Lord has of his abounding goodness answered the prayers of his in worthy creatures in the behalf of fine weather wind in the easterly quarters – Horses at plough in the Wainhousefield – Gurr Bob David and I built a wheat stack in the 10 acres against the hay stack with the 7 acres and a few sheeves of the 10 acre wheat there was 6 loads in the 7 acres – Eastone and his wife and Beal in the 10 acres Evenden and his wife and Dann in the Esquirefield T Hoad and his Family at Hodges – Wm went to the other farms a harvesting etc I cannot keep a proper account of the goers and comers I so often forget and seldom know when they happen but Mr Lower went home on Monday last his daughter is still here

Thursday 4
Most excellent harvest weather – Horses at Plough – Bob went to plough in the Room of Harry and Harry David and Gurr with the oxen fetched 4 loads of wheat from the Esquirefield into the home barn – T Hoad and his family have done at Hodges and went on in the 10 acres rest as yesterday Father and I went to Mayfield to my aunts funeral Wm went to work at the

280   THE OXLEY FARM DIARIES

other farms

Friday 5
Warm sunny weather as yesterday wind in the northeast – Horses and oxen 5 carts Wm Hoad Harry Gurr Old Gurr Wm and David mouling Carried 50 loads of lime and mould 10 pr cart into the 8 acres I helped Wm load chiefly – all the reepers as yesterday I believe Father went to the other farms etc Elizabeth Lade came here to night I suppose to see Mrs Lade I don't know – Mr Everden and his wife finished their part of reeping

Saturday 6
Warm still weather as usual – Horses and oxen carried 44 loads as yesterday David missed one load by reason of Master Wisdom ordering their cart home last night David went and borrowed Wm Harmers in the room Father and I after wards helped them the wheat from Hodges is 4 loads and one load from the Esquirefield to the home Barn – Old Dann finished reeping the Esquirefield T Hoad Esstone and Beal finished reeping the 10 acres

Sunday 7
Delightful weather. – Father mother and Martha Lower (who is gone home) rode and Wm David and I walked to Heathfield Chapel in the morning Wm and I stayed the afternoon the Revd Mr Watson from Wivelsfield preached from the 5th Verse of the 1st chapter of the 1st Epistle to the Thessalonians in the morning and from Job the 10th chapter part of the 2 verse 'show' me wherefore 'etc' – Father I Wm and David went to Stonehose in the evening Mr Watson preached from Zechariah the 13th chapter and the 1st verse 'In that day etc' the Revd Mr Press is gone on a visit into Wales for six weeks as far as Haverford west that lays on the coast of the Irish sea I suppose 300 miles from here – Elizabeth and Hannah Verral went to Herstmonceux Chapel I suppose all day

Monday 8
A warm day wind east chiefly – Horses and oxen 5 carts Wm Hoad Harry Gurr Old Gurr David and I carried 50 loads of lime and mould see Friday last – T Hoad and Eastone mowed some clover in the 9 acres – Beal spreading lime and mould in the 8 acres – and Old Guy who has been threshing peas in the CB 4 or 5 days last week was there to day I cannot find time to set things down as they should be I shall miss the visitors and the out goers

Tuesday 9
Not so warm morning as yesterday nearly the same afterwards wind in the north Horses and oxen carried 55 loads see yesterday and Friday – T Hoad and Eastone mowing litter[?] in the Furze wood hill Eastone broke his scythe and he whent to chopping hops with Old Guy in the Brook Old Guy finished threshing the peas Beal as on yesterday – Mr Purstglove sent there team after 200 of Kiln Faggots Wm is gone to Battle Market J T Lade sleeps here to night

Wednesday 10
A warm sunny day – Horses and oxen Wm Hoad H Gurr Old Gurr David and I finished carrying the lime and mould from against the oast into the 8 acres 24 loads to day and 199 before is in all 223 we afterwards carried the 10 acre wheat into the Home Barn 5 loads Wm and Eastone and T Hoad cleaned the peas in the CB 13 sacks and 1 bushel – Wm afterwards helped us the others where chopping hops

Thursday 11
Foggy weather – Horses at plough in the 8 acres oxen do with the wheel plough in the Wainhousefield T Hoad and Eastone reeping spring wheat in the Gutterfield – Old Guy chopping hops Beal at I forget what – Father and I went to The Halfmoon Market

Friday 12
Weather nearly as on yesterday in the morn … Horses and oxen workmen and all nearly as on yesterday

Saturday 13
Some rain – Horses and oxen at plough T Hoad and Eastone mowing oats in the 12 acres Beal chopping hops and binding spring wheat Old Guy chopping young hops

Sunday 14
Misty rain in the morning a warm day Father mother Wm David I Elizabeth Hannah and the maid went to Heathfield Chapel in the morning Father Wm David I Elizabeth and Hannah stayed the afternoon – Mr Chittenden from Bri[gh]ton preached from Isiah 27th chapter and the 13th verse in the morning and from Phillipians the 1st chapter and the 21st verse in the afternoon

Monday 15
A warm day Horses and oxen as on Thursday T Hoad and Eastone

Tuesday 16

Warm day not many clouds – David went to plough in my room T Hoad and Eastone finished the 12 acres oats and I helped them measure some of their reeping – I measured some reeping for Mr H Purstglove on Saturday last and some for Mr J Pattenden on Monday last

Wednesday 17

Cloudy day some rain towards night the wind which has been rather calm the few weeks past was rather brisk in the evening from the north – Horses at plow all the rest except Father Wm and I were on hoping T Hoad dries them Wm went to Hailsham Market I went to Mayfield

Thursday 18

Misty rain nearly all day wind northwards Horses finished plowing the 8 acres 2 time carried the spring wheat with the oxen and sett the waggons in the Lodge afterwards all hoping except Guy who was on threshing in the HB

Friday 19

Cloudy misty weather wind in the northly quarters Horses and oxen at plough Old Guy threshing wheat – all the rest on a hoping

Saturday 20

Cloudy not much rain wind in the north – Horses and oxen at plough till noon afterward the horses carried 6 pockets of hops to Cade Street and the oxen carried 10 sacks of peas to Wood corner all the rest on a Hoping

Sunday 21

A mild warm day some clouds wind in the north Father mother Wm David I Elizabeth Hannah and the maid went to Heathfield Chapel in the morning Wm David and I and Elizabeth stayed the afternoon the Revd Mr Dicker preached from Romans the 9th chapter the 30th and following verses in the afternoon and from Daniel the 9th the 24th verse in the morning – Father I Wm and David were at Stone House this evening Mr Dicker preached from Deuteronomy the 15th chapter and the 1st and 2 verses

Monday 22

A cold wind the former part of the day not many clouds wind in the north – we put the hoping of to day and carried 9 loads of oats from the 12 acres to the CB and fetched a load of litter from the Furze wood to the home mowing oats in the 12 acres Beal leaving[?] spring wheat – Old Guy chopping Hops etc close – the men were Wm Hoad T Hoad Eastone Beal Gurr Wm Burges Wm David I Harry and Bob the women were Mrs Dann Ruth Dann and Harriot Bradford – Both teams 2 waggons

Tuesday 23
Cloudy morning afterwards some sun – wind in the north – Bob and Harry at plough with the horses in the Wainhousefield – Wm Hoad and Gurr mowed the Grinets oats and began the Kiln field oats rest chiefly hoping Old Guy is threshing wheat in the Home Barn when I do not mention his name Eastone and Beal pull the poles and I measure

Wednesday 24
Bright sunny day Horses at plough the further part of the Croft – Gurr and Wm Hoad mowing oats and pulling poles hoppers picked part of their time in the Poundfield garden and part of their time in the Croft we thought they were not ripe in the Poundfield they are very slite in the Croft – Father went to Mayfield I being rather idle and not having much time for this job I do not keep so good account of things of this sort as I did for I had quite forgot that the Martins burnt & emptied a kiln of lime last week It was emptied on Friday last by the oxen and Horses and all the men except Old Guy and the pole pullers assisted J T Lade has also sleept here some five nights I have forgot when

Thursday 25
Misty rain all the morning finished the Croft and Brook hop gardens 121 bushels and went into the Poundfield again Gurr and Wm Hoad went to mowing oats again Horses at plough in the Croft we are a going to grub the Croft for wheat

Friday 26
Windy showery day wind in the SW Horses at plough in the Alley in the Croft Wm Hoad and Gurr mowing oats in the Kilnfield Old Guy threshing hoppers etc

Saturday 27
A very wett day carters with the Horses carried 9 pockets of hops to Cade Street Old Gurr went to threshing wheat with Old Guy in the Home Barn all the rest a hopping but did not do much it was such wett weather

Sunday 28
Some clouds rather cold day Wind in the Northwest – Father Mother I William David Elizabeth and Hannah went to Heathfield Chapel in the

morning Wm David and I stayed the afternoon Mr Chittenden from Brighton preached from Genesis the 28th chapter and the verse in the morning and from the 89 Psalm the 15th Verse in the afternoon

Tuesday 30
A frost in the morning and some sun afterwards cloudy wind north and west wards Wm Hoad and Harry who are the carters at plough in the Croft Old Gurr stripping otherwise pulling poles in the croft hoppers etc

Wednesday 1 Oct
Fine cloudy day Horses warpping in 8 acre field Old Gurr stripping poles in the croft garden David afternoon Wm jobbing morning picking hops after Father gone too Bellhurst

Thursday 2
A cold day wind in the northeast – Horses at plough – Old Gurr stripping poles – David is a gentlemans footman to day waiting on Mr T Tourle Esquire and his wives Father who came here yesterday rest hoping

Friday 3
Frosty morning a fine day a cold evening Father Old Gurr and the carters carried the Grinnetts oats 3 loads this afternoon Horses were at plough before hopers finished the Poundfield gardens this evening there was 3160 bushels of hops in that garden

Saturday 4
A sharp frost in the morning a sunny day wind NE some rain – Horses at plough in the 8 acres oxen carried 2 loads of oats from the Old Archer garden where we were to day picking the gentlemen are gone to day

Sunday 5
A cold day wind northeast wards Horses and oxen carrying oats from the Kilnfield to the C.B. I think it was 7 loads but I am not certain the Blacksmith and Gamekeeper helped our men to day harvesting – Hoppers and pole peelers as usual

Weather and wind nearly as yesterday Father mother Wm David Elizabeth and Hannah went to Heathfield Chapel in the morning Wm I and Elizabeth stayed the afternoon – Mr Gurnets from Hailsham preached from the 28th chapter of Isiah the 16th verses in the morning and from John the 10th chapter and the 27th verse in afternoon David went to stonehouse this evening

Summertree Farm, Bodle Street Green.

Summertree Farm

Monday 6
Cold weather Horses at plough in the 8 acres oxen harvesting finished carrying oats hopers as usual

Tuesday 7
The weather was Mere[379] mild than yesterday Horses at plough Old Gurr and Wm Harmers men mowing barley Eastone helped them finish it after we finished hoping in the Archer Garden – I helped Wm and David lay it on Beal went to gathering Bullice – Beal and Eastone pulled poles and I measured this hoping T Hoad dryed the hops finished picking to day about noon there was 3160 bushels in the Poundfield 121 in the Croft and Brook and 599 in the Archer in all 3880 bushels this hoping

Wednesday 8
A windy day – Horses at plough Old Gurr Wm David Bob and I carried the barley with the oxen from the Kilnfield to the H Barn T Hoad Eastone Beal and Wm Harmers men mowing tares in the 13 acres Horses loaded one load up – paid the hoppers to night 2½d pr bushel

[379] More.

Thursday 9
More cloudy than yesterday – the men mowed and loaded the tares etc I do not know how many loads because I was not at home to day I went to Mayfield on my business

Friday 10
Horses harrowing Wm Hoad sowed The Bushy field with wheat – Old Gurr and David with the oxen were healing the chalk with faggots and drawing the poles out of the Croft into the Poundfield T Hoad digging up of Potatoes Beal and Eastone threshing tares in the HB I at nothing in particular I do not think that I shall any account of these things any longer but shall have business of my own to attend too
I shall now turn book into a book of account on my own business seeing if have not time to attain to the above particulars and instead of saying any thing
about Bucksteep and Cold Hodges Farms I may perhaps make some remarks on Summertree and Sandhole Farms

23 October 1817
J T Lade and I entered on Summertree and Sandhole Farms November we have sowed the 10 acres with Thick sett wheat and 7 acres of the 9 acres and 5 acres with some Brown wheat from the Priory and the 5½ acres field with brown Cobham Wheat in all about 27½ acres of wheat for this year and we have Sowed the remainder of the 9 acres with Winter Tares which is about 2 acres NB Did agree with Martin Gurr for his son Thomas to Bound him and give him 1.s a week as wages and also that the might have all the regular holidays fron Old Michealmas to new Lady lide – but its not suiting J T Lade we do give his father 7s per week for his board

NICHOLAS OXLEY DIARY 1821, 1822 & 1823

An account of Work etc done on Sandhill, Comwish and Pilly Farms since Jany 2nd 1821 paid for by me Nicholas Oxley

Wednesday 3 January
Ruben Baker and Benjamin Cat with the Horses fetched 3 tons of Beach from Pevensey to Bodle street Green It was very Cold snowy weather

Thursday 4
Horses kept Holiday Carters threshing for Mrs Waters

Friday 5
Horses Carring Dung into little Pilly Hop Gardens

Saturday 6
Finised Carring Dung into Hop garden about 70 Loads tredeled[380] all the Garden afterwards carried 9 Loads into Pilley Hop Garden

Monday 8
Horses Began Plowing in the Hoads field

Tuesday 9
Carried Old Master Tedham into the Workhouse

Wednesday 10
Plow with Horses etc

Thursday 18
I cannot remember every particular between this Date and the above Sent the Carters and Horses to Mrs Waters to Day

Tuesday 13 February
Between this day and Jan 10th the Horses have plowed the Pilly plat about an Acre and the Pilley Hop garden about 1600 Hill 8 feet by 4 feet plants and the Hoads field at Sandhill 5½ acres and about 1¼ acres for Hops in the Old Sandhill Hop garden field. Also they have Ploughed the Midle crocers[381] 5½ and fetched some Mould from Christian River into the Friched field at Pilley also the Boy has Wipt one of the Horses eyes out which Horse had but one that one Eye before consequently is now Blind. Also the Stonehorse has Lamed himself in his pen one night after which the Horses

---

[380] Treddled (spread dung).
[381] Crokers.

did not work for a few days and the Carters sett up some Low faggots to the Pilly Wagon Lodge and cutt some sticks to sett out Hops with the Stonehorse soon got well after which they had G Guy to helpt them (the Carter) remove 1700 Hop poles from the Calves Meadow hop Garden into the Pilly Hop garden and 3500 poles into the Wish meadow Hop garden the Old poles that would not do again they fetched one load to my House and One load up into the Sandhill Hay plot Also they have Harrowed that part of the Old Sandhill Hop garden field which is plowed up for Hops with the little Horse Harrows a part of one Day G Guy hass turned two Mixons of Dung and mould one in the Old Sandhill Hop garden field and one in the road just by it Master John Catt and Boys have been cutting part of the Slip Shaw except about 2½ hours 1 day he helped me sett out Hops The 7 year old Cow calved at Conwish about the 26th of January a Cow Calf Paid the appraisement to Mrs Waters February 2nd at Beastons Mr John Waters my Land Lord died Tuesday February 7th and left the Sandhill etc Conwish to Mrs A Maria Waters and Family and the Pilly to Mr Ths Waters and Family Lent Mrs Waters the Oxen to Carry a Hay to the Workhouse Feb 2nd and they have had them for a few things besides not worth mentioning which are all the particular that I can remember

Wednesday 14
Horses plough the downs—G Guy holeing hops – Master Catt at work for Mrs Waters

Thursday 15
Same as yesterday.

Friday 16
Horses began Plow Hops in the West Meadow Hop garden G Guy helped Mrs Waters men cleaning Oats

Saturday 17
Horses and Carter went Lewes with Corn for Mrs Waters Oxen went with them a little way G Guy Holing Hops

Monday 19
Horses fetched 8 Bu of Mortar from Mr Burges's Rushlake green and 300 of Bricks from Mr Goldsmith the Brick Kiln to Pinnick below Mr Tedhams on the Parrish accounts afterwards at plow in the West Meadow Hop garden G Guy finished holing[382] hops about noon afterwards was diging hops in

[382] Poling.

Sandhill Farm

the West meadow Hop garden Mr Wm Grant and his Boy Joe began dig Hops there to day

Tuesday 20
Horses finised ploughing the West meadow Hop garden Wm Grant Joel Grant and G Guy Diging Hops there G Guy broke the Handle and one speon of the spud that he worked with Settled with Wm Burges he hass trimmed the frute tree at Sandhills and has dug that garden and planted some Peas and Beans he worked there 13¾ Days at 1s/6d per day which amounted to £1:0:6d Also he has worked about 8 days in my Sandhole Garden which comes to 12s all which I have paid him Forgot to mention the Horses sometime ago cleared the Pilly plat Shaw of every thing except the poles which were not all shaved there wass 84 House Faggots 115 Kiln Ditto 71 Thatch rods and 13 fence poles which we removed into the Pilly fostel The Horses have had 1 sack & 1 Bus of Oats Since the Second of January from Summertree and Sandhole

Wednesday 21
The horses began Plough up Hops in the Calves Meadow Hop garden at Pilly Charles Hook who lives at Summertree helped them something more

than half the Day pooking out and Chopping up and lumping the Hop Roots Master Grant his son Joel and G Guy Diging Hops as yesterday Settled with Master Catt for Cutting part of the Slip Shaw there wass 575 House Faggots 950 Ruff and 275 Best Kiln Faggots 25 of 14 feet 1225 of 13 feet 1475 of 12 feet and 187 of 10 feet Hop poles 30 Bush Faggots 66 Alders and Sally[383] fence poles 55 Ash poles 4 Poles for Kiln rensellers 1000 Thatch Rods 150 stakes 125 Binders. 20 Lew Faggots and 900 Hop sticks Also paid him for 1 Day and 2 hours work and paid him for his Boy Benjamin 7 weeks at 3s/6d per week up to this day Mrs Water's men had the Oxen to fetch some Barley from Dallington Henry Hoad brought a Cart Load of Potatoes from Summertree with his Horses consisting of 19 Bushels This Winter hitherto hass paid off very well indeed ispaciously[384] this month so that the roads are dry enough for packing in trade and it is dry enough to go almost any wear with low shoes Slipers so that Mr Moor is not right in his almanack for this year about weather for this month.

Thursday 22

Horses at Plough as yesterday and Charles Hoad helping them Wm Grant his son Joel and G Guy Diging Hops as yesterday Ruben Baker had 1 Bu of Wheat from the Sandhole Barn There wass shocking news brought to our Ears today from Dallington that Mr William Dunk a Farmer at Dallington was thrown from his Horses and Killed between Netherfield Gun and Darvel hole coming from Battle

Friday 23

Wm and Joel Grant and G Guy all as yesterday Horses draw some of our Summertree Corn up to Windmill Hill to go to Lewes tomorrow and fetched 4 Sacks of Spring Tares home from Bellhurst to sow Horses had 2 Bu Oats from Summertree

Saturday 24

Ruben Baker with two of the Horses and Henry Hoad with the 4 Summertree Horses went to Lewes to Mr Jesse Cooks with 2 Loads of Wheat at 11£ per Load and 15 Sacks of Peas at 28s per quarter and fetched home 120 Sacks of Oats for my Father Thomas Oxley Also I Bought 2 Tubs of Wheel Grease one for Summertree Business one for me both cost £1:17s:0d A new Chaff cutting Knife 5s 6d and 4 new pair of Horse Chains

---

[383] Salix Willow.
[384] Especially.

wt 63½ lbs at 6d per lb £1:11:9d I went to Lewes on Fathers Horse Wm Grant and his son Joel began Dig hops in the Pilly Hop garden G Guy finised the West meadow Hop Garden and Dug two Alleys at the Pilley Master Catt hass been to work for Mrs Waters threshing Clover and finised yesterday afterward he and his Boy Wm where a Hedging for Me to day and a part of yesterday

Monday 26
Horses and Oxen and all the Men and Boys (except G Guy who was not at work to day) Removed Mrs Water's Wheat stack in to the Pilly Barn

Tuesday 27
It having Freezed to much for Plough last night the Carters and Horses and C Hook removed the straw from where the Wheat Stack stood into the Pilly yard and fetched all the 13 feet Hop poles from the Pilly plat Shaw into the West Meadow Hop Garden Consisting of 177 poles afterwards Master Catt helped the Carters with the Horses filling up the Hop holes with Dung and Mould in the Old Sandhole Garden in the afternoon G Guy was not at work NB Sent C Hook home to Summertree after he had loaded the above mentioned straw for I thought of their ploughing up Hops if it wass not for the Frost The Horses had 4 Bu of Oats

Wednesday 28
Horses Carters and Master Catt filling up the Hop holes with Dung and Mould till the Frost wass to much gone away there wass 28 loads of Dung and Mould in the Old Sandhill Hop garden field Mixon they afterwards Carried in 5 loads from the Mixon of Dung and Mould in the Road and carried 6 loads of Horse Dung to mix with the Mould that lay against the other Mixon in the road G Guy wass not at work to day It has been fine weather nearly all month till to Day it has snowed and Rained nearly all day so that it is dirtyier to night than it has been afore for a month or more

Thursday 1 March
Horses at Plough in the Dawn G Guy Diging Hops in the Pilly Hop garden I bought a new Handbill of Jn Oxley Cost 2/9 and Planted some Potatoes Onions

Friday 2
Horses at Plough a little while in the Dawn and finised plowing the Calves Meadow hop garden which is to be Grubed up. G Guy Diging hops in the Pilly Hop garden It hass been almost continuously Wett weather since last Wednesday it is now very Dirty

Saturday 3
Wett weather nearly all Day but not a hasty rain The Horses did not do any thing but sett the Broad Wheel Waggon into the Pilly Lodge Ruben Baker the Carter and his Mate Benjamin Catt Grinding Malt at Mrs Waters's Malt Mill and Fetched some Water for the Women ready for Brewing and Cutt some Chaff for the Horses and had a Horse shod etc G Guy not at work to Day Master John Catt and his Boy have been Threshing for Mrs Waters all the Week. Horses had 1 Bu of Oats tonight

Sunday 4
Dirty Showry weather

Monday 5
Verry Dirty rather Cold Wind removed from the Southwest to the Northeast cloudy nearly all Day Horses began plow in the upper crocers because it wass to Wett in the Dawn G Guy Diging Hops in the Pilly Garden Horses had 4 Bu of Oats to night they have about 6 Bu of Oats per week and the Summertree Horses about 5 Bu per per week My Brother John Pattenden and I found out to night that one of the Summertree Cows which sockels 2 Claves[385] hass got the Red Water[386]

Tuesday 6
Cloudy morning very Wett afternoon Horses at Plough in the upper Crocers G Guy Diging Hops at Pilly only the rain made him leave of I made a little Cart for Thomas in the afternoon

Wednesday 7
A very Warm pleasant Day but very Dirty Master Thos Hoad killed a fat Sow which was shut up when we weaned her Pigs about the 8th of December (a little sow) hass been a fatting about 3 Months and Weighed 47 stone 6lbs Horses at Plough in the upper Crocers G Guy finised Diging Hops at Pilly about noon and came home and told me that the last 3 yearling Heifer had just calved a Bull Clalf at Comwish the maid and I and Master Grant and he went and milked her and left the calf and she doing very well G Guy was afterwards Grubing Hops in the Calves meadow Hop garden at Pilly Master Grant who hass been several days at work at Priory was this Day Gaping and Brushing up Hedges for me at Sandhill and

---

[385] Suckles two calves.
[386] Redwater (babesiosis) is a tick-borne infection that is usually fatal to cattle. Babesiosis is commonly called 'Red Water' as it causes the urine to develop a red colour.

Sandhole Farms I wass at Mr Noakes's Dallington to night and had a verry wett journey home My Father was there also and I went with him home but did not go in

Thursday 8
Warm pleasant weather the fore part of the Day but very Wett from 2 O'Clock till about 5 O'Clock in the afternoon The Wind has of late been chiefly Downwards We left the Heifer that calved yesterday as far as we could tell doing verry well but this morning when Master Richard Batton (Mrs Waters's Bailey Man[387] who wass to fodder all the stock for me till lady day) was Foddering he perceived the Heifer that calved yesterday had thrown her Bed out[388] he immediately sent for me and I went and he soon put it in again and Sowed it in and she now seems doing very well Horses at Plough in the upper Crocers G Guy was not at work for me today J T Lade and myself fetched a Steer and a Heifer of mine from the Pilly to the Sandhole Close and J T Lade drove 16 Ewes in Lamb of our summertree stock into my Comwish fields by way way of exchange of Keep and accommodation on both sides I went to the Half Moon Market in the afternoon Bought of My Brother John Pattenden 3 Bu of Clover Seed at £1:1s per Bushel and of Mr Jas Pinyon 1 Quarter of Rye grass for One Pound £

Friday 9
Dull Cloudy weather some Rain in afternoon and Evening Horses finised Ploughing the Upper Crocers about Noon and finised their day at plough in the Dawn G Guy grubing Hops I had 1 Bu Hd 1 Bu wheat for a Grist

Saturday 10
Verry Dirty some sun and some rain Generally Cloudy Horses at Plough in the Dawn G Guy Grubing Hops Master Catts Children shaving Hop poles in the Slip Shaw Settled with Master Grant and G Guy for their work Horses had 2 Bu of Oats to night I Gave for Hop diging this year for Slips 6d per Hundred and for the stack Rows 12d per Hundred in the West meadow Hop garden and 7d per Hd for slips and 14d per Hd for Stack Rows in the Pilly Hop Garden

---

[387] Bailiff, here in the sense of 'one who superintends the husbandry of a farm for its owner or tenant' (OED).
[388] Suffered a uterine prolapse.

Sunday 11

A Drying Day except a little shower about noon Mr Press Preached from Isaiah the 59th Chapter and the latter part of the 19th verse 'When the enemy shall come in like a flood the Spirit of the Lord Shall lift up a standard against him' the Summertree and Sandhole sheep began lamb to day at Cornwish One Lamb came to Day

Monday 12

A Warm pleasant Drying Day with some Clouds and a foggy morning Ruben Baker with one Horse Carried a sack of Trefoil seed from Bucksteep to Egypt [Farm] and fetched 3 Bushels of Clover seed from Egypt to Sandhill I sowed the last part of the Hoads field with Tares for the Horses and some Trefoil and Clover mixed together for seeds and the Horses Harrowed them in in the forenoon and the Horses went to clearing off Hop roots from the Calves Meadow Hop garden in the afternoon G Guy Grubbing Hops there wass one more Lamb came this afternoon there wass a meeting to night at the Green to take into consideration the propriety of getting the Tithes Lowered but there was nothing in particular done only that Mr Jarvis and Mr Potter were to go to London on the Parish Charge to see the Trust about it Horses Had 4 Bu of Oats to night

Tuesday 13

A foggy morning a warm sunshining day and a Foggy Evening Wind in the Southwest and West Horses at plough in the Dawn G Guy grubing Hops Master Button Dryed some of Mrs [Walters's] wheat on the Oast to Day with my Coal

Wednesday 14

Very Warm Pleasant weather there wass not a Cloud to be seen one time this after noon Horses carried a Load of Pea Haulm from Sandhill to Pilly in the morning and cleared the Hop Roots out of the Calves meadow Hop Garden afterwards G Guy finised Grubing of them I went to Hailsham Market

Thursday 15

A Frosty morning some Cloud a very pleasant Day Ruben Baker sowed the Calves Meadow Hop Garden that wass but which may be here after called the Calves Meadow field with Early Gray Peas which I had from Summertree and the Horses Harrowed them in Benjamin Catt and I Backed 70 fence and ash Poles out of the Slip Shaw G Guy mixed up a little Dung and mould in the Road (the account of which rec February 28th) till about

11 O'clock afterwards sharping Hop Poles by the Hund[?] I went to the Halfmoon Market in the afternoon and exchanged 4 Sacks of Barley for 5 sack of Oats with Mr James Harmer and I afterwards Bought 15 Sacks of Oats of Mr Everest of Gardener street at 19s per Quarter the best Sow went to Hog to J Harmer's Boar

Friday 16
Weather as yesterday – Ruben Baker and Benj Catt his mate Master Catt and G Guy with the Horses and a pair of Oxen finised putting Dung and mould in the Holes for the Hops in the Old Sandhill Hop garden there wass 62 loads of Dung and mould put into the Holes in all 28 loads of Dung and Mould from the Mixon in the same field and 34 loads from the Mixon in the Road and there wass about 2 loads from that Mixon left

Saturday 17
Pleasant weather Horses at Plough in the Dawn Master Catt threshing for Mrs Waters G Guy putting Mould over the Dung and Mould where the Hills are to be in the Old Sandhill Hop garden in the forenoon not at work in the afternoon Summertree people put 30 Bu of Potatoes for Me in to the Sandhill Barn and brought 20 Bu more to My House Horses had 1 Bu of Oats to night I went to the Book Making at the Green tonight we made an 8s/6d book for the Half year Poor Rate

Sunday 18
Stormy Windy weather Wind in the Northwest Mr Press is very ill with the Quinsey[389] Mr Parris from Ninfield preached in his room from Isaiah the 25th chapter and the 6th Verse in the morning but wass not any of us there in the afternoon

Monday 19
Stormy Windy weather as yesterday Horses at Plough in the Dawn The next Best Heifer Calved about noon a Bull Calf G Guy as on Saturday forenoon all day to day Mr Gower from Blackstock Mr Tho Hall Mr Christmas from Heathfield Mr Tho Waters and My Father T Oxley looked over the Farms today on purpose to divide the Rent He placed £31:10s to the Pilly and £33:10s to the Sandhill and Comwish The Horses had 4 Bu of Oats to night – NB J Harmer sent 5 sacks of Oats to Sandhill

Tuesday 20
Weather about as yesterday Horses finised Plowing the Dawn for Oats and

---

[389] Quinsy; a bacterial infection of the throat.

Drawed 350 Hop pole out of the Pilly plat Shaw into the Pilly Hop garden and carried 35 Alder and Willow and 45 Ash poles to Master Daws and had the Narrow Wheeled Waggon to Bodle Street to be mended G Guy as on Saturday and yesterday and gapping the Hedges to keep the sheep in the Cornwish fields they have been verry troublesome of late by getting out altho they have verry good keep Mrs Waters men had a pair of my oxen to day Summertree Heifer calved to Day a Bull Calf

Wednesday 21

Cold weather some small showers Wind Northward it has been verry Windy and stormy these last few days Horses Harrowing in Tares in the Middle Crocers 2 of Master Catts Boys drove them Ruben Baker sowed the Tares and sowed them to thick so there was not enough by about a Bushel G Guy as on Monday Master Catt cutting Hop setts at Bucksteep for me I went to Burwash to see Mr Philcox the Lawyer about the Tithes on my farms but could not make any sense of him The Summertree Old Cow calved this morning a Bull calf

Thursday 22

Not so windy as it hass been but was stormy Ruben Baker sowed the upper Crocers with the Oats which I had from J Harmer last Monday which he says are long tailed wights and he also sowed the Rye Grass I had of J Pinyon Horses did not quite finis Harrowing the field today G Guy planting Hop setts in the forenoon afterwards finised filling up the Hop holes and went to Chopping the spits to pieces which come out of the Hop holes[390] Charles Hook planting Hops with G Guy in the forenoon and began Dress Hops at Pilly in the afternoon Joel Grant laying out Hop setts 6 for a Hill before G Guy and C Hook and opening hops before Charles Hook Master Catt cleaning for Mrs Waters and Master Grant went to Cutting Hop setts in his room Messrs Henry Blackman and Jesse Jarvis come here and went around the Parish to Day with a notice respecting the Tithe had a sack of Oats of Mrs Waters and sowed about ½ a Bushel to finis the field with The Horses had the rest

Friday 23

A Cold Frosty morning a still warm sunny Day Cloudy part of the evening the Wind shifted about from the North to the Southwest Ruben Baker fetched one Bu of Tares from the Priory to finis the Middle Crocers with Horses finised Harrowing the upper and middle Crocers and Ruben with

[390] Spits: small pieces of wood which break off the bottom of the hop pole.

one Horse carried 15 Sacks to Mr C Everest's Gardener street to put the Oats in which I bought of him Master Grant Cutting Hop setts at Bucksteep Wm Catt carried 5 of Master Harmers sacks home to Batsford and fetched our 4 sacks home in the morning afterwards helping Joel Grant opening Hops Charles and G Guy planting and Dressing Hops

Saturday 24
Verry much the appearance of Rain all Day from the Southwest Cloudy afternoon Wind in SW Horses at Plough for Father in his 13 acres G Guy C Hook Master Grant Joel his son and Wm Catt planting and Dressing Hops and Cutting Hop setts see yesterday Settled with Master Ruben Baker to night he hass been ill with Master Ruben Baker to night he hass been my Carter from the Day I took Pilley Comwish and Sandhole farms till this day at 15s per Week also settled with Martin Grant for work done on both Farms or Bussiness It began to Rain this evening

Sunday 25
Verry Wett weather nearly all Day and a Wett evening the Wind towards night shifted from the Southwest to the North I stayed at home all Day such a thing as I have not done before for some Years on a Sabbath Day Henry Hoad went to Chapel in the morning I understand that Mr Press is much Better he hass been ill with the Quinsey in his Throat and for six Days and six nights did neither Eat or Drink anything he Preached to Day

Monday 26
Cloudy dirty morning showry Day Frosty morning the Wind removed back to the Southwest Henry Hoad left the Summertree Horses yesterday and took my Horses and Ruben Baker left them. Benjamin Catt that went Mate with my Horses for 3s:6d per week came this Day to live in my Houses to go mate with my Horses for his Board and the Parish to Clothe him and I am to have 40s for the year thus much for that matter Horses Drawed the Broad Wheeled Waggon to Bodle street to be repaired took the narrow wheeled Waggon and fetched home 15 sacks of seed Oats from Mr Everists Gardener street and fetched 25 House Faggots from the Pilly to Master Grant R Baker and Wm Grant threshing in the Sandhole Barn G Guy Ditching in the Old Sandhill Hop garden Martin Catt wood cutting and Hedging at Pilly Horses had 4 Bu of Oats to night

Tuesday 27
Stormy Weather Henry Hoad with the Horses fetched the Broad Wheeled Waggon home from Bodle street and 10 Alder poles from the Master Daws which he did not like to except see last Tuesday Baker Grant and Ben

Wednesday 28

A verry Wett forenoon and a cloudy afternoon the [Wind] Southwest and south and in the evening in the East Horses did nothing all Day Carters Boseling jobs Workmen threshing G Guy I saw nothing of all day

Thursday 29

Cloudy and but little rain all Day Wind Southwest Horses at nothing Carters Boseling and G Guy choping turfs to pieces in the young Hops in the forenoon I sent him to Gravel Diging in the afternoon on the Parrish account I believe all the rest were threshing but not for me only because I have none as yet to myself

Friday 30

A verry fine Day and but very few clouds a Cold keen air in the afternoon and evening Wind in the Westerley Quarters Carters Boseling Master Grant and Master Baker finised threshing Oats this morning about half past eight o'clock in the Sandhole Barn afterwards they were Dressing Hops in the Westmeadow Hop garden. Joel Grant all day and Wm Catt ½ day opening hop hills Horses had 4 Bu Oats

Saturday 31

A verry Wett forenoon some sunshine in the afternoon with some Rain and Hail Still morning and Windy part of the afternoon the Wind suddenly changed about 2 O'clock from the Southwest to the Northwest Harry Cutting Potatoes in the Sandhill Barn R Baker part of the afternoon Ditto afterwards they helped T J Lade clean some Oats in the Sandhole Barn Master Grant wass not at work for us today and R Baker did but ½ the Day

Sunday 1 April

A verry pleasant sunny Day Wind westwards Mr Press wass not quite recovered from the effects of his illness to day he preached in the morning from Hebrews his Tex wass 'The Just shall live by Faith' it wass a noble discourse I heard him much to profit providentially there was a Minister out from Kent there this morning who undertook to preach this afternoon his subject wass upon the cure of Naamans Leprosy 2nd Kings 5 chapter etc

Monday 2

Showry Weather Henry Hoad and Benjamin Catt with the Horses fetched

Catt threshing in the forenoon Carters and all Hop dressing in the afternoon I went with the little Sow to Hog Mr J Harmers Boar. My Biggest Heifer Calved in the Sandhole Close this morning a Bull Calf some Hop roots home from the Pilly and carried a load of Hay from the Sandhill to the Comwish and fetched a load of Wheat straw from the Pilly to the Sandhill Barn Ruben Baker Sharping new Hoppoles in the Pilly Hop garden in the forenoon Dressing Hops in the Westmeadow Hop garden in the afternoon Wm Catt helped him Master Catt and Boys finised Wood cutting and Hedging about the Pilly fostel and in the Pilly meadow against the Calves meadow field (late HG) today etc

Tuesday 3
Verry Windy and some storms Wind Northwest West and Southwest Henry Hoad and Ben Catt Charles Hook Silas Brook (and Boy) J T Lade Wm Catt and Ruben Baker finised Dressing My Hops in the Wmeadow H gardens which is all the Hop Dressing I have to do this year I mean that I have now finised Hop Dressing for this year Master John Catt began Cutt Hoath in the Slip

Wednesday 4
A very still warm pleasant Day Wind upward My Horses and Carters were at work for Father to Day Master Baker helped gett in the Sandhole Wheat stack Wm Catt Ditto They Killed all the Ratts that they saw but there wass not above 10 or 12 Rats in all no young ones Master Catt cutting Hoath Horses had 4 Bu of Oats etc

Thursday 5
Weather as yesterday except a shower in the afternoon and it wass more Windy than yesterday The Carters and Wm Catt with the Horses sowing Oats and seeds and Harrowing in the Dawn Master Catt as on yesterday NB I lett him have 2os in part for his works today Ruben Baker Sharping Hoppoles Etc NB Sowed the least part of the Dawn with Trefoil seed only and Long tail white Oats and Harrowed it two wints or four Draught

Friday 6
Warm pleasant weather Wind upwards and Westwards R Baker and I sowed the rest of the Dawn with Oats Trefoil and Clover seeds mixed but the Horses did not quite finis Harrowing the seeds by reason of one of the Horses Trooper by name having a very great cold so that they could not gett on with their work Jn Catt Cutting Hoath

Saturday 7
There was some heavy rain in the night which made it rather smeary[?] this morning A verry warm growing Day not much sun Wind Southwest and Northwest Horses removed some Hop poles from the Slip shaw into the

Westmeadow Hop garden R Baker Helped them I did not see any thing of Master Catt in the Hoathy field Mrs Wilmshurst of Warbleton I believe that she wass eldest daughter of the Revd George Gilbert she has been verry comfortable in mind and soul during her long and severe Illness and I believe hass now undergone a Happy change May the Lord keep me from sin and lead me and guide me into all Truth all my life long that I may be prepared for the solemn approach of Death and be made meet the dwell with Christ in Glory when my time here on Earth is over — —

Sunday 8

Warm pleasant Weather Mr Press is now pretty well recovered from his Illness he preached this morning from Zechariah 9 chapter and the 11 Verse 'But as for thee also' etc

Monday 9

Verry Growing Weather Horses Finised Harrowing the Dawn and where afterwards at harrowing in the Hoads field R Baker sowed the bigest part of of the Hoads field with Oats I had of Mr Everest he and Benjamin Catt and one of the Horses shimed part of my garden and I sowed it with early Gray peas in the afternoon etc Master R Winchester wass here to Day and Mended the Chaff cutting Box and began make a Ladder Master Catt and his boy William threshing for Mrs Waters

Tuesday 10

Verry pleasant weather Horses finised Harrowing the Hoads field H Hoad sowed the seeds ½ Trefoil and ½ Clover Master Baker cutting turfs to pieces in the Old Sandhill Hop garden

Wednesday 11

There was a small shower early this morning and it wass some what windy southwest – a warm pleasant Day some clouds very growing weather I sowed the Pilly Plot with Barley and H Hoad sowed it with Clover seeds only Horses shimed it over twice with Mr J Lades great shim and Harrowed it once with the little Horse Harrows M Baker finised the job he wass about yesterday and mowing he was afterwards sharping new Hop poles in the Westmeadow Hop garden We have now finised our sowing for this Spring so that I have this year sowed and what wass sowed before I took The Farms 13½ Acres of Wheat 6¼ Acres of Spring Tares 2 Acres of Peas 15¾ acres of Oats 1 Acre of Barley 1 Acre of Clover 2¾ of Trefoil 9½ Clover and Trefoil Mixed and 4½ Acre of Rye grass Also we have planted 1678 Hills of Hops and there is 5¼ Acres of Hops to Pole Also there is 8 Acres of seeds to Mow this summer and 4 Acres of Old seeds to feed off or mow as may seem more proper this the particulars of My Arible land this year and If you wish to find out you must look book for a few weeks back up to this time The Old seeds are in the Freehold field at the Pilly and the seeds to mow are in the Gravelpitt field and lower 5 acres at Comwish the Wheatfields are the lower Crocers the Barnfield at Comwish and the upper 5 acres

Thursday 12
Windy stormy weather rather Cold Carters R Baker Wm Catt and Joel Grant with the Horses shiming the young Hops Mr Wm Harmer fetched me 3 sacks of Oats and took from Summertree in my name 2 sacks of Barley I went to Chapel this afternoon and Mr Press preached Mrs Wilmshurst's Funeral sermon from 118 Psalm the 18 & 19 & 20th Verses

Friday 13
Cold Windy and Stormy weather Wind West and Northwest Horses Dredging the Hollow meadow Flatfield etc Master Baker sharping hop poles in the West Meadow Hop garden

Saturday 14
Showry weather Cold and Windy from the Southwest Horses Dredging the House Meadow the Old field and Pilly meadow Master Baker sharping old hop poles ready for poling in the West meadow Hop gardens I went to Heathfield fair with a pair of Oxen and 2 Heifers and their Calves Master T J Lade went with me and drove a cow and calf it was a verry Dull Fair we sold one of my Heifers and calf to Mr Jn Trill of Dallington for 11£ 10s and Drove all the rest home again Benjamin Catt had my Old Blind Horse by the name of Pedler to the Fair about noon for sale J T Lade sold the Horse to Master Barnett for £3: 15s to be taken out in Chalk[391] The four year old Cow Calved a Bull calf this morning in the Sandhill flatt field

Sunday 15
Showry weather as yesterday Mr Press preached from Jeremiah the 8th Chapter and the last Verse

Monday 16
Verry pleasant weather the Wind Southwest wards Horses Dredged the Comwish pasture field and the Old Sandhill field and fetched a load of Litter from the Pilly to Sandhills Yard Master Baker as on Saturday G Guy

---

[391] To be chalked up? sold on credit?

whoom I have imployed on the Roads for some days I have sett to turning up of Mould in the gravel Pitt on my account today Mr Arthur Russell the School Master and assessor was here to night respecting my Horses I have made entry of six 4 for Sandhill and 2 for Sandhole and gave notice that I have left off keeping one

Tuesday 17
Some showers Wind Westwards Horses and Carters Carried some Hay from Sandhill to Comwish and some Oat straw from Comwish to the Pilly and some Kiln Faggotts from Pilly to Sandhole Lime Kiln and some Old Faggotts from the Kiln to Mrs Waters Ruben Baker poling Hops in the Westmeadow Hop garden G Guy as on yesterday Master Catt finised Mrs Waters's threshing at the Pilly this afternoon and I sett him to poleing Hops in the Pilly Hop garden I went with the Least Sow to Mr Jas Harmers and She went to Hog to his Boar

Wednesday 18
Showry weather Wind in the West Horses Carters and One pair of Oxen and G Guy faggot carring Master Catt and R Baker Hoppoling etc

Thursday 19
Cold Showry a winterly weather Wind in the Southwest It hass now much the appearance of a back ward spring the Lord knows what is best for us and it is a Great Mercy to be enabled to Bow with submission to his Almighty Will I find that I am continually in need of the powerful Influences of his sweet and Heavenly spirit to Inable me to lie pasive in his Hands and know no will but his Carters G Guy Horses and Oxen yesterday etc and to Day removed all the House Faggots that we're left at the Pilly to Master Catts and Master R Bakers who live in the Pilly house namely 90 Faggots to Catts and 83 Faggots to Bakers and 60 more House faggots from the Slip Shaw to Master Catts and 17 more Ditto to R Baker and 125 Best Kiln Faggots from Ditto to Master Catts and 50 more Ditto to Master Bakers And 200 House Faggots from the Slip Shaw to Mrs Waters's which in all 150 House and 125 Best Kiln Faggots to Master Catts 100 House and 50 Best Kiln Faggots to Master Baker and 200 House Faggotts to Mrs Waters's which I believe is all the House Faggots I shall sell this spring Master Baker and Master Catt Hop poling

Good Friday 20
Showry weather it Thundered Lightened Rained and Hailed this evening which bring to My remembrance that solemn event which Happened just

1787 years ago to Day if our accounts are right which this Day is sett appart to commemorate the Dieing Love and Sufferings of that precious Redeemer who died 'the Just for the unjust that he might Bring us to God' 1 Peter 3 chapter part 18 verse which wass the Part that was preached from by Mr Owen from Tunbridge Wells at Heathfield Chapel to day Being wett and dirty the Horses did not work to day Carters went to Chapel and drove a Cow and Calf from the Lower Sandhole Close to Comwish and drove my Cow and the best Calf to Summertree to weand the Calf Mr Jn Pattenden sent his Mare to Horse G Guy Mouling and Gaping see last Monday rest as yesterday the Wind wass Southwest south and southeast in the day but a remarkable still calm evening except what hass been before written

Saturday 21
A verry pleasant Day chiefly cloudy Wind Northeastwards Horses Carters a pair of Oxen and G Guy with the Broad wheeled Waggon Removed 100 House Faggots from the Slip Shaw to the Sandhill hay plat (to be used by either Mrs Waters or us as circumstances may require) and all the rest of the House Faggots in the shaw Consisting of 195 they removed to my House All the House Faggots I had this year wass 770 Hop poles as on yesterday

Sunday 22
A Cold Northeasterly wind but pleasant weather with some Clouds Mr Press preached at the Heathfield Chapel this morning from the first part of the 10th Verse of the 3rd Chapter of Philippians and at Bucksteep in the evening from 1st Peter 1st Chapter the 11th Verse A verry precious sermon Mr Barnett fetched his Blind Horse away that he Bought of me at Heathfield Fair

Monday 23
A still warm Cloudy Day wind chiefly Northeast Horses removed 412 Hop pole from in and about the Pilly meadow into the Pilly Hop garden and two Loads of 12 feet poles from the slip shaw into the West meadow Hop garden Catt poleing Hops at Pilly and Baker in the West meadow Hop garden G Guy wass not at work for me today anywhere Two of the Winchesters repairing the Sandhill Waggon Lodge Doors to Day etc

Tuesday 24
After a Showry night a still warm Day some clouds Wind in the Southwest Henry and Benjamin with the Horses and 1 pair of oxen removed all the rest of the Hop poles from the Slip Shaw to the West meadow Hop garden

and two Loads of Kiln Faggots from the Slip Shaw to our Lime Kiln I helped them unload I thought of G Guy helping but he did not come Master Catt hass finised poleing the Pilly Hop garden and began part of the West meadow Hop garden and he and Master Baker were both there to Day Hop poleing Master R Winchester finised making a Ladder and mended a Bed steddle for me to Day etc

Wednesday 25

After a warm growing night a verry warm pleasant Day scarce any clouds Wind in the South Mr J T Lade helped the Carters and Horses and Oxen Carring Kiln Faggots as yesterday I helped unload Master Catt and Master Baker poleing Hops in the Westmeadow Hop garden I believe G Guy hass left me we did not well agree about the price of his work I gave him 1s/6d per Day and he wanted more

Thursday 26

A verry warm pleasant Day some clouds It Lightened verry sharp and verry frequent this evening but not much thunder and but little rain Wind in the South and East finised clearing the Slip Shaw except some of the Bush faggots and removed the Kiln Faggots from the Pilly meadow etc to the Lime Kiln there was nearly 200 so that I have this year about 1260 Ruff Kiln Faggots this year which are all removed to the Lime Kiln and about 107 the Remainder of the Best Kiln Faggots where stacked up in the Sandhill Hog plot to Day and 16 Bundles of Thetch rods where laid up in the Sandhole Bullock Lodge and some of the fence poles to lay them up on rest of the Fence pole stakes Binders etc in the Sandhill Hog plot 3 Bundles of Thetch rods in the Sandhill granary and one in my privy which makes the 20 Bundles in all I had about 79 fence poles in all this year there wass 13 Sally poles at Pilly but somebody hass stolen 3 of them and the Carpenters have had 3 of them to Day for Mrs Waters fencing so that there is but 7 there now and Master Daw hass had 25 of the others One Carpenter making Barrows and repairing Hoads gates at Comwish and Sandhill Master Winchester Ditto There repairing the Barn etc at Summertree and Sandhole Farms Hop polers as usual Master T J Lade helped the Carters to Day

Friday 27

Some clouds in the morning Clear warm sunny afternoon Wind Southwest and West Carters Joel Grant and I with the Horses and 2 shims shimming the young Hops Hop polers as usual Mr John Pattendens Mare went to

Horse the Second time to night My Wives Mother came to see her this afternoon Our Maid Sarah Pettitt went away ill on Good Friday the same Day her Brother Samuel Died I understand she hass kept being worse ever since

Saturday 28
A warm Day some Clouds Wind in the Northeast Carter with the Horses finised shimming the young Hops and Drawed the Verrows[392] ready for planting potato's Catt and Baker poleing Hops etc My Cousin Lower (Martha Lower) from Chiddingly came to see me to Day

Sunday 29
A Bright sunny Day Cold Northeast Wind Mr Press preached at Heathfield Chapel from Ephesians the 6 chapter the middle part of the 12th Verse in the morning I heard him Gladly I wass not there in the afternoon H Hoad wass there I understand the Mr Press preached a Funeral sermon for Samuel Pettitt Junior from a Text he had choosd himself whilst living Ecclesiastes the 11th Chapter and the 9th Verse

Monday 30
Cold Cloudy Day and verry Windy great part of the Day Wind Northeastwards Horses and one pair of Oxen removed 100 of House Faggots from the Sandhill Hog plot to Mr S Waters the Shoemaker at Rushlake Green and 350 Old Hop poles from the Pilly Hop garden home to My House and one Load from the Westmeadow and Hop garden Ditto Catt and Baker finised poleing for Me for the year in the Westmeadow Hop garden to night Mrs Baker and Mrs Message began the Hops at Pilly to Day

Tuesday 1 May
A cloudy day not so cold as yesterday wind northeast – early this morning about 2'oclock Henry was called up to go for the Doctor for Mrs Waters who was this morning between 5 & 6 o'clock delivered of a girl – and my glover or runt cow calved a bull calf about the same time – Henry Hoad with 3 horses and a pair of oxen removed some of Mrs Waters wheat from the Pilly Barn to Mr John Heads mill her man Richard Button Helped him – Benjamin call with one pair of oxen rolling in the Crocker – Catt & Baker poling hops in the Sandhole hop garden which is between J T Lade and me put 3 calves in my Sandhill Brook to night—

[392] Furrows.

Wednesday 2
A still warm day mostly cloudy some sun wind south – the ground is now prity dry – Henry Hoad with the horses harrowed the wheat at Comwish Ben Catt rolling in the Crockers and the barley in the Pilly plat

Thursday 3
A very warm day some thunder and lightening which were very distant in the afternoon some rain at night about 6 o'clock – Wind south and east – H Hoad with my horses harrowed the Sandhole 10 acre wheat – Ben Catt rolling in the Dawn at Pilly

Friday 4
A warm day some distant thunder in the afternoon some dark clouds around the south and east quarters – wind downwards – Horses cleared the Westmeadow hop garden of old hop poles – We have finished poling the Sandhole hop garden about noon potatoing in the Summertree 9 Acres in the afternoon

Saturday 5
A warm day some clouds wind southern Horses shiming the Pilly hop garden – Master Catt and Master Baker cleaning wheat for Mrs Waters J T Lade Master Grant his son Joel & Wm Catt planting potatoes in my young hops – Crowherst came to see one of my cows with a bad udder to night – he gave her a drink and said that the udder must be stougest[393] in warm water twice a day etc

Sunday 6
A warm day but a cooling air and some clouds wind southwest – Mr Press was gone to Battle Mr Parris preached in his room from the 2nd Epistle of Peter the 1st chapter the middle part of the 1st verse viz ' to them that have obtained like precious faith with us' in the morning – we borrowed Mrs Waters cart to day and put one of my cart horses to draw us to Chapel.

Monday 7
Cloudy and not quite as warm as it was a few days ago wind southwest. – Henry Hoad with the team removed 2 loads of Mrs Waters wheat from the Pilly to Mr T Balcombs Rushlake – and some hay from Sandhill to Comwish – Ben boseling Grant Catt and Baker with 2 of their boys Wm & Joel Planting potatoes in my young hops

[393] Staunched.

Tuesday 8
Cold cloudy day with some sleet rain great part of the day wind southwest – Henry & Ben with 1 horse & cart picking up chucks in the Westmeadow hop garden and fetched home till the rain obliged them to leave of Master Grant Joel Grant Master Catt Wm Catt and Master Baker finished planting potatoes among my young hops about noon – Master Baker helped the carters setting up old hop poles – and all the rest of the finished planting potatoes in our Summertree 9 Acres in the afternoon

Wednesday 9
A warm pleasant day some but not many clouds wind downwards – Harry Ben & Wm Catt finished picking up chucks in the W_m_w Garden with one Horse and cart – Lent 2 horses to the Summertree team who with my broad wheel waggon fetched a load of chalk from Hailsham their waggon being under repair at the wheelers – NB I rode one of the summer tree mares to market J T Lade with 4 summertree and 4 of my oxen were at plough on the Roads to day between Christion river and Pagham The Old Hands helped him – Master Catt & Master Baker gaping & severing out waterings etc.

Thursday 10
A mild day some cloud and some rain wind southwest – Horses fetched about 2½ tons of beech and laid a little above end lime kiln – Master Catt and his boy Wm and Master Baker chopping Hops at Pilly

Friday 11
Somewhat cold and cloudy wind southwest Horses as yesterday – the rest finished the Pilly garden about noon afterwards at work among the young hops Put 4 cows into Old Seeds in the Freehold field to night first time turning out this year

Saturday 12
A mild day chiefly cloudy some little rain but scarce perceptible wind southwest – carters oiling the harnesses and Mr S Fox mended them – Baker Catt and Wm Catt at work among the young hops chopping about the Hills etc I went to Burwash Fair with some Beech but could not sell it was so very dull

Sunday 13
Showery weather wind westward Mr Press preached from 1 Peter 5 Cha 6 verse in the morning

Monday 14
Showery wind westward – Master Baker & Joel Grant with the carters and horses shiming in the Westmeadow Hop Garden Master Catt chopping hops in Do.

Tuesday 15
Showery wind westward strong Henry with 3 horses and C Hook with 3 horses fetched a load of chalk from Jevington Chalk Pitt – Ben and Silas the boys picking up chalk put off the forenoon from my Pilly meadow Catt and Baker casting up dung in the Comwish Yard

Wednesday 16
Stormy weather wind west – Horses fetched a load of beech – Catt & Baker throwing dung and mould in the Sandhill hop garden field and fattfield in the forenoon – Chopping hops in the Westmeadow hop garden in the afternoon – I sold a pair of oxen a heifer & calf and a 3 year old steer to Mr Arcoll for 48£ to day

Thursday 17
Wett and dirty weather all day wind westward – Horses fetched a load of chalk from Hailsham Ben and the oxen at plough on the Roads same as on the 9th inst Catt turning dung in the Old Sandhill field and worked on the Roads in the afternoon – Baker turning dung with Master Catt till noon threshing with Master Grant in the Sandhole Barn

Friday 18
Some clouds in the morning afterwards a warm drying day wind upwards – Henry and the horses with C Hook and 3 of Summertree Horses fetched a load of Summertree chalk Baker Carters Horses & Oxen removed 70 loads of dung from the Pilly yard into the Pilly fostell – Wm Catt and I drove the beast which I sold last Tuesday to Mr Acolls

Saturday 19
A warm pleasant day some clouds wind upwards & downwards towards evening chiefly still – Wm Catt with the other men as yesterday but He removed 80 loads of dung My last cow calved this morning

Sunday 20
A cool air some clouds and some sun wind northeast – Mr Press preached at Chapel this morning from Mathew 7th Cha 21st verse and in the evening at Bucksteep from Acts 16th chapter 14 & 15 verses

Monday 21
Cold cloudy weather wind upward Horses went for chalk with 3 of Summertree Horses Benjm & Silas shiming hops in the Westmeadow hop garden Catt and Baker chopping hops there Also – It seems a very backward spring for almost every thing

Tuesday 22
A cold windy day some clouds wind upwards Horses went for chalk as yester day – Catt & Baker hop chopping – Benjn and Silas shiming hops in the Sandhole hop garden – Master Baker planted some potatoes & french beans in my garden last night which I had almost forgotten – J T Lade and I settled with Mr Noakes for his Summertree & Sandhole Rent to day

Wednesday 23
A cold sleet rain and cloudy nearly all day Wind northeast – Henry and Master R Button (Mrs Water's man) with the horses removed some wheat from Dallington to Mr Balcomb's Rushlake and brought some home for Mr Waters they were not quite all day – Master Baker and Master Catt finished turning up dung at Comwish – and trunking in the young hops Ben picking potatoes at Summertree

Thursday 24
A cold drying northeast wind some clouds – Horses went for chalk – Catt & Baker finished trunking and they were afterwards chopping hops – Mr James Pattenden from Burwash and his wives father come here this afternoon and brought my runt for 9£ for me to have the money in 2 mont[hs] at outside upon condition that Mrs Waters at Rushlake should have the calf when it is fatt and for me to take the money of it from her – I was very loth to sell the cow but they very much wanted her and I did not know as I should make so much of her any other way – My Cherry Cow went to bull to my fathers bull to night

Friday 25
Somewhat warmer to day than it has been for a few days past but it is cold for the time of the year some rain at night the wind shifted from the northeast to the southwest Horses and 3 of Summertree horses carried 30 Bu of Mrs Waters potatoes to Mr Ades Jevington and fetched chalk home – Catt & Baker chopping hops – Ben weeding

Saturday 26
A very cold cloudy morning some snow and rain in the afternoon wind Northwest North and Northeast and very cold – There has been sharp

frosts several mornings past – Horses went for chalk and carried 30 Bu more of potatoes see yesterday – Catt and Baker not at work on my farm Benjn & Wm Catt weeding at Comwish – Masons repairing the foundations of my house to day etc Messrs T Lades and John Pattendens mare went to horse

Sunday 27
A clear cold frosty morning cold showery day wind upwards Mr Press preached at Heathfield Chapel from the 17th chapter of John the 6th verse in the morning I was not there in the afternoon

Monday 28
Frosty morning cold showery weather Wind upwards – Horses bringing Kiln Faggots out of the woods to our Sandhole Kiln on the Summertree account oxen gravelearing The Road men had them 2½ days last week but I sent no men with them – 2 Summertree carts and 4 oxen were with them to day a man and a boy Do Catt and Baker gaping about the Pilly meadow Freehold and Comwish field etc part of the day – chopping hops in the Sand hole garden afterwards – Masons finished their jobs to night – Jas. Harmer's mare went to horse to night

Tuesday 29
Cold morning showery weather not so cold in the day as it has been wind northwest – Horses as yesterday – Catt & Baker on the Sandhole ground at work Boys weeding at Comwish – put the cows into the Old field this morning

Wednesday 30
Somewhat warmer and no rain to day some clouds wind eastwards forgot to mention there was some distant thunder last Saturday Sunday and Monday – Horses went for chalk to day first load with joined horns on Summertree boys weeding men on Sandhole farm

Thursday 31
A warm day some cloud wind east and northeast – Horses went for chalk Ruben Baker and the oxen graveling with The Summertree and Mr Veness oxen – Master Catt is gone to London to see his daughters Boys Weeding

Friday 1 June
A warm summer like day wind as yesterday – All as yesterday except Ben shining with Silas in the Sandhole hop garden & Joel carting in his room – Father sent his mare to horse to night

Saturday 2
Quite a summers day wind many ways The vegitution has altered wonderfully for the better Horses & carters went to Amberstone for chalk – Baker and the oxen gravelling weeders etc

Sunday 3
Cool and cloudy morning and a warm day wind many ways – Mr Press preached at Heathfield Chapel from the 2nd chapter the first Epistle of Peter the 24th verse in the morning

Monday 4
A warm shower this morning and a warm sunny day wind downwards – What hath God wrought! we had almost like to murmer at the late service and unpleasant weather – but how can we be thankful enough for his goodness he hath removed his judgement which we deserved and visited us with mercies – Blessed be his Great name
'Oh for grace our hearts to soften!
Teach us! Lord at length to love
We alas! Forget too often
What a friend we have above
But when home our souls are brought
We will love thee as we ought'
Newton Horses began plough up the Freehold field side Mrs Morsey and Mrs Gurr weeding – Master Catt not come home – rest on Summertree account – Mr Tindal mare went to horse

Tuesday 5
Mild weather some clouds wind westward Horses at plough in the Freehold field at Pilly oxen Do with them – rest on Summertree account etc except Fanny or Mrs Gurr who finished weeding my Hoadsfield this afternoon afterwards she was in the Summertree 12 acres

Wednesday 6
Mild weather cloudy and somewhat the appearance of rain this afternoon wind west – Horses at plough Master J Easton who has worked some days on the Roads was to day ditching in my Hoads Brook – Brought 5 Bad locks[394] at the Market to day they cost 0 10s 2d

Thursday 7
Mild weather some clouds wind west – Horses & oxen at plough (NB I

[394] Padlocks.

have but 3 horses & one pair of oxen) J Cotton Finished ditching about ½ past one O'clock afterwards Chopping among the young hops – Master Catt returned from London last night he was at work among the young hops to day – no others on my account – fetched the calves out of my Hoads Brook and put them into the Sandhole 7 acres to night for change of keep shut my heifers calf up to weand last night and let Mrs Waters have a cow to day the first time

Friday 8
There was some rain in the night and a shower this morning and it rained quite fast to day between the hours of 10 & 2 O'clock the wind shifted from the northwest to the northeast and somewhat colder than yesterday – but little sun all day – Tom finished ploughing the Freeholdfield and fetched some chalk from Amberstone – Easton & Catt at work among the young hops before the rain came and after the rain Catt turned a little mixon of mould in the Sandhole platt and Easton casting up mould below my house in the road Sandhill side – Wm Catt (the boy) boseling jobs for me & women Mr Trill Lade told me to night that his bull broke in among my cows last Monday or Tuesday morning and put my Kicking Cow to bull she is a good cow for milk otherwise I should rather she had not gone to bull

Saturday 9
I understand but I was not up soon enough to see that there was a frost in the night it was a clear morning afterwards cloudy and some rain in the evening – Wind removed from the northern back to the northwest not much warmer than yesterday Henry and Ben (the carters) Master Catt and Master Easton with 2 of my carts and 1 pair of oxen & cart from Summertree removed 73 loads of dung from the Sandhill Close to the Flattfield

Sunday 10
Showery weather wind upwards Mr Press preached from Acts 2nd chapter 17th & 18th verses in the morning and from Epherions the 2nd chapter 13th verse in the afternoon

Monday 11
Cold showery weather wind upwards Carters not at work – R Baker and Wm Catt with the turn in their room[395] to day removing 66 loads of dung

[395] Took their turn.

Master Catt & Master Easton filled the carts see Saturday last above – put one of my calves into the Sandhole seven acres to day among the others

Tuesday 12
A dirty morning a drying day not much rain chiefly cloudy wind upwards – Horses went for chalk – Master Catt Master Baker and Master Easton with the oxen at road work down at Christion river put the cows into the Flatt field to night first time

Wednesday 13
Not much sun nor much rain nor much wind nor very warm now very cold but a little of all – wind upwards – Henry & Ben with the horses removed 11 loads of dung shovelling see last Saturday – and fetched 4 loads of gravel from the crossways and laid one against the stable door 1 against Mrs Waters Court Gate and 2 in the track before my fore door – Catt Baker & Easton with the oxen and cart with my fathers oxen and 3 carts gravelling below Bennetts House removed the gravel from crossways

Thursday 14
A clear sunny morning some clouds in The day somewhat cold for summer wind upwards Horses removed 31 loads of dung at Pilly see May 18th 70 loads & 19th 80 loads in all 181 loads of Ruff dung made in the Pilly yard and 139 loads in the Sandhill yard this year – (see opposite page) Catt Baker & Easton with the oxen gravelling on the roads with my fathers oxen & carts

Friday 15
A cold cloudy morning afterwards warm summer like weather still mild evening wind upwards horses shiming – Carters and Master Grant Wm Catt with them in both hop gardens – Catt Baker & Easton with the oxen as yesterday

Saturday 16
A cold cloudy morning some sleet rain in the afternoon windy towards night wind upwards and cold – All the teams and men as yesterday

Sunday 17
Cold cloudy weather some sun wind upwards Mr Press preached from Romans the 14th chapter the 3 first words of the 22nd verse at Heathfield Chapel in the morning (namely) 'Hast thou faith' – and from Galatians the 1st Chapter and the 23rd & 24th verses at Bucksteep in the evening

Monday 18
A very cold cloudy morning some sun in the afternoon wind upwards – Horses harrowed the the Freehold field and fetched some chalk from the 5 Bell river Master Catt Master Baker and Master Grant began mow seeds today in the lower Comwish 5 acre field Easton and some Road men laid a stone pinnock across the road below Mr Bennett's House against Christion river J T Lade Wm Catt & Joel Grant had my oxen with the Summertree oxen ploughed the sides of the road along by my Sandhill hop garden hedge

Tuesday 19
Some cloud and some sun wind upwards borrowed fathers violet mare & 6 Summertree oxen and sett them to work with my 3 horses and one pair of oxen with 4 carts removed 48 loads of drift sand and mould from the Christion river into the Freehold field Henry Hoad shelved the carts Ben Catt & Joel Grant drove between Master J T Lade and Easton filled the carts mowers finished mowing my seed about 4 O'clock this afternoon and began the Summertree seeds Wm Catt boseling jobs

Wednesday 20
Much the same weather today as yesterday all the men the same as yesterday except G Guy and Wm Catt helping grub the stubs and fill the cart NB it was somewhat warmer than yesterday

Thursday 21
Not quite so warm as yesterday wind upwards – Baker Catt and Grant finished mowing Summer tree seeds this morning before 7 O'clock afterwards Master Baker helped the moulders – Catt and Grant chopping the young hops – Teams as on yesterday and Tuesday they removed 48 loads Tuesday 50 loads yesterday and 40 loads to day 138 loads in all

Friday 22
A warm sunny forenoon cloudy afternoon wind upwards Horses fetched [a] load of chalk from Amberstone this forenoon haying in the afternoon Master Lade Master Baker Silas Brook (Ben Catt H Hoad the carters) Joel Grant Dame Grant and Fanny Gurr haying this afternoon in my 5 acres carried 3 loads which is all there was to the Sandhill rickstede did not unload any – Catt his boy Willm and master Grant hop chopping – Eastone shovelling in the Westmeadow hop garden and dug a por[396] hole at the

[396] Post.

flatfield Hive gate[397] against the road Master Winchester the carpenter sett up a new post there – My wife went with her brother & sisters to Ticehurst to the Funeral of their uncle Robert Pattenden who died last Friday and was brought to Burwash to be buried this afternoon

Saturday 23
Cold cloudy weather nearly all day some sleet rain wind upwards – Horses & carters mouling in the Freehold field etc carrying hay in the afternoon all the men and boys except Eastone helped two loads of hay out of the Gravelpittfield and unloaded the 3 loads we loaded up yesterday Henry Hoad stacked all the 5 loads of seed hay in the Sandhill rick stedle – In the forenoon all the men were as on yesterday except Baker who was spreading mould in the Freehold field

Sunday 24
Not so cloudy as yesterday wind upwards Mr Press preached at Heathfield Chapel from Romans the 3rd Chapter the 28th verse in the morning

Monday 25
Cold weather some sleet rain it is hitherto a remarkable cold summer so that sometimes it is almost like winter and at the times for a short time perhaps the sun shines so warm it makes us quite cheerful the wind has kept very steady in the northeast for some time past and chiefly very cold when the sun does not shine – Horses fetched home some Summertree chalk oxen with them Do Master Catt chopping young hops Master Baker spreading mould in the Freehold field Eastone not at work rest on Summertree account except Wm Catt who was with his father as above

Tuesday 26
We had more sun to day than we have had for a few days past otherwise the weather was much the same – R Baker & Henry Hoad with the horses & two carts removed 20 loads of mould from the Christian river to the Freehold field – Ben helpt his father & brother chopping young hops rest as yesterday

Wednesday 27
A cold cloudy morning some sun in the afternoon wind northeast wards – H Hoad and R Baker as yesterday they removed 20 loads to day and with what was removed on the 19th 20th & 21st Inst is 178 loads in all from the Christian river to the Freehold field Catt and two boys chopping &

[397] Heave-gate.

shoveling hops at Pilly Eastone not at work as I have seen – E Erry thatched the Sandhill hay stack – some body has put the calves in my Comwish field

Thursday 28
The weather was more mild to day than it has been for some days the wind has been up wards and very cold for 3 weeks past so that things have made but small improvement in growing particularly the seeds grass oats & fruits I have not seen one May Bug all the spring – Through mercy there is now an appearance of better weather the wind changed this afternoon about 4 O'clock from the north east to the southwest – Horses began plough up the 5 acres – Wm Catt chopping hops Catt shovelling hops Eastone Do R Baker spreading mould & chopping hops etc E Erry thatched a cone of hay at Pilly & mended the stall

Friday 29
Warm day not many cloud wind downwards but very still – Horses plough – Master Catt & Master Baker with my oxen & a pair of Summertree oxen gravelling etc on the roads at Christian River Eastone & Will Catt finished chopping and shovelling Hops etc

Saturday 30
A warm day wind south & southwest The ground has been very dry and the roads very dusty but there is now at this very time (8 O'clock evening) A still warm gentle pleasant shower – Horses at plough – Will Catt spuding chisttes in the Flatfield Baker Catt & Eastone with 3 carts gravelling etc

Sunday 1 July
Cloudy & smory walking mild weather and some little sun wind southern Mr Press preached at Heathfield Chapel this morning from Jerimiah 3 chapter   Verse

Monday 2
Mild weather it rained nearly all day and if any but very little sun all day The wind is got back to the northeast again Horses at plough Master Catt not at work boy at Summertree – Baker & Eastone gravelling one of my carts and one Summertree cart etc

Tuesday 3
Very cold cloudy weather for the time of the year some sun wind northeast – Horses at plough Easton & Baker clearing out Pilly & Comwish barns etc Killed 2 rats – Master Catt not at work NB It was a Wet morning

Wednesday 4
Warmer weather and more sun than yesterday wind northeast & northwest – Horses finished plough in the 5 acres for a fallow – Baker & Eastone at Padgham to day on the road account – Catt shovelling up dung at the great doors of the barn etc

Thursday 5
A pleasant day wind west wards – Horses harrowed the 5 acres etc – Baker and Eastone as yesterday – Catt & oxen gravelling Master Winchester the carpenter pulled up the comwish barns floor etc

Friday 6
A warm sunny morning some rain in the afternoon cloudy evening wind west and southwest Baker Eastone Carters & Horses removed 52 loads of mould from the lower hindland of the 5 acres up into the field – Catt cleared the Comwish Barn out The 4 year old cow went to bull F[?] Lades bull

Saturday 7
Cold & cloudy some rain afternoon & evening wind northeast – Baker Eastone etc 48 loads see yesterday – Catt diging up mould before my house little more the ½ day rest time gardening for Mrs Waters

Sunday 8
A mild day some clouds wind northeast & northwest – Mr Press preached from Romans 8 Chapter the & verses[398] in the morning Brother William Oxley was at Chapel to day with his mistress & young mother etc they went to Bucksteep and I spent part of the afternoon with them

Monday 9
Cloudy and some rain this morning a fine afternoon wind northwest & west – Horses went for Beach for Comwish Barn to lay under the new floor – Summertree horses Do Do Master Catt boseling chiefly mould spreading in the 5 acres Wm his boy Do ½ day on Sandhole which J T Lade keeps account on Eastone & Baker with a pair of Summertree and a pair of my oxen graveling on the roads

Tuesday 10
A warm pleasant day some clouds wind westerly quarters – Horses began

---

[398] Gaps left in the original.

sturr[399] the Freehold field – Wm Catt was with H Hoad with the horses Ben Catt J T Lade Baker & Eastone moulding in the 5 acres removed 50 loads NB J T Lade and Ben were not moulding all day Winchesters felled some trees for repairs on the Pilly farm to day Master Catt was gardening for Mrs Waters – Summertree sheep were shorn to day at Bucksteep – My w[h]ite sow farrowed this morning 2 very small live pigs and 3 dead ones 2 of them midling size and 1 very large a sort of double pig 5 in all – two living and three dead

Wednesday 11
A warm sunny day cloudy evening wind chiefly southwest and west but still – Horses at plough on yesterday – Catt Baker Eastone & Ben Catt removed 66 loads of mould in the 5 acres – with Summertree and my oxen see yesterday

Thursday 12
Mild still weather some clouds wind northeast Horses Henry Hoad and Wm Catt at plough – Catt Baker & Eastone with Ben Catt the under carter with Summertree and my oxen mouling removed 66 loads in the 5 acres see yesterday & Tuesday – Settled with Master Catt to night for all his and his boys work up to this night

Friday 13
A warm summer day not much wind Horses sturring or ploughing in the Freehold field with Fathers wheel plough ½ day and ½ day ploughing in tares in the middle Crocers Joel Grant was with them ploughing in tares – rest as on yester day removed 58 loads of mould – Master Launkhurst (and road men) chopping among the young hops & hoeing up potatoes

Saturday 14
Warm weather some but not much rain in the afternoon wind southwest chiefly calm Henry Hoad and Wm Catt with the horses shiming hops – moulders removed 70 loads – Thursday Master Launkhurst chopping among the young Hops & hoeing up the potatoes – Settled with Master Baker for his work to night

Sunday 15
A warm day it rained from about 10 O'clock till about ½ past 3 O'clock a heavy shower made the road quite dirty where they had been dirty – Wind blowed harder than it has done lately from the southwest – Mr Press

[399] Stir, harrow.

preached at the Heathfield Chapel this morning from the 125 Psalm the first verse and at Bucksteep in the evening from Ephesians the 6th Chapter the 18th & 19th verses

Monday 16
A warm sunny day wind upwards and still – Summertree and my teams fetched 2 loads of beach to Comwish Barn Eastone and Wm Catt spreading mould in my Comwish 5 acres – The rest began mow the Sandhole Barn Meadow to day – Master Launkhurst hoeing up potatoes

Tuesday 17
A warm sunny day cloudy evening wind southwest – Horses carters sowed the Pilly hop garden with turnips and harrowed them in and ploughed the headlands and finished sturing the Freehold field (first time) sturing) – etc Eastone helped emty the Lime Kiln on Summertree account ½ day – rest time spreading mould see yesterday – Wm Catt Summertree account all day Baker Catt & Grant finished mowing the Sandhole meadows etc and began my house meadow this evening – Master Launkhurst hoeing up potatoes Putt the horses in the Comwish field – and took a calf of fathers to keep and put it among mine at Comwish

Wednesday 18
A warm day wind northeast Horses & Carters ploughing in tares see last Friday – Joel Grant helpt them – Eastone and Wm Catt spreading mould in the 5 acres Master Launkhurst among the young hops mowers finished the house meadow & began the Hollow Meadow

Thursday 19
A very warm day wind eastward Horses as yesterday Wm Catt with them [k]nocking off sowthistle heads – Eastone spreading mould before noon took up part of a fence at Comwish and haying in the afternoon I have not seen any thing of Master Launkhurst to day I believe he was not at work for me to day – I understand that Master Launkhurst is unwell which I did not know when I wrote the above

Friday 20
Warm weather some little rain not much wind east and other quarters – Horses ploughing in tares Joel Grant & Wm Catt as on yesterday with them The mowers finished the hollow meadow last night or to day morning and mowed part of the Old Sandhill field and began the Pilly meadow to day – Eastone at work on the Summertree account Grass did not hay near to fast as yesterday forgot there was some thunder in the night and cloudy to day

Saturday 21
Mild weather cloudy and some rain wind chiefly southwest – Horses as on yesterday – Wm Catt has finished nocking off Sowthistle heads so he was on Summertree account to day – Mowers finished mowing grass in the Pilly meadow to night Eastone on Summertree account except a short time while I helped him making lime lump places in the Freehold field – Finished the Sandhole haying to night R Bakers wife turned part of the Hollow meadow hay for me this afternoon which is all the haying that has been done on my farms since Thursday – We have had some nice warm showers for the corn grass and vegetation the turnips were sowed last Tuesday morning I saw were some of them up this afternoon

Sunday 22
A very wett morning cloudy till noon some sun and some clouds afternoon wind southwest – The rain prevented our going to Chapel in the forenoon so we went this afternoon My wife etc etc in Mrs Waters cart and she with us Mr Press Preached from Colossians the 1st Chapter the 12th and 14th verses

Monday 23
Showery weather wind wind south west – Horses carters and Joel Grant ploughing in tares J T Lade Eastone Baker and Ben emptying the Lime Kiln put 3 loads in the Freehold field and 2 loads in the Pilly meadow and afterwards haying Bakers wife Do and cocked the House Meadows[400]

Tuesday 24
Showery weather wind southwest & south a short time – Horses finished plowing in Tares in the Middle Crocers – Eastone Catt & Baker with Ben mouling in the 5 acres remove 52 loads and J T Lade and the loaded up 2 loads of hay from the House Meadow in the afternoon – Wm Catt & Joel Grant with the horses

Wednesday 25
Weather continues showery unpleasant haying weather – Wind southwest – Eastone Henry and Ben with the horses mouling removed 40 loads of mould out of the Brook and road in to the 5 acres – Baker mowing Greenweed in the Flattfield rest on Summertree account

Thursday 26
Showery weather – wind west Horses carters boseling and haying –

[400] Heaped the hay into haycocks.

Eastone mould spreading & haying Baker mowing Greenweed and haying loaded up one load from the House Meadow and and loaded 2 loads see Tuesday – rest on Summertree account

Friday 27
Warm morning some clouds and rain in the middle of the day wind west – Horses Boseling and harrowing the Freehold field – Mrs Grant Mrs Baker and Ben Catt turned the hay in the Pilly meadow in the forenoon – Master Eastone and I haying in the Hollow Meadow and get it all in good order and should have set to getting of it up in short time afterwards but the rain came and we where forced to abandon our desire till another opportunity did no more haying afterwards – Eastone & Ben spreading mould in the 5 acres in the afternoon all the rest on Summertree account

Saturday 28
A dull cloudy day a very few drops of rain about noon some sun in the evening wind still and at times scarce perceptible chiefly upwards – Eastone and the Carters with the horses & oxen removed 38 load of mould from the Headlands of the 5 acres out into the field – Baker mowing green weed in the Flattfield Bakers wife and Mrs Grant haying ½ day all the rest on Summertree account till night about 4 O'clock the Summertree folk and rest sett too and loaded all the hay in the Hollow meadow up on 3 waggons and sett them in and against the Comwish rick steddle to be unloaded at a suitable opportunity – Settled with Master Eastone to night

Sunday 29
A warm sunny day cloudy and a few drops of rain in the evening wind southwest Mr Press preached at Heathfield Chapel this morning from 2nd Epistle to the Thessulonions the 3rd chapter and the 1st verse – There was a seal[401] to Mr Press's ministry received in as a member to our church to day, Hannah Kemp of Warbleton daughter to Mr Kemp of Warbleton near Punnetts Town – May the Lord confirm in heaven what we have this day done on earth and may all our souls be comforted in the Holy Ghost and may he add unto our number many more of such as shall be eternally saved!!

Monday 30
Very wett weather all day wind south west – Horses plowing up mould in the 5 acres in the morning and Eastone with them but it being so wett and

[401] Reward.

dirty they did not do any thing else for me

Tuesday 31
Foggy all day and some rain wind southeast Horses and carters removed 28 loads of mould out of the Green lane into the Freehold field – Baker spreading Mould – Catt loping trees on Pilly farm rest on Summertree account

Wednesday 1 August
Cloudy some rain and sun towards night Wind westwards – Carters horses Eastone and Baker mowing in the 5 acres removed 50 loads Master Catt finished his job and helped them a little while Wm Catt spreading Dame Baker and Dame Grant haying ½ day – all of us and Summertree people cleared the Sandhole field of one large load of hay and unloaded the 3 loads that were loaded up on Saturday

Thursday 2
This is the Best Haying Day we have had for many Day still Wind upwards some Clouds in the evening Henry Hoad and Master Catt unloaded the Hay we loaded up last night and finised the stack at Comwish in 4 loads Wm Catt wass with them they were afterwards Haying at Pilly Ben Catt Eastone and Baker with the Horses removed 39 loads of Mould in the 5 acres ½ day ½ day Haying at Pilly Dame Grant and Dame Baker all Day long Streeter ½ Day Fanny Gurr part of the afternoon and Master Lade and Master Grant helping them a while cleared the Pilly Meadow of about 5 loads of Hay and stacked it all up in the Pilly Rick steddle which finised my Haying for this year It hass been verry unfavourable weather all the Haying but I believe by keeping off it well waited on we have got it nearly all up in good fair order I sold some oats for Mrs Waters at market to Day for 19 shillings

Friday 3
Cloudy and some Rain and but little sun still weather Wind Northeast and East and Southeast chiefly Carters and Easton Moulding in the 5 acres removed 55 loads Mr R Winchester the Carpenter wass here to day all day seeing about laying the new Floor at Comwish Barn etc Mr Burges the Mason wass there about laying the Foundations Sold some Wheat this morning to Mr Balcomb at 12£ 12s per Load Catt Baker and Grant began mow Trefoil in the 9 acres at Sandhole namely the Kiln field

Saturday 4
A warm sunny Day Wind Eastwards And southeast Carter Eastone with

Horses as yesterday removed 50 loads rest workmen as on yesterday

Sunday 5

A warm summers Day Wind Eastwards etc Mr Press wass gone to London to day Mr Parris preached at Heathfield Chapel in his room to day from the 104 Psalm the 34th Verse in the morning

Monday 6

Not so warm and more cloudy than yesterday some appearance of approaching rain at time to Day Wind in the Westerly Quarters chiefly Horses at Plough shiming the 5 acres first time Eastone with the Oxen and Cart Moulding removed 21 loads into 5 acres from the Lower Headland and out of road along by the Hop gardens Hedge above Master Grant Our 3 Yearling Heifer wass lost last Saturday and found to Day in the new Cattle Yard in Dallington Parish

Tuesday 7

A warm sunny Day some Clouds and some rain Wind southwest chiefly Horses at Plough Oxen Eastone and Joel Grant carried 11 Quarters of Mrs Waters's Oats from the Pilly Barn to Mr Everest's Gardener Street I sold them to him last Thursday at Half Moon Market for 19s per Quarter Baker Catt and Grant cleaned them yesterday a second time Wm Catt his Boy spreading mould in the 5 acres to Day he wass a looking after the Heifer[402] all day yesterday rest on the Summertree account to Day

Wednesday 8

A verry Wett Day Wind Southwest Horses at Plough part of the Day Eastone and Wm Catt spreading mould part of the Day rest on summer tree account

Thursday 9

Showry Weather Wind Southwest Horses at Plough Eastone and Wm Catt finised spreading mould in the five acres about noon there hass been 755 Loads of mould carried out and spread in that field this year which hass heald[403] it almost all over and it is late in the year. Wm Catt went to spreading mould in the Freehold field and Eastone went to work Diging a fresh Watering at the Sandhole Close in the afternoon My Other Sow farrowed to night I sett up with her and she finised about midnight only 4 Wite Pigs all living and doing well

[402] Searching for the heifer.
[403] Covered.

Friday 10
Showry Weather Wind Southwest Horses at Plough Eastone road work with the Oxen ½ Day and ½ Day Diging watering at Sandhill Close Wm Catt finised spreading mould ½ Day. And ½ Day at Summertree all the rest at Summertree Carpenter sawing for Comwish Barn

Saturday 11
Showry Weather Wind Wist etc Horses at Plough Eastone Diging Watering etc all the rest on Summertree account Carpenters as yesterday

Sunday 12
One Shower about ½ past 4 O'Clock rest fine Weather Wind Westwards chiefly Mr Press preached at the Heathfield Chapel this morning from the 1st Epistle Thessalonians 1 chapter the 4th 5th and 6th Verses and from the 1st Epistle of Timothy 1 chapter part of the 11th Verse viz 'the Glorious Gospel of the blessed God' at Bucksteep in the evening

Monday 13
Some Couds rain in the evening Wind Westerley Quarters Horses at Plough All the rest on Summertree account Masons and Carpenters at Comwish Barns Floor

Tuesday 14
Wett weather nearly all day Wind as yesterday Carter finised their field rest as on yesterday Summertree People took their 2 Calves away from among mine at Comwish Carpenters all day Masons ½ day

Wednesday 15
A Drying Day Winds upwards Horses began start the Freehold field the 2nd time Carpenters laying the Barn Floor at Comwish the Masons finised their work yesterday about noon they were at work of Mrs Waters's well to day My Brother David and I had Fathers Colt what we weaned a few Days ago into Fathers Grimes Brook Carpenters etc

Thursday 16
Warm Growing Weather wind southwest etc Horses harrowed the middle Crocers rest at Summertree

Friday 17
Warm weather some Rain Wind many ways Horses Harrowed the 5 Acres etc

Saturday 18
A warm Close Cloudy day and but little wind Wind Westwards Horses at Plough and Eastone with the Oxen spreading Lime in the Freehold Field rest began mow peas at Summertree etc

Sunday 19
A clear warm summers Day Wind upwards Mr Press preached at Heathfield Chapel from Acts the   chapter latter part of the 26th Verse in the morning and from Acts the 3rd Chapter and the 22nd and 23rd Verses in the afternoon

Monday 20
Quite a summers Day Horses at Plough Mowers finised mowing the Summertree peas and began mow mine in the C M field[404] at Pilly the Summertree Folk carried all theirs to Day I believe there was 10 small loads of 7½ acres Carpenters

Tuesday 21
Still warm day Horses at Plough Eastone finised spreading Lime with the Oxen in the Freehold field and collected the Bark together and laid up in the Pilly Lodge Mowers finised mowing peas about noon at work on the Summertree account afterwards carpenters etc Mr Catt helpt Eastone etc

Wednesday 22
Verry warm Wind upwards – Horses plough Eastone finished spreading lime about noon collected the bark together and laid up in the Pilly Lodge in the afternoon went to Pevensey for Coals Wm Catt went with them Broak a Hind Exel[405] there Ben tending Hogs at Summertree Eastone Hoeing turnips etc Carpenters on Both farms etc

Thursday 23
Warm still Day Horses at plough Eastone Master Catt and Wm Catt hoeing Turnips Carpenters etc rest on Summertree account

Friday 24
Warm weather Horses Carters unloaded the coal at the Pilly Oast Finised sturring the Freehold field and began Middle Crocers Eastone Master Catt Wm Catt and Master Launkhurst Hoeing Turnips etc Master Catt began reap the Lower Crocers tonight Carpenters etc Master Pankhurst put a

---

[404] Calves Meadow.
[405] Axle.

New Exel Tree to the narrow Wheel Waggon

Saturday 25
A Close Foggy and Cloudy Day Wind West and Southwest but little sun there hass been scarce any clouds to be seen all the week till to Day Horses at Plough in the Middle Crocers till noon Easton and Launkhurst finised Hoeing turnips and began chop the young Hops till noon wen they were all a Pea Harvesting Built a stack of 4 Loads in the Pilly Rick steddle and put 1 Load in the Barn 5 loads in all of from 2 Acres of Ground the Calves Meadow field Catt and Boy Reeping etc There wass shocking news Brought to our ears this morning of the Death of Master Wm Catt senior of Bathhurst in this Parish whilst Master Henty and he wass youking a Cow to prevent her getting out after she wass lett loose the inraged Beast turned round with great force and struck Master Catt on his Head Just above his forehead and broke a great Hole in his scull so that he never spoke afterward this wass done last night about 7 O'Clock and he Died this morning about six O'Clock he wass Master Catts Father that works for me and lives in my Pilly House what an uncertain thing is Life and how awful to Die out [of] Christ and what a mercy to have Good Hope through Christ to the former sudden Death is sudden Distruction to the Latter sudden death is sudden Glory I believe Master Catt wass a Good Man he seemed a great Lover of the Truth but never for much conversation he always attended very steaddy at Heathfield Chapel and wass there twice last Sabbath Day

Sunday 26
Cloudy and some Misty rain Wind Southwest Mr Press preached of Heathfield Chapel in the morning from 1 Chapter Phillipians the 6th Verse

Monday 27
Cold Cloudy Weather some rain Wind Northeast some little sun at times in the afternoon Horses at Plough in the Middle Crocers Catt and Boy a Reeping Pankhurst Mowing Errey thatched the Pea stack

Tuesday 28
Dull Cloudy weather and some rain and verry cold Northeast Wind The difference between this Day and all last week is surprising last week it wass so verrry Hot and this week it is so Cold and Winterley Horses Plough in the Middle Crocers Henry went to Master Catts funeral this afternoon and I went to Plough in his room see last Saturday Catts Boys Reeping

Reaping and binding

Wednesday 29
Wett weather all most All Day wind Northeast the Carters and Horses wass a going to Moul the Bond in the Sandhill Close if it had not rained Catt and Boys could not Reep so they threshed some Peas in the Pilly Barn

Thursday 30
A warm Foggy morning some little sun in the afternoon Wind SW Horses at Plough in the Calves Meadow field at Pilly a Pea Gratten Catt and Boys Reeping

Friday 31
Showry weather Wind SW All as on yesterday

Saturday 1 September
Cloudy Day some rain Wind chiefly Southwest Horses went for Beach and left it on Bodle Street Green Catt and Boys Threshing Peas and Reeping at Pilley

Sunday 2
A mild pleasant Day Wind Northwest and West Mr Press preached a Funeral sermon for Master Wm Catt senior at the Heathfield Chapel this morning from Matthew the 24th Chapter the 44 verse see last Saturday a week ago yesterday My Dear Wife was this night about 4 minits before 10 O'clock by My Clock which I believe is about 25 minnits to fast which makes it about ½ past 9 O'clock of real time or there abouts Dilivered of A Male Child which is My second son Mr Bidwell at Rush lake Green wass her Doctor and Mrs Fanny Gurr wife of Henry Gurr is her nurse Oh that the Life that is spared and the Life that is given May both be the Lords to the salvation of both of their poor immortal souls – Amen

Monday 3
A warm Day some Clouds Wind South Henry Hoad by playing the rogue with Father's Bellhurst Men last Saturday had one of his Eyes hurt with a pebble stone so that he could not see to hold plough to day so Stephen Gurr Fathers under Carter wass at Plough with My Horses in the Middle Crocers in his room Henry wass at other jobs in the forenoon and afternoon he and I with the Oxen removed a Load of Wheat shieves from the the Lower Crocers into the Pilly Barn and loaded up a Load of Peas halm and brought up to the Sandhill Barn Master Catt and Boys finised Reeping the Lower Crocers and began the Comwish Barnfield

Tuesday 4
Showery weather Wind Southwest Henry Hoad and Ben Catt with the Horses at Plough in the Middle Crocers Catt and Boys Reeping in the Comwish Barnfield

Wednesday 5
Warm weather some little Rain Wind Northwest Horses at Plough part of the Day Master Catt and I cleaned the 3 sacks of Peas at Pilly 3 sacks of Head and about 1 Bu of tail peas his Boys were Reeping all Day Dame Grant and Dame Baker laying on Oats in the upper Crocers Master Catt and the Carters with the Horses removed them in 5 Loads in to the Pilly Barn Carpenters at work at the Pilly Oast

Thursday 6
Some rain but not Bad Harvest weather My Horses and Carters helped the Summertree people build a Wheat stack at Sandhole afterwards they Cleared the lower Crocers of the Wheat 5 Loads and 1 before makes 6 in all Catt and Boys Reeping Carpenters Etc Mr Pankhurst Began Mow Oats in the Hoads field ½ Day began about noon

Friday 7
Showry weather Wind Southwest Henry Hoad mowing Oats along with R Pankhurst in the Hoads field Benjamin had the wheel plow to the Wheelers for them to make a new one afterwards helped his Father ½ Day Reeping at Comwish

Saturday 8
A Wett forenoon some Thunder of sea wards some sun afternoon Wind Southeast chiefly Henry and Pankhurst began Mow Barley in the Pilly plat Ben with his Father Reeping Master Catt and Boys threshed some new wheat at Pilly whilst it rained

Sunday 9
Showry weather more sun than yesterday Wind south a verry Blusterous evening Mr Press preached at Heathfield Chapel this morning from Hosea the 2nd Cha and the Verse and at Bucksteep in the evening from Ephesians the 1st chapter and the Verse

Monday 10
A verry Wett Stormy Day Wind Southwest Men did little or nothing verry Bad Harvest weather

Tuesday 11

A Drying Westerley Wind Henry and Pankhurst mowing oats in the Dawn etc etc Ben with his Father and Boys Reeping etc

Wednesday 12

Cloudy Showry weather got up a Load of Wheat sheeves in the morning they were mowing and Reeping etc afterwards put 2 Loads of sheeves into the Comwish Barn to night but not in good order

Thursday 13

Showry Weather Pankhurst finised mowing Oats Henery and Ben Reeping with Master Catt and Boys till noon when Pankhurst Master Catt Ben and I with the Horses Built a Wheat stack of 6 Loads at Comwish in the afternoon

Friday 14

Verry Showry weather but little Harvesting done Henry with the Horses Carried some wheat straw from Pilly to Comwish to Thatch the Wheat stack with and removed 8 sacks of Oats for Mrs Waters from the New Castle House at Dallington to Mr Bidwell the Doctor at Rushlake Green It is verry Wett Harvest and by all appearance a Great deal of Corn must be spilt

Saturday 15

Some Rain but on the whole a better Day than we have had any one before some Days the Wind is more upwards Carters Pankhurst Catt and Boys finised My Reeping for the year and got up one Load and turned the Pilly plat Barley and the Hoadsfield Oats etc

Sunday 16

Cloudy and some few Drops of Rain Wind NW Mr Press preached at Heathfield Chapel

Monday 17

Showery Weather but not so Bad as it hass been Wind NW We began Hop to Day in the West Meadow Hop garden Master Catts Drys at Pilly Oast Master Eastone etc Rd Pankhurst Pulled poles to 8 Bins Carters and Horses Carried the Barley from Pilly plat to Sandhill Wm Winchester one of the Hoppers and they got up 2 Loads of Oats from the Dawn and put into the Pilly Barn in the afternoon Wm Catt with My Oxen and Cart Carries the hop to the Oast etc NB finised Wheat Harvest this morning Master Erry thetched the Wheat stack

Tuesday 18
Showry Weather Wind NW Horses Carters and I Carried the Barley yesterday from the Pilly plat to the Sandhill Barn that was done yesterday I have made a mistake about it's being to day they Carried the Oats from the Hoads field to the Comwish and 2 More Loads of Oats from the Dawn to the Pilly to Day Summertree team Helped us in the afternoon Master Streeter and Wm Winchester and I laid on etc there wass 7 loads in the Hoadsfield

Wednesday 19
Showry Weather Wind W Horses and Carters Bosseling Hoppers as usual

Thursday 20
Showry Weather finised Harvest this afternoon

Friday 21
Showry Weather Horses and Carters Bosseling I Bought a Rider[406] to night of Mr Sweetman the Glover for 10£

Saturday 22
Showry weather Horses and Carters Bosseling It hass been a verry gagery Harvest and I doubt not but that a Great Deal of Corn is spilt but through Mercy I hope there is none of Mine that will catch much hurt.

Sunday 23
Showry Weather Mr Press preached at Heathfield to day

Monday 24
Showry Weather Horses and Carters carried 7 Pockets of Hops to Cate Street[407] this morning and fetched some Oats from Dallington for Mrs Waters and fetched some trees from the Old field to Pilly fostel the Hopers finised My West meadow Hop garden and began the Sandhole garden to night etc etc Carpenters at Pilly etc

Tuesday 25
Showry Weather Horses began Warp in the 5 Acres with the 2 bar plow

Wednesday 26
Showry Weather Horses at Plough etc Mr H Hoad was unwell Master Baker went to Plough in his room to Day

[406] Horse for riding.
[407] Cade Street.

Thursday 27
Horses at Plough

Friday 28
Horses at Plough

Saturday 29
Horses at Plough

Sunday 30
Mr Press is gone to London and Mr Parris Preached at Heathfield Chapel in his room

Monday 1 October
Horses at Plough etc

Tuesday 2
Horses at Plough etc

Wednesday 3
Horses at Plough etc Hopers finised the Sandhole garden and began my Pilly garden There is 2 More Bins than there wass when they wass in My other Hop garden J T Lade helpt pull poles see Monday 17th September

Thursday 4
The weather has been showry many Days past Wind Southwest it wass Wett weather to Day other wise they would have finised Hoping to Day Horses at Plough

Friday 5
Better weather than we have had lately finised Hoping about noon Horses at Plough Pole pullers throwed some Old Hop bines over into the Pilly yard this afternoon etc

Saturday 6
A pleasant Day Horses at Plough in the Free hold field Master Catt and Boys striping and stacking Hop poles at Pilly Master Baker threshing at Cornwish

Sunday 7
Cloudy but verry little rain Mr Press preached at Heathfield Chapel and at Bucksteep to day My wife and I had our second Child Baptised to Day His name is Othniel see pages 1st - 613 v Josh 15 - 17 v

Monday 8
Showry Weather Master Catt and Harry laying Hops Master Baker and Ben Catt threshing Wheat at Comwish

Friday
Moved to the Sandhills House etc We growed about 39:3:14 Hops this year and Sold some at 46s per Hd in London and the rest at home some for 42 and some for 45 shillings per Hundred [weight] Bought 4 Steers coming 3 years old at Mayfield fair for 38£ and a Heifer of My Father for 11£ and 14 lambs and 7 Old sheep of J T Lade from Summertree Farm for 15£.15s Also exchanged a Horse for a Colt at Battle Fair with Drowley and Gave 8 Guineas the Boot and whilst we were settling his men exchanged the Colt for another not so large nor worth so much as what we Dealt for by 3 or 4£ So no more Dealings with Mr Drowley Horse Cheater Henry went to Mr Maningtons at Wighter for about a fortnight he Bargained to stop the winter but would not but come Back to me again giving Mr Mannington and me both bad usage R Baker hass been with the Horses ever since Henry Hoad first left them since the wheat sowing they have been at Bosseling jobs Agreed with R B for 2s per week till Lady tide Master Catt hass Cutt a little shaw in the upper Crocers against Mr Lade's Huglets Wood and a Little against the Curlsdown in the same field and mend the Hedges between the Middle Crocers and the Huglets wood also cutt part of the Shaw at the Bottom of the Pilly Meadow and Made the Hedge against the Road at Christians River and moved the Hedge along the Top of the Pilly hop Garden and made the Hedge on the Eastside and along the Bottom of Ditto Master Grant Made a new Ditch and made that part of the Hedge the Bellongs to me on the North side of the Old field against Mr T Lades Bakhouse field he also made the Hedge on the West side of the same field against the slips and the High road Master Sellen made the Hedge and cutt the shaw in the slips against the High Road Master Grant Cutt and Grubed the Hedge between the upper and the lower Comwish fields and Henry Hoad made the Hedge between the Lower Comwish field and the Five Acres and Master Catt made a Little piece of Hedge and cut the Fright[408] about and against the Pond at Comwish which is all the Wood cutting I have had done this Winter Master Catt and his Boys have done the threshing up the Pilly Barn and Henry Hoad at the Comwish Barn and the Carters and he in the Home Barn at least principally so I hope the Lord will

[408] Frith.

inable me to bear all with patience This is an uncommon Bad year with me It seems as if I should not grow but verry Little more than Corn enough for My Family and Workmen's Consumption Although I Bought all my seed wheat last Auttumm and not sold any only to my Work men!!!
February 12 1822 Nicholas Oxley

1822

Monday 28 January
Both sows went to Hog

Saturday 9 February
Began Fatt 7 old Ewes with turnips and Barley

Monday 11
A yearling Calf struck and Died

Sunday 24
A yearling lamb Died A fine day one of My Fatting Ewes had a lamb

Monday 25
Horses at Plough in the 9 Acres at Comwish one of Summertree Horses with them

Tuesday 26
Ditto

Wednesday 27
Removing Mould from the Road in the 3 Acres 2 Men and a Boy with Horses and Oxen

Thursday 28
Ditto

Friday 1 March
At Plough

Saturday 2
2 Men and a Boy with Horses and Oxen remove Loads of Good root Dung from the Pilly plat into the Pilly Hop garden

Monday 4
Plough

Tuesday 5
A Man and 2 Boys Removing Wood and Clearing the shaws in the Upper Crocers NB Master Baker the Carter hass been Ill some Days so that Henry Hoad hass been Obliged to work with the team in his room

Wednesday 6
Windy Wett weather all Day we have not had so much Rain before a long

time It hass been an uncommonly fine winter but little rain and verry trifulling of Frost or snow since Christmas

[*Thursday 7*]
Windy but not much rain Sent a Hog to the workhouse it weighed 39 stone 2 lbs Henry Hoad with the Horses went with it and did some other Boseling jobs Master Catt and His Boy Ditching in the Road against the Sandhill Hop Garden he had 2 Bu of wheat and 1 Bu of Oats to Day Master Nicolls Hop diging My Cherry Cow Calved a Bull Calf Ben Catt Hunting after a Bacon rack My Wife Bargained with one of Master John Avards Girls for a Maid for to come here at Ladetide[409] but how and on what condition I know not

Friday 8
Showry weather Horses at Plough Catt and Nicolls as yesterday Master G Jack Grant and Easton finised Diging Summertree Hops and where afterwards Diging Hops in my West Meadow Hop garden

Saturday 9
Horses finished ploughing the 9 acres & carried Master Grant 25 faggots etc Master Catt and his boy and Wm Burgess 15 sacks & 2 Bu of wheat the last of the wheat at the Pilly for this year – Nicolls Eastone Grant & his boy Joel hop digging Showery windy weather

Sunday 10
Windy & wet forenoon – The Colly heifer which I brought of my father in the autumn last calved a cow calf this afternoon

Monday 11
Gentle showers

Friday 22
I forgot the particulars of every day between this day and the day named above but they have carried 30 loads of Good Old Rott Dung and 40 loads of New rough Dung into the Pilly hop garden etc and yesterday Summertree team and mine sowed oat seed and harrowed the Lower Crocer to day my carters and team worked for them in their 10 acres sowing oats and peas – etc etc uncommonly mild pleasant weather the wheats on the ground look nicely

[409] Lady Day: 25 March.

Monday 15 April

Since this time above mentioned we have sowed the 9 acres at Comwish with oats and seeds etc Master Catt has cut 1564 Hoath Faggots etc and other men and boys with him have finished digging and dressing all the hops and began pole etc Henry Hoad left me at Lady tide after having lived with me (excepting a fortnight that he went to Wighten) for 3 years by half yearly bargains altering his wages and settling with him every ½ year giving him the liberty to go away every time before we bargained again – Also Mary Tedham left us after having lived with us about 42 weeks My youngest child Othniel has been very ill with inflammation on his lungs but is now through mercy better – sold on the 13th inst to Mr Arcoll 13 Tay sheep a pair of oxen a pair of steer and a 4 year old barren of my stock and an old barren cow of the Summertree stock for 55£ !!

April 15

The five year old cow calved a cow calf

Sunday [21 or 28] April

The Cherry Cow went to my fathers bull

Tuesday 7 May

Between this and last 15th April Master Catt hass cut the hoath at the bottom of the Freehold 1211 faggots which makes 2775 Hoath Faggots in all – All of which the Summertree people have took away.

1823

Monday 29 September
Cowden Work

Master Hutchinson & Benjamin Morley with 3 horses at plough warping the 5 acre Hodges – James Martin & James Bray warping the 4 acre Hodges – John Martin & Jerry Longley with the oxen warping in the Prinkle field – Master Bray & his boy threshing wheat – Master Bradford & his son Tom pulling poles – Finished hoping to day & paid the hoppers off at 2d per bushell

Tuesday 30

A showery day – Hutchinson his mate & 3 horses sowing roling & harrowing tares about 3½ acres in the Colvers – Martin threshing oats – Oxen plough in the Prinkle field Bray & his boys threshing wheat – Bradford stripping hop poles – my brother & I sold 4 rams[?] & a barren cow to Mr Noakes for 48£ 10s from the marsh

Wednesday 1 October
Wett day – Hutchinson Morley & Horses at plough – Jo Martin threshing oats Bray & his boy threshing wheat – Js Martin and Jerry bagging hops

Thursday 2
Horses at harrowing in the tares in the Colvers and carried 11 sacks & 12 Bu wheat to Wd Mill Oxen plough in the Prinkle field – Bray & boys threshing wheat Jas Martin threshing oats – Bradford stripping hop poles – Showery frosty morning John Pattenden & Mr Gorringe were here to day

Friday 3
Horses at plough in Squirefield Oxen Do in the Prinkle field – Bray & boys threshing Jas Martin helped them clean up some seed wheat in the afternoon – Jas Martin threshing oats in the morning – Bradford stripping hop poles – I paid my Warbleton hoppers to night at Bucksteep – A Court Leet was held to day at Windmill Hill my brother David and I were there

Saturday 4
Fine weather Horses at plough In the Squirefield Oxen Do in The Prinklefield Jas Martin threshing oats my brother and he & I finished putting up the hops – Bray & boys threshing wheat – Bradfords stripping poles – P Pankhurst chipping[410] and altering the strike plough etc Hetty Bradford who has lived with us since Lady tide as our Maid servant lost her mother on last Wednesday and went to see her father told my wife today she wants to leave us for good and all

Sunday 5
Showery weather

Monday 6
Showery weather Horses & carters sowing & harrowing in wheat in the 4 acres Browning Oxen finished warping the Prinkle field Bray & his boys threshing wheat – James Martin boseling oats one more lamb this is the 13th lamb dead Bradfords stripping hop poles

Tuesday 7
A fine day Horses & carters sowing & harrowing wheat in the Blackmans – Oxen dung carrying about the house – Jas Martin spreading lime in the Squirefield – Bradford stripping hop poles Bray & boy threshing – Masters

[410] Chepping.

Prinkle Farmhouse today

Thomas & Holman apprised me out of the Sandhills & Pilly farms Mr Wm Isted took the Sandhills & Mr Wm Waters Mr Thomas slept here last night one more lamb Dead – the 14th

Wednesday 8
Fine weather – Horses at plough warping in the Squirefield – Oxen cleared the Pilly & Sandhill of all my old tackling and carried it to Frankwell to be sold at their sale – Bray & boys threshing and cleaning wheat – Jas Martin spreading lime & scouring out lot furrows Bradford

Thursday 9
Showery – Horses warping Oxen dunging Bray & boys threshing peas – James Martin & Tom Bradford threshing oats

Friday 10
Showery weather – Horses at plough Oxen boseling – Threshers etc

Saturday 11
Showery weather – same as yester day except Master Bray and boys cleared

the peas – My brother David and I went to Bourne Fair and brought 19 twotoothed ewes at 19s each 28 lambs at 11s each & 1 Ram for 42s

Sunday 12
Showery weather

Monday 13
Showery weather – Master Hutchinson & Ben Morley with the Horses sett off to London with Mr Wm Harmer Thos Harmer my Fathers my Brothers and my own hops Oxen Helped them up to Windmill Hill etc Bray Boys fetched the sheep home from our Marsh which we bought at Bourne Fair Rest boseling

Tuesday 14
Some what better weather than we Have had this last few days – Bray & Boys threshing wheat rest digging up potatoes My father and my Brother David sett off to London to day with my horse and cart

Wednesday 15
Some rain – John & Jerry with the Oxen carried 100 tress[411] of Wheat straw to Ashburnham place …… Bray & Boy threshing rest digging up potatoes etc.

END OF DIARY

---

[411] Trusses, bundles.

APPENDIX 1: ACCOUNTS

After page 265 (23rd October 1817) the diary changes format. Nicholas begins the next page with all that is on Table 1 below and carries on for the next 13 pages, with a few of the actual pages of the diary left blank.

The individual tables are reproduced here and numbered Tables 1-14.

TABLE 1

Received by Nicholas Oxley for Summertree and Sandhole Bussiness between J T Lade and I in 1817 since October		£	s	d
Decr 15th	Recd of Mr T Oxley the money that was paid him over and above the amount of the appraisement	2	11	9
	Received of Martin Catt 1/2 years rent	1	10	-
1818	Recd of Mast Hoad 1/2 years rent Due Michas	1	-	-
Sept 30th	Recd of Mr Gill Banker for hops	79	8	6
Oct 3rd	of Mast D Honeysett for 2 Bu(shels) Peas		17	6
13th	of Mr Noakes for Taxes			
	1 Poor Rcd[?] At 10s in the pound	2	10	-
	Way Tax settled up to Michas 1818		10	-
	Land Tax settled up to Michas	3	8	2
	of Mr Purstglove bill for sheep	65	-	-
*NB	NB One third of the expenses for the lease to be paid by Mr Noakes and to be out sett in the first half years Rent	3	1	11 1 farthing

APPENDIX 1: ACCOUNTS

TABLE 2

1817	Account between J T Lade and I	£	s	d	
Oct 25th	Paid John Catt for 3 days work at 2s 6d		7	6	
Nov 1st	Paid Master Gurr for his son Tom 9 days at 14d per day		10	6	
8th	Paid Master Gurr for his son 6 days		7	-	
15th	Paid Master Gurr for his son 6 days		7	-	
	Paid Master Wm Grant for mowing and raking 3½ acres of stubble at 3s 6d pa		11	9	Out by 6d
22nd	Paid Master Gurr for his son 6 days		7	-	
	Bought a book for keeping accounts at Battle		8	-	
24th	Paid my Father for 24 bushels of seed wheat at 12s per bushel	14	8	-	Correct
	And for 16 bushels of seed wheat at 10s per bushel	8	0	-	Correct
	And 3 bushels of oats at 3s per bushel		9	-	Correct
	And 5 bushels of Tares at 11s per bushel	2	15	-	Correct
29th	Paid Master Gurr for his son		8	-	
Dec	Paid John Fox for an Iron Spade		4	6	
	Paid G Guy for mowing 8 acres of stubble at 2s 6d per acre	1	-	-	
	Many other things an wooden spade		5	-	
	A hand saw		4	-	
	An old sack		1	-	
	Hammer and Pincers		3	6	
	3 Large gimblets and an old trug basket			10	
6th	Paid Master Gurr for his son Toms work		6	-	
13th	Paid Master Gurr for his son Toms work		8	-	
					...continued

*13th	Paid my father for his paying for the lease of Summertree and Sandhole Farms	9	5	10
	and for his paying our appraisement	4	4	-
	Do for a stamp		10	½
	and for his paying half of Mrs Pankhurst bill to the amount of 3 0 10½	1	10	5¼
17th	Paid Mr Daw for a haycutter handle			1½
20th	Paid Master Gurr for his son Tom		6	-
25th	Paid him to the 28th inst		8	-
26th	Paid Mr Waters for 4 bushels of oats		12	-
		48	8	¼

APPENDIX 1: ACCOUNTS

TABLE 3

		£	s	d
	Money paid away to workmen and done myself & as a balance against J T Lade's work NB If I do and pay for than J T Lade has done he must balance the remainer between both			
1817				
Dec 25th	about 7 days work myself at 2/6 p/day		17	6
	Paid J Eastone 5 day at 2/6 per day		12	6
1818				
Jan 3rd	Paid Master Foot 4½ days work at 2/6		11	6
10th	Cash		12	-
18th	Cash		9	-
	Paid Jn Catt for foddering at Sandhole up to Jany 19th		2	-
24th	Paid Master Foot Cash		12	-
31st	Cash		14	-
Feb 7th	Cash		7	-
	Settled with Master Foot day work to March 14th 1818			
Mar 21st	Paid Master Foot cash		7	6
Apr 3rd	Paid Master Foot off to do no more work at present for us			
Apr 7th	Paid Master Grant cash towards his Hop poling	1	-	-

TABLE 4

	Money paid away continued	£	s	d
		48	8	¼
Jan 1st	Paid to Wm Isted for a dung cart	8	-	-
	and for 3 Horse Harrows	4	-	-
	and for a Strike Plough	1	-	-
	and for a seed cord and whip		7	-
	and for a Hind Harness bitt etc	1	5	-
12th	a dung spud		2	-
	and a ox yoke off Mr Wm Isted		6	-
13th	Paid Mr T Oxley for a lock and			
	2 keys		2	10
	Paid Jn Oxley the Blacksmith his bill	2	15	6
	Paid Master Catt for trussing straw		2	-
	Paid him for sowing tares		1	-
31st	Paid Mr Stone for 10 sacks	1	16	-
	Do half lb sack nettering[?]			7
Feb 7th	Paid Wm Grant cash towards his work	1	1	-
	Paid Mast. Foot cart 2 days day work		5	-
10	Brought ¼ to Bowder and 5 lbs shott		2	9
13th	Wm Grant wood work and	£	s	d
	hedging			
	35 rods hedges and no ditch at 4d		11	8
	per Rod			
	11 in with a ditch at 7d per Rod		6	5
	275 hop poles cutting & shaving at		4	7
	20d ph			
	15 fence poles at 1/2d per pole			7½
	58 House Faggots at 4s per hd		2	6
	200 Kiln Faggots at 3s per hd		6	-
	12 stakes at 6d per hund			3
	102 sally plants at 4d per hd			4
	Planting Do			6
	10 Bush Faggots at ½d faggot			5
	Total amount	1	13	1¼
	Paid him before	1	1	-
21st	Paid him the remainder		12	1¼
	Paid Master Foot ½ days day work		3	9

... continued

APPENDIX 1: ACCOUNTS

Mar-07	Paid him back for his hop digging		6	-
7	Settled with him for digging 3560 Hill of hops at 20d per hundred and 2012 at 2s per hundred £4 19s 7d J T			
	Lade paid him £1 9s 0d and I paid him	3	10	7
14th	Paid Foots 4 days day work at 2/6		10	-
	see the other side Paid J Eastone 5 days at 2/6		12	6
	which is altered Paid Foots 4½ days at 2/6		11	3
	Paid Wm Isted for sundries		3	-
21	Paid Master Lambhurst 1 Day		2	-
		75	19	10½

TABLE 5

Money paid away between J T Lade & I continued from the last page

1818					
Mar 24th	Paid Tom Gurr wages	75	19	10½
25th	Paid Master Lambhurst 2½ days day work at 2 shillings per day		3	-
			5	-
28th	Paid Wm Isted for Sundrys	1	3	-
April 3rd	Paid Master Foot 8 day at 2/6 per day	1	-	-
	Settled with Master Master Foot paid him for sharping hop poles (2475) at 5d per Hd		10	6
	also for day work 5 1/2 days		4	3
14th	For 40 bushels of potatoes	2	-	-
17th	Paid Wm Grant or 6 1/2 days day work		16	3
	Do for sharping poles 275 at 5d per hund.		1	1
	Do for Childrens picking up stones		2	-
April 27th	Settled with Mr Thom Oxley			
	2 Qr Black Oats at 22s per Qr	2	4	-
	3 Qr Do at 22s Do	3	6	-
	39 bushels of peas at 6s per bus.	11	14	-
	Stakes and thatch rods		7	10
	1 dozen of Oxbows		3	6
	15 Qr scotch white oats 27 pr Qr	20	5	-
	5 Qr Black Oats at 28 pr Qr	7	-	-
	2½ Bu Trefoil	1	17	6
	A cart Mare	8	8	-
	½ a years Poor Tax	21	4	-
	The Whole Amount	76	9	10
29th	Paid Master Crouch for tailing sheep		1	-
May 3	Paid Master Catt cash due to him		3	-
15	Paid Master Grant for poling the hops at 1/6d per hundred	4	3	7½
	Also paid him for sharping			

... continued

APPENDIX 1: ACCOUNTS

16th	75 new poles at 5d per hundred		3	1½
16	Paid Master Catt one weeks work		15	-
22	Paid him Do Do		15	-
30th	Paid him Do Do		15	-
	Paid Master Grant 7 days work		17	6
	Bought a half bushel and a bottle etc		3	9
June 28th	Paid Master Grant 9 days work	1	2	6
	Paid him for some more etc		15	6
	Paid Master Catt part 6 days work		11	6
		169	**8**	**3½**

TABLE 6

1818	Money paid away between J T Lade & continued from the last page	£	s	d
		169	8	3½
June 27th	Paid Master Catt one week		15	-
	Paid Mrs Catt and Mrs Baker for tieing the hops 300 at 1¾ rest [?] at 9d	2	2	6
29th	Paid the Lime burners	1	6	-
July 9th	Paid Mr Coleman's man for Swallers going to horse	1	3	6
10th	Paid Dame Hoad ½ day haying			6
11th	Paid Dame Baker 1 day & two ½ days		2	-
	Paid Master Catt 12 ½ days d work	1	11	3
	Paid Lime burners	1	6	-
Aug 19th	Settled with Master Dann for reeping 3 acres 1 Q 17 rods of wheat at 12s per acre	2	-	-
	Allowance for beer and 1 days work was paid for by J T Lade		3	-
	Settled with Wm Burges for reeping 1 a 3 Q 25 r acres of wheat at 12s per acre		16	10½
Aug 25th	Settled with Master Grant for Sundry work and harvesting	9	10	-
	Reeping 6 acres of oats and 6 acres of Barley at 2/6 per acre	1	10	-
	to 2 days work at 2s 3d per day		4	6
	to allowance for beer		3	-
	Do settled with Master Catt the same day for Sundry work and harvesting J T Lade and his boy also up to this day	6	2	0¾

... continued

APPENDIX 1: ACCOUNTS

27th	paid him 9s out of £6 11s 0¾d				
	Settled with Master Daw for Sun dry work and harvesting for		5	12	-
	J T Lade and me				
Sept 2nd	Gave Master Pettitt for stopping the fire at our Lime Kiln			3	-
	Paid Master D Honeysett Cash		2	10	-
14th	Paid Mrs Baker for reeping				
	1 a 0 qr 16 r of wheat at 12s			13	3
	4 ½ days day work			4	6
	paid her her hopping money 19s 3d at 2d per Bu		1	19	4
	Paid Mrs Stedham 17s 17d		1	15	2
			210	18	8¾

TABLE 7

1818		£	s	d
	Money paid away between J T Lade & I continued from the last page	210	18	8¾
Sept 14th	Paid to Mrs Catt her hoping money			
	Picked 17..10. at 2d per Bu	1	15	8
	Mrs Grant Do 1..3..3	2	6	6
	Do for other work by herself and children		7	2
	Mr Hoad Do 18..6..	1	17	-
	J & D Honeysett Do 1..17..0	3	14	-
	West & Winchester 13..9..	1	7	6
	Do gave them in the room of a supper		0	6
	Gave Ann for her hoping		1	6
	Paid Master Grant for 14 days hop drying at 4s 6d per day	3	13	-
	Paying 31 hundred 23[?] Of hops at 5d		13	-
	Boys work up to 12th Inst		11	-
29th	Paid Master Catt for pulling poles etc	2	4	-
	Paid Master Collins for burning lime	1	6	-
Oct 3rd	Settled with Mr D Honeysett for Threshing 15 Qr 6 Bu of wheat at 4s per Qr	3	3	-
	Do for threshing 15 Qr 2 Bu peas at 2/6d		15	-
	Do for 4¼ days day work at 2/6d per day		10	7½
	Allowance for dinner for cleaning		2	2
7th	Brought a pair of swipes and a sive off Mr Wm Isted	1	6	-
8	Expense of of warnings[?]		6	-
	Brought a new half bushel		9	6
13th	Paid Mr Noakes half years rent	55	0	-
	Paid Mr Reed for catching rats		3	6
	Paid Mr Wm Isted for a pairs of swips and a sive	1	6	-
	Brought 15 ewes at Bourn Fair at 35s 6d	26	12	6
		319	4	2½

APPENDIX 1: ACCOUNTS

TABLE 8

1818		£	s	d
	Nicolas Oxley pays since the last settling paid more than J T Lade 25th October	58	5	11½
Nov 13th	Paid the half year Poor tax Due Michas 1818	27	-	-
14th	Paid Master Grant for work	10	18	7½
	Paid Master Catt Do Do	6	3	3
30th	Paid Mr Cole the Tythe for our Farms	29	2	6
	Paid Mr Smith the Way Tax Due Michas	5	6	-

TABLE 9

1818	Recieves since our settling	£	s	d
Dec 9th	The account of all the money Recd. before this	241	7	11

APPENDIX 1: ACCOUNTS

TABLE 10

1818		£	s	d
	Dr (Debitors) and Cr (Creditors) to J T Lade & I			
March 10th	Mr Wm Dray Dr (debtor) to a pair of oxen	19	-	-
April	Paid to J T Lade cash	19	-	-
	Th Oxley Dr 6000 hop poles at 9d per Hd			
	Do Do 1800 Do	2	18	6
	Mr T Harman Dr 5000 hop sets at 9d per Hd	1	17	6
April 6th	Mr Dorsett Dr 6000 Hop setts	3	-	-
	Mr Woodhams Dr 100 Hop setts		1	-
	Mr Barton Dr 1200 Hop setts		12	-
	Mr John Robbins for 3 sacks of wheat	6	-	-
	Mr R Reeves for 2 sacks of wheat	4	-	-
	Mr John Pattenden 6 sacks of wheat	12	-	-
	Mr John Reeves 1 sack of peas	1	15	-
	Mr Body 2 sacks of peas	3	10	-
	Mr Bray 2 sacks of peas	3	10	-
	Mr S Fox 2 Bushels of peas		15	6
	Mr S Burgess Junr 2 sacks of peas	3	10	-
	Mr Mercer 2 sacks of peas	3	10	-
1821	Nicholas Oxley Dr (Debtors)	£	s	d
March 26th	Mr Wm Grant 25 House Faggots		8	-
April 19th	Mrs Waters 200 House Faggots	3	4	-

...continued

	Master John Catt 150 House and			
	125 Best Kiln Faggots	3	8	-
May 17th	Master Baker 100 House and			
	8s paid cash for the Kiln Faggots	1	12	-
July 17th	50 Best Kiln Faggots			
Omitted	he paid in part for the rest £0 10s 0d			
	the 20th March Mr Stephen Daw 45			
	Ash and 25 Alder and Willer poles at 6d	1	5	-
30th	Mr Stepen Waters 100 House Faggots	1	14	-
June 17th	Peter Pankhurst Cash	1	-	-

APPENDIX 1: ACCOUNTS

TABLE 11

			£	s	d
1821		The Apprisement of Sandhill Combish and Pilly Farms in the Parish of Warbleton in the County of Sussex from Mrs Maria Waters to Nicholas Oxley Jany 2nd 1821 consisting of all the stock and tackling of woodland ploughings &			
		Woodlands & Hoath			
		Copes in the Oldfield and Slipshaw	20	-	-
		Slips Hoath	10	-	-
		Wood Ground in the Calves Meadow downfield	2	2	-
		Wood in all the Crocers	5	-	-
		Wood in the Pilly meadow Shaw	7	-	-
		Hoath and Wood in the Freehold field etc	7	8	-
		Woods at Sandhill and Comish	13	10	-
		All the Woods and Hedge Rows	65	-	-
		4190 Hills in West mead Garden			
		9600 Poles Do			
		3900 Poles in Pilly Garden			
	Graveled	Do 1630 Hills			
		6800 Poles in Calvesmead			
		Do 2740 Hills			
		20300 Poles in all Gardens at 7s per hundred	71	1	-
		Manures Plowing & C			
		Dung Maxim 7 yards by 7 Yds nearly 1 yard thick 73 loads	8	8	-
		21 yards Dung at Comish	3	-	-
		50 loads of Dung & Mould in old Sandhill Garden Field	3	15	-
		50 Loads of Dung and Mould in Flatt Field	3	-	-
		Dung at Stable Hog hounds and house & C	1	-	-
		42 loads of Dung in Wertes Mead our hop garden	4	4	-

...continued

20 Loads of Dung and Mould Do	1	10	-
4 Loads of Lime in Comish field	10	10	-
Fatching and spreading	8	-	-
1 Kiln of Lime from Sandhill Kiln 4½ loads at £4 12s 6d per load	20	16	3
400 loads of Mould in lower Comish field at 4d per load	6	13	4
Carried Over	70	16	7

APPENDIX 1: ACCOUNTS

TABLE 12

1821				
	Manures brought over	70	16	7
	Plowings & C			
	9 Acres 3 Times Plowed	18	18	-
	Sowed 13½ acres Wheat 37 Bushels at 7s per Bushel	12	19	-
	Sowing and Harrowing Do	3	7	6
	16 Acres of Wheat Straw			
	except 1 load shaw carried to Dallington			
	13½ Acres Oat Straw by Lump	28	10	-
	4½ Acres of Peas Halm			
	Whole Manures and Plowing and so on	134	11	1
	Omited 4½ Acres 2 times plowed & Crockers	6	6	-
	Half manures & C	140	17	1
	2 Kilns Lime 1 crop off	23	2	6
	200 Loads Mould in Crockers			
	1 Crop off at 2d per load	1	13	4
	150 Loads Dung and Mould			
	in Dawn lime Crop off	6	11	3
	90 Loads Dung in Hoads Field	6	15	-
	50 Loads in Do Calves Meadow Hop			
	Garden 1 Crop off	3	15	-
	1 Load Lime in Flat Field			
	from Ades Kiln 1 Crop off	2	12	6
	4 Cart Loads Ashes Crop Hay off		8	-
	Whole Amount of Half Manares	44	17	7
	Hay Rick at Pilly	18	-	-
	Hay Rick at Comish	5	-	-
	Hay Rick at Sandhill	40	-	-
	Clover Halm at Pilly	1	-	-

...continued

STOCK			
4 Oxen Pirt and Lively	63	-	
March & January			
3 Heiffers in Calf	32	-	-
A Steer 3 yers old	12	-	-
4 Cows in Calf	45	10	-
Stone Horse Prince	19	10	-
Captain Rising 9 years old	15	-	-
Trooper 5 years old	20	-	-
Pedler 11 years old	2	10	-
Whole amount of Stock	209	10	-

APPENDIX 1: ACCOUNTS

TABLE 13

1821		£	s	d
	Husbandry Implements			
	6 inch Wheel Waggon 2 shids pan Squat Double Rods &C	24	-	-
	2 Narrow Wheel Waggons rods Neb &C	25	10	-
	2 Dung Carts Rods and Nebs	10	-	-
	1 Old Do Neb & C	2	2	-
	1 Roller Neb and Rods	3	-	-
	Hop Cart 2 Corn Rakes & C		7	-
	2 Hop Edgets	4	-	-
	1 Do Do	1	1	-
	One 2 Farrow Plow	6	-	-
	1 Foot Plow	2	-	-
	1 Old Broad Share Plow	1	5	-
	1 Strike plow 1 old Foot Do	1	5	-
	2 Ox Harrows	2	-	-
	1 Hook Harrow	2	-	-
	5 Horse Harrows	4	-	-
	A quantity of coals in Oast	2	10	-
	32 yds Oast Hair at 15d per yard	2	-	-
	Hop Sieve and Bagging hoop		5	-
	Coal sifters and hoe		4	-
	4 Chain Harnesses 2 quiler Harnesses 7 collars 6 bits	10	-	-
	Pair plow chains		4	-
	4 Ox yokes and 4 chains	3	-	-
	6 Pole Bins		6	-
	Wheel Barrow		6	-
	5 Oast grabes	1	-	-
	3 Shovels 2 Spades 2 Hops Pitchers 1 Spud 2 Hop Dogs 2 Wedges Bittle 1 large 2 small	1	8	-

...continued

Hop Openers &C		
Hammer pinchers chaff		
sieve carry combs pail oat		
chest lanthorn cart whip and	1	2	-
sundries of old harness &C		
12 Prongs		18	-
7 Hay rakes		3	6
Carried over	112	6	6

APPENDIX 1: ACCOUNTS

TABLE 14

1821	Husbandry Implements	£	s	d
	Continued			
	I brought over	112	6	6
	2 Sheep Racks 1 Trough		7	6
	1 Large Scale Beam and			
	Scales	1	5	-
	4 Half Hundreds 1 Quarter one 14lb			
	One 7lb One 4lb one 2lb one 1lb weights	1	15	-
	2 old Whippens 1 Slip Strap		3	-
	1 Pair Trais Hamre Woods		1	-
	Seed Lipp and Strap		4	-
	Pertatoe Mill		6	-
	Pair Waggon Ropes		15	-
	2 Chissels 2 Augers Goge			
	Mallot & C		2	-
	3 Hop Bills and Long Spud		2	-
	A quantity of old iron			
	Stub Sythe and old pair			
	Harn woods 2 single Ox			
	yokes 2 back straps Belly	1	-	-
	gurt and sudries in Granney			
	Chaff cutting Box		5	-
	Whole Amount Husbandry	118	12	-
	Impliments and Tackling			
	Omitted Maxim 15 loads in			
	Old Sandhill field Dung and Mould	3	4	6
	28 Do in Road			
	Carrying Mould together in road		1	6
	Carrying and Stacking hop			
	Bines	1	10	-
	Kiln of Chalk	10	10	-
			...*continued*	

	15	6	-
Woods and Hedgerows	65	-	-
Hop poles	71	1	-
Whole Manures	156	3	1
Half Manures	44	17	7
Hay	64	-	-
Stock	209	10	-
Tackling & C	18	12	-
Whole Amount of Inventory	729	3	8

2 *February 1821*

Paid the whole amount of the before mentioned Inventry to Mrs Meria Waters at Beastons [Beestons] in the presence of Messrs Thomas Oxley Thomas Hall Henry Harcot Waters and Mr Benjamin Waters and Received a Stamp for the same in regular Order £729..3s..8d

Nicholas Oxley

APPENDIX 2: THE PROSECUTING SOCIETY OF HEATHFIELD AND WARBLETON

by Teresa Whetstone

At the end of the 18th Century, property owning individuals began forming Prosecuting Societies across the Country. Their aim was to raise funds to pay rewards for information leading to the successful prosecution and conviction of thieves and felons. The Societies held AGMs, had accounts and even enjoyed dinners. The Clerk of the Society would have made use of local newspapers to advertise the rewards. The Clerk's names would usually follow details of the reward. For example, in 1828, F.H. Gell was Clerk to the Alfriston Prosecuting Society and in 1836, Edward Verral was the Clerk of the Hamsey, Barcombe and Chailey Prosecuting Society.

The earliest mention in the British Newspaper Archive of a Sussex Society is in West Hoathly in 1798 and the last found mention of a similar Society is at Storrington in 1885. It would appear that these societies became less necessary after the establishment of the first Public Police Force in 1829.

It is likely that the Oxley family were members of the 'Prosecuting Society of Heathfield and Warbleton.' Nicholas Oxley writes in his diary 'Father went to the Club at the Star Inn, Heathfield for Prosecuting Thieves.'

The Sussex Advertiser 19th November 1827 had a notice about the theft of a Bay Nag Mare stolen from Mr Thomas Barton's Stable. 'A reward of 3 Guineas was offered over and above the reward allowed by the Heathfield and Warbleton Prosecuting Society.'

On the 13th October 1828, the Sussex Advertiser carried a notice of a Five Pound Reward over and above the reward offered by the Prosecuting Society of Heathfield and Warbleton following the theft of a 'Strong, black, six year old riding horse' stolen from the field belonging to Mr Thomas Crismas of Heathfield.

It would appear that the Heathfield and Warbleton Society could still have been in existence as late as 1857. The Sussex Advertiser records the attempted prosecution of an elderly labourer from Heathfield, Thomas Sands for damaging the hedge of Mr William Cole, the Crown Inn, Heathfield. According to another labourer, Peter Marson also of Heathfield, he saw 'the prisoner walking along the road near Mr Cole's hedge with a small bundle of wood under his arm.' He also saw him break a binder from the hedge. As the Prosecution was unable to put a price on the value of the binder, the case was dismissed. According to the Court Reporter, 'Mr Cole was a member of a Prosecuting Society and was therefore bound to prosecute.'

REFERENCES:

ESRO and WSRO hold information about a few Prosecuting Societies including:

- Ewhurst and Bodiam Prosecuting Society. Minute Book 1823-1849 NRA 29495. Parish of Ewhurst Other Records includes lists of members and resolutions of inaugural meeting 1823. ESRO: PAR 324/26/2/1. 'The Society was formed at a meeting at the Red Lion Inn Bodiam in 1823. As well as the two parishes its benefits were extended to Brede High Farm (in Ewhurst, Udimore detached and Sedlescombe) and to Messrs Levett and Henley's property in Sandhurst.'
- West Hoathly. Account and Minute Book 1798-1820 ESRO: NRA 29495
- Pulborough Prosecuting Society. WSRO: PHA/9518
- Arundel Society for the Prosecution of Felons. 1796-1952. WSRO: Holmes Campbell MSS
- Wisborough Green Prosecuting Society. Rules and List of Subscriptions. 1820 WSRO: PAR/210/43/3
- Steyning Society for the Protection of Property and Prosecution of Thieves. Minute Book 1818-1847. WSRO: Add MS 2961
- West Tarring Society for Prosecuting Felons, Thieves and Other Offenders. Accounts and Membership List. 1813-1849 WSRO: Add Mss 45622
- Storrington Prosecuting Society. 1828-1885. Includes photocopies of handbills and a photograph of George French Mant, Clerk and Treasurer of the Storrington Society. Records held in the West Sussex Constabulary Records, Steyning Divisinln. WSRO: POL/W/S
- British Newspaper Archives

APPENDIX 3: 1816: THE YEAR WITHOUT A SUMMER

Adapted from the Wikipedia article of the same name, retrieved 18 November 2023; reproduced under the terms of the Creative Commons Attribution-ShareAlike 3.0 Unported License and the GNU Free Documentation License.

The year 1816 is known as the Year Without a Summer because of severe climate abnormalities that caused average global temperatures to decrease by 0.4–0.7°C (0.7–1°F). Summer temperatures in Europe were the coldest of any on record between the years of 1766 and 2000. This resulted in major food shortages across the Northern Hemisphere.

Evidence suggests that the anomaly was predominantly a volcanic winter event caused by the massive 1815 eruption of Mount Tambora in April in the Dutch East Indies (modern-day Indonesia). This eruption was the largest in at least 1,300 years (after the hypothesized eruption causing the volcanic winter of 536); its effect on the climate may have been exacerbated by the 1814 eruption of Mayon in the Philippines.

DESCRIPTION

The Year Without a Summer was an agricultural disaster. Historian John D. Post has called this 'the last great subsistence crisis in the Western world'. The climatic aberrations of 1816 had their greatest effect on most of New England, Atlantic Canada, and parts of western Europe.

The aberrations are now generally thought to have occurred because of the April 5–15, 1815, Mount Tambora volcanic eruption on the island of Sumbawa, Indonesia. The eruption had a volcanic explosivity index (VEI) ranking of 7, a colossal event that ejected at least 100 km3 (24 cu mi) of material. It was the world's largest volcanic eruption during historic times, comparable with the Minoan eruption in the 2nd millennium BC, the Hatepe eruption of Lake Taupō at around 180 AD, the eruption of Paektu Mountain in 946 AD, and the 1257 eruption of Mount Samalas.

Other large volcanic eruptions (with VEIs of at least 4) around this time were:

- 1808, the 1808 mystery eruption (VEI 6) in the southwestern Pacific Ocean
- 1812, La Soufrière on Saint Vincent in the Caribbean
- 1812, Awu in the Sangihe Islands, Dutch East Indies
- 1813, Suwanosejima in the Ryukyu Islands, Japan

- 1814, Mayon in the Philippines

These eruptions had built up a substantial amount of atmospheric dust. As is common after a massive volcanic eruption, temperatures fell worldwide because less sunlight passed through the stratosphere.

According to a 2012 analysis by Berkeley Earth Surface Temperature, the 1815 Tambora eruption caused a temporary drop in the Earth's average land temperature of about 1°C. Smaller temperature drops were recorded from the 1812–1814 eruptions.

The Earth had already been in a centuries-long period of global cooling that started in the 14th century. Known today as the Little Ice Age, it had already caused considerable agricultural distress in Europe. The Little Ice Age's existing cooling was exacerbated by the eruption of Tambora, which occurred near the end of the Little Ice Age.

...

EUROPE

As a result of the series of volcanic eruptions, crops had been poor for several years; the final blow came in 1815 with the eruption of Tambora. Europe, still recuperating from the Napoleonic Wars, suffered from food shortages. The impoverished especially suffered during this time. Low temperatures and heavy rains resulted in failed harvests in Great Britain and Ireland. Families in Wales traveled long distances begging for food. Famine was prevalent in north and southwest Ireland, following the failure of wheat, oat, and potato harvests. In Germany, the crisis was severe. Food prices rose sharply throughout Europe. With the cause of the problems unknown, hungry people demonstrated in front of grain markets and bakeries. Later riots, arson, and looting took place in many European cities. On some occasions, rioters carried flags reading 'Bread or Blood'. Though riots were common during times of hunger, the food riots of 1816 and 1817 were the highest levels of violence since the French Revolution. It was the worst famine of 19th-century mainland Europe.

Between 1816 and 1819, major typhus epidemics occurred in parts of Europe, including Ireland, Italy, Switzerland, and Scotland, precipitated by malnourishment and famine caused by the Year Without a Summer. More than 65,000 people died as the disease spread out of Ireland and onwards to Britain.

APPENDIX 4: FAMILY TREES AND BIOGRAPHICAL NOTES

Family trees and notes prepared by Jayne Adams
Sussex Family History Group

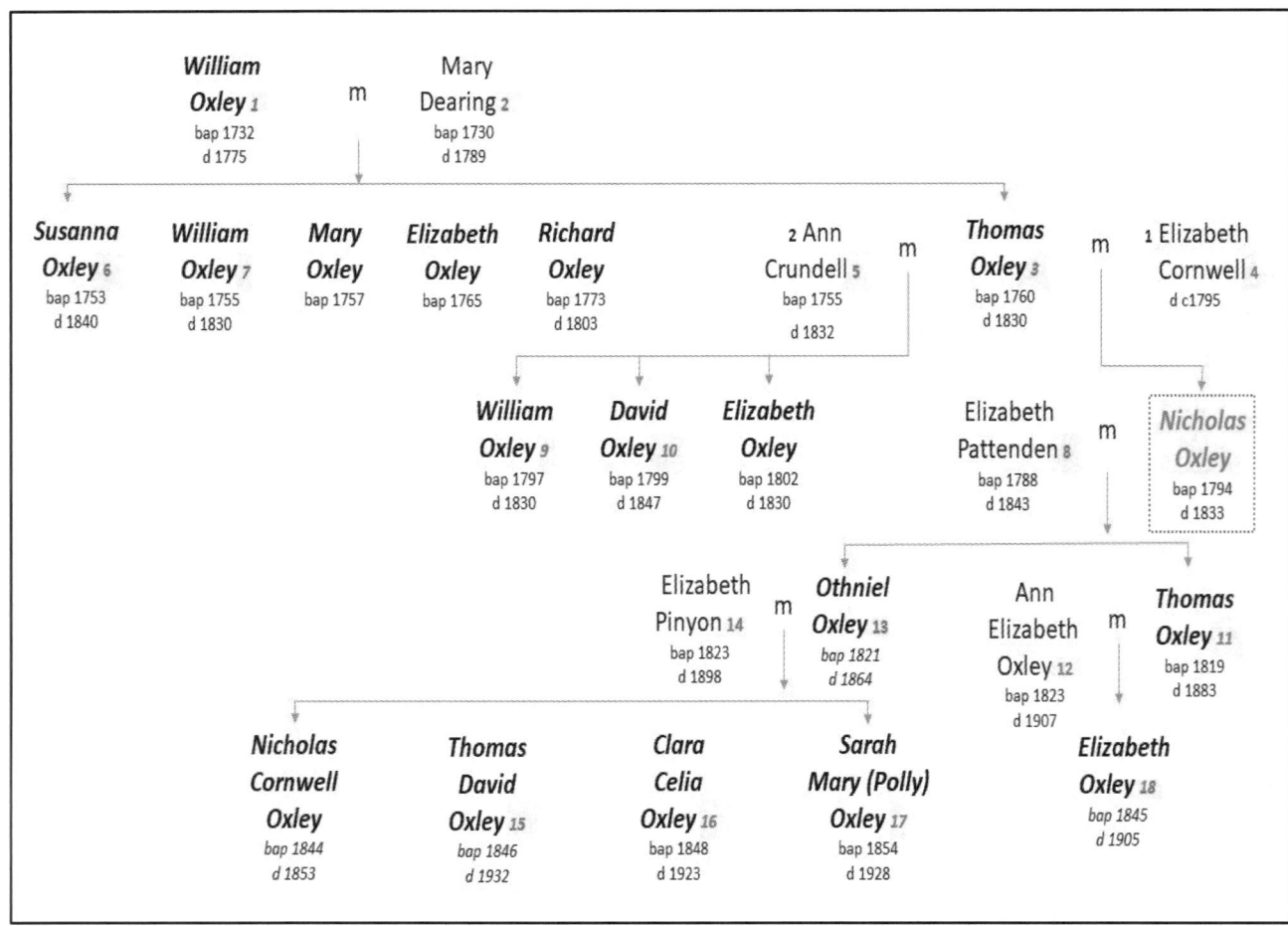

APPENDIX 4: FAMILY TREES

NICHOLAS OXLEY: NOTES

1. There are several birth entries for a William Oxley in the Heathfield area at this time. Based on William and Mary's elder daughter (b 1753) being named Susanna, it is a plausible evaluation to conclude that William (bap Heathfield in 1732) was likely to be the son of Richard Oxley and Susannah Traish (married Heathfield 1722). William married Mary Dearing in Heathfield in 1751.

2. The daughter of John Dearing and Dorothy Mepham

3. Thomas was a tenant farmer in the Warbleton area, with the Brighton Gazette of 10th February, 1825, recording his lease of Coldhodges and Frosts Farm in Warbleton. Thomas married twice, firstly to Elizabeth Cornwell and secondly to widow Ann Bland née Crundell

4. Date and place of Elizabeth's birth is uncertain but likely to be c1760. She is likely to be the daughter of Robert Cornwell and Elizabeth Diplock, and the sister of Nicholas Cornwell (1755-1815). This conclusion is based on the will of Nicholas Cornwell who left a legacy in his will dated 1815 to his 'nephew, Nicholas Oxley' in 1815. Also, the marriage of Thomas Oxley to Elizabeth Cornwell was witnessed by one Nicholas Cornwell. The marriage of Nicholas Cornwell to Lucy Chatfield was witnessed by one Elizabeth Cornwell, which could have been either his mother or his sister.

5. Daughter of Stephen Crundell and Mary Tuppeny of Brenchley in Kent. Ann was the widow of John Bland when she married Thomas Oxley at All Saints, Heathfield on 29th March 1796. Previous marriage to John Bland was by licence on 6th November 1779, with the marriage taking place on 7th November 1779 at All Saints, Brenchley – witnesses Stephen Crundell and John Twort.

6. Baptised at All Saints Heathfield on 5th Jan 1753. Married to John Morris in Heathfield, 1788.

7. Married Martha White 1st May 1778 at All Saints, Heathfield, the daughter of Lilley White and Martha Piper. Buried at Heathfield Chapel.

8. Married Nicholas Oxley, farmer of Warbleton, at St Mary the Virgin, Warbleton in 1818 by licence – sureties on the licence were Nicholas Oxley and Thomas Oxley. Witnesses to the marriage – John Pattenden and Elizabeth Oxley. Elizabeth was the daughter of John Pattenden and Elizabeth Gorringe of Herstmonceux. Elizabeth was baptised in Warbleton on 28th October 1788.

9   William was a miller in Herstmonceux. He married Elizabeth Bonter on 11th December 1822 at Ninfield with the consent of the bride's parents. Elizabeth was a schoolmistress in Herstmonceux.

10 David Oxley was a farmer in Chalvington. Married Mary Deadman in 1845. Mary was previously a servant in his employ as per the 1841 census.

11 Thomas Oxley married his 1st half-cousin, Anne Elizabeth Oxley, daughter of William Oxley (see 15) and Elizabeth Bonter, in Herstmonceux in 1845. The family emigrated from England in 1856, settling in Syracuse, New York, USA. Thomas was a teacher of music and a teacher of the violin, and was buried in the Woodlawn Cemetery in Syracuse in 1883.

12 Anne Elizabeth Oxley died in Syracuse, New York, in 1907. She is buried in the Oakwood Cemetery, Syracuse. In the US Federal Census of 1860, Anne Elizabeth is also recorded as a teacher but with no indication as to what subject she taught.

13 Othniel Oxley married Elizabeth Pinyon in Wartling in 1854. Othniel undertook a variety of occupations. The 1851 census records him as a farmer of 315 acres in Cowden; the 1861 census records him as an Overseer of Roads, and at his death in 1864 his will records him as a Tea Dealer from Herstmonceux. He is buried at All Saints, Herstmonceux.

14 Elizabeth Pinyon was born in Wartling in 1823, the daughter of Thomas Pinyon, a farmer from Wartling and later Ashburnham, and Nancy Cruttenden. Elizabeth is buried at All Saints, Herstmonceux.

15 Thomas David Oxley was married twice, first to Mary Ann Eaton (daughter of George and Mary Eaton of Guestling) and secondly to Jane Elizabeth Howland (daughter of William and Jane Howland née Saxby of Folkestone). Thomas was a wheelwright/carpenter who spent the latter part of his life, from the 1880s onwards, in Folkestone in Kent. He is buried in the Cheriton Road Cemetery in Folkestone.

16 Married William Lewis Henry Hunniset b 1846 Herstmonceux.

17 Sarah Oxley was born in Wartling in 1851. Her baptism document records her name as Sarah Margaret Oxley, however she went by the names Sarah Mary and/or Polly during her life. Sarah married Philip Richard Murton, a native of Perranarworthal In Cornwall, in Catsfield in 1895. She lived in Cornwall with her husband, a domestic gardener,

during their married life but after her husband's death she returned to the South East of England to be with her brother and his family. Sarah is buried in the Cheriton Road Cemetery in Folkestone.

18 Elizabeth Oxley was born in 1845 in Ninfield. She emigrated with her parents to Syracuse, New York. Elizabeth never married and died in 1905. She is buried in the Oakwood Cemetery, Syracuse.

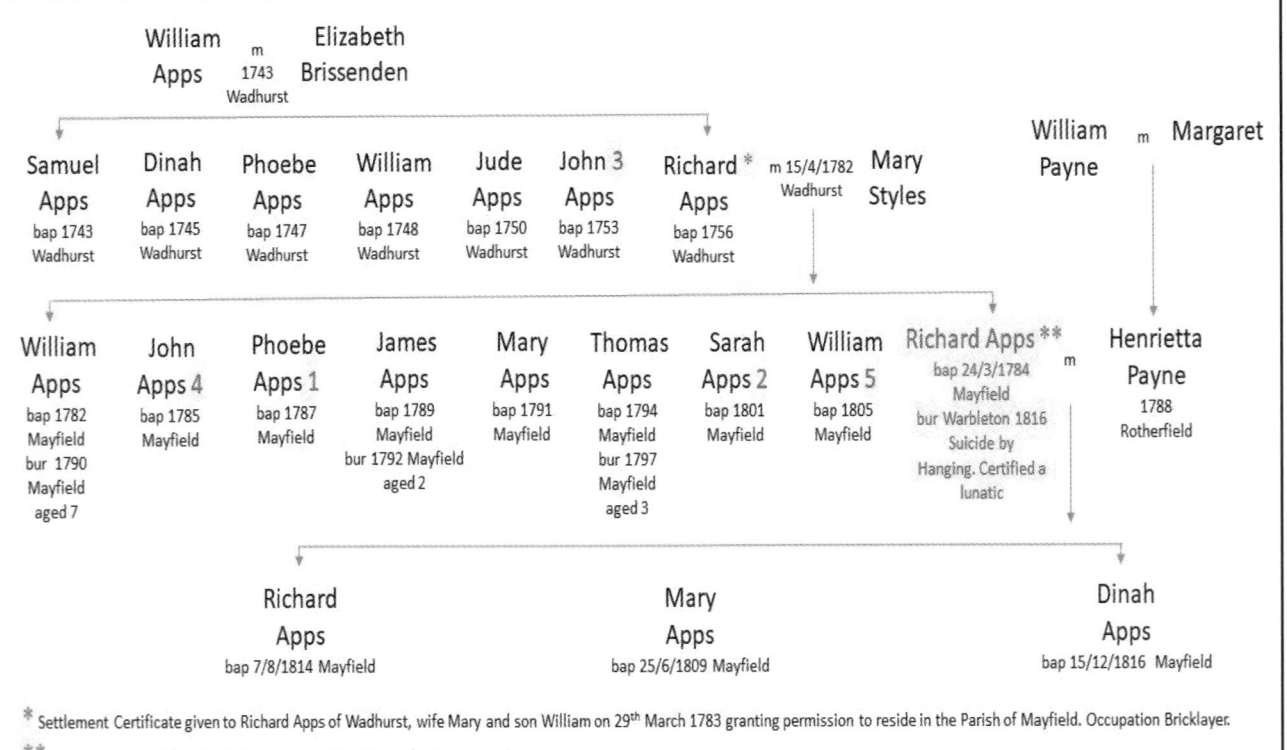

APPENDIX 4: FAMILY TREES

APPS (2)

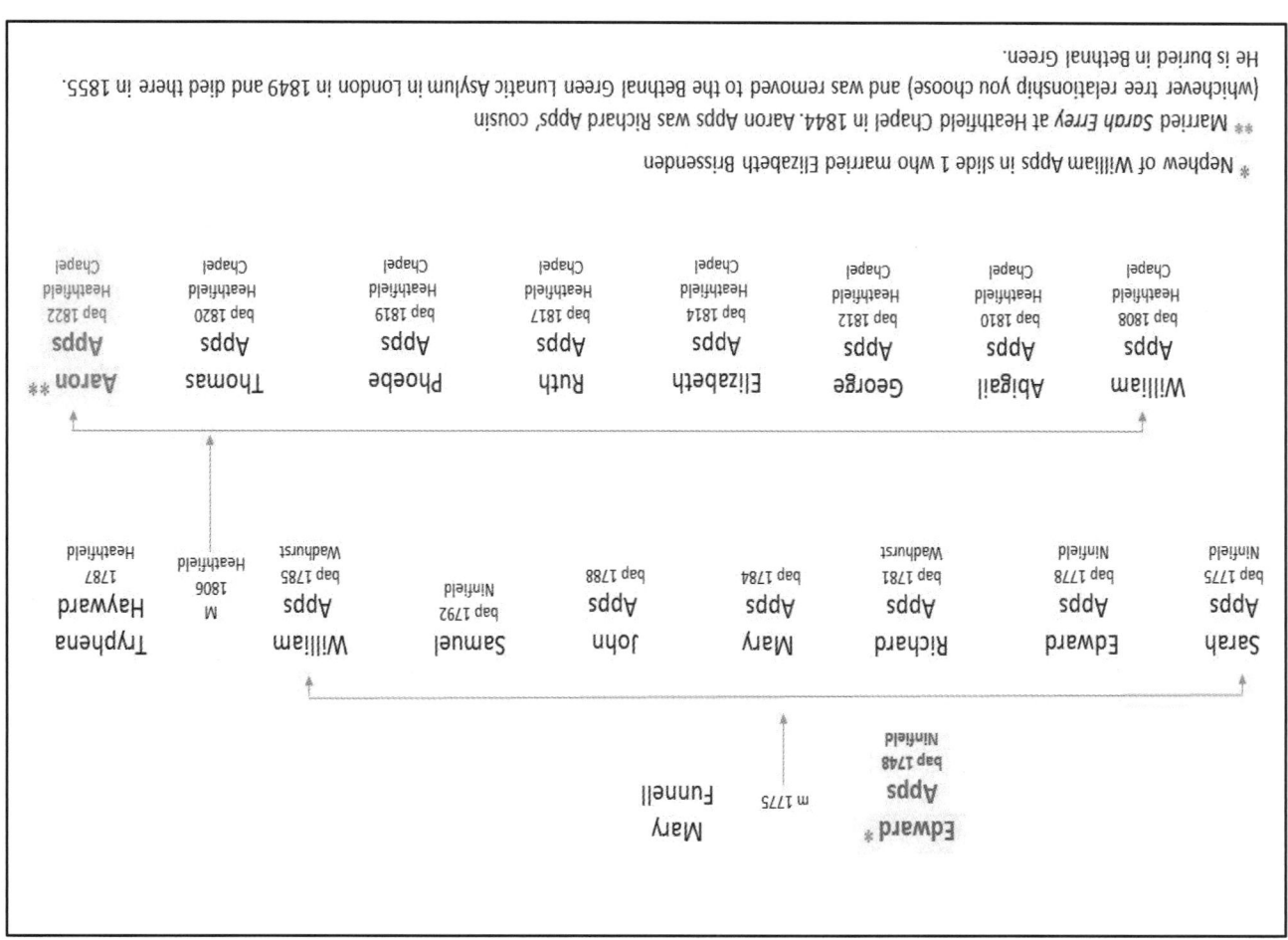

* Nephew of William Apps in slide 1 who married Elizabeth Brissenden
** Married *Sarah Errey* at Heathfield Chapel in 1844. Aaron Apps was Richard Apps' cousin (whichever tree relationship you choose) and was removed to the Bethnal Green Lunatic Asylum in London in 1849 and died there in 1855. He is buried in Bethnal Green.

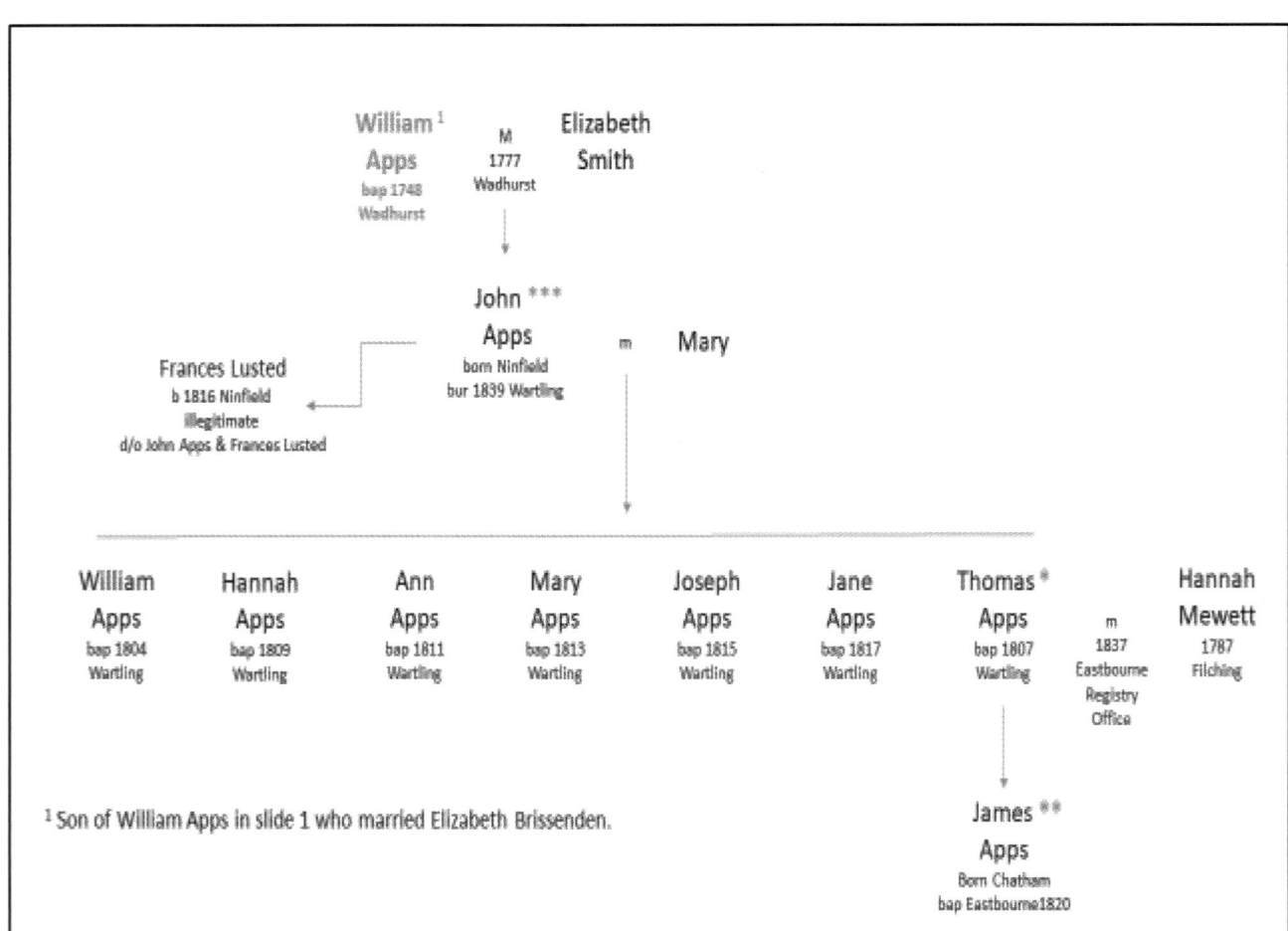

APPS (4)

* Settlement Examinations of James and Thomas Apps - 1858

Examination of **Thomas Apps** of Bexhill, pensioner; born and baptised at Wartling, son of **John Apps of Ninfield**, labourer, son of **William Apps of Ninfield**; John Apps died in 1840; TA aged 51 and joined the Marines in 1826 and served 21 years, has been home for 10 years last Oct; married Harriett Mewett at Eastbourne registry office in Feb 1837; son James Apps born at Chatham and baptised at Eastbourne; father **John Apps lived in a cottage in Wartling** now belonging to Messrs George and Thomas Sinnock of Hooe; Thomas Apps lived in a cottage in Meads, Eastbourne belonging to George Head for five years six months, then rented house at Meads from Thomas Rason, then to Crowlink, East Dean; has lived at Bexhill for 15 months

** Examination of James Apps: aged 19 on 13 Nov 1857; son of Thomas Apps, who lives at Little Common, Bexhill as a pensioner; mother Harriett Mewett, daughter of Robert Mewett of Filching in Jevington, shepherd to Mrs Noakes of Wannock in Jevington; Jams Apps joined the East Sussex Artillery Militia in Dec 1855. Married Harriett Leaney in 1859.

*** 9th June 1807 – "Warrant to apprehend John Apps of Wartling" for the bastard daughter of Frances Lusted, singlewoman, born at Ninfield poorhouse, 6 Nov 1806. The child's name was Frances and she was baptised on 14/12/1806 at St Mary's Ninfield.

BLAND (1)

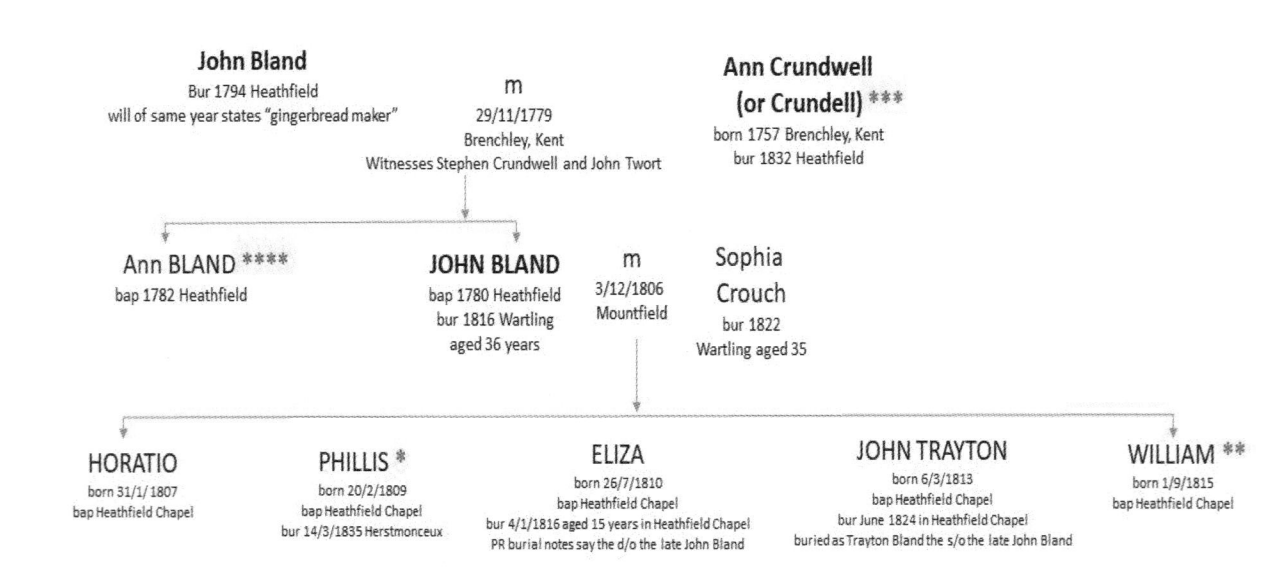

* married RICHARD HOAD (s/o **Thomas Hoad** and **Ann Honeysett** – see slide 2) on 19/7/1827 in Herstmonceux. Had 2 children - Ann Hoad born 1829 & Thomas Hoad born 1833. Richard Hoad was married for a 2nd time in 1836 in Herstmonceux to one Sarah Chapman. In the 1841 census he is living at Golden Cross, Herstmonceux and in 1851 at Lower Road Herstmonceux. His occupation is cited as *"a looker over stock in the marsh"*.

** married MARY BRISTOW (d/o Thomas Bristow) in Brighton in 1839.
In the 1841 census he is living in Brighton with his wife and two children – Emily b 1838 and William b 1845. His occupation looks like *"Land Chairman"*

*** d/o William Crundwell and Elizabeth Thrummings. Second marriage to **THOMAS OXLEY** in 1796 – see slide 2

**** married **SIMON SELMES** in Warbleton in 1806. Simon's first was marriage to Benedicta Barrow. Simon died in 1809. Ann's second marriage was to **JOHN TRILL LADE** in 1815 in Warbleton.

APPENDIX 4: FAMILY TREES

BLAND (2)

```
THOMAS         m    Elizabeth
OXLEY         1792  Cornwell
East Hoathly        died 1795
        |
    NICHOLAS OXLEY
      born 1794
    bap Heathfield Chapel


THOMAS     m    Ann Crundwell (or Crundell)
OXLEY     1796         BLAND
        Heathfield    Born 1758
                      died 1832
        |
   ┌────────────────┬──────────────────┐
WILLIAM OXLEY    DAVID OXLEY      ELIZABETH OXLEY
  born 1797       born 1799         born 1802
bap Heathfield Chapel  bap Heathfield Chapel  bap Heathfield Chapel
```

* The d/o Richard Honeysett and Ann Sharood. PR marriage notes say Thomas Hoad was a "sawyer" and 21 years old at marriage, Ann was 17 and was married with the consent of Richard Honeysett. Thomas lived at Stunts Green and Golden Cross, Herstmonceux in the 1841, 1851 and 1861 census'.

```
THOMAS HOAD        m        Ann
  b 1785        16/9/1806   Honeysett *
Herstmonceux    Herstmonceux  bap 1788
                            Herstmonceux
        |
    RICHARD        m        PHILLIS
     HOAD       19/7/1827    BLAND
    B 1807     Herstmonceux
  Herstmonceux
        |
   ┌──────────────┐
  ANN           THOMAS
  HOAD           HOAD
 b 1829         b 1833
```

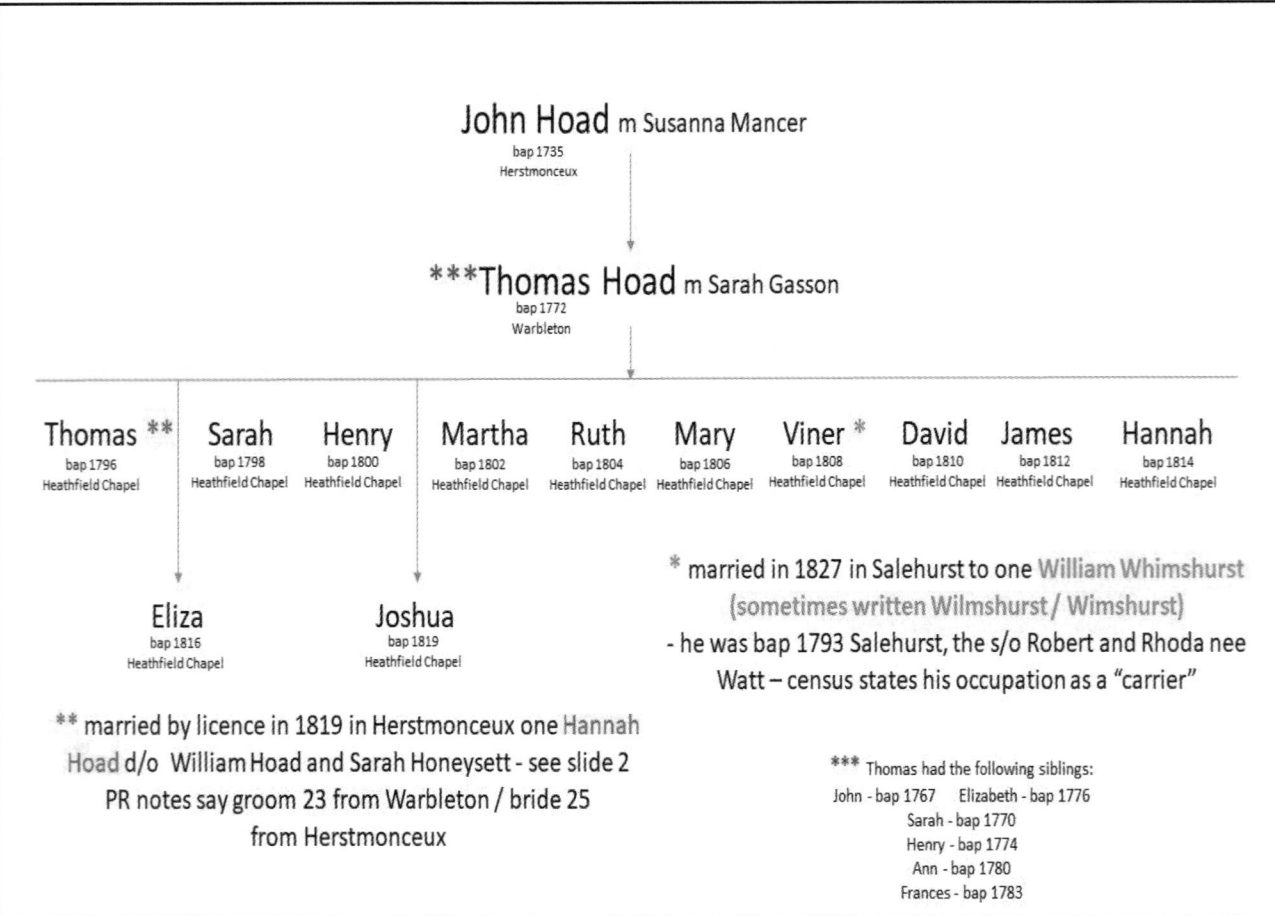

APPENDIX 4: FAMILY TREES

HOAD (2)

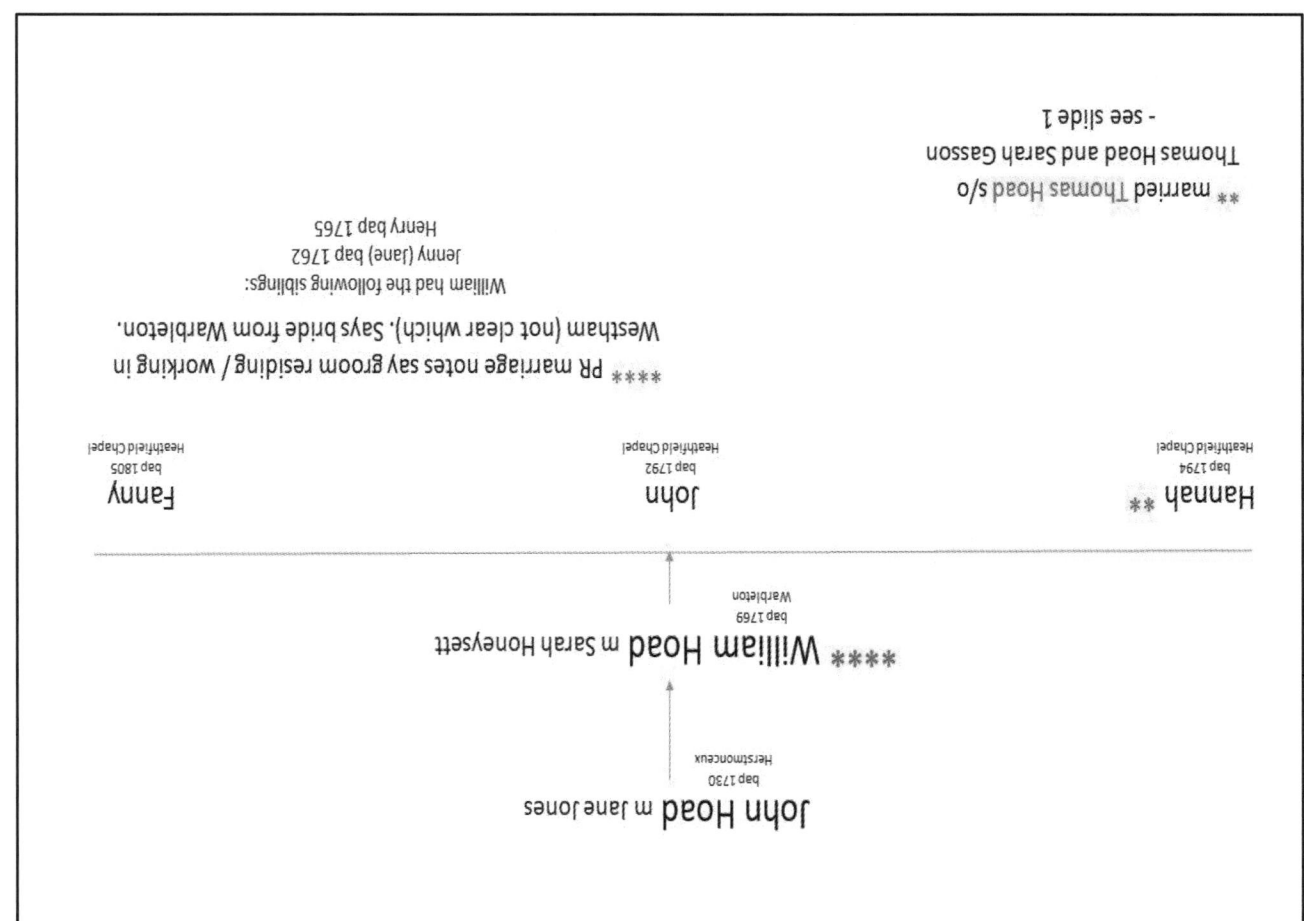

John Hoad m Jane Jones
bap 1730
Herstmonceux

William Hoad m Sarah Honeysett ****
bap 1769
Warbleton

**** PR marriage notes say groom residing / working in Westham (not clear which). Says bride from Warbleton.

William had the following siblings:
Jenny (Jane) bap 1762
Henry bap 1765

** married Thomas Hoad s/o Thomas Hoad and Sarah Gasson - see slide 1

Hannah **
bap 1794
Heathfield Chapel

John
bap 1792
Heathfield Chapel

Fanny
bap 1805
Heathfield Chapel

381

HONEYSETT

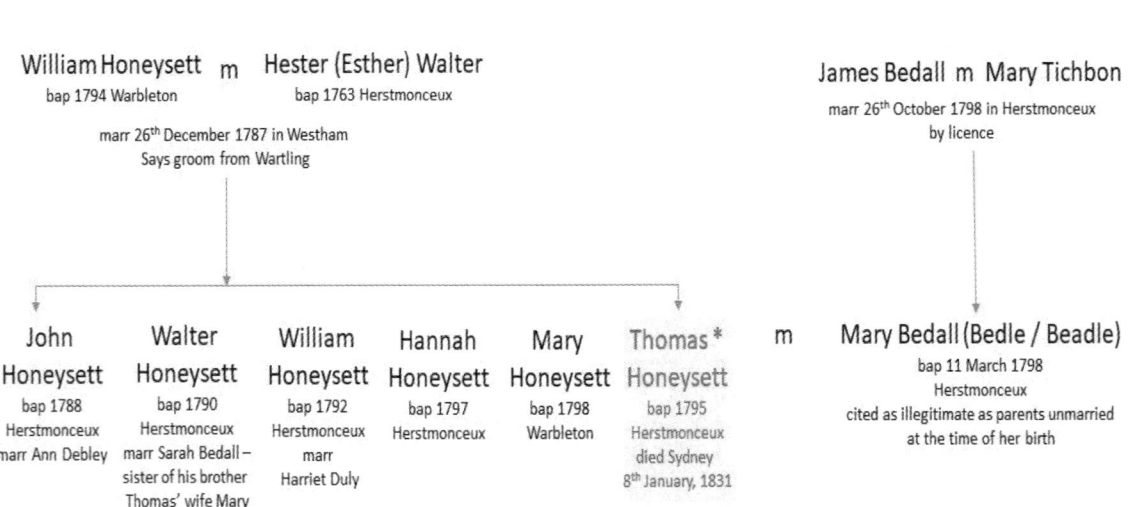

* According to the Convict Records Index in Australia, Thomas Honeysett's occupation in England was *"blacksmith"*

THOMAS HONYSETT: NOTES

On 24th March 1817 a Thomas Honeysett of Warbleton, aged 21, was tried at the Horsham Assizes charged with having shot at Samuel Pettit, also of Warbleton, with a pistol with the intention of murdering or maiming him because Samuel had informed on some illegal gin shops. Despite pleading not guilty Thomas was convicted by the jury and sentenced to be hanged; however he was later reprieved and given transportation for life. Thomas was transferred to Horsham gaol before being taken to Portsmouth and serving time on the prison hulk Leviathan before leaving on the transport ship Larkins for New South Wales on 20th July 1817, arriving in Port Jackson (now Sydney) on 22nd November 1817. The master of the Larkins was Henry R. Wilkinson, and the ship was guarded by detachments of the 46th and 48th Regiments under the command of Captain John Brabyn. The convicts did not disembark until 2nd December 1817, when the ship's surgeon, William McDonald, stated in his medical journal 'the whole of the convicts were disembarked clean and healthy when His Excellency Governor MacQuarie inspected them in person.'

The surgeon's log makes fascinating reading. Only 3 men had died during the voyage, but how true Mr McDonald's statement actually was is hard to tell, because on arrival several convicts made an official complaint of ill treatment, and also that the boxes they had brought on board with them had been plundered. An enquiry was held and it was found that the boxes had been stowed below for safe keeping and had been broken open by other prisoners. No further action resulted from the enquiry. The prisoners were then distributed out to Windsor, Liverpool, Bringelly and the Hunter Valley.

On 27th December, 1821, Thomas is on the list of convicts taken up to Newcastle as per the ship 'Elizabeth Henrietta'. The Land and Stock Muster of 1822 shows 'Thomas Honidett' as a convict in the government employ at Newcastle. It appears that Thomas Honeysett was not willing to toe the line and serve out his sentence without incident, because on October 2nd, 1824 he and a convict named Joseph Hinton were both tried for stealing a bag of flour. Their punishment was to be sent to the harsh penal colony of Port Macquarie with two additional years on their sentences.

In March 1821 Francis Allman was appointed commandant of the new penal establishment at Port Macquarie. The Governor's instructions to Allman informed him that the principal objective in establishing a settlement at Port Macquarie was to secure a secondary place of punishment for the worst description of convicts, especially those convicted of crimes after their arrival in the colony. By October 1821 there were 92 convicts at Port Macquarie. Convict employment was grouped according to the level of skill and the severity of punishment. Those assigned to hard labour were part of chain gangs, or employed in agricultural work and public works construction. By 1825 Governor Brisbane felt that Port Macquarie was no longer suitable as a penal settlement due to the ease of escape from the establishment, and he also believed that the area was ready to be opened to free settlers. The effort to close Port Macquarie was taken up by Brisbane's successor Governor Darling in 1828.

The 1828 NSW census shows that Thomas must have got up to other shenanigans, or he may have been relocated, because at the time of the census he was incarcerated on the prison hulk 'Phoenix' in Sydney harbour, apparently due to his 'rebelliousness'. It is not clear what form this rebelliousness took. The Phoenix hulk was the first floating prison used in Australian mainland waters. Between 1825 and 1837 it was moored in Sydney Harbour at Lavender Bay, known then as Hulk or Phoenix Bay, as a sobering symbol, according to Governor Brisbane, of the 'strength and terror' of the colony's police. It housed up to 260 prisoners at a time, including those awaiting trial, convict witnesses giving evidence, invalid convicts waiting for a ship to Port Macquarie Invalid Station, and those under colonial sentence of re-transportation. As with other prison hulks around the world, the human cargo on board was a source of cheap labour. Apparently, convicts on the Phoenix worked from dawn to dusk, predominately in 'shore parties', quarrying stone, cutting timber, building fortifications, reclaiming land and working in dockyards.

Three years later Thomas was dead. Records say he is buried in Sydney, but no other details exist regarding the exact location.

LADE

The Lade family of Warbleton were descended from a family originally spelt both Lad and Ladd, originally from Kent, who were 'of good antiquity in this county, in several parts of which they were possessed of lands as early as Edward the 1st.'s reign, which still bear their name'. In the reign of King Edward the IV, a branch settled at Eltham. One of them - John Ladd (died in 1527) – had a son Thomas who settled at Barham, where many of his descendants lie buried. John's grandson, Vincent Lad, died in 1625, leaving several sons, of whom Robert the eldest, who first spelt his name Lade, was a barrister-at-law at Grays Inn, and recorder of Canterbury, who was granted arms (see below) by Sir William Segar. Robert was the ancestor of the Lades, of Boughton, whilst Thomas, a younger son, was ancestor of the Lades, of Warbleton, in Sussex.

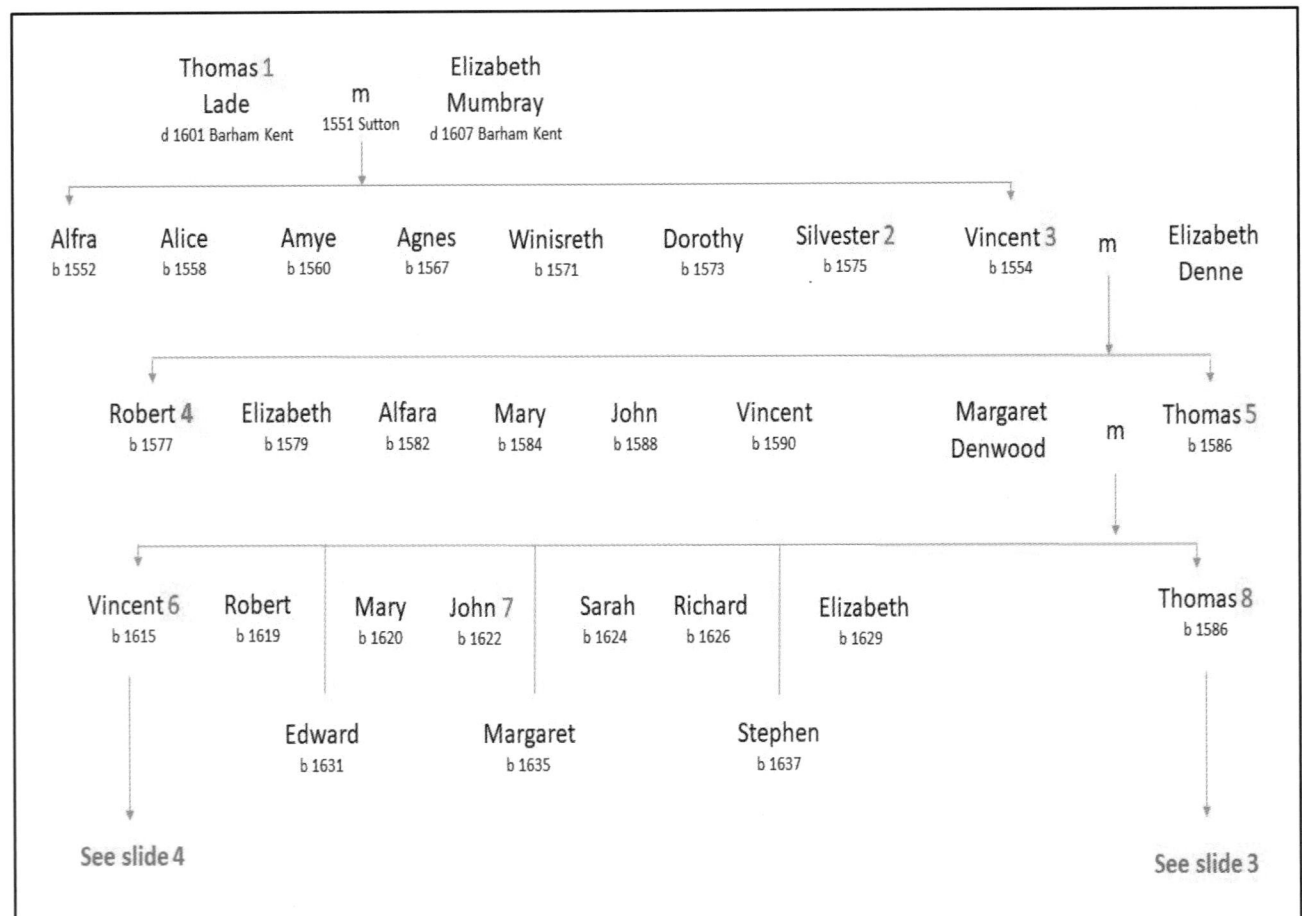

LADE (3)

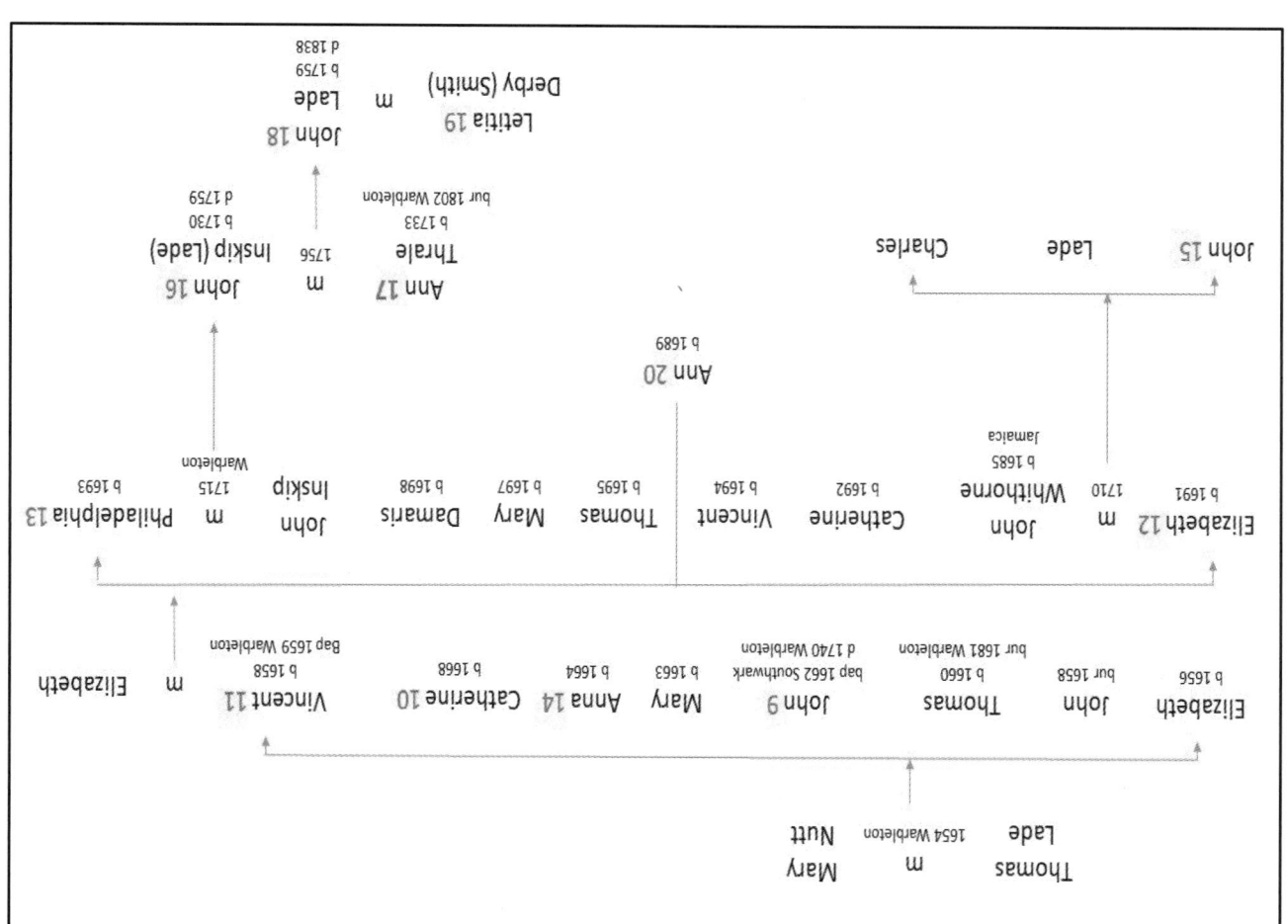

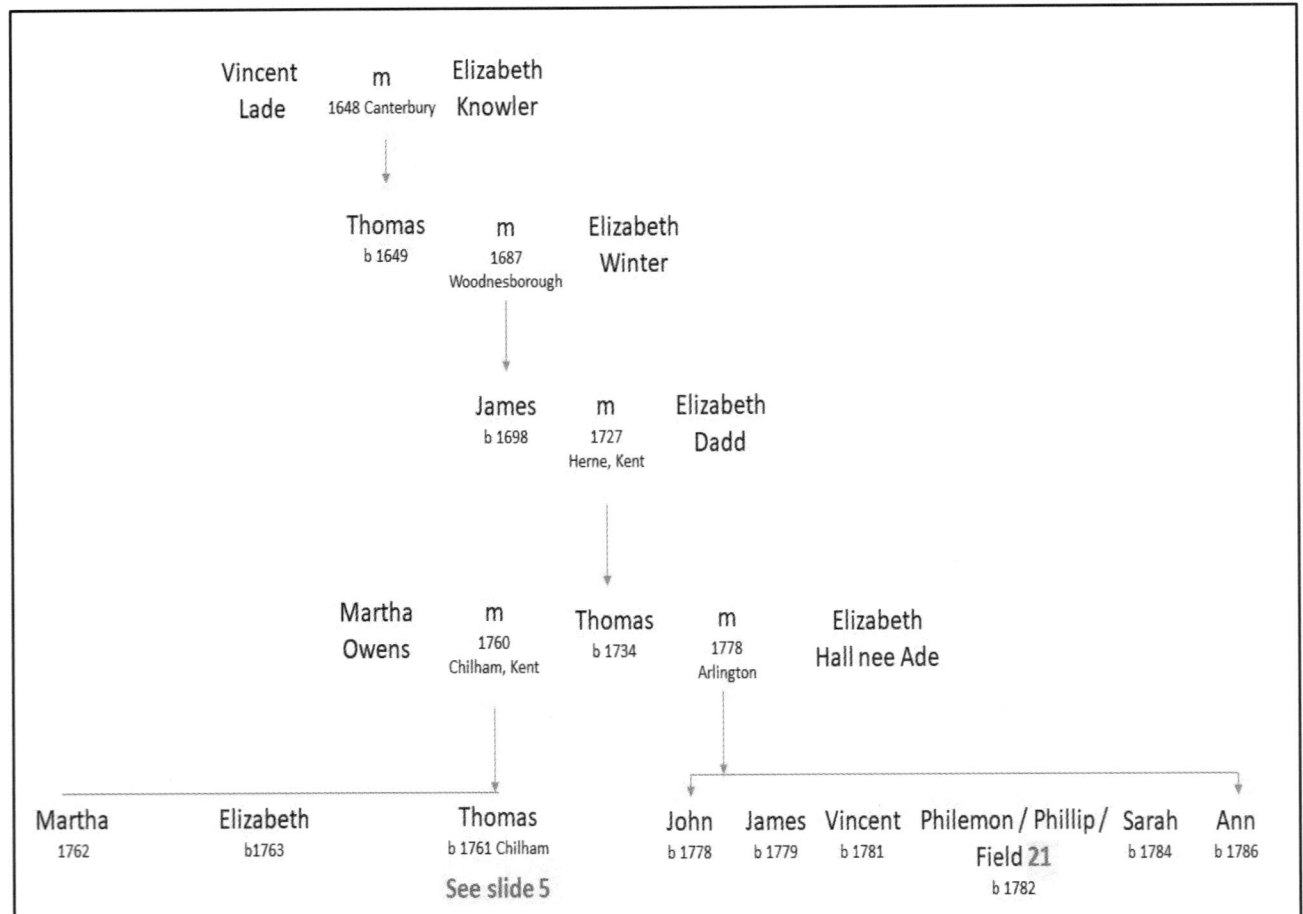

APPENDIX 4: FAMILY TREES

LADE (5)

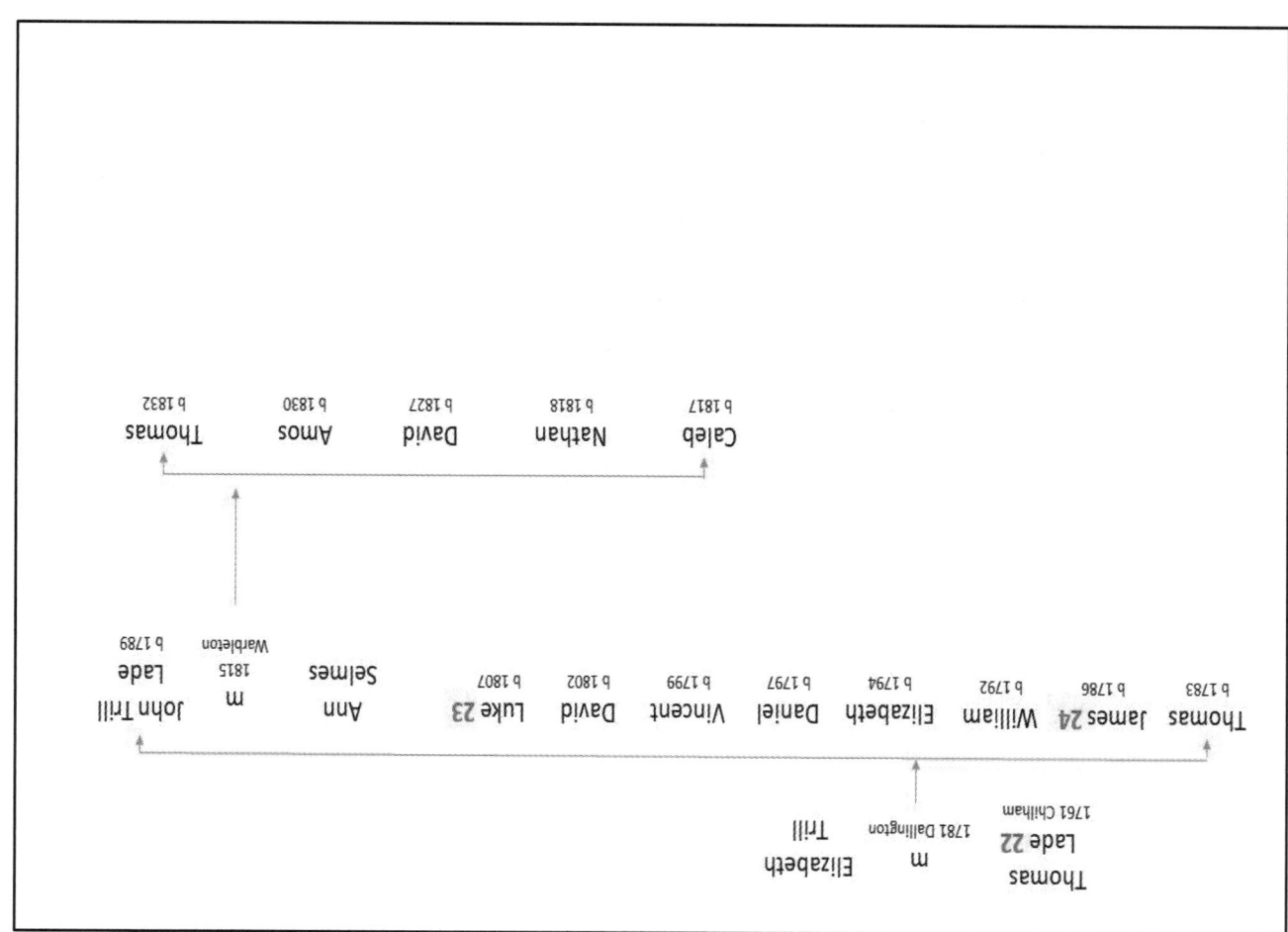

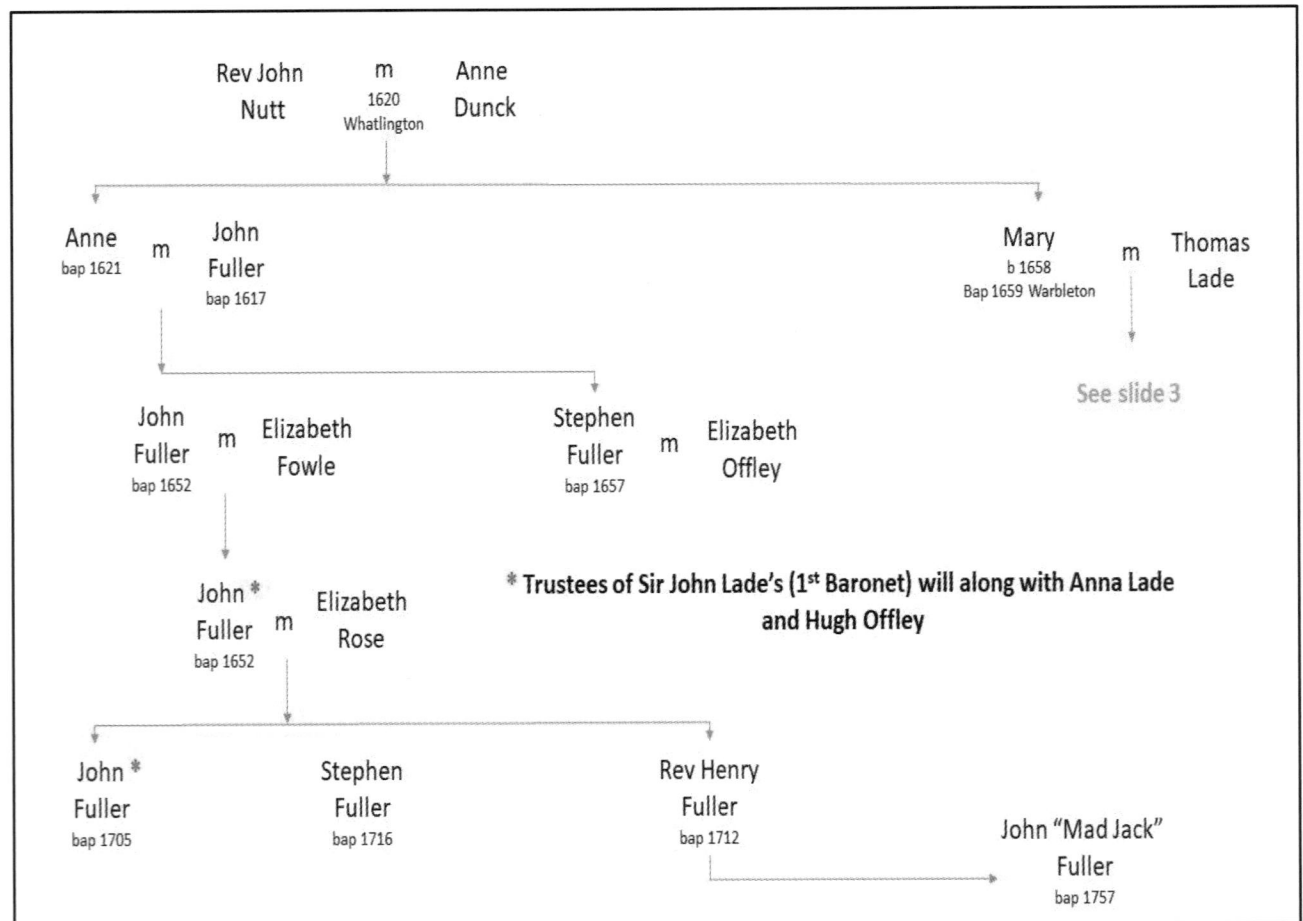

LADE: NOTES

1. Thomas Lade of Barham, Kent died 15th March 1601. He married Elizabeth sister and heir of Thomas Mumbray of Sutton, near Dover.

2. His daughter Silvester married Vincent Nethersole of Wilmingswold, Kent

3. Vincent Lade died 27th August 1625. He married Elizabeth, daughter of Vincent Denne of Denhill in Kent by whom he had four sons. John and Vincent left no issue.

4. Robert Lade was a barrister of Grays Inn in London. Robert, who married Mary, daughter of William Lovelace of The Fryars in Canterbury, was the ancestor of the Lades of Canterbury.

5. Thomas died 28th May 1660. He married Margaret, daughter of William Denswood of Ebbsfleet.

6. Vincent Lade of Barham married Elizabeth, daughter of Thomas Knowler of Canterbury.

7. John Lade of Barham married Hannah Cloak, daughter of Walter Cloak of Winchop near Canterbury. John died in 1682 in Addisham in Kent. John and Hannah had 4 daughters – Mary, Sarah, Margaret and Anne.

8. Thomas Lade died in Selmeston in 1668. He married Mary Nutt in Berwick in 1658, the daughter of the Reverend John Nutt and Anne née Dunck.

9. John Lade, born in Warbleton in 1662, made a fortune as a brewer in Southwark. He purchased an extensive estate in Southwark and added some lands in Sussex to those he inherited in Warbleton. He was MP for Southwark 1713-22 and 1724-27; in 1730 he was made a baronet i.e. Sir John Lade of Warbleton (1st baronet 1st creation). The Fuller papers contain reports on the Sussex estates owned by Lade from 1729-40, and there are scattered references thereafter on the proceedings of the Court of Chancery into whose hands Lade's executors placed the estate after his death. The Fullers of Brightling Park managed Lade's Sussex estate for over 25 years before his death. Sir John was JP for the county of Surrey.

Sir John died unmarried.

His great nephew, John Whithorne - see item 15 (grandson of his brother Vincent – see item 11) was in line to inherit the baronetcy as well as Sir John Lade's fortune, but his behaviour, as an Oxford undergraduate and subsequently, led Sir John to debar him, in 1739, from his fortune and awarded him a token 20 shillings a week, payable each Monday morning. John did inherit the baronetcy, however, and changed his name to Lade. John Whithorne had matriculated at University college in 1738, aged 17, and ran up large debts in the town. By 1739 he had been given a commission as a Lieutenant in Colonel Robinson's Regiment of Marines. He died in 1748 and left no issue. In Sir John Lade's will, subsequent to the fortune disinheritance of Whithorne, the main part of the estate and rents were to go to Lade's great nephew, the young John Inskip – only son of John Inskip of Uckfield and Lade's late niece Philadelphia – see item 13 – also a grandson of his brother, Vincent Lade. John Inskip was to be kept out of the main inheritance until he was 26. Until then Lade put the estate in the care of four trustees, his sister Anna Lade, John Fuller snr, Hugh Offley of Possingworth (husband of his sister Catherine) and John Fuller jnr. For this major task they were each to receive £100. Inskip was to have £50 for his education until the age of 14, £100 from then until 18, £300 to 21, and £1000 a year until he was 26; however, this was on the proviso he also changed his name to Lade; failure to do so would debar him from the estate. John Inskip, now John Lade, became baronet on 17 March 1758. He died from complications after a leg amputation as a result of falling from a horse - from The Fuller Letters, Crossley & Saville

10 Catherine Lade married Hugh Offley, son of Thomas Offley and Elizabeth Bathurst. Hugh was born in 1672 at Possingworth Manor, Waldron, and died on 29 Jun 1746 at age 74. They had one child - Elizabeth Offley - who married Stephen Fuller, who was the grandson of Reverend John Nutt and Anne Dunck, Anne Dunck's sister, Mary Nutt, having married Thomas Lade – see item 8. Stephen and Elizabeth had three children – Thomas, John and Elizabeth. In addition Stephen Fuller was the great, great uncle of 'John, mad Jack, Fuller'

12 Elizabeth Lade married John Whithorne of Jamaica, West Indies.

14 Anna Lade married John Roberts (sometimes spelt Robards) 'gent of Warbleton' in Warbleton in 1656. John was the son of Harbor Roberts/Robards 'gentleman deceased'.

17 The Parish Register entry in Warbleton for the burial of Lady Ann Lade – in Warbleton 31 March 1802 - notes that she was brought from St. Albans.

18 John Lade was born posthumously and became Sir John Lade, 2nd

Baronet of Warbleton. He was a prominent member of Regency society, notable as an owner and breeder of racehorses, an accomplished driver, associated with Samuel Johnson's circle (it is said that Dr Johnson was consulted on his upbringing), and one of George IV's closest friends.

19 Letitia Derby (or Smith, the sources are unclear) was a woman of uncertain origins who, prior to being discovered by the royal circle, was likely a member of the working class in the Drury Lane district, and possibly a servant in a brothel (letters of Fanny Burney). Subsequently she befriended and was probably the mistress of the highwayman 'Sixteen String Jack Rann'. After Jack Rann was hanged in 1774, she became the mistress of the Duke of York. After that it is said that her looks and her seat on a horse and skills as a driver attracted the attention of Sir John Lade and they were married in 1787 after a long affair and in spite of family disapproval. It is also said that Lade and Rann knew each other well, as Rann went to races and had once been coachman of Hester Thrale's sister; however, it cannot be definitely proven.

After Letitia's death, Sir John retired to farm in Sussex, and continued to receive his pension. His relative, Dorothy Neville, the writer and horticulturist, wrote of him, 'my poor crazy cousin' as it seems he was dependent on the kindness of a court functionary and on hints dropped in suitable ears. Queen Victoria, when a young girl and fresh to the throne, records in her diaries that she discovered that she was paying 'a Sir John Lade, one of George IV's intimates'.

20 Anne Lade was baptised in Warbleton in 1689. She was married twice – Thomas Wandell (druggist) and William Nutt of Marshalls in Maresfield.

23 Luke Lade married Ann Reeves, the daughter of John Reeves of The Stream, Chiddingly and brother of Robert Reeves, also of The Stream, Chiddingly.

24 This is the 'James Lade from Chiddingly'. He married Rebecca Reeves, sister to his brother Luke's wife Ann, and also daughter of John Reeves – see above. NB: Rebecca and Ann had sisters Sarah and Ruth Reeves, and it is Rebecca, Sarah and Ruth that Nicholas is referring to when, in 1815, he says 'Great number of visitors the chief of which are Mr James Lade & wife, Sarah & Ruth Reeves, George Ellis, Thos Goldsmith, Chiddingly'. The Reeves girl's other sister, Mary Glyde Reeves, married John Patttenden.

APPENDIX 4: FAMILY TREES

PATTENDEN

Pattenden Family Tree

1671 - 1843

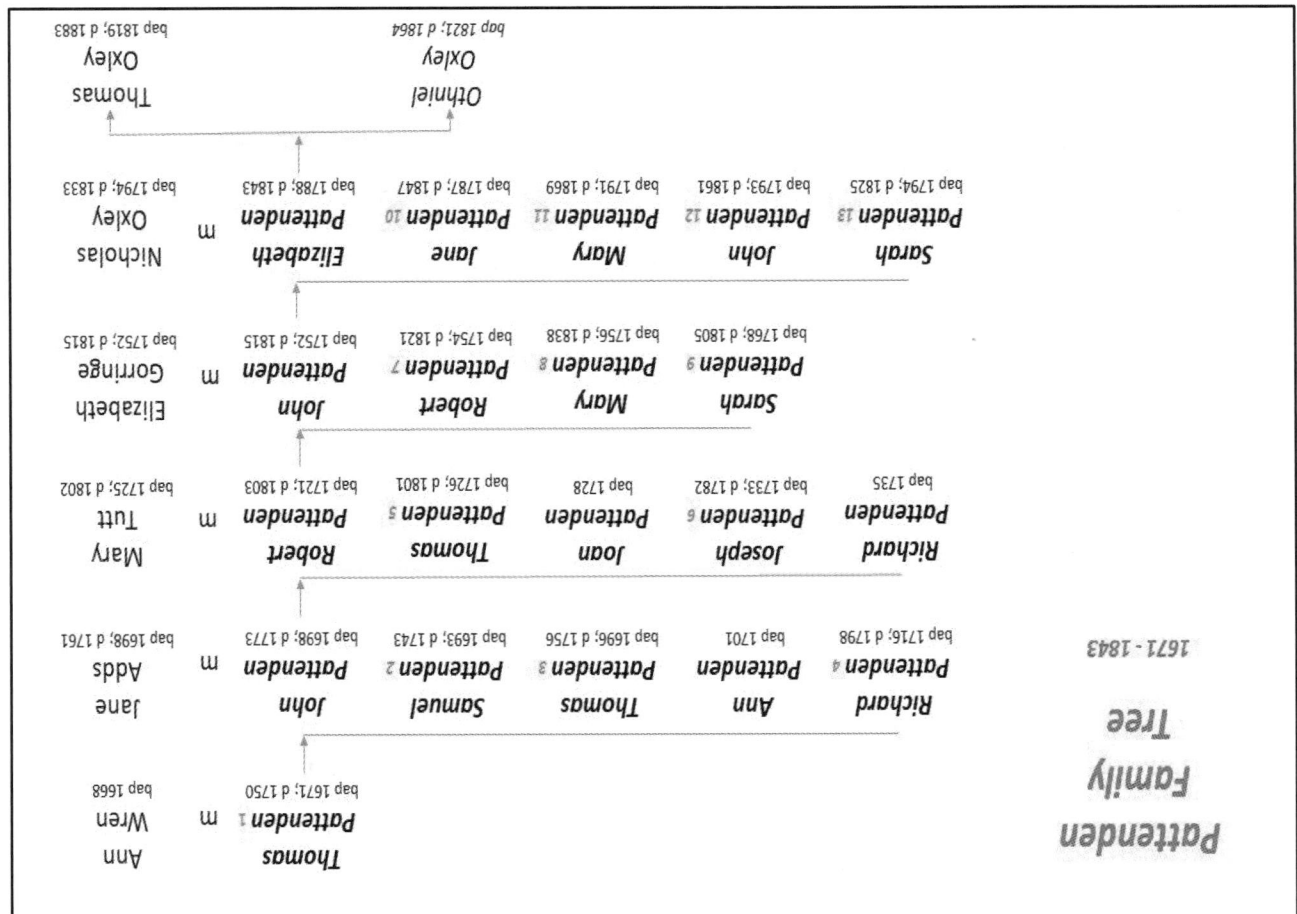

PATTENDEN NOTES

1 Thomas Pattenden was the son of Thomas Pattenden (1642-95) and Joan née Adames (1642-1713), who are recorded as living at Mowle in Waldron, Sussex
2 Married Elizabeth Waggonne (1691-1752) from East Grinstead, Sussex
3 Married Sarah Bysshe (1696-1732) from Burstow, Surrey
4 Married Mary Clark
5 Married Elizabeth West, baptised 1732 in Wartling
6 Married Ann Edwards, baptised 1731 in Burwash
7 Robert Pattenden (bap 1754), was Elizabeth Pattenden's uncle - brother of her father John. Robert married 4 times, firstly to Mary Blundell; secondly to Frances Squires; thirdly to Margaret Moon and lastly to Ann Martin. Robert Pattenden owned Batemans in Burwash from 1787 until his death in 1821. Prior to 1787 he is recorded as living at and paying land tax for, Maunders in Hailsham. Robert was the father of Elizabeth's cousin, James Pattenden (1797-1850), who is also mentioned in the diary.
8 Married John Colbran(d), baptised 1753 in Wartling
9 Married Stephen Stace
10 Married James Harmer, baptised 1783 in Herstmonceux, Sussex
11 Unmarried and lived under independent means in the Rushlake Green area
12 Married Fanny Cheal from Warbleton
13 Married Daniel Lade, baptised 1797, Herstmonceux

APPENDIX 4: FAMILY TREES

REV. JOHN PRESS

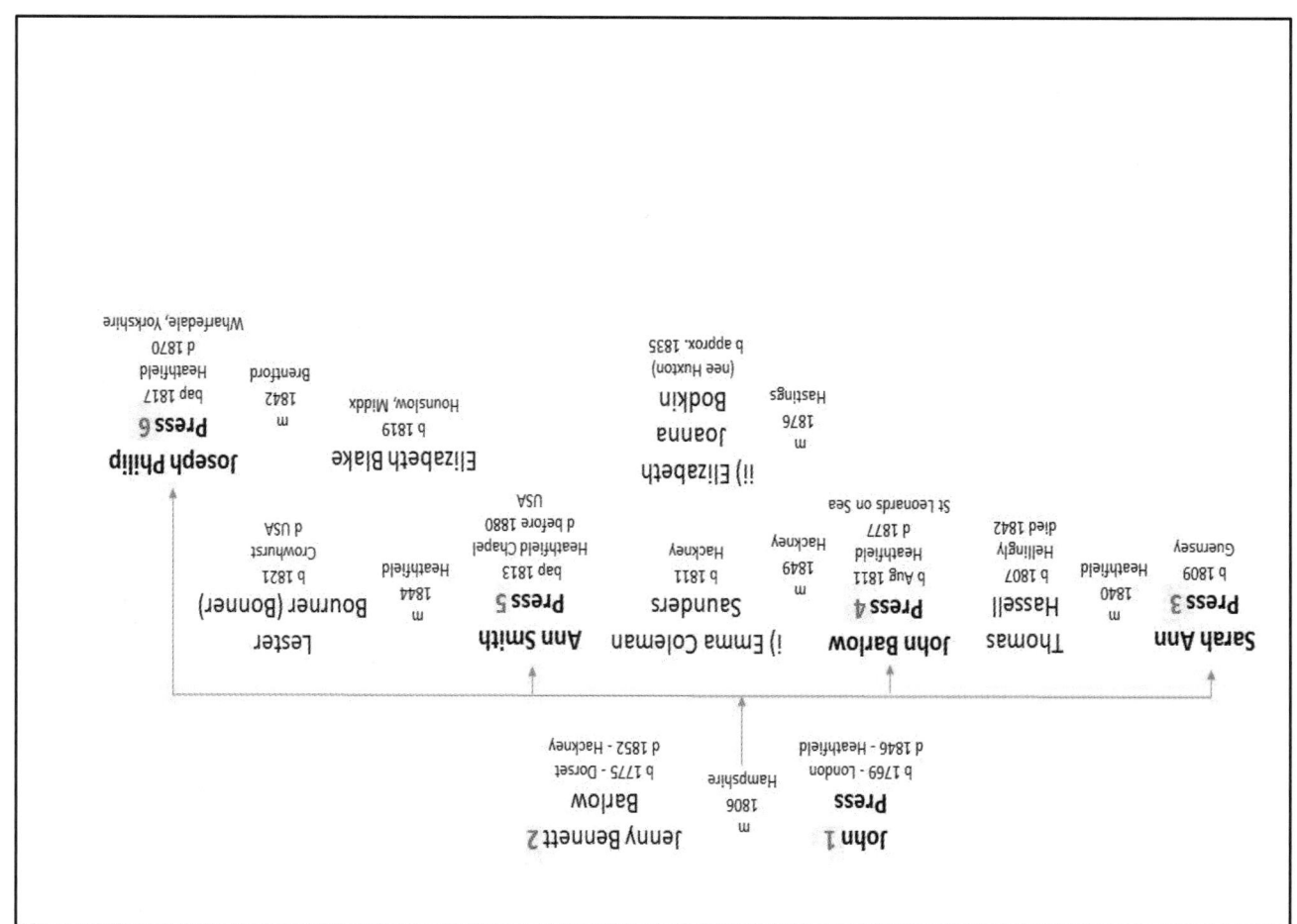

REV. JOHN PRESS: NOTES

1 John Press was born in London (location unspecified) in 1769. His father died when John was eight years old and he was subsequently given into the care of his uncle, who employed John in accounts/bookkeeping. In his younger days, according to the memoir about him published in 1847 (a year after his death), he is described as being 'a determined philosopher of the Epicurean School' who 'gave himself up, without stint, to every pleasure to which his depraved nature impelled him.'

Around this time he lost his uncle, after which he was 'apprenticed', although it does not specify at which occupation. It does state, however, that his Master 'appears to have been, in every respect, similar to his uncle; so the best interests of the lad were wholly neglected.' Apparently, John continued 'in the same course of ungodly living and worldly pleasure.'

John is said to have had 'high health, a cheerful disposition, and no small amount of intelligence. Hence, his society was courted.' It seems John had a friend, or acquaintance, who attended Methodist and dissenting chapels, and he invited John to accompany him on one particular evening. According to the memoir, it seems John was very affected by his impressions that 'towards the close of the sermon he sank down prostrate in the pew, overcome by his emotions.' After this it seems that 'he abandoned his ungodly companions... and cast in his lot with the people of God.'

Prior to coming to Heathfield, it appears that John spent some time on the Island of Guernsey where his first child, Sarah, was born in/around 1809. John's memoir states 'The Reverend John Press, formerly of the Island of Guernsey...' 'It appears he came to Heathfield on 23rd February, 1811. Then, following on from that, the memoir states that 'on April 23rd, 1829... after 18 years as assistant to the late Reverend George Gilbert of Heathfield in Sussex was ordained pastor of the Independent Church of Christ', with Rev Harris of Lewes, Rev Drury of Shoreham, Rev Evans of London, Rev Bannister of Arundel, Rev Edwards of Hanover Chapel, Brighton, Rev Thornton of Bognor, Rev Smith of Lindfield and the Rev Lefevre of Cuckfield officiating in various capacities.

The memoir states that John died in Heathfield, surrounded by his family, at a quarter past two in the afternoon of August 2nd, 1846. He

APPENDIX 4: FAMILY TREES

is buried in the grounds of Heathfield Chapel. It appeared he also owned Crowhurst Bridge Farm as well as being trustee in possession of the Heathfield Chapel and Chapel Cottage.

2 Jenny Bennett Barlow (aka Jane), was born on Nov 20th 1775 and baptised on 25th Nov at St Nicholas Street Independent Chapel, Weymouth, Dorset, the daughter of John and Sarah Barlow.
In the 1841 census Jane/Jenny is recorded as living at Chapel Cottage, Heathfield, with her daughter Ann. Her husband John is recorded as being at 'Brickhouse' in Burwash at that time, residing, for whatever reason, at the house of James Lade.
According to the 1851 census, she was living with her widowed daughter, Sarah (cited as a 'Draper's widow'), at 2, Widow's Retreat, St John's, Hackney, London. Jane/Jenny died in Hackney in 1852.

3 Sarah Ann Press was born on the Island of Guernsey in 1809. She married Thomas Hassell (a Grocer/Draper born in 1807 in Hellingly) in Heathfield in 1840 and they lived at 'Nevills' in Heathfield prior to Thomas's death in 1842. No issue.

4 John Barlow Press was born in Heathfield in 1811. He was a Commercial Clerk. He married twice – first to Emma Coleman Saunders and secondly to Elizabeth Joanna Bodkin née Huxton. John and Emma had two children – Lilla and Emma.

5 Ann Smith Press was born in Heathfield in 1813. She married Lester Bourner or Bonner who was a Limeburner and later a Miller. They emigrated to the United States in the 1850s, living in Ohio, Iowa and Missouri. Ann and Lester had six children – Stephen, Frank, Frederick, William, Fannie and Lilly.

6 Joseph Philip Press was born in Heathfield in 1817. He was a warehouseman/merchant and married one Elizabeth Blake. They lived in London and later in the West Riding of Yorkshire where he eventually died in 1870. Joseph and Elizabeth had seven children – Jane, Harriet, Fanny, William, Alfred, Frank and Mary.

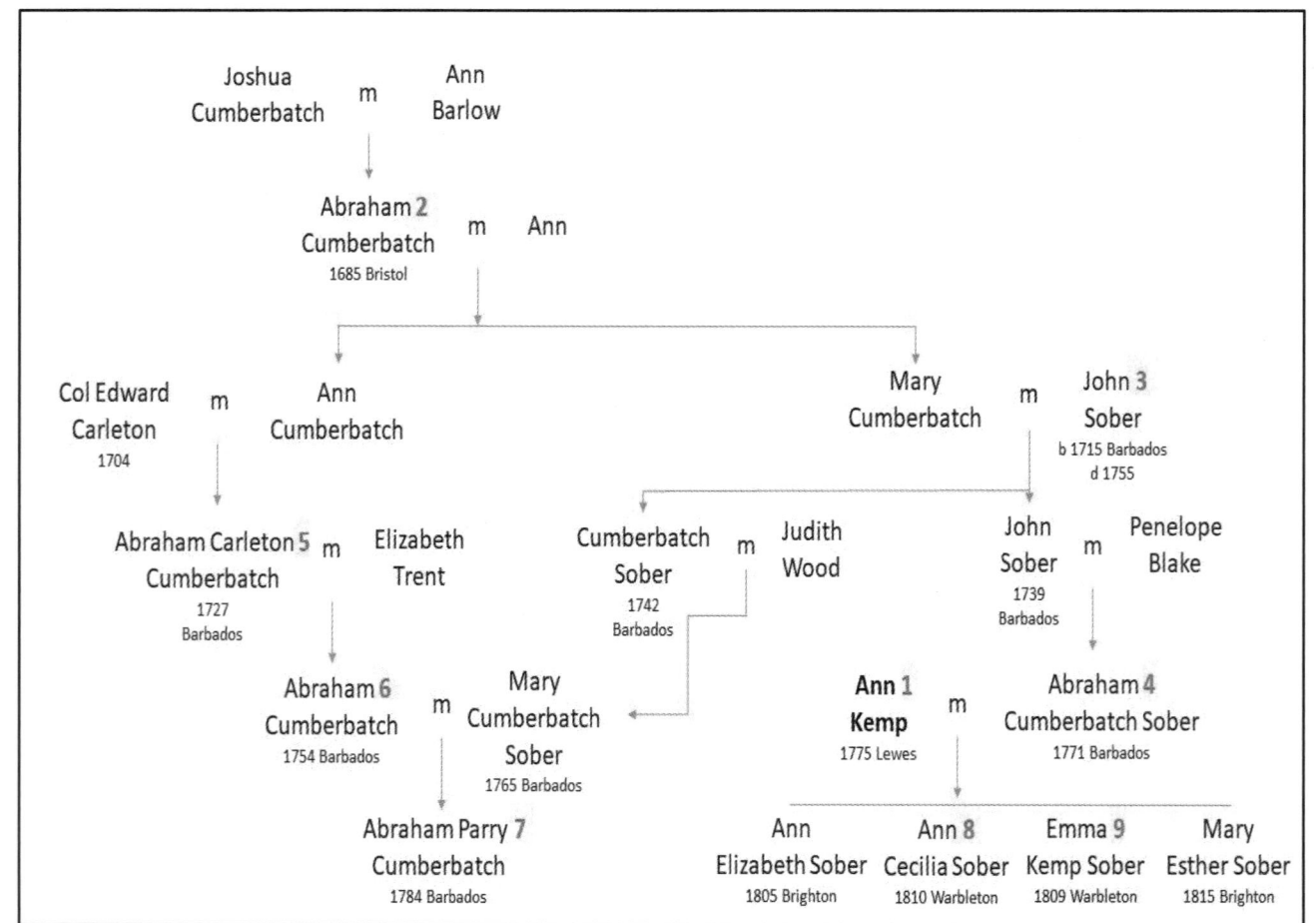

SOBER: NOTES

1. This is the Honourable Lady Sober – no 's'. Ann Kemp was the daughter of Thomas Kemp MP for Lewes, who lived in Lewes Castle and Herstmonceux Place. She married Abraham Cumberbatch Sober and her brother was Thomas Read Kemp also an MP. Ann had two sisters – Grace who died in 1775 and Elizabeth who was born in 1773. I believe it is Elizabeth Kemp that is 'Mrs Sober's sister'. Also, It seems that Kemp Town in Brighton was named after Thomas Read Kemp who conceived and developed it.

2. Abraham Cumberbatch, son of Joshua Cumberbatch, merchant and Horner, is cited as owning Cleland and the farm plantations in Barbados. His wife's full name is not recorded. He had a considerable fortune and no son to carry on the name.

3. John Sober, of The Castle, St Peter, Barbados, married Mary Cumberbatch. It seems that John made his money from slavery. He married for a second time to Mary Wilcox. John Sober purchased slaves in Africa and traded them on the Barbados sugar plantations for rum to export to New York. It was a lucrative business, it seems, but prices fell when Barbados had enough slaves & the Colonies produced their own liquor. John & his son Cumberbatch Sober owned the Mount Gay Rum Factory in St Peters, Barbados. Sober or Sobers is still common name in Barbados, and most black descendants who carry that name are descendants of former slaves who took the surname of their masters, including, perhaps, Gary Sobers the cricketer.
An extract from John's will is as follows:
John Sober, late of the p. of St. Peter in the Island of Barbados, now of Little Bursted, co. Essex, Esq. Will dated 12 Oct 1751. My father-in-law Nich. Wilcox of Bdos Esq., Edwd: Clark Parish of L., Esq, Abr. Carleton Cumberbatch and Joseph Lindsey, both of Bdos, Esqres. on T. all my sugar work plantations and personal estate. 200 negroes, 100 cattle and 10 horses to be kept on my estate, 60 a. to be planted in provisions, negroes to be well fed and clothed, and casks to be made.
John is buried in St Paul's Cathedral, London

4. Abraham Cumberbatch Sober married Ann Kemp d/o Thomas Kemp MP for Lewes. He was a fellow of Trinity College Cambridge and in the King's Dragoon Guards. At 26 he is shown as managing a Barbadian plantation called Ellis Castle aka Clement Castle. He is died in Lewes and was buried on 16/12/1813 in Woodnesborough, Kent. His

will was proved in Lewes 07/04/1814. The will is very simple and left everything to his wife Ann née Kemp, carefully described as the daughter of Thomas Kemp MP. He was also on the Committee of the British and Foreign Auxilliary Bible Society for the County of Sussex, which was chaired by his brother-in-law Thomas Read Kemp, who was also President. The 'The Sober sale' that Nicholas refers to is the sale of Stonehouse in Warbleton (now a hotel, I believe) which occurred in April 1815.

5   Abraham Carleton Cumberbatch inherited Cleland and the farm plantations and other estate under the Will of his grandfather, Abraham Cumberbatch. He assumed the surname Cumberbatch in fulfilment of the terms of the said Will. Married Elizabeth Trent, daughter of Lawrence and Jane Trent. He was a Member of the Council of Barbados for thirty years. He made his Will on 26 April 1785 intending shortly to leave for England. He died there on 25 July 1785 and was buried in Bristol Cathedral by the Precentor on 30 July. A tablet to his memory erected on the north wall of the Choir Vestry of the Cathedral records that he bore a long and painful illness with uncommon patience and fortitude, and came to England in hopes of receiving benefit from a change of climate.

6 & 7 Abraham Cumberbatch, born 1754, married Mary Cumberbatch Sober, daughter of Cumberbatch Sober. She was his second cousin. After his death she married 20 August 1797 William Smith Forth of the King's Dragoon Guards. Abraham Cumberbatch inherited Cleland and The Farm, and was for some years a Member of Council of Barbados. He went to live in England and died of a malignant fever at his seat Fairwater, near Taunton, on June 16, 1796 in his 42nd year. A tablet to his memory is on the north wall of the north choir of Bristol Cathedral, erected by his widow. His only child and heir was Abraham Parry Cumberbatch, born in Barbados, baptised 29 November 1784. He married Charlotte, daughter of Robert Burnett Jones on 31 October 1805. She died 15 January 1818, and he married secondly, Caroline Chaloner by whom he had children. Their son, Abraham Parry Cumberbatch, died at Tunbridge Wells October 1840 aged 56. The actor Benedict Cumberbatch is descended from this line.

8. Ann Cecilia Sober born in Warbleton married the Reverend Allen William Chatfield in Brighton in 1833. An anonymous diary entry speaks of their marriage:

June 25: Immediately after breakfast we got ready and took a Fly as far

APPENDIX 4: FAMILY TREES

as the Old Church, that we might see Miss Anne Sober & Mr Allan Chatfield married. Mr Martland married them and Mr Mitford gave the bride away, it was a most interesting ceremony, quite painfully exciting.

9. Emma Kemp Sober born in Warbleton married John Reveley Mitford in Cropthorne, Worcester in 1832

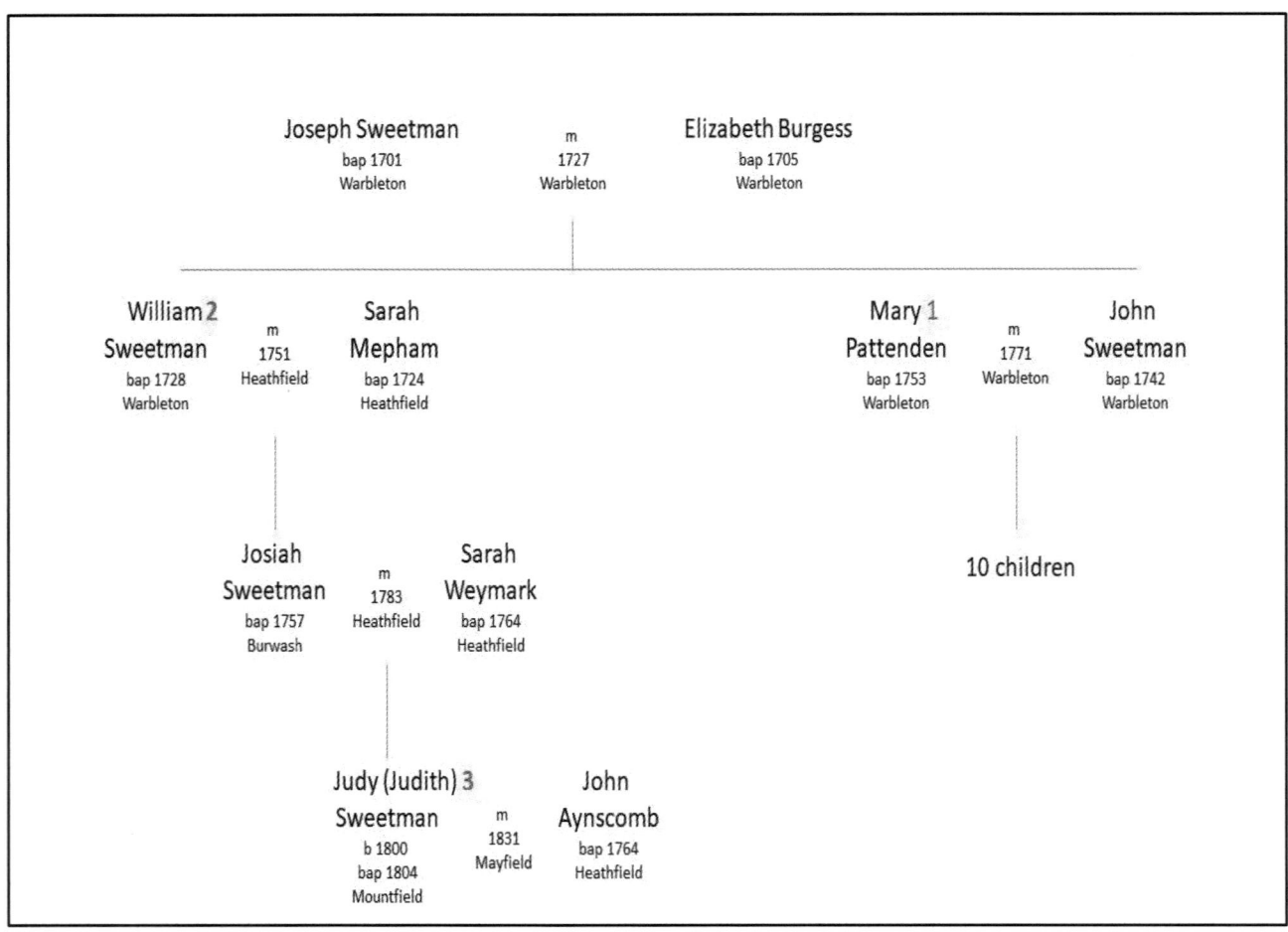

JUDITH SWEETMAN: NOTES

1. Mary's sister, Elizabeth Pattenden, bap 1759, married John Winchester, who was witness to John and Mary's marriage, along with one Mary Saunders.

2. William's youngest brother, John Sweetman, married Mary Pattenden in Warbleton in 1771. Mary Pattenden was related to Nicholas's wife Elizabeth Pattenden. Both were descended from John Pattenden and Jane Adds. John and Jane had a son Robert Pattenden who was Elizabeth Oxley's grandfather. John and Jane's son Thomas Pattenden was Mary's father.
William's brother, Joseph Sweetman, bap 1735 in Warbleton, married Mary Alfree. One of their children was Lenny Sweetman bap 1771 who married Samuel Pettit, the man who shot at Thomas Honeysett, reputedly with a horse pistol

3. It seems Josiah and Sarah Sweetman moved around the county a fair bit with children being born in varying towns. I do not think it is wrong to believe that Judy Sweetman was working in the Warbleton/Herstmonceux area prior to her marriage to John Aynscomb considering a lot of her close family were living there. However, the piece of information that reinforces this is that in 1823 she gave birth to an illegitimate child – Caroline Sweetman – fathered by my 1st cousin 5x removed, Thomas Hayward. The bastardy examination dated 15th July 1823 names Thomas Hayward of Herstmonceux as father to her female bastard child. Thomas Hayward lived at Limes Cross – a stone's throw from Windmill Hill

Judith Sweetman married John Aynscomb in Heathfield on 9th October 1831.

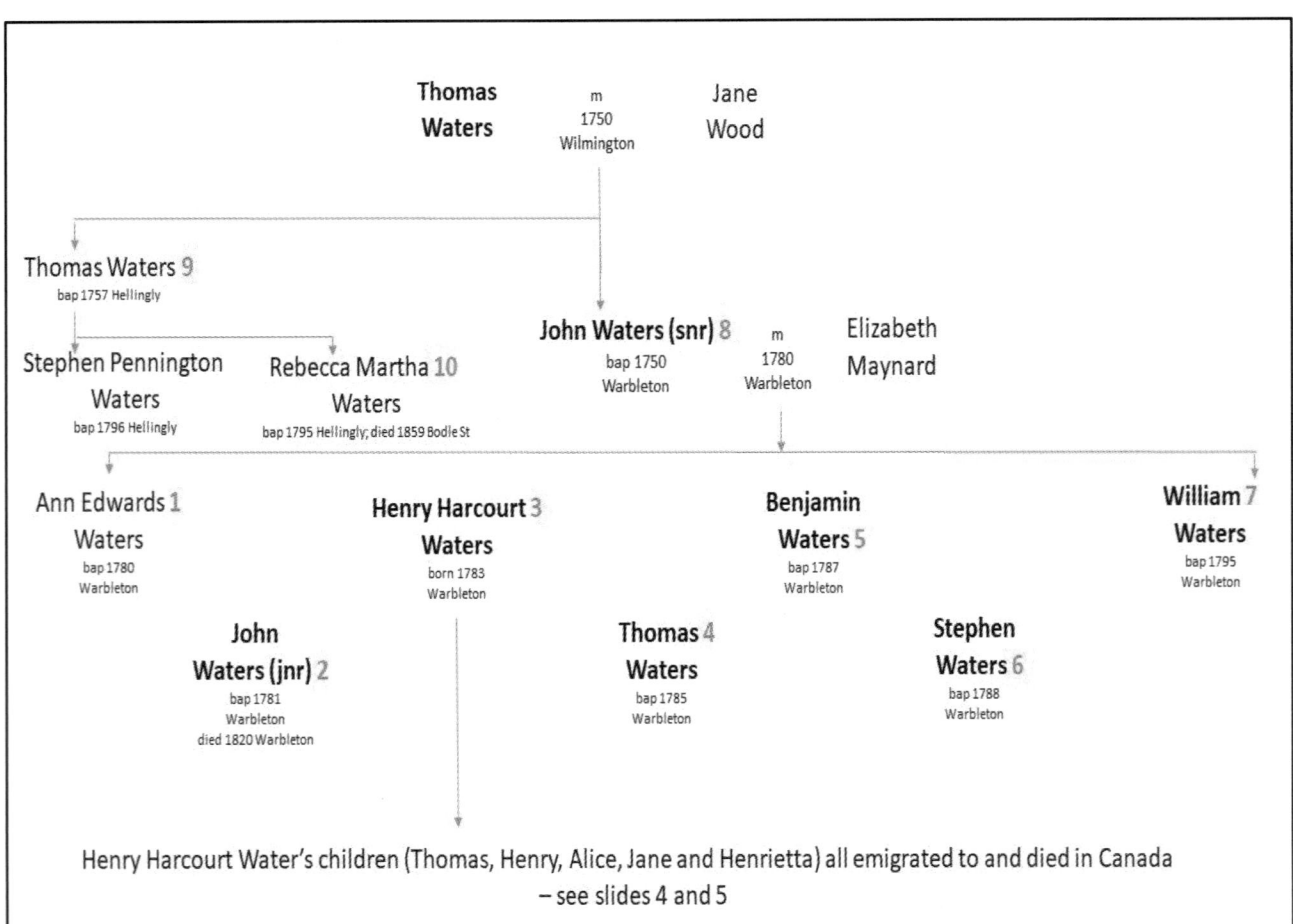

WATERS: NOTES

1. Ann Edwards Waters married my 4x great uncle, John Haffenden, s/o my 5x great grandparents, James Haffenden and Ann (née Unstead), in Heathfield on 2/3/1802.

2. John Waters married Anna Maria Colbrand Hall in Hellingly on 16/6/1807. The marriage licence states 'John Waters farmer from Warbleton, and Anna Maria a spinster from Hellingly. The sureties were pledged by John Waters and John Haffenden, yeoman farmer from Heathfield.'

3. Henry Harcourt Waters married Elizabeth Kitchener, widow, née Crowhurst, on 12/1/1808 in Hailsham. The marriage licence states 'bachelor 24 Draper, Hailsham, Elizabeth Kitchener widow of Hailsham. Witness - John Haffenden, yeoman from Heathfield'

4. Thomas Waters married Ann Martin on 16/2/1819 in Warbleton. The marriage document states 'bachelor of this parish.' Witnesses were Thomas White junior and Elizabeth Waters.

5. Benjamin Waters married Frances Gorringe on 13/5/1817 in St Giles in the Fields Middlesex. The marriage licence states 'bachelor from Warbleton.'

6. Stephen Waters married Sarah Thomson on 26/5/1810 in Heathfield. The marriage licence states 'bachelor from Warbleton – yeoman. Sarah, 20, married with consent of John and Sarah Thompson, farmers from Heathfield.' Sureties given by Stephen Waters and James Thompson, yeoman from Heathfield.

7. William Waters married Sarah Lade on 6/6/1823 in Herstmonceux. The marriage document states 'bachelor from Warbleton'. Bride 'of this parish.' i.e. Herstmonceux.

8. John Waters's second marriage was to widow Lydia Cheesman (née Elford) on 29/11/1796 in Warbleton. The marriage licence shows both bride and groom as widow and widower. Sureties – John Waters and John Fisher, gentleman from Lewes.

9. Thomas Waters married Jane Gorringe on 29/3/1780 in Hellingly. The marriage licence states bride 18 years and married with consent of guardians – Pennington Gorringe, yeoman of Heathfield and William Pennington Gorringe, Yeoman of Westham. Thomas and Jane's son was Stephen Pennington Waters

10. Rebecca Martha Waters married John Farmer on 23/3/1826 in Warbleton. The marriage licence states 'bride 30 years old from

Warbleton. Groom 33 years old, a bachelor from Catsfield.' John Farmer was born in Ninfield in 1793, the son of James Farmer and Mary, née Powell.

APPENDIX 5: NICHOLAS OXLEY LAST WILL AND TESTAMENT

THE LAST WILL AND TESTAMENT OF NICHOLAS OXLEY 27TH DECEMBER 1830

This is the last will and testament of me Nicholas Oxley of the parish of Wartling in the County of Sussex, yeoman, having the disposition of such temporal estate as it hath pleased almighty God of his goodness to bestow upon me. First, I order and direct that all such just debts that I shall owe at the time of my decease, my funeral expenses, and the costs and expenses of proving this my will, shall be fully paid and satisfied by my executors hereinafter named from and out of my personal estate. I give and bequeath unto my beloved wife Elizabeth Oxley, the sum of six hundred pounds to be paid twelve calendar months next after my decease to and for her own use and benefit. Also I give and bequeath unto my wife, the said Elizabeth Oxley, my household furniture to the amount and value of fifty pounds, the same to be valued by some proper person to be chosen by my executors. And my will is that the last mentioned legacy shall be in lieu of interest on the first mentioned legacy for the first year next after my decease. I give unto my brother David Oxley of Warbleton, farmer, and to my brother-in-law, John Pattenden, of the same place, farmer, and to my brother-in-law, James Harmer of Wartling, farmer, and to their executors and administrators forever, upon trust, all that my freehold messuage and tenement and the outbuildings, gardens and premises thereto belonging, situate and being in the parish of Herstmonceux and now in the occupation of Charity Collins. Also, I give upon further trust unto them the said David Oxley, John Pattenden and James Harmer, their executors and administrators, all that my freehold piece or parcel of Marshland with its appurtenances thereto, belonging, situate and being in the parish of Herstmonceux, known by the name of the Iron Croft, containing by estimation two acres, be the same more or less, and now in the occupation of Richard Hoad. Also, I give unto them the said David Oxley, John Pattenden and James Harmer, all the rest, residue and remainder of my goods, chattels, effects, monies, sureties for money, rights, credits and personal estate, whatsoever and wheresoever after payment of my just debts, funeral and testamentary expenses, the aforesaid legacy or sums of six hundred pounds and household furniture to the amount of fifty pounds as before directed. I give unto the said David Oxley, John Pattenden and

James Harmer their executors and administrators forever, upon the several trusts nevertheless herein declared or expressed of, and direct the same / that is to say / upon trust, that they the said David Oxley, John Pattenden and James Harmer or the survivor of them and their executors, and administrators of such survivors, do and shall as soon as conveniently may be after my decease as they or he shall in their or his discretion think proper, absolutely sell and dispose of my freehold estates before mentioned either by public auction or private contract for the best price that they or he can obtain for the same. And I do declare that the receipt of my said Trustees or the survivors of them or the survivor of either of their respective executors or administrators, shall be a good and sufficient title to the said estates to the purchaser or purchasers thereof without such purchase or purchases serving to the application or non-application of such purchase money. And further upon trust, I do hereby order and direct my said trustees to sell and dispose of all such part or parts of the said residuum of my personal estate as shall be of a saleable nature, for the most money and best price that can be obtained for the same, either by public auction or private contract, and either together or in lots or parcels as they, my said trustees or survivors of them or the executors or administrators of such survivor, shall also in their discretion think proper. Re the monies arising from the sale or sales thereof, together with such monies or debts as shall from part of the said residuum of my personal estate, to dispose thereof as follows. I order and direct my trustees, the survivors of them, or their executors or administrators of such survivors, in the first place to put or place out at interest, on Government or real security, the sum of four hundred pounds, and that the interest, dividends or proceeds arising by the same, be paid by them, my said trustees, to Elizabeth Oxley my wife during the term of her natural life. And upon further trust, I do order and direct my said trustees to divide all the rest, residue and remainder of my personal estate, with the produce of my real estate, which I give and bequeath to my son Thomas Oxley and my son Othniel Oxley and to any other children or child that may hereafter be born to me of my wife the said Elizabeth Oxley within ten months after my decease, to be equally divided between and amongst all my surviving children, share and share alike, provided nevertheless, and my will is, that in case my children or either of them shall be under the age of twenty one years at the time of sale of the disposition of the said residue of my estate, my will and meaning is then that the parts or shares or part or share of such minors or minor of the residue of my estate still owing them, or his minorities or minority, be put or placed out at interest by and in the names or name of my trustees or trustee or their executors or administrators, on some good and sufficient security, and the interest and dividends therefrom arising from time to time, be received and or paid and applied for the benefit of such minors or minor as aforesaid by my trustees or survivors of them or the executors and administrators of such survivors, in such manners that they or he shall in their or his discretion think most proper until such children or child shall attain to the age of twenty one years respectively. And at the death of my wife the said Elizabeth Oxley, my will is that my trustees, or survivor or the survivors of them, or the executor or administrator of such survivors, upon further trust, do their will in the aforesaid sum of four hundred pounds, and divide the same equally between my surviving children, or the issue lawfully born to either of them who may die before their mother, such issue to respectively take the part of the same equally amongst them if more than one to which his or their parent or parents would be entitled if living. And if it should so happen that all my children should die before their mother and not have lawful issue, then I give the said sum of four hundred pounds unto Elizabeth Oxley my wife for her use and benefit absolutely. And in case all my children should die in their minority then I give the whole interest of my estate unto the said Elizabeth Oxley my wife during the term of her natural life, and at her death I give the whole principal sum thereof as follows: one half to the Oxley family to be divided into two equal shares, one share thereof to my brother David Oxley, and the other share to the children of my late brother William Oxley, the same to be divided equally amongst them or their respective lawful issue; the other half I give to the Pattenden family to be divided into three equal shares, the first share, or one third part thereof, to John Pattenden, the second share to the two children of James Harmer, namely Henry Harmer and Harriet Harmer, equally between them or their respective lawful issue, and the third share to the two sons of Daniel Lade of Cowbeach, born to him by his first wife, the late Sarah Pattenden, namely to Luke Lade and Levi Lade, equally between them or their respective lawful issue. And I do hereby nominate, constitute and appoint the said David Oxley, John Pattenden and James Harmer joint executors of this my last will and testament, and also guardians of my said sons Thomas Oxley and Othniel Oxley during their respective minorities, and I do hereby expressly declare and direct that they my executors and trustees shall not be charged and chargeable with, or accountable for, any more of my monies, estates or effects, or any part thereof, than they shall respectively actually receive or come to their respective hands by virtue of this my will, nor with or for any loss which may happen of such monies, estates or effects or any part thereof, so as such loss do not happen by or through their wilful default or neglect, nor shall either of them, my said executors or trustees, to be answerable or accountable for the other of them or for the acts, deeds, receipts, defaults or disbursements of the other of them, but each of them for himself and for his own acts, deeds, receipts, defaults and disbursements only, and further it shall and may be lawful to and for my said executors and trustees, to retain to and reimburse themselves respectively from and out of my monies and personal estate all such loss, costs, charges, damages and expenses as they shall respectively sustain, bear, pay, expend, or be put unto in the execution of this my will or in anywise relating thereto. Lastly I hereby revoke all former wills by me made and declare this and this only to be my last will and testament. In witness thereof, I the said Nicholas Oxley have hereunto set my hand to the first three sheets thereof, the whole being sustained in four sheets of paper, on this twenty seventh day of December in the year of our Lord one thousand eight hundred and thirty ..... Nicholas Oxley ... signed sealed published and declared by the above named Nicholas Oxley, the testator of and for his last will and testament in the presence of us, who in his presence, in his request, and in the presence of each other, hereunto subscribe our names as witnesses thereto:

William Tayler   Thomas Vinell   James Sweetman

Proved at London 17th December 1833 before the judge by their oaths John Pattenden and James Harmer, two of the executors to whom administration was granted, having been first sworn by Commission duly to administer. Power reserved of making the like grant to the other executor David Oxley whom he shall apply for the same

APPENDIX 6: FAMILY NAMES INCLUDED

Many named individuals feature very frequently in the diaries, sometimes hundreds of times. Including them in a standard page index would be impractical and unhelpful. A dual approach is adopted here.

SURNAMES FEATURING VERY FREQUENTLY IN THE DIARY

Baker
Beal
Bland
Brook
Cat
Cornford
Dann
Daw
Delves
Easton
Farmer
Foster
Fox
Fuller
Goldsmith
Grant
Gurr
Guy
Hall
Harmer
Hoad
Hoath
Hodges
Honeysett
Isted
Jarvis
Lade
Marten
Martin
Morfey
Oxley
Pankhurst
Pattenden
Phillips
Press
Pursglove
Reed
Reeves
Russell
Selmes
Smith
Sobers
Trill
Verrall/Verel(l)
Waters
Winchester

PAGE INDEX TO OTHER SURNAMES

Adams 44, 48, 88, 92, 132, 145, 219, 221
Adds 78
Ades 264, 309
Akehurst 61
Apps 150
Arcoll 308, 337
Ashe 226
Ashley 147
Atree 93
Avard 336
Balcombe 14, 92, 274
Barker 6, 81

Barnes 21, 25, 73, 149
Barnett 75, 158, 236, 301, 303
Barns 99, 141, 161, 167, 251
Barrow 162
Bartlett 127, 134
Barton 92, 148, 237-49
Bates 240
Batup 61, 63
Beaufay 37
Beecham 88
Beedle/Beadle 52, 61
Beeny 179
Bennett 68, 72, 131, 145, 150, 313-14
Best 14
Bidwell 328, 330
Blackford 56, 84
Blackman 38, 45, 63, 125, 235, 238, 296, 338
Blackpole 90
Blucher 26
Bodeham 88
Body 217
Bornor 156
Bradford 283, 337-39
Bray 60, 246, 267, 337-40
Brocks 75
Browne 99
Buckland 73, 137
Burgess 288, 336
Burt 181
Buss 63, 65, 149
Button 65, 294, 305, 309
Callis 146
Capper 210
Chandler 192
Chittenden 38, 100, 281, 284
Christmas 51, 75, 82-5, 161, 270, 295
Clement 148
Cole 190

Collins 92-3, 103, 110, 188, 194, 230-33
Cook 139
Cooks 290
Cooper 152, 233
Cooter 124
Cornwell 157, 235, 273, 278
Couchman 25, 95, 99, 113, 131, 146, 190, 216-17
Counts 59, 68
Cramp 159
Creel 84
Crouch 18, 30, 69, 80, 223, 250, 265-66
Crowhurst 111, 147, 213, 242-43
Curtis 21, 33, 101, 103, 144
Dalloway 227
Diamond 71, 109, 145-47
Dice 24
Dicker 282
Dirkel 26
Dorsett 179
Dowland 273
Dray 149
Drew 188
Drowley 333
Drury 64
Dunk 196-97, 252, 273, 290
Eastland 140-41, 234
Edman 264
Edmonds 147
Effick 95
Elfick 72, 97
Ellis 59, 63, 69-71, 77, 97, 212
Errey 134, 326
Erry 22, 36, 141, 211, 225-26, 248, 316, 331
Eton 11
Evenden 24-30, 156-57, 161, 172, 180-89, 192-96, 276-79
Everest 41, 43, 110, 177, 197, 295, 297, 300, 323

APPENDIX 6: FAMILY NAMES INCLUDED

Field 78
Fluorance /Flurence 67, 68
Ford 268
Forkhouse 180
Fowle 123, 137, 145
Fowler 130
Fox 141
Friston 92
Gain 49, 97, 203
Gander 6-11, 188
Garnett 256
Gell 67
Gilbert 7, 35, 38, 74, 134, 221, 300, 399
Gillick or Gillard 151
Gorringe 65, 338
Gower 141, 159-63, 253, 295
Gray 161-62
Gurnets 284
Haffenden 110, 152
Harman 201, 217, 240, 274
Harris 58, 72, 92
Hayward 185
Head 305
Henty 326
Hilder 71-73, 260
Holder 88
Holland 209, 264
Holman 339
Hook 289, 291, 296-97, 299, 308
Howses 211
Hugh 155
Hutchinson 337-38, 340
John 141
Johnson 180
Judge 26, 30
Kemp 133, 156, 159-60, 164, 166, 175, 179, 181, 195, 219, 257, 273, 276, 321
King 237
Kirby 148, 238

Knight 169, 243, 275
Lambhurst 95
Lanhard 24
Latham 87, 103, 106, 119, 179, 191, 193
Launkhurst 318-19, 326
Leeves 245-50
Lloyd 21 71, 149, 247
Lower 278
Luck 138, 177
Lullham 22
Lusted 161
Mannington 85, 131, 144, 153, 165, 224, 333
Martel 159
Mepham 63, 92, 143, 151, 253
Merricks 256
Message 5, 9-10, 12, 15, 305
Morres 74
Morris 149
Morrys 143
Morsey 311
Nathan 65, 120
Newington 24, 68
Newman 56, 72-3, 81, 152-53, 197, 256
Noakes 27, 56-8, 87, 223, 262, 267, 278, 293, 309, 338
Over 141
Owen 303
Pain 47, 75
Pardon 205
Parker 36, 59, 66, 110, 112, 117
Parris 90, 278, 295, 306, 323, 332
Peers 141
Peter 130
Pettit 74, 134, 233, 305
Philcox 127, 296
Pinyon 24, 34, 132, 217, 278, 293, 296
Piper 4, 5
Pitcher 149

Pledwell 127
Pocock 21, 71
Pook 95, 97, 134-37
Preston 140, 156, 197
Purley 157
Randell, Randle 196, 271, 273
Reed 54, 71-2, 82, 88, 116, 130, 141, 146, 188, 191, 205
Reinsford 127
Richardson 51, 78, 128, 139, 141
Robbins 31-2
Robins 86, 95
Rouds 88
Saunders 63, 135, 140
Scrace 70-1, 74, 149, 181
Sellen 333
Soland 52
Soper 57
Squires 23, 55, 72-3, 103, 190, 269
Standen 7, 17, 73, 80, 92, 104, 257
Stanford 23, 42, 71, 84, 98-9, 147, 156, 169, 208, 277
Start 176, 238
Steer(s) 53, 61, 84, 94, 110, 114, 123, 152, 179, 187, 189, 251, 266
Stodhart 199
Stone 15
Streeter 322, 331
Sweetman 331
Tailor 58, 120
Tanner 20
Tedham 287-88, 337
Thomas 339
Thompsetts 192
Thompson 6
Thomsett 64
Thorp 209, 238
Ticehurst 192, 252
Tindal 311

Tomlins 18
Tourle 42, 208, 284
Usher 236
Ven 147
Veness 85, 91-2, 170, 188, 197, 206, 208, 310
Venus 12, 93, 125
Vicker 94
Viger 68
Vinn 152
Vion 84
Wallis 153
Walters 56, 58, 72, 84, 126-28, 132, 140, 142, 294
Warner 95, 101, 193, 233, 242-43, 276
Watson 274, 280
Weller 15
Wenhams 70
Wethers 49
Whisham 22
Whitman 6
Wilkes 199
Willis 147
Wilmshurst 136-36, 142-43, 146, 151, 155, 163, 165-66, 196, 201, 300-01
Wisdom 25, 259
Woods 44
Woodham(s) 60, 198
Woodhouse 158
Wooten 108
Wratten 198
Wratton 188
York(e) 43, 148, 160-61, 164, 169-70, 174-77
Young 114